RECENT AMERICA: A HISTORY

Book One: 1900–1933

RECENT AMERICA: A HISTORY

Book One: 1900–1933

Book Two: Since 1933

Book One: 1900-1933

RECENT
AMERICA

A History

HENRY BAMFORD PARKES

VINCENT P. CAROSSO

New York University

THOMAS Y. CROWELL COMPANY

New York, Established 1834

Library of Congress Catalog Card Number: 63-9192

TYPOGRAPHY BY LAUREL WAGNER

COVER DESIGN BY THOMAS RUZICKA

Manufactured in the United States of America by Vail-Ballou Press, Inc., Binghamton, N.Y.

Preface

Although any division of history into periods must be somewhat arbitrary, there are good reasons for regarding either the Spanish-
American War of 1898 or the accession to the Presidency of Theodore
Roosevelt in 1901 as the beginning of a new epoch in the development of
the United States. American history since these two events has been dominated by many of the same trends, and the people of the United States
have been confronted by many of the same basic problems. An equally
significant dividing line is the year 1933, when the newly elected administration of Franklin D. Roosevelt assumed the responsibility of alleviating
the numerous social and economic problems arising from the grave economic crisis facing the nation. The legislation that followed Roosevelt's
inauguration radically altered many previously held conceptions of the
proper role of the federal government in promoting the general welfare.

The later nineteenth century was a period of rapid expansion in both
agriculture and industry, with little awareness of the consequent growth
of economic inequality and insecurity. During the twentieth century the
chief factor causing social change has been the continued growth of
machine technology and of the large corporation as the characteristic
institution of machine civilization; furthermore, the American people have
become increasingly concerned about the economic, social, and political
problems which this growth has presented. Thus, the main trend in American political history during the twentieth century has been the prolonged
attempt of the American people to cope realistically with these problems.

During the nineteenth century the United States enjoyed complete
security against any possible attack from abroad and was able to indulge
in the luxury of isolation in foreign affairs. The twentieth century, on the

other hand, has witnessed the emergence of the United States as a world power, and its gradual assumption of the responsibilities of leading the free world in defense against Communist aggression.

Both of these twentieth-century trends are of enormous and lasting importance in this era of increasing momentum. History moves more rapidly than at any earlier period. Attitudes and opinions need constant revision, and doctrines firmly established only a decade ago appear already to require change.

Our purpose has been to present a clear and reasonably comprehensive account of recent American history in terms intelligible to both the college student and the general reader. Our central theme has been the political and economic development of American society. We have also given considerable attention to social, cultural, and intellectual changes and have sought to relate these to the main lines of American development. But our central emphasis has been upon political and economic changes at home and on the growth of American interests and responsibilities abroad.

Any historical account that aims to be more than a lifeless chronicle of events must necessarily reflect the point of view of the historian; and while we have sought to achieve strictest factual accuracy and to present opposing interpretations fairly, we have not tried to suppress our own judgment of events. We believe that both the movement toward greater governmental supervision of the economy and the assumption by the United States of international responsibilities, despite numerous errors and failures, have been necessitated by historic trends too powerful to be resisted. And we feel that, with wise statesmanship, they promise a better life not only for Americans but for all mankind.

We should like to express our thanks to Professor John Morton Blum of Yale University and Professor John D. Hicks of the University of California at Berkeley for the care with which they read the entire manuscript and for their many invaluable suggestions. We are indebted also to Mrs. Julanne Arnold and Mr. Philip Winsor of the Thomas Y. Crowell Company for editorial advice and services far beyond the call of duty, and to Mr. Irving Katz, a doctoral candidate at New York University, for assisting us in checking the bibliographies. Rose Carosso helped by typing a large part of the manuscript, and several of our colleagues gave us the benefit of their expert knowledge.

H.B.P.
V.P.C.

New York City
December, 1962

Contents

Preface   v

I THE HERITAGE OF THE NINETEENTH CENTURY AND THE EMERGING PROBLEMS OF THE TWENTIETH

Foreword   3

I The State of the Nation in 1900: Material Aspects   11

THE REGIONS OF THE UNITED STATES   *11*
THE AGE OF THE CORPORATION   *21*
THE CONDITION OF THE WORKING CLASS   *31*
THE PROBLEMS OF AGRICULTURE   *36*
Suggested Readings   *43*

2 Domestic and Foreign Politics at the Turn of the Century   49

PARTY STRUCTURE AND ORGANIZATION   *49*
POLITICAL CONTROVERSIES   *58*
THE UNITED STATES BECOMES A WORLD POWER   *65*
Suggested Readings   *76*

3   The New Society   81
    ETHNIC PROBLEMS   83
    THE FORMATION OF PUBLIC OPINION   89
    NEW INTELLECTUAL AND ARTISTIC TRENDS   97
    Suggested Readings   106

4   The Progressive Movement   109
    PROGRESSIVE IDEALS   109
    THE MUCKRAKERS   110
    POLITICAL THEORY   113
    MUNICIPAL REFORMERS   115
    STATE REFORMERS   119
    THE EIGHTEENTH AMENDMENT   125
    THE NINETEENTH AMENDMENT   126
    Suggested Readings   127

5   The Administration of Theodore Roosevelt,
    1901–1909   131
    PRESIDENTIAL LEADERSHIP   131
    ROOSEVELT AND THE TRUSTS   136
    ROOSEVELT AND THE COAL STRIKE   139
    LEGISLATION, 1901–1905   141
    THE ELECTION OF 1904   142
    PURE FOOD AND CONSERVATION   144
    THE PANIC OF 1907   146
    ROOSEVELT'S FOREIGN POLICY   150
    Suggested Readings   165

6   William Howard Taft and the Split in
    the Republican Party, 1909–1912   172
    TAFT AS PRESIDENT   174
    TAFT AND THE TARIFF   175
    THE BALLINGER-PINCHOT CONTROVERSY   178
    THE SPEAKERSHIP FIGHT AND THE ELECTION OF 1910   180

CANADIAN RECIPROCITY   *184*
THE REFORMS OF THE TAFT ADMINISTRATION   *185*
TAFT AND FOREIGN POLICY   *187*
THE ELECTION OF 1912   *189*
Suggested Readings   *196*

7   Woodrow Wilson and the New Freedom, 1913–1917 199

WOODROW WILSON'S CAREER TO 1912   *199*
THE LEGISLATION OF THE NEW FREEDOM, 1913–1914   *209*
FURTHER DOMESTIC REFORM, 1915–1917   *218*
FOREIGN POLICY, 1913–1917   *221*
Suggested Readings   *229*

II   THE ERA OF WORLD WAR I,

1914–1921

8   From Neutrality to Belligerency, 1914–1917   237

THE OUTBREAK OF WAR   *237*
AMERICAN DIPLOMACY, 1914–1916   *249*
PREPAREDNESS   *260*
THE ELECTION OF 1916   *264*
WAR   *266*
Suggested Readings   *270*

9   The United States at War, 1917–1918   273

THE TASK OF PREPARATION   *273*
AMERICAN NAVAL AND MILITARY ACTIVITIES   *287*
WILSON'S WAR AIMS   *292*
Suggested Readings   *294*

10   Peace and the Return to "Normalcy," 1919–1921   297

WILSON'S TASK   *297*
THE PEACE CONFERENCE   *299*
THE FIGHT FOR RATIFICATION   *306*

THE RETURN TO "NORMALCY" *311*
THE ELECTION OF 1920 *314*
Suggested Readings *317*

III   THE REPUBLICAN ERA, 1920–1933

II   Republican Politics and Policies, 1921–1929   323

STALWARTS AND PROGRESSIVES IN CONGRESS *323*
WARREN GAMALIEL HARDING *327*
CALVIN COOLIDGE *338*
Suggested Readings *353*

12   Economic Developments, 1921–1929   358

AN ERA OF PROSPERITY *358*
THE DEVELOPMENT OF THE CORPORATION *360*
MONOPOLY PRACTICES *363*
CHANGES IN THE CHARACTER OF ECONOMIC ACTIVITY *366*
SOME NEW INDUSTRIES *373*
THE LABOR MOVEMENT *385*
AGRICULTURE *389*
FOREIGN TRADE AND INVESTMENTS *392*
Suggested Readings *398*

13   Social and Cultural Trends   406

AN AGE OF MATERIALISM *406*
THE INCREASE OF CRIME *409*
THE GROWTH OF INTOLERANCE *411*
PROHIBITION *415*
CRITICS OF AMERICAN SOCIETY *416*
LITERATURE AND THE ARTS *418*
Suggested Readings *427*

14   Foreign Policy, 1921–1933   432

ISOLATION OR COOPERATION? *432*
Suggested Readings *454*

15 Herbert Hoover and the "Great Depression,"

1929–1933 458

THE ELECTION OF 1928 *458*
HERBERT HOOVER *464*
AGRICULTURAL RELIEF *466*
THE TARIFF *468*
THE WALL STREET CRASH AND THE ONSET OF THE
    DEPRESSION *470*
THE FIRST TWO YEARS OF THE HOOVER ADMINISTRATION *484*
THE ELECTION OF 1932 *492*
Suggested Readings *500*

Index 507

PART I THE HERITAGE OF THE NINETEENTH CENTURY AND THE EMERGING PROBLEMS OF THE TWENTIETH

Foreword

In 1789, when Washington took office as first President under the federal Constitution, the United States covered an area of about 800,000 square miles between the Atlantic Ocean and the Mississippi River and had a population of nearly 4 million. An overwhelming majority of the population was concentrated along the Atlantic Seaboard; settlers between the Mississippi and the Appalachians had to face the hostility of savage Indian tribes, the British in Canada, and the Spaniards in Louisiana. There were only six cities with more than 8,000 inhabitants,[1] and their combined population amounted to only 3 per cent of the total population of the republic. Shipowners in New England, New York, and Pennsylvania had grown rich on trade with Europe and the West Indies and were beginning to establish contacts with India and China, but American manufacturing was still insignificant, because the Industrial Revolution had not yet commenced. There were only three banks in the whole country,[2] and none of them did business outside the state in which it was located.

Methods of communication were primitive; roads were merely dirt tracks. To travel from Massachusetts to Georgia required at least a month. Agriculture was the normal occupation of at least nine-tenths of the

---

[1] Philadelphia, Boston, New York, Baltimore, Charleston, and Salem (Massachusetts).
[2] The Bank of North America (in Philadelphia), the Bank of New York, and the Bank of Massachusetts (in Boston).

population, and except among the planters of the southern states, it was practiced primarily for subsistence rather than for trade. The typical American of that era was an independent freeholder who produced almost all the necessities of life for himself and who was dependent upon marketing his crops locally for little more than the money needed for the payment of his taxes, the repayment of his debts, and the purchase of some luxury articles.

By the year 1900 the United States had grown in size and wealth with a rapidity unprecedented in history. Successive acquisitions from France, Spain, Great Britain, and Mexico had extended its territories westward as far as the Pacific, giving the republic a total area of more than 3 million square miles. Since every section of this vast country had been colonized, it was no longer possible to trace any continuous frontier line between inhabited and uninhabited areas. Meanwhile, through purchase (Alaska, 1867), occupation (Midway, 1867), annexation (Hawaii, 1898), and war with Spain, the United States had extended its sovereignty and interests throughout the Pacific, in the Caribbean, and as far north as the Arctic Ocean. In 1900, the population amounted to nearly 76 million. One-third of this population now lived in cities with more than 8,000 inhabitants, and there were nineteen cities each of which had more than 200,000 inhabitants, with a combined population of more than 11½ million. Nearly 200,000 miles of railroad had been built and, save for a very few lines, all of them were physically integrated into a national railway system. There were 10,382 banks. The application of science to technology and the consequent development of mining and manufacturing had created an industrial system with an extraordinary productivity and complexity. Agriculture was now the occupation of less than half the population, and the American farmer concentrated on raising staple crops for sale to the cities of America and Europe. There were more than half a million factories and workshops, which employed more than 5,300,000 workers and turned out products with an annual value of more than $13 billion. And the annual value of American foreign trade totaled nearly $2 billion. The national wealth—the total value of all property in the United States—was $88 billion, and the national income amounted to nearly $18 billion.

This vast growth had been accomplished without fundamentally changing American institutions or the American view of life from what they had been since the earliest days of the republic. A civil war had been fought to vindicate the authority of the federal union and to crush sectional independence. Nevertheless, the federal Constitution which had been drafted for the original thirteen states in 1787 had undergone only minor changes, and by the year 1913 thirty-five new states had been successfully incorporated into it. Americans still cherished the doctrines of freedom and equality proclaimed by their eighteenth-century predecessors; they still believed that society should encourage individual initiative, tolerate diversities of opinion, and allow no caste or class distinctions; they still felt that the United States had been destined to excel other nations in its devotion to democracy and in its youthful spirit of optimism and enterprise.

The material growth of the United States had, however, resulted in an economic and social structure fundamentally different from that of the eighteenth century. The industrial system had created a number of new problems which threatened, if ignored for too long, to undermine democratic institutions and to involve the country in dangerous and destructive conflicts. If the American people were to solve these problems without doing violence to American traditions, they would be required to display political talents of a high order.

The typical American of 1789 gained his livelihood from his own land by his own labor and was almost independent of the market. The typical American of 1900 was dependent for his livelihood upon a complex economic system which was international in scope and the workings of which were beyond the control of any individual or group of individuals. Any sudden change or interruption in the delicate mechanisms of the world market might result in large-scale distress and unemployment. A sudden fall in values on the New York Stock Exchange meant that factories throughout the country closed their gates; a growth in the agricultural production of Asia and South America meant that farmers in the United States were unable to pay their mortgage obligations. This economic insecurity was to be, in every industrialized nation, the most acute problem of the twentieth century. There was, however, no agreement among either economic experts or ordinary citizens as to what attitude should be adopted—whether industrial crises should be left to adjust themselves automatically, in accordance with the principles of laissez-faire economics, or whether governments should enforce some positive program of amelioration or control.

In the United States of 1789 there were no great extremes of wealth and poverty. With the exception of the Negro slaves, only a small fraction of the population was wholly without property, and there was no class of men so rich as to constitute a menace to democratic institutions.

By 1900, on the other hand, the United States seemed to many persons to be in danger of falling under the rule of a small oligarchy. The leaders who had created and organized the new industrial system had acquired great wealth and economic power and were able to exercise a dangerous degree of control over the institutions of government. At the other end of the social scale a large urban proletariat had developed, whose earnings were insufficient to give them an adequate standard of living. Meanwhile, in both the South and the West, the farmers, who were not receiving their fair share of the national income, believed that their economic difficulties were the result of privileges acquired by the big financiers and industrialists.

According to calculations made in 1890, one-eighth of the population owned seven-eighths of the wealth, and 1 per cent of the population owned more than did the other 99 per cent together. Champions of the existing order defended these conditions on the ground that wealthy industrialists were, by their enterprise and organizing ability, increasing the productivity of the economic system and thereby benefiting all classes. Reformers, on the other hand, regarded this inequality as inconsistent with American democratic ideals and believed that, if it remained uncorrected, the result would be a growth of bitter class conflicts.

In the United States of 1789 there was an apparently limitless supply of cheap land and undeveloped natural resources. For a century thereafter America had remained a country of opportunity, where an individual, by going west, might hope to acquire economic security. By 1900 most of the nation's agriculturally available lands and the most valuable mineral deposits had been transferred to private ownership; farming had become a precarious and often unprofitable occupation. Henceforth the people of the United States would be required to husband their surviving natural resources with a care which had not hitherto been considered necessary. Unless future generations were to be condemned to poverty, a constructive program of conservation must be enforced.

The United States of 1789 had few political and economic ties with other countries. Europe was six weeks' voyage distant; and if the United States developed its own manufacturing system and prevented any European interference with the affairs of the Western Hemisphere, it could hope to isolate itself from the Old World and thereby avoid destructive wars and alien political influences. By 1900 the United States had established important political and commercial connections with all parts of the world, both its farmers and its manufacturers exported an important proportion of their products, and American prosperity interlocked with that of Europe. Isolation was now impossible unless drastic changes were imposed upon the American economic system. Mechanical inventions were, moreover, bringing America steadily nearer to Europe and to the Far East: by the 1930's the Atlantic could be crossed within five days by sea and within twenty-four hours by air, and by radio and telegraph happenings in Europe became known in the United States a few minutes after they occurred. The United States was therefore compelled to play a more active role in international politics, for now its interests were intimately affected by the ambitions and conflicts of the European and Far Eastern powers.

The American people of 1789, in spite of the differences of interest and viewpoint between the southern and the northern states, were remarkably homogeneous. With the exception of some 757,000 Negroes, who had no political rights, Americans were predominantly Anglo-Saxon in race and Protestant in religion. They had been educated in the political philosophy of the English Whig tradition, and their political disputes were normally provoked by its application, not by any fundamental conflict of principle. With few exceptions, they spoke the same language, professed similar beliefs, and cherished similar ideals.

The United States of 1900, on the other hand, had become a melting pot containing representatives of almost every race in the world. More than 20 million immigrants had entered the country during the nineteenth century, and during the last two decades of that century an increasing proportion of them had come from the countries of eastern and southern Europe, whose political and religious traditions were very dissimilar to those of native-born Americans. The Protestant Anglo-Saxon tradition was still predominant, but its control was no longer undisputed. Although the new racial groups could immeasurably broaden and enrich American culture, their growth, not always welcomed by the descendants of the earlier immigrants, threatened to provoke racial and religious conflicts. A similar problem was presented by the emancipation of the Negroes, who had become legally free as a result of the Civil War but who continued to suffer from economic, educational, and social disabilities. Meanwhile the traditions of eighteenth-century America were being modified by the growth of urbanization. While rural America remained faithful to its old mores, new attitudes—rationalistic, skeptical, and libertarian—developed in the cities. Two cultures, one traditional and the other cosmopolitan, existed side by side; and it was becoming increasingly difficult for the adherents of one to understand or tolerate the other.

Suggested Readings

The number of books and articles on the history of the United States in the twentieth century is already very large and every indication points to its growing still larger. The purpose of the bibliographies at the end of each chapter is to suggest some of the more important works that bear on the subjects treated in the text, to indicate where the reader can go to carry on his investigation of a particular subject in greater detail, and to point out differing interpretations.

The standard bibliographical reference for the history of the United States is Henry P. Beers, ed., *Bibliographies in American History* (rev. ed., New York, 1942). Oscar Handlin, *et al.*, *The Harvard Guide to American History* (Cambridge, Mass., 1954) is the most recent general bibliography of American history and, for most purposes, supplants the one-time classic, Edward Channing, *et al.*, *Guide to the Study and Reading of American History* (rev. ed., Boston, 1921). A shorter and highly useful reference is the recent compilation of about 10,000 annotated titles on American history by Roy P. Basler, *et al.*, *A Guide to the Study of the United States of America* (Washington, D.C., 1960). Annual publications—books, articles, documents, etc.—are listed in Grace G. Griffin, *et al.*, *Writings in American History* (Princeton, N.J., and elsewhere, 1902–   ). Three specialized bibliographies which merit particular attention are Maurice F. Neufeld, *A Bibliography of Labor Union History* (Ithaca, N.Y., 1958), Edward E. Edwards, *Bibliography of the History of Agriculture in the United States* (Washington, D.C., 1930), and Henrietta M. Larson, ed., *Guide to Business History* (Cambridge, Mass., 1948). Since there is no general bibliography for the economic history of the United States, Miss Larson's *Guide* is especially useful, for it includes brief, critical evaluations of many works in economic history. Lorna M. Daniells, comp., *Studies in Enterprise* (Boston, 1957) and John G. B. Hutchins, "Recent Contributions to Business History: The United States," *The Journal of Economic History*, XIX (March 1959), 103–21, cite the most significant works to appear since the Larson *Guide*. A brief bibliographical essay on the most important works published on the economic history of the United States in the twentieth century between 1945 and 1959 is Thomas C. Cochran, "Recent Contributions to Economic History: The United States, the Twentieth Century," *The Journal of Economic History*, XIX (March 1959), 64–75. For foreign affairs and diplomacy the standard reference is Samuel F. Bemis and Grace G. Griffin, eds., *Guide to the Diplomatic History of the United States, 1775–1921* (Washington, D.C., 1935).

Edwin R. A. Seligman and Alvin Johnson, eds., *The Encyclopaedia of the*

Social Sciences (15 vols., New York, 1930–34) contains numerous articles pertinent to developments in America during the twentieth century. James T. Adams, ed., *Dictionary of American History* (5 vols., New York, 1940) and Richard B. Morris and Henry Steele Commager, eds., *Encyclopedia of American History* (rev. and enl. ed., New York, 1961) are convenient references. The former contains brief articles on numerous incidents, issues, and other developments; the latter lists chronologically the major events and the basic "facts" of American history, and also includes a few topical summaries on various subjects.

The lives and contributions of distinguished men and women are collected in Allen Johnson and Dumas Malone, eds., *Dictionary of American Biography* (22 vols., New York, 1928–44) and in two supplementary volumes. Together these volumes summarize the lives and activities of some 14,500 Americans. Oscar Handlin, ed., *The Library of American Biography* (Boston, 1954–) is a series of brief, readable, up-to-date biographies of important figures in American history. Biographical sketches of twentieth-century secretaries of state up to 1925 are collected in Samuel F. Bemis, ed., *The American Secretaries of State and Their Diplomacy* (10 vols., New York, 1927–29). Norman A. Graebner, ed., *An Uncertain Tradition: American Secretaries of State in the Twentieth Century* (New York, 1961) contains biographical sketches of the fourteen men who held the post from John Hay through John Foster Dulles.

New publications, book reviews, and important articles bearing on twentieth-century developments appear regularly in a number of journals. Among the most important are the following: *American Historical Review* (New York and elsewhere, 1895–); *Mississippi Valley Historical Review* (Cedar Rapids, Iowa, 1914–); *American Quarterly* (Minneapolis and elsewhere, 1949–); and *American Heritage* (New York, 1954–). The latter is a beautifully illustrated publication that appears six times a year. Also useful, though more specialized, are the *Journal of Economic History* (New York, 1941–); *Business History Review* (Boston, 1954–); *Agricultural History* (Chicago and elsewhere, 1910–); *Political Science Quarterly* (New York, 1886–); *Journal of Modern History* (Chicago, 1929–); *Journal of the History of Ideas* (Lancaster, Pa., 1940–) and numerous other regional journals, such as *The New England Quarterly* (Orono, Me., 1928–), *Pacific Historical Review* (Glendale, Calif., and elsewhere, 1932–), and the *Journal of Southern History* (Baton Rouge, La., and elsewhere, 1935–).

The most recent multivolume comprehensive history of the United States is Henry Steele Commager and Richard B. Morris, eds., *The New American Nation Series* (New York, 1954–). This set supplants the old-time classic of Albert B. Hart, ed., *The American Nation: A History* (26 vols., New York, 1904–8). An effort to cover comprehensively the nonpolitical developments of American life from the beginning to the outbreak of World War II is Arthur M. Schlesinger and Dixon Ryan Fox, eds., *A History of American Life* (13 vols., New York, 1927–48). The many volumes in Allen Johnson, ed., *The Chronicles of America* (50 vols., New Haven, Conn., 1918–21) have been brought down to 1945 by the addition of six supplementary volumes under the editorship of Allan Nevins (New Haven, Conn., 1950–51). Daniel J. Boorstin, ed., *The Chicago History of American Civilization* (Chicago, 1956–) is a new series of brief studies, some topical and others chronological, which, when completed, will cover the entire history of the American people. Four volumes published in 1957 and 1958 cover developments between 1885 and 1945. The set by the long-time political columnist of the New York *Herald Tribune*, Mark Sullivan, *Our Times* (6 vols., New York, 1926–35) is a sprightly account of the experiences of "an average American" from 1900 to 1925.

More specialized comprehensive histories in progress and pertinent to developments in the twentieth century include the last three volumes in Henry David, *et al.*, *The Economic History of the United States* (9 vols., New York, 1945–); Wendell H. Stephenson and E. Merton Coulter, eds., *A History of the South* (10 vols., Baton Rouge, La., and Austin, Tex., 1948–); and Sumner Welles and Donald C. McKay, eds., *The American Foreign Policy Library* (25 vols., Cambridge, Mass., 1945–). Each volume in the latter set discusses briefly the historical development of American policy and relations with one or more countries. An excellent analysis of the nature, developments, and influence of American economic thought from colonial times to 1933 is Joseph Dorfman, *The Economic Mind in American Civilization* (5 vols., New York, 1946–59).

There is no single collection of sources and documents devoted exclusively to the twentieth century, though many of the standard compilations contain some relevant material. Among the more useful and convenient ones are Henry Steele Commager, ed., *Documents of American History* (5th ed., New York, 1949); Ruhl J. Bartlett, ed., *The Record of American Diplomacy* (New York, 1950); Joseph T. Lambie and Richard V. Clemence, eds., *Economic Change in America: Readings in the Economic History of the United States* (Harrisburg, Pa., 1954).

An indispensable compilation of carefully prepared statistical information on many aspects of American society and its economy is U.S. Department of Commerce, Bureau of the Census, *Historical Statistics of the United States, 1789–1945* (Washington, D.C., 1954). See also the carefully prepared statistical summaries and critiques in U.S. Congress, Hearings Before the Joint Economic Committee, *Employment, Growth, and Price Levels* (Washington, D.C., 1960). A convenient reference for current statistical information is the annual volume of the U. S. Department of Commerce, Bureau of the Census, *Statistical Abstract of the United States.*

I

The State of the Nation in 1900:
Material Aspects

THE REGIONS OF THE UNITED STATES

The United States is a continental area rather than a single country; and its government, unlike the governments of almost all European nations, has never been entirely centralized. The various regions into which the country is divided have a common language and similar institutions, but they differ from one another in their geographical and economic characteristics and in the attitudes and values of their inhabitants. Political parties in the United States have always been coalitions of different groups from different regions, whose alliances have often been based on expediency or on tradition rather than on common principles; and political conflicts have defined themselves along regional lines at least as often as along class lines.

Since the establishment of the federal Union, however, there has been a strong trend toward centralization. The different regions have been drawn together by the building of the railroads, by the construction of a national telegraph and telephone system, by the growth of large-scale industries producing standardized commodities, by the spread of financial control by the banking institutions of the Northeast, by the migratory habits of the population, and in the twentieth century, by two great wars and a worldwide depression of unprecedented severity. The growth of economic integration has led to a corresponding, but slower, increase in the powers of the federal government. In 1789 the country was partially united by political ties, but the thirteen separate states had few economic bonds with one another. In 1900, on the other hand, the unity of the different sections was much greater economically than politically or psychologically.

The Industrial Middle West

In the nineteenth century the allied occupations of mining and manufacturing had become the most important part of the American economic system and, along with speculation in rural and urban real estate, the chief source of American wealth. Originally developed in the Northeast close to the Atlantic Seaboard, mining and manufacturing gradually moved into the middle-western region across the Appalachians. Important industries were still located in southern New England, New Jersey, and New York; but by 1900 the most important branches of American heavy industry were to be found along the western slopes of the Appalachians, extending from Pennsylvania south along the mountain ranges as far as Alabama, and west through the states of Ohio, Michigan, Indiana, and Illinois to the shores of the Great Lakes.

The character of this region was determined by its mineral deposits. Western Pennsylvania was the original center of oil production. In northeastern Pennsylvania, in the valleys of the Schuylkill and the Susquehanna, were 480 square miles of the hard, smokeless coal known as anthracite. By 1920 more than a million persons were concentrated in this region. Deposits of soft bituminous coal occurred throughout the whole Appalachian area from Pennsylvania down to Alabama and could often be dug out of hillsides without sinking mines; iron could be mined in the same areas. Pittsburgh, lying in the heart of the mining area, connected by river with the Gulf of Mexico and by canal with the Great Lakes, became in the later decades of the nineteenth century the chief center of heavy industry in the United States.

Toward the end of the century heavy industry began to spread southward, and Birmingham, Alabama, became another center of steel production. Meanwhile the richest iron deposits in the world had been discovered along the western shores of Lake Superior, in Minnesota, lying in ranges above the surface of the ground so that the ore could be shoveled into cars without any of the apparatus of mining. The exploitation of these ranges drew branches of the steel industry northward, industrial areas growing up closer to the Great Lakes at such places as Youngstown, Ohio, and Gary, Indiana. In the twentieth century another industry, the making of automobiles, grew to enormous proportions, and this, with its affiliate manufactures, centered at Detroit. Meanwhile Chicago had become the metropolis of the whole agricultural region which lay farther to the west; the greatest railroad terminal in the world and the principal marketing center of grain and cattle, it specialized in industries closely affiliated with farming, such as meat packing and the manufacture of agricultural implements.

By the end of the nineteenth century this middle-western region, which had grown with such overwhelming rapidity, was not only the heart of the new industrial economy; since the Civil War it had also largely dominated the politics of the country. Its economic development had given wealth and power to a group of industrialists who had, for the most part, started life without hereditary advantages and had risen to supremacy by their own ruthless energy, skill, and ambition. Closely allied to these industrial chieftains and similar to them in character and veiwpoint were the political leaders who controlled the Republican party in the Middle West; and from the accession of General Ulysses S. Grant until the assassination of President William McKinley (with the exception of the eight years of Grover Cleveland's two administrations), it was the Middle West which provided the country with its Presidents and which, in alliance with the GOP's eastern bosses, largely determined the policies of the nation's majority party.

At the same time, the laboring population of the Middle West was, in the later years of the nineteenth century, subjected in some areas to an industrial feudalism unparalleled elsewhere either in the United States or in western Europe. The mines and factories of Pennsylvania, Ohio, and Illinois were largely manned by immigrants from southern and eastern Europe. They composed a bewildering mixture of Czechs, Slovaks, Serbs, Croats, Slovenes, Ukrainians, Poles, and Russians, who spoke different languages, worshiped in different churches, and came from countries where their standards of living had often been very low. As a result of the handicaps of the workers and of the cooperation among the industrialists, the local government, and the police authorities, conditions in many of the mining and factory towns were often a travesty of American democratic ideals and institutions. And whenever the laboring population ventured to struggle for better conditions, the conflict was often violent and bloody.

The Agricultural Middle West

Adjacent to this industrial region, but very different from it, was the principal agricultural section of the country. With the westward gravitation of the American economy, agriculture had gone ahead of industry; and though large sections of all the eastern and middle-western states remained largely agricultural, the centers of agricultural production were, by the year 1900, west of the Mississippi River, with Iowa the richest agricultural state in the union. The agricultural region had four subdivisions: the corn belt stretched from Ohio west into Iowa; Wisconsin and Michigan were the chief dairy centers; a part of Kansas and Nebraska, narrowly restricted by climatic conditions, produced winter wheat; and Minnesota and the Dakotas produced spring wheat. Chicago, Minneapolis, St. Paul, St. Louis, Kansas City, Cincinnati, and Buffalo, the only cities found in this agricultural region, served as markets and distributing centers and specialized in meat packing and flour milling. But for the most part it was a region of small towns and rolling prairies, the monotony of which was almost unbroken by hill or forest.

The inhabitants of this vast area had a considerable uniformity of outlook. They were for the most part either of New England descent or of Scandinavian or German stock, with similar religious traditions and cultural traits. The typical farming unit of less than 150 acres was operated by a single family, often with the aid of a hired man and of the migratory laborers who came only for the harvest season. It was an area of a Protestantism which often became puritanical and of a democracy which was perhaps more deeply rooted in economic and social conditions than elsewhere in the United States. It prided itself on its devotion to American ideals. Since no part of the country had fewer direct economic or cultural ties with the rest of the world, in the twentieth century this region was the chief center of the demand for an isolationist foreign policy.

Its enrollment in the struggle to prevent any extension of slavery and to preserve the Union had caused this agricultural region to combine with the industrial sections in support of the Republican party; but after the slavery issue had been settled, agriculture derived few advantages from the combination. Republican policies were devoted primarily to the benefit of industry and finance; and the farmers felt themselves exploited by the railroads which transported their products, the merchants who bought those products, the industrialists who sold them machinery, and the bankers who loaned them money. After the Civil War there was never any permanent political realignment; but a series of waves of agrarian insurgency swept over the agricultural regions, some of which led to the formation of progressive blocs within the Republican party, while others threatened to put an end to Republican predominance. In the 1880's Kansas was particularly noted for a fanatical antagonism to big business. In the twentieth century Wisconsin became the chief example in the United States of progressive ideals translated into practical politics, and the spring wheat section of Minnesota and the Dakotas, where the farmers had to contend with so many forms of natural catastrophe—frost, drought, hail, rust, invasions of grasshoppers, and a long five-month winter—became a new home of insurgency.

The Northeast

With the growth of the country the chief sources of wealth had moved west, but the ownership and control of that wealth had largely remained in the East. By 1900 the centers of industry were in the Middle West, and the chief agricultural region was west of the Mississippi River; but financial predominance still belonged to the banking institutions of the Atlantic Seaboard cities. And as the industrial system developed, the powers of the eastern bankers tended to increase.

The northern and middle Atlantic Seaboard had been predestined to greatness by its location, which enabled it to control the flow of commerce between Europe and the Middle West; and early in the nineteenth century its leading cities—Boston, New York, Philadelphia, and Baltimore —had become rivals for supremacy. Victory rested finally with New York, as a result of its superb natural harbor at the mouth of the Hudson River, the building of the Erie Canal linking it with the Great Lakes, and subsequently its railroad connections with the West. Commercial supremacy was followed by financial and cultural leadership: after the Civil War New York began to surpass Boston and Philadelphia as the headquarters of banking, and to become the intellectual capital of the nation. By the end of the century it was the home of America's leading financiers and industrialists, and the center of numerous economic empires whose properties extended into every state in the Union. It was the headquarters also of the publishing business, of the chief aesthetic and intellectual organizations, and of the numerous instrumentalities by which public opinion might be influenced or controlled.

Scattered over the eastern states were agricultural sections, settled during the Colonial period, where the inhabitants had retained strongly marked traditions and characteristics. In the New England countryside much of the old Yankee spirit had survived; New England farmers were still hardworking, frugal, self-reliant, and taciturn. The whole New England region, however, had since the Civil War been decreasing in relative importance. Farming in this region had largely ceased to be a profitable occupation, and between 1880 and 1920 the acreage of cultivated land in New England was cut in half. Southern New England became the most highly urbanized area in America. Similar to rural New England in the conservatism of its inhabitants, though more prosperous, were the agricultural sections of upper New York State and New Jersey, while in the fertile valleys of central Pennsylvania the German communities which had been established early in the eighteenth century still lived in isolation from the modern world.

The great cities, however, dominated the whole northeastern region, and by the end of the nineteenth century they had become conglomerations of all the innumerable races and religions in the American melting pot. Important industries were still located along the seaboard, in spite of the fact that almost all the materials for them had to be imported from other sections. New England retained its supremacy in textiles, although there was increasing competition from the South; the cities of northern New Jersey specialized in silk, leather, and oil-refining; New York was the chief center of the clothing industry. Before the end of the nineteenth century, these and other industries began to attract millions of immigrants from Italy and eastern Europe and from French Canada, so that here, more than in any other section of the United States, the Anglo-Saxon and Protestant traditions of the eighteenth century seemed likely to be obliterated. In New England, by 1920, one-quarter of the population was foreign-born, and nearly two-thirds had at least one parent who had been born abroad. The immigrants did not attain social or financial equality with the old families, but immigrant and Catholic influences soon began to predominate in the city governments. In New York City the processes of the melting pot were even more rapid. The most cosmopolitan city in the world, it contained colonies of almost every ethnic group in existence. Restless, tolerant, and heterogeneous, New York epitomized all the newer forces in American life.

The South

The Middle West and the Northeast, devoted to industry, agriculture, and commerce and finance, were united by close economic ties and, to a large degree, by a common allegiance to the Republican party—an allegiance created by the Civil War and never fully broken, though sometimes threatened by subsequent disagreements. By contrast, the other sections of the United States—the South, the Rocky Mountain region, and the Far West—were less integrated into the economic and political structure of the country.

The eleven states which during the Civil War had composed the Confederacy, along with the three or four border states—together including nearly one-third of the area and nearly one-third of the population of the United States—differed markedly from every other part of the country. They were united by their bitter memories of the Civil War and of Reconstruction, by the poverty which had resulted from the war, by their preoccupation with the racial problem (about one-third of the population of the South was Negro), and by the common ancestry and traditions of their white inhabitants (in 1910 only 2.5 per cent of the population of the South was foreign-born).

The South contained several clearly marked subdivisions. The heart of the whole section and the location of its chief economic and racial problems was the cotton belt which stretched from Georgia and South Carolina westward into Texas. The states farther north practiced a more variegated agriculture and were less affected by the color question. Texas, an empire in itself, larger than, and potentially almost as rich as, any European nation except Russia, was as much western as southern in its psychology and economic conditions. The Appalachian and Ozark regions, making up parts of almost every southern state, had scarcely been touched by any changes since the beginning of the nineteenth century.

If agriculture in the Middle West was handicapped by being an individualistic economy in a society increasingly dominated by big corporations, agriculture in the South was suffering not only from this same disadvantage but also from the crushing damages, both material and psychological, which had been inflicted during the Civil War and the period of Reconstruction. Although southern leaders devoted themselves to rebuilding their society with an extraordinary energy, the South was to remain for a long period the victim of extreme poverty (due partly to its own social and cultural outlook and institutions) and of the cultural ills resulting from poverty.

Traditionally, the South was an agrarian section, putting the interests of agriculture above those of industry and priding itself on its gracious way of life and its freedom from the materialism and pecuniary standards which prevailed in the North. Defeat in war had, however, been followed by the decay of the southern tradition. Northern industrial corporations extended their operations to the South. At the same time, following the Reconstruction period, leadership in the South was assumed by men who abandoned the traditions of the plantation aristocracy and believed that the South should now adopt the business methods of the North. In the latter part of the nineteenth century, under this "Bourbon" rule, the South began rapidly industrializing—a process accompanied by the low wages, the child labor, and the close connections between government and business that had characterized the earlier stages of the Industrial Revolution elsewhere.

A majority of the southern population continued, however, to be agricultural; and they suffered, especially in the cotton belt, from a poverty rivaling that of the peasants of backward eastern European and Asiatic nations. Not only were the southern farmers, both white and Negro, exploited by the southern bankers, merchants, and landlords who had taken power after Reconstruction, but all classes in the South were the common victims of the results of the war—the destruction of the southern economy in the war, northern control of the federal government and of industry and transportation after the war, and the economic weaknesses of the system of cotton production itself. The poverty of the rural South meant, in turn, that it was severely handicapped with respect to health and public education. Any drastic reformation was rendered difficult by the pervasive and apparently insoluble problem of race. The white population of the South was largely determined to keep the Negro in subordination. And though the decade of the 1890's saw a widespread agrarian revolt against "Bourbon" control, the belief of most white people in the South that their racial unity and social institutions must be preserved made any substantial reorganization of southern society impossible.

The Rocky Mountain Region

Socially, the South differed markedly from the Northeast and the Middle West, but geographically the main dividing line in the United

States was not that along which the Civil War had been fought but that which divided all the eastern sections from the West. Running through the Dakotas, Nebraska, Kansas, Oklahoma, and Texas was the line which separated the agricultural lands of the East from the arid West. Here, for the first time, the American settler in his progress across the continent met an environment which demanded fundamental changes in his economic methods. The plantation and the homestead were both unadapted to a country where the average rainfall was less than twenty inches a year.

Although the region of the Great Plains, the Rocky Mountains, and the western plateaus beyond the Rockies made up nearly 30 per cent of the total area of the United States, in 1900 it had only a little more than 2 per cent of the population, and this proportion did not greatly increase during the next forty years. Successful agriculture, necessary for a substantial population growth, required larger farms than the 160-acre homestead which settlers had become accustomed to in other regions, and it required also a collective planning of irrigation, such as was alien to the laissez-faire individualism of nineteenth-century Americans. A number of homesteaders, tempted by an occasional year of heavy rainfall, had attempted farming in the Great Plains, but with disastrous results. Throughout the whole region, the Mormons in Utah, thanks to a wise regulation of water rights, were almost the only white people who had developed a successful agriculture.

Except in Utah this was mainly a country of cattle ranches and mining camps. The 1880's were the great age of cattle breeding, when herds could be driven almost freely across the plains from Texas as far as the Canadian border, and when the cowboy, borrowing his costume and his way of life from Mexico and living with a picturesqueness and a spaciousness rare in the annals of the Anglo-Saxon pioneer, won for himself a permanent place in American legend. Subsequently, barbed wire put an end to the open range, and overproduction, overcropping of the grass, and the severe winter of 1886–87 ruined many of the cattle owners, though much of the country between the Great Plains and the Pacific was still devoted to cattle and sheep.

The other chief occupation of this region was the mining of silver, gold, copper, and lead. Exploitation of the mineral wealth of the western plateaus began during the Civil War, and prospectors, particularly in the silver mines of Nevada, occasionally became millionaires. But some of the mines were quickly exhausted; and ghost towns, built within a few months and deserted almost as rapidly, became a characteristic feature of the mining regions. The workers in these western mines were a nomadic people, often without family ties and habituated to the violence and the occasional lawlessness which flourished in this sparsely settled country. Their labor organizations, unlike those of the industrial East, were easily converted to revolutionary doctrines.

The Pacific Coast

In contrast with the East, almost all the West was arid—an aridity which culminated in the desert of Arizona, where the rainfall, over an area of nearly seventy thousand square miles, averaged less than three inches a year. The Indian tribes who still lived on the southern plateaus in New Mexico and Arizona had achieved a better permanent adaptation to their environment than had the more recently arrived Europeans. Close to the Pacific, however, along both sides of the coast ranges, water was more plentiful, although artificial irrigation was usually necessary; and the population of these areas, first settled by citizens of the United States in the 1840's, continued to grow rapidly.

California, after the decline of its gold production in the 1850's, found a more permanent basis for prosperity in fruit and vegetable farming. The coastal plain and the Imperial Valley east of the mountains in southern California, and the Great Valley in northern California, were as intensively cultivated as any part of the United States. Land ownership in the two valleys was monopolized by a few individuals and corporations—a relic of the Spanish heritage; and the work was performed by tenant farmers and by migratory laborers, many of whom were Japanese, Chinese, Hindu, or Mexican. The exploitation of agricultural labor and the rivalry between white and oriental farmers created a complex agrarian problem peculiar to California. By the turn of the century and increasingly thereafter, German, French, Italian, and other European immigrants acquired farmlands and cultivated more and more of the state's grape, fruit, and vegetable crops.

Meanwhile the state was becoming famous for its climate, and in the twentieth century hundreds of thousands of retired farmers and businessmen throughout the nation chose it as the home of their old age. California was at once the end of that march to the West—begun three hundred years earlier at Jamestown and Plymouth—and the beginning, perhaps, of a new historic process which would make the Pacific the chief center of world civilization. Here everything was grandiose and both the idealisms and the eccentricities of the American people assumed exaggerated colors.

In the Pacific Northwest there was more sobriety. Washington and Oregon had a climate closely resembling that of northwestern Europe, the original home of the majority of the American people. Those states had been settled democratically on the homestead principle. Potentially, through the development of water power, this was one of the richest areas in America, but in 1900 it could still consider itself as the last frontier. Prosperous farming regions were being developed in the Columbia basin, around Puget Sound in Washington, and in the Willamette Valley in Oregon. But lumbering, the first stage in the exploitation of virgin country, continued into the twentieth century to be the chief business of the region.

THE AGE OF THE CORPORATION

More than any previous epoch in history, the nineteenth century was a period of rapid change, especially in the economic field; and the structure of American society was, in certain respects, radically different in 1900 from what it had been in 1789. Individualistic private property and small-scale production had steadily decreased in importance, and economic power had been acquired by vast corporations, each of which was owned by thousands of stockholders and gave employment to thousands of workers. By the end of the nineteenth century these great aggregations of capital had acquired a dominant position in American economic life. In 1900 two-thirds of all manufacturing was done by corporations; and by 1960 the proportion had increased to more than nineteen-twentieths. Just as in Europe the twelfth and thirteenth centuries were the age of feudalism and the seventeenth and eighteenth centuries were the age of absolutism, so in the United States the twentieth century will probably go down in history as the age of the corporation.

The characteristic feature of the new economic system was the mass production of standardized commodities. In place of small factories producing mainly for local markets, there developed large industrial organizations turning out goods in quantities sufficient for a nationwide market. This was made possible by new scientific inventions, by the growth of mechanization, and by the discovery of new sources of energy, water power giving way to steam and later to oil and electricity. Every effort was made to develop more efficient and more economical methods of production. Industrialists encouraged scientific research and began finally to organize private research departments of their own, careful studies were made of methods for economizing labor, and the division of labor and the building of machinery with interchangeable parts were carried to almost fantastic extremes.

The development of the corporation system began in the Northeast as early as the beginning of the nineteenth century, but until after the Civil War its growth in other areas of the country was impeded by the lack of a national market and the opposition of the two agrarian sections, the South and the West. The war, however, gave supremacy to the North, and the close of hostilities was followed by a very rapid growth of industry. Industrialists enjoyed the support of a government which protected them both from opposition at home and from foreign competition. They found it easy to obtain labor, as a result of large-scale immigration from Eurpoe. They were often able to borrow capital from European investors. They could exploit the enormous natural resources of a continent still largely undeveloped. And for the sale of their products they had a larger internal market than any other industrialized nation in the world.

A corporation was, in theory, a cooperative enterprise in which ownership was divided among a number of stockholders, and management was entrusted to their elected representatives. Actually, however, most of the big industrial combinations of the post-Civil War period were created and dominated by single individuals, and it was not until after they had died or retired that the corporation passed beyond the stage of personal rule. Before the Civil War the chief sources of wealth had been foreign trade and the ownership of real estate. After the war the immense opportunities for industrial development were seized by a group of ambitious entrepreneurs—such men as Rockefeller in oil, Carnegie and Frick in steel, Vanderbilt, Hill, and Harriman in railroads, McCormick in agricultural machinery, Havemeyer in sugar, Duke in tobacco—some of whom had started life without hereditary advantages. They came to constitute a new plutocracy, whose wealth quickly surpassed that of the older mercantile and landowning aristocracies. Their less successful fellow-citizens were dazzled by their triumphs but alarmed by their newly-found power.

There were considerable variations in the methods by which these men achieved supremacy as well as in their standards of economic morality.

Some of them, like Andrew Carnegie and John D. Rockefeller, were genuine industrial entrepreneurs, whose wealth came initially from the efficiency with which they organized production, although it was subsequently enlarged through diversified investments. Others were primarily financiers, who bought control over industries which others had created and who built their fortunes by combining corporations into more powerful units and by manipulating stock prices to their private advantage. All of them were alike, however, in the ruthlessness with which they sought power and crushed opposition, in their conviction that society had no right to interfere with their activities and that any methods, however unscrupulous, might justifiably be adopted for their protection, and

Three representatives of the concentration of economic power and the age of the corporation at the turn of the century. Left to right, Charles F. Steele, a brilliant corporation lawyer who became a partner in Morgan's banking firm; James J. Hill (center), the builder of the Great Northern Railway; and George F. Baker, the head of the First National Bank of New York, a powerful financial institution specializing in large corporate accounts. (Brown Brothers)

in their belief that the pursuit of wealth was a noble activity, beneficial to society as well as to themselves. This attitude was an expression of the dominant ethos of nineteenth-century American civilization, derived partly from the Puritanism which had condemned pleasure and extravagance and had declared that devotion to one's work was pleasing to God, and partly from the doctrines of laissez-faire economics which saw in the enlightened self-interest of each individual an instrument for promoting the common interest of all. These doctrines received new confirmation after the Civil War from the social philosophy expounded by the Yale sociologist and economist William Graham Sumner, who applied to economic life many of the ideas originally set forth by Charles Darwin in his *The Origin of Species* (1859). According to this "social Darwinism" the biological principles of survival were equally applicable to the operation of the economic system.

The building of huge industrial corporations and the bitter competitive battles which characterized the struggles of the entrepreneurs to achieve wealth and power were accompanied by an increase in the authority of the investment bankers, most of whom were located either in New York or Boston. The investment bankers undertook to provide capital for industry by managing the sale of stocks—a function industrialists could not easily undertake themselves at a period when a large proportion of the capital was supplied by European investors. And in order to protect the interests of the stockholders, the bankers gradually began to assume some degree of supervision over the management of corporations, and in cases of bankruptcy, to undertake the responsibility for the necessary reorganization. Banking firms, particularly the most powerful of them, the House of Morgan, began to be represented on the directorates of an increasing number of railroads and manufacturing corporations; and this common banking supervision by means of "interlocking" directors was an important factor in checking competition and bringing about what the bankers described as a "community of interest."

Corporations and the Government

The growth of the big corporations would have been impossible if they had not received legal protection and governmental assistance. The American Constitution had been planned largely for the protection of property rights, in accordance with the eighteenth-century theory that life, liberty, and property were the three natural rights of man and that the arbitrary

deprivation of any one of them was tyranny. A series of judicial interpretations subsequently enlarged the conception of property rights, giving
to corporations the same protection as to individuals and defining any
drastic government regulation of corporate business as a violation of
property rights. The growth of large-scale corporations could thus take
place within a legal framework which had originally been created for
the security of individual property owners.

The immunity of business from political interference acquired added
justification from the economic theory of laissez faire. This theory, first
elaborated by Adam Smith and subsequently built into a philosophical
system by Herbert Spencer, whose writings had an enormous influence
in the United States, declared that the mechanisms of the free market,
regulated by the interplay of supply and demand, would guide the activities of each individual into the channels where they would be socially
most useful. The doctrine of laissez faire was used by American businessmen to justify their freedom from political interference; continuous progress, they declared, was dependent upon unchecked freedom for individual
enterprise. The successful entrepreneur must be protected from the envy
of the poorer classes in the community, who lacked the industry and
ability needed for acquiring wealth and who sought compensation for
their economic failure through political action.

In reality, however, American businessmen never adopted the doctrine
of laissez faire completely or consistently; they used it as an instrument
for repelling interference and opposition. The real attitude of American
business was that it was the function of government to assist and encourage
economic development. The prevalent belief was that if business entrepreneurs enjoyed freedom and protection, the benefits of their activities
would percolate down to all sections of the population. The correct
method of improving the condition of the workers and of other under-
privileged classes was not to legislate directly for their benefit but to
encourage business expansion.

A corporation was an artificial creation that came into existence through
the granting of a charter by the government. Under the American federal
system, however, it was the states and not the federal government which
gave corporation charters, although after a corporation had been created
it could do business throughout the Union and enjoyed the protection of
the federal Constitution. In the 1880's there was considerable alarm at
the growth of monopoly, so that a number of states passed antitrust laws
limiting the powers granted through corporation charters. On the other

hand, the state of New Jersey deliberately altered its corporation laws in order to encourage business entrepreneurs to apply for New Jersey charters. This step was taken at the suggestion of James B. Dill, who pointed out that the state could increase its revenues and solve its financial difficulties by going into the business of selling charters. Henceforth a group of businessmen could obtain a New Jersey charter for almost any purpose and with very few restrictions in return for payment of a fee of twenty cents for every thousand dollars of capitalization.

In the establishment of freedom for business enterprise two amendments to the Constitution, the fifth and the fourteenth, were of particular importance. The Fifth Amendment prohibited the federal government from depriving individuals of life, liberty, or property except by due process of law, while the Fourteenth Amendment, enacted after the Civil War nominally to protect the Negro population in the South, extended the same prohibition to the state governments. Judicial interpretation of the Fourteenth Amendment, beginning in the year 1886, extended the due process clause, originally intended merely as a ban on confiscation, to cover any regulation of corporations which might prevent them from earning what the judges considered to be a reasonable profit.

The same purpose was secured also through judicial interpretations of the commerce clause in the Constitution. According to the Constitution, the federal government might regulate interstate commerce, but commerce which was not interstate remained, it was implied, under the control of the state governments. A very narrow judicial definition of the regulatory powers given to the federal government coupled with the fact that state governments were unable effectively to control corporations manufacturing products for a nationwide market, created a borderland between federal and state authority in which industrial corporations seemed able to enjoy almost complete independence.

Industrial corporations not only enjoyed legal protection; they also expected and obtained direct assistance from the federal government. The tariff, raised during the Civil War to increase revenues and left high in spite of treasury surpluses after the war, protected American industry from foreign competition and, by enabling corporations to charge higher prices, acted as an indirect subsidy. The tariff was a violation of the rules of laissez-faire economics; but economists who insisted that laissez faire should be applied consistently and that free trade should therefore be established were regarded by most businessmen with almost as much hostility as were the advocates of government ownership or control. The federal government had at its disposal, moreover, all the natural resources of the undeveloped West, and until the end of the nineteenth century the dominant idea was that these resources should be transferred to private ownership quickly and on generous terms. Homesteads were given freely to farmers; but the major part of the mineral and timber resources of the West became the property of corporations, partly through gifts to the transcontinental railroads and partly through lax administration of the homestead regulations.

The Decline of Competition

In the nineteenth century the majority of the American people believed in freedom for business enterprise, but they believed also in the preservation of competition. According to the laissez-faire doctrine, only constant competition could provide a stimulus for economic growth and guarantee the consumer against unjustly high prices. The growth of corporations led necessarily, however, to a decrease in competition. The need for aggregations of capital large enough to finance the building of the new large-scale machinery caused some industrial units to combine with one another, while others were driven into bankruptcy by cutthroat price cutting. As the economic system developed, industrial organizations became larger and fewer, and the processes of combination seemed to be leading toward the creation of a few great monopolies which would enjoy absolute power over large areas of American life. Most businessmen disliked competition, which exposed them to the dangers of price wars, whereas by combining they could keep prices high and thereby increase their profits. With the decrease in the number of units in any branch of industry, combinations became proportionately easier to arrange.

Combinations were effected in a number of different ways. Several corporations might be completely merged into one large corporation. Industrialists might make pooling and price agreements with one another, dividing the market and charging the same prices. A number of corporations might transfer their stock to a small committee, which was to hold it as trustees for the stockholders. (This device, invented in 1882 by the lawyers of Standard Oil, led to the original trust, though the word *trust* was later applied, more loosely, to any industrial combination.) A single holding company, dominated by one individual or group of partners, might own a majority of the stock in a number of other corporations. One banking firm might secure sufficient power over several industrial corporations to enforce agreement and "community of interest." Interlocking directorates might place different corporations under the control of the same individuals. Or one corporation might acquire such a dominant position in a particular industry that it could dictate policies to its competitors and threaten them with a price war if they refused to comply.

It could be argued that the decline of competition was economically beneficial, that numerous small competing industrial units could not serve the public as effectively as could a few corporations. But these large-scale corporations did not always have sufficient inducements to share the benefits of combination with the consumer. The decline of competition meant that there was no longer automatic control over the price system; combination often made it possible for corporations to exploit the consumer through high prices. The evils of this situation were, moreover, intensified during periods of economic depression. Whereas competitive industries had to maintain production and cut their prices, the big corporations tended to maintain their prices and to restrict production, a policy which, by causing greater unemployment, increased the length and severity of the depression.

Public opinion was, in general, opposed to combination, the most vocal opponents of it being the small-scale producers who had to compete with the large corporations; and beginning in 1890, when the Sherman Antitrust Act was passed, the federal government tried to preserve competitive conditions. Effective trustbusting, however, presented many problems. Some economic enterprises, such as the railroads and the public utilities that supplied electricity and telephone and telegraph services, were natural monopolies, where competition would involve wasteful duplication of equipment. Since large-scale production appeared to be economically desirable in most branches of industry, it was difficult to decide at what point the disadvantages of combination began to outweigh the advantages of the increase in size. Furthermore, when an industry had passed under the control of a small number of powerful corporations, legal prohibitions of combination became almost impossible to enforce, because it was easy for corporation managers to make private price agreements with one another which were beyond the reach of the law.

The Growth of Inequality

The building of the corporations was accompanied by a number of financial malpractices. By legal theory, a corporation was the common property of its stockholders, but in actuality the average small stock-holder was incapable of exercising any effective supervision over corporation policies. In the nineteenth century most corporations were dominated by individuals, who were apt to manipulate the finances of the institution for their own personal advantage. This domination might be secured through outright ownership of a majority of the stock, through such a wide diffusion of stock ownership that the various small stockholders were unable to unite in the protection of their interests, or through "pyramiding," building a structure of holding companies by which an individual might control one relatively small corporation which owned a majority of the stock in some larger corporation, which, in turn, might own stock in another still larger corporation. Thus, corporation directors could often secure for themselves an exorbitant share of the profits of the business by, for example, voting themselves excessive salaries or forming independent companies owned wholly by themselves, from which the corporations they directed would then proceed to buy commodities at excessive prices.

The most prevalent of financial abuses, and the most far-reaching in its consequences, was the watering of stock. When several small industrial units were merged into one large corporation, the owners who were being bought out would frequently receive an excessive price for their properties and the bill would be paid by increasing the capitalization of the new corporation and persuading the general public to buy the newly issued stocks. It became customary to fix the capital value of a new corporation in terms not of the real cost of its properties but of the profits which it might be expected to make. As Andrew Carnegie once expressed it, "they throw cats and dogs together and call them elephants." Thus, unscrupulous financiers made gains at the expense of the small investors, whose stocks were decreased in value, and ultimately of the consuming public, whose purchases created the dividends which the newly created stocks were expected to earn.

This financial buccaneering, which usually conformed to the letter of the law but occasionally crossed the line from legal to criminal, was perhaps the most spectacular feature in the building of the large corporations. But in spite of the indignation it provoked, it was by no means the most important of the problems created by the new economic structure. To a large degree it was a symptom of growing pains, an accompaniment of rapid economic development, which ceased after an industry had reached its appropriate size and become stabilized. Questions of greater permanent importance were presented by the increase of class and regional inequalities.

The growth of large-scale industry made it increasingly difficult for even the more ambitious and enterprising of the workers to achieve economic independence. Urban society in the United States began becoming stratified along class lines, with a clear line of demarcation between the salaried or property-owning business classes and the propertyless working class.

American society was also divided along sectional lines. Ownership and control of the big corporations was usually concentrated in the Northeast, even when their material properties and equipment were in the South or the West; and the development of corporate industry and of the powers of the investment bankers increased the relative wealth of the Northeast at the expense of that of other sections of the country. The privileged position of the Northeast, due originally to its priority in industrial and financial development, was strengthened after the Civil War by the railroads, whose freight rates tended to discriminate against the South and the West, and by certain policies of the federal government —in particular, by the tariff. The exploitation of the South and the West by northeastern industry and finance resulted in considerable disparities in the wealth and living standards of the different sections. By the 1930's sixteen northeastern and middle-western states, with 53 per cent of the population and only 21.2 per cent of the area of the United States, owned at least 80 per cent, and probably more than 90 per cent, of the total wealth of the country. According to the census of 1930, their share of the national income amounted to 66 per cent. The average northerner had nearly twice as much in bank deposits as the average westerner, and more than five times as much as the average southerner. After 1930, however, economic trends, combined with the policies of the New Deal, led to a reduction in these sectional disparities. By 1960 the sixteen northeastern and midwestern states contained 49 per cent of the total population, and their share of the national income had dropped to 53 per cent.

Every decade gave the big corporation a more commanding position in American economic life. The individual entrepreneurs who played the dominant role in the later years of the nineteenth century had no comparable successors in the industries they had created; the descendants who inherited their wealth tended to become a leisured *rentier* class, divorced from the actual management of industry. After a corporation had been built, it usually became an impersonal institution, controlled by a kind of corporation bureaucracy which tended to be self-perpetuating and to acquire an *esprit de corps* and an institutional loyalty of its own.

The giant corporation of the twentieth century, with its array of stock-holders, directors, salaried executives, technicians, and wage earners, was a kind of economic empire, an *imperium in imperio*, endowed by American constitutional law with a semi-independence of the political authorities and enjoying enormous powers over both its own employees and the general public. The position of these leviathans was in some ways comparable to that of the big feudal principalities in the kingdoms of the Middle Ages. And one of the primary problems of twentieth-century American society was to find some method of ensuring their subordination to democratic principles and to the interests of the general public.

THE CONDITION OF
THE WORKING CLASS

At the end of the nineteenth century the number of wage earners in industry, mining, transportation, and commerce was about 15 million. Industry was employing an increasing number of women, whose average wage was considerably less than that received by men, and there were 1.7 million child workers under sixteen years of age. The increase in the national income resulted in a rise in the living standards of the workers, but their gains were much slower and less spectacular than those of the business classes.

The general movement of both prices and wages was upward, with wages usually rising somewhat more quickly. In 1899, hours of labor averaged about nine and a half a day. Early in the twentieth century the workers in a number of different industries obtained an eight-hour day, but this reduction was by no means general.

These gains in wage and hour conditions were offset by a number of disadvantages. Work, though concentrated in a shorter period, was becoming more intense. The function of the average factory worker was to tend a machine, the movement of which could be speeded up by the factory management, and his pace was no longer governed by the natural rhythms of the human body. Industrial accidents had become frequent, especially in mining and transportation.

The workers had no security of employment, and the impersonal processes of the economic system, with its alternation between booms and depressions, might at any moment deprive him of the wages which were his sole source of livelihood. During the economic crisis of the 1890's, for example, at least one-sixth of the working class were unemployed. The growth of absentee ownership, with factory managers becoming the salaried agents of stockholders, meant that there was no longer much personal contact or sense of mutual obligation between employer and and employee. The workers were, moreover, crowded into the slum tenements of the rapidly growing cities, where poverty meant far more serious deprivations than in rural areas.

The dominant belief in the nineteenth century was that the state had no responsibility for the welfare of the working class. The owners of industry should have absolute power to hire and dismiss workers as they chose and to decide what wages they could afford to offer. The standard of living of the working class should be regulated by the law of supply and demand. It was assumed that the processes of the economic system would sufficiently reward honesty, industry, sobriety, and intelligence; and the comforting idea that workers were themselves to blame for any misfortunes which they suffered and that even in times of depression deserving men could always find employment was very prevalent. This attitude was applied not only to unemployment but also to industrial accidents. By common law doctrine, generally accepted until the twentieth century, an employer had no responsibility for injuries suffered by his workers if they were due to the ordinary hazards of the occupation, to contributory negligence, or to negligence on the part of fellow-workers.

Such an economic philosophy was too contrary to the realities of the situation to be accepted permanently. The interplay of supply and demand would not result in economic justice unless there was a reasonable degree of equality between the buyer and the seller of a commodity. There was no such equality between the employer who bought labor power and the individual worker who sold it. Unsanitary slum areas and low standards of living meant, moreover, that the health of all classes in the community might be endangered and the vitality of future generations undermined. Despite the belief of property owners that each individual should be held responsible for himself, the welfare of all social groups was, in the last resort, interdependent. Before the end of the nineteenth century a growing realization of this had caused a few states, most notably Massachusetts, to pass laws limiting hours of labor for women and children and prohibiting dangerous machinery and fire hazards. Such legislation was, however, always liable to be declared unconstitutional, as a violation of the rights of property and of freedom of contract, by both federal and state courts. The United States remained, in general, two or three generations behind most of the European countries in its acceptance of the principle of social responsibility for individual welfare.

The Growth of Trade Unionism

It was to be expected that the American workers, like those of the European countries, would organize trade unions to protect their interests and provide for collective bargaining over wages and hours. The growth of trade unionism in the United States was, however, slower than in Europe, so that until the 1930's the proportion of workers who belonged to unions remained considerably less. There were a number of reasons for this difference. Working-class wages and standards of living, although very low, were generally higher in America than in any European nation. Most American industrialists were, moreover, bitterly opposed to unionism. Since they regarded it as an interference with the rights of property and represented it as a device by which agitators extracted dues from the workers and thus became salaried union officials—an attitude generally shared by the courts—they used methods of both force and conciliation to crush the unions.

The organization of the working class was hampered also by numerous racial, linguistic, and religious barriers and by differences of interest between skilled and unskilled labor. The stream of immigrants from Europe, continuing until World War I, was always liable to sweep away any trade union established among unskilled workers who could easily be replaced. Much of the immigration from eastern Europe in the late nineteenth century was more docile than the earlier immigration from northern Europe and the British Isles and less responsive to union organizers. For these reasons almost the only unions which achieved any permanent successes were those representing skilled workers, which were able to acquire a strong bargaining position by restricting their membership to specialized crafts.

A new epoch in American labor history began in 1886 when some of these unions organized the American Federation of Labor (AFL). The guiding spirit in the new organization was Samuel Gompers, an immigrant from England, of Dutch-Jewish descent, who acted as president every year except one until his death in 1924. Gompers and his friend Adolph Strasser controlled the cigar-makers union, where for some years they had been putting into practice their belief in "pure and simple" trade unionism. This theory held that unions should concentrate on winning immediate gains in wages and hours and should gain strength by strict discipline and the steady accumulation of financial reserves. As Strasser told a Senate committee in 1883: "We are all practical men. We have no ultimate ends. We are going on from day to day. We are fighting only for immediate objectives—objects which can be realized in a few years."

The new unionism insisted on centralized control by salaried officials, prohibited strikes not sanctioned by the central authorities, and required a regular payment of dues to build up strike funds and make possible the payment of sickness, accident, and death insurance benefits. The AFL had a steady growth, winning the adherence of every important union except the four railroad brotherhoods. But although its membership grew frow 548,321 in 1900 to 2,020,671 in 1914, it never included more than a relatively small proportion of the American working class.

The primary object of every AFL union was to induce the employers to recognize the union as the collective bargaining agent for the workers. The unions attempted to achieve this object by strikes, accompanied by picketing, and also by urging consumers to boycott firms which did not employ union labor. Most AFL unions hoped to establish a "closed shop," which meant that a person who was not a member of the union could not work in the factory in question and, hence, that any abandonment of collective bargaining would be impossible. Employers, on the other hand, demanded the preservation of the "open shop," which they often preferred to call euphemistically the "American plan." The AFL disliked strikes, except when they were necessary to win union recognition, and it declared itself opposed to the use of any form of violence. This repudiation of violence was, however, not always respected by some of its constituent unions.

Unlike the trade union movement in Europe, the AFL never joined forces permanently with any political organization. It formally repudiated socialism in 1894, and because so many of its leaders and nearly half of its members were Roman Catholics, the Church's antisocialist position was reflected in the federation's political and economic activities. Gompers and his leading lieutenants accepted the capitalist system, but at the same time they insisted that there were inevitable conflicts of interest between the capitalist class and the working class. The political program of the union was to fight for social reforms which would be of benefit to the workers. In the early 1900's it declared that its policy was to support its friends, whether in the Republican or Democratic parties, and to punish its enemies. In practice, however, the AFL's leadership was not as nonpartisan as Gomper's statement suggests: though some of its leaders continued to support the Republicans, after 1906 the AFL's "top level" became increasingly committed to the Democratic party.[1]

The AFL had considerable success in winning benefits for its members in the form of higher wages, the eight-hour day, and establishment of collective bargaining. Representing, however, only the "labor aristocracy," it had little concern for the welfare of the masses of unskilled workers who remained outside its ranks. Its closed shop policy, although necessary as a safeguard of collective bargaining, could easily lead to abuses, since it meant that union officials virtually had the right to supply factories with new workers when they were needed and to decide who could, or could not, obtain employment. The AFL was, in fact, endeavoring to establish a series of labor monopolies—a policy exemplified also in the attempt of certain unions which had won the closed shop to restrict their membership by means of strict apprenticeship rules and high initiation fees. Moreover, the officials of the AFL, receiving large salaries and elevated above the class to which they had originally belonged, tended to develop into a privileged bureaucracy, whose interests were in some respects different from those of the workers whom they supposedly represented. A labor monopoly could thus be as opposed to the general welfare as could a capitalist monopoly.

After the rise of the AFL a number of employers were willing to accept collective bargaining, realizing that the workers had genuine grievances and that, if they could voice their grievances through a responsible trade union organization, the result might be an increase in industrial efficiency. A majority of the big industrialists, however, including the directors of all the basic mass-production industries, remained uncompromisingly opposed to unionism.

The powers of the unions were, moreover, narrowly restricted by the courts, particularly through the use of the injunction to limit or prohibit picketing and to forbid any public appeal to boycott firms employing nonunion labor. An injunction was a court order forbidding certain actions on the ground that they would cause loss or damage to individuals of a kind which could not afterwards be remedied through legal procedure, and persons who disobeyed an injunction were liable to prosecu-

[1] Marc Karson, *American Labor Unions and Politics, 1900–1918* (Carbondale, Ill., 1959).

tion for contempt of court and were not allowed the right to a jury trial. The broad uses to which the injunction could be put were shown in the Bucks' Stove and Range Company case of 1907 and the Danbury Hatters' case of 1908, in which the officials of the AFL were forbidden to include these firms in their "We Don't Patronize" list or to make any reference either in print or by word of mouth to their refusal to employ union labor.

In 1900 the labor movement counted 791,000 members, only a small part of the 15 million nonagricultural workers in the United States. About 60 per cent of the unionized workers under the jurisdiction of the eighty-two unions affiliated with the AFL; the others were members either of the conservative railroad brotherhoods or of small, unaffiliated unions, several of which espoused radical or revolutionary ideas. A spectacular, though temporary, increase in union membership between 1900 and 1904 (from 791,000 to 2,000,000) was accompanied by much hostility and bitterness between workers and employers and attracted national attention; and the vigor and determination with which unions and workers sought to secure better wages and hours and recognition of the right to bargain collectively resulted in numerous work stoppages. Between 1900 and 1903 the number of these stoppages increased from 1,839 to 3,648. These figures established a new record, although the late nineteenth century had seen bitter labor struggles.

THE PROBLEMS OF AGRICULTURE

The decades after the Civil War brought a remarkable development in the country's agriculture. The colonization of the West and the application of science to farming resulted in a great increase in production and a corresponding decrease in the need for human labor. This agricultural progress, without which the growth of industry would have been impossible, did not, however, bring prosperity to the farmers who were responsible for it; on the contrary, the farm population suffered during the later years of the nineteenth century, and again after World War I, from a depression which had harmful effects on the whole American economy.

The rapid expansion of agriculture after 1865 was due to a number of different factors: the need of both European countries and the new urban areas in America for American agricultural products; the opening of the

West by the railroads; and the Homestead Act of 1862, with the large number of Civil War veterans, native Americans from the eastern states, and immigrants from northern Europe who were eager to take advantage of it. During the next thirty years vast areas in the states west of the Mississippi were transformed into farmland. Between 1860 and 1900 the total acreage of American farms increased from 407 to 840 million, and the total value of farm properties increased from $8 to $20 billion. In 1900 there were 5.75 million farms and 10.25 million persons engaged in agriculture as either owners, tenants, or hired laborers.

Equally remarkable was the progress in agricultural methods. Seeds and animals were steadily improved by a series of importations and breedings. Such artificial fertilizers as nitrogen, potash, and phosphate were used for improving the quality of the soil. The knowledge of scientific agricultural methods was diffused among the farm population through the land-grant colleges set up under the Morrill Act of 1862, the agricultural experiment stations established by the Hatch Act of 1887, and the itinerant farmers' institutes financed by the state governments and supervised by the U. S. Department of Agriculture.

Meanwhile the successive inventions of the mechanical reaper, the binder, and the threshing machine had, by the 1880's, mechanized the whole process of harvesting, from cutting the grain to bagging the kernels, and by the end of World War I the development of the tractor made the horse almost unnecessary. Between 1830 and 1900 the total amount of labor needed for producing a bushel of wheat was reduced from 183 to 10 minutes; between 1850 and 1895 production per labor unit increased 500 per cent. In the twentieth century other developments—the telephone, the automobile, good roads, electric lighting and electric apparatus, and the radio—along with the great expansion of selling by such mail-order houses as Sears, Roebuck and Montgomery Ward, greatly increased the amenities of farm life and destroyed much of its traditional isolation.

To the farmers themselves the growth of mechanization was by no means wholly beneficial. It meant that they had sacrificed their economic security and independence. In the eighteenth century farmers fed and clothed themselves and made their own houses and implements. The twentieth-century farmer, on the other hand, was a part of an intricate economic structure. His higher standards of living greatly increased his need for money, so that he now had to find markets for a much larger proportion of his products. Furthermore, in order to obtain the harvesters and the tractors which promised to reduce his labors, he very frequently had to go into debt. The farmer tended increasingly to concentrate on the production of a single staple crop, all of which he sold, and to buy all his necessities rather than raise them himself. Instead of grinding his own grain and baking his own bread, he now sold his wheat and bought his bread. His life was, in consequence, more leisurely but also much more precarious. The insecurity of it, moreover, was increased by the extension of his market to Europe. The total annual value of American agricultural exports in the 1890's averaged about $660 million. One-third of the American wheat crop was exported. It was, indeed, the American farmer who, by producing this surplus beyond domestic needs, enabled the American economic system to pay the interest on the capital invested in it by Europeans and who thus contributed materially to the rapid expansion of industry.

The economic difficulties from which the American farmer so frequently suffered were due, in the first place, to international competition. In the later years of the nineteenth century there was a rapid growth of agricultural efficiency in Russia, India, and South America, which resulted in falling prices and a tendency toward the overproduction of basic foodstuffs. At this period American industry was producing mainly for the domestic market, so that it was possible for Congress to give it protection by means of tariff duties. The tariff could, however, be of no assistance to the farmer, and its effect was to raise the prices of the manufactured products he bought.

In the second place, the farmers were in a much weaker position than the industrialists because they were unable to form combinations to limit the effects of competition. Except among the California fruit and vegetable growers, there was no important tendency toward large-scale methods in farming. The average farm at the end of the century contained only 146.6 acres, and on it could be applied the most improved scientific methods with no great outlay of capital. Since the farmers were unable to unite with one another to limit production but were forced to compete with one another, they found themselves caught in a vicious circle, in which greater production meant lower prices and lower prices led to further increases in production. Between 1870 and 1900, for example, American wheat production increased 250 per cent while the price of wheat per bushel dropped from 105.3 to 62 cents. Increased production and lower prices were, in themselves, socially desirable; but unfortunately American large-scale industry had been able to escape from the cycle of competition by adopting monopolistic practices of restricted production and high prices. The decrease in farm prices was thus not compensated by any equivalent decrease in industrial prices, the result being that the farmers' share in the national income tended to grow smaller. The ultimate result was an absolute overproduction of farm products, which reached its peak in the 1920's.

In the third place, the farmer was constantly victimized by other groups in the community who had been able to escape the effects of competition or who enjoyed political or legal protection. His grain was stored first in elevators which were—in the nineteenth century—largely owned by a small group of men who combined to keep their charges high. It was shipped to market by the railroads, whose charges were also high. Finally it was sold to the terminal elevator operators at the big grain markets, who were likely to exploit the farmers further. As the crowning touch to the grievances of the farm population, many of these operators were in the habit of speculating on "futures" in the Chicago wheat pit and could sometimes make millions by doing so. Moreover, the agricultural machinery used by the farmers was, after 1902, usually bought from the International Harvester Company, one of the most powerful trusts in the country. When the farmers needed credit—and they frequently required short-term loans in anticipation of their harvests—they had to go to local merchants, moneylenders representing eastern creditors, or private individuals with funds to lend. In the decades following the Civil War money was expensive: interest rates fluctuated between 8 and 12 per cent, sometimes even higher.

The grievances of the farm population were especially acute from 1870 through 1890. This was a period of deflation, which appears to have been caused chiefly by the failure of gold production to keep pace with the growth of the economic system. The main burden of the consequent fall in prices was borne by farmers and small businessmen, since industry was able to protect itself through combination. The result was a steady growth in farm indebtedness and in tenancy. By 1900, 31 per cent of all farms carried mortgages, the proportion being even higher in such rich agricultural states as Iowa and Wisconsin. Since national banks were forbidden under the National Bank Act of 1863–64 to lend on farm mortgages, this function was assumed principally by investment trusts, which were owned mostly by easterners and which, especially in the 1880's, carried on elaborate advertising campaigns to persuade farmers to borrow. The proportion of farms operated by tenants in 1900 was 35.3

per cent. The landlords were, in many cases, themselves farmers; and many of the tenants were sons, brothers, or former hired men of their landlords, who expected eventually to become owners. But if the tenure ladder often led upward, it could also lead downward, many owners losing their properties through mortgage foreclosures. An appreciable part of the farm population lived migratory lives, renting farms for two or three years only and then, unable to pay their landlords, moving elsewhere with little hope of finding permanent homes.

The only bright feature in the farm situation was that, as a result of the growth of population and the march of industry westward, real estate values were steadily rising. There were, for example, lands in Iowa worth $7 an acre in 1877, which by 1914 were selling at $200. In eastern Nebraska, increasing land values yielded two New York landowners returns which ranged from 10.9 per cent (1880) to 6.5 per cent (1900). Between 1870 and 1900, the profits these men earned from their Nebraska lands were greater than the returns they would have received had they purchased railroad bonds or common stocks.[2] Although not all landholders profited so from rising values, most owners could normally expect to be able to sell at a profit, thus providing for their old age.

Meanwhile agriculture in the South was faced by additional problems resulting from its heritage of slavery and the Civil War. Cotton continued to be the basis of the southern economy, tobacco and sugar being the only other important commercial crops. The production of cotton remained unmechanized, and the labor it required was almost as great in the twentieth century as before the Civil War. More than half the cotton crop was sold to Europe, cotton being the largest single item in the American export trade, where the South had to face the growing competition of India and the Sudan. By 1876 the crop was again as large as in 1859; between 1876 and 1914 it increased by 300 per cent, a process inevitably accompanied by steadily falling prices.

Before the Civil War cotton for world trade had been grown principally on big slave plantations. The financial losses incurred during the war, the abolition of slavery, and the crushing taxation of the Reconstruction period largely destroyed the plantation system and led to the parceling of the plantations into small farms. Between 1860 and 1900 the number of separate farm properties in the South increased from 700,000 to 2.5 million. In 1900 about 55 per cent of these farms were operated by

[2] Allan G. Bogue and Margaret Beattie Bogue, " 'Profits' and the Frontier Land Speculator," *The Journal of Economic History*, XVII (March 1957), 19, 23.

owners, roughly 1.2 million of them being white, and 180,000 Negro. Of the tenant farmers, who numbered about 1.13 million, slightly more than half were Negro. The size of the average farm was smaller in the South than in the West; the tenant, moreover, operated less than the owner, and the Negro farmer less than the white. The average holding of the white tenant farmer was 84 acres, that of a Negro tenant farmer only 40 acres.

Both the tenant farmers in the cotton belt and also many of the smaller owners suffered from a crushing poverty unequaled among any other group in the United States. They operated almost universally without capital, on a basis of indebtedness to their landlords or to the local merchants. Nearly half the tenant farmers were sharecroppers, who used tools, animals, and seeds supplied by the landlord and who were required, in return, to give him half their crop. A majority of the remainder operated on a basis of share-tenancy, under which the tenant owned the tools and animals but the landlord supplied the seeds and received from one-quarter to one-third of the crop. A large number of both the tenants and the owners were, moreover, compelled to take goods on credit every spring from the local merchants, who acquired, in return, liens on their crops. The interest rates were excessive, sometimes reaching 40 per cent, and there was also a large difference in price between goods sold for cash and goods advanced on credit. The viciousness of the system was increased by the insistence of the landlords and the merchants that farmers concentrate on a single cash crop so that they might be better able to pay their debts. In the cotton belt, therefore, little was cultivated except cotton, and the farmers were often unable to grow their own food or to improve the quality of the soil by introducing a more variegated agriculture.

Yet if the landlords and local merchants victimized the farmers, it was not because they themselves were, by choice, an exploiting class. Equally with the farmers they were the victims of southern poverty and of the uncertainties of the single-crop system. Bad debts were frequent, and the local merchants and landlords were themselves usually in debt to wholesalers, who, in turn, were usually in debt to northern bankers and manufacturers. The result was that the average income of the southern farmer was less than half that of farmers elsewhere and that the number of tenant farmers steadily increased both relatively and absolutely. By 1930 the proportion of tenancy in the South had risen from 45 to 55 per cent, and the number of tenant farmers to 1.79 million.

The grievances of the farmers found expression in a series of waves of agrarian insurgency, which culminated in the campaign of William Jennings Bryan for the Presidency in 1896. After 1896, however, the position of the farmers began to improve, and until World War I it seemed possible that the agricultural problem might be gradually solving itself. The opening of the Transvaal gold mines and the use of the new cyanide process for mining precious metals increased the amount of money in circulation. State governments and, finally, the federal government established stricter control over the railway and public utility corporations and made it more difficult for them to exploit the farm population. The farmers themselves organized cooperatives which acquired ownership of county elevators and which, though more slowly, began to handle the marketing of farm products.

There was, moreover, a decline in the rate of growth of both the farm population and farm production, the result being an increase in farm prices. Between 1900 and 1910, 3 million persons left the rural areas to seek employment in the cities. The number of persons employed in agriculture reached its peak in the census of 1910, with a figure of 10.42 million, and then began to decrease. Crop production per capita declined after 1906. Between 1900 and 1910 the production of grain increased by only 1.7 per cent, while the value of the grain crop rose by 79.8 per cent; during the same period the number of cattle dropped from 41 million to 36 million, while their value rose by 42 per cent.

Just at a time when the rate of agricultural production was declining, the domestic market for farm goods was increasing. In 1910 there were 12 million more people living in cities than there were in 1900. This 40 per cent increase in the size of the urban population was caused by native births, immigration, and the migration of rural workers to urban centers. The result was that between 1900 and 1914 declining supplies and increasing demand caused farm prices to rise. During this period the real income of the farm population, measured in terms of purchasing power, increased at the rate of 1.3 per cent a year.

Unfortunately this steady improvement was ended after World War I. The demand of Europe for almost unlimited supplies of American foodstuff led to a sudden expansion of crop production, millions of new acres being put under the plough. For a period the farmers enjoyed high prices and were encouraged to borrow heavily. The restoration of peace in Europe and the subsequent growth of economic nationalism abruptly ended this agricultural boom, so that during the 1920's and 1930's the plight of the farmers was even worse than it had been before 1896.

Suggested Readings

The influence of geography upon the course of American history is stressed in a number of works, among them: Ellen C. Semple and Clarence F. Jones, *American History and Its Geographic Conditions* (rev. ed., Boston, 1933); Albert P. Brigham, *Geographic Influences in American History* (Boston, 1903); Isaiah Bowman, *The New World* (4th ed., New York, 1928); J. Russell Smith and M. Ogden Phillips, *North America* (rev. ed., New York [1942]); and Nathaniel S. Shaler, *United States of America* (2 vols., New York, 1894). Wallace W. Atwood, *The Physiographic Provinces of North America* (New York [1940]) and Howard W. Odum and Harry E. Moore, *American Regionalism* (New York [1938]) emphasize the varied character of the nation's sections. The influence of geography upon economic development is treated in Harold H. McCarty, *The Geographic Basis of American Economic Life* (New York [1940]). Regional economic development in the twentieth century is expertly treated in Carter Goodrich, *et al.*, *Migration and Economic Opportunity* (Philadelphia, 1936).

More specialized regional studies include Walter P. Webb, *The Great Plains* (Boston, 1931). Webb's thesis on the development of this region is closely examined in Fred A. Shannon, *et al.*, *Critiques of Research in the Social Sciences III* (New York, 1940). The geography of the Great Plains is analyzed also in James C. Malin, *The Grassland of North America: Prolegomena to Its History* (Lawrence, Kans., 1947).

Sectional and geographical influences in the South are appraised in Howard W. Odum, *Southern Regions of the United States* (Chapel Hill, N.C., 1936); and Rupert B. Vance, *Human Geography of the South: A Study in Regional Resources and Human Adequacy* (Chapel Hill, N.C., 1932). Geographic influences along with other intersectional factors which have affected the history of the modern South are analyzed in Walter P. Webb, *Divided We Stand* (New York [1937]); and for the post-1920 period in Thomas D. Clark, *The Emerging South* (New York, 1961).

Thomas Le Duc, "Recent Contributions to Economic History: The United States, 1861–1900," *The Journal of Economic History*, XIX (March 1959), 44–63, appraises carefully the major works on the economic history of the United States published between 1945 and 1959.

The post-Civil War background to the agricultural developments of the twentieth century is carefully appraised in Fred A. Shannon, *The Farmer's Last Frontier: Agriculture, 1860–1897* (New York, [1945]). Murray R. Benedict, *Farm Policies of the United States, 1790–1950: A Study of Their Origins and Development* (New York, 1953) is largely concerned with twentieth-century developments. Agricultural statistics are interpreted in Harold Barger and Hans H. Landsberg, *American Agriculture, 1899–1939* (New York, 1942). The most recent comprehensive history of the nation's land policies is Roy

M. Robbins, *Our Landed Heritage: The Public Domain, 1776–1936* (Princeton, N.J., 1942). Twentieth-century developments are detailed in E. Louise Peffer, *The Closing of the Public Domain: Disposal and Reservation Policies, 1900–1950* (Stanford, Calif., 1951).

Agricultural developments in the South are discussed in a number of works, including Robert P. Brooks, *The Agrarian Revolution in Georgia, 1865–1912* (Madison, Wis., 1914) and Rupert B. Vance, *Human Factors in Cotton Culture* (Chapel Hill, N.C., 1929), an excellent study of the region's living conditions. General histories which are also useful include the old but still valuable study of Holland Thompson, *The New South* (New Haven, Conn., 1919). Among the more recent volumes, C. Vann Woodward, *Origins of the New South, 1877–1913* (Baton Rouge, La., 1951) is especially good. See also such works as Paul H. Buck, *The Road to Reunion, 1865–1900* (Boston, 1937); William T. Couch, ed., *Culture in the South* (Chapel Hill, N.C., 1934); Jonathan Daniels, *A Southerner Discovers the South* (New York, 1938), especially for the more modern period; and Benjamin B. Kendrick and Alex M. Arnett, *The South Looks at its Past* (Chapel Hill, N.C., 1935). The influence of the antebellum heritage upon postwar developments is well told in Wilbur J. Cash, *The Mind of the South* (Garden City, N.Y., 1941). Marjorie A. Potwin, *Cotton Mill People of the Piedmont* (New York, 1927) is a specialized and able presentation of this subject, while Thomas D. Clark, *Pills, Petticoats and Plows: The Southern Country Store* (Indianapolis, 1944) is a lively discussion of this important economic institution between 1865 and 1915.

The agrarian discontent of the latter years of the nineteenth century is treated generally in Chester M. Destler, *American Radicalism, 1865–1901: Essays and Documents* (New London, Conn., 1946). The best and most comprehensive study of Populism is John D. Hicks, *The Populist Revolt* (Minneapolis, 1931). A different view of the Populist movement is seen in Carl C. Taylor, *The Farmers' Movement, 1620–1920* (New York [1953]) and Allan G. Bogue, *Money at Interest: The Farm Mortgage on the Middle Border* (Ithaca, N.Y., 1955). Among the numerous studies of Populism on the state level and biographies of important Populist leaders, C. Vann Woodward, *Tom Watson, Agrarian Rebel* (New York, 1938) deserves special note.

The third volume of Victor S. Clark, *History of Manufactures in the United States* (3 vols., New York, 1929) is old but still standard. A very useful one-volume collection of essays is John G. Glover and William B. Cornell, eds., *The Development of American Industries* (rev. ed., New York, 1946). Post-Civil War industrial developments are discussed briefly in Burton J. Hendrick, *The Age of Big Business* (New Haven, Conn., 1919). Nonagricultural developments between 1860 and 1917 are ably covered by Edward C. Kirkland, *Industry Comes of Age* (New York, 1961) and Harold U. Faulkner, *The Decline of Laissez Faire* (New York, 1951), volumes VI and VII of Henry David, *et al.*, *The Economic History of the United States*. Much briefer but very useful and not limited to economic developments alone is Samuel P. Hays, *The Response to Industrialism, 1885–1914* (Chicago, 1957). See also John Moody, *The Masters of Capital* (New Haven, Conn., 1919); Walter W.

Jennings, *Twenty Giants of American Business: Biographical Sketches in Economic History* (New York, 1953); and Stewart Holbrook, *The Age of the Moguls* (Garden City, N.Y., 1953). Allan Nevins, *The Emergence of Modern America, 1865–1878* (New York, 1927) contains several chapters on the economic life of the people during these years. Ida M. Tarbell, *The Nationalizing of Business, 1878–1898* (New York, 1936) and the section on the United States in George W. Edwards, *The Evolution of Finance Capitalism* (London, 1938) are also useful. The industrial changes in the post-Civil War South are treated in Broadus Mitchell and George S. Mitchell, *The Industrial Revolution in the South* (Baltimore, 1930). Statistical accounts of the performance of American industry include National Industrial Conference Board, *A Graphic Analysis of the Census of Manufactures, 1849–1919* (New York, 1923) and Edmund E. Day and Woodlief Thomas, *The Growth of Manufactures, 1899 to 1923* (Washington, D.C., 1928), a statistical study by the Bureau of the Census. The National Bureau of Economic Research, Inc., has sponsored a number of important statistical studies, such as Solomon Fabricant, *Employment in Manufacturing, 1899–1939* (New York, 1942), and by the same author, *The Output of Manufacturing, 1897–1937* (New York, 1940); William H. Shaw, *Value of Commodity Output Since 1869* (New York, 1947) and the same author's *Finished Commodities Since 1879: Output and Its Composition* (New York, 1941); and Arthur F. Burns, *Production Trends in the United States Since 1870* (New York, 1934). See also Willford I. King, *The Wealth and Income of the People of the United States* (New York, 1915).

The most recent account of the patent laws is Floyd L. Vaughan, *The United States Patent System: Legal and Economic Conflicts in American Patent History* (Norman, Okla., 1956).

Technology and inventions and their role in the mechanization of American industry are studied in Waldemar Kaempffert, ed., *A Popular History of American Inventions* (2 vols., New York, 1924); Holland Thompson, *The Age of Inventions* (New Haven, Conn., 1921); and John W. Oliver, *History of American Technology* (New York, 1956).

There is no general history of American business. A brief effort to summarize some of the most important developments is Thomas C. Cochran, *Basic History of American Business* (Princeton, N.J., 1959). A number of studies, however, are useful. Thomas C. Cochran and William Miller, *The Age of Enterprise: A Social History of Industrial America* (New York, 1942) appraises the social consequences of industrialism since 1828, but in greater detail after 1865. Norman J. Silberling, *The Dynamics of Business* (New York, 1943) discusses such factors as prices, interest rates, etc., on business developments since the eighteenth century, but with emphasis on twentieth-century developments. Norman S. B. Gras, *Business and Capitalism* (New York, 1939) contains useful chapters on industrial and financial capitalism, while Norman S. B. Gras and Henrietta M. Larson, *Casebook in American Business History* (New York, 1939) is a useful collection of case histories of a number of important businessmen and firms.

Sigmund Diamond, *The Reputation of the American Businessman* (Cambridge, Mass., 1955) samples and weighs the editorial reaction to the deaths of six leading businessmen. The ideas of business leaders are discussed generally in Edward C. Kirkland, *Dream and Thought in the Business Community, 1860–1900* (Ithaca, N.Y., 1956), and more specifically in Thomas C. Cochran, *Railroad Leaders, 1845–1890: The Business Mind in Action* (Cambridge, Mass., 1953). The influence of business ideas and views upon the social and intellectual currents of the times is discussed in Irwin G. Wyllie, *The Self-Made Man in America: The Myth of Rags to Riches* (New Brunswick, N.J., 1954). A number of the socioeconomic and intellectual conflicts of the years 1865 to 1901 are discussed in Sidney Fine, *Laissez Faire and the General Welfare State* (Ann Arbor, Mich., 1956). Matthew Josephson, *The Robber Barons: The Great American Capitalists, 1865–1901* (New York, 1935) is a lively account of the methods employed to achieve wealth and power by some of America's leading entrepreneurs. Equally strong in its attack upon the methods businessmen used to accumulate their wealth is Gustavus Myers, *History of the Great American Fortunes* (3 vols., New York, 1910–11). Sidney Ratner, *New Light on the History of Great American Fortunes: American Millionaires, 1892–1902* (New York, 1953) attempts to correct and modify some of the conclusions in Myers.

The trust problem and its consequences are detailed in a number of important works, including Jeremiah W. Jenks and Walter E. Clarke, *The Trust Problem* (5th ed., rev. and enl., Garden City, N.Y., 1917); Eliot Jones, *The Trust Problem in the United States* (New York, 1921); John Moody, *The Truth about the Trusts: A Description and Analysis of the American Trust Movement* (New York, 1904), an especially useful description of the trust movement at the turn of the century; William Z. Ripley, ed., *Trusts, Pools and Corporations* (rev. ed., Boston, 1916), a summary of the growth of the major combinations during the latter decades of the nineteenth century; Henry R. Seager and Charles A. Gulick, Jr., *Trusts and Corporation Problems* (New York, 1929); and Myron W. Watkins, *Industrial Combinations and Public Policy* (New York [1927]).

The basic work on the history of American labor is John R. Commons, et al., *History of Labour in the United States* (4 vols., New York, 1918–35). Among the many one-volume histories, Joseph G. Rayback, *A History of American Labor* (New York, 1959) is the most recent. Other similar studies include Selig Perlman, *A History of Trade Unionism in the United States* (New York, 1922); Herbert Harris, *American Labor* (New Haven, Conn., 1938); Marjorie R. Clark and S. Fanny Simon, *The Labor Movement in America* (New York [1938]); Leo Wolman, *The Growth of American Trade Unions, 1880–1923* (New York, 1924); and Foster R. Dulles, *Labor in America: A History* (2d rev. ed., New York, 1960). The second volume of Philip S. Foner, *History of the Labor Movement in the United States* (New York, 1955) covers the period indicated by its subtitle, *From the Founding of the American Federation of Labor to the Emergence of American Imperialism*.

Among the more specialized works, see Norman J. Ware, *The Labor Movement in the United States, 1860–1895* (New York, 1929); Marc Karson,

American Labor Unions and Politics, 1900–1918 (Carbondale, Ill., 1959); Edward Berman, *Labor and the Sherman Act* (New York, 1930); Henry David, *History of the Haymarket Affair* (New York, 1936); Terrence V. Powderly, *Thirty Years of Labor* (Columbus, Ohio, 1889), the reminiscences of an important labor leader; Felix Frankfurter and Nathan Green, *The Labor Injunction* (New York, 1930); George G. Groat, *The Attitude of American Courts in Labor Cases* (New York, 1911); Alpheus T. Mason, *Organized Labor and the Law* (Durham, N.C., 1925), especially good on the Sherman and Clayton acts; and Susan M. Kingsbury, ed., *Labor Laws and Their Enforcement* (New York, 1911), which details the major labor legislation before 1929, emphasizing Massachusetts. See also Louis Adamic, *Dynamite: The Story of Class Violence in America* (New York, 1931); John A. Fitch, *The Causes of Industrial Unrest* (New York, 1924); Robert Hunter, *Violence and the Labor Movement* (New York, 1914); and Samuel Yellen, *American Labor Struggles* (New York, 1936).

The founding and history of the American Federation of Labor is detailed in Selig Perlman and Philip Taft, *History of Labor in the United States, 1896–1932* (New York, 1935) and Lewis L. Lorwin and Jean A. Flexner, *The American Federation of Labor* (Washington, D.C., 1933). See also Samuel Gompers, *Seventy Years of Life and Labor* (2 vols., New York, 1925), an important autobiography, and Rowland H. Harvey, *Samuel Gompers* (Stanford, Calif. [1935]).

The political and socialist aspects of the labor movement are treated in Nathan Fine, *Labor and Farmer Parties in the United States, 1828–1928* (New York, 1928); Marguerite Green, *The National Civic Federation and the American Labor Movement, 1900–1925* (Washington, D.C., 1956); Howard H. Quint, *The Forging of American Socialism: Origins of the Modern Movement* (Columbia, S.C., 1953) for the years 1886 to 1901 and David A. Shannon, *The Socialist Party of America: A History* (New York, 1955) for the period 1901–52. On the I.W.W. see Paul F. Brissenden, *The I.W.W.: A Study of American Syndicalism* (New York, 1919). See also William D. Haywood, *Bill Haywood's Book* (New York [1929]), his autobiography.

Clarence E. Bonnett, *Employers' Associations in the United States* (New York, 1922) is a useful study on this subject.

Labor's earnings are discussed generally in Paul H. Douglas, *Real Wages in the United States, 1890–1926* (Boston, 1930) and in a number of other studies, including Joseph M. Viau, *Hours and Wages in American Organized Labor* (New York, 1939); Robert G. Layer, *Earnings of Cotton Mill Operatives, 1825–1914* (Cambridge, Mass., 1914). See also Paul Blanshard, *Labor in Southern Cotton Mills* (New York [1927]).

Among the many studies of labor's efforts to organize some of the principal industries see Charles A. Gulick, *The Labor Policy of the United States Steel Corporation* (New York, 1924) and John Mitchell, *Organized Labor* (Philadelphia [1903]).

The above references indicate the nature of some of the more specialized literature covering the material developments in American life at the turn of the century. For more detailed references see some of the recent economic history texts, most of which contain critical bibliographies, such as Gilbert C. Fite and Jim E. Riese, *An Economic History of the United States* (Boston, 1959); Donald L. Kemmerer and C. Clyde Jones, *American Economic History* (New York, 1959); Edward C. Kirkland, *A History of American Economic Life* (3d ed., New York, 1951); George Soule and Vincent P. Carosso, *American Economic History* (New York, 1957), and Harold F. Williamson, ed., *The Growth of the American Economy* (2d ed., New York, 1951).

2

Domestic and Foreign Politics

at the Turn of the Century

PARTY STRUCTURE AND ORGANIZATION

The chief danger of party politics is that, ceasing to be merely a means by which the will of the electorate can be translated into action, it may become an end in itself. Parties may maintain the loyalty of their members and endeavor to win elections not in order to carry into action a body of political ideals but merely to obtain the rewards of office. A degeneration of this kind was very apparent in the United States after the Civil War. As the differences of principle which had originally separated the Republicans and the Democrats were forgotten or became unimportant, each party tended to become a body of professional politicians primarily interested in patronage and offices. Political leaders tended to degenerate into political bosses, and political parties into political machines.

The Republicans were normally the dominant party, winning seven of the nine presidential elections between 1868 and 1900. The Democrats were always, however, a formidable opposition, winning control of Congress occasionally and electing Grover Cleveland to the Presidency in 1884 and again in 1892. The party system thus justified itself by ensuring that officeholders were never exempt from criticism and could not afford to ignore the wishes of the electorate. Party rivalries, however, rarely reflected any of the fundamental political divisions in American life, and there was little difference in the policies which each party adopted when in office.

Probably the most important political division in the United States was the conflict of interest between business and agriculture—a division which had appeared immediately after the establishment of the federal government in the opposing beliefs of Hamilton and Jefferson. This natural line of division had been destroyed by the Civil War. The attempt of the southern planters to extend slavery to the western territories and their subsequent secession from the Union had separated the two agrarian sections, the South and the West, and had brought about the alliance of eastern industrialists and western farmers in the Republican party. This realignment of forces continued long after its original cause—slavery— had been abolished. The Republican party, although dominated by middle-western and eastern industrialists and financiers, was able to retain its western agrarian supporters by appealing to their memories of the Civil War—a political tactic known as "waving the bloody shirt"—and by generous distributions of pensions to veterans of the Grand Army of the Republic.

If, however, the Republican party continued to be a heterogeneous combination of conservative eastern bankers and corporation magnates, radical western farmers, and idealists originally attracted to it by the crusade against slavery, it could claim to be relatively coherent by contrast with the Democratic party. After the Civil War the Democrats became the party of white supremacy in the South, including both conservative Bourbon leaders who represented the interests of southern industrialists and landlords, and agrarian radicals who championed the cause of the southern farmers. To these mutually hostile southern groups were added a number of corrupt city machines in the North, particularly the Tammany machine in New York, a few northern financiers and industrialists whose viewpoint was little different from that of the conservative Republicans, and a number of western farmers whose interests were identical with those of their Republican neighbors.

In theory, the two parties advocated different principles. The Republicans, for example, were traditionally in favor of a strong federal government and a high tariff; the Democrats were the party of states' rights and a low tariff. After the Civil War, however, these differences had little reality. The states' rights question lost its importance; and although the Democrats still professed to believe in a low tariff, Democratic congressmen were usually willing to support a high tariff when it gave protection to industries in which their constituents were interested. Actually, each party was a coalition of different sectional groups with discordant interests, held together by the doctrine of party regularity. The party allegiance of individuals was frequently determined not by political principle but by the traditions of their families, by the section in which they lived, and in many cases by their ethnic origins. The vote of the northern Negroes, for example, was almost solidly Republican; the Irish vote, on the other hand, went mainly to the Democrats. In the North and West the Republican party was usually the party of respectability, whereas the Democrats were the party of revolt; in the South, on the other hand, the reverse was true. Each party had a conservative wing and a radical wing and could swing in one direction or the other to conform to the tendencies of the electorate.

Local Government

The various units of local government—the states, counties, cities, and townships—were from some points of view even more important than the federal government. Local government, having control over such matters as public health, education, protection against crime, and regulation of economic activity, affected the ordinary citizen more intimately and in more varied ways than did the federal government. Although the issues decided at Washington were of more fundamental importance, national political parties were based on the local organizations; hence, when local politics was corrupt, federal politics could not wholly escape contagion. In the latter part of the nineteenth century the degree of corruption in many of the local governments was very great. Political bosses and political machines exercised great powers and rarely used them to promote the general welfare. The electorate was frequently unable or unwilling to maintain effective control over the officeholders.

The best local government was probably in rural New England, where the town meeting had retained its vitality. The township system had spread also to parts of the Middle West but had not acquired much importance there. Outside New England the chief units of local government, below the state governments, were the counties and cities, of which the latter, owing to their greater wealth and population, were the more important. New York City, for example, had by the end of the nineteenth century a budget larger than those of London, Paris, and Berlin combined, larger even than those of the central governments of some of the smaller European countries. A city government consisted usually of a mayor and a council or a board of aldermen. In the latter part of the nineteenth century the powers of the councilmen and aldermen had been steadily decreasing, and those of the mayors had been growing larger. The legal forms of city government, however, did not usually correspond to the real situation: at the end of the century almost every city in the United States was controlled by a political machine.

The rank and file of a city machine consisted of party workers, whose duty was to secure votes for their party in the districts for which they were responsible, and who expected, in return, to receive jobs on the city payroll. The boss who controlled a city machine did not usually hold any official position himself; generally he was a self-made man, with little education, who controlled the city government from behind the scenes. The mayor was often a mere figurehead, put forward by the machine because of his vote-catching powers and apparent respectability. Some city bosses enriched themselves at the public expense, but most of them cared for power rather than for money. And although they could never afford to be scrupulous in the methods by which they kept their machines in office, some of them had a genuine desire to provide government as good as the system allowed.

The votes which elected a city machine into office might be due partly to its party label or to recognition of whatever genuine services to the city it might have performed. However, there were much ballot-box stuffing, intimidation or bribery of voters, and numerous other kinds of fraud. Another significant source of machine votes lay in protecting the poorer families in the city from starvation, finding jobs for them, and giving them assistance when they were accused of violating the law. Social services of this kind, although they might have been better performed by the state or national government or by philanthropic organizations, answered a genuine need, especially among the immigrant population; and it was not surprising that city politicians could thereby win in slum areas a loyal support scarcely weakened by proofs of corruption or bad administration.

In addition to votes, a machine also needed money, much of which was obtained corruptly. City officeholders were required to contribute a part of their earnings to the machine, in return for which they could usually augment their official salaries by various forms of petty graft. The chief opportunities for petty graft arose through laws and regulations reflecting the moral principles of the community rather than its practices. Laws limiting the sale of liquor or prohibiting prostitution could, for example, usually be evaded by paying graft to the appropriate local authorities. Occasionally this condonation of activities which society regarded as immoral developed into an alliance with definitely criminal elements.

Besides the petty graft obtained from lawbreakers, city machines also gathered money from wealthy businessmen. Through its ability to grant contracts for official buildings and supplies, to change tax assessments, and to impose police regulations of numerous kinds, a machine could easily be extortionate. Businessmen, moreover, often wanted favors. The money which passed between business interests and city machines could be regarded either as blackmail or as bribery, and in many cases it was probably both. The accepted idea in the nineteenth century was that such payments were purely blackmail and that all the dishonesty was usually on the side of the politicians.

There were occasional revolts against a city machine. Machines were likely to grow too confident, to allow too many criminals to escape punishment, and to increase excessively the costs of city government. Under such conditions a reform administration might be elected to office. Almost invariably, however, the machine returned to power at the next election, chastened by its temporary separation from the city payroll but not fundamentally changed. Reform administrations were likely to alienate businessmen by being too honest, the poorer classes by failing to give them that protection from individual misfortune which they had received from the machine, and the general public by insisting on a strict enforcement of puritanical legislation. The members of a reform party were, moreover, amateurs, who lacked the skill of the professional politicians of the machine and who were apt to grow tired of political activity. Experience showed that reforms were temporary but that the machine was permanent.

The State Machines

In most of the state governments conditions were similar. The state machines were, however, less carefully organized than the city machines and more likely to disintegrate. The state bosses were usually men of a very different type from the city bosses, although they exercised similar functions. The state boss was usually a man of old American stock, wealthy and well educated. He did not have the preference displayed by the city bosses for remaining in the background, being very frequently a member of the United States Senate. Probably the strongest of the state machines was the Republican machine in Pennsylvania which, under a succession of able leaders—Simon Cameron, Matthew Quay, and Boies Penrose—controlled the state from the Civil War until after Warld War I. The fraudulent methods by which this machine gathered votes were notorious.

The Republican party in New York State was similarly boss-controlled, although it had to face a strong Democratic opposition, based on the Tammany machine in New York City, which could occasionally win control of the governorship. In 1915, at the New York State constitutional convention, Elihu Root recalled how "for many years Conkling was the supreme ruler in this state; the governor did not count, the legislature did not count; comptrollers and secretaries of state and what not did not count. It was what Mr. Conkling said; and in a great outburst of public rage he was pulled down. Then Mr. Platt ruled the state; for nigh upon twenty years he ruled it. . . . I don't criticize the men of the invisible government. . . . But it is all wrong." What Root said of New York might, at the turn of the century, have been said with equal truth of a majority of the other states in the Union.

The state governments resembled the city governments also in the prevalence of corrupt financial connections between government and business. Businessmen insisted, with much justice, that the payments they made to state legislators were a form of blackmail. Moorfield Storey declared in 1894 that "when a state legislature meets, each large corporation within its reach prepares for self-defence, knowing by bitter experience how hospitably attacks upon its property are received in committee and on the floor." State legislators would introduce what were known as "strike bills," limiting the rights of business corporations. These were not intended to pass, but they would frighten corporation directors into distributing bribes.

On the other hand, the powers enjoyed by corporations were often excessive. In the 1880's and 1890's a number of state governments, from New Hampshire in the East to California in the West, were virtually the property of railroad corporations. In Pennsylvania the representative of the Pennsylvania Railroad actually sat alongside the legislators in the state capitol and instructed them how to vote. Corporation magnates were frequently indifferent to party distinctions and were willing to do business with whatever party happened to be in power. As Jay Gould expressed it, during the period when he controlled the Erie Railroad: "In a Republican district, I was Republican; in a Democratic district, I was Democratic; and in a doubtful district, I was doubtful; but I was always Erie."

The Federal Government

The federal government was always considerably more honest than the local governments, yet in the latter part of the nineteenth century it exhibited similar tendencies toward boss and machine rule and corrupt connections between politics and business. The dishonesty of local politics inevitably infected federal politics. There were, moreover, certain features of the American form of government which tended to encourage irresponsibility and inefficiency.

Since every congressman had to retain the support of his own state, it was necessary that he secure special benefits for his constituents. He must endeavor to get tariff protection for commodities produced in his state, arrange that federal money be spent in the state, and obtain appointments to the federal payroll for his supporters. Much congressional activity took the form of bargaining among various congressmen, who would agree to support one another in the furthering of their various local interests. The most notorious example of this system was the annual rivers and harbors bill, under which federal money was appropriated for making improvements in different parts of the Union. Such distributions of federal money were known as the "pork barrel." A result of the system was that few congressmen, especially in the House of Representatives, could afford to oppose the party leaders, because they would be punished for their independence when the party was in power by being deprived of their share of federal "pork" and federal patronage.

Strong leadership by the President, the only elected authority who represented the national interest and not merely a local interest, was the best remedy for the weaknesses of the federal government, but between 1865 and 1901 only one President, Grover Cleveland, was willing to exercise such leadership. The Republican Presidents were generally willing to allow the party leaders in Congress to determine government policies. Before 1901, when Theodore Roosevelt began to reassert presidential initiative, the real authority in Washington was divided among the President, the Speaker of the House of Representatives, and a small group of senators.

The House of Representatives was the weaker of the two houses of

Congress, chiefly because the two-year term of its members, as contrasted with the six-year term of the senators, made it more difficult for them to assert their independence of party leaders. Most of the real work of the House was not done in its public debates but in the committees, which considered bills before they were submitted to the House as a whole and which were virtually able to kill any proposals of which they disapproved. The Speaker, who was nominated by the caucus of the majority party and then elected at the beginning of each term by the House, was able after 1889 to exercise virtually dictatorial powers. In that year the Republican Speaker, Thomas B. Reed, confronted by a strong Democratic opposition, carried through a revision of the rules. Henceforth the Speaker made all the committee appointments given to members of the majority party, being able to punish opponents by giving them unimportant assignments. Through his control of the rules committee he could decide what business the House was to discuss, and by refusing to recognize members who wished to speak or to entertain motions which he chose to regard as "dilatory," he could guide all proceedings on the floor of the House. Reed, generally known as "Czar Reed," dominated the House until his retirement in 1899. Similar powers were exercised by Joseph G. Cannon, Speaker from 1901 until 1911, a convinced conservative of great political shrewdness, whose general attitude was that any change was likely to be for the worse.

The Senate, on the other hand, was one of the ablest legislative bodies in the world. The six-year term of the senators, the prestige of many of them, and their jealously guarded right of unlimited debate gave them a personal independence not enjoyed by members of the House. Although the Senate always contained men of great ability, it was often, however, at the end of the nineteenth century, dangerously out of contact with popular sentiment. The system of election by state legislatures made many senators the nominees of the party bosses and of powerful business corporations rather than of the people. It contained so many men of great wealth that it was sometimes referred to as the "millionaires' club"; many of its members were themselves business magnates, and others were corporation lawyers who continued to receive regular retainers from their employers after their election to the Senate. Chauncey Depew of New York, for example, was a director of seventy different corporations, from which he derived $50,000 a year in fees alone. Such men spoke as the political agents of economic interests, of railroads or steel or oil, rather than as representatives of the states.

The two leading senators at the end of the century were Nelson W. Aldrich of Rhode Island, the Republican floor leader, and Mark Hanna of Ohio, the friend and adviser of President McKinley. Both these men had qualities of statesmanship, and Hanna at least believed that business magnates should develop a stronger sense of responsibility for the welfare of the workers. Both of them, however, were essentially aristocratic in their political philosophy, distrusting democracy and advocating government by and for men of wealth. Both of them, moreover, were millionaires, with numerous interests in street railroads, mines, and other industries.

Between the Civil War and the end of the century, financial questions probably occupied more of the time and attention of Congress than did any others, and the tariff and veterans' pensions were the two pivots of Republican party strategy. The tariff, raised to provide revenue during the Civil War, remained high after the war on the theory that the manufacturing costs of European industry were lower than those of American industry; free trade, it was claimed, would compel American producers to reduce wages to the lower levels prevalent in Europe. Actually, however, the tariff was generally higher than was needed to achieve this purpose; it enabled American industry not only to pay higher wages than were paid in Europe but also to charge high prices from American consumers. Some American industries, such as steel, continued to receive tariff protection long after they had begun to compete successfully with European industries in European markets. No coherent national tariff policy was ever adopted; the tariff was a local question, tariff bills being constructed by means of trading between congressmen, each of whom wanted protection for the industries in the district he represented. And although the Democratic party was, in theory, in favor of tariff reductions, chiefly because of the influence of the cotton planters, whose prosperity depended on foreign markets, Democratic congressmen would often vote for those tariff bills which gave protection to their own constituents.

The revenues derived from the tariff were spent in the same manner as they were collected, each congressman being anxious that federal money be distributed in his district. Although the debt of the federal government was reduced from nearly $2.7 billion in 1865 to less than $1.1 billion in 1895, there was a treasury surplus almost every year, so that considerable sums were available for appropriation. Some $11 or $12 million was spent each year through the annual rivers and harbors bill; but when the Republicans were in power, the preferred method of distributing money was through veterans' pensions. The political advantage, everywhere except in the South, of giving pensions to veterans of the northern armies was obvious; and by 1937 a total of nearly $8 billion had been spent on this purpose.

POLITICAL CONTROVERSIES

The Agrarian Crusade

Although each of the major political parties was dominated by conservative interests, the traditional conflict between business and agrarian groups continued, though it now ran counter to the line of demarcation between Republicans and Democrats. During the late nineteenth century the insurgent agrarians constituted a radical wing of both parties and also made several attempts to form a farmer-labor combination which would be the basis of a third party. This agrarian revolt was of such import that its effect upon the nature and course of America's political development and upon the structure of the national parties was apparent far into the twentieth century.

In the 1870's farmers' organizations known as Granges had spread through the Middle West and had been mainly responsible for a series of state laws that regulated the railroads but were finally destroyed by a Supreme Court decision of 1886. The early 1880's was a period of greater prosperity, but for a decade following 1887 the prairies were parched by droughts and swept by hot, dry winds, and a series of bad harvests revived the movement of agrarian insurgency with greater vigor. Two farmers' organizations, the Southern Alliance and the Northwestern Alliance, grew rapidly; and in 1889 and for several following years representatives of the two alliances held political conventions and put forward political programs. They demanded government ownership of railroads, telephones, and telegraph; control of currency by the government instead of by the banks; and currency inflation by both the coinage of silver and an increase in paper money. For the relief of their credit difficulties they put forward a subtreasury plan under which the government was to establish warehouses where farm products could be held for a year, producers meanwhile receiving loans up to 80 per cent of the value of their products. They proposed also the popular election of senators, the initiative, and the referendum; and in the hope of attracting labor support, they urged an eight-hour day for government employees and the abolition of such private detective agencies as the Pinkertons.

Prior to the elections of 1892 the two alliances held a convention at Omaha, at which they combined to form a Populist, or People's, party, and named General James B. Weaver as the party's presidential candidate. Weaver won a popular vote of 1,041,600 and an electoral vote of 22. Two years later the Populist vote in the congressional elections increased to 1,471,600, and it seemed that it might become a permanent factor in American politics.

These expectations were frustrated in 1896, when the Democratic party adopted the issue of free silver and captured the bulk of the Populist vote. Gold had been made the sole basis of the American currency in 1873. The Bland-Allison Act of 1878, which was superseded in 1890 by the Sherman Silver Purchase Act, had provided for the purchase and coinage by the government of limited quantities of silver; but in 1893 Grover Cleveland had induced Congress to repeal the Sherman Act. The abandonment of silver was opposed by the owners of western silver mines, who wanted to raise silver prices, and also by western agrarians, who believed that an increase in the quantity of money in circulation would raise farm prices and lighten the burdens of debtors. A combination of the two groups persuaded the Democratic convention of 1896 to repudiate Cleveland and to adopt as the chief proposal of its platform the free and unlimited coinage of silver at a ratio to gold of sixteen to one.

William Jennings Bryan, a thirty-six-year-old lawyer and newspaper editor from Nebraska who had served one term in Congress and had for two years been preaching the gospel of free silver throughout the South and West, swept the convention with his famous "cross of gold" speech and was nominated for the Presidency on the fifth ballot. The Democratic platform contained few of the other demands of the Populists, but the free silver issue and the eloquence of Bryan were sufficient to win most of them to the Democratic standard.

The Republican convention of that year was dominated by Mark Hanna, who secured the nomination for his friend William McKinley of Ohio. The campaign aroused a bitterness of class feeling such as had been equaled only in 1800 and in 1828. The issue of free silver became merely a symbol of the hostility between agrarianism and big business. Bryan, tall, handsome, eloquent, and magnetic, too simple to be ranked as a statesman but too honest to be condemned as a demagogue, traveled 18,000 miles and delivered 600 speeches, arousing everywhere a crusading fervor among his agrarian supporters. He was the spokesman of those egalitarian aspirations which had formerly been championed by Jefferson and Jackson. The business classes, on the other hand, saw in Bryan a dangerous and anarchical revolutionary and rallied round McKinley as the representative of business prosperity and economic sanity. Hanna raised a huge campaign chest, and his supporters threatened that if Bryan were elected, farm mortgages would not be renewed, business orders would be canceled, and factories would be closed. McKinley was elected President by a popular vote of 7,107,000 and an electoral vote of 271, as against 6,533,000 and 176 for Bryan. The silver issue was afterward buried by the Gold Standard Act of 1900.

After 1896 agrarian insurgency assumed milder forms. The merger of the Populists with the Democrats and the defeat of Bryan ended agrarian hopes of winning control of the federal government, and a period of rising farm prices and greater prosperity caused the discontent of the farmers to become less bitter and fanatical.

The Regulation of Big Business

The grievances of the farmers and of small businessmen against the big corporations could not be altogether ignored by Congress, in spite of the generally conservative sentiments of that body. The economic theory of laissez faire prohibited government regulation of business, but it declared also that competition must be maintained; and the growth of the trusts meant that many economic enterprises were ceasing to be competitive. Railroad practices and the methods used in building such corporations as Standard Oil were, moreover, causing great indignation not only among agrarian radicals but also among conservatives. In the 1880's, therefore, Congress began to take the first hesitating steps toward regulation of big business. It established a mild degree of government control over the railroads, appointing a special commission for that purpose; and it endeavored to preserve competition between industries which were not naturally monopolistic.

The Supreme Court invalidation of the Grange Laws in 1886 made it plain that only the federal government could regulate the railroads, and in 1887 Congress passed the Interstate Commerce Act. The act declared that railroad rates must be published and must be reasonable, endeavored to preserve some degree of competition by forbidding the railroads to make pooling arrangements for the division of traffic, and prohibited rebates, drawbacks, rate discriminations between long and short hauls, and other devices for giving advantages to certain businesses or localities. An

Interstate Commerce Commission of five members was appointed to supervise railroad practices and prosecute violations of the act, and shippers who had been charged unjust rates were to appeal to the commission for redress.

The Interstate Commerce Commission was, however, a futile body until invigorated by President Theodore Roosevelt. The membership of the commission was conservative, and it was denied adequate power by the courts. In the maximum freight case of 1897 the Supreme Court declared that it could not fix maximum rates, and in the Alabama Midland case of the same year the Court prevented it from exercising effective control over long and short haul discriminations. Out of sixteen cases brought before the Supreme Court under the Interstate Commerce Act before 1901, fifteen were won by the railroads.

The function of preserving competition was undertaken by the federal government in 1890. A number of state governments had already enacted antitrust laws and established stricter supervision over the issuance of corporation charters; but since other states had failed to take action or, like New Jersey, were deliberately making themselves refuges for corporations, these state laws could not be very effective. The Sherman Antitrust Act, enacted in 1890, declared that "every contract, combination in the form of trust or otherwise, or conspiracy, in restraint of trade or commerce among the several states, or with foreign nations" was illegal. Persons who conspired to monopolize any branch of commerce were to be fined or imprisoned. Federal district attorneys were to see that the act was enforced, and persons who had been injured by combinations in restraint of trade were to sue for damages. Congress did not intend that the act should apply to labor unions but decided that it was unnecessary to make this exemption a part of the law.

During the administrations of Harrison, Cleveland, and McKinley the government made no serious attempt to enforce the Sherman Act against the trusts; it did, however, pervert the act into a weapon against trade unionism, most notably in the injunction it obtained against the American Railway Union during the Pullman strike of 1894. In eleven years federal law officers brought eighteen suits under the Sherman Act, and succeeded in winning ten of them. These ten victories were scored not against any of the big trusts but against the Addyston Pipe Company, two railroad associations, three local associations of coal dealers, and four trade unions. Twenty-two suits were brought by private persons, of which only three were successful.

During this period the two most important Supreme Court decisions under the Sherman Act were in the E. C. Knight Company case of 1895 and the Trans-Missouri Freight Association case of 1897. The Knight case was an attack on the sugar trust. The government showed that the sugar trust controlled 95 per cent of the sugar refining business; it failed, however, to prove that a monopoly of manufacturing was also a monopoly of interstate commerce, and on this ground the trust was acquitted by the Supreme Court. In the Freight Association case, on the other hand, the Court agreed that any combination in restraint of interstate trade was illegal, even though it could be argued that such a combination was "reasonable." This case suggested that the Court would be willing to enforce the act if the government would act vigorously and present its evidence adequately.

Before the accession of Theodore Roosevelt to the presidency, therefore, federal action to curb business abuses remained wholly futile. Certain processes had been initiated, however, which twentieth-century administrations would make more effective. A division had been made between those economic enterprises that were naturally monopolistic and should, therefore, be under direct government regulation, and those that were naturally competitive and in which the government should act to enforce competition. The principle had been established that, where regulation was necessary, it should be performed by a commission with partly administrative and partly judicial functions. A number of legal difficulties to effective regulation had also become apparent. It was almost impossible to define clearly what was included in "interstate" commerce, what was meant by the rule that railroad rates must be "reasonable," or what was meant by the prohibition of combinations in "restraint of trade." In practice the concrete meaning of these phrases depended on the attitude of the courts, which thus acquired increased powers.

Political Changes in the South

Populism had especially important consequences in the South, where it sought to overthrow the Bourbon oligarchy of landlords, merchants, and industrialists which dominated the region in the 1880's. The rapid growth of the Southern Alliance at this time was due not only to the grievances which the hard-pressed farmers, tenants, and workers of the South shared with those of the West—falling agricultural prices and the growth of mortgages and tenancy—but also to their indignation against the "Bourbon aristocracy" which, in the opinion of many southern Populists, was "trying to coerce the people into perpetual submission to the dictation of the Northeast, and to their debasing exactions." [1] In addition to the standard agrarian demands of the times—easier credits, strict regulation of railroads and other corporations, abolition of child labor, and protective legislation for factory workers—the southern Populists wanted a greater expenditure of money for public education and various other reforms on the state level designed to curb such abuses as the use of convict labor. The realization of these objectives, especially those of the more radical agrarians like Thomas E. Watson of Georgia, who called upon the farmers and workers of both races to join the Populist party, was complicated by the color question, which the Bourbons used to safeguard their hold over the Democratic party.

The Bourbon planters and businessmen controlled the Democratic party in the South through a number of devices, such as taxation and literacy qualifications for voting and heavy representation for the former plantation areas, which enabled them to out-vote the small farmers who constituted a majority of the white population. Even though the Democratic party ignored the opinions and aspirations of nearly all its non-Bourbon members, most whites continued to support it because they were afraid that joining a third party would divide the white vote and lead to "Negro domination." The Republican party, consisting of white farmers in the mountains and Negroes who held federal offices, was generally unimportant except in North Carolina. The Negroes were not legally disfranchised, but few of them dared to exercise their right to vote unless they were encouraged to do so by white politicians.

In the congressional elections of 1890 Southern Alliancemen captured the Democratic party from its Bourbon leaders in South Carolina, Georgia, and Tennessee, electing governors in each of those states and also in North Carolina, where they had formed an alliance with the Republicans. Besides these outstanding victories, forty-four Alliancemen won seats in Congress and many others were elected to legislative offices in their states. The Southern Alliance achieved most of these victories by taking over the Democratic state organizations, except in a few instances when it worked through the Republican party. The effort of these agrarians to break the Bourbon hold over the Democratic Party precipitated bitter political conflicts throughout the South, with both sides employing bribery and

[1] Quoted in C. Vann Woodward, *Origins of the New South, 1877–1913* (Baton Rouge, La., 1951), p. 252.

intimidation to capture the Negro vote. In this competition, the Bourbon landlords, who could often bring their Negro tenants and sharecroppers to the polls in gangs, proved more successful than their agrarian opponents. By employing these and other similarly unscrupulous tactics, and by repeatedly warning the white voters that supporting the Populists would result in "Negro rule," the Bourbons were able to defeat the Populist party in 1892 and 1896 and to frustrate many of the more democratic aspirations of its leaders.

With the collapse of southern populism after 1896, most of its supporters returned to the Democratic party and joined the Bourbons in adopting legal methods for permanently disfranchising the Negroes. Devices by which this might be accomplished had already been adopted in Mississippi. In 1890 that state enacted a law restricting the vote to those who had paid a poll tax eight months before the election and had resided in the same district for at least a year. In 1892 a literacy test was added, requiring every voter to be able to read and interpret part of the federal constitution. Similar laws were subsequently adopted in all southern states. Since these regulations were likely to disfranchise white as well as colored citizens, Louisiana in 1898 added a "grandfather clause," giving the vote to anybody whose father or grandfather had been a voter before 1867.

The grandfather clause was invalidated by the United States Supreme Court in 1915, but the purpose of these regulations—defined by Carter Glass at the Virginia Constitutional Convention of 1901 as "discrimination within the letter of the law"—was achieved through their administration by white Boards of Registry. It was easy for these boards to declare all Negroes—even if, as sometimes happened, they were professors in Negro colleges—to be illiterate. The bulk of the colored population was thus effectively disfranchised. In Louisiana, for example, there were 130,344 Negro voters in 1896 and only 5,320 in 1900. In the twentieth century there was a slow increase in Negro voting in the southern cities, where the Negro population often had able leaders and the white population was relatively liberal. By 1960 1,361,000 southern Negroes, 28 per cent of those of voting age, were registered as voters. But throughout the rural areas the Negroes mostly remained disfranchised and, in general, accepted their exclusion apathetically.

After 1900, though a number of Populists continued to hold office and authority in the South, their influence was negligible. The cause of reform was now taken up by the progressives, most of whom came from the urban middle class. Like the Populists, the southern progressives of the first decade of the twentieth century directed their attack against the Bourbon landlords and industrialists who controlled the political and economic life of the South. But whereas the Populists had also been concerned with improving the plight of the Negroes, the progressives were staunch defenders of white supremacy, chiefly interested in improving the lot of the poor whites by providing them with better educational opportunities and by protecting them from monopolists.

THE UNITED STATES BECOMES
A WORLD POWER

The Growth of Power Politics

Throughout the earlier decades of the nineteenth century American foreign policy had been generally isolationist. With the exception of such interludes as the War of 1812, the war with Mexico, and an occasional outbreak of nationalistic excitement, it had also usually been pacifistic. With vast undeveloped territories at home, the United States had no economic motives for expansion abroad and little reason far taking any active part in the affairs of Europe. Once independence had been secured and the nation's chief interest was no longer focused on foreign affairs, American diplomacy no longer attracted the first-rate men it had during the first quarter of the nineteenth century. As foreign affairs declined in importance, the diplomacy of the United States was conducted mostly by amateurs, so that it never acquired the professional traditions of European foreign offices. Indeed, the very need for a foreign service was questioned. In 1889 the New York *Sun* called the diplomatic service "a costly humbug and sham . . . a nurse of snobs" and suggested that "Congress should wipe out the whole service." During the 1890's, however, interest in overseas expansion and the growing awareness that the United States must play a more significant role in world affairs emphasized the need to reconsider the role and position of the foreign service. The first indication of this change occurred in 1894 when President Grover Cleveland elevated the legations at London, Paris, Berlin, and St. Petersburg to the rank of embassies. The following year new appointment and promotion policies were established for the consular service. This was another step in the direction of creating a professional career foreign service.

The one permanent feature of American foreign policy was the

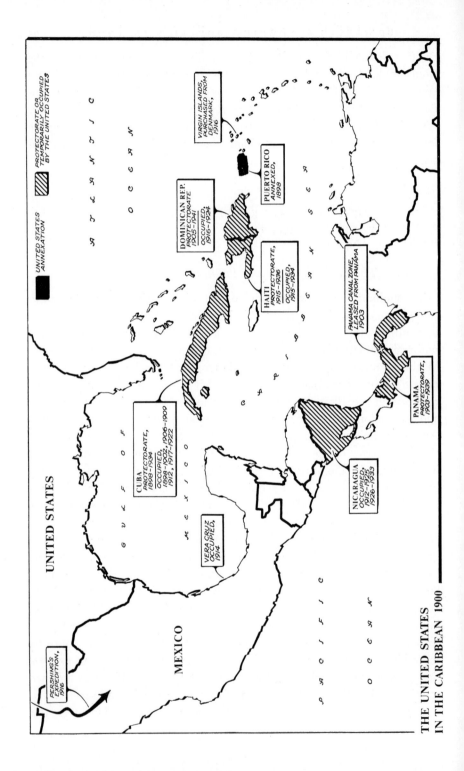

UNITED STATES

MEXICO

PERSHING'S
EXPEDITION,
1916

GULF OF MEXICO

VERA CRUZ
OCCUPIED,
1914

CUBA
PROTECTORATE,
1898–1934
OCCUPIED,
1898–1902, 1906–1909
1912, 1917–1922

NICARAGUA
OCCUPIED,
1912–1925,
1926–1933

NICARAGUA
PROTECTORATE,
1916–1939

PANAMA
PROTECTORATE,
1903–1939

PANAMA CANAL ZONE,
LEASED FROM PANAMA
1903

HAITI
PROTECTORATE,
1915–1936
OCCUPIED,
1915–1934

DOMINICAN REP.
PROTECTORATE,
1905–1941
OCCUPIED,
1916–1924

PUERTO RICO
ANNEXED,
1898

VIRGIN ISLANDS,
PURCHASED FROM
DENMARK,
1916

CARIBBEAN SEA

ATLANTIC OCEAN

PACIFIC OCEAN

UNITED STATES
ANNEXATION

PROTECTORATE OR
TEMPORARILY OCCUPIED
BY THE UNITED STATES

**THE UNITED STATES
IN THE CARIBBEAN 1900**

Monroe Doctrine. The United States would always oppose any attempt by a European power to acquire new possessions in the Western Hemisphere. Prior to 1895, however, the United States had not usually intervened in diplomatic disputes between Latin American republics and European powers, even when such disputes involved the use of force. And the continued independence of the Latin American countries had been due not so much to the Monroe Doctrine as to the sea power of Great Britain. From the time that those countries had won their independence from Spain, Great Britain had established close economic connections with them and had consistently been interested in preventing its European rivals from acquiring control of them. The dependence of the Monroe Doctrine on British control of the Atlantic was not, however, generally appreciated in the United States.

During the last two decades of the nineteenth century there was a growing sentiment in the United States in favor of a more aggressive foreign policy. American foreign trade was rapidly increasing; and although American industrialists were, in general, opposed to policies of war and imperialism, American politicians believed it was their duty to capture new foreign markets for American exports. The leading European powers, Great Britain, France, and Germany, were rapidly building or increasing their empires and beginning to engage in competition for military and naval supremacy. Americans were both infected by their example and alarmed lest their own security be threatened by this growth of aggressive power politics. The writings of such English imperialists as Rudyard Kipling had great influence in the United States; and such men as John Hay, Senator Henry Cabot Lodge, Theodore Roosevelt, and Whitelaw Reid of the New York *Tribune* were eager that their own country assert itself as a competitor of the European imperialisms. Similar ideas of nationalistic greatness were propagated by the popular newspapers developed by Joseph Pulitzer and William Randolph Hearst. Another proponent of an assertive foreign policy was Alfred T. Mahan, appointed lecturer in naval history at the Naval War College at Newport, Rhode Island in 1885, who for years employed his profound knowledge of naval history to urge the building of a strong American navy, and who was largely responsible for the fact that by 1900, with sixteen battleships completed or under construction, the navy of the United States was surpassed only by those of Great Britain and France.

In the 1880's and 1890's the United States government began to evince greater interest in Latin America, largely in the hope of increasing trade.

Attempts were made to promote Pan-American unity under the leadership of the United States. The chief prophet of Pan-Americanism was James G. Blaine, Secretary of State under President Harrison, who presided over the first Pan-American Congress in 1889. Such advances, however, received little response south of the Rio Grande until after World War I. The Latin American republics were generally suspicious of the United States, fearing its superior strength and believing that their own Catholic and Hispanic traditions might be endangered by Yankee economic penetration.

The anxieties of the Latin American countries were increased in 1895, when the United States made a most challenging assertion of its leadership in the Western Hemisphere. After Great Britain had refused to allow a boundary dispute between Venezuela and British Guiana to be settled by arbitration, Richard Olney, Secretary of State under President Cleveland, informed the British Prime Minister, Lord Salisbury: "Today the United States is practically sovereign on this continent, and its fiat is law upon the subjects to which it confines its intervention. Why? . . . It is not because of the pure friendship or good will felt for it. . . . It is because, in addition to all other grounds, its infinite resources combined with its isolated position render it master of the situation and practically invulnerable as against any or all other powers." The dispute was finally settled peacefully, with Great Britain submitting to arbitration. And since the British now decided to accept United States supremacy in the Caribbean area, the final result was a marked improvement in Anglo-American relations.

The War with Spain

The growing imperialist psychology of the American people found overt expression in 1898 in the war with Spain. In 1895 a rebellion against Spanish rule broke out in Cuba. At that time $50 million of American capital was invested in Cuba, but American business interests had no sympathy with the movement for Cuban independence and little desire that the United States become involved in the conflict, so long as their present interests and future opportunities in the island were not threatened. Western and southern farmers, on the other hand, many of whom were still chafing from the defeat of William Jennings Bryan's free silver plank in 1896, saw in a war with Spain an excellent opportunity to get Congress to accept their program for monetary inflation. Since many of them were also Protestants, they had another reason to go to war against Catholic Spain. Meanwhile there developed a considerable popular sentiment in favor of United States intervention on behalf of the rebels. This sentiment was stimulated by stories of atrocities committed by Spanish authorities —stories which were circulated by agents of the Cuban nationalists and by the newspapers of Pulitzer and Hearst, who were then engaged in a fierce circulation rivalry. The battleship *Maine* was sent to Havana to protect United States citizens, and on February 15, 1898, the ship was blown up, either by an internal explosion or by a mine. To this day, the exact cause of the disaster has not been determined.

The Spanish authorities were accused, wholly without evidence, of having caused the explosion, and President McKinley demanded that Spain agree to an armistice and accept United States mediation. The Spanish government was willing to comply, but it could not do so immediately because of Spanish public opinion. Meanwhile popular sentiment in the United States was demanding war; and McKinley, who wanted peace but who also had to consider the next election, was not strong enough to resist it. On April 11 he sent a message to Congress, in which he minimized the evidence that Spain was apparently preparing to accept the American demands and hinted that war had become necessary. On April 19 Congress declared war and pledged itself that Cuba should be liberated. The main causes of the war were the crusading ardor of the American people, in which motives of idealism and self-aggrandizement were curiously mingled, and the desire of a small but influential group of imperialists to use this opportunity for the expansion of American power and economic interests. Perhaps the best explanation why America went to war was supplied by Senator John C. Spooner in May, 1898: "I think . . . possibly the President could have worked out the business without a war, but the current was too strong, the demagogues too numerous, the fall elections too near."

The war was being fought to free Cuba, but its first episode was an attack on another Spanish possession, of which most Americans had never heard. Theodore Roosevelt, Assistant Secretary of the Navy, left in charge of the Navy Department for a single afternoon in February, had seized the opportunity to send orders to the Asiatic fleet that if war came it should proceed at once to the Philippines. Accordingly, in late April the fleet sailed, and on May 1 Admiral George Dewey won the battle of Manila Bay. In June American troops arrived, subsequently capturing the city of Manila, while elsewhere Filipino nationalists under Emilio Aguinaldo expelled Spanish officials and declared the Philippines an independent republic. Meanwhile there had been a successful naval and military invasion of Cuba, followed by the occupation of Puerto Rico; and on August 12 Spain sued for peace.

By the Treaty of Paris, signed on December 10, 1898, Cuba was to become independent and the United States acquired Puerto Rico, the Philippines, and the island of Guam in the Pacific, paying $20 million to Spain in compensation for the Philippines. This adoption of an imperialist policy, which meant that for the first time the United States was assuming dominion over colonial peoples who were not to be admitted to the full benefits of American citizenship, was opposed by the Democrats and by a number of New England Republicans. When the treaty was submitted to the Senate, it obtained the necessary two-thirds majority by only one vote. In the presidential election of 1900, Bryan, who was again nominated against McKinley, based his campaign on the issue of imperialism, demanding that the Philippines be immediately freed. But although Bryan opposed Old World colonialism for the United States, he shared the views of many Americans who believed it was necessary to safeguard the nation's access to world trade, commerce, and markets. McKinley was, however, elected by a slightly increased majority over his vote in the previous election, receiving 7,219,530 popular votes and 292 electoral votes, as against 6,358,071 and 155 for Bryan.

American Colonial Policy

The elaboration of an American colonial policy was largely the work of Elihu Root, who, after a long career as a New York lawyer, was appointed Secretary of War in 1899. Root's primary task was to make those drastic reforms in the organization of the army which the war had shown to be necessary, but he also took charge of overseas possessions. The primary purpose of American colonial administration was to train the colonial peoples for self-government on the American model. It was never unduly deferential to American business interests. But although the colonial policy of the United States was probably more liberal and enlightened than that of any other imperialist power, it could never overcome the natural dislike of the subject races for alien rule.

Cuba remained under American control for three and a half years, with General Leonard Wood as governor. Wood separated church and state, built schools, and reorganized the finances. Yellow fever, the causes of which had been discovered by Dr. Walter Reed and the Cuban physician Carlos Finlay, was stamped out by Major William C. Gorgas. Meanwhile a Cuban constitutional convention was meeting, and future relations between Cuba and the United States were being defined in an amendment to the military appropriations bill of 1901, written by Root and introduced into Congress by Senator Orville Platt. By the Platt Amendment the United States was to have the right to intervene in Cuba, when necessary, in order to maintain order and preserve Cuban independence. The Cuban government was not to permit any foreign power to secure control over the island or to acquire debts in excess of its capacity to pay. On May 20, 1902, Cuba became autonomous. Since the island was primarily dependent on the sugar industry, President Roosevelt negotiated a treaty by which Cuban sugar was admitted into the United States at 20 per cent less than the regular tariff schedule. On three occasions danger of revolution or civil war caused American troops or marines to be landed; and from 1906 until 1909, briefly in 1912, and again from 1917 until 1922 Cuba was partially controlled by United States officials.

Puerto Rico and the Philippines, under the Organic acts passed by Congress, were to be similar in status to the thirteen colonies before 1776. Each was to have a governor and a council appointed by the President and an elected legislature. According to the legal formula defining their status worked out by the Supreme Court, they were to be dependencies of the United States and not a part of it, their native inhabitants being American nationals but not American citizens. They did not have the full protection of the Bill of Rights, and unless Congress decided otherwise, they would be outside the American tariff wall. According to the Supreme Court the "fundamental" provisions of the Constitution, but not its "formal" provisions, applied to them. The chief "fundamental" provision was the right not to be deprived of life, liberty, or property except by due process of law, while the "formal" provisions included such rights as that to trial by jury.

Within its area of 3,670 square miles, Puerto Rico in 1898 had a population of about a million and by 1930 of more than a million and a half. In the generation preceding the great depression, Puerto Rican progress was disappointing. The death rate, quickly cut in half, created new population pressures, and by 1930, with one-third of the total government expenditures devoted to the school system, only half the children of the island were being educated. There were frequent conflicts between the government and the legislature; and American control intensified the island's economic problems. After 1902 Puerto Rico was inside the American tariff wall, and American corporations began to acquire ownership of sugar and tobacco plantations. By 1928 the total foreign investment, mostly from the United States, was $176 million, and 89 per cent of Puerto Rican foreign trade was with the United States. Meanwhile four-fifths of the population were without land of their own, and the island had become dependent for its livelihood on the export of sugar, tobacco, coffee, and fruit. In 1929 the average rural family in Puerto Rico was earning only $6.71 a week; and in the following year, when the depression cut down its export trade, 60 per cent of the population were unemployed and without means of support.

In the Philippines, American rule was more beneficial. These islands, more than 3,000 in number, had an area of 114,400 square miles, and a population amounting in 1903 to 7,635,426 and in 1930 to 12,082,000. The decision to retain them, rather than allow them to become independent, was due partly to a well-founded belief that their inhabitants were not yet fitted for self-government and partly to economic considerations. President McKinley explained to a group of Methodist ministers that "there was nothing left for us to do but to take them all, and to educate the Filipinos, and to uplift and civilize and Christianize them, and by God's grace do the very best we could by them as our fellow men for whom Christ also died." Other members of the government were more impressed by the suggestion that the Philippines would be a convenient base for trade with China and also by the probability that, if the United States surrendered them, they would be annexed by Germany.

A number of the Filipinos, headed by Emilio Aguinaldo, had expected independence; and for three years, from 1899 until 1902, an American army of 70,000 men—four times as large as that which had invaded Cuba—was engaged in crushing the Filipino nationalists. This prolonged guerrilla warfare cost 4,300 lives and was accompanied by numerous atrocities committed by both sides. In 1899 a commission headed by Jacob Gould Shurman was sent to prepare the way for the establishment of civilian government, and in 1900 a second commission was sent under the presidency of William Howard Taft, who in that same year was appointed the first civil governor. Congress passed the Organic Act in 1902, and the first legislature was elected in 1907.

The success of American rule was due largely to the work of Taft, who served as governor until December, 1903, and who became extremely popular among the Filipinos. By 1921 the rate of illiteracy had dropped from 85 to 37 per cent, and the number of school children had risen from 5,000 to more than 1,000,000. Cholera and smallpox were wiped out, and the infantile death rate in Manila was cut from 80 to 20 per cent. The government encouraged the growth of small landholdings and restricted the right of corporations to acquire land. Taft solved one of the most difficult problems of the islands, the wealth and power of the Catholic clergy, by visiting Rome and arranging for the purchase by the government of 400,000 acres of church lands and their sale to Filipino farmers on easy terms. As preparation for self-government, the number of Filipinos in the government service was steadily increased.

Progress toward autonomy became much more rapid after 1913 under the Democratic administration of Woodrow Wilson. Francis Burton Harrison, appointed governor of the islands by President Wilson, increased the number of Filipinos in the civil service, reducing the number of Americans from 2,623 in 1913 to 614 in 1921. He also gave the Filipinos a majority on the appointive commission and established government ownership of railroads and other economic enterprises. In 1913, moreover, the Underwood Tariff established complete free trade between the Philippines and the United States. In 1916 the Jones Act promised independence as soon as the Filipinos seemed to be ready for it, gave the suffrage to all literate males, and substituted an elective senate for the appointive commission.

The liberality of American rule did not prevent the Filipinos—or at least the more vocal of them—from wanting to govern themselves; and their desire for independence won increasing support in the United States. The United States derived few economic benefits from possession of the islands, either directly or through the development of trade with China; and American statesmen soon began to realize that they were a military liability. They were more than 6,000 miles from the American coast, and in the event of war with Japan it would be almost impossible to defend them. As early as 1907 Theodore Roosevelt, who had been more responsible than any other American for the conquest of the Philippines, had come to the conclusion that it had been a mistake.

In addition to Puerto Rico and the Philippines, the United States also owned the island of Guam, taken from Spain in 1898, and a part of the island of Samoa, known as Tutuila, taken by agreement with Great Britain and Germany in 1899; possessions destined to be more significant were Alaska and the Hawaiian Islands. Alaska, with an area of 590,000 square miles, had been purchased in 1867; but until the end of the century when, first, gold and, subsequently, copper, coal, and iron, were discovered, it remained unimportant. It was given the status of a territory in 1912 and became a state in 1959. The eight Hawaiian Islands, having an area of 6,406 square miles, had come under the control of immigrants from the United States, who set up a government in 1893, and secured annexation by the United States in 1898. Hawaii was given territorial rights in 1900, and statehood in 1960. The population was preponderantly of Chinese, Japanese, and Filipino descent, though the sugar and fruit plantations which were the islands' main sources of wealth were mostly owned by Americans.

The Open Door in China

Another indication of America's growing interest in world politics was the promulgation by John Hay of the "Open Door" policy in China. At the end of the nineteenth century the Chinese empire was apparently beginning to dissolve, and much of its territory was being carved into spheres of influence by the European powers and by Japan. In the Open Door policy the United States expressed its opposition to this process; America wished to preserve the territorial integrity of China, in the interests both of the Chinese themselves and of Americans who had commercial interests in the Far East.

The Open Door policy developed out of a proposal originally made by the British. Great Britain handled 65 per cent of China's foreign trade and had large investments in the Yangste Valley. Alarmed by French, Russian, and Japanese encroachments upon Chinese territory, in 1898 London suggested that the United States join Great Britain in demanding equal commercial opportunity for all nations in all parts of China. The United States refused this proposal, and Great Britain then adopted a different policy. Alarmed by the growing power of Germany, she proceeded to make agreements with her leading rivals in the Far East—with Japan in 1902, France in 1904, and Russia in 1907. John Hay had, however, been impressed by the British suggestion; and when he became Secretary of State, he resolved to add to it the concept of protecting Chinese territorial independence.

In 1899, in the first of the Open Door notes, Hay asked the leading European powers to adopt the principle of commercial equality for all nations within the spheres of influence they controlled in China. In 1900 when a group of fanatical Chinese, the Boxers, began to attack foreigners, the leading Western powers, including the United States, sent a joint military expedition to protect their citizens and suppress the Boxers, subsequently levying a heavy indemnity on the Chinese government. Fearing that the European powers might take advantage of the situation to annex part of China, Hay issued in July, 1900, the second of the Open Door notes, in which he urged not only commercial equality for all nations in China but also the territorial integrity of the Chinese empire.

In theory the Open Door policy, like the Monroe Doctrine, represented an admirable combination of idealism and self-interest. It would benefit the Chinese by protecting them from foreign conquest; it would benefit the Americans by enabling them to share in the commercial and industrial development of the Far East; and it would check the growth of imperialist rivalries and hostilities by preventing the European powers from excluding one another from any part of China. Unfortunately the United States was not strong enough to enforce the Open Door by itself, nor were the American people sufficiently interested in Far Eastern affairs to undertake the responsibilities of carrying out a positive policy. And although the European powers professed respect for the principles of the Open Door, they adopted qualifications and limitations which deprived their adherence of any practical reality. The United States hoped on several occasions that Great Britain would join it in defending the Open Door; but once the British had come to terms with their leading rivals, their primary interest in the Far East was to protect their own holdings in the Yangtse Valley. Successive administrations were to attempt for forty years to uphold the Open Door, which soon acquired the sanctity of a tradition; but their successes were dubious and their failures frequent. Nonetheless, whatever its political shortcomings as a basis for the formulation of a realistic Far Eastern policy, one sufficiently flexible to meet the changing conditions of that area, it did allow the United States, for a time at least, the opportunity to augment its interests and power in the Orient.

The emergence of the United States as a world power at the turn of the century was a dramatic event of worldwide import. The extent to which the consequences of our "splendid little war" with Spain altered America's position, interests, and responsibilities throughout the world was perceived only imperfectly by most people at the time. This is understandable, for the transformation of the United States from a hemispheric to a world power occurred abruptly, almost without warning. Nonetheless the events of 1898 and those which followed them marked the end of an era in American foreign relations, just as the great changes wrought by the technological and industrial developments of the last thirty-five years of the nineteenth century meant the end of many old, established economic patterns and practices and the development of new and more complex ones. The decade of the 1890's was a great dividing line for the diplomatic, economic, and political history of the United States. But the decade was equally significant for the many changes which were taking place in the ethnic character of the people, in their social relationships, and in their ideas regarding the purpose and function of democratic government.

Suggested Readings

Among the many books that treat parties and politics, Charles E. Merriam and Harold F. Gosnell, *The American Party System* (4th ed., New York, 1949) is most useful. Wilfred E. Binkley, *American Political Parties: Their Natural History* (3d rev. and enl. ed., New York, 1958) surveys the major changes and ideas underlying the parties. Consult also Denis W. Brogan, *Government of the People* (new ed., New York, 1944); Charles A. and William Beard, *The American Leviathan* (New York, 1930); Harold R. Bruce, *American Parties and Politics* (3d ed., New York [1937]); E. Pendleton Herring, *The Politics of Democracy* (New York [1940]); Claudius O. Johnson, *Government in the United States* (6th ed., New York, 1956); J. M. Mathews, *The American Constitutional System* (2d rev. and enl. ed., New York, 1940); James Bryce, *The American Commonwealth* (New York, 1888) is a classic, containing numerous insights into the working of the political system. Harold J. Laski, *The American Presidency* (New York [1940]) is an excellent collection of essays on various aspects of this office.

On the subject of corruption in American politics, see Samuel P. Orth, *The Boss and the Machine* (New Haven, Conn., 1919) and R. C. Brooks, *Corruption in American Politics and Life* (New York, 1910). Harold F. Gosnell, *Boss Platt and his New York Machine* (Chicago [1924]) is a useful study of an important political boss with national influence, while Walton E. Bean's *Boss Ruef's San Francisco* (Berkeley and Los Angeles, 1952) details the career of one of America's most unique city bosses. Austin F. Macdonald, *American City Government and Administration* (5th ed., New York, 1951) is a useful text on urban government and its problems. A recent study of the impact of social and economic change upon both Chicago and Illinois is Ray Ginger, *Altgeld's America, 1892–1905: The Lincoln Ideal versus Changing Realities* (New York, 1958). Herbert Croly, *Marcus Alonzo Hanna* (New York, 1912) is a useful biography with much pertinent information on the alliance of business and politics. See also Thomas P. Beer, *Hanna* (New York, 1929). The political ideas of the period are surveyed in Edward R. Lewis, *American*

Political Thought from the Civil War to the World War (New York, 1937)
and in Charles E. Merriam, *American Political Ideas . . . 1865–1917* (New
York, 1920).

There are a number of texts covering the constitutional history of the United
States that treat the problems of the federal judiciary after the Civil War. A
useful one is Alfred H. Kelly and Winfred A. Harbison, *The American Con-
stitution: Its Origins and Development* (rev. ed., New York, 1955). See also
such standard works as Ernest S. Bates, *The Story of the Supreme Court* (New
York [1936]); Charles A. Beard, *The Supreme Court and the Constitution*
(New York, 1912); and Charles E. Hughes, *The Supreme Court of the United
States* (New York, 1928). An especially useful study is Charles Warren, *The
Supreme Court in United States History* (rev. ed., 2 vols., Boston, 1935).
See also Benjamin N. Cardozo, *The Nature of Judicial Process* (New Haven,
Conn., 1922); Edward S. Corwin, *The Twilight of the Supreme Court* (New
Haven, Conn., 1934) and the same author's, *The Commerce Power versus States
Rights* (Princeton, N.J., 1936); and Felix Frankfurter, *Mr. Justice Holmes and
the Constitution* (Cambridge, Mass. [1927]). On Holmes and Brandeis, see
also Alfred Lief, ed., *The Dissenting Opinions of Mr. Justice Holmes* (New
York [1929]) and the same editor's *The Social and Economic Views of Mr.
Justice Brandeis* (New York [1930]). Brandeis' legal thought and the operations
of the Supreme Court are revealed further in Alexander M. Bickel, *The Un-
published Opinions of Mr. Justice Brandeis* (Cambridge, Mass., 1957). On
Holmes, see also Dorsey Richardson, *Constitutional Doctrines of Justice Oliver
Wendell Holmes* (Baltimore, 1924). A good study of Cardozo is Joseph P.
Pollard, *Mr. Justice Cardozo* (New York [1935]). Alfred Lief, ed., *Public
Control of Business: Selected Opinions by Harlan Fiske Stone* (New York
[1940]) is useful and specialized. Feliz Frankfurter and James M. Landis, *The
Business of the Supreme Court* (New York, 1927); and Charles Warren,
Congress, the Constitution and the Supreme Court (new rev. and enl. ed.,
Boston, 1935) are also pertinent.

Many of the titles cited in the bibliographical essay at the end of Chapter 1
are useful also for the political consequences emerging out of the social and
economic changes of the times. See, for example, Samuel P. Hays, *The Response
to Industrialism, 1885–1914* (Chicago, 1957), which is brief and contains an
excellently selected bibliographical essay, and the more detailed volume of
Harold U. Faulkner, *Politics, Reform and Expansion, 1890–1900* (New York,
1959). On the various aspects of the agrarian revolt, see especially Alex M.
Arnett, *The Populist Movement in Georgia* (New York, 1922); William D.
Sheldon, *Populism in the Old Dominion* (Princeton, N.J., 1935) and Paul H.
Buck, *The Road to Reunion, 1865–1900* (Boston, 1937). Paul Lewinson, *Race,
Class and Party* (New York, 1932) is especially good. See also Francis B.
Simkins, *The Tillman Movement in South Carolina* (Durham, N.C., 1926) and
the excellent study by C. Vann Woodward, *Tom Watson* (New York, 1938).
Solon J. Buck, *The Granger Movement* (Cambridge, Mass., 1913) and the
same author's *The Agrarian Crusade* (New Haven, Conn., 1920); John B.
Clark, *Populism in Alabama* (Auburn, Ala. [1927]); Frederick E. Haynes,

Third Party Movements since the Civil War (Iowa City, Iowa [1916]); Richard Hofstadter, *The Age of Reform* (New York, 1956); and Eric F. Goldman, *Rendezvous With Destiny* (New York, 1952) treat the farmer's protests less sympathetically than John D. Hicks, *The Populist Revolt* (Minneapolis, 1931).

There is no biography of Bryan that is superior in every respect, and William Jennings Bryan, *Memoirs* (Philadelphia, 1925) leaves much to be desired. Among the more useful biographies, the following deserve note: Paxton Hibben, *The Peerless Leader: William Jennings Bryan* (New York [1929]); John C. Long, *Bryan, The Great Commoner* (New York, 1928); Morris R. Werner, *Bryan* (New York [1929]); and Wayne C. Williams, *William Jennings Bryan* (New York, 1936). See also the perceptive essay on Bryan in Richard Hofstadter, *The American Political Tradition and the Men Who Made It* (New York, 1948) and the first part of Eric F. Goldman's, *Rendezvous with Destiny*, cited above. The most recent detailed analysis of Bryan's career as a national figure is Paul W. Glad, *The Trumpet Soundeth: William Jennings Bryan and His Democracy, 1896–1912* (Lincoln, Nebr., 1960).

On the early regulation of business, A. H. Walker, *History of the Sherman Law* (New York, 1910) although old is still useful, while Hans B. Thorelli, *The Federal Antitrust Policy: Organization of an American Tradition* (Baltimore, 1955) presents a more detailed and up-to-date account of the evolution of antitrust policy to 1903. An especially useful account of the many conflicts involved in formulating regulatory legislation for the growing size and influence of American business is Sidney Fine, *Laissez Faire and the General Welfare State: A Study of Conflict in American Thought* (Ann Arbor, Mich., 1956).

Most of the standard texts in diplomatic history contain the basic details of the foreign policy of this period and suggestions for further reading. See, for example, such works as Thomas A. Bailey, *A Diplomatic History of the American People* (6th ed., New York [1958]), especially excellent for its bibliographical notes, and Samuel F. Bemis, *A Diplomatic History of the United States* (4th ed., New York [1955]). More detailed surveys of the modern post-1898 period include J. H. Latané, *America as a World Power, 1897–1907* (New York, 1907), a volume in the old *American Nation* series. Carl R. Fish, *The Path of Empire* (New Haven, Conn., 1919) covers the same ground in less detail. See also Archibald C. Coolidge, *The United States as a World Power* (New York, 1908); and the recent studies by Foster R. Dulles, *America's Rise to World Power, 1898–1954* (New York, 1955) and Ernest R. May, *Imperial Democracy: The Emergence of America as a Great Power* (New York [1961]). The latter is a superb analysis of the events of the 1880's and 1890's that led to the recognition of the United States as a first-rate nation, including an especially astute and perceptive study of the causes leading to the war with Spain.

A recent, specialized appraisal of an important figure's views on American foreign policy is William M. Armstrong, *E. L. Godkin and American Foreign Policy, 1865–1900* (New York, 1957).

The growth of an Anglo-American accord in foreign policy is appraised in Lionel M. Gelber, *The Rise of Anglo-American Friendship, 1898–1906* (London, 1938) and in the more recent study by Charles S. Campbell, Jr., *Anglo-American Understanding, 1898–1903* (Baltimore, 1957).

On American expansion into the Pacific, see the excellent study by A. Whitney Griswold, *The Far Eastern Policy of the United States* (New Haven, Conn., 1938); J. M. Callahan, *American Relations in the Pacific and the Far East, 1784–1900* (Baltimore, 1901); and Tyler Dennett, *Americans in Eastern Asia* (New York, 1922).

The events of the Spanish-American War are interestingly recorded, largely in the words of the men who were in Cuba, and beautifully illustrated, in Frank Freidel, *The Splendid Little War* (Boston, 1958). The war's most famous battle is told by A. C. M. Azoy, *Charge!: The Story of the Battle of San Juan Hill* (New York, 1961). The causes and course of the war are summarized in William E. Leuchtenburg, "The Needless War with Spain," *American Heritage*, VIII (February 1957), 33–41, 95. Old, detailed, and still dependable is French E. Chadwick, *The Relations of the United States and Spain: The Spanish-American War* (2 vols., New York, 1909–11). Walter Millis, *The Martial Spirit* (New York, 1931) is sound, interesting, and revisionist, while Julius W. Pratt, *The Expansionists of 1898* (Baltimore, 1936) is a scholarly and most useful account of the causes of this conflict and the acquisition of Hawaii. Chapter I of George F. Kennan, *American Diplomacy, 1900–1950* (Chicago, 1951) appraises carefully the implications of American diplomacy on the origins, course and consequences of this war. The influence of public opinion and the press is detailed in Marcus M. Wilkerson, *Public Opinion and the Spanish American War* (Baton Rouge, La., 1932) and in Joseph E. Wisan, *The Cuban Crisis as Reflected in the New York Press, 1895–1898* (New York, 1934). William A. Swanberg, *Citizen Hearst* (New York, 1961) is a careful, detailed biography which contains much useful information on Hearst's early career.

The acquisition and administration of the newly acquired territories is discussed in a number of works, including William H. Haas, ed., *The American Empire* (Chicago [1940]); Richard F. Pettigrew, *The Course of Empire* (New York [1920]); Elihu Root, *The Military and Colonial Policy of the United States* (Cambridge, Mass., 1916); Albert K. Weinberg, *Manifest Destiny* (Baltimore, 1935); William F. Willoughby, *Territories and Dependencies of the United States* (New York, 1905); Leon Wolff, *Little Brown Brother: How the United States Purchased and Pacified the Philippine Islands . . .* (New York, 1961); William H. Anderson, *The Philippine Problem* (New York, 1939); William C. Forbes, *The Philippine Islands* (rev. ed., Cambridge, Mass., 1945); José S. Reyes, *Legislative History of America's Economic Policy toward the Philippines* (New York, 1923); Moorfield Storey and Marcial P. Lichauco, *The Conquest of the Philippines* (New York, 1926); Dean C. Worcester and Ralston Hayden, *The Philippines: Past and Present* (New York, 1930); Brookings Institution, *Porto Rico and Its Problems* (Washington, D.C., 1930); Russell H. Fitzgibbon, *Cuba and the United States, 1900–1935*

(Menasha, Wis., [1935]); Leland H. Jenks, *Our Cuban Colony* (New York [1928]); Ralph S. Kuykendall and A. Grove Day, *Hawaii: A History from Polynesian Kingdom to American Commonwealth* (New York [1948]); Earl S. Pomeroy, *Pacific Outpost: American Strategy in Guam and Micronesia* (Stanford, Calif. [1951]); Foster R. Dulles, *America in the Pacific* (2d ed., New York, 1938).

American interest in China is detailed in Mingchien J. Pao, *The Open Door Doctrine in Relation to China* (New York, 1923); Westel W. Willoughby, *Foreign Rights and Interests in China* (rev. and enl. ed., Baltimore, 1920); and reevaluated in Chapter II of George F. Kennan's *American Diplomacy, 1900–1950* cited above. Consult also Tyler Dennett, *Americans in Eastern Asia* (New York, 1922).

Economic interests and foreign policy are treated in Benjamin H. Williams, *Economic Foreign Policy of the United States* (New York, 1929) and more recently in the first two chapters of the challenging and provocative study of William Appleman Williams, *The Tragedy of American Diplomacy* (Cleveland and New York, 1959).

The Latin American policy of the United States has been the subject of many works. Dexter Perkins, *The Monroe Doctrine, 1867–1907* (Baltimore, 1937) is indispensable for the period its title indicates. See also G. H. Stuart, *Latin America and the United States* (5th ed., New York [1955]).

The rise of a new naval consciousness late in the nineteenth century is discussed in the biography of one of the "big navy" men of the times in William D. Puleston, *Mahan: The Life and Work of Captain Alfred Thayer Mahan* (New Haven, Conn., 1939); and it is expressed also in Mahan's own memoirs, *From Sail to Steam: Recollections of Naval Life* (New York, 1907). A good general account of the U. S. Navy's history is Harold and Margaret Sprout, *The Rise of American Naval Power, 1776–1918* (Princeton, N.J., 1939). Gordon C. O'Gara, *Theodore Roosevelt and the Rise of the Modern Navy* (Princeton, N.J. [1943]) is a detailed and careful statement of Roosevelt's efforts on behalf of a "big navy."

A number of biographies of important figures in the diplomacy of this period are very useful. Among these, consult Tyler Dennett, *John Hay* (New York, 1933); William R. Thayer, *The Life and Letters of John Hay* (Boston, 1915); Hermann Hagedorn, *Leonard Wood* (New York, 1931); and the detailed and highly able study by Philip C. Jessup, *Elihu Root* (2 vols., New York, 1938). On Root, see also the brief but excellent biography by Richard W. Leopold, *Elihu Root and the Conservative Tradition* (Boston, 1954). On Taft in the Philippines, see the first volume of Henry F. Pringle, *The Life and Times of William Howard Taft* (2 vols., New York [1939]).

3

The New Society

THE DEVELOPMENT OF INDUSTRY brought about far-reaching changes in the outlook and way of life of the average citizen. The older rural America had been a country of independent farmers and small businessmen. It had encouraged self-reliance, thrift, and versatility, and had promoted a strong sense of private property. The new society stimulated traits of a different kind. Its typical members were wage or salary earners in large organizations and were not independent property-owners. Even when they had property, it was frequently in the form of paper securities which entitled them to dividend payments but which gave them little control over any branch of economic activity. Instead of living in their own houses, they often lived in rented apartments; and instead of performing themselves most of the varied activities needed for the maintenance of life, they devoted themselves to a single job and relied for almost all their needs on the paid labor of other people. Thus the new industrial society promoted interdependence, and the old individualistic viewpoint of rural America had to be drastically modified.

Many of the changes in American ways of living can be summarized in the word *urbanization*. The proportion of urban Americans had been steadily increasing ever since the foundation of the republic. In 1790 only about one-twentieth of the American people lived in places with more than 2,500 inhabitants. By 1900 the proportion had risen to two-fifths, and by 1960 to more than three-fifths. (If all suburban areas were included, according to new criteria put forth by the Census Bureau, then in 1960 close to 70 per cent of all Americans were urban.) More than one quarter of the total population was now massed in seven great urban areas in and around the cities of New York, Chicago, Philadelphia, Boston, Detroit, Los Angeles, and Cleveland. Urban habits and ideas were, moreover, spreading rapidly through the rural areas.

For average middle-class citizens and for the more highly paid members of the working class, the new industrial society brought a vast improvement in standards of living. They enjoyed more comforts, more leisure time, and more access to facilities for recreation and for cultural appreciation. Life in the cities was in some ways more insecure and more conducive to anxiety than the life of the older rural and small-town America, but it was incomparably richer and more varied in the opportunities it offered for material and cultural development. Nevertheless, for a long time the evils associated with rapid urban growth were so conspicuous that they seemed almost to outweigh its advantages.

Most American cities were allowed to grow haphazardly, with little social planning or control. Real estate interests and speculative builders were generally left free to do as they pleased. In the late nineteenth century city expansion meant chiefly the building of rows of middle-class houses and of working-class tenements that had little air or sanitation and were designed to crowd as many families as possible into the smallest possible space. Little was done to secure open spaces for fresh air and recreation or to take advantage of rivers and other natural features. The congestion of slum areas quickly became appalling. Generally it was not until after irreparable harm already had been done that municipal authorities began to try to find remedies.

Gradually it became apparent that the old laissez-faire principles were no longer applicable, and city governments began to assume new responsibilities. They provided citizens with fresh water and with garbage disposal, established professional police and firefighting forces, made regulations for the protection of public health, set up relief agencies for assistance to the poor, and endeavored to plan further urban growth. Meanwhile a growing number of private citizens were aroused to take action against slum poverty and crime, and social work was becoming a recognized profession. By 1900 more than a hundred settlement houses had been set up in slum areas, Hull House in Chicago and the Henry Street Settlement in New York City being the best known, and social-work leaders like Jane Addams and Lillian Wald were becoming militant crusaders for government action to improve conditions.

ETHNIC PROBLEMS

Immigration

The economic growth of the United States was accompanied and made possible by a large-scale immigration which fundamentally altered the ethnic composition of the American people. Between 1820 and 1920 some 35 million immigrants entered the United States, though not all of them remained in the country permanently. This constituted the largest movement of people in all history.

Before 1890 the majority of the immigrants came from northern and western Europe, especially from Germany, Scandinavia, Great Britain, and Ireland. With the exception of the Irish, these groups were mainly Protestant and were accustomed to relatively high economic and cultural levels. Again with the exception of the Irish, they settled mostly in the rural areas of the United States. After 1890 the stream of immigrants began to flow mainly from southern and eastern Europe, from Italy and the Austrian and Russian empires, and also from French Canada. These later arrivals were Catholic, Greek Orthodox, or Jewish in their religious beliefs. Coming from relatively backward countries, they were frequently illiterate; and although they came mostly from rural areas in their homelands, lack of money made it necessary for most of them to become urban wage earners when they reached the United States. The two peak years of immigration were 1907 and 1914, in each of which more than 1.2 million persons were admitted.

By 1921, when the door to immigration began closing, the United States was no longer a predominantly Anglo-Saxon nation: it had become a combination of almost every people in the world. In 1790 more than 90 per cent of the white population was either English or Scotch-Irish. By 1920, according to the national origins quota, the English and Scotch-Irish element in the population had been reduced to 42.7 per cent, while some other estimates made it considerably lower. Every part of the country except the South had large immigrant colonies, the largest concentrations being in the industrial cities of the Northeast and the Middle West.

The immigrant groups supplied the bulk of the manual labor for building the railroads and for mining and manufacturing. They could often contribute to American society a color and emotional warmth that was

Italian immigrants arriving at Ellis Island, in upper New York Bay. Between 1911, when this picture was taken, and 1920 more than 1.1 million Italians left their homeland to establish new lives for themselves in the United States. (Brown Brothers)

lacking among the more dour and reserved Anglo-Saxons. And though it would be a long time before many of their members rose to leadership in federal politics or in industry and finance, some of them were soon playing important roles, despite economic and educational handicaps, in science and technology and in learning and the arts. Their arrival made the United States a new kind of nation—a nation bound together, not by community of race, history, and tradition, but by common hopes and ideals for the future and a common allegiance to the principles of human freedom and equality.

These principles, unfortunately, were not always respected. Because most human beings cannot easily conquer distrust for others whose racial and cultural past they recognize as different from their own, the older ethnic stocks were liable to regard the newcomers as a potential menace to American institutions, so that there were periodic outbreaks of racial and religious intolerance. The prevalent belief was that the immigrants must be assimilated and Americanized as rapidly as possible. Their languages and customs were treated as signs of inferiority, and they were encouraged to abandon their native traditions and to adopt the mores and beliefs of the dominant Anglo-Saxon, Protestant, and capitalistic culture.

The excessive rapidity of this Americanizing process, as imposed in the schools and by public opinion, created some difficult problems of adjustment. The majority of the immigrants were only too eager to become Americanized, but the process was often superficial, leading to the abandonment of much that was valuable in their previous heritage and to the acquisition only of undesirable American characteristics. This was particularly true of the children of immigrants. Regarding their parents' customs as signs of inferiority, they often became emotionally separated from them and grew up with little religious or family discipline. The prison rate among the foreign-born was only one-third of the national average, but among their children it was higher than the average. Crime and gangsterism flourished especially in those urban slum areas where one ethnic community intermingled with another and where the disintegration of cultural traditions was therefore especially rapid. The cause was not, as was too often assumed, the unrestricted admission of immigrants but the imposition upon them of a forced and superficial process of Americanization. As the journalist Jacob Riis pointed out, the important question was not what the immigrant was doing to America but what America was doing to the immigrant.

The Beginning of Restriction

Hostility to unrestricted immigration began to develop before the end of the nineteenth century. The most justifiable reasons for limitation were those presented by American labor organizations, which maintained that the flow of immigrants made it difficult to establish effective trade unions and to maintain high wage levels. Other factors in the demand for restriction were the strong popular prejudice against the Catholic Church and the belief of many people of Teutonic descent in the inherent inferiority of southern and eastern European groups. There were also allegations, which had no sufficient justification, that radical beliefs were prevalent among the immigrants.

Starting in 1875, the federal government began to exclude various undesirable characters, especially criminals and persons suffering from serious diseases. On several occasions Congress passed bills imposing literacy tests, but these were killed by presidential vetoes on the ground that they would discriminate unfairly against the natives of backward countries. Although presidential opposition to the literacy test was finally overridden by Congress in 1917, it was not until 1921 that the United States completely abandoned its traditional policy and imposed limitations upon the number of immigrants.

Special problems were presented by immigration from Asia, which encountered strong popular racial prejudices. Chinese immigrants had begun entering California before the Civil War, and many of them were employed in the building of the transcontinental railroads. Since they were willing to accept very low living standards, they were regarded by white workers as dangerous competitors. Any further immigration of Chinese laborers was temporarily forbidden in 1882, and the ban was made permanent in 1902. Chinese immigrants were not allowed to be naturalized, though Chinese born in the United States ranked, of course, as American citizens.

More complicated was the question of the Japanese, who began to come to California in the 1880's. Some of them became tenant farmers, and like the Chinese, they antagonized their white competitors by their industry and low standards of living. But when the California state legislature began to pass laws discriminating against them, the Japanese government protested. The problem was partially settled by the Gentlemen's Agreement of 1907, by which the government of Japan promised to stop the movement of Japanese laborers to the United States. But Japan continued to feel aggrieved by the race prejudice of which its people were the victims.

The Negro People

Far more difficult than any of the problems resulting from immigration were those confronting the Negro population. The position of the Negro in American civilization was a matter of peculiar complexity as a result of the barriers created by color prejudice and the heritage of slavery, the Civil War, and Reconstruction.

The number of Negroes in the United States in 1900 was 8,833,994, 11.6 per cent of the total population. The proportion had amounted to 19.3 per cent in 1790, and continued to decrease until 1920. The diminution, however, did not continue after the restriction of immigration, since the birth-death ratio of the Negroes differed little from that of the whites. The bulk of the Negroes were concentrated in the South, although they began to migrate northward in the twentieth century. In 1900, 90 per cent of them were in the South, where they constituted 32.3 per cent of the total population.

Of these southern Negroes, more than four-fifths were engaged in agriculture. The proportion of owners among Negro farmers had been increasing, amounting in 1900 to about one-quarter, most of the remainder being sharecroppers. But standards of living were extremely low: nearly half the Negro families lived in one-room cabins. The landlords of the Negro sharecroppers often prided themselves on caring for the welfare of their dependents, like the slave owners before the Civil War, and would help them when they suffered from sickness or a bad harvest. But the possibilities of fraud in such a relation were great. Most of the sharecroppers were in debt to their landlords and were bound to the soil until the debt was paid off. The increase of Negro ownership, moreover, was not maintained in the twentieth century; by 1935 the proportion of owners among the Negro farmers had dropped to one-fifth.

The educational development of the Negroes in the South was largely at the mercy of the white officials on the county boards of education. Segregation in the schools, as in transportation and many other areas of social life, was enforced by the "Jim Crow" laws of the southern states, and in theory the Negroes were entitled to equal facilities. This "separate but equal" doctrine was accepted by the Supreme Court in the case of *Plessy v. Fergusson* in 1896, the contention that segregation meant inequality being brushed aside as a mere subjective opinion without factual support. But in practice the Negro schools were far inferior to those of the white children. As late as 1930, the South was spending $45.63 for each white child and only $14.95 for each Negro child. Negroes received help, however, from private philanthropy, especially from the Rosenwald and Peabody foundations, while Congress passed an amendment to the Morrill Act in 1890 which resulted in the establishment of seventeen Negro land-grant colleges. The rate of Negro illiteracy dropped from 80 per cent in 1880 to only 5 per cent in 1960. But most of the one hundred and eight Negro colleges were either theological or mechanical institutes, and even the better institutions were severely handicapped by lack of money.

The most lamentable result of the inferior status of the Negro people was the prevalence of lynching. Originating in frontier communities where there was no adequate police protection, lynching had spread to the black belt in the South after the Civil War. According to figures compiled by Tuskegee Institute there were 4,733 lynchings between 1882 and 1950: 3,444 of Negro men and 84 of Negro women, the remainder being of white people. Nearly 90 per cent were in the South, and the worst year was 1892, when there were 292 lynchings. After 1900 the growth of more enlightened attitudes produced a slow but steady decrease; 1901 was the last year in which there were more than 100 cases, and 1926 the last year in which there were more than 30. In the 1950's there were only two for the whole decade.

In the South it remained difficult for Negroes to find occupations outside agriculture and personal service. Most forms of wage labor were preempted by white workers, and the southern trade unions were mostly hostile to the Negroes. The North, however, offered more opportunities; and although there was discrimination in housing, so that Negro families were mostly confined to urban slum areas, jobs were more plentiful and more varied. Through the twentieth century there was a steady movement among the Negro population from agriculture into the cities and from the South to the Northeast. By 1950 more than half of them were living in cities, more than a third of them were living in the North, and a considerable Negro business and professional class had emerged.

After the Civil War the Negro population had been encouraged by northern political leaders to expect full equality with the whites and rapid political, economic, and cultural progress. The failure of the Reconstruction experiment led to the formulation of more modest aspirations. The chief Negro spokesman of this period was Booker T. Washington, who founded Tuskegee Institute in 1881. Washington declared that the Negroes could solve their racial problems only by winning the respect of white people through hard work, sober conduct, and skill in agriculture and mechanics. He remained for many years the most influential Negro leader. In the twentieth century, however, younger Negro intellectuals began to attack Washington's program as too humble and too passive. The chief spokesman of this more militant viewpoint was W. E. Burghardt DuBois, a Harvard-trained scholar who became a professor at Atlanta University. Whereas Washington had argued that "the race, like the individual, that makes itself indispensable, has solved many of its problems," DuBois insisted that "persistent manly agitation is the way to liberty." This change of attitude led to the formation in 1910 of the National Association for the Advancement of Colored People (NAACP), which organized a long series of struggles to secure the rights supposedly assured to Negroes by the Constitution.

THE FORMATION OF PUBLIC OPINION

The Churches

In the twentieth century, as at earlier periods, the religious beliefs and moral values of a majority of the American people were derived, directly or indirectly, from the teachings of the Protestant churches. There were more than one hundred and fifty different Protestant denominations, though more than half the church members were Methodists or Baptists. Disagreements about the details of belief and practice were less emphasized than in the past, and there was a significant trend toward denominational cooperation in the pursuit of common objectives. This was exemplified in the formation, in 1908, of the Federal Council of Churches.

The later years of the nineteenth century had been a difficult period for the Protestant clergy. Most of them had been accustomed to regard the Bible as the inspired word of God, while their ethical teaching had reflected the economic individualism of the middle class, with much emphasis on the virtues of thrift and hard work. Each of these attitudes was now under attack. The authority of the Bible was undermined by the theory of evolution, as presented in Charles Darwin's *Origin of Species*, first published in 1859, and by the growth of the so-called "higher criticism" of the biblical record. Meanwhile belief in the virtues of economic individualism was less easy to maintain in the new industrial economy, which seemed to require a different approach to the problems of social justice.

A growing number of clergymen accepted the Darwinian hypothesis and found ways of reconciling it with Christian beliefs by arguing that much of the Bible should be interpreted allegorically rather than literally. God, they declared, was ultimately responsible for evolution, but he worked more slowly and less directly than had formerly been believed. Having abandoned the doctrine of the literal truth of the Bible, some modernist clergymen went on to deny all the supernatural elements in Christian theology and to reinterpret religion as an ethical attitude rather than a system of beliefs. These tendencies horrified religious conservatives, who, because they continued to insist on the authenticity of the biblical record, became known as "fundamentalists." During the twentieth century there was continued conflict between the two points of view; and while modernism in one form or another spread among wealthier and better-educated groups in urban areas, many rural churches, especially in the South, remained belligerently fundamentalist.

Concern with the problems presented by the growth of industrialism led to the formulation of the "social gospel." This originated in the 1880's among clergymen working in urban areas who were shocked by the living conditions of the working class. They declared that the Christian ethic had hitherto been interpreted too individualistically and that the churches should work for a reformed social order in which labor would no longer be exploited. Probably the most influential exponent of the social gospel was Walter Rauschenbusch of the Rochester Theological Seminary, author of *Christianity and the Social Crisis* (1907) and other books. It is difficult to estimate the concrete effects of this movement; Sunday sermons often have little influence on the weekday activities of the laity. But this new interpretation of Christian morality undoubtedly contributed to the strength of the progressive movement. Especially significant was the social creed adopted by the Methodist Episcopal Church in 1908, which called for the "most equitable division of the products of industry that can ultimately be devised," the reduction of hours of labor, and other economic reforms. It was subsequently adopted, with only minor changes, by the Federal Council of Churches.

A more indisputable indication of the strength of Protestantism was the growth of the prohibitionist movement. Spearheaded by the Anti-Saloon League, which was founded in 1895, this movement was supported especially by the Methodist, Baptist, and Presbyterian churches. By 1916 nineteen states had adopted total prohibition, and many others had passed local-option rules, with the result that three-quarters of the United States, containing half the population, was legally "dry." Passage of the Eighteenth Amendment followed in 1919. On the other hand Protestant attempts to maintain Sabbath-day observance and enforce other traditional blue laws had little success.

Meanwhile the immigration of Irish, Italians, Poles, south Germans, and other Catholic peoples, as well as the growth of parochial schools and Catholic colleges, was steadily increasing the strength of the Roman Catholic Church. By 1910 Catholics numbered 17 million, 17 per cent of the total population. Their ecclesiastical leadership continued to be largely Irish, though this caused some resentment among later immigrant groups.

Anti-Catholic prejudice continued to be a factor in American politics, especially in rural areas in the South and Middle West. Many old-fashioned

Protestants still believed that the Pope was antichrist and was conspiring to dominate America, an attitude that found expression in the late nineteenth century in the American Protective Association, and after World War I in the Ku Klux Klan. It flared up in the presidential election of 1928, in which the Democratic candidate, Al Smith, the first Catholic to be nominated by either major party, was heavily defeated and even failed to carry five of the traditionally Democratic southern states. On the other hand, religious issues were kept more in the background in the election of 1960, which gave America its first Catholic President in John F. Kennedy.

The Catholic Church found it easier than most Protestant churches to adapt itself to economic changes, since it had never been closely identified with economic individualism and had its own social gospel dating back to the teachings of the medieval scholastics. Officially, it was critical of strict laissez-faire doctrines and affirmed the duty of the government to protect the laboring classes and bring about social justice. On the other hand, it was vigorously opposed to socialism. This liberal attitude was not always reflected in the statements of Catholic ecclesiastics, some of whom were strongly conservative; but on the whole the Church in America gave its support to moderate economic reforms. Most American Catholics belonged to the working class, and Catholic influence was strong in the trade union movement.

On questions of personal morality the Church, however, remained firmly conservative. It was opposed to divorce and to artificial methods of birth control, and it favored the censorship of books and plays it regarded as inculcating immorality. The efforts of the Church to maintain legislation in accord with its ethical beliefs and to secure some measure of state support for its parochial schools continued through the twentieth century to present difficult problems of church-state relations.

Education

The ideal of free public education for all had won general acceptance during the nineteenth century, though it did not immediately become a reality. Thirty-two states had adopted compulsory education laws by 1900, and all forty-eight (the last being Mississippi) had acted by 1918. Most states began by requiring only two or three years' attendance at a grammar school, but the number of years was steadily extended, and states began to assume responsibility for providing secondary as well as primary education. By 1900 78 per cent of all children between the ages of five and seventeen were attending school, and by 1936 the proportion had risen to 84. The cost of public education, which had amounted to $9.23 per pupil in 1870, had increased by 1930 to $74.38. One of the results of this impressive growth was a fall in the national illiteracy rate to 11 per cent in 1900 and 4.3 per cent in 1930. But since education remained under the control of state and other local authorities, facilities varied considerably in different parts of the country. Rich states like New York, New Jersey, and California were able to spend about five times as much per pupil as the more poverty-stricken sections of the South.

The public school system was rightly regarded as one of the foundations of American democracy, not only because of the need for a literate electorate but also because the passage of most American children through the same schools promoted a sense of national unity and helped to weaken class and race distinctions. It was principally in the schools that the children of immigrants learned American ways and won acceptance into the American community. But the vast quantitative expansion of the system was accompanied by some lowering of standards. The main emphasis was placed on the education of children of average intelligence, and not enough was done to develop the talents of those with special gifts. Nor did the respect which the American people felt for education extend to the profession responsible for it. Teachers had a relatively low social status and were generally underpaid. City and state authorities often seemed to be more willing to spend money on elaborate buildings and athletic equipment than on adequate salaries. As late as 1900, the salary of the male teacher averaged only $42.14 a month, less than that of many manual laborers, while women teachers earned even smaller salaries. Since it was difficult to support a family on such earnings, relatively few men cared to enter the profession; the proportion of women teachers was 70 per cent in 1900 and rose to 85 per cent by 1920.

Meanwhile the need for trained teachers was met by the growth of normal schools and schools of education, and some training in educational methods gradually became a prerequisite for permanent appointment. Largely through the influence of the educational philosophy of John Dewey, progressive-minded teachers began to lay less emphasis on the dogmatic inculcation of fixed principles and ideas, to substitute "learning by doing" for learning by rote, and to connect the schools more intimately with society through the study of contemporary social institutions. These developments were strongly opposed by conservatives, who complained that in emphasizing the study of methods the schools of education seemed to be forgetting the importance of subject matter, and they criticized the progressives for underrating the need for intellectual discipline.

The development of the college system paralleled that of the public schools. In the later nineteenth century the financial resources of the colleges were enormously increased through the growth of tax-supported state universities, land grants made by the federal government under the Morrill Act of 1862, and gifts from rich men. By 1900 there were some 500 colleges, with a student enrollment of 237,000. The right of women to higher education was now generally recognized, and by 1900 they made up a quarter of the total number of undergraduates. By 1931 the number of institutions of higher learning had increased to 931, of which 262 were public, 205 private, and 464 denominational. College students numbered more than a million, faculty members exceeded 90,000, the money spent on higher education approached $500 million a year, and the total value of college properties and endowments was more than $3.5 billion.

The older American colleges had emphasized the study of classics and theology, one of their primary purposes being to provide the churches with a learned ministry. After the Civil War, with the growing importance of the sciences, college curricula and methods of instruction were revolutionized. The leader of the educational reformers was Charles W. Eliot, president of Harvard from 1869 to 1909. Eliot, who was himself a scientist, broadened the college curriculum by introducing numerous new subjects, and established the elective system, under which undergraduates, instead of confining themselves to a single course of study, were allowed considerable freedom of choice among different subjects. Critics of the elective system complained, with considerable reason, that it caused many undergraduates to acquire only a smattering of information in a bewildering variety of different fields without gaining real mastery in any of them; but in the beginning it was a useful weapon for breaking down the supremacy of the traditional disciplines.

A less controversial new development was the growth of facilities for postgraduate training and research. At Harvard President Eliot vitalized the professional schools of law and medicine and made them an integral part of the university. Almost as influential were the innovations made by Daniel Coit Gilman, president of the Johns Hopkins University from 1875 until 1912. Copying methods of higher education that had developed in Germany, Gilman established a graduate school in which students participated with professors in the work of seminars and were expected to devote themselves to research in order to obtain a doctorate. The innovations made by Eliot and Gilman quickly spread to other universities. Learning and research were also stimulated through the establishment of associations of scholars in all the major fields of knowledge and through the endowment by rich men of numerous libraries, museums, laboratories, research institutes, and research fellowships. No longer considered merely teaching institutions, colleges and universities were expected not only to transmit existing knowledge but also to add to it. Henceforth American universities made increasingly important additions to all branches of the natural and social sciences.

Not all the new developments in higher education were healthy. An unduly large proportion of the available money was spent on buildings (many of them in an unfunctional pseudo-Gothic), largely because millionaire contributors and college presidents wanted to leave concrete memorials of their generosity and statesmanship. Academic freedom was endangered both by the powers of state legislatures over the state universities and by the eagerness of private colleges to extract endowments from rich men; and instructors holding opinions considered radical were occasionally dismissed. In American universities, unlike those of Europe, control was vested not in the faculties but in bodies of trustees, so that administration was largely divorced from teaching. Another new development which, though adding to the excitement of college life, was not conducive to high academic standards was the growth of organized athletics. Introduced from England after the Civil War, football had acquired a new character, rougher and more complicated than its English model, and had been adopted by most American colleges before the end of the century. Baseball, which had become a national sport during the Civil War, became almost equally popular, as also did basketball, which was invented at the YMCA college at Springfield, Massachusetts, in 1891. In the twentieth century, with the growth of alumni enthusiasm that often approached hysteria, some colleges seemed in danger of degenerating into mere adjuncts to athletic stadiums.

The Press

Prior to the development of the radio after World War I, Americans derived their knowledge of national and world affairs mainly from newspapers. Since the American press never became national, each city of any size relied primarily for its news on papers which were published locally and gave considerable attention to local events. In 1900 the United States had 2,226 daily newspapers with a total circulation of 15 million and 14,000 weeklies with a total circulation of 42.5 million. Half of all the world's newspapers were published in the United States.

Through most of the nineteenth century the leading newspapers had expressed the tastes and opinions of individual editors, but with the growth of journalism into a big business the press became less personal. In the twentieth century there was less competition, and ownership began to consolidate, national newspaper chains being created by such men as William Randolph Hearst and Edward W. Scripps. At the same time the financial resources of the press increased as a result of larger circulations and a rapid growth of advertising, and this made possible a considerable improvement in the mechanism of production and the efficiency of news gathering. A more comprehensive news service was provided through the establishment of the Associated Press and other independent news-gathering agencies.

The growth of popular daily newspapers with enormous circulations was largely due to the work of Joseph Pulitzer and William Randolph Hearst. Pulitzer, an immigrant from Hungary who had come to the United States without financial resources in 1864, acquired the New York *World* in 1883. He built up its circulation by printing lurid news stories, but used its editorial columns to campaign for liberal reforms and honesty in government. Hearst, who had inherited a fortune from his father, a California mining millionaire, became owner of the New York *Journal* in 1895. The two men became bitter rivals and were soon competing with each other in stirring up the popular hysteria which contributed largely to the war with Spain. Each paper soon ran up its circulation to the unprecedented figure of more than a million. Since they printed rival versions of an early comic strip featuring a character known as the Yellow Kid, their sensationalist methods became known as "yellow journalism." Pulitzer continued to support liberal causes until his death in 1911. During the first half of his career, Hearst, while always belligerently nationalistic, attacked big business and advocated reforms verging on socialim, but after World War I he swung over to conservatism. He acquired a large chain of papers, most of which he continued to control until his death in 1951.

Other entrepreneurs copied the methods of Pulitzer and Hearst, and many of the smaller papers, unable to withstand this kind of competition, went out of business or merged with others. After 1900 the num-ber of daily and weekly newspapers began to decrease, dropping to 10,000 by 1950; and in some cities the entire press came under the owner-ship of a single syndicate. Thus the chief agencies of informing the public were coming under the control of wealthy entrepreneurs who might be expected to use their influence to oppose progressive attitudes. Insofar as they slanted news reports and appealed to mass prejudices, they were poisoning public information at its source. On the whole, however, elec-tion returns during the twentieth century seem to indicate that news-papers had less influence over public opinion than might have been ex-pected.

A small but distinguished group of papers continued to supply reasona-bly complete and accurate news coverage. *The New York Times*, con-trolled after 1896 by Adolph Simon Ochs, generally lived up to its slogan of giving "all the news that's fit to print," as did some other journals in other sections of the country. Unfortunately even the best American newspapers did not circulate widely outside the cities where they were produced, and there were many sections of the country which remained alarmingly uninformed about world affairs.

A similar trend toward mass production and circulation was manifested in the magazine field. The most influential nineteenth-century maga-zines were generally sober and conservative in tone and appealed only to highly educated readers. But the 1890's saw the advent of new popular magazines which printed good fiction and accurate news stories but which were sold at a low price and aimed at a wide circulation. The pioneers in this field were Edward Bok, Frank A. Munsey, and John Brisben Walker; but the most vigorous of the new publishers was S. S. McClure, who began in 1893 to issue a magazine named after himself which sold for only ten cents. Another influential new magazine was *The Saturday Evening Post*, which achieved a circulation of 2 million early in the twentieth century and held it for several decades.

During the first decade of the twentieth century these new cheap magazines continued to maintain high literary standards and to have a healthy influence on public opinion. In particular, they sponsored the muckraking movement, which did much to stimulate the reforms of the progressive era. Later in the century they generally swung over to a more conservative position, and their fiction, news stories, and editorials tended to glorify the businessman and the mores of the American middle class. In part this reflected a popular reaction against muckraking, though it may also have been a response to advertising pressure from business interests. A number of high-priced monthlies such as *Harper's*, *Scribner's*, *The Forum*, and *The Atlantic*, continued, however, to present a more realistic attitude toward the contemporary scene, while an influence out of proportion to their small circulations was exercised by two liberal weeklies, *The Nation* and *The New Republic*.

NEW INTELLECTUAL AND ARTISTIC TRENDS

Paralleling the transformation of the United States from a predominantly rural and agrarian society to one largely urban and industrial was a corresponding change in intellectual attitudes and beliefs. Early Americans had mostly believed that social institutions and ethical standards should be guided by laws of nature either revealed by God or discovered by human intelligence. Since these laws of nature were not subject to change, social and moral values were essentially fixed and did not vary in different environments. Americans had also believed that individuals should be responsible for their own welfare, both spiritual and economic, and that paternalism was likely to undermine their moral strength. This faith in individualism, originally derived partly from the religious doctrines of Protestantism and partly from the theories of eighteenth-century liberal politics and laissez-faire economics, was strengthened by the influences of the American environment with its abundance of cheap land, and its relative freedom from the social, racial, and religious intolerance of the Old World. In the American world before the rise of big business, it was relatively easy to justify the popular belief that the welfare of each individual depended largely on his own efforts, and that if he failed to prosper it was usually because of his own weaknesses.

Social Darwinism

In the later nineteenth century both the traditional faith in fixed truths and values and the confidence in individualism began being challenged. Truths and values, it was now affirmed, might vary in different situations and should be viewed as dynamic rather than static, relative rather than absolute. Men might often suffer from poverty and unemployment through causes wholly outside their own control, and the simple individualistic moral code of earlier generations was no longer an adequate guide. Individual welfare required positive intervention by social agencies. The main reason for these changes of viewpoint was the growth of the new industrial economy, but an important intellectual influence was exercised by the theory of evolution. Darwinism promoted a dynamic conception of values and implied that they should be regarded not as absolutes but as instruments in man's struggle to master his environment.

The application of the evolutionary theory to the workings of human society was known as Social Darwinism. Before the end of the nineteenth century this had brought about far-reaching changes of intellectual attitudes. In its initial manifestations, however, it seemed to promote conservative rather than progressive conclusions. Darwin had argued that the struggle for existence between different species was the chief factor in evolution. This emphasis on the value of struggle was used by the English philosopher Herbert Spencer to justify economic competition and laissez faire. Unrestricted competition would guarantee continued progress, while state action tending to protect the weak and unfit against the strong and better adapted was contrary to natural law and would do more harm than good. Spencer's ablest American disciple was William Graham Sumner, professor of political and social science at Yale from 1872 until his death in 1910. A brilliant, belligerent lecturer and writer, Sumner devoted much of his life to defending economic individualism and attacking humanitarian reformers who proposed to check the struggle for existence. Although Sumner was too honest and independent a thinker to be merely an apologist for big business—he incurred much hostility by attacking the protective tariff, which he correctly regarded as contrary to genuine individualism—his main importance was in providing new arguments to justify old-fashioned capitalism.

Another form of Social Darwinism glorified conflict between races and nations. The notion that mankind was divided into biologically distinct racial groups, some of which were superior to others, had been popularized by various European pseudoscientists, especially by the Frenchman Arthur de Gobineau. The racists quickly adopted Darwinism and began to argue that the higher races should preserve their biological purity and should have no humanitarian compunctions about conquering and exploiting their weaker neighbors. Racist thinking was too contrary to American ideals to strike any deep roots in the United States; but it began to spread during the 1880's and took the form of claiming some inherent superiority for so-called Anglo-Saxons, or sometimes for all people of Teutonic stock. Advocates of American imperialism, such as Theodore Roosevelt before he assumed the Presidency, argued mostly in Darwinian terms, declaring that the United States should prepare itself for world leadership and should be ready to assume "the white man's burden" of governing backward peoples, such as the Filipinos. Racist doctrine was also influential in the movement for ending the unrestricted immigration of allegedly inferior ethnic groups, such as those from southern and eastern Europe.

Toward the Welfare State

A more important new trend in social and economic theory was the growing emphasis on social responsibility for individual welfare. This made a sharp break with the traditional individualism of American thought, and prepared the way for the reforms of the progressive and New Deal eras. Its exponents retained the Darwinian belief in evolutionary change, but insisted that man should consciously guide and plan his own development instead of submitting to natural processes. In the words of the sociologist Lester Frank Ward, there was "no natural harmony between natural law and human advantage." Because a laissez-faire economic system did not necessarily promote human progress, its operations should be regulated and modified by government intervention.

Probably a majority of professional economists remained faithful to laissez-faire doctrines, insisting that these represented absolute truths and were valid for all societies. But a growing number of younger men revolted against this fatalistic approach. When the American Economic Association was founded in 1885, its original draft of principles affirmed that the state was "an agency whose positive assistance is one of the indispensable conditions of human progress" and that "the doctrine of *laissez-faire* is unsafe in politics and unsound in morals." Among the spokesmen of this viewpoint were Richard T. Ely, of the University of Wisconsin, who believed that economic processes should be modified by Christian ethics, and Simon Nelson Patten, of the University of Pennsylvania, who suggested that the United States was moving toward a new economy of abundance in which the classical principles would no longer be valid. Another group of economists, of the so-called historical or institutionalist school, believed that the primary function of the economist was not to formulate general principles but to analyze what actually

happened, often showing that this was vastly different from what, according to classical principles, was supposed to happen. These included
John Rogers Commons, of Wisconsin, who made pioneer studies of
American labor history, and Wesley Clair Mitchell, of Columbia University, who emphasized the need for statistics and used them to elucidate
the business cycle, which had hitherto been regarded as a kind of act
of God which man could not hope to control. A more radical institutionalist was Thornstein Veblen, who made a number of highly critical
studies of big business practices and gloomily predicted that as the
ownership of industry became more consolidated, it would end in the
establishment of some kind of militaristic and imperialistic dictatorship.

Meanwhile, outside academic circles the American people were becoming increasingly receptive to proposals for economic change. A wide
influence was exercised by Henry George, whose *Progress and Poverty*
appeared in 1879. George argued that as civilization advanced, the mass
of the people were increasingly impoverished, and suggested that the
main cause of injustice was the private ownership of land and natural
resources by a small group of landlords. His remedy was a "single tax"
on land, to give back to the community that part of the land's value
which was not derived from the labor of the owner. This was oversimple;
but many readers who did not accept George's positive proposals were
awakened to the need for some kind of reform by reading his books.
Another significant trend was the popularity of socialist utopias. The
first of them, Edward Bellamy's *Looking Backward*, published in 1888,
had an enormous sale and inspired numerous imitations. However, relatively few Americans were converted to socialism. A Socialist party was
formed in 1901, and its leader, Eugene Debs, was widely respected for his
integrity and idealism; but the party vote in presidential elections never
made it a serious contender against the older parties. At its greatest
strength, in the elections of 1912 and 1920, its supporters numbered less
than a million. Yet many people who did not accept the socialist program
were made aware of economic injustices by reading socialist literature.

Pragmatism

Contemporary with these new tendencies in social theory was a new
philosophical movement, which was of equal importance in changing
traditional ideas. This was the movement known as pragmatism or instrumentalism.

Philosophy, originally treated in American colleges as subordinate to theology, began developing as an independent discipline in the 1880's. Initially, most American teachers of philosophy were strongly influenced by German idealism, which affirmed the unity of the universe and regarded it as an expression of the divine mind. Pragmatism, on the other hand, originated in America and displayed an American concern for practical utility and an American belief in the freedom and uniqueness of every individual. The pragmatist approach to philosophy originated in the 1870's in the writings of Charles Sanders Peirce, and its best-known exponent was William James, who turned to philosophy late in life after devoting himself primarily to psychology. Similar views were developed in more detail and with more philosophical elaboration in the writings of John Dewey, who preferred to call himself an instrumentalist.

Pragmatism affirmed that thinking was subordinate to action, that the real function of the mind was to serve as a guide for successful behavior, and that all ideas should be judged by their practical consequences. The true significance of any general proposition was to be discovered by inquiring what it meant in terms of human action. It was thus a theory about the human mind rather than about the nature of the universe, though in other writings James presented more general views of human life. He insisted that this was an open universe in which nothing was predetermined—God was not omnipotent—and in which man was free and his decisions made a real difference to the course of future events. Every event was in some way unique, and general laws were, at best, mere approximations to the truth. Perhaps the main weakness of pragmatism was its failure to establish criteria for moral and social values, for which reason it was criticized by more conservative thinkers on the ground that it weakened traditional standards without putting any sufficiently definite new ones in their place.

The most valuable consequence of pragmatism was to encourage a critical examination of traditional beliefs. By applying to general principles the test of practical efficacy, it made both their virtues and their deficiencies more evident. Its influence was especially important in education, where it resulted in the theory of "learning by doing." Instead of inculcating truth dogmatically, teachers should encourage their pupils to discover truths themselves through practical experiment. Pragmatism also had significant effects on jurisprudence. In this field it caused students of the law to abandon the belief that the courts were engaged in interpreting immutable constitutional principles and to inquire instead into the actual social consequences of court decisions. William James's friend Justice Oliver Wendell Holmes viewed the judiciary with a wholesome skepticism, declaring that "the prophecies of what the courts will do in fact, and nothing more pretentious, are what I mean by the law." His conclusion was that the courts should allow governments more freedom to experiment with new kinds of legislation. Meanwhile, Roscoe Pound, of the Harvard Law School, was teaching that jurisprudence "must be judged by the results it achieves, not by the niceties of its internal structure; it must be valued by the extent to which it meets its ends, not by the beauty of its logical process." He advocated "putting the human factor in the central place and relegating logic to its true position as an instrument." This pragmatist approach was exemplified by Louis D. Brandeis, whose practice was to show the real meaning of judicial decisions by examining in detail their economic and social consequences. Legal pragmatism thus brought American constitutional theory into closer contact with the realities of twentieth-century life.

The broader implications of pragmatism were even more important. It reflected, and gave support to, the American distrust of dogmatic systems of belief, and the American confidence in individual freedom and in a bold experimentalism. The twentieth century would see many other countries come under the rule of groups of fanatics who affirmed the absolute truth of some system of ideas and refused to allow any dissent from it. The American way, as illustrated in the progressive movement and in the New Deal, was very different. Instead of adopting some unitary theory of social development, American reformers concentrated on practical needs and were willing to make any experiments that looked promising and to abandon them if they failed to produce desirable results. This flexible and modest approach to social problems, thoroughly pragmatist in spirit, precluded all dangers of dictatorship and civil war, and enabled the United States to make more genuine progress by peaceful methods than other countries did by revolution.

New Trends in the Arts

As in social and philosophical thought, so also in literature and art the end of the nineteenth century saw a sharp break with traditional attitudes. The new writers and painters began to deal directly with the new urban and industrial society, and were denounced by aesthetic conservatives for their lack of reticence, their pessimism, and their apparent preference for ugliness rather than beauty.

Prevalent literary and aesthetic standards had never been lower than in the later nineteenth century. Popular taste demanded conformity with conventional beliefs and sentimental romanticism. In the 1890's the accepted leaders of American poetry were such figures as Thomas Bailey Aldrich and Richard Watson Gilder, who produced diluted imitations of Alfred Tennyson; while the chief tendency in the novel was toward historical romance, as exemplified in the works of Thomas Nelson Page, Winston Churchill, S. Weir Mitchell, F. Marion Crawford, and Mary Johnston. Similar tendencies were upheld in painting by the National Academy of Design, whose members liked to produce large historical or mythical pictures, often featuring idealized nudes. Writers and artists were expected to produce a type of beauty that had nothing to do with reality. Great figures were by no means lacking, notably Mark Twain and Henry James in the novel, and Thomas Eakins and Winslow Homer in painting; but they lacked an audience with adequate critical taste to understand them fully. Readers laughed at Mark Twain's humor, but failed to appreciate his underlying pessimism about human life; and most of them were bewildered by James's subtle analyses of human character.

The movement toward realism was initiated by William Dean Howells, who wrote novels about typical middle-class characters confronting typical problems. His reticence about sexual relationships and his optimistic insistence that "the more smiling aspects of life . . . are the more American" prevented him from being fully realistic, but he gave support and encouragement to most of the younger men. A much sharper break with the so-called "genteel tradition" came about at the turn of the century. Writers began to abandon the conventions of English and German romanticism, which had dominated American literature through most of the century, and to imitate the French and Russian realists, especially Emile Zola and Leo Tolstoy. They were strongly influenced by the materialistic and antireligious doctrines of nineteenth-century scientists and by the gloom provoked by the evils of industrialism. They began to describe the society in which they lived with a remarkable frankness and a lack of respect for accepted moral standards. These new attitudes were represented particularly in the writings of Stephen Crane, Frank Norris, and Theodore Dreiser. Crane and Norris both died young, but Dreiser lived to become a major figure of twentieth-century literature. His first novel, *Sister Carrie*, appeared in 1900, though the book's irreverent attitude toward traditional morality caused such antagonism that he did not publish his second novel until 1911. In poetry similar tendencies were represented by Edwin Arlington Robinson, who published his first volume in 1896 but—in spite of the outspoken admiration of Theodore Roosevelt—did not achieve adequate recognition until after World War I.

During the first dozen years of the twentieth century these trends were not carried much further, possibly because many intellectuals became preoccupied with the progressive movement and the struggle for reform. Writers like David Graham Phillips and Upton Sinclair dealt with political and social problems on a relatively superficial level, and were joined by Winston Churchill, hitherto known as an author of historical romances. The most widely known novelist of the period was probably Jack London, who called himself a revolutionary socialist but who was also influenced by Nietzschean doctrines of master races and supermen. Of humble origin and mostly self-educated, London was significant as representative of new trends in American life, but he was too undisciplined to achieve permanent importance. The two best novelists whose work belonged largely to the early twentieth century were women whose subject matter was regional rather than national and who did not attempt to cope with any of the major problems of national life. Edith Wharton analyzed the ethical and social standards of old New York families with aristocratic pretensions, while Ellen Glasgow wrote similarly about the old families of Richmond, Virginia.

New beginnings in painting paralleled those in literature. At the end of the nineteenth century a number of young artists, the most prominent being Robert Henri and John Sloan, began to portray urban scenes with the same harsh fidelity to fact that Norris and Dreiser were introducing into fiction. Displaying strong social consciousness and radical sympathies, their work marked an abrupt break with the conventional belief that art should be concerned only with "beauty." The group achieved notoriety in 1908 when eight of them held a joint exhibition in New York. Conservative critics referred to them as the "Ashcan School" and the "Revolutionary Black Gang" and complained that they "deliberately and conscientiously paint the ugly wherever it occurs." But they were excellent craftsmen, and the vigor and gusto with which they rendered American life made them most stimulating influences on the art of the twentieth century.

The architectural equivalent of realism was functionalism, which represented an attempt to find a new American style appropriate to the new society. Most late nineteenth-century American architects had copied earlier European styles with little consideration for appropriateness or practical convenience and had covered their buildings with ostentatious and irrelevant ornamentation. In revolt against these false values, pioneers like Louis Sullivan and his pupil Frank Lloyd Wright insisted that the form of a building should reflect its function, made a bold and frank use of new materials, and abandoned much of the ornamentation. The new functionalist approach was beginning to make headway in the 1880's, but the Chicago Exposition of 1893, with its dazzling array of buildings in classical and Renaissance modes, restored the prestige of the older styles, which retained their dominance until after World War I. Government buildings continued to be mostly classical, churches and universities were mostly Gothic, while the private homes of rich families were often copied from Renaissance palaces. The work of the functionalists was studied in Europe, where it had a wide influence in some countries, but for a long time it had little effect on building in America.

Thus new tendencies in several different aesthetic fields were taking shape before the turn of the century, but for a long time they had a kind of underground existence and so did not begin to dominate the cultural scene until after World War I. The accepted intellectual leaders of American society in the universities and in magazine and book publication paid little attention to the growth of realism and continued to preach optimism, respectability, and artistic and ethical conservatism. There was, however, one figure, born into high social position and endowed with great intellectual talents and wide learning, whose attitude toward modern society was fully as pessimistic as that of the new novelists and artists. After a lifetime largely divided between teaching and writing history at Harvard and associating with the nation's political leaders at Washington, Henry Adams concluded in his *Education* that the high moral and political standards bequeathed to him by his ancestors had no place in the chaotic and predatory world of the new industrialism, that the changes which had befallen America might fairly be measured by the differences between President Washington and President Grant, and that the transition from the organic unity of the medieval period to the disintegrated multiplicity of modern society might well be regarded as decay rather than as progress.

Suggested Readings

Three volumes in the *History of American Life* series cover social changes around the turn of the century: Arthur M. Schlesinger, *The Rise of the City, 1878–1898* (New York, 1933); Ida Tarbell, *The Nationalization of Business, 1878–1898* (New York, 1936); and Harold U. Faulkner, *The Quest for Social Justice, 1898–1914* (New York, 1931). Nelson M. Blake, *A Short History of American Life* (New York, 1952) is a useful survey.

On the beginnings of organized charity, see Robert H. Bremner, *From the Depths: The Discovery of Poverty in America* (New York [1952]) and Frank D. Watson, *The Charity Organization Movement in the United States* (New York, 1922). Jane Addams, *Twenty Years at Hull House* (New York, 1922) is an interesting memoir.

Marcus L. Hansen, *The Immigrant in American History* (Cambridge, Mass., 1940) and Carl Wittke, *We Who Built America* (New York, 1939) are standard works on immigration. Oscar Handlin, *The Uprooted* (Boston, 1951) describes immigrant experiences. Francis J. Brown and Joseph S. Roucek, eds., *Our Racial and National Minorities* (New York, 1937) is a useful survey. Opposition to the immigrant is described in John Higham, *Strangers in the Land: Patterns of American Nativism* (New Brunswick, N.J., 1955). For the movement to limit immigration, see William S. Bernard, ed., *American Immigration Policy* (New York [1950]) and Roy L. Garis, *Immigration Restriction* (New York, 1927).

There are an immense number of books dealing with white-Negro problems. John Hope Franklin, *From Slavery to Freedom* (New York, 1947) and E. Franklin Frazier, *The Negro in the United States* (New York, 1949) are general surveys. Gunnar Myrdal, *An American Dilemma* (2 vols., New York, 1944) is an exhaustive study of race relations. Booker T. Washington stated his beliefs in his *Up From Slavery* (New York, 1901) and in *My Larger Education* (New York, 1911). For William E. B. Du Bois see his *Black Folks, Then and Now* (New York [1939]). Different aspects of Negro life are described in Melville J. Herskovits, *The American Negro* (New York, 1928); Dwight O. W. Holmes, *The Evolution of the Negro College* (New York, 1934); Vernon Loggins, *The Negro Author* (New York, 1931); Carter G. Woodson, *The History of the Negro Church* (Washington, D.C., 1921); Arthur F. Raper, *The Tragedy of Lynching* (Chapel Hill, N.C., 1933); and Sterling D. Spero and Abram Harris, *The Black Worker* (New York, 1931). For the Negro in politics, see Harold F. Gosnell, *Negro Politicians* (Chicago [1935]); Paul Lewinson, *Race, Class and Party* (London, 1932); William F. Nowlin, *The Negro in American National Politics* (Boston, 1932); and Elbert L. Tatum, *The Changed Political Thought of the Negro, 1915–1940* (New York [1951]).

There is no definitive history of American religion, but William W. Street,

The Story of Religion in America (2d rev. ed., New York [1950]) is the most useful survey. See also Anson P. Stokes, *Church and State in the United States* (3 vols., New York, 1950). Useful books on the changing attitudes of the Protestant churches include Aaron I. Abell, *The Urban Impact on American Protestantism, 1865–1900* (Cambridge, Mass., 1943); Charles H. Hopkins, *The Rise of the Social Gospel, 1865–1915* (New Haven, Conn., 1940); and Henry F. May, *Protestant Churches and Industrial America* (New York [1949]). For the history of Catholicism in America, see Theodore Maynard, *The Story of American Catholicism* (New York, 1941), and for changes in attitude, consult Robert D. Cross, *The Emergence of Liberal Catholicism in America* (Cambridge, Mass., 1958).

The standard work on the public school is Ellwood P. Cubberly, *Public Education in the United States* (rev. and enl. ed., Boston [1934]). For the colleges, see Charles F. Thwing, *A History of Higher Education in America* (New York, 1906). Merle E. Curti, *Social Ideas of American Educators* (Paterson, N.J., 1959) is a stimulating analysis. Richard Hofstadter and Walter P. Metzger, *The Development of Academic Freedom in the United States* (New York, 1955) is a standard work. See also Howard K. Beale, *Are American Teachers Free?* (New York [1936]).

The history of the press is covered in Frank L. Mott, *American Journalism* (rev. ed., New York, 1950), and for periodicals, see the same author's, *A History of American Magazines* (4 vols., New York, 1930–57). For biographies of leading figures, consult Oliver Carlson and Ernest S. Bates, *Hearst* (New York, 1936); Don C. Seitz, *Joseph Pulitzer* (New York, 1952); and the works cited in Chapter 2 on the press and the Spanish-American War.

In intellectual history, Merle Curti, *The Growth of American Thought* (New York, 1951) is a standard work. Ralph H. Gabriel, *The Course of American Democratic Thought* (2d ed., New York [1956]) is also very useful. Richard Hofstadter, *Social Darwinism in American Thought, 1860–1915* (New York, 1944) treats all the main trends during the period covered. Morton G. White, *Social Thought in America* (New York, 1949) deals with leading thinkers of the early twentieth century. Also useful are Oscar Cargill, *Intellectual America: Ideas on the March* (New York, 1948) and Henry S. Commager, *The American Mind* (New Haven, Conn., 1950). For Darwinism, see Stow Persons, ed., *Evolutionary Thought in America* (Princeton, N.J., 1950).

Economic theory is covered in Joseph Dorfman, *The Economic Mind in American Civilization* (5 vols., New York, 1946–59). Sidney Fine, *Laissez Faire and the General-Welfare State: A Study of Conflict in American Thought, 1865–1901* (Ann Arbor, Mich. [1956]) is a useful study. For socialism, see D. D. Egbert and Stow Persons, eds., *Socialism in American Life* (Princeton, N.J., 1952). Useful biographies of economic thinkers include Charles A. Barker, *Henry George* (New York, 1955); Joseph Dorfman, *Thorstein Veblen and His America* (New York, 1934); Arthur E. Morgan, *Edward Bellamy* (New York, 1944); and Harris E. Starr, *William Graham Sumner* (New York, 1925).

Philosophical development is covered in Herbert W. Schneider, *A History of American Philosophy* (New York, 1946) and William H. Werkmeister, *A History of Philosophical Ideas in America* (New York [1949]). For pragmatism and instrumentalism, see Sidney Hook, *John Dewey* (New York, 1939); George R. Geiger, *John Dewey in Perspective* (New York, 1958); Edward C. Moore, *American Pragmatism* (New York, 1961); Ralph B. Perry, *The Thought and Character of William James* (Boston, 1936); and Philip P. Wiener, *Evolution and the Founders of Pragmatism* (Cambridge, Mass., 1949).

Robert Spiller, *et al.*, *Literary History of the United States* (3 vols., New York, 1948) is the standard work on literary history. Van Wyck Brooks, *New England: Indian Summer* (New York, 1940) and the same author's, *The Confident Years, 1885–1915* (New York, 1952) deal vividly but uncritically with American writers rather than with what they wrote. James D. Hart, *The Popular Book: A History of America's Literary Taste* (New York, 1950) is a useful supplement. For analyses of leading figures, see Oscar Cargill, *The Novels of Henry James* (New York, 1961); Everett Carter, *Howells and the Age of Realism* (Philadelphia [1954]); and Bernard De Voto, *Mark Twain's America* (Boston, 1932). Dorothy Dudley, *Forgotten Frontiers: Dreiser and the Land of the Free* (New York, 1932) deals largely with the battle for freedom of expression.

Oliver W. Larkin, *Art and Life in America* (rev. and enl. ed., New York [1960]) is the standard work on all the visual arts. For painting, see also Virgil Barker, *American Painting* (Boston, 1950), and for architecture, consult James M. Fitch, *American Building* (Boston, 1948). Lewis Mumford, *The Brown Decades* (2d rev. ed., New York [1955]) deals sketchily but perceptively with art during the late nineteenth century. Charles C. Baldwin, *Stanford White* (New York, 1931) and Hugh Morrison, *Louis Sullivan* (New York, 1935) are useful biographies.

4

The Progressive Movement

PROGRESSIVE IDEALS

The thirteen years between the accession to the Presidency of Theodore Roosevelt in 1901 and the outbreak of World War I in 1914 were a period of great social, political, and economic reform, generally known as the progressive era. The growing discontent of large sections of the American people with political corruption and economic oligarchy now began to find more statesmanlike leaders and more realistic objectives than in the 1880's and 1890's and to achieve practical results in municipal, state, and federal legislation.

The progressive leaders accepted American traditions: they believed in individual freedom, in democracy, and in private property, and although they advocated public supervision of business practices, they were opposed to any form of socialism. But they felt that the realization of American ideals required an extension of government activities. Whereas the dominant idea of the nineteenth century had been that freedom and democracy could best be achieved by leaving men alone and restricting the government to the negative function of preventing them from injuring one another, the progressives argued that the achievement of freedom and democracy now required positive action by the government. What they wanted to do was to use government to restore the freedom and opportunities that had been curbed by the rapid industrial and business concentrations of the late nineteenth century. The progressives were disturbed at and apprehensive about the tremendous power which big business wielded and to which organized labor aspired. Like the farmers and the reformers of the Middle West, the middle-class urban progressive resented his loss of social position, prestige, and influence, and was shocked to see the changes industry and the new immigration had wrought upon society. Most of the progressives began by viewing social evils in moral terms: they were horrified by the dishonesty of individual politicians and business leaders. They were, however, gradually forced to recognize that the causes of this dishonesty were to be found in social and economic conditions as well as in individual corruption and that the remedy was social and economic reform.

The chief purposes of the progressive reforms were, in politics, to revitalize democratic institutions by destroying the powers of bosses and machines and by making government officials more directly responsible to the people; and, in economics, to restore opportunity and establish public control over big business in the interests of the farmer, the worker, the small businessman, and the general welfare, present and future, of the American nation.

THE MUCKRAKERS

An important part in arousing public opinion to the need for reform was played by a group of journalists generally known as the muckrakers —a word first applied to them by Theodore Roosevelt in a moment of irritation in 1906. The muckraking movement began almost by accident. In October, 1902, S. S. McClure, one of the ablest of the publishers producing low-priced popular magazines, printed an article exposing political corruption in St. Louis, which had been written by Lincoln Steffens in collaboration with Claude H. Wetmore. In the following month appeared the first installment of Ida Tarbell's *History of the Standard Oil Company*, which had been contracted for two years earlier. The wide attention attracted by these two articles showed McClure that there was now a large audience for documented and accurate exposés of political and economic abuses. Similar work had been done earlier by Benjamin O. Flower, editor of *The Arena* since 1889, and by Henry Demarest Lloyd, whose study of Standard Oil, *Wealth against Commonwealth*, had appeared in 1894. But these earlier publications had caused relatively little excitement.

Having discovered the commercial possibilities of muckraking, Mc-
Clure went on to publish a number of similar articles, of which the most
important were a series of analyses of political corruption in different
city and state governments by Lincoln Steffens, and a study of railroad
practices by Ray Stannard Baker. As the circulation of *McClure's* soared,
other popular magazines quickly began to imitate it. *Everybody's* joined
the muckraking movement in 1903, *Collier's* in 1905, *The American* and
The Cosmopolitan in 1906, and *Hampton's* in 1907. The supremacy of
McClure's did not survive the secession of its leading contributors in
1906; and in the later stages of the muckraking movement the leadership
belonged to *Collier's*, which was ably edited by Robert J. Collier with
the assistance of Norman Hapgood and Mark Sullivan, and which by
1912 achieved a circulation of more than a million.

Among the most important works of the muckrakers were Thomas
W. Lawson's *Frenzied Finance*, Charles E. Russell's exposé of the beef
trust, and Ben Lindsay's study of crime among young people, all of
which were published in *Everybody's;* Samuel Hopkins Adams' analysis
of the patent medicine business in *Collier's;* and David Graham Phillips'
articles on *The Treason of the Senate* in *The Cosmopolitan*. Not all the
muckrakers were equally conscientious. Lawson was a Wall Street operator anxious to advertise his own activities, and Phillips' articles were more
sensational than accurate. But the majority of the muckrakers, particularly
those who wrote for *McClure's*, were scrupulously careful to tell the
truth and to base everything they wrote on lengthy and detailed re-
searches.

The movement ended before 1914. The public eventually tired of it,
and their confidence in the reliability of the muckrakers was weakened
by a growth of sensationalism. Furthermore, by enacting some reform
legislation and investigating other obvious abuses, Congress deprived the
muckrakers of their monopoly in exposing society's evils. A more important factor, however, seems to have been advertising pressure. Since
the average low-priced magazine was sold for less than its cost of production, it could not survive without advertisements. When business leaders
began to refuse to buy advertising space in magazines whose editorial
policies they disliked, there was usually a change in editorial policy.
After 1912 or 1913 popular magazines very rarely printed anything offensive to big business.

Of the muckrakers themselves, a number grew more conservative.
After World War I Mark Sullivan developed into a champion of busi-

ness freedom and an enemy of state regulation, and Ida Tarbell turned from excoriating John D. Rockefeller to glorifying a new kind of business leadership represented by United States Steel's Judge Elbert H. Gary and Owen D. Young. Lincoln Steffens, on the other hand, concluded that it was society rather than individuals which needed to be changed and that in capitalist society corrupt politicians were often less hypocritical and more realistic than those who prided themselves on their honesty. Believing that what was needed was a union of political and economic leadership which would make corruption unnecessary, he became in the 1930's one of the most influential of the American "fellow travelers" of the Communist party.

Contemporary with the muckraking journalists were a number of writers who exposed similar abuses through the medium of fiction. Their work rarely had any great literary value and was quickly forgotten; but much of it exercised considerable influence on public opinion. The best-known of the muckraking novels was Upton Sinclair's *The Jungle*, published in 1906. This was written to advocate socialism, but what caught public attention was a section describing the filth of the meat-packing factories in Chicago. The book sold 150,000 copies within a year of publication and helped to bring about the Meat Inspection Act of that year. Another best-selling socialist novelist was Jack London, whose studies of the class struggle and prophecies of proletarian revolution were incongruously mingled with Nietzschean doctrines of the superman and with a belief in the supremacy of the Aryan race. Among other muckraking novels were Winston Churchill's *Coniston*, Robert Herrick's *Memoirs of an American Citizen*, Booth Tarkington's *In the Arena*, Brand Whitlock's *The 13th District*, and William Allen White's *The Old Order Changeth*, the majority of which were published in 1905 and 1906. The literature of protest and exposure, however, was not limited to the writings of the muckrakers. It found expression in many novels of the period, such as William Dean Howells' *Through the Eye of the Needle* (1907), which, like his earlier work *Traveller from Altruria* (1894), was a gentle but serious criticism of contemporary social and economic conditions. Despite the country's great material progress and prosperity and the many new comforts technology and science provided to more and more people, the nation's literary record during the first decade of the twentieth century provided little evidence to indicate that the promise of a happier and more satisfying life was being fulfilled.

POLITICAL THEORY

The muckraking journalists and novelists were concerned primarily with specific abuses. The formulation of more general historical and sociological theories that would provide the progressive movement with a theoretical basis and help define its ultimate purposes came more slowly, although the groundwork had already been laid by the new liberal Protestant theology, the social gospel movement, and the writings of some of the academic economists, sociologists, philosophers, and political theorists. A number of these men expressed the belief that it was the proper function of government to provide its citizens with an environment which would yield them the greatest opportunity for self-improvement. While the influence of these intellectual trends and controversies is difficult to assess, the importance of the idea of opportunity and the necessity of restoring it to the people was central to progressive thought.

The intellectual foundations of the progressive movement were not entirely indigenous. Many twentieth-century reformers, like their predecessors in the middle decades of the nineteenth century, looked to the Old World for ideas and guidance in trying to solve the problems facing an increasingly urban and industrial nation. Just as William Graham Sumner, Andrew Carnegie, and the other exponents of free enterprise had borrowed and propagated the ideas of Herbert Spencer and the Manchester school of economists, now a number of American progressives borrowed the ideas and programs of English liberals and Fabian socialists who indicted the ugliness, immorality, and materialism of predatory capitalism and summoned the well-educated to inaugurate and lead the reform movement. Similarly, American reformers borrowed from Germany the economic thought of the institutionalist and historical economists, with their emphasis upon the positive state and its obligations to promote the national welfare.

If Europe provided American reformers with much food for thought, it supplied them also with many practical examples, because almost everywhere in Europe, programs to extend social democracy were being put into effect quite often in far more advanced stages than in the United States. Germany's experiment with social legislation covering sickness, accident, and old-age insurance, labor legislation limiting hours for

women and children, improved factory inspection, and the establishment
of industrial courts to adjust wage disputes attracted the attention of
many reformers in the United States. Between 1905 and 1914 similar
laws were being enacted by a liberal administration in Great Britain.
Switzerland continued its social reform program without impairing or
curbing the people's desire to exercise their democratic privileges directly whenever possible. The worldwide social and democratic reform
movement of the early years of the twentieth century stimulated many
Americans to examine more carefully the condition of democracy in
their own country.

In the later years of the progressive era writers began to reinterpret
American history with a view to emphasizing the influence of economic
forces and stripping American traditions of much of the aura of sanctity
with which they were surrounded. This new approach to the American
past was foreshadowed in J. A. Smith's *Spirit of American Government,*
and in Gustavus Myers' *History of the Great American Fortunes,* both
of which were published in 1907. The most important of the historical
iconoclasts, however, was Charles A. Beard, who published his *Economic
Interpretation of the Constitution* in 1913. Beard's book purported to
show in detail the precise economic interests of the members of the
Constitutional Convention of 1787 and deduced that their primary intention had been to protect the mercantile and financial classes from
radical legislation sponsored by the agrarian interests.[1]

Writers who attempted to guide future political development included
Walter Weyl, whose *New Democracy* appeared in 1912, and a younger
man, at this period a moderate socialist but subsequently a champion of
laissez faire, Walter Lippmann, who published his *Preface to Politics* in
1912. The most influential work of this kind, however, was Herbert
Croly's *Promise of American Life,* published in 1909. Adapting the
Hamiltonian belief in a strong federal government to twentieth-century
conditions, Croly argued that large business corporations must be accepted as economically desirable but that they must be subjected to
federal control. The Sherman Act should be repealed, but at the same
time the powers of big business should be counteracted through the
growth of a strong trade union movement. In other words, the correct

---

[1] This interpretation of the Constitution was not seriously challenged until 1956,
when Professor Robert E. Brown published a detailed analysis of Beard's work and
concluded that it required considerable revision. See *Charles Beard and the Constitution* (Princeton, N.J., 1956).

policy was not to abolish special privilege but to give privileges to everybody. Croly's thesis owed much to the ideas expressed by Theodore Roosevelt and foreshadowed the first phase of the New Deal of Franklin Roosevelt.

This semisocialist point of view was supported by one section of the progressive movement but was opposed by others who believed that the growth of large corporations was caused not by their superior economic efficiency but merely by the superior opportunities for self-enrichment which they offered to unscrupulous financiers. The most influential exponent of this second point of view was perhaps the Boston lawyer Louis D. Brandeis. Brandeis argued that beyond a certain point the growth of centralization, both in politics and in economics, resulted in inefficient administration and was incompatible with individual freedom and initiative. Brandeis wished to prevent the "curse of bigness" and restore effective competition by prohibiting, through federal regulation, any corporation from controlling more than 30 per cent of any industry. The political leaders of the progressive movement were divided between these two conflicting economic philosophies, Theodore Roosevelt, for example, inclining more to strong federal action, and Woodrow Wilson and Robert La Follette leaning more toward the ideas elaborated by Brandeis.

MUNICIPAL REFORMERS

Though the progressive movement originated in the municipal and state governments of the Middle West and borrowed from the Populist tradition, it was much more than a revival or extension of the older agrarian reform crusade. During the first decade of the twentieth century, progressivism broke through its regional confines and moved out in all directions, until by 1910 no state or section was entirely free from its influence; and all over the country had sprung up reform movements which endeavored to destroy the manifestations of political and economic corruption. Since the degree of honesty on the federal level was dependent in part upon conditions in local politics, municipal reform bore significantly upon progressivism on the national level. Indeed, progressive reformers often began by attacking corruption in city and state government before they were drawn into national politics.

The leadership of the progressive movement, unlike that of the Populists, was assumed by middle-class urban reformers. Many of them were lawyers, journalists, and small businessmen who belonged to one or the other of the two major parties but were alike in their opposition to machine politics. In Boston, for example, the reformers included members of every major religious group—Protestants, Catholics, and Jews; among them were representatives of the old humanitarian reform impulse of the nineteenth century and advocates of the new concept of the welfare state. Within their ranks were to be found college professors, clergymen, feminists, and labor leaders. The reforms they advocated were as diverse as their social, religious, and occupational origins. The influence of the urban middle class upon progressive reform in the East was duplicated in the cities of the Middle West and on the Pacific coast. In California, the progressive fight against all forms of monopoly and special privilege originated in San Francisco and Los Angeles, the state's two largest cities, and was led by and received its greatest support from the moderately wealthy professional and business classes. To be sure, there were regional and local differences. What was deemed an imperative reform in one city was relegated to secondary importance in another, and often the means employed to effect change were different too. In California, for example, the reform element was as determined to crush labor's efforts to control politics as it was to oust the Southern Pacific Railroad and the other private interests. But the pressure which carried all of these reformers to success was supplied almost everywhere by the same group —the middle class.

An important role in the progressive movement, particularly in the enactment of social welfare legislation, was played by women's organizations, which were growing rapidly in size and influence. The General Federation of Women's Clubs had been formed in 1889, and the membership of the organizations affiliated with it increased from 50,000 in 1898 to more than a million in 1914. Also of great importance was the growth of social work, which made many middle-class citizens aware for the first time of the darker side of industrial society and which was responsible for much of the local legislation of the progressive era. Settlement houses for social work in slum areas, modeled after Toynbee Hall in the East End of London, had first been established in the 1880's. By 1900 there were about a hundred such projects, the most prominent being Hull House in Chicago, founded by Jane Addams in 1889, and the Henry Street Settlement in New York, founded by Lillian D. Wald in 1893.

In the city governments the main purposes of the progressives were to destroy the powers of the political bosses and machines and to end the corrupt influences of business interests, particularly of the street-railroad, gas, and electric companies. The progressives were, however, constantly hampered by the lack of complete municipal home rule and by the fact that many of the public utility corporations were too large for municipal control. Finding that cities could not achieve good government as long as the state legislatures remained corrupt, many of the municipal reformers were gradually compelled to extend their activities to state politics.

The most famous of the city reformers was Tom Johnson of Cleveland, who had a capacity for winning popularity and affection, and a refreshing freedom from the fanaticism that too many reformers were sometimes guilty of displaying. Johnson had himself been a street-railroad magnate, who had made money by the usual corrupt methods and who thus had the advantage of possessing an intimate knowledge of business practices. A porter on a train is said to have induced him to read a book by Henry George, and Johnson found George's arguments unanswerable. As a result he became converted to the reform movement. Johnson served as mayor of Cleveland from 1901 until 1909. His primary objective —municipal ownership of public utilities—was vetoed by the Ohio government, and the state authorities also prevented him from increasing the taxes paid by the street-railroad corporations and from building municipal lines to compete with them. When Johnson ran as candidate for the state governorship, he was defeated. In spite of these failures, however, Cleveland under his rule won the reputation of being the best-governed city in the United States. Johnson gathered round him able disciples, notably Newton D. Baker, who succeeded him as mayor, and Frederic C. Howe; and he publicized and dramatized all the problems of municipal government. Reformers from all over the United States visited Cleveland to study Johnson's methods.

During the same period there were a number of other municipal reformers who attracted national attention, most notable of whom was, perhaps, Joseph W. Folk of St. Louis. Under the rule of the city boss, Edward R. Butler, a group of financiers had bought a railroad franchise from the city council with a bribe of $250,000, and then had sold their franchise to the existing railroad corporation for $1,250,000. Folk, elected district attorney in 1901, secured twenty convictions against those responsible for this particularly reprehensible street-railroad manipulation.

Equally spectacular was the crusade against the boss of San Francisco, Abraham Ruef. Unlike most other city bosses at the turn of the century, Ruef was a college and law school graduate and a highly cultivated individual. His interest in politics began as a reformer but practical experience caused him to lose his earlier idealism. In 1901, he joined forces with groups of disgruntled workers who, angry with the incumbent administration for its antilabor activities during a recent strike, formed the independent Union Labor party in the hope of electing a labor mayor. Ruef had no interest in the workers' grievances or in the party, except as an instrument for his own selfish interests. He selected Eugene R. Schmitz, the president of the San Francisco Musician's Union, to run for mayor, and succeeded in getting him elected three times. With Schmitz in the mayor's office and, after 1905, with an inexperienced, incompetent, and dishonest board of supervisors for legislators, graft and corruption became widespread, permeating almost every area of the city's government. Ruef was at first careful to keep within the law by disguising his activities through his law office, but in 1905 the supervisors, learning of the lucrative fees and retainers which Ruef received from the utility companies and other businessmen he represented before the city, insisted on participating in the profitable "attorney fees" business. An arrangement was worked out whereby Ruef divided the money he received among the supervisors and the mayor, keeping a fourth of it himself. The open and widespread corruption of the administration shocked the city's respectable elements, among them Fremont Older, the editor of the San Francisco *Bulletin*. With the aid of two lawyers, Francis J. Heney and Hiram W. Johnson, the detective William J. Burns of the United States Secret Service, and the financial support of millionaires Rudolph Spreckels and James D. Phelan, Older succeeded in getting Ruef convicted for bribery. In December, 1908, Ruef was sentenced to fourteen years in the state penitentiary. However, the business leaders behind Ruef—the owners of the street railroads, the other public utility companies, and the Southern Pacific Railroad—all proved to be beyond the reach of the law.

Among other cities which had notable reform administrations were Toledo and Milwaukee. The former was governed from 1897 to 1904 by "Golden Rule" Jones and from 1904 to 1913 by Brand Whitlock. Milwaukee elected a socialist mayor in 1910 and continued until 1939 to keep socialists at the head of its government because of their honesty and in spite of their political ideals.

New Ideas in Municipal Government

The chief new ideas in municipal government were the commission and city manager plans. The advantages of these plans were that they avoided the division of responsibility between the mayor and the council or board of aldermen, got rid of the numerous elective positions upon which the powers of political machines had been largely based, and made possible a nonpartisan administration concerned merely with municipal needs and divorced from national party politics. Commission government originated at Galveston, Texas, in 1901, when a destructive flood made efficient administration more necessary than usual. In 1907 the plan was adopted, with improvements, by Des Moines, Iowa, which henceforth took a leading place in the movement for better city government. In 1913 Dayton, Ohio, adopted the commission system and added a city manager to act as executive and be responsible to the commission. By 1921 there were perhaps five hundred cities that had adopted some form of commission government, most of them having commissions with five members. Other improvements in city government included the growth of municipal ownership of public utilities, the public letting of contracts, and planning of cities.

Although few cities were wholly unaffected by these municipal reforms, there were a number which continued to be dominated by machines. The three largest cities in the country—New York, Chicago, and Philadelphia—continued to suffer from corruption and misgovernment; and even in the 1930's there were still some city machines, such as the Hague machine in Jersey City and the Pendergast machine in Kansas City, which exhibited all the vices that had been characteristic of municipal government in the 1880's and 1890's.

STATE REFORMERS

In the state governments the progressives worked for changes in the electoral system that would make officials more directly responsible to the people. Likewise, they attempted to destroy the corrupt powers of business corporations, particularly the big railroads, and to enact social legislation protecting the working class from insecurity and exploitation. Though they were constantly impeded by the judiciary, both state and federal, which was likely to regard reforms as violations of the rights of property, some notable reforms were accomplished.

The outstanding progressive leader in state politics, the heir of the Populist tradition and an example of the college-educated reformer, was Robert M. La Follette of Wisconsin. After a prolonged struggle with the railroad and lumber interests, which, by bribing the convention, twice prevented him from securing the Republican nomination for governor, La Follette won the nomination and the election in 1900 and was reelected in 1902 and 1904. In order to prevent the old Republican machine from regaining control of the state, La Follette built up a powerful organization of his own, which continued to dominate the state of Wisconsin long after his own death. He sought advice constantly from intellectuals and social scientists and effectively collaborated with the staff of the state university. As governor, La Follette succeeded in enacting a long series of reforms, which became known as the "Wisconsin Idea" and made Wisconsin the chief example of progressivism in the United States. The Wisconsin Idea included taxation of the railroads, fixing of railroad rates on a basis not of the capitalization of the railroad corporations but of the real physical value of their properties, income and in-

As senator from Wisconsin (1906–25) and presidential candidate of the Progressive party of 1924, Robert M. La Follette was a belligerent opponent of big business and economic privilege. (Culver Pictures, Inc.)

heritance taxes, laws regulating insurance and banking practices, laws limiting hours of labor for women and children, a workmen's compensation law, creation of a state forest reserve, and establishment of primary elections for the choice of party candidates for office. In 1906 La Follette went on to the United States Senate. Denounced by his enemies as a self-righteous fanatic, he was regarded by his friends as the greatest champion of liberalism in the United States; and as the spokesman of the rural Middle West, La Follette reminded the nation that despite the farmer's apparent prosperity, his difficulties were great.

No other state governor achieved such an imposing series of reforms as did La Follette; but there were a number who adopted at least part of the Wisconsin Idea. Two municipal reformers became state governors, Joseph W. Folk governing Missouri from 1904 to 1908 and Hiram W. Johnson governing California from 1910 to 1916. Each of them was able to rescue the state administration from control by the railroads, Missouri having hitherto been dominated by the Missouri Pacific and the Burlington, and California by the Southern Pacific. New Hampshire elected a reform governor to curb the Boston and Maine Railroad's power over that state. In 1908 a reform administration took over the government of Vermont and, after a bitter fight with the state legislature, forced it to enact regulatory legislation of various kinds. One of the most notable progressive administrations in the East was that of Woodrow Wilson, who was elected governor of New Jersey in 1910. Building upon the traditions and the labors of earlier reformers, such as George Record of Jersey City and Everett Colby's "New Idea Republicans," Wilson used his two years in office to put through a number of laws limiting the powers of the political machines and regulating corporation charters, thereby driving holding companies out of New Jersey and forcing them to find a new sanctuary in the state of Delaware.

Similar reform programs were carried out in other sections of the country. In the Middle West, governors Albert B. Cummins of Iowa and John A. Johnson of Minnesota followed the La Follette tradition and inaugurated similar reform programs of their own. Governors Jeff Davis of Alabama, James K. Vardaman of Mississippi, and Hoke Smith of Georgia campaigned against monopolies, discriminatory railroad rates, the entrenched power of the ruling Bourbon oligarchy, and the "foreign" corporations of the Northeast which they claimed were exploiting their people. The progressive leaders of the South championed the interests of the poor whites, but as white supremacists they were firmly opposed to guaranteeing the Negro his political rights. In Texas, Governor James Stephen Hogg secured legislation to prohibit railroad companies from issuing watered stock and to regulate the lines more effectively through a strong railroad commission. During his administration similar efforts were made to regulate other corporations and to safeguard the public from corrupt business practices.

Another progressive achievement in state politics, which helped to create two national reputations, was regulation of the insurance companies. The insurance business had hitherto been conducted purely for private profit, at great expense to the policyholders and with little security. In Massachusetts Louis D. Brandeis showed that during the fifteen-year period between 1890 and 1905, the insurance companies had received more than $61 million from policyholders, had paid out less than $22 million, and had retained less than $10 million in reserve. The balance had been taken in salaries by the directors of the companies. Brandeis was able to secure rigid state regulation of insurance practices and to make possible the transfer of much business to savings banks, which sold insurance at relatively low cost. This achievement, along with his prolonged fight against the corrupt financing of the Morgan-controlled New York, New Haven & Hartford Railroad, his services in settling the garment workers' strikes, and his numerous other activities as the "people's counsel," caused Brandeis to be regarded by all conservatives as a dangerous radical and led to his appointment to the Supreme Court in 1916 by Woodrow Wilson.

In New York, insurance practices were even more scandalous. The funds of the three big companies were used by their directors for Wall Street speculation, salaries of $150,000 a year were paid, and each company was accustomed to set aside nearly $1 million a year for bribing officials. The situation became public knowledge in 1905, when there was a struggle for control of the Equitable among a number of financiers, chiefly the railroad magnate Edward H. Harriman and the street-railroad manipulator Thomas Fortune Ryan. The New York *World* started a campaign against the companies, forced the governor to appoint the Armstrong Committee to investigate them, and secured as counsel for the committee a forty-three-year-old lawyer hitherto unknown to the general public, Charles Evans Hughes. Hughes's success in exposing the practices of high finance led to his election to the governorship in 1906. As governor, he secured several changes in the insurance laws: a new statute mutualized the insurance companies, made the directors responsible to the policyholders, prohibited speculation in insurance company funds, and limited directors' salaries. These changes, however, less drastic than the measures enacted in Massachusetts, did not end abuses since the policyholders had no real control over the directors. Among the other reforms enacted during the four years Hughes was governor were the Moreland Act, which empowered the governor's office to investigate the administration of city and county governments, the creation of an effective and responsible public service commission with power to investigate and determine rates and other operating procedures, the tightening of the state's gambling laws, and the promotion of conservation. Hughes's effective leadership and administration of the state's government caused President William Howard Taft to appoint him to the United States Supreme Court in 1910 and made him a promising presidential prospect.

New Ideas in State Government

The progressive movement was responsible for a number of new political devices, of varying utility, which were intended to strengthen popular control over the state governments. Most of these originated in the West and had originally been suggested by the Populists in the 1890's. The leading crusader for reforms of this kind was William S. U'Ren of Oregon.

The initiative, which allowed 5 per cent of the citizens of a state to demand consideration of a proposal for a new law, and the referendum, which allowed such proposals to be submitted to direct popular vote, were adopted by South Dakota in 1898 and by Oregon in 1902, and were ultimately established in twenty states. The recall of elected officials by popular vote was adopted by Oregon in 1908 and subsequently by ten other states. Eight states, moreover, allowed the recall of judges, and Colorado made it possible for a popular vote to overrule certain judicial decisions. The results of the initiative, the referendum, and the recall, however, in spite of the violent controversy these measures excited, proved insignificant.

More important was the adoption of the direct primary, allowing popular choice of party candidates and thereby restricting the powers of the party conventions, which had so often been controlled by bosses and open to bribery by business interests. Originating with the Democratic party in the South, the primary began to spread into the North after 1903, when it was adopted in Wisconsin, and by 1915 it had been established in thirty-seven states. The use of the primary for the choice of presidential candidates began in Oregon in 1910 and had been adopted in twenty states by 1920. Since, however, the final choice had to be made by the national convention, the party members of each state could only indicate their preference and must allow considerable discretion to their delegates. Presidential primaries, therefore, had little value. The primary system was also extended to the choice of U.S. senatorial candidates. By 1912 twenty-nine states had compelled their state legislatures, in the choice of senators, to follow the popular decision indicated in the primaries. This led in 1913 to the Seventeenth Amendment, which established direct election of senators.

To curb the powers of business interests, most of the states established public utility commissions which regulated, with varying and often dubious effectiveness, the rates and practices of railroad, telephone, and electric corporations. They also imposed legal restrictions on the granting of public utility franchises. Bribery of state officials was diminished by antilobbying and corrupt-practice laws, by the reduction of the number of elective positions, and by the adoption of civil service rules; and more efficient use of state revenues was achieved by the establishment of budget systems.

In the protection of workers, the most important advance for the benefit of injured workers was represented by workmen's compensation acts establishing insurance systems to which employers were compelled to contribute. The first such law was passed in Maryland in 1902, and similar laws had been adopted in forty-two other states by 1920. A number of states also established safety and health codes for the protection of industrial workers and adopted old age pension and mothers' assistance plans. More controversial were the attempts to impose maximum hours and minimum wages. The Supreme Court decision in the Lochner case of 1905 appeared to prohibit wage and hour legislation; but in 1910 and 1917 Oregon laws fixing maximum hours, first for women and later for male factory workers, were upheld. In 1912 a minimum wage law for women was enacted in Massachusetts, and by 1923 this example had been followed by fourteen other states and in the District of Columbia. In 1923, however, the District of Columbia law was invalidated by the Court in *Adkins v. Children's Hospital,* and in 1925 and 1927 the Court also voided the Arizona and Arkansas laws. The attitude of the Court toward wage and hour laws continued to be very uncertain, with the Court reversing itself on these questions several times.

Supreme Court opposition also prevented any effective prohibition of child labor. A number of states passed laws restricting child labor and appointed departments of labor or industrial boards to supervise enforcement, but prohibition of child labor by any one state would handicap its industries in competition with those of other states. In 1916 Congress passed the Keating-Owen Act which—like federal laws directed against the white slave and narcotics traffics—prohibited the entry into interstate commerce of products made by child labor. This law was voided by the Supreme Court the following year in the case of *Hammer v. Dagenhart*. Opponents of child labor then turned to constitutional amendment as the only method of reform, but to this day have been unable to secure ratification by a sufficient number of states.

THE EIGHTEENTH AMENDMENT

Associated with progressivism in local politics were two movements which eventually resulted in amendments to the federal constitution: the prohibition movement, and the woman suffrage movement. Both of these had originated in the middle of the nineteenth century, but both of them gained impetus from the swing toward reform in the progressive era, although only the second of them was clearly in harmony with progressive ideals.

The attack on alcoholic liquors had begun in New England and the Middle West early in the nineteenth century. The state of Maine, for instance, had adopted a prohibition law before the Civil War. From the beginning, prohibition was closely associated with the Protestant churches. Working in cooperation with the Methodist, Baptist, and Presbyterian churches as the chief forces in the movement were two organizations: the Women's Christian Temperance Union, founded in 1879 under the leadership of Frances Willard, and the Anti-Saloon League, founded in 1895.

The prohibitionists publicized the very real evils of the saloon, especially its associations with prostitution and with vote-buying by corrupt political machines. Their cause was strengthened by the rapid increase in the consumption of liquor in the latter decades of the nineteenth century: between 1878 and 1898 per capita consumption more than doubled. The areas of rural Protestantism, in the South and the Middle West, were most responsive to prohibitionist propaganda. In the South the movement was strengthened by the desire of the white race to enforce temperance upon the Negroes. The cities, on the other hand, where immigrant and Catholic influences were strong, remained hostile. The movement also received considerable support from wealthy businessmen who were anxious to increase the efficiency of their employees.

The Anti-Saloon League was not content with the usual propaganda against the abuse of liquor. Under the leadership of Wayne B. Wheeler and W. H. Anderson it organized the prohibitionists into a pressure group with lobbies in Washington and in the state capitals. By 1908 it had a hundred offices and was spending $400,000 a year. Through asking only that politicians vote as "drys," without inquiring whether they lived as "wets," it carried the movement to eventual victory, but it also contributed considerably to the growth of political hypocrisy.

Five states—Maine, New. Hampshire, Vermont, Kansas, and North Dakota—adopted prohibition before 1900. Between 1907 and 1916 fourteen other states, eight of them in the South and six in the West, followed their example. In March, 1913, Congress adopted the Webb-Kenyon Act which prohibited the shipment of liquor into dry territory. Other states passed local option rules, which enabled counties and municipalities to adopt prohibition; and every state except two introduced propaganda against liquor into its school system. By 1916 three-quarters of the area of the United States, containing half the population, was legally dry, and only the cities still resisted the movement.

A prohibition amendment was first submitted to Congress in 1913; but it was not until World War I, which necessitated the economizing of foodstuffs and the greatest possible industrial efficiency, that Congress capitulated. The Eighteenth Amendment passed Congress in 1917, was ratified by every state except Connecticut and Rhode Island, and was declared a part of the constitution in January, 1919. Congress passed, over Wilson's veto, the Volstead Act in October, 1919, which defined liquor prohibited by the terms of the Eighteenth Amendment as containing more than 0.5 per cent alcohol. Enforcement began on January 1, 1920.

THE NINETEENTH AMENDMENT

The abolition of legal and economic differences between the sexes was everywhere an accompaniment of the growth of industrialism, which made it possible for many women to become independent wage earners. This movement was particularly rapid in America, especially in the West, where pioneering conditions had resulted from the beginning in a greater degree of sexual equality than existed in Europe.

After the Civil War there was a steady increase in the number of women employed outside their own homes. In 1870, 1.3 million women, 11.8 per cent of the total number, were gainfully employed in non-agricultural occupations, but about half of these were in domestic service. By 1920 the number employed had increased to 7.3 million, 21.3 per cent of the total number. More than one-fifth were married, and only one-quarter were in domestic service. The average wage of women was still, however, only about three-quarters that received by men.

In spite of considerable opposition, women began to assert their right to enter any of the professions and to combine marriage with a professional career. As a result the states began to pass laws giving women control over their own property and removing other legal restrictions. But the suffrage was the most important right from which women were excluded, since the vote would bring with it the possibility of remedying other grievances through legislation. The first woman suffrage association was founded in 1869 by Elizabeth Cady Stanton and Susan B. Anthony. In the twentieth century the chief leaders of the movement were Carrie Chapman Catt and Dr. Anna Howard Shaw, who adopted methods of peaceful persuasion. In 1912, however, another section of the movement, headed by Alice Paul, introduced the militancy practiced by Mrs. Emmeline Pankhurst and the suffragettes in Great Britain.

Four states—Colorado, Idaho, Wyoming, and Utah—adopted women suffrage before 1900. Between 1910 and 1914 eight more states, all of them west of the Mississippi, followed their example; and in 1916 a woman, Jeanette Rankin of Montana, was elected to Congress. The leaders of the movement demanded a federal amendment; and in the campaign of 1912 they won the support of Theodore Roosevelt, while Wilson expressed sympathy but recommended that the question be left to the individual states. After Congress rejected the proposed amendment in 1914, the woman suffrage leaders campaigned against all legislators who had voted against it when they ran for reelection. They claimed to have secured the defeat of forty-three of them. World War I weakened the opposition, and the Nineteenth Amendment was added to the Constitution in 1919.

Suggested Readings

The intellectual foundations of the progressive movement are treated in a number of works. One of the most thoughtful and influential contemporary statements is Herbert Croly, *The Promise of American Life* (New York, 1909).

Walter Lippmann's two books, *Drift and Mastery* (New York, 1914) and *Preface to Politics* (New York, 1913), and Walter Weyl, *The New Democracy* (New York, 1912) are equally significant revelations of the progressive mind. Consult also Simon Patten, *The New Basis of Civilization* (New York, 1907); Louis D. Brandeis, *Other People's Money* (new ed., New York [1934]) and the same author's *The Curse of Bigness* (New York, 1934). See also Alfred Lief, *Brandeis* (New York, 1936). For an interesting journalistic retrospect, see John Chamberlain, *Farewell to Reform* (New York, 1932). More recent appraisals include David W. Noble, *The Paradox of Progressive Thought* (Minneapolis, 1958); Morton G. White, *Social Thought in America: The Revolt Against Formalism* (New York, 1949); Daniel Aaron, *Men of Good Hope: A Story of American Progressives* (New York, 1950); and Walter Johnson, *William Allen White's America* (New York, 1947). The influence of British ideas is appraised in Arthur Mann, "British Social Thought and American Reformers of the Progressive Era," *Mississippi Valley Historical Review*, XLII (March 1956), 672–92. Not limited to the first decade of the twentieth century, but indispensable for their interpretations of the progressive era are Eric F. Goldman, *Rendezvous with Destiny: A History of Modern American Reform* (New York, 1952); Richard Hofstadter, *The Age of Reform: From Bryan to F.D.R.* (New York, 1955); and Henry Steele Commager, *The American Mind* (New Haven, Conn., 1950). See also the appropriate chapters in Sidney Fine, *Laissez Faire and the General Welfare State* (Ann Arbor, Mich., 1956); Richard Hofstadter, *Social Darwinism in American Thought, 1860–1905* (Philadelphia, 1944); Louis Hartz, *The Liberal Tradition in America* (New York, 1954); and Arthur Ekirch, Jr., *The Decline of American Liberalism* (New York, 1956).

The influence of religious reform upon the progressive era is discussed in Charles H. Hopkins, *The Rise of the Social Gospel in American Protestantism, 1860–1915* (New Haven, Conn., 1940); Henry F. May, *Protestant Churches and Industrial America* (New York, 1949); Edward A. White, *Science and Religion in American Thought: The Impact of Naturalism* (Stanford, Calif., 1952); and Sidney Warren, *American Free Thought, 1860–1914* (New York, 1943). See also the more specialized study of Ira V. Brown, *Lyman Abbott, Christian Evolutionist: A Study in Religious Liberalism* (Cambridge, Mass., 1953) and Brand Whitlock's reminiscences, *Forty Years of It* (New York, 1914).

The contributions of economists is treated in the third volume of Joseph Dorfman's *The Economic Mind in American Civilization* (5 vols., New York, 1946–59) and in the same author's *Thorstein Veblen and His America* (New York, 1934). More specific is James R. Everett, *Religion in Economics: A Study of John Bates Clark, Richard T. Ely and Simon Patten* (New York, 1946). See also the autobiographies of Richard T. Ely, *Ground Under Our Feet* (New York, 1938); Edward A. Ross, *Seventy Years of It* (New York, 1937); and John R. Commons, *Myself* (New York, 1934).

Literary influences can be traced in many of the works cited above and in greater detail in Alfred Kazin, *On Native Grounds* (New York, 1942) and Oscar Cargill, *Intellectual America* (New York, 1941).

The most detailed study of the muckrakers is Cornelius C. Regier, *The Era of the Muckrakers* (Chapel Hill, N.C., 1932). Also useful is Louis Filler, *Crusaders for American Liberalism* (2d ed., Yellow Springs, Ohio, 1950). Ray Stannard Baker, *American Chronicle* (New York, 1945) is the autobiography of an important muckraker. See also Oswald G. Villard, *Memoirs of a Liberal Editor* (New York, 1939) and Mark Sullivan, *The Education of an American* (New York, 1938). Some of the writings of the muckrakers are collected in Arthur and Lila Weinberg, eds., *The Muckrakers* (New York, 1961).

Harold U. Faulkner's two studies, *The Quest for Social Justice, 1898–1914* (New York, 1931) and *The Decline of Laissez Faire, 1897–1917* (New York, 1951) contain pertinent material, while George E. Mowry, *The Era of Theodore Roosevelt, 1900–1912* (New York, 1958), though covering more than the progressive movement, contains the best summary of the recent scholarship on all aspects of the movement. A more detailed account of the period 1909 to 1916 is George E. Mowry, *Theodore Roosevelt and the Progressive Movement* (Madison, Wis., 1946). One of the very best intellectual analyses of the progressive period as seen through three of its chief figures is Charles Forcey, *The Crossroads of Liberalism: Croly, Weyl, Lippmann and the Progressive Era, 1900–1925* (New York, 1961). One of the earliest efforts to describe the decade of reform was Benjamin P. DeWitt, *The Progressive Movement* (New York, 1915). Claude G. Bowers, *Beveridge and the Progressive Era* (New York, 1932) is the biography of an important reformer. See also Charles A. Beard, *Contemporary American History* (New York, 1919), a collection of essays interpreting the progressive era.

One of the best studies of municipal corruption and reform is Walton E. Bean, *Boss Ruef's San Francisco: The Story of the Union Labor Party, Big Business and the Graft Prosecution* (Berkeley and Los Angeles, 1952). Consult also Arthur Mann, *Yankee Reformers in the Urban Age* (Cambridge, Mass., 1954), a regional rather than urban study, but it contains much information on Boston's reformers. Lincoln Steffens, *The Shame of the Cities* (New York, 1904); Tom L. Johnson, *My Story* (New York, 1911); Fremont Older, *My Own Story* (New York, 1926); and Frederic C. Howe, *The City: The Hope of Democracy* (New York, 1905) are also useful for what they reveal on urban problems.

Among the best studies of Progressivism on the state level are George E. Mowry, *The California Progressives* (Berkeley and Los Angeles, 1951); Ransom E. Noble, Jr., *New Jersey Progressivism before Wilson* (Princeton, N.J., 1946); and Winston A. Flint, *The Progressive Movement in Vermont* (Washington, D.C., 1941). See also Robert S. Maxwell, *La Follette and the Rise of the Progressives in Wisconsin* (Madison, Wis., 1956); and the contemporary works of Frederic C. Howe, *Wisconsin, An Experiment in Democracy* (New York, 1912) and Charles McCarthy, *The Wisconsin Idea* (New York, 1912). For the role of the poor whites in the South, see A. D. Kirwan, *The Revolt of the Rednecks; Mississippi Politics, 1876–1925* (Lexington, Ky., 1951). Two other important biographies of progressive reformers on the state level include Eric F. Goldman, *Charles J. Bonaparte, Patrician Reformer: His Early Career*

(Baltimore, 1943) and Louis G. Geiger, *Joseph W. Folk of Missouri* (Columbia, Mo., 1953). Robert C. Cotner, *James Stephen Hogg* (Austin, Tex., 1959) is a detailed account of the life of a Texas reform governor. Robert M. La Follette, *Autobiography* (Madison, Wis., [1913]) is important and quite complete, but it should be supplemented by the more recent biography of Belle C. La Follette and Fola La Follette, *Robert M. La Follette* (2 vols., New York, 1953). Consult also Frederic C. Howe, *The Confessions of a Reformer* (New York, 1925), a revealing autobiography.

The most recent and comprehensive appraisal of the reform impulse in the Middle West is Russell B. Nye, *Midwestern Progressive Politics: A Historical Study of Its Origins and Development* (East Lansing, Mich., 1951). There is valuable material on the middle-western farmer in the progressive movement in the first part of Theodore Saloutos and John D. Hicks, *Agricultural Discontent in the Middle West, 1900–1939* (Madison, Wis., 1951).

State reforms are discussed in several older works, including William B. Munro, *The Initiative, The Referendum, and the Recall* (New York, 1912); Charles A. Beard, ed., *Documents on State-wide Initiative, Referendum and Recall* (New York, 1912); Ellis P. Oberholtzer, *The Referendum in America* (new ed., New York, 1911); and Allen H. Eaton, *The Oregon System* (Chicago, 1912).

There is no general study of the impact of feminism and its role in the reform impulse. An old and brief, though highly competent, account is the chapter in Arthur M. Schlesinger, *New Viewpoints in American History* (New York, 1922). Two early accounts are James P. Lichtenberger, ed., American Academy of Political and Social Science, *Women in Public Life* (Philadelphia [1914]) and Eugene A. Hecker, *A Short History of Women's Rights . . .* (New York, 1910). Some of the best information is to be found in the biographies and memoirs of the leaders themselves. Among these, some of the most useful ones are: Mary Earhart, *Frances Willard: From Prayers to Politics* (Chicago, 1944), an excellent, perceptive, and informative biography; Josephine Goldmark, *Impatient Crusader: Florence Kelley's Life Story* (Urbana, Ill., 1953); Robert L. Duffus, *Lillian Wald: Neighbor and Crusader* (New York, 1938) and Wald's own memoirs *The House on Henry Street* (New York, 1915); Mary G. Pick, *Carrie Chapman Catt: A Biography* (New York, 1938); and Jane Addams, *My Friend Julia Lathrop* (New York, 1935) and Addams' memoirs, *Forty Years at Hull House* (Chicago, 1910).

The most recent general account on prohibition is Herbert Asbury, *The Great Illusion: An Informal History of Prohibition* (Garden City, N.Y., 1950). Older but still useful are Ernest H. Cherrington, *The Evolution of Prohibition in the United States of America* (Westerville, Ohio, 1920) and John A. Krout, *The Origins of Prohibition* (New York, 1925). Specialized studies include Peter H. Odegard, *Pressure Politics: The Story of the Anti-Saloon League* (New York, 1928); Justin Steuart, *Wayne Wheeler, Dry Boss* (New York [1928]); and the recent and detailed state study of Gilman M. Ostrander, *The Prohibition Movement in California 1849–1933* (Berkeley and Los Angeles, 1957).

5

The Administration of
Theodore Roosevelt, 1901-1909

On September 14, 1901, President William McKinley died as a result of wounds inflicted eight days earlier by Leon Czolgosz, a demented anarchist, who approached the President at a reception in the Pan-American Exposition's Temple of Music and fired two shots at him. McKinley's death brought Theodore Roosevelt to the White House. Few realized the extent to which the office and functions of the Presidency would be altered by the succession of this young and energetic Chief Executive.

PRESIDENTIAL LEADERSHIP

Born on October 27, 1858, of a comfortably prosperous and cultivated New York family of Dutch origins, Theodore Roosevelt was "a sickly and timid boy" who suffered from more than the usual number of childhood illnesses, including a severe asthmatic condition which, for a time, limited his activities. His eyesight was so poor that it made him clumsy and awkward, and, as he stated in his *Autobiography*, "while much of my clumsiness and awkwardness was doubtless due to general characteristics, a great deal of it was due to the fact that I could not see and yet

The delight of the cartoonist and a hero to many Americans, Theodore Roosevelt brought youth and vitality to the White House. (Brown Brothers)

was wholly ignorant that I was not seeing." When he was nearly fourteen years old he was fitted for glasses. The results were extraordinary. "I had no idea," he writes, "how beautiful the world was until I got those spectacles." Despite his infirmities and nearsightedness, Roosevelt's energetic, strong-willed, and education-conscious father "refused to coddle" him and, when he was twelve years old, told him that he should prepare himself "to do the rough work of the world" by building up his body.[1] There then followed a strenuous program of directed gymnastics and exercises. Too fragile to attend even private schools regularly, Roosevelt's formal education, until he entered Harvard in 1876, was entrusted almost entirely to the family, private tutors, continuous and purposeful self-study, and two extensive trips to western and central Europe and the Middle East. After graduating from Harvard in 1880, where he continued to improve his health while earning a Phi Beta Kappa key, Roosevelt enrolled at Columbia University to study law but soon found politics more interesting than his studies and quickly abandoned the latter.

His political career, much to the chagrin of his family, began in 1882 when he was elected to the New York State Assembly. After three terms

---

[1] Quoted in Carleton Putnam, *Theodore Roosevelt: The Formative Years, 1858–1886* (New York [1958]), pp. 56, 80, 72,

at Albany, where he showed marked ability for engaging in controversy but little of the progressivism he was to display as President, he refused renomination; the Republican party did not press him to run again. Somewhat disillusioned by his initial experience in politics, unhappy with Blaine's nomination as the GOP standard-bearer in 1884, and greatly saddened by the deaths, on the same day, of his first wife and his mother, Roosevelt went west to raise cattle on his ranch in the Dakota Territory. By 1886 he was back in New York City campaigning as the Republican candidate for mayor. Defeated by the Democratic party's iron millionaire, Abram S. Hewitt, and finding few influential friends or supporters among the state's Republican bosses, Roosevelt remained out of office until 1889, when his good friend Henry Cabot Lodge of Massachusetts prevailed upon President Benjamin Harrison to appoint him to a federal office. Harrison obliged with a relatively insignificant $3,500 a year job on the Civil Service Commission, a post Roosevelt held until 1895. The job may have been an unimportant one when Theodore Roosevelt accepted it, but he soon made it into a significant and newsworthy one. Under his administration the Pendleton Act of 1883, which had established the federal civil service, was enforced vigorously, examinations were improved, and in the election of 1892, when the long-accepted though illegal practice of collecting campaign funds from federal employees was exposed, Roosevelt and the commission fought to stop it. Though the Republicans lost to Grover Cleveland that year, the Democratic President, pleased with Roosevelt's record on the commission, kept him at his post.

Roosevelt remained in Washington until 1895 when, at the request of New York City's Mayor William L. Strong, he resigned to head the city's police commission and to rid the police force of corruption. In 1897, again as a result of Lodge's efforts, McKinley appointed Roosevelt Assistant Secretary of the Navy, an office which gave him the opportunity to gratify another of his strong interests—a big navy. Roosevelt resigned this office in 1898 to serve in the army and take part in the invasion of Cuba, and then returned to New York, where he received a hero's welcome. Tom Platt, the state's Republican boss, searching for a respectable candidate who was not associated with the corruption and scandals of his party, arranged Roosevelt's nomination for governor. Elected by the slight majority of 17,794 votes, Roosevelt so annoyed Platt and the other party chieftains by imposing taxes on corporate franchises, enforcing the civil service system, and replacing the state superintendent of insurance, that the bosses feared he would wreck the machinery through which they controlled the party and the state. In order to get rid of him, Platt boosted Roosevelt for the Vice Presidency in 1900. His candidacy was supported by other state bosses who wished to annoy Mark Hanna, the real leader of the Republican party; it also evoked wide popular enthusiasm. Hanna, who suspected that Roosevelt did not share McKinley's reverence for big business, accepted Roosevelt as Vice President with reluctance, referring to him as "that damned cowboy" and asking his fellow bosses if they did not realize that there would be "only one life between that madman and the presidency." Roosevelt himself was not at all enthusiastic about his candidacy or the prospect of presiding over the Senate with almost no authority or voice over its deliberations. After the election, expecting to be shelved by the party leaders once his term was over, he planned to resume his career as a writer (by this time he had already written several quite respectable works on American history and popular accounts of his experiences as a rancher, hunter, and soldier),[2] or to renew another one by reading and studying law with the Chief Justice of the United States.

Czolgosz's bullet put into the White House the youngest President that the United States had ever had and the first President since Abraham Lincoln who was capable of real statesmanship. Full of energy and enthusiasm, this advocate of the "strenuous life" brought a new vitality to the Executive office and an enlarged view as to the nature and proper limits of presidential leadership and authority. There were few subjects, if any, that did not attract his interest or upon which he failed to express an opinion. Unlike McKinley, who deferred to the Congress, Roosevelt believed the President was "the steward of the people" and "bound to serve the people affirmatively." He saw himself in the Jackson-Lincoln tradition, not as a Buchanan type. "A strong people," he once said, "need never fear a strong man or a strong government; for a strong government is the most efficient instrument, and a strong man the most efficient servant of a strong people. It is an admission of popular weakness to be afraid of strong public servants and of an efficient governmental system." Roosevelt believed that the powers of the President should be greatly increased, declaring that "it was not only his right but his duty to do anything that the needs of the Nation demanded, unless such action was

[2] *The Naval War of 1812* (1882), *Thomas H. Benton* (1887); *Gouverneur Morris* (1888), *The Winning of the West* (6 vols., 1889–96), *Ranch Life and the Hunting Trail* (1888), *Hunting Trips of a Ranchman* (1886), *The Rough Riders* (1900).

forbidden by the Constitution or by the laws." His desire for power and his belief in a strong President were based upon the idea that it was the duty of the Chief Executive to act in behalf of the public welfare. He was able to win popular support for his activities by his talent for dramatizing them and coining singularly vivid phrases. Roosevelt once stated that he did not use words "to be subtle or original," but as "instruments" aimed "to make the plain everyday citizen understand . . . the things which I regard as essential to good government." His ability to express the prevailing mood and sentiment of the people, his understanding, appreciation, and skillful use of publicity and the press (he was on excellent terms with the White House press corps and cooperated with them in handling news releases, while they, in turn, reciprocated by publicizing his every activity), and his keen political sense and astute handling of political affairs brought him great popularity and made him an extraordinarily effective politician.

Fundamentally a conservative, he believed that change was inevitable, but that it should be "gradual . . . within established institutions" and achieved not by reckless or thoughtless actions but by "adapting, managing, and administering." Uncertain whether he was a "conservative radical" or a "radical conservative," he was convinced that "the only true conservative is the man who resolutely sets his face toward the future."[3] Roosevelt believed that political and economic stability could be maintained by instituting moderate reforms. He had no desire to alter the existing system of capitalism, but his strict moral code was shocked by the low ethical standards prevalent in business and by the apparent conviction of the corporate magnates that they should be independent of the laws and the government. He believed that if business were not compelled to conform to higher standards, American capitalism would be endangered by a growth of revolutionary sentiments. To avoid radical reform from the bottom, it was necessary to administer conservative reform from the top. According to one expert, Roosevelt stands as one of the "giants of American conservativism" because he succeeded "in shaping the old truths of conservativism to the new facts of industrialism and democracy."[4] Yet Roosevelt's ability to work with and through the Old Guard Republican leaders, and the frequent discrepancy between his words and his deeds—the former often being much more radical

[3] Quoted in John Morton Blum, *The Republican Roosevelt* (Cambridge, Mass., 1954).
[4] Clinton Rossiter, "The Giants of American Conservativism," *American Heritage*, VI (October 1955), 56.

than the latter—caused many of the progressives, particularly Robert La Follette, to denounce him as dishonest and insincere. Such accusations derived support from two factors—Roosevelt's capacity for self-deception, which sometimes caused him to violate promises and change policies without admitting it; and the egotism which prevented him from being just to men against whom he cherished personal grudges.

The changes made by Roosevelt in the functioning of the economic system were, in fact, meager. His real importance was that he was the first President since the Civil War to insist on the principle of government supremacy over business. By his varied intellectual and aesthetic interests, moreover, which had been equaled among American presidents only by Thomas Jefferson, and by the energy with which he both preached and practiced the "strenuous life," he did much to elevate the tone of American politics. His most dangerous weaknesses, on the other hand, were his passion for militarism, his leaning toward imperialism, and his belief in the superiority and responsibilities of the Anglo-Saxon peoples.

Roosevelt's accession to the Presidency caused considerable alarm in business circles, but Roosevelt declared at once that he proposed to follow in the footsteps of his predecessor and to cooperate with Hanna and with the Old Guard Republican leaders in Congress, Senator Nelson W. Aldrich and Speaker Joseph G. Cannon. He retained the somewhat mediocre cabinet inherited from McKinley, which was headed by Secretary of State John Hay. However, because Hay was now old and feeble, Roosevelt relied for advice chiefly on Elihu Root, the Secretary of War, recognizing that Root's capacity for dispassionate analysis provided a valuable check on his own impulsiveness. In 1904 William H. Taft returned from the Philippines to succeed Root, and in the following year Root succeeded Hay. During Roosevelt's second term, he, Root, and Taft, who were united by close friendship as well as by political agreement, liked to regard themselves as "the three musketeers."

ROOSEVELT AND THE TRUSTS

In spite of Roosevelt's promise to follow McKinley's policies, big business quickly discerned that he intended to interpret his duties in a different spirit. His first message to Congress (December 3, 1901) was a lengthy and studiously moderate document, the most important feature of which was a statement that "in dealing with the big corporations we call trusts we must resolutely purpose to proceed by evolution and not by revolution." "We do not wish to destroy corporations; but we do wish to make them subserve the public good." "The biggest corporation like the humblest private citizen must be held to strict compliance with the will of the people as expressed in the fundamental law."

It soon appeared that Roosevelt intended these phrases as more than soothing generalities. In March, 1902, he ordered Attorney General Philander C. Knox to bring suit under the Sherman Act, hitherto almost a dead letter, against the Northern Securities Company, which had been established by James J. Hill of the Great Northern Railway Company, Edward H. Harriman of the Union Pacific and Southern Pacific lines, and J. P. Morgan. This gigantic holding company, chartered in New Jersey, was formed in 1901 to prevent Harriman from competing with the Hill-Morgan combination. In order to give his lines an independent connection with the Middle West, Harriman had sought to capture control of the Chicago, Burlington and Quincy. Foiled in this effort, Harriman began to buy Northern Pacific stock in the hope of capturing it from Hill and Morgan. In one hour, on May 9, 1901, the value of the stock rose from $350 to $1,000. When the rival groups found eventually that they had bought from speculators 78,000 more shares than actually existed, they agreed to pool their interests in a new corporation, the Northern Securities Company, which monopolized the railroad facilities of the Northwest.

Roosevelt's sudden action against this new business combination was the first time that the United States government had shown any serious desire to enforce the Sherman Act, and hence caused great indignation on Wall Street. Morgan, for example, regarding Roosevelt as a kind of rival rather than a superior authority, urged him to send "your man to my man" to arrange a settlement. The resentment of the railroad men was even more extreme. "It really seems hard," complained Hill, "when we look back on what we have done—in opening the country and carrying at the lowest rates, that we should be compelled to fight for our lives against the political adventurers who have never done anything but pose and draw a salary."

In 1904, by a vote of five to four, the Supreme Court decided against the Northern Securities Company. This verdict, although it affirmed the supremacy of the federal government over big business, did not alter substantially the railroad situation of the lines involved. The Hill interests were left in control of the Northern Pacific, but Hill and Harriman continued to act in accordance with the "community of interest" theory.

The Department of Justice then went on to attack a number of other trusts, among them Standard Oil, the American Tobacco Company, the E. I. Du Pont powder trust, and the Swift meat-packing trust. During Roosevelt's seven and a half years in office, the administration secured in all twenty-five indictments and eighteen bills in equity.

The economic results of this trustbusting crusade, however, scarcely justified the furor it excited. In some instances, such as United States Steel's acquisition of the Tennessee Coal and Iron Company and the government's investigation of the International Harvester Company, the corporations and the administration worked out mutually satisfactory "gentlemen's agreements" whereby the firms could avoid prosecution if they corrected illegal practices and abided by the government's recommendations.[5] Court decisions compelled a number of trusts to dissolve themselves into their component parts, but it could not transfer these parts to new ownership. Hence, there was no real revival of competition. "Community of interest" arrangements, beyond the reach of court action, took the place of legal ties as the method by which business magnates maintained high prices and limited production. The Sherman Act, moreover, was gradually weakened by the Supreme Court. The act had originally defined combination in restraint of trade as criminal action; but in the Northern Securities case both the government and the Court agreed that the defendants should be immune from criminal penalties— a step which caused Oliver Wendell Holmes, recently appointed a justice by Roosevelt, to vote with the minority. Although, moreover, the Court originally agreed that the Sherman Act forbade all combinations, it subsequently decided that it should apply only to those which were "unreasonable." In the Standard Oil and American Tobacco cases, which did not reach the Court until 1911 and 1912, the justices declared that only "undue" restraint of trade was forbidden. This adoption of the rule of reason meant that the ultimate authority over business now belonged to the Court rather than to the government.

Roosevelt recognized the inadequacy of trustbusting as a method for reforming the economic system. Making a distinction between good trusts and bad trusts, he declared that "we draw the line against misconduct, not against wealth." Unlike Bryan and many Democratic party leaders who wished to prevent any corporation from controlling more than 50

[5] Robert H. Wiebe, "The House of Morgan and the Executive, 1905–1913," *American Historical Review*, LXV (October 1959), 49–60.

per cent of an industry, Roosevelt believed that big business should be accepted, but that it should be subordinated to the public interest. During his second term he urged that corporations be licensed and regulated by the federal government instead of by the state governments and that various specific malpractices be prohibited, but bills to that effect were rejected by the Senate. He believed, however, that the most important questions involved were not so much economic as political and legal. "When I became President," he declared in his *Autobiography*, "the question of the method by which the United States Government was to control the corporations was not yet important. The absolutely vital question was whether the Government had power to control them at all." "These men demanded for themselves an immunity from governmental control which, if granted, would be as wicked and as foolish as immunity to the barons of the twelfth century."

ROOSEVELT AND THE COAL STRIKE

Roosevelt's next intervention in the workings of the economic system involved labor, and it was equally unprecedented. The largest single union in the AFL, the United Mine Workers, was founded in 1890 and was organized as an industrial union, comprising all the workers in the industry, rather than as a craft union. Begun among the workers in the bituminous mines, by 1900 it had extended its activities to include the hard-coal miners as well.

The miners of anthracite coal were among the most exploited groups in the United States. Their wages averaged $560 a year, their employment was very irregular, their families received no compensation in cases of death or injury, and they lived in company houses and had to buy at company stores. The railroad magnates who operated the coal fields had a feudal attitude toward their workers which shocked even Mark Hanna and J. P. Morgan. A remarkably able and dynamic young labor leader, John Mitchell, succeeded in recruiting the miners into the United Mine Workers' Union; and in the summer of 1900 they struck for higher wages. Since a coal shortage might endanger the reelection of McKinley, Mark Hanna persuaded the operators to grant a 10 per cent increase in wages.

In March, 1902, the United Mine Workers asked for union recognition, a nine-hour day, guarantees that the coal dug would be accurately weighed, and a 20 per cent increase in wages. In May, 1902, after the operators had refused to negotiate, 150,000 miners went on strike. There was considerable popular sympathy for the miners, and this was increased when the principal employer, George F. Baer of the Reading and Philadelphia, declared in reply to a letter urging him to end the strike that "the rights and interests of the laboring man will be protected and cared for—not by the labor agitators, but by the Christian men to whom God in His infinite wisdom has given the control of the property interests of this country." The arrogance of the mine owners and the able leadership of John Mitchell won for the strikers the support of President Roosevelt.

By the autumn, when there was danger of a scarcity of coal, Roosevelt resolved to intervene—not, as Cleveland had done in the Pullman strike, to support the employers but to enforce negotiation. He called representatives of both sides to a conference at the White House, but the operators refused to negotiate with Mitchell, whom they regarded as no better than a criminal. Roosevelt then made plans to send the army into the coal fields to dig coal, and meanwhile Elihu Root induced J. P. Morgan to support arbitration and to put pressure on the mine owners. The owners finally consented to arbitration by a government commission; and although they would not allow labor to be officially represented on the

NO MOLLY-CODDLING HERE

Actually a moderate conservative, President Theodore Roosevelt alarmed many big businessmen by insisting on the principle of government supremacy. (Culver Pictures, Inc.)

commission, they made no objection when Roosevelt appointed a trade union leader but called him an "eminent sociologist."

The decisions of the commission were that the union should not win formal recognition as bargaining agent for its members, but that the workers should receive a nine-hour day and a 10 per cent increase in wages, they should have their own checkweighmen at the scales, and a board of conciliation should be established to negotiate future disputes. The settlement was followed by a large increase in the union's membership and ten years of peace in the coal fields. During the next eighteen years the United Mine Workers steadily gained in strength and benefits. In 1912 the workers won another wage increase after a month's strike, and in 1916 they secured an eight-hour day and union recognition. By 1920 the union's membership numbered 370,000 workers, about half the total number of miners in the country. After 1920, however, it failed to hold these gains, and until 1933 its membership steadily declined.

LEGISLATION, 1901–1905

During Roosevelt's first term relatively little legislation of major significance was enacted. One of the most important laws which the Congress passed was the Newlands Act of 1902, which established the Reclamation Service and provided for the establishment of irrigation projects by the federal government with money derived from the sales of public lands. By 1915 a million and a quarter acres of arid land in the West had thus been opened to agriculture.

In 1903 Roosevelt secured from the Congress the creation of a Department of Commerce and Labor, which included a Bureau of Corporations. Congressional opposition to this measure was overcome when Roosevelt made public a series of telegrams sent by a Standard Oil executive, which revealed the corrupt connections between big business and certain senators. Also in 1903 there was passed, with the approval of the railroads, the Elkins Act which forbade the giving of rebates on freight rates and declared that corporations receiving rebates were to be fined for each offense. How strictly the act would be enforced, however, remained to be seen. In 1907 Judge Kenesaw Mountain Landis ordered a Standard Oil affiliate in Indiana to pay a fine of $29.24 million for accepting a series of rebates; but this decision was reversed for technical reasons by a higher court, and the company was acquitted.

THE ELECTION OF 1904

The chief reason for Roosevelt's relative caution in pushing legislation during his first term was his fear that he might not be renominated. But his leadership of the Republican party was strengthened by the death of the ailing Mark Hanna in February, 1904; and in the summer of that year he secured the party nomination for a second term without opposition. The Republican platform that year was a relatively conservative document, reflecting the influence of the party's stalwarts but, at the same time, extolling Roosevelt's accomplishments.

The Democrats, abandoning Bryan and unable to interest their former two-time leader, Grover Cleveland, adopted as their candidate a relatively unknown, conservative easterner, Judge Alton B. Parker of New York. Parker demanded and secured from the Democratic leadership a major concession when he asked them to recognize "the gold standard as firmly and irretrievably established." In the hope that he would help fill the party's campaign chest, the Democrats nominated the wealthy octogenarian and former West Virginia senator, Henry G. Dawes, for Vice President. No longer demanding a radical and inflationist monetary policy or an income tax, and standing on "the essential principles of Democratic faith," including a low tariff, enforcement of the antitrust laws, anti-imperialism, and Philippine independence, the Democratic party hoped to secure the support of the business community. But the corporation magnates, in spite of the unpredictable Roosevelt, still preferred the Republicans and contributed lavishly to that party's campaign fund, Harriman giving a quarter of a million dollars and Standard Oil a hundred thousand.

Roosevelt carried every state save twelve in the South and was re-elected by a popular vote of 7,628,834 to 5,084,491 and an electoral college vote of 336 to 140. Debs, the Socialist nominee, received 402,283 votes; and Tom Watson, nominated by the surviving Populists, received 114,753. The Republicans also won large majorities in both houses of Congress. Immediately after the election Roosevelt made a statement which he afterwards regretted: "Under no circumstances," he declared, "will I be a candidate for or accept another nomination."

During his second term Roosevelt was much more outspoken in his denunciations of big business than he had been previously. In his December, 1905, message to the Congress he outlined the need for more social and economic legislation, emphasizing the necessity for more effective railroad regulation, especially in the matter of fixing rates. Public opinion was strongly behind the President on this issue, and T.R., realizing how long and how often the people had been thwarted in trying to curb rebates, rate discrimination, and other equally unethical practices, proposed to satisfy the public's demand for more effective railroad legislation.

The Hepburn Act, passed in 1906, revitalized the Interstate Commerce Commission and gave it real authority over the railroads. Roosevelt's original proposals, which were more drastic than the act as finally passed, were accepted by the House of Representatives, where Speaker Cannon, in spite of his own conservatism, considered it his duty to cooperate with the administration; but they were vigorously opposed by the conservative Republicans in the Senate. In order to save the bill, Roosevelt was forced to agree to a compromise.

In its final form the Hepburn Act extended the authority of the commission over all forms of transportation, forbade the giving of railroad passes except to railroad employees, required the railroad corporations to divorce themselves from their ownership of coal fields, and gave the commission power, when there were complaints by shippers, to reduce unreasonable rates. Rate reductions were, however, to be subject to judicial review and were not to go into effect until the courts had agreed that they were reasonable, although the burden of proof was placed on the railroads and not on the commission. The authority thus given to the courts was denounced by progressives, who wanted some clearer definition of what constituted a reasonable rate; and La Follette urged that the commission be empowered to assess the physical value of the railroad properties, so that the rates might be judged in relation to the capital really invested in them rather than to their nominal capitalization, which included so much watered stock.

The Hepburn Act proved to be more effective than the progressives had anticipated: within two years of its enactment there were nine thousand complaints by shippers against unreasonable railroad practices. But few of these related to rates, and it was doubtful whether the commission had acquired effective power to force reductions. In 1910, however, the powers of the commission were further extended by the Mann-Elkins Act, which gave the commission authority over the telephone and telegraph systems, and allowed the commission to suspend rate increases until it had been decided whether they were reasonable. Passage of the act was hastened by an announcement on the part of the railroad companies that they proposed to increase rates, and in 1911 this increase was prohibited by the commission. La Follette's proposal for a physical valuation of railroad properties was accepted by Congress in 1913.

PURE FOOD AND CONSERVATION

Two other important laws passed in 1906 were the Meat Inspection Act and the Pure Food and Drug Act. Chemical experts in the pay of the state and federal governments, originally appointed to serve the interests of the farmers, had for some years been investigating the widespread adulteration of foods by manufacturers and the selling of harmful patent medicines; and popular indignation had also been provoked by a number of startling disclosures, particularly those made by Harvey W. Wiley, chief chemist of the U. S. Department of Agriculture. However, the Senate had previously rejected several pure food bills on the old principle of *caveat emptor*. The patent medicine interests, moreover, were well protected from newspaper criticism by means of an unscrupulous use of advertising pressure.

The pure food crusaders won Roosevelt's support in 1905, but Congress again refused to take action. In the spring of 1906, however, after Roosevelt read Upton Sinclair's *The Jungle*, he appointed a commission to investigate conditions in the packing houses, and the commission reported that the reality was even worse than Sinclair's lurid descriptions of it. When the meat-packing interests succeeded in blocking a bill providing for government inspection of the packing houses, Roosevelt made public some of the findings of the commission, with the result that the sales of canned meat immediately dropped by one-half. In June, 1906, popular indignation forced Congress to accept the Meat Inspection bill and, at the same time, a Pure Food and Drug bill which prohibited the sale of harmful foods and ordered that foods and medicines be correctly labeled. This was a step in the right direction, although as a result partly of weaknesses in the act and partly of inadequate enforcement it by no means ended the selling of adulterated or harmful products. In the 1930's the patent medicine interests were still fighting against stronger legislation, and not until 1938 did Congress pass a more effective Pure Food, Drug and Cosmetic Act.

Another even more vital national problem to which Roosevelt drew attention was the need to conserve and use effectively the country's natural resources. In 1879 the United States Geological Survey was established, and under the directorship of Frederick H. Newell it studied the nation's surviving natural wealth on the public lands. In 1887 a forestry division was established in the Department of Agriculture. In 1891 followed the Forest Reserve Act, which authorized the President to retain public ownership of timber lands. Beginning in 1891, some 36 million acres had been so reserved by Harrison, Cleveland, and McKinley, and had been placed under the supervision of the General Land Office. As soon as Roosevelt entered the White House he indicated his interest in promoting forestry, irrigation, and conservation measures. In 1901 he called upon Newell and Gifford Pinchot of the Forest Service to help him with the forestry and irrigation sections of his first message to the Congress. In addition to stressing the "imperative business necessity" of safeguarding the country's forest, mineral, and water resources, Roosevelt, at Pinchot's suggestion, also recommended that the forest reserves be taken out of the Department of Interior and placed under the immediate supervision and control of the Bureau of Forestry. Roosevelt believed that too many government officials followed "the habit of deciding, wherever possible, in favor of private interests against the public welfare" and hoped that he could inculcate in them a different point of view. In this he was ably and energetically assisted by Pinchot, who devoted himself to the cause of conservation with a zeal which approached fanaticism, and by James R. Garfield, who became Secretary of the Interior in 1907.

The conservation program was aided also by some of the muckrakers who, beginning in 1902, exposed and publicized land thefts involving thousands of acres of government land. Aided by public opinion on his side and spurred on by Pinchot and other conservationists, Roosevelt, despite the opposition of certain influential senators and congressmen, succeeded in carrying out most of his program. Between 1906 and 1908 he added about 148 million acres to the forest reserves, by then called the National Forests, and, as of February 1, 1905, placed under the control of the Bureau of Forestry. Roosevelt included in his reserve program not only genuine timberlands but also—with dubious legality and in spite of protests in Congress—lands which contained coal, phosphates, and waterpower sites. Roosevelt explained his action by saying: "I acted on the theory that the President could at any time in his discretion withdraw from entry any of the public lands of the United States and reserve the same for forestry, waterpower sites, for irrigation, and for other public purposes. Without such action it would have been impossible to stop the activity of the land thieves." Roosevelt's interest in public ownership of water power was indicated also by his veto of a bill which would have allowed a private power company to build a dam at Muscle Shoals on the Tennessee River.

Because Roosevelt was anxious that the state governments cooperate with the federal government in conservation, in 1908 he called a White House conference of state governors. The conference recommended that the federal government retain ownership of all public lands containing minerals and that ownership of the surface of the soil be separated from ownership of the subsoil. Roosevelt failed to secure supporting legislation from Congress, though his activity had an important effect in awakening public opinion to the seriousness of the problem and led to the appointment of conservation commissions in forty-one of the states.

THE PANIC OF 1907

Roosevelt's denunciation of the "malefactors of great wealth" grew steadily more bitter throughout his second term; and when, in October, 1907, the stock market suddenly slumped and there were numerous bankruptcies, the financiers accused the President of having provoked it by undermining business confidence. Roosevelt retaliated by stating that the financiers had precipitated a banker's panic by their "speculative folly and flagrant dishonesty" and had used the crisis to try to discredit his administration.

The panic, which started on October 22 with the failure of the Knickerbocker Trust Company in New York City, was the result of careless speculation, financial and business mismanagement on the part of certain prominent individuals whose speculations alarmed investors and frightened depositors, and the inelasticity of the nation's credit and currency, which prevented the federal government and the national banks from enlarging the supply of paper money to help deserving and sound banks meet the demands of their depositors. The total amount of paper money in circulation (gold and silver certificates and United States and Treasury notes), as well as the notes issued by the national banks, was determined by law or other considerations which bore little, if any, relationship to the needs of an expanding economy. In times of crisis, such as the autumn of 1907, the scarcity of currency aggravated further an already strained and precarious credit situation. Sound banking institutions were threatened with runs and were often unable to raise enough money to meet the demands of their depositors, even though they possessed excellent securities and other collateral in their vaults.

The nation's financial plight was also in part the result of the fact that a number of the larger New York City banks held in their vaults deposits from banks all over the country. In order to earn interest on their excess reserves, the out-of-state banks deposited these funds with New York City banks, which used these deposits to lend to stock market speculators and other investors. The result was that the reserves of the New York banks and their correspondents all over the United States were closely tied to the financial and stock market operations of a few Wall Street institutions. Anything which caused an unforeseen run on the reserves of these pivotal banks, such as exceptionally heavy withdrawals by depositors, forced them to call in their loans. If, in order to meet the demand of their depositors, they were forced to sell securities, their action might precipitate a money panic and an unwarranted drop in the price of stocks on the exchange, with heavy losses. The very efforts which the banks were forced to employ to meet the demands of their clients tightened credit and the money supply just at the time when they should have been loosened. Unable to borrow, banks were forced to suspend payment. The psychological effect of such action caused other depositors to demand payment from their banks, thus creating a full scale money panic, even though economic conditions were generally sound. This is precisely what occurred when the Knickerbocker Trust Company, after paying out $8 million in one day, was forced to suspend payments. Runs on other trust companies followed.[6] To stop the panic, the bankers called on J. P. Morgan for assistance, and under his forceful and able leadership a committee was formed to devise a plan of action. Secretary of the Treasury George Cortelyou cooperated closely with the Morgan committee, and ordered $35 million of government funds to be deposited in the national banks, thus providing them with money to lend to the sound trust companies which were, or seemed to be, getting into difficulties. For nearly a month Morgan led his committee and the New York banking community safely through one crisis after another until the problem of the trust companies was resolved and the Wall Street panic

[6] John A. Garraty, "A Lion in the Street," *American Heritage*, VIII (June 1957).

ended. Frederick Lewis Allen characterized Morgan's actions during the month's crisis as those of a "one-man Federal Reserve Bank."

One episode during the panic shows how far Roosevelt was from being an economic radical. The brokerage house of Moore and Schley was in financial difficulties, and its collapse threatened to cause further bankruptcies on Wall Street. The house owned $5 million of stock in the Tennessee Coal and Iron Company, for which it was unable to find

J. P. Morgan, the leading and most influential investment banker in America before World War I, is shown here leaving the office of his famous banking house, on the corner of Broad and Wall streets in New York City. (Brown Brothers)

purchasers, except at such disastrously low prices as to cause its downfall. J. P. Morgan decided that the situation could be saved if Tennessee Coal and Iron was purchased by United States Steel. He sent Gary and Frick to ask Roosevelt for a guarantee that the purchase would not be followed by a prosecution under the Sherman Act; and without learning all the details Roosevelt gave his assent. United States Steel thereupon added Tennessee Coal and Iron to its properties at a price of $45 million. Enemies of big business declared that Morgan and Gary had deliberately made use of the crisis to acquire Tennessee Coal and Iron for much less than its real value and that they had misled Roosevelt as to the facts of the situation. That Roosevelt later came to suspect Morgan had out-witted him was suggested by the extraordinary vehemence with which he defended what he had done and by the fact that he never forgave Taft for permitting Attorney-General Wickersham to file an antitrust suit against the United States Steel Corporation in 1911.

The worst of the Wall Street panic was over by mid-November, after which recovery and prosperity followed rapidly. During the crisis the banks were hit hard. The total number of bank suspensions, which in-creased from 90 in 1907 to 153 in 1908, was not exceeded until the depression of 1920. Unemployment in the manufacturing and transpor-tation industries increased from an estimated 3.5 per cent in 1907 to 12 per cent in 1908. There had been many panics before, but the crisis of 1907 not only was particularly severe but also pointed out the danger-ous inelasticity of the nation's money supply and credit system.

The need to reform the system had been evident for some time, though little had been done about it. With the memory of the frightful events of the month of October still fresh in mind, the Congress moved quickly to enact legislation to prevent similar crises in the future. On May 30, 1908, the Aldrich-Vreeland Act was passed to increase the elasticity of the currency by empowering the national banks to issue emergency notes secured by state and local government bonds and acceptable commercial paper. Far more important was the act's provision creating the National Monetary Commission "to inquire into and report to Congress . . . what changes are necessary or desirable in the monetary system of the United States or in the laws relating to banking and currency." On January 8, 1912, after nearly four years of careful and detailed research and some forty volumes of studies, the commission, made up of expert economists and historians assigned to study the development and operation of the

American and foreign banking systems, reported to Congress. Its recommendations were used in drawing up the Federal Reserve Act, which became law the next year.

During his last year in office Roosevelt sent a series of messages to Congress, attacking the misdeeds of business and asking for more government regulation, denouncing the conservatism of the courts, recommending federal legislation to regulate stock market speculation, and proposing income and inheritance taxes. The programs and legislation which Roosevelt asked Congress to enact in his messages of December, 1907, and January, 1908, indicate that he had moved considerably to the left of his earlier administration. His interest in promoting labor's welfare by curbing the use of the antistrike injunction and advocating an eight-hour work day and better workmen's compensation laws foreshadowed the advanced reform program of the "New Nationalism" of 1910 and 1912. His approaching retirement, however, deprived him of effective control over legislation. His program and reforms were far too radical for the conservative majority in the Congress, so that in spite of the increasingly progressive temper of the country at the time, the Republican leadership ignored almost all of Roosevelt's 1908 and 1909 recommendations.

When Roosevelt left the White House in 1909, the rift in the Republican party between the progressives and the conservatives, which was to plague his successor and tear the Republican party apart in 1912, was already evident. Within the next three years, progressives in and out of Congress adopted and elaborated the social and economic philosophy and many of the proposals of Roosevelt's last year to build their own reform program. Roosevelt can hardly be held responsible for inaugurating the Republican schism, for as George E. Mowry observes, "it would have developed with or without his aid," but Roosevelt's words and actions, especially in 1907 and 1908, certainly "abetted it." [7]

ROOSEVELT'S FOREIGN POLICY

Imperialist Tendencies

The foreign policy of the progressive era seems, from some points of view, to be inconsistent with the dominant tendencies of domestic poli-

[7] George E. Mowry, *The Era of Theodore Roosevelt, 1901–1912* (New York [1958]), p. 225.

tics. At home the period from 1901 to 1914 was marked by liberal reforms intended to protect democracy from the powers of big business; but in foreign affairs the United States played the part of a great power and developed imperialist tendencies which often appeared to be serving the interests of American industry and finance. Many of the leading progressives, such as President Roosevelt, Senator Albert J. Beveridge, Herbert Croly, and Willard D. Straight, a founder of the *New Republic*, were among the most ardent champions of a large navy and a vigorous foreign policy. On the other hand, conservatives like Senator Nelson W. Aldrich and business tycoons like Andrew Carnegie, the men with whom Roosevelt was fighting over his domestic reform program, were strongly opposed to imperialism and militarism. But what these apparently conflicting tendencies within the progressive movement had in common was that both imperialism and militarism were marked by an extension of the powers of the federal government, which assumed more positive functions than in the past.

The three Presidents of the progressive era pursued quite different objectives in their foreign policy, though all of them recognized the need to promote America's foreign trade. Roosevelt was a believer in the leadership of the Anglo-Saxon race, in the need for the use of force in settling international disputes, and in the therapeutic value of war; in foreign affairs he thought primarily of increasing the military strength and security of the United States. During the Taft administration economic considerations predominated; the government advocated "dollar diplomacy" and endeavored to secure new foreign markets for American trade and investments. Wilson, on the other hand, was a moralist, who deplored the influence of financial interests on foreign policy and believed that the United States should use its strength to promote democracy, amity, peace, trade, and the rule of law in international affairs.

Yet in spite of these marked differences in viewpoint, the policies actually adopted by the Roosevelt, Taft, and Wilson administrations differed little from one another. Throughout the whole of the progressive era the United States claimed certain rights of suzerainty over the Caribbean region and was actively concerned with the affairs of Europe and the Far East. One of the main considerations dominating American foreign policy during the first decade of the twentieth century was an increasing concern about the effect of power politics and imperialist rivalries in other parts of the world upon the international position of the United States. Roosevelt, for example, was convinced that the United States now had to consider national security more carefully than in the past, and, in particular, had to strengthen the Monroe Doctrine in order to prevent any European power from acquiring a dangerous position in the Caribbean region.

A significant development in Latin American foreign policy during the progressive era—the growth of the practice of intervention in the Caribbean republics—has been attacked as a form of economic imperialism. It is true that it often served the interests of American bankers and industrialists; but the chief reason that caused Roosevelt, Taft, and Wilson to adopt this policy, in spite of the differences in their ideals, was the fear of economic and political encroachment by European powers, particularly Germany. This policy had, however, the unfortunate result of antagonizing and alarming all the Latin American nations, South American as well as Caribbean. What the United States lost by its interventionist policy, through the growth of Latin American hostility, may have been more important than what it gained by it.

The Panama Canal

During the Roosevelt administration the most important episode in American foreign policy was the construction of the Panama Canal. The building of a canal across Central America was of vital importance to American security since it would enable the navy to move quickly between the Atlantic and the Pacific. Without a canal the United States would be compelled to maintain a first-class navy on both oceans. The need for it had been dramatized by the voyage of the battleship *Oregon* around Cape Horn during the Spanish-American War. Although Roosevelt deserves credit for the building of the canal, his handling of the diplomatic problems involved showed a marked disregard for the rights of weaker nations and caused bitter resentment throughout Latin America.

The building of a canal across Central America had been considered at the time of the acquisition of California; and in 1850, by the Clayton-Bulwer Treaty, the United States and Great Britain had agreed that the proposed canal should be jointly controlled by the two countries and should not be fortified. The project subsequently was dropped until after the war with Spain. Secretary of State John Hay then opened negotiations with Great Britain for a revision of the Clayton-Bulwer Treaty; and in November, 1901, by the Second Hay-Pauncefote Treaty (the British had rejected the amendments the Senate had appended to the first one), it was agreed that the United States might construct, control, and fortify a canal, but that ships of all nations should use it on equal terms and that the United States government should guarantee its neutrality.

The next step was to decide whether to build the canal across Nicaragua or the isthmus of Panama, then under Colombian sovereignty. Unsuccessful attempts had been made in both places: in 1889 a French company, headed by Ferdinand de Lesseps, went bankrupt trying to dig a canal across Panama; and a few years later, lack of funds forced a group of Americans to abandon construction of a Nicaraguan canal. After the Spanish-American War, President McKinley appointed a commission headed by Rear Admiral John G. Walker to survey both approaches. In November, 1901, after two years of study, the commission reported in favor of a Nicaraguan canal, largely because of the exorbitant price of $109 million demanded by the New Panama Company, the French corporation which had taken over DeLesseps' abandoned properties in Panama. Besides DeLesseps' improvements the company also held the concession which the famous engineer had acquired from the Colombian government in 1880, authorizing him to build a waterway across the isthmus. This concession, however, was to expire in 1904; and the New Panama Company, realizing its holdings would become worthless if the Nicaraguan canal were built, was anxious to sell out to the United States government. In 1902, it reduced its price to $40 million, the approximate value which the Walker commission had estimated the company's assets were worth. Theodore Roosevelt, a longtime enthusiast of a Central American canal, had originally endorsed the Nicaraguan route, but after succeeding to the Presidency, he shifted his support to the Panama site. The reasons which motivated Roosevelt to change his mind aroused considerable speculation; and for a long time it was generally believed that his decision had been influenced by the lobbying activities of the New Panama Company, especially the $60,000 it had contributed to the GOP's campaign fund in 1900. Subsequently, however, the publication of Roosevelt's letters revealed that it was the opinion of America's leading scientists and engineers, nearly all of whom had always opposed a Nicaraguan canal, which led the President to alter his decision. The views of these experts caused the Walker commission to reconsider its earlier recommendation, and after further study, the commission issued a second report on January 18, 1902, in which it reversed its previous position and endorsed Panama as "the most practicable and feasible route."

With Roosevelt and the Walker commission in favor of the Panama site, the New Panama Company directed its American representative, Thomas Nelson Cromwell, a prominent and influential New York City attorney, to win Senate approval for acquiring the site. Cromwell's lobbying activities on Capitol Hill, which had been going on for several years already, were greatly assisted early in 1901 by the arrival in the United States of Philippe Bunau-Varilla, a French engineer who had worked with DeLesseps and, after the collapse of that enterprise, had assisted in establishing the New Panama Company, of which he was an important stockholder. These two men carried on an energetic campaign to win Congress's and the people's approval of the Panama route. While Cromwell concentrated his attention upon Mark Hanna and other influential legislators, Bunau-Varilla dilated effectively on the dangers of volcanic eruptions in Nicaragua. Their efforts were finally rewarded on June 28, 1902, when the Senate passed the Spooner Act. The canal was to be built across Panama, and the New Panama Company was to receive $40 million; but if the government of Colombia refused to grant its consent and cede to the United States in perpetuity the land for the canal "within a reasonable time and upon reasonable terms," the Nicaraguan route was to be substituted.

In January, 1903, by the Hay-Herran Convention, the government of Colombia agreed to lease a canal zone to the United States for 99 years in return for $10 million in cash and an annual rental of $250,000. The Colombian Congress, however, refused to ratify the convention. It was alarmed by the sacrifice of its sovereignty over the canal zone and was angry with the New Panama Company for selling its canal concession without asking Colombia's consent. Colombia insisted that it ought to receive an additional $10 million out of the $40 million to be paid to the company. There was some justification for this, since the company's concession would expire in eight months. When Hay refused to consent to this proposal, the Colombian Senate adjourned without acting upon the Hay-Herran Convention. Roosevelt was mightily indignant with the attitude of the Colombians, whom he described, in private, as "those contemptible little creatures in Bogotá" and as "foolish and homicidal corruptionists."

Colombia's rejection of the convention meant that the canal would be built across Nicaragua and that the New Panama Company would not get its $40 million. Bunau-Varilla and Cromwell then proceeded to finance and engineer a revolution in Panama, assuring the Panamanians that if they declared their independence from Colombia, the United

States would assist them. They also pointed out that the money from the sale of the canal zone would then go to Panama instead of to Colombia. Roosevelt does not appear to have participated in the conspiracy; but he guessed and approved of what Cromwell and Bunau-Varilla were planning and, interpreting liberally certain provisions of the Bidlack-Mallarino Treaty of 1846 between the United States and Colombia (then known as New Granada), he ordered United States warships to proceed to Panama to prevent any interference with traffic across the isthmus and to protect American rights. Some hours before the revolution began, the State Department cabled the American consul at Panama for news of it. On November 3, after the Panamanians had been informed by a cable from Bunau-Varilla that the American navy was on its way, they revolted. Colombian troops were prevented from reaching Panama by a United States warship, and on November 6 the United States recognized the independence of the new republic.

A week later the government of Panama appointed Bunau-Varilla as its American representative; and on November 18, 1903, by the Hay–Bunau-Varilla Treaty, the United States leased the canal zone in perpetuity for $10 million in cash and an annual rental of $250,000. The New Panama Company thereupon obtained the $40 million. The identity of the stockholders to whom the money was paid has never been revealed. Roosevelt insisted that they were French citizens, but there were persistent accusations, which have never been disproved, that the rights of the New Panama Company had been acquired by Wall Street financiers.

The behavior of the United States government caused indignation throughout Latin America. There was little justification for the support given by Roosevelt to the Panamanians since there was no pressing reason for beginning the canal before 1904, when the concession held by the New Panama Company would expire. Cromwell and Bunau-Varilla had succeeded in maneuvering Roosevelt into a violation of the rights of Colombia for the benefit of the unknown stockholders whom they represented. Roosevelt, moreover, increased the resentment of Colombia when, in a speech at Berkeley, California, in 1911, he declared flatly: "I took the Canal Zone and let Congress debate." In 1914 Secretary of State Bryan negotiated a treaty with Colombia by which the United States government agreed to pay $30 million in compensation and expressed "sincere regret that anything should have occurred to interrupt or mar the relations of cordial friendship." However, the Republicans in the Senate succeeded in defeating ratification, as a slur on Roosevelt. But as Colombia's continued hostility proved to be harmful to American commercial interests, in 1921, when American businessmen were anxious to obtain oil concessions from the Colombian government, a new treaty was negotiated and ratified. The United States government made no expression of regret but paid Colombia $25 million.

Construction of the canal by the United States Army Engineers Corps began in 1904. Progress was at first disappointingly slow. But a primary difficulty—the prevalence of tropical diseases—was finally removed by the work of Dr. William C. Gorgas, and after 1908, when Colonel George W. Goethals was given sole authority, building proceeded rapidly. The first ocean vessel passed through the canal in 1914, and the work was completed in 1920, the cost being $275 million for the canal itself and $113 million for the fortifications. In 1912 Congress decided that United States ships engaged in coastal trade should be exempt from paying taxes and passed the Panama Tolls Act, but this measure, attacked by the railroads and denounced by Great Britain as a violation of the Hay-Pauncefote Treaty, was repealed by Congress in 1914 during the Wilson administration.

Intervention in the Caribbean

The importance of the Panama Canal to American security made it necessary for the United States to guard the approaches to the canal and to prevent European powers from acquiring positions in the Caribbean. The Caribbean republics suffered from frequent revolutions, which were likely to endanger the lives and properties of foreign citizens. Also, they often defaulted on their foreign debts. There was, therefore, danger that European powers might intervene to protect their commercial and financial interests. Roosevelt concluded that to avert the possibility of such intervention, the United States must, when necessary, intervene itself. As the British government had pointed out, this was a logical deduction from the claims made by Secretary of State Richard Olney during the Venezuela boundary dispute of 1895.

In his message to Congress of December 2, 1904, Roosevelt declared that "Chronic wrongdoing, or an impotence which results in a general loosening of the ties of civilized society may in America, as elsewhere, ultimately require intervention by some civilized nation, and in the Western hemisphere the adherence of the United States to the Monroe Doctrine may force the United States, however reluctantly, in flagrant cases of such wrongdoing or impotence, to the exercise of an international police power." This assertion that the United States ought to police the Western Hemisphere, which became known as the Roosevelt Corollary, had never, in the nineteenth century, been regarded as justified by the terms of the Monroe Doctrine. The Latin American nations generally disliked it and put forward an alternative doctrine, named after Luis Drago, Minister of Foreign Affairs for Argentina, according to which any kind of armed intervention for the collection of debts and the protection of foreigners, whether by the European powers or by the United States, should be regarded as contrary to international law.

Defenders of the practice of intervention have argued that it was justifiable not only on grounds of national security but also because it brought good government and economic and social improvement to the Caribbean area. There appears to be considerable truth in this assertion, but it should be added that the good government was not always appreciated by the natives of the Caribbean republics and that intervention was generally accompanied by the use of force. And although economic and financial imperialism was not the original cause of interventionism, it was certainly one of its consequences. Debts due by Caribbean republics to European investors were frequently transferred to American bankers, who acquired a dominating position in the Caribbean area; and United States intervention was likely to result in the maintenance of conservative governments and in the suppression of radical movements hostile to foreign capitalists. Opponents of the Roosevelt Corollary had, therefore, some reason for believing that it had perverted the Monroe Doctrine into an instrument of United States financial hegemony.

Roosevelt's practices, in foreign policy as in internal affairs, were milder than his public utterances, and it was not until after he had left the White House that intervention became a habit. Roosevelt's moderation was partly due to the influence of Elihu Root, who became Secretary of State in 1905 and who had a strong appreciation of the value of Latin American goodwill.

In 1902, when Venezuela refused to compensate foreigners for losses they had suffered during a civil war, British, German, and Italian warships blockaded the Venezuelan coast. Roosevelt urged the different governments to submit to arbitration and, in moderate but firm language, he warned them that the United States would not tolerate their acquisition of any American territory. Since Germany's attitude was particularly intransigent, Roosevelt gave added meaning to his words by strengthen-

Secretary of War (1899–1904), Secretary of State (1905–9), and senator from New York (1909–15), Elihu Root was one of the ablest conservative leaders in twentieth-century America. (Brown Brothers)

ing the fleet in the Caribbean and alerting Admiral Dewey to be prepared for action, if necessary. Throughout this crisis Roosevelt's objective was to defend the Monroe Doctrine and to avoid American involvement, both of which he succeeded in achieving by skillful personal diplomacy. Finally, in February, 1903, Britain and Germany agreed to end their blockade and to allow the Hague Tribunal to settle their claims, which, with Roosevelt's approval, it did the next year.

In 1905, on the other hand, Roosevelt intervened in the Dominican Republic. Unable to pay its debts to European bondholders and threatened by attack from European powers, the Dominican government was persuaded to sign a treaty by which an American receiver-general was to collect its customs duties and supervise the spending of them. The United States Senate refused for two years to ratify the treaty, but Roosevelt ignored this rebuke. American marines took charge of the republic until 1907, by which time its revenues had been doubled and the claims of its foreign creditors had been almost halved. Roosevelt then withdrew the marines, declaring that he had "put the affairs of the island on a better basis than they had been for a century." This may have been true; but it should also be pointed out that the claims of the European creditors had been transferred to New York bankers, who henceforth controlled the economic development of the republic, and that the Dominicans themselves continued to prefer self-government, however bad, to government by the United States. Again in 1906 Roosevelt sent American troops to Cuba, in accordance with the Platt Amendment, to prevent civil war, and the island remained under American rule until 1909.

The Far East

In the Far East Roosevelt, Taft, and Wilson all continued to support the policy, first enunciated by John Hay, of preserving the Open Door and protecting the territorial integrity of China. American diplomacy in the Far East was, however, not conspicuously successful, partly because the American people were not sufficiently concerned about the independence of China to use force in its defense and partly because China was now threatened not merely by European powers but by a new and aggressive Asiatic imperialism, that of Japan. The United States was, moreover, in no position to invite Japanese hostility, because of fear of attack on the Philippine Islands.

In February, 1904, the Russo-Japanese War began. Since Russia was regarded in the United States as the more aggressive and imperialistic of the two powers, American sympathy was with Japan. The Japanese won a series of naval and military victories, but it was doubtful whether their resources would be sufficient for a long war. Roosevelt, aware of the necessity of maintaining the balance of power in the Far East, was anxious that peace be concluded before Japan was exhausted. Russia consented to accept American mediation, and the delegates of Russia and Japan conferred at Portsmouth, New Hampshire. With Roosevelt's assistance a treaty was agreed upon in September, 1905, by which Japan acquired control over Korea (Roosevelt and Root had agreed to this in July, 1905, when the secret Taft-Katsura memorandum was signed) and made other economic and territorial gains in southern Manchuria and on the southern half of Sakhalin Island. Roosevelt later asserted that in the course of the war he had warned France and Germany against intervening in order to deprive the Japanese of the fruits of their victory, but no record of such a warning has survived.

The war left Japan the dominant power in the Far East, and it was followed by Japanese economic control of a large part of southern Manchuria, which was legally a part of China. It began to seem that if the

United States wished to maintain the Open Door, it had been a mistake
to support Japan against Russia. After the war there was, moreover, a
growth of bad feeling between Tokyo and Washington. Believing that
they ought to have received better terms at the Treaty of Portsmouth
(they had demanded an indemnity and all of the island of Sakhalin), the
Japanese blamed the United States for having interfered to deprive them
of both. They also resented the increasingly outspoken opposition of the
white population of California to Japanese immigration.

There was an outburst of indignation in Japan when, in October, 1906,
the San Francisco Board of Education issued an order segregating Oriental children in the public schools of the city. This action angered the
Japanese, who protested it as a violation of their 1894 treaty rights and
the agreement of 1900, whereby Japan voluntarily limited the number
of its nationals emigrating to the continental United States. No provision
had been made, however, to prevent Japanese from entering the United
States via Canada, Mexico, Hawaii, or the Canal Zone. Roosevelt met the
dangers of the Japanese protest in a realistic spirit. Although he had no
legal power over the school system of San Francisco, he summoned the
municipal authorities to Washington and persuaded them to rescind the
segregation order. In return for their cooperation, Roosevelt secured an
amendment to the Immigration Act of 1907, whereby the President could
"prevent the immigration of aliens who . . . are or may be excluded
from entering the United States." In this way, the door was closed to
Japanese immigration to the United States via Mexico, Canada, Hawaii,
and the Canal Zone. Then Roosevelt induced the Japanese government,
by the Gentlemen's Agreement of 1907, to pledge itself to issue no more
passports for laborers to come to the United States. To demonstrate the
power of the United States and to impress upon the Japanese that he was
"not afraid of them and that the United States will no more submit to
bullying than it will bully," he sent the sixteen battleships of the American navy on a tour round the world, in the course of which they stopped
at the port of Yokohama and exhibited American naval strength to the
Japanese. Finally, by the Root-Takahira Agreement of 1908, Japan and
the United States agreed to maintain the "existing *status quo*" in the
Pacific area, to respect each other's territorial possessions, and to uphold
the Open Door. The agreement tacitly accepted Japan's control over
Manchuria, and to that extent, in the opinion of some students, it marked
a retreat from the policy of John Hay, Japan's promise to obey the Open
Door being more academic than real. If this opinion is correct, then

Roosevelt had decided to accept Japanese penetration into China in return for security for the Philippines.

The almost simultaneous emergence of the United States and Japan as world powers during the 1890's and the first decade of the twentieth century so altered their political and military relationships in the Far East that by the time Roosevelt left the White House in 1909, the two countries, despite the agreements of 1907 and 1908, found themselves increasingly opposed to each other on many issues which each nation regarded as vital to its interests and security. Japanese ambitions in Asia ran counter to the Open Door policy and to America's insistence upon the territorial integrity and independence of China. Meanwhile, Japan saw in the United States's efforts to preserve a balance of power in the Far East one of the chief obstacles to the fulfillment of its ambitions. The diplomats of both countries henceforth found the task of trying to accommodate the growing conflicts of interest between the two countries increasingly difficult.

Europe

Roosevelt's interest in imperialism was accompanied by an equally strong desire to use the power of the United States to preserve peace and promote international stability. "If we are to be a really great power," he once declared, "we must strive in good faith to play a great part in the world. We cannot avoid meeting great issues. All that we can determine ourselves is whether we shall meet them well or ill." Unlike many of his contemporaries, Roosevelt realized that the events of 1898 had made isolationism neither practicable nor realistic. The United States had worldwide interests which required it to exercise its influence whenever an international crisis threatened to disturb the peace and equilibrium of the world. And because Roosevelt had a realistic grasp of the international rivalries, ambitions, and aspirations of the great powers, he was able to steer American policy along a course which both safeguarded national interest and augmented national prestige.[8] "Let us . . . make it evident," Roosevelt declared, "that we use no words which we are not prepared to back up with deeds, and that while our speech is always moderate, we are ready and willing to make it good." Roosevelt's enlarged view of America's role in world politics, the new problems resulting from the recently acquired empire, and the imperial and national rivalries of the

[8] Howard K. Beale, *Theodore Roosevelt and the Rise of America to World Power* (Baltimore, 1957).

great powers all combined to draw the United States into closer diplomatic relations with the European states. Meanwhile those states showed a new concern for American opinion.

During the Spanish-American War, Great Britain, faced with imperial troubles in Asia, Africa, and the Near East and concerned with the rising power of Germany in Europe and on the high seas, was the only major European state friendly to the United States. Germany, France, and most of the other continental powers were sympathetic to Spain. Britain's difficulties were complicated by its disinclination to become overly involved in European politics and by the fact that its global empire provided ample opportunity for conflicts of interest. As a result, Britain welcomed the opportunity to cultivate the friendship of the United States. In the Hay-Pauncefote Treaty of 1901 Britain yielded to American pressure on fortifying the Panama Canal. Two years later the dispute over the boundary line between Canada and Alaska was settled, again in favor of the United States. Eight years later, in 1911, Roosevelt wrote his old friend Alfred Thayer Mahan that "The settlement of the Alaskan boundary settled the last serious trouble between the British Empire and ourselves as everything else could be arbitrated. . . ." [9] By 1914 all the remaining controversies had been ended: in 1910 the United States and Britain accepted the decision of the Hague Tribunal (confirmed in 1912 by joint convention) on American use of the Newfoundland fisheries; in 1911 Britain, Russia, Japan, and the United States agreed to limit and then regulate pelagic sealing in the North Pacific; and in 1914 the Panama tolls question was settled. The growing rapport between the United States and Britain led some people to believe that a secret alliance or some other similar commitment had been reached. There was nothing of the sort, either formal or informal. The Anglo-American *rapprochement* of these years was the inevitable result of the worldwide changes in the distribution of power brought about by the rise of the United States, Germany, and Japan and the growing awareness that the United States and Great Britain shared similar interests and that their security rested on common foundations. Increasing friendship, moreover, did not prevent strong differences of opinion or sharp criticism. But the differences were always resolved amicably and the criticisms mostly forgotten.

In May, 1904, one month before the Republican convention met to

[9] Quoted in Charles S. Campbell, Jr., *Anglo-American Understanding, 1898–1903* (Baltimore, 1957), p. 347.

nominate Roosevelt for President, Mulai Ahmed er Raisuli, the Berber chief and brigand, whose open defiance of the young and ineffective sultan kept Moroccan affairs in a state of near anarchy, raided the Tangier villa of Ion Perdicaris, kidnaped its wealthy proprietor, and demanded a considerable amount of ransom money. Samuel R. Gummere, the consul general of the United States, believing Perdicaris, a former resident of the United States, to be an American citizen, called upon the State Department for a man-of-war to strengthen his demands for Perdicaris' release. Roosevelt complied at once by sending the four ships of the Atlantic squadron to Tangier. When it became obvious that Raisuli was promoting his own personal power and fortune at the expense of the United States, Roosevelt ordered the European squadron to join the South Atlantic one at Tangier and called upon France "to lend her good offices." At the height of the crisis, as American public opinion and the press were demanding punishment for Raisuli's insults to the national honor, the State Department learned that the American-born Perdicaris had become a naturalized Greek in 1862. For Roosevelt and the State Department to admit to such an error just when the Republican convention was in session at Chicago, at a time when Perdicaris' fate was the chief topic of public attention, and when the honor of the nation had been committed, would have been too humiliating even to contemplate. Roosevelt and Hay, therefore, decided to say nothing and carry on.[10] Meanwhile the French Foreign Office, aided by a French loan, persuaded the sultan to accept Raisuli's demands. When Raisuli proscrastinated in fulfilling his part of the agreement, Secretary Hay, after consulting with Roosevelt, telegraphed Gummere: "This Government wants Perdicaris alive or Raisuli dead." The administration's telegram had no effect in Morocco, but it transformed the unenthusiastic and listless Republican convention into a cheering and jubilant pro-Roosevelt one. Waving the "big stick" in behalf of Perdicaris did not serve the national interest, but it did acquaint the American newspaper reader with Moroccan politics, and prepared him for another more serious crisis in that region.

Less than a year later, when Kaiser Wilhelm II visited the sultan at Tangier in 1905 and delivered one of his aggressive speeches, the dispute between Germany and France over the economic control of Morocco threatened to provoke a general European war. In 1904 France and Eng-

[10] The details of the Perdicaris incident, which remained secret until 1933, are taken from Barbara W. Tuchman, "Perdicaris Alive or Raisuli Dead," *American Heritage*, X (August 1959), 18–21, 98–101.

land had settled their colonial differences and agreed to cooperate and support each other in Africa. Germany, disturbed by the growing *rapprochement* between France and Great Britain and resenting the fact that Berlin had not been invited to participate in deciding Morocco's fate, demanded an international settlement in the hope of securing a diplomatic *coup* by embarrassing France. Since the United States, along with all the major European powers, had been one of the signatories of the 1880 agreement guaranteeing the rights of foreigners in Morocco, the German Foreign Office called upon Roosevelt to intervene. Realizing that America's interests in Morocco were negligible and that intervention in European politics violated the principles of the Monroe Doctrine as much as European intervention in the affairs of the Western Hemisphere, Roosevelt accepted nonetheless and sent two American representatives to the conference which met at Algeciras on January 16, 1906. He explained his action on the grounds of promoting peace and protecting American interests by strengthening the Open Door principle. The settlement negotiated at Algeciras provided a preview of the power alignment of 1914 and ended in a diplomatic defeat for Germany —a result to which the United States had not contributed but by which it was by no means displeased, since German ambition in the West Indies and in the Far East and the aggressive speeches of the German Kaiser were causing slowly increasing alarm in the United States. The United States Senate ratified the Algeciras Convention and, at the same time, reaffirmed the nonintervention principle by asserting that participation in the conference did not mean that the United States intended "to depart from traditional American foreign policy."

Meanwhile Roosevelt worked to promote world peace by encouraging the settlement of all international disputes by arbitration. In 1907 the United States and forty-four other nations accepted Tsar Nicholas II's invitation to participate in a second Hague conference (originally proposed by Roosevelt in 1904, but delayed because of the Russo-Japanese War). This conference, like the first one held in 1899, failed to limit armaments, but established a number of new rules of warfare and denied creditor nations the right of armed intervention in states which had defaulted on their debts unless such states refused to accept settlement by arbitration. The American proposal for a permanent world court to determine the legal merits of cases brought before it was rejected because no one could agree on what nations or how many should be represented on the high tribunal.

Adherence to the Hague proposals varied and their enforcement depended upon each nation's desire to abide by them. But despite the failures at the Hague, the desire to ensure peace by eliminating the occasion for wars continued. In 1908 and 1909 Elihu Root negotiated treaties with twenty-five nations for the arbitration of any controversies about minor questions. In 1911 Taft negotiated treaties with Great Britain and France for the arbitration of all disputes, major or minor; but the Senate, under the leadership of Henry Cabot Lodge, amended them so thoroughly that they became meaningless. Finally Bryan in 1913 and 1914 negotiated thirty "cooling-off" treaties, according to which all disputes should be submitted to commissions of investigation, and there should be no resort to war for twelve months after the beginning of a dispute.

Suggested Readings

The most useful one-volume life of Roosevelt, Henry F. Pringle, *Theodore Roosevelt: A Biography* (New York, 1931), is regarded by many historians as unduly critical in tone. William H. Harbaugh's, *Power and Responsibility: The Life and Times of Theodore Roosevelt* (New York, 1961) is a recent effort to correct some of Pringle's earlier interpretations by showing the important and permanent contributions of the Rough Rider. The early years of T. R.'s life and career are detailed in the first of a proposed four-volume biography by Carleton Putnam, *Theodore Roosevelt: The Formative Years, 1858–1886* (New York [1958]). A light, interesting, but very sound account of the many-faceted T. R. is Edward C. Wagenknecht, *The Seven Worlds of Theodore Roosevelt* (New York, 1958). A brief but highly significant "interpretation of the purposes and methods of . . . [T. R.'s] career" is John M. Blum, *The Republican Roosevelt* (Cambridge, Mass., 1954). The private life of T. R.'s clan is expertly and interestingly detailed in Hermann Hagedorn, *The Roosevelt Family of Sagamore Hill* (New York, 1954). Older biographical studies include Joseph B. Bishop, *Theodore Roosevelt and His Time as Shown in His Letters* (2 vols., New York, 1920); Walter F. McCaleb, *Theodore Roosevelt* (New York, 1931); William R. Thayer, *Theodore Roosevelt: An Intimate Biography* (Boston [1919]); Lawrence F. Abbott, *Impressions of Theodore Roosevelt* (Garden City, N.Y., 1919); and William D. Lewis, *The Life of Theodore Roosevelt* (New York?, 1919). Indispensable for Roosevelt's career is Elting E. Morison and John M. Blum, eds., *The Letters of Theodore Roosevelt* (8 vols., Cambridge, Mass., 1951–56). Also useful and convenient are Albert B. Hart and Herbert R. Ferleger, eds., *Theodore Roosevelt Cyclopedia* (New York [1941]) and Hermann Hagedorn, ed., *The Theodore Roosevelt Treasury: A Self-Portrait from His Writings* (New York [1957]). Consult also Lewis Einstein, *Roosevelt: His Mind in Action* (Boston, 1930).

Among the many memoirs, diaries, and collections of letters by friends and other contemporaries, the following deserve special attention: Lawrence F. Abbott, ed., *The Letters of Archie Butt* (Garden City, N.Y., 1924); *Taft and Roosevelt: The Intimate Letters of Archie Butt* (Garden City, N.Y., 1930); *Selections from the Correspondence of Theodore Roosevelt and Henry Cabot Lodge, 1884–1918* (2 vols., New York, 1925); and Owen Wister, *Roosevelt: The Story of a Friendship* (New York, 1930). T. R.'s own *An Autobiography* (New York, 1913) and his *The New Nationalism* (New York, 1910) are indispensable for the man's views and self-revelation.

By far the best and most knowledgeable account of the period 1900 to 1912 is George E. Mowry, *The Era of Theodore Roosevelt, 1900–1912* (New York, 1958) and for the period after 1909 especially, the same author's *Theodore Roosevelt and the Progressive Movement* (Madison, Wis., 1946). For an interestingly written general account of this decade, see Walter Lord, *The Good Years* (New York, 1960). Older and briefer is Harold Howland, *Theodore Roosevelt and His Times* (New Haven, Conn., 1921), volume XLVII in *The Chronicles of America*. Also useful are the appropriate chapters in Samuel P. Hays, *The Response to Industrialism, 1885–1914* (Chicago, 1957); Claude G. Bowers, *Beveridge and the Progressive Era* (New York, 1932); Matthew Josephson, *The President-Makers* (New York, 1940); and volumes I–III of Mark Sullivan, *Our Times* (6 vols., New York, 1926–35). Roosevelt as a conservative is detailed in Blum, cited above, and also in Clinton Rossiter, *Conservativism in America* (New York, 1956).

A number of memoirs, diaries, and biographies of important national figures should also be consulted. Among the more useful ones are: Philip C. Jessup, *Elihu Root* (2 vols., New York, 1938) and the much briefer but equally competent biography by Richard W. Leopold, *Elihu Root and the Conservative Tradition* (Boston, 1954); Nathaniel W. Stephenson, *Nelson W. Aldrich* (New York, 1930); Ray Ginger, *The Bending Cross: The Biography of Eugene V. Debs* (New Brunswick, N.J., 1950); Belle Case La Follette and Fola La Follette, *Robert M. La Follette* (2 vols., New York, 1953) and La Follette's own *Autobiography* (Madison, Wisc. [1913]); Merlo J. Pusey, *Charles Evans Hughes* (2 vols., New York, 1951) and the briefer but equally valuable and interesting biography by Dexter Perkins, *Charles Evans Hughes and American Democratic Statesmanship* (Boston, 1956); Hermann Hagedorn, *Leonard Wood* (2 vols., New York, 1931); L. White Busbey, *Uncle Joe Cannon* (New York [1927]); and the less satisfactory Champ Clark, *My Quarter-Century of American Politics* (2 vols., New York, 1920). See also the excellent biography of George W. Perkins by John A. Garraty, *The Right Hand Man* (New York, 1960).

The trust problem and the growth of business combinations are discussed in many of the works cited in Chapter 1, including Eliot Jones, *The Trust Problem;* William Z. Ripley, *Trusts, Pools and Corporations;* John Moody, *The Masters of Capital;* Stewart H. Holbrook, *The Age of the Moguls;* Harold U. Faulkner, *The Decline of Laissez Faire, 1897–1917;* Sidney Fine, *Laissez Faire and the General Welfare State;* Henry R. Seager and Charles A. Gulick, *Trust and Corporation Problems;* and Henry D. Lloyd, *Wealth against Com-*

monwealth. Special attention is called to the only general account of business developments in the twentieth century, Thomas C. Cochran, *The American Business System . . . 1900–1955* (Cambridge, Mass., 1957). Among the more important business and industrial histories and biographies, see James H. Bridge, *The Inside History of the Carnegie Steel Company* (New York, 1903); Abraham Berglund, *The United States Steel Corporation* (New York, 1907); George B. Harvey, *Henry Clay Frick* (New York, 1928); Charles A. Gulick, *The Labor Policy of the United States Steel Corporation* (New York, 1924); Burton J. Hendrick, *The Life of Andrew Carnegie* (Garden City, N.Y., 1932); Ernest D. McCallum, *The Iron and Steel Industry* (London, 1931); Harvey O'Connor, *Steel Dictator* (New York [1935]); and Ida M. Tarbell, *The Life of Elbert H. Gary* (New York, 1925). On the oil industry, see the excellent first volume of several more to follow by Harold F. Williamson and Arnold F. Daum, *The American Petroleum Industry, 1859–1899* (Evanston, Ill., 1959). A popular account, but not always accurate, is John T. Flynn, *God's Gold: The Story of Rockefeller and His Times* (New York [1932]). The best biography of Rockefeller is Allan Nevins, *Study in Power: John D. Rockefeller, Industrialist and Philanthropist* (2 vols., New York, 1952), a major revision of the author's earlier *John D. Rockefeller: The Heroic Age of American Enterprise* (2 vols., New York, 1940). The most careful and detailed account of the Standard Oil empire is Ralph W. Hidy and Muriel E. Hidy, *Pioneering in Big Business: History of the Standard Oil Company (New Jersey), 1882–1911* (New York, 1955). It corrects and supplements the older Ida M. Tarbell, *History of the Standard Oil Company* (2 vols., New York, 1904). Other useful industrial studies include Horace Coon, *American Tel and Tel* (New York, 1939) and Noobar R. Danielian, *A.T. and T.* (New York [1939]); Frank L. Dyer and Thomas C. Martin, *Edison* (New York, 1929); and Henry G. Prout, *A Life of George Westinghouse* (New York, 1921). See also Raymond C. Miller, *Kilowatts at Work: A History of the Detroit Edison Company* (Detroit, 1957); Forrest McDonald, *Let There Be Light: The Electric Utility Industry in Wisconsin, 1881–1955* (Madison, Wis., 1957); Carl B. Glasscock, *The War of the Copper Kings* (Indianapolis [1935]); Harvey O'Connor, *The Guggenheims* (New York [1937]); Glenn L. Parker, *The Coal Industry* (Washington, D.C. [1940]); Jules I. Bogen, *The Anthracite Railroads* (New York [1937]); Walton H. Hamilton and Helen R. Wright, *The Case of Bituminous Coal* (New York, 1925); Eliot Jones, *The Anthracite Coal Combination . . .* (Cambridge, Mass., 1914); William T. Hutchinson, *Cyrus Hall McCormick* (2 vols., New York, 1930–35); John W. Jenkins, *James B. Duke* (New York [1927]); and Harper Leech and John C. Carroll, *Armour and His Times* (New York, 1938).

The best account of early trust policy is Hans B. Thorelli, *Federal Antitrust Policy: Organization of an American Tradition* (Baltimore, 1956). Also useful is James D. Clark, *The Federal Trust Policy* (Baltimore, 1931).

Railroad developments are discussed in many books; among the most useful is George R. Taylor and Irene D. Neu, *The American Railroad Network, 1861–1890* (Cambridge, Mass., 1956) on the physical integration of the lines.

Still useful are the older, general account of John Moody, *The Railroad Builders* (New Haven, Conn., 1919) and the study by William Z. Ripley, *Railway Problems* (Boston [1913]). Financial and corporate changes are discussed in Edward G. Campbell, *The Reorganization of the American Railroad System, 1893–1900* (New York, 1938); William Z. Ripley, *Railroads: Finance and Organization* (New York, 1915); Frederick A. Cleveland and Fred W. Powell, *Railroad Promotion and Capitalization* (New York, 1909); and William Z. Ripley, *Railroads: Rates and Regulation* (new ed., New York, 1927), all of which are useful. Oscar Lewis, *The Big Four: The Story of Huntington, Stanford, Crocker, and Hopkins* (New York, 1938); Robert E. Riegel, *The Story of the Western Railroads* (New York, 1926) and James B. Hedges, *Henry Villard and the Railways of the Northwest* (New Haven, Conn., 1930) should also be consulted. Two important biographies of railroad leaders are George Kennan, *E. H. Harriman* (Boston, 1922) and Joseph G. Pyle, *The Life of James J. Hill* (2 vols., Garden City, N.Y., 1917).

Finance banking and investment capitalism as seen by the Pujo Committee is described in Louis D. Brandeis, *Other People's Money and How the Bankers Use It* (New York, 1914) and through the eyes of the 1930's in Frederick Lewis Allen, *The Lords of Creation* (New York, 1935). The influence of Morgan on American finance is detailed, though not always accurately, in Lewis Corey, *The House of Morgan* (New York, 1930). The financier's career is surveyed in its entirety in Frederick Lewis Allen, *The Great Pierpont Morgan* (New York, 1949) and more appreciatively by his son-in-law Herbert L. Satterlee, *J. Pierpont Morgan: An Intimate Portrait* (New York, 1939). The activities of a Morgan partner are covered in Thomas W. Lamont, *Henry P. Davison* (New York, 1933) and in John Garraty, *Right Hand Man*, cited above. Another, somewhat hostile account of high finance and the career of James Stillman is John K. Winkler, *The First Billion: The Stillmans and the National City Bank* (New York, 1934).

Many of the books cited previously on American labor are also useful for the problems and controversies of the Roosevelt administration, but see especially Howard L. Hurwitz, *Theodore Roosevelt and Labor in New York State* (New York, 1943) and Robert J. Cornell, *The Anthracite Coal Strike of 1902* (Washington, D.C., 1957), the most recent, detailed account of this affair.

On conservation, see John Ise, *United States Forest Policy* (New Haven, Conn., 1920); Charles R. Van Hise and Loomis Havemeyer, *Conservation of Our Natural Resources* (New York, 1930); and J. Leonard Bates, "Fulfilling American Democracy: The Conservation Movement, 1907–1921," *Mississippi Valley Historical Review*, XLIV (June 1957), 29–57. A recent study that emphasizes the role of the "scientists and technicians . . . to the development and use of natural resources" is Samuel P. Hays, *Conservation and the Gospel of Efficiency: The Progressive Conservation Movement, 1890–1920* (Cambridge, Mass., 1959). Also very useful are Louise E. Peffer, *The Closing of the Public Domain: Disposal and Reservation Policies, 1900–50* (Stanford, Calif., 1951) and Arthur B. Darling, ed., *The Public Papers of Francis G. Newlands* (Boston, 1932). The views of a zealous conservationist are expressed in Gifford Pinchot,

The Fight for Conservation (New York, 1910) and the author's excellent memoirs, *Breaking New Ground* (New York [1947]). Nelson M. McGeary, *Gifford Pinchot: Forester Politician* (Princeton, N.J., 1960) is the most recent study of this aspect of Pinchot's career, and Martin L. Fausold, *Gifford Pinchot: Bull Moose Progressive* (Syracuse, N.Y., 1961) also contains pertinent information. Rodney C. Loehr, *Forests for the Future: The Story of the Sustained Yield as Told in the Diaries and Papers of David T. Mason, 1907–1950* (St. Paul, Minn., 1952) and Carl Schenck, *The Biltmore Story* (St. Paul, Minn., 1955), the memoirs of a German forester who founded the first school of forestry in the United States, are also important. Theodore Roosevelt's own development as a conservationist, beginning with his boyhood experiences, is interestingly told in Paul R. Cutright, *Theodore Roosevelt the Naturalist* (New York, 1956).

On the Pure Food Act see Harvey W. Wiley's own experiences as expressed in his *An Autobiography* (Indianopolis, 1930) and the detailed account in Oscar E. Anderson, Jr., *The Health of a Nation: Harvey W. Wiley and the Fight for Pure Food* (Chicago, 1958).

One of the most important books on Roosevelt's foreign policy is the carefully researched and suggestive study of Howard K. Beale, *Theodore Roosevelt and the Rise of America to World Power* (Baltimore, 1957). Older but still useful is J. H. Latané, *America as a World Power* (New York, 1907), but see also the pertinent parts of the more recent study by Foster R. Dulles, *America's Rise to World Power, 1898–1954* (New York, 1955). See also Alfred L. P. Dennis, *Adventures in American Diplomacy, 1896–1906* (New York, 1928). The effects of the emergence of America as a world power and of T.R. upon Washington's diplomatic corps are interestingly portrayed in Nelson M. Blake, "Ambassadors at the Court of Theodore Roosevelt," *Mississippi Valley Historical Review*, XLII (September 1955), 191–206. Some of the ideological foundations of Roosevelt's militarism are appraised in John P. Mallan, "Roosevelt, Brooks Adams, and Lea: The Warrior Critique of the Business Civilization," *American Quarterly*, VIII (Fall 1956), 216–30. The progressive attitude in foreign policy is analyzed in William E. Leuchtenburg, "Progressivism and Imperialism: The Progressive Movement and American Foreign Policy, 1898–1916," *Mississippi Valley Historical Review*, XXXIX (December 1952), 483–504. See also the relevant pages of Herbert Croly, *Willard Straight* (New York, 1924). The role of economics in foreign policy is appraised generally in Benjamin H. Williams, *The Economic Foreign Policy of the United States* (New York, 1929). Roosevelt's navalism is best described in Gordon C. O'Gara, *Theodore Roosevelt and the Rise of the Modern Navy* (Princeton, N.J., 1943). Consult also William D. Puleston, *The Life and Work of Alfred Thayer Mahan* (New Haven, Conn., 1943). Specialized and valuable is Oulten J. Clinard, *Japan's Influence on American Naval Power* (Berkeley and Los Angeles, Calif., 1947).

Among the numerous works on Roosevelt and the Caribbean, see especially the following: Dexter Perkins, *The United States and the Caribbean* (Cambridge, Mass., 1947) and the same author's *The Monroe Doctrine, 1867–1907*

(Baltimore, 1937); Howard C. Hill, *Roosevelt and the Caribbean* (Chicago, 1927); Dana G. Munro, *The United States and the Caribbean* (Boston, 1934); Chester L. Jones, *Caribbean Interests of the United States* (New York, 1916) and the same author's two other studies, *The Caribbean since 1900* (New York, 1936) and with Henry K. Norton and Parker T. Moon, *The United States and the Caribbean* (Chicago [1929]).

Interventionist policies are detailed also in a number of more specialized works, including: Carl Kelsey, *The American Intervention in Haiti and the Dominican Republic* (Philadelphia, 1922); Melvin M. Knight, *Americans in Santo Domingo* (New York, 1928); Arthur C. Millspaugh, *Haiti under American Control* (Boston, 1931); and Sumner Welles, *Naboth's Vineyard: The Dominican Republic* (2 vols., New York, 1928). See also J. Fred Rippy, *The Caribbean Danger Zone* (New York [1940]) for a valuable summary and appraisal of American policy.

Panama and the canal diplomacy is expertly handled by Mary W. Williams, *Anglo-American Isthmian Diplomacy, 1815–1915* (Washington, D.C., 1916). This excellent study should now be supplemented with J. A. S. Grenville, "Great Britain and the Isthmian Canal, 1898–1901," *American Historical Review*, LXI (October 1955), 48–69. See also the excellent account by Dwight C. Miner, *The Fight for the Panama Route: The Story of the Spooner Act and the Hay-Herran Treaty* (New York, 1940). The strategic and wartime significance of the canal is appraised in Norman J. Padleford, *The Panama Canal in Peace and War* (New York, 1942). Consult also William D. McCain, *The United States and the Republic of Panama* (Durham, N.C., 1937); J. Fred Rippy, *The Capitalists and Colombia* (New York [1931]); and E. Taylor Parks, *Colombia and the United States* (Durham, N.C., 1935).

The building of the canal has been most recently treated in W. Storrs Lee, *The Strength to Move a Mountain* (New York [1958]), "a reassessment of the significance of the American accomplishment a half century ago." Older and still useful is the excellent account by Gerstle Mack, *The Land Divided* (New York, 1944). See also Joseph B. and Farnham Bishop, *Goethals, Genius of the Panama Canal* (New York, 1930); Hugh G. Miller, *The Isthmian Highway* (New York, 1929); Miles P. Du Val, Jr., *And the Mountains Will Move* (Stanford, Calif., 1947); Marie D. Gorgas and Burton J. Hendrick, *William Crawford Gorgas: His Life and Work* (Garden City, N.Y., 1924); and the more recent study of John M. Gibson, *Physician to the World: The Life of General William C. Gorgas* (Durham, N.C., 1950).

Latin American policy is expertly surveyed in Samuel F. Bemis, *The Latin-American Policy of the United States* (New York, 1943). See also G. H. Stuart, *Latin America and the United States* (5th ed., New York, 1955).

The growing *rapprochement* between Britain and the United States is most recently detailed in Charles S. Campbell, Jr., *Anglo-American Understanding, 1898–1903* (Baltimore, 1957), but see also Lionel M. Gelber, *The Rise of Anglo-American Friendship, 1898–1906* (New York, 1938).

American and Canadian relations are treated in Percy E. Corbett, *The Settlement of Canadian-American Disputes* (New Haven, Conn., 1937) and in greater detail in Charles C. Tansill, *Canadian-American Relations, 1875–1901* (New York, 1943). Allan Nevins' biography of *Henry White: Thirty Years of American Diplomacy* (New York, 1930) is also pertinent.

The standard and most satisfactory survey of Far Eastern policy is A. Whitney Griswold, *The Far Eastern Policy of the United States* (New York, 1938). More detailed analyses of specific problems include Mingchien J. Bau, *The Open Door Doctrine in Relation to China* (New York, 1923). On this subject, also consult the detailed analysis by Charles S. Campbell, Jr., *Special Business Interests and the Open Door Policy* (New Haven, Conn., 1951). There is also material of value in Charles F. Remer, *Foreign Investments in China* (New York, 1933). Two different views on the Open Door policy are to be found in chapters II and III of George F. Kennan, *American Diplomacy, 1900–1950* (Chicago, 1951), and chapters I and II of William A. Williams, *The Tragedy of American Diplomacy*, both cited previously. Also useful is Paul H. Clyde, *International Rivalries in Manchuria, 1689–1922* (2d rev. ed., Columbus, Ohio, 1928). Imperial rivalries between 1844 and 1928 are summarized in David E. Owen, *Imperialism and Nationalism in the Far East* (New York, 1929). American policy is seen here against the European background. See also Tyler Dennett, *Americans in Eastern Asia* (New York, 1941).

Japanese-American relations have been treated in numerous specialized works, including Payson J. Treat, *Diplomatic Relations between the United States and Japan, 1895–1905* (Stanford, Calif., 1938); Tyler Dennett, *Roosevelt and the Russo-Japanese War* (New York, 1925); Thomas A. Bailey, *Theodore Roosevelt and the Japanese-American Crisis* (Stanford, Calif., 1924) and the pertinent pages in the same author's *America Faces Russia* (New York, 1950). Rodman W. Paul, *The Abrogation of the Gentlemen's Agreement* (Cambridge, Mass., 1936); Eleanor Tupper and George E. McReynolds, *Japan in American Public Opinion* (New York, 1937); Elmer C. Sandmeyer, *The Anti-Chinese Movement in California* (Urbana, Ill., 1939); and Yamato Ichihashi, *Japanese in the United States* (Stanford, Calif., 1932) are equally valuable.

American participation in the Algeciras Conference is detailed in Eugene N. Anderson, *The First Morocco Crisis, 1904–1906* (Chicago, 1930). On Algeciras, as well as German-American relations in world politics, see Alfred Vagts, *Deutschland und die Vereinigten Staaten in der Weltpolitik* (2 vols., Berlin, 1935). On American participation at the Hague conferences, see James B. Scott, *The Hague Peace Conferences of 1899 and 1907* (2 vols., Baltimore, 1909).

6

William Howard Taft

and the Split in the

Republican Party, 1909-1912

THOUGH ROOSEVELT WAS UNABLE to get Congress to enact any of the legislation he recommended to it during 1907 and 1908, he was, nonetheless, able to dictate the nomination of his successor. As much as he enjoyed being President, Theodore Roosevelt was dedicated to the two-term tradition. And while he once wrote that he disapproved of a President's choosing his "political legatee," as Jackson had done with Van Buren, Roosevelt was convinced that the only way to prevent his own renomination was to find a successor who would support and extend "my policies." Because of his immense popularity and his astuteness in handling Republican politicians, and because of the control always enjoyed by a GOP President over the southern delegates to the convention, Roosevelt had no difficulty in getting it to endorse his candidate. His own preference was Elihu Root, Secretary of State since 1905, but Root was sixty-three years old and liable to attack on account of his defense of the infamous "Boss" Tweed in 1873 and his long career as a wealthy corporation lawyer. After considering and rejecting the claims of Charles Evans Hughes, the governor of New York, Roosevelt secured the nomination for William Howard Taft on the first ballot. For Vice President the delegates registered their independence of the White House by choosing conservative New York Congressman James S. Sherman. The Republican convention praised Roosevelt's and the GOP's achievements since 1896, while it endorsed a conservative platform that bore little resemblance to the advanced reforms Roosevelt had advocated in 1907 and 1908 and the party's leaders had chosen to ignore. Progressive Republicans left the Chicago convention with little hope in their party's platform. Neither Roosevelt nor Taft was satisfied with the compromises and the equivocation involved in the party's position on the tariff, conservation, business and railroad regulation, and use of the injunction against labor unions.

The Democratic party, remembering the disastrous results with the conservative Parker in 1904 and finding no readily apparent sure-winner within its ranks, for the third and last time nominated William Jennings Bryan, his running mate being a rather obscure city solicitor from Indianapolis, John Worth Kern. The Democratic platform, like the GOP's, reflected the compromises necessary to bridge the differences between the conservative and liberal elements in the party, but on several issues it was far more outspoken than the Republican. Bryan and the Democrats put themselves on record clearly for a downward revision of the tariff, stricter enforcement of the Sherman Antitrust Act, and a vigorous trustbusting crusade against business combinations which verged on monopoly; they called for more effective regulation of the railroads and, if necessary, government ownership of the major interstate carriers, and for a federal income tax; and they demanded a strong and effectively enforced antiinjunction law, which caused Gompers and the AFL to abandon their traditional nonpartisanship and endorse the Democratic party's labor plank officially. The Democrats also asked for a federal corrupt practices act, publicity of campaign expenditures, and laws prohibiting corporations from contributing to political campaign funds and publicizing and placing limitations upon similar bequests by private individuals. But in the end, the Democratic party program, despite the talk of reform, strict enforcement of government regulations against corporate wealth and malpractices, and more legislation for the public good, was very similar to Roosevelt's program, incorporating many of his 1907 and 1908 proposals to the Congress. And in the case of Bryan's demand for a federal corrupt practices act making it illegal for corporations to contribute money to political campaigns, the Roosevelt administration had enacted the first such law in 1907, shortly before the election.

In addition to the Socialist party, which ran Eugene Debs again as its candidate, and the Populists, who for the last time presented a presidential candidate by nominating Thomas E. Watson, there were the usual minor parties (Prohibitionists, United Christians, and Socialist-Labor) and William Randolph Hearst's National Independent party. The latter, apart from promoting the political ambitions of its publisher-founder, tried to steer a liberal and progressive course to the left of Bryan and Roosevelt without embracing Deb's socialism.

After a rather dull and ineffectual campaign, Taft was elected President by a popular vote of 7,679,076 to Bryan's 6,409,106, and an electoral vote of 321 to 162. The Republicans retained substantial majorities in both houses of Congress. The popular vote for Debs was 420,890 and for Watson 29,146. In 1909, at the age of fifty-one, Roosevelt left office and on March 23, 1909, departed for a fifteen-month visit to Africa and Europe, returning in June, 1910.

TAFT AS PRESIDENT

Roosevelt's energy and versatility and his talent for inspiring newspaper headlines had made him for seven and a half years the focus of public attention. Almost any successor would have seemed, by contrast, tame and uninspiring. Taft therefore began his administration under a severe handicap; nor did he have the political cleverness or the capacity for leadership needed to surmount it. Honest, good-humored, placid, and likable, he had been a capable, industrious, and loyal subordinate; but he had too little force or subtlety of character to fill the highest place. By temperament he was better suited for a judicial or an administrative post than for an executive position.

Born in Ohio in 1857, Taft had been in public office since 1881, a year after his graduation from Yale University Law School; but of the nine posts he had filled, eight had been appointive and only one elective. He had been solicitor general under Harrison, a federal judge, governor-general of the Philippines, and Secretary of War. His own strongest wish was to serve on the Supreme Court, to which Roosevelt had three times offered to appoint him; but he had allowed himself to be persuaded by his wife and his wealthy half-brother, the Ohio businessman Charles P. Taft, to aim instead at the Presidency. He shared some of Roosevelt's progressive inclinations and endeavored to follow in Roosevelt's footsteps; but he differed from Roosevelt in his greater respect for the letter of the Constitution, for the legal rights of property, and for the principles of laissez-faire economics. Taft had little sympathy with Roosevelt's view of a strong, interventionist federal government. Instead of extending presidential initiative as Roosevelt had done, he preferred to follow the constitutional principle that Congress should make the laws and the President should enforce them. In some respects, his administration was perhaps more fruitful in progressive legislation than was Roosevelt's; but Taft received little of the credit for it and finally found himself branded by public opinion as a supporter of reaction.

Taft was, moreover, unfortunate in assuming the Presidency at a time when the Republican party was splitting into two factions, one conservative and the other insurgent. Under Roosevelt the conservatives had dominated Congress, and Roosevelt had worked in cooperation with the conservative leaders, Senator Nelson W. Aldrich and Representative Joseph G. Cannon. By 1909, however, the growth of progressivism in the state governments had led to the formation of a progressive bloc in Congress. There was now a group of progressive Republicans, headed by La Follette in the Senate and George W. Norris of Nebraska in the House, who were bitterly opposed to Aldrich and Cannon and were hoping for presidential support. Confronted by a dilemma which only a man of the greatest political subtlety could have overcome, Taft continued to cooperate with the conservatives without making an effective effort at placating the progressives. He was thereupon denounced by the latter as a tool of predatory business interests.

TAFT AND THE TARIFF

The problem that first brought the Republican split in Congress out into the open was the tariff. There had been no changes in the tariff schedules since the Dingley Act of 1897, which popular sentiment now felt to be too high and too favorable to big business. Roosevelt had not dared to handle the question, partly because he knew the difficulty of securing reductions and partly because he felt that he did not sufficiently understand financial questions. He therefore bequeathed the problem to his successor. The Republican platform of 1908 promised that the tariff would be revised, and Taft made it plain that, in his opinion, revision meant reduction. He thereupon called a special session of Congress immediately after his inauguration to undertake the task. The House of Representatives quickly passed the Payne bill providing for considerably lower schedules; but when the bill reached the Senate, Aldrich and the Senate Finance Committee proceeded to insert some eight hundred amendments, most of which were increases. For eleven weeks Aldrich's proposals were attacked by a group of progressives, including La Follette of Wisconsin, Jonathan P. Dolliver and Albert B. Cummins of Iowa, Albert J. Beveridge of Indiana, Joseph L. Bristow of Kansas, and Moses Clapp of Minnesota. It became very apparent during the debates that

THE EASY UMPIRE

"He slugs me every chance he gets, and you can't or won't see it."

President Taft antagonized progressives in Congress by showing too much deference to the conservative leader, Senator Nelson W. Aldrich of Rhode Island. (Culver Pictures, Inc.)

whereas the progressives had genuinely studied the question, the conservatives had merely written into the bill the wishes of the manufacturers and did not understand their own proposals. The progressives had been hoping for support from Taft; but apart from persuading the Senate Finance Committee to adopt a 1 per cent tax on the earnings of corporations, support the income tax, and make some extensions in the free list, Taft left the question in Aldrich's hands. "I don't much believe," he told La Follette, "in a President's interfering with the legislative department while it is doing its work."

Aldrich's bill finally passed the Senate, and most of his proposals were subsequently accepted by the House, although Taft's belated intervention while the bill was in the conference committee did result in lowering some rates. Taft, whose own views on the tariff were far closer to those of the progressives than those reflected in the final bill, again disappointed the progressives by refusing to veto the bill; and the Payne-Aldrich tariff became law on August 5, 1909. While Taft admitted that the final draft of the measure contained serious faults, he called it, nonetheless, "a very scientific bill," one that he could defend as fulfilling his campaign promise of a downward revision. The progressives felt otherwise. To La Follette, it was "the most outrageous assault of private interests upon the people recorded in tariff history." The final judgment, including that of most tariff experts, is that the Payne-Aldrich bill was essentially protective. Of the schedules in the Dingley Act, 650 had been lowered, 220 had been raised, and 1,150 had been left unchanged. The progressives maintained, however, that the reductions had been made only on such commodities as coal, lumber, hides, iron, steel, and oil, where there was no possibility of foreign competition, and that many of the increases would enable big business to exact higher prices from the consumer. The schedules for wool and sugar, for example, were particularly resented. Other features of the act were the corporation tax and the establishment of a commission to study the tariff scientifically and, when necessary, recommend changes. Taft particularly approved of the last measure, but the commission proved to be of little value and was abolished by the Democratic majority in 1912.

The unpopularity Taft had incurred by failing to put pressure on the conservatives was greatly increased when, in a most unfortunate speech at Winona, Minnesota, he described the act as "the best tariff bill that the Republican Party has ever passed." There was wide agreement when Senator Dolliver described the President as "an amiable man, completely surrounded by men who know exactly what they want." Far more serious than the tariff fight itself was the growing conviction in progressive circles in and out of Congress that Taft had abandoned Roosevelt's policies and had joined Aldrich and the other defenders of eastern corporate wealth. The Winona speech brought the insurgents' resentment against Taft out in the open. Here was a clear indication of the dissatisfaction of an important segment of the party. Instead of trying to assuage it, Taft ignored it.

THE BALLINGER-PINCHOT CONTROVERSY

Another of Taft's political misfortunes was a controversy over conservation which started as an interdepartmental quarrel and ended as a national debate with serious political repercussions, far beyond the issue of conservation. Roosevelt had withdrawn lands from public entry by Executive order. Taft regarded this method as of doubtful legality and preferred to act through Congress, which in 1910 passed a series of nine laws, separating ownership of the surface from ownership of the subsoil and adding a number of timber, mineral, oil, and waterpower sites to the lands reserved for permanent government ownership. After promising to reappoint James R. Garfield as Secretary of the Interior, Taft replaced him by Richard A. Ballinger, a former mayor of Seattle, who was distrusted by the progressives because he had many anticonservationist friends and because he had formerly been a corporation lawyer. Ballinger, believing that Roosevelt had acted illegally, restored to public entry certain waterpower sites in Montana and Wyoming which had been included by Roosevelt among the lands placed in reserve. His action was bitterly opposed by Gifford Pinchot, who resented Ballinger's holding the job his friend Garfield had held under Roosevelt and had hoped to keep in the Taft administration. Moreover, Pinchot regarded the cause of conservation as more important than obedience to the letter of the law or than the private interest.

Ballinger also incurred the enmity of Louis R. Glavis, an official of the General Land Office. Some 5,280 acres of coal land in Alaska were claimed by the Cunningham syndicate of Seattle, which was supposed to be affiliated with the Morgan and Guggenheim interests. As Glavis investigated this claim, he came to believe that Ballinger, who had formerly served as attorney for the Cunningham syndicate, was trying to have the claim validated without sufficient inquiry. Pinchot supported Glavis' accusation. Taft and Attorney General George B. Wickersham examined the charges made against Ballinger by Pinchot and Glavis and came to the conclusion that Ballinger was entirely honest—a verdict with which later students of the question have usually agreed.

Instead of accepting Taft's decision, however, Pinchot and Glavis proceeded to make their suspicions public. In November, 1909, *Colliers' Weekly* published Glavis' criticisms against Ballinger's administration of the Interior Department, initiating a series of violent attacks on Ballinger by progressive journalists and congressmen, who declared that the Department of Interior had been turned over to the Guggenheims. In January, 1910, Iowa's progressive Senator Dolliver read to the Senate a letter attacking Ballinger which he had received from Pinchot, who was now prepared, if not anxious, to sacrifice his own job as head of the Forest Service for the cause of conservation. Taft then had no alternative but to dismiss Pinchot and Glavis for breaking the rules of official discipline. Ballinger was exonerated by a congressional investigation, but realizing that he had lost the public's confidence, he resigned shortly thereafter.

The Ballinger-Pinchot controversy, in spite of the various administrative and policy changes which followed, did little to promote an enlightened and coordinated program to manage the nation's resources wisely and effectively. Because this fight was widely, though mistakenly, interpreted and publicized as a struggle between the forces of evil and virtue, the whole affair "obscured rather than clarified conservation problems" and perpetuated numerous misconceptions which "remained a millstone around the necks of those who wanted to think clearly and act concretely about specific conservation problems." [1] But if the Ballinger-Pinchot controversy contributed little toward modern conservation policies, its political consequences were highly significant. The episode strengthened the belief of the progressives that the Taft administration was controlled by big business and that it had repudiated Roosevelt's policies protecting the people against the interests; by widening the gulf between the administration and the progressive and insurgent Republicans in the Congress, it thus contributed to the party's split in 1912; and it accelerated and aggravated the growing estrangement between Taft and Roosevelt.

[1] Samuel P. Hays, *Conservation and the Gospel of Efficiency: The Progressive Conservation Movement, 1890–1920* (Cambridge, Mass., 1959), p. 170.

THE SPEAKERSHIP FIGHT AND
THE ELECTION OF 1910

The growing strength of the Republican insurgents was exhibited in March, 1910, when they succeeded in stripping Speaker Joseph Cannon of the semidictatorial powers he exercised over the House of Representatives. During the campaign and election of 1908 Taft, on several occasions, decried Cannon's "reactionaryism" and indicated that he favored curbing the Speaker's authority. But when the time came for him to use his influence against Cannon's election to the speakership, Taft held a conference at which Senator Aldrich and the equally conservative chairman of the House Ways and Means Committee, Henry C. Payne, warned him that he was jeopardizing tariff reform. Taft then dropped his opposition to Cannon, thus permitting his selection. The progressives, who had always regarded the arch-conservative Cannon as one of their particular enemies, continued their opposition to him, especially since Cannon indicated he would continue to discriminate against the insurgents by opposing them at every opportunity. The insurgents were supported by the journalist Mark Sullivan, who organized a press campaign to arouse public opinion against the dictatorial Speaker. Meanwhile the struggle over the Payne-Aldrich tariff and the wrangle over conservation were alienating the progressives in Congress from Taft so that when the insurgents challenged Cannon a second time in March, 1910, the President took no part in the fight, even though he had disapproved of Speaker Cannon's tactics during the tariff debate.

The "March Revolution" was headed by George W. Norris of Nebraska, who had come to Congress in 1903 at the age of forty-one as an orthodox Republican but had rapidly been disillusioned by what he saw there. Norris and his insurgent band succeeded in winning a majority vote for a proposal that the Rules Committee, which determined what business should be discussed by the House, be enlarged to fifteen and be elected by the members of the House instead of being nominated by the Speaker and the minority leader, and that the speaker be excluded from membership. The power of the Speaker to control legislation was diminished further the following year when appointments to all standing committees were transferred to the Ways and Means Committee. The diminution of the Speaker's power over legislation was an insurgent victory which, like the tariff and conservation issues, reflected Taft's political ineptness, vacillation, and inability to exercise effective leadership. To the progressives, it was another example of the President's loyalty to the conservative Old Guard. Taft, who had always suspected the motives, if not the honesty, of many of the progressives in his party, now interpreted the rising insurgency in the GOP as unmistakable proof that they were out to discredit him and to scuttle his administration.

The final rupture between the President and the insurgents in Congress occurred in the spring of 1910 when Taft, cooperating closely with Aldrich and other party stalwarts, worked for the election of "orthodox Republicans" in his party's primaries. In one state after another, in Iowa, Kansas, Nebraska, Wisconsin, California, and Washington, the well-financed, regular party machine, aided by recently formed "Taft Republican" clubs, campaigned against the insurgent candidates. In February, 1910, just as a number of influential midwestern progressive leaders were starting their campaign to get Roosevelt to lead their cause, the former President, after ten months of hunting big game and collecting specimens, terminated his African expedition at Gondokoro, in northern Uganda. From then on, as he moved northward from Africa to Europe, where he spent two months being feted and honored, Roosevelt's friends kept him constantly informed of the GOP's troubles and the struggle for control of the party that was going on between Taft and the progressives. By the time he returned to the United States on June 18, 1910, a number of progressive leaders were organizing "Roosevelt Republican" clubs to promote his nomination to the Presidency in 1912. Once in the United States, Roosevelt was immediately besieged by men such as Gifford Pinchot who believed that Taft was betraying the cause of progressivism and that it was Roosevelt's duty to return to active politics. Roosevelt, however, had resolved, in fairness to Taft, not to abandon the President, who still hoped he could count on his former chief's support and friendship. Moreover, Roosevelt did not want to do anything to aggravate the Republican schism. Early in June he promised Taft he would avoid all political controversies and "make no speeches or say anything for two months." Yet by the end of the month, and in spite of his promise, Roosevelt was already involved in the forthcoming election.

Still vigorous and relatively young, Roosevelt had quickly found the position of an unemployed former President with no political future an exceedingly irksome one. Nor was he sufficiently magnanimous to recognize that Taft might have had good reasons for adopting different methods and choosing different advisers. The two men had begun to move apart on the day Taft took office. Whatever innovations Taft had made in presidential policies Roosevelt interpreted as a direct or an implied rebuke to himself; furthermore, Taft had angered Roosevelt by failing to reappoint more than two members of Roosevelt's cabinet, and many of the friends of both men had encouraged them to feel suspicious of each other. After returning to America, Roosevelt continued to give Taft at least his nominal support for about eighteen months. He was, however, unable to remain in retirement, and his utterances became increasingly radical.

During the summer of 1910, Roosevelt hoped that his decision to participate in the midterm elections by speaking on behalf of all moderate Republican candidates would unite the party and prevent the national calamity (as he regarded it) of a Democratic victory in the November elections. His efforts to compromise the factional conflict which was tearing the GOP apart were sincere, but the differences between the conservatives and the progressives were too deep-seated to be easily reconciled. Between June and November of 1910 Roosevelt spoke in favor of both conservative and progressive Republicans. At the request of Governor Charles Evans Hughes he supported a proposal for adopting primary elections in New York. When the proposal was defeated by the conservative Republicans, Roosevelt's irritation with the Old Guard increased. After Taft had nominated Hughes to the Supreme Court, Roosevelt cooperated with the President in fighting the New York bosses again. This time they won and secured the nomination of Henry L. Stimson for governor. Roosevelt supported Taft's position on the Payne-Aldrich tariff in an article in *The Outlook,* approved some of the administration's conservation policies, and endorsed the candidacies of Henry Cabot Lodge for the United States Senate, Warren G. Harding for the governorship of Ohio, and certain other "orthodox Republicans." These tactics he hoped would placate the more conservative East. But in his speaking tour through the progressive Middle West, nominally undertaken to support the Republican party, the doctrines Roosevelt advocated were almost identical with those of La Follette and the insurgents.

In a speech at Osawatomie, Kansas, on September 31, 1910, Roosevelt outlined an advanced program of political, social, and economic reform which he called the "New Nationalism" and the "Square Deal." In this speech, which was widely cheered by the progressives and bitterly criticized by the conservatives, Roosevelt advocated the necessity, indeed the obligation, of the federal government's participating actively in promoting human welfare and social justice. "I mean," he explained, "not merely that I stand for fair play under the present rules of the game but that I stand for having the rules changed so as to work for a more substantial equality of opportunity and of reward for equally good services." The changes in the rules which Roosevelt specified as necessary included not only such economic reforms as he had supported when President—federal regulation of corporations, conservation, revision of the tariff, income and inheritance taxes, labor codes, child labor regulation, and publicity for contributions to campaign funds—but also the whole western program of political reform—primaries, the initiative, the referendum, the recall, and the recall of judicial decisions. The inclusion of this last item, which Roosevelt supported by vigorously denouncing the conservatism of the judiciary, was especially alarming to Republican stalwarts. Human rights, Roosevelt maintained, should never be subordinated to those of property, for "every man holds his property subject to the general right of the community to regulate its use to whatever degree the public welfare may require it." [2] Though Roosevelt's speeches and actions during the summer and autumn of 1910 were intended to breach the split in the Republican party, the results proved disastrous. Besides being censured by both conservatives and progressives for trying to be all things to all men, he was forced to admit that the issues dividing his party were far more serious than he had realized. Each side distrusted the other and neither indicated real interest in compromise.

The election of 1910 resulted in huge Democratic and insurgent victories. The Democrats won a substantial majority in the House of Representatives, their first since the Cleveland administration, and elected twenty-six governors, including many in normally Republican states, such as Nebraska, Colorado, New Jersey, New York, Connecticut, Massachusetts, Ohio, and Indiana. Progressive Republicans controlled Michigan, Wisconsin, and most of the states west of the Mississippi. The Senate remained Republican by seven seats, but this meant little, since there were enough insurgents who, by voting with the Democrats, could deprive the regular GOP of effective control over that body. Just as the election dashed Republican confidence, it buoyed Democratic hopes. The voters had rejected Taft and the conservatives but had given few indications they had swung over to Roosevelt. Many of the men for whom

[2] Quoted in George E. Mowry, *Theodore Roosevelt and the Progressive Movement* (Madison,Wis., 1946), p. 143.

he had campaigned (for example, Stimson and Beveridge) were defeated, whereas La Follette, whom he had ignored while campaigning in Wisconsin, even though he had appropriated many of "Fighting Bob's" policies, won a smashing victory. Roosevelt, like Taft, had good reason to be displeased with the outcome of the midterm elections. For the victorious Democrats, even though they too suffered from intraparty divisions, the election signified the promise of a new era and an opportunity to influence national policy. The Democratic tide, moreover, had swept into office many new men, such as governors Woodrow Wilson of New Jersey and Judson Harmon of Ohio, and elevated to national prominence others, such as Champ Clark of Missouri, who became Speaker of the newly elected House of Representatives. Once Bryan, the Democratic party's undisputed leader since 1896, stated that he would not be a candidate in 1912, the Democrats, with no recognized leader, prepared to face a major fight to determine the man and the program to succeed the Nebraskan's midwestern populist-progressive credo. Meanwhile, the remainder of Taft's term was occupied chiefly by constant conflict between the President and a Democratic and insurgent Republican Congress.

CANADIAN RECIPROCITY

Taft suffered still another disappointment through the failure of a reciprocity agreement he negotiated with Canada. This measure, which provided for free trade in food products and for reductions in the duties on manufactured articles, aimed to alleviate some of the burdens and ill-will brought about by the Payne-Aldrich Act of 1909. It also reflected Taft's interest in tariff reform. The agreement was immediately denounced by the American farmers and the progressives from the Middle West as favoring American industry at the expense of American agriculture. Then the protectionists, who had little to fear from the measure but who opposed any rate reductions, joined the farmers in denouncing it. The agreement ultimately was accepted by the House and the Senate, though it was Democratic votes rather than Republican or progressive ones that put it through. Champ Clark, the new Democratic speaker of the House, declared he was for it because he hoped "to see the day when the American flag will float over every foot of the British North American possessions clear to the North Pole." Similar announcements were made in the newspapers of William Randolph Hearst. These imperialis-

tic sentiments aroused Canadian opposition and enabled Canadian manufacturers to secure a rejection of the treaty by the Ottawa Parliament.
Taft's effort to secure Canadian reciprocity earned him nothing but the
animosity of the American farmer, most of whom voted Republican, and
the ill-will of the conservatives—manufacturers and businessmen—whose
support he needed desperately.

THE REFORMS OF
THE TAFT ADMINISTRATION

Despite the political strife between conservatives and progressives
which prevailed during Taft's Presidency, his administration achieved
some important reforms. And even though his inclinations were conservative, Taft at first loyally supported the progressive movement, except in
those instances when he believed that progressive demands were blocked
by legal obstacles or that the President had no power to act. Aldrich and
the Senate conservatives, moreover, were astute enough to understand
the growing power of progressivism and to realize the need for making
some concessions.

The Taft administration, for example, brought ninety suits against large
corporations under the Sherman Act, as contrasted with Roosevelt's
record of forty-four. Among the trusts attacked were the American
Sugar Refining Company, the International Harvester Company, the National Cash Register Company, General Electric, and United States Steel.
The suit against United States Steel was based on its purchase of Tennessee Coal and Iron—a procedure which, however justifiable, was politically
unfortunate since it was bitterly resented by Theodore Roosevelt. This
case did not reach the Supreme Court until 1920, by which time the
trustbusting crusade had been obliterated by World War I; and it ended
in a legal victory for United States Steel. To permit Washington to regulate big business more effectively, Taft proposed that the federal government charter all corporations involved in interstate commerce and that
the Congress establish a special regulatory body to supervise their activities. The Congress ignored this proposal entirely.

Both Taft and the progressives favored more effective railroad regulation, but despite this common interest five months of bitter congressional
wrangling between the regular and insurgent Republicans on Capitol
Hill accompanied the writing of the Mann-Elkins Act; and when the

bill finally passed both houses of Congress (June 18, 1910), the rift between the President and the progressives was greater than it had been before. The law broadened and strengthened the powers of the Interstate Commerce Commission by empowering this body to prevent the railroad companies from changing their rates without first securing approval in the courts. In addition to giving the ICC more effective means to regulate the railroads, the progressives wrote into the act a provision making the commission also responsible for regulating telephone, telegraph, wireless, and cable companies.

Another of Taft's recommended reforms, the postal savings bank bill of June, 1910, had results similar to those of the Mann-Elkins Act: although strongly supported by the progressives in Congress and bitterly opposed by most conservatives and by the private banking interests, by the time the bill became law, the rift between the President and the progressives had grown even wider. The law, as finally passed, provided for 2 per cent interest on deposits (3 to 5 per cent was the rate paid by most private savings banks), the progressives' amendment to the bill calling for a 2¼ per cent rate being defeated. Displeased with the concessions the final bill made to the private banking interests, the progressives voted against the bill and blamed Taft.

Between 1910 and 1913 several other important reforms were achieved. The Publicity Act of 1910 and another law in 1911 required that expenditures in federal political campaigns, as well as the sources from which the parties derived financial support, be made public. In 1912 Alaska was organized as a territory and New Mexico and Arizona were admitted as states, the admission of Arizona being notable for an unsuccessful attempt by Taft to prevent the state from adopting in its constitution a clause providing for the recall of judges. In 1913 the parcel post system was established, and Congress created a separate Department of Labor with cabinet status to "foster, promote, and develop the welfare of the wage earners of the United States; to improve their working conditions, and to advance their opportunities for profitable employment." The creation of an independent Department of Labor within the federal Executive satisfied a demand which went as far back as 1865. The Sixteenth Amendment, authorizing an income tax, was passed by Congress with Taft's support in 1909 and ratified in 1913. Here was a major reform, one which would make it possible for the federal government to pay for the numerous social and welfare services the people were increasingly demanding of it. Although Taft supported the amendment and worked to influence Ohio's ratification, his efforts received little public attention and were not appreciated by the liberal-progressive bloc in Congress. Though Congress in 1910 passed the necessary legislation which ultimately led to the Seventeenth Amendment providing for the popular election of senators, which was ratified in 1913, Taft was little interested in this reform and took no part in promoting its passage. Taft, however, supported several other reform measures which were enacted during his administration, such as the creation of a Federal Children's Bureau, passage of the Mann White Slave Traffic Act, and laws protecting miners and railroad workers.

Taft's long-time interest in good administration led him to promote efforts to improve the operation of the federal departments and to attempt to reduce the cost of running the national government. At his request in 1910, Congress established a commission on efficiency and economy to study the entire administrative structure of the federal government and to recommend reforms. But congressional indifference, party strife, and increasing political discord between the President and Congress prevented Taft from implementing the commission's recommendations, one of which, the establishment of a national budget, was enacted ultimately in 1921.

By most standards, Taft's record of reform was a commendable one. But because of his political ineptitude, his inability and unwillingness to advertise himself and his policies effectively, and his failure to appreciate the necessity of cooperating with and winning the support of the increasingly powerful progressive elements in his party, he received considerable criticism and little credit for his accomplishments. As George E. Mowry points out, Taft was too disposed "to adopt a hard-and-fast position" and lacked the "facility for running with the reform hares and hunting with the conservative hounds." [3]

TAFT AND FOREIGN POLICY

Latin America

The imperialistic implications and economic expansionism which emerged during the Roosevelt era became more explicit during the Taft

[3] George E. Mowry, *The Era of Theodore Roosevelt, 1900–1912* (New York [1958]), p. 266.

administration. Taft's Secretary of State, Philander C. Knox, a believer in what he himself called "dollar diplomacy," set out to promote America's commercial relations with other parts of the world and to secure and enlarge economic opportunities for American financiers. The most obvious examples of this policy occurred in Central America.

In 1909, when a revolution in Nicaragua, which was supported by United States mining interests, overthrew President José S. Zelaya, Secretary of State Knox was quick to recognize the new regime. In 1911 he negotiated treaties providing for United States control over the finances and customs of Nicaragua and Honduras, including the right of American intervention to implement the treaties, but he was unable to persuade the Senate to ratify them. Finally in 1912, when there was another revolutionary movement in Nicaragua, which threatened to overthrow a president friendly to the United States, the Taft administration sent marines to assist in maintaining order. An American citizen was appointed to supervise the finances of Nicaragua, and American bankers took control of its national bank. The marines did not finally leave Nicaragua until 1933. Taft's policy in Nicaragua and Honduras was hardly a new one, except insofar as it stressed economic rather than political or strategic reasons for intervention. Aside from the economic consideration, it followed very clearly the precedents established by Roosevelt's agreement with Santo Domingo in 1905.

In some respects Taft did not take as firm or as expansive a view of the strategic and political interests of the United States in the Western Hemisphere as had Roosevelt. In 1911, when a private Japanese company negotiated to purchase 400,000 acres of land off Magdalena Bay in lower California, Taft showed very little concern. Though nothing came of the Japanese plan, largely because of the hostility of a large segment of the American press and the disapproval of the State Department, Senator Henry Cabot Lodge used the incident to introduce a Senate resolution extending the principles of the Monroe Doctrine to include non-European states and private foreign corporations. On August 2, 1912, by a vote of 51 to 4, the Senate approved what came to be known as the Lodge Corollary, whereby the United States would look upon with "grave concern the actual or potential possession" of "any harbor or other place in the American continents . . . so situated that the occupation thereof for naval or military purposes might threaten the communications or safety of the United States." The principle of the Lodge Corollary enlarged the scope of the Monroe Doctrine and provided additional means for the State Department to intervene in the affairs of Latin America.

The Far East

In the Far East, the Taft administration reversed Roosevelt's policy of coming to terms with Japan and attempted to promote "dollar diplomacy" more energetically by making the Open Door a reality. Largely as a result of the influence of Willard Straight, an American diplomat who had served for some years as consul in Manchuria, Taft and Knox attempted for four years to secure opportunities for American capital in the Chinese empire, including Manchuria. They challenged the control exercised by Japan and by the "consortium" of European powers—Britain, France, and Germany—over different parts of China by insisting that American bankers should be permitted to participate in making loans to the Chinese government and to invest in Chinese railroad projects. This policy antagonized the various powers already entrenched in China, and though, largely through Taft's efforts, United States participation in the consortium was finally secured (May, 1911), it did not result in any considerable American investment chiefly because American bankers were reluctant to risk their money in the Far East, especially in view of the fact that they were not welcomed by the other banking and business interests there. "Dollar diplomacy" was intended to serve the interests of American industry and finance. In this instance, however, it was not supported by those interests which were expected to benefit by it. Two weeks after Wilson entered the White House, Secretary of State Bryan informed the members of the Six-power Consortium that the United States would not participate in the proposed Chinese loan because, as Wilson declared later, the proposed arrangements would have come very close to affecting "the administrative independence of China itself." "If we had entered into the loan," Wilson told his cabinet, "we would have got nothing but more influence in China and lost the proud position which America secured when Secretary Hay stood for the open door." [4]

THE ELECTION OF 1912

Formal preparations for the presidential campaign of 1912 began on January 21, 1911, when the National Progressive Republican League was

[4] Quoted in Arthur S. Link, *Woodrow Wilson and the Progressive Era, 1910–1917* (New York [1954]), pp. 83, 84.

organized. The progressives planned to capture the Republican party and to prevent Taft from being nominated for a second term. La Follette, the most prominent of the midwestern insurgents and the leader of the region's fight against the GOP's conservatism in the Senate, hoped to become the beneficiary of a progressive victory, and in the summer he launched a campaign for the Republican nomination. Roosevelt still refrained from attacking Taft, and he refused to join the Progressive Republican League. Moreover, he was convinced that La Follette was incapable of winning the GOP nomination from Taft. Until the autumn of 1911, Roosevelt repeatedly declared that he did not want to be President again and that he had not the slightest idea of becoming a candidate.

Many of the progressives, however, preferred Roosevelt to La Follette. The glamour of Roosevelt's name and his immense personal popularity made him a much stronger candidate than La Follette who, despite his energy and his Senate record, remained a regional rather than a national figure, the spokesman of the farmers and the small businessmen of the Middle West. Roosevelt's relatively conservative record as President attracted many moderate reformers who regarded La Follette as too radical and too doctrinaire. While Roosevelt's recent speeches had won the approval of the western insurgents, he continued also to have close associations with certain wealthy easterners who were willing to give him financial support—particularly George W. Perkins of the House of Morgan and the newspaper publisher Frank Munsey. The event which caused Roosevelt seriously to consider running against Taft for the GOP nomination occurred in October, 1911, when the government instituted suit against the United States Steel Corporation for absorbing Tennessee Coal and Iron, and when Taft made a speech (which Roosevelt interpreted as a personal reference) denouncing the more radical reformers as "political emotionalists" and "neurotics." From this time on, Roosevelt's interest in the Republican nomination grew more and more pronounced, as his personal resentment against Taft broke all bounds. Meanwhile La Follette's presidential hopes, which even his most loyal and dedicated supporters doubted he could realize, collapsed on February 2, 1912, when—as a result of overwork and his daughter's serious illness—he lost control of himself during a speech before the Periodical Publishers Association of America at Philadelphia and continued talking, with little tact and complete incoherence, until most of his audience had gone. A week later, on February 10, by arrangement with Roosevelt, a group of seven Republican state governors invited him to become a candidate, and two weeks later Roosevelt declared, "My hat is in the ring."

The fight between Roosevelt and Taft for the Republican nomination was a deplorable exhibition of mudslinging. Roosevelt bitterly denounced the man whom he himself had selected for the Presidency as feeble, incompetent, and ungrateful, and implied that Taft's primary obligations were not to the American people but to himself. Taft, with more sense of personal decency but equal lack of dignity, apologized for attacking Roosevelt by telling the public that "even a rat in a corner will fight." The party convention met at Chicago in June, 1912. From those states, thirteen in number, which had adopted the presidential primary, three-quarters of the delegates were for Roosevelt, including those from Taft's home state, Ohio. The conservatives, however, had a majority of the delegates from the other states; and the administration could, as usual, count on the support of the delegations from the South. There were rival delegations from Indiana, Michigan, and Wisconsin; and the credentials committee, which had been appointed in 1908 and was controlled by the conservatives, decided these disputes in favor of the Taft delegations.

At the first meeting of the convention when Elihu Root, the candidate of the conservatives, was elected chairman, and it became obvious that the progressives had failed in their effort to capture the party. Roosevelt ordered his supporters to leave the convention, and Taft was then renominated on the first ballot, the vote being as follows: Taft, 561; Roosevelt, 107; La Follette, 41; Albert B. Cummins, 17; Hughes, 2. Three hundred and forty-nine delegates refused to vote. For Vice President, the nomination went to James S. Sherman, the incumbent. Whether a different decision in the case of the disputed delegations would have given Roosevelt a majority is problematical. Although Roosevelt was unquestionably supported by a majority of the rank and file of the Republican voters, it would be unjust to accuse the conservatives of having deprived him of the nomination by fraud. They had merely used the traditional methods of manipulating the party machinery, which had been employed by Roosevelt himself in securing the nomination for Taft in 1908. Roosevelt, however, declared that Taft was a beneficiary of a "successful fraud," that he had "no claim to the support of any Republican on party grounds," and that he had "forfeited the right to win the support of any honest man on moral grounds."

Roosevelt's supporters met again at Chicago on August 5 to launch the Progressive party. The convention was a curious mixture of western insurgents who liked Roosevelt's principles, wealthy easterners who liked his personality, and social reformers of all kinds, including many from what Roosevelt had once called the "lunatic fringe." Not all the insurgents who had favored Roosevelt at the GOP convention, however, were prepared to join the third party. A number of them, such as Senator Cummins of Iowa and all but one of the state governors who had asked Roosevelt to run, refused to bolt; others, such as La Follette, came out for Wilson.[5]

After a keynote speech by former Senator Beveridge of Indiana, Roosevelt was nominated for the Presidency, with Hiram Johnson of California as his running mate. When Roosevelt arrived in Chicago to accept the nomination, he told reporters that he felt like a bull moose; and the bull moose was adopted as an appropriate symbol for the new party. The proceedings ended in a spirit of religious enthusiasm: Roosevelt concluded his speech of acceptance by declaring that "we stand at Armageddon, and we battle for the Lord," and the convention then sang "Onward, Christian Soldiers."

From the viewpoint of practical politics, the Bull Moose movement was a disastrous mistake. Primarily the expression of a single man's ire and ambition, the party had no permanent vitality; and after failing to recapture the Presidency, Roosevelt killed his party by deserting his followers. Years later Amos Pinchot attributed the failure of the Progressive party to the fact that "it had an aspiration and no issue . . . no described, understandable program for transforming its reveries into facts." [6] The only results of the movement were to make it inevitable that the Democrats would win the 1912 election and to leave the conservatives in complete control of the Republican party. When the progressives returned to republicanism, they found they had lost influence and prestige through their temporary desertion and were further than before from capturing the party machinery.

But though the party was short-lived, the advanced social and economic reforms it proclaimed in its platform supplied progressivism with a program upon which it could build for the future. To be sure, many of the planks in the Bull Moose platform—such as direct primaries, women's suffrage, more effective corrupt practices legislation, and the

[5] Eugene H. Roseboom, *A History of Presidential Elections* (New York, 1957), pp. 364-65.

[6] Amos R. E. Pinchot, *History of the Progressive Party, 1912-1916* [ed. by Helene Maxwell Hooker] (New York, 1958), p. 229.

initiative, referendum, and recall—had been advocated before; others did no more than demand "responsible government" as well as attack "invisible government" and "the unholy alliance between corrupt business and corrupt politics." What was significant in the Progressive party platform of 1912 in terms of the future was the proposals aimed to safeguard "human resources through an enlightened measure of social and industrial justice." Among the legislation recommended were laws prohibiting child labor and regulating industrial practices to prevent "accidents, occupational diseases, overwork, involuntary unemployment"; others "fixing . . . minimum safety and health standards for the various occupations" and setting "minimum wage standards for working women," as well as an eight-hour day for both men and women workers; and those devising a program of "social insurance" to protect "home life against the hazards of sickness, irregular employment, and old age." These and the other proposals in the Bull Moose platform, such as those demanding broader and more effective regulation of business, as well as certain statements Roosevelt made during the campaign, indicated that he had moved considerably to the left since the days he had occupied the White House. Much of the philosophy underlying the progressive program he espoused in 1912 looked forward to the reform legislation of the 1930's.

The Democrats met at Baltimore on June 25 with high hopes, realizing full well that the Republican split would help them materially in their effort to capture the White House. The talk of a Democratic victory in the November elections brought forth a number of candidates, all willing this year to sacrifice themselves for the party's welfare. Representative Oscar W. Underwood of Alabama, the chairman of the Ways and Means Committee, Joseph W. Folk, the former progressive governor of Missouri, and Judson Harmon, the governor of Ohio, were considered serious contenders for the nomination. Besides these three men, there was the usual number of favorite sons, such as Governor Thomas R. Marshall of Indiana. Bryan, present as a member of the Nebraska delegation, remained the leading figure in and the titular head of the party, but his leadership was opposed by the eastern conservative wing of the party which had promoted Parker in 1904. Still, Bryan's attitude was important and it would influence the decision of the convention. The two leading candidates were Champ Clark of Missouri, who, except for one term, had been a member of the House of Representatives since 1893, and Governor Woodrow Wilson of New Jersey, whose political career was but two years old. As Democratic leader of the House, Clark had joined with the insurgents in the fight against Cannon and, after the Democratic victory in the election of 1910, had been elected Speaker. Though his association with practical politics exceeded Wilson's by far, neither his record nor his public statements indicated he possessed the qualities necessary for the Presidency.

When the Democratic convention began to ballot for the presidential nomination, Clark led with 440½ votes. Wilson was second with 324. Bryan, however, had determined that no candidate should win the nomination who was supported by Tammany or by such Wall Street Democrats as the banker August Belmont and the street-railroad magnate Thomas Fortune Ryan. After the tenth ballot, when the New York delegation gave its votes to Clark, it appeared as if Wilson's chance for the nomination was through. With 556 of the convention's 1,088 votes, Clark had more than a majority, though not enough to meet the required two-thirds to win. Discouraged and ready to admit defeat, Wilson was persuaded to hold on to his delegates a little longer. Chairman Underwood did likewise. Then, on the fourteenth ballot, Bryan, after accusing Clark of being too closely associated with Wall Street and Tammany Hall, shifted to Wilson. But even this move, though gratifying, did not improve Wilson's position appreciably, except to provide his supporters and convention strategists time to negotiate for more votes. Wilson moved ahead slowly for twenty-seven more ballots. Then, on the forty-second ballot, the boss-controlled Illinois delegation turned over its votes to him. Finally, on the forty-sixth ballot, after Underwood gave him his votes, Wilson secured the nomination.[7] When Underwood refused the Vice Presidency, the convention nominated Governor Thomas R. Marshall of Indiana. With Wilson's nomination, the leadership of the Democratic party passed into the hands of an energetic and determined progressive statesman.

Because the sentiment of the electorate in 1912 was predominantly progressive, the campaign was mainly a contest between Roosevelt and Wilson. Alike in their conviction that democracy must be revitalized by limiting the powers of the large corporations and of the political bosses, the two men differed in their ideas as to the purposes and extent to which government intervention was required and in the remedies that they advocated. Roosevelt's "New Nationalism" accepted the Hamiltonian principle of a strong, powerful government and, as Herbert Croly

[7] Link, *op. cit.*, pp. 12–13.

had indicated earlier in *The Promise of American Life*, recognized the big corporations as economic necessities. Roosevelt advocated establishing federal regulation over these large business units, thus greatly extending the powers of the federal government and using it as a vehicle through which to achieve social and economic justice. Wilson, on the other hand, preached a "New Freedom," a program in the Jeffersonian tradition of states' rights. Wilson's social and economic ideas at this time were influenced by Louis D. Brandeis, a native Kentuckian and Harvard Law School graduate whose legal efforts in defending the people against the vested interests had gained for him the title "the people's lawyer." Brandeis' progressivism and economic liberalism caused him to fear monopoly, what he called "the curse of bigness," and it squared well with Wilson's own thought at this time. During the latter part of the campaign Brandeis supplied Wilson with many of the ideas which found expression in the New Freedom, such as Wilson's demand that the growth of big corporations must be limited, competition reestablished, the rights of the small businessmen protected, and the powers of the state governments preserved. Wilson's underlying idea in 1912 was that the federal government should be used to guarante and safeguard the people's freedom; Roosevelt argued that "the power of government" should be employed to "exalt the lowly and give heart to the humble and downtrodden." [8] Thus, despite certain surface similarities between the New Freedom and the New Nationalism, such as the need for tariff, banking, and trust reform, there was a fundamental and highly important difference in the progressive philosophy which these two men elaborated. The progressive debate which occurred between Wilson and Roosevelt during the campaign of 1912 was, as Eric F. Goldman has pointed out, "the first time the two major candidates for the Presidency were progressives, and . . . the first time a major split in reform doctrine was being argued before a national audience." [9]

From the election figures it does not appear that many voters changed their party allegiance; Wilson received the regular Democratic vote, while the Republican vote was divided between Roosevelt and Taft. With a popular vote of 6,286,214, 42 per cent of the electorate, Wilson won forty states with an electoral vote of 435; in only 14 of these states, however, did he have a clear majority over both his opponents. Roose-

---

[8] Quoted in Mowry, *Theodore Roosevelt and the Progressive Movement*, p. 278.
[9] Eric F. Goldman, *Rendezvous with Destiny: A History of Modern American Reform* (New York, 1953), p. 216.

velt had a popular vote of 4,126,020 and an electoral vote of 88, carrying Pennsylvania, Michigan, Minnesota, South Dakota, Washington, and 11 out of the 13 California votes. Taft, with a popular vote of 3,483,922, won only 8 electoral votes, those of Utah and Vermont. The election also marked a big increase in the Socialist vote, with Debs securing a popular vote of 897,011. The Socialist-Labor candidate, Arthur E. Reimer, polled 29,079; Eugene W. Chaffin, the Prohibitionist, secured 206,275. In addition to winning the Presidency, the Democrats also elected twenty-one state governors and won majorities in both houses of Congress.

With Wilson's election, the Democratic party captured the White House for only the third time since the Civil War, its previous victories being those of Grover Cleveland in 1884 and 1892. Wilson, moreover, was the first southerner to be elected since Zachary Taylor in 1848. Combined with the crucial role of the southern delegates in nominating Wilson, this meant that for the first time in more than a half century the South would have a voice in formulating national policies. In this respect, as Arthur S. Link has pointed out, the election of 1912, like the one which brought Jefferson to power in 1800, "effected an important shift in the geographical control of the federal government." [10] Aware of the opportunities for Executive leadership with which the election provided him and determined to exercise the kind of "constructive statesmanship" he had been advocating before college and public audiences for many years, Wilson entered the White House in March, 1913, with no political debts to prevent him from fulfilling his campaign promises to the people. The election had indicated that a majority of the voters demanded reform; and Wilson was determined to gratify their desires in this direction.

Suggested Readings

Many of the books cited in Chapter 5 are pertinent for developments during the Taft administration. The most recent general survey of the Taft years is in George E. Mowry, *The Era of Theodore Roosevelt 1900–1912* (New York, 1958). For the years 1909–14, see also the fourth volume of Mark Sullivan, *Our Times* (6 vols., New York, 1926–35) and Charles A. Beard, *Contemporary American History, 1877–1913* (New York, 1929), a collection of essays interpreting the progressive period. Also useful is Mark Sullivan, *The Education of an American* (New York, 1938). Many of the biographies and memoirs cited

[10] Link, *op. cit.*, p. 24.

in Chapters 4 and 5 are equally relevant for the light they shed on Taft and his times.

The best biography of Taft is Henry F. Pringle, *William Howard Taft* (2 vols., New York, 1939). A briefer and less carefully researched one is Herbert S. Duffy, *William Howard Taft* (New York, 1930). Much interesting detail, especially on Taft before he entered the White House, is to be found in Mrs. Taft's memoirs, *Recollections of Full Years* (New York, 1914).

The Payne-Aldrich Tariff is discussed in most of the general accounts, biographies, and memoirs pertinent to these years cited above and in Ida M. Tarbell, *The Tariff in Our Time* (New York, 1911), a study inspired by the progressive attack on the tariff. See also the relevant chapters in Frank W. Taussig, *The Tariff History of the United States* (8th rev. ed., New York [1931]); the same author's *Free Trade, The Tariff and Reciprocity* (New York, 1920); and Nathaniel W. Stephenson, *Nelson W. Aldrich* (New York, 1930).

On the Ballinger-Pinchot controversy, see Alpheus T. Mason, *Bureaucracy Convicts Itself: The Ballinger-Pinchot Contoversy of 1910* (New York, 1941); the older study by Rose M. Stahl, *The Ballinger-Pinchot Controversy* (North-ampton, Mass., 1926); and Gifford Pinchot, *The Fight For Conservation* (New York, 1910), as well as many of the books cited in the conservation section of Chapter 5.

Insurgency and the speakership fight are well covered in Kenneth W. Hechler, *Insurgency: Personalities and Politics of the Taft Era* (New York, 1940) and Blair Bolles, *Tyrant from Illinois: Uncle Joe Cannon's Experiment with Personal Power* (New York, 1951). See also L. White Bushey, *Uncle Joe Cannon* (New York [1927]), Richard L. Neuberger and Stephen B. Kahn, *Integrity: The Life of George W. Norris* (New York, 1937), and the pertinent chapters in Norris' autobiography, *Fighting Liberal: The Autobiography of George W. Norris* (New York, 1945); and Claudius O. Johnson, *Borah of Idaho* (New York, 1936). The most recent biography of Borah is Marian C. McKenna, *Borah* (Ann Arbor, Mich., 1961).

The fight for Canadian reciprocity is detailed in L. Ethan Ellis, *Reciprocity, 1911: A Study of Canadian-American Relations* (New Haven, Conn., 1939).

On Taft's Latin American foreign policy, see Scott Nearing and Joseph Freeman, *Dollar Diplomacy* (New York, 1925); Emory R. Johnson, *History of Domestic and Foreign Commerce of the United States* (Washington, D.C., 1915); Isaac J. Cox, *Nicaragua and the United States, 1910–1927* (Boston, 1927); and Dana G. Munro, *The Latin American Republics* (New York [1960]).

Developments in the Far East are detailed in John G. Reid, *The Manchu Abdication and the Powers, 1908–1912* (Berkeley, Calif., 1935) and in Herbert Croly, *Willard Straight* (New York, 1924). See also many of the books cited in the foreign policy section of Chapter 5. On Mexican developments, see the references in Chapter 7.

The Republican party split in 1912 and the election of that year are covered in numerous works, including Oscar K. Davis, *Released for Publication* (New York, 1945), the memoirs of a Theodore Roosevelt manager in 1912; Victor Rosewater, *Back Stage in 1912* (Philadelphia, 1932); and William Jennings

Bryan, *A Tale of Two Conventions* (New York, 1912). Amos R. E. Pinchot, *History of the Progressive Party, 1912–1916* (New York, 1958) is the account of the party's rise and decline by an active participant in those events, and Martin L. Fausold, *Gifford Pinchot: Bull Moose Progressive* (Syracuse, N.Y., 1961) contains much valuable material on its subject's political activities between 1909 and 1917. See also Benjamin P. De Witt, *The Progressive Movement* (New York, 1915). The most analytical, brief account is to be found in Chapter I of Arthur S. Link, *Woodrow Wilson and the Progressive Era, 1910–1917* (New York [1954]).

7

Woodrow Wilson and

the New Freedom, 1913-1917

WOODROW WILSON'S CAREER TO 1912

When Woodrow Wilson entered the White House on March 4, 1913, he had only two years of experience in active politics behind him. At the time, many of his supporters scarcely expected he would be a strong President. Almost no one foresaw the influence his policies and ideas would exercise on the course of American and world history, not only during his lifetime, but for many years thereafter. But as events soon proved, Wilson as President was to dominate Congress and to dictate the policies of the government even more decisively than Theodore Roosevelt had done. From 1913 until 1919 much of the history of the United States and the world was determined mainly by the personality and mental development of Woodrow Wilson.

Of Scotch-Irish ancestry and the descendant of Presbyterian ministers on both sides of his family, Wilson was born in Staunton, Virginia, in 1856. He grew up in a devout family which placed great store upon duty, religion, moral principles, and education, and upon their efficacy in influencing and determining practical affairs. The academic and religious background of his family and the fact that he grew up in the South during the Civil War and Reconstruction were important influences upon Wilson's life and outlook. He inherited a highly complex character marked chiefly by a tenacious strength of will that often made him inflexible, a gift for eloquence that inspired men's hopes, and a moral idealism which caused him to view the world in terms of a battle between good and evil. He could dominate men from his study or from the platform by inspiring them with his own faith in justice, freedom, and democracy and his own uncompromising hatred of whatever obstructed the forces of righteousness. An idealist in his belief that religious, intellectual, and moral forces could be employed to shape a better world, Wilson also understood practical politics, possessing, as one commentator has phrased it, "an instinctive grasp of realities which enabled him to preserve the vital balance between ideals and practice."

But he had also many of the defects of his qualities. Narrow both in his intellectual interests and in his sympathies, he was often lacking in the detailed social and economic understanding needed for making his ideals effective. While he craved warm affection from a few intimate friends, he was often unable to return it. As a result, to many people he appeared reserved, distant, and coldblooded. Moreover, he was often tactless and ineffectual in handling individuals in personal contact. He showed little sympathy for, or ability to forgive, human error. He loved mankind, but he had little use for most men. His faith in the justice of his own ideals and in his ability to understand, express, and execute the will of the people was apt to degenerate into obstinacy and self-righteousness and to make him feel that those who opposed him were opposing God. Though he made many concessions and indicated on numerous occasions that he could work out compromises and though, as one of his biographers has stated, he was and remained "eminently educable," he preferred too often to break rather than to bend. Despite Wilson's great strength of character, his determination to succeed, and his courageous, capable, and dedicated leadership, he failed to realize fully many of his hopes and ideals because he possessed insufficient subtlety and far too little humility. The combination of qualities which dominated his character predestined him to tragedy.

After attending Davidson College in North Carolina for a year, he entered Princeton, graduating in 1879. His family had hoped that he would become a minister like his father, but Wilson never showed any signs of being attracted to the pulpit. Since his real interests lay in the practice and administration of government and in public affairs, he determined to study law. "The profession I chose was politics," he wrote in 1883;

"the profession I entered was the law. I entered the one because I thought it would lead to the other. It was once the sure road; and Congress is still full of lawyers." With this view in mind, Wilson prepared to study law at the University of Virginia. Upon graduating in 1882, he practiced for a year in Atlanta, but quickly found the *"pettinesses"* of the profession and his "humdrum life . . . in slow, ignorant, uninteresting Georgia" so dissatisfying that he decided to enter Johns Hopkins. "My plain necessity," he confided to a friend, "is some profession which will afford me a moderate support, favourable conditions for study, and considerable leisure; what better can I be, therefore, than a professor, a lecturer upon subjects whose study most delights me?" At Johns Hopkins he studied American history and government, and in 1885 was awarded a Ph.D. For his dissertation he used his recently published and widely acclaimed first book, *Congressional Government: A Study in American Politics*. Primarily an analysis of the practical operations of the federal government, emphasizing the shortcomings which resulted when the legislature was permitted to encroach upon the Executive, it extolled the British cabinet system and suggested various reforms to improve the American system.

Between 1885 and 1902, when he became president of Princeton University, Wilson taught and wrote on American history and politics at Bryn Mawr, Wesleyan, and, after 1890, at Princeton. An inspiring lecturer and a popular teacher, Wilson was at his best when delivering formal lectures before a large class. His courses were always filled to capacity and his lectures often applauded. Experience before the classroom and self-study gave him the assurance and practice which made him the popular, articulate, and distinguished public speaker the nation came to know after 1910. Wilson also attracted considerable attention during his years as a professor by his writings—books, essays, and articles in popular magazines like *Harper's* and *The Atlantic Monthly*.[1] His interest in the actual workings of government and in contemporary issues and his ability to express himself clearly, forcefully, and with considerable

[1] In addition to *Congressional Government*, Wilson's more important books in political science included a popular textbook on comparative government, *The State* (1889), which he referred to as a "dull fact book"; a collection of essays, *An Old Master and Other Political Essays* (1893); and the lectures he delivered at Columbia University and published under the title *Constitutional Government in the United States* (1900). On American history he wrote *Division and Reunion* (1896) and the five-volume *History of the American People* (1902). His collection of essays, *Mere Literature* (1896), covered, besides historical subjects, his thoughts on writing and the art of expression.

elegance assured him a much larger audience than most academicians can command. His popularity and reputation as a teacher and writer led the trustees of Princeton University to elect him president unanimously in 1902.

In this position Wilson's forceful personality and moving speeches began to attract increasing national attention. He was uninterested in economic questions at this period; and although his democratic sentiments were unimpeachable, he was hostile to Bryanism and showed little sympathy for or understanding of the need for the kind of reform which many progressives were advocating. Admiring the type of leadership produced by the English parliamentary system, Wilson proclaimed the importance of political honesty and idealism in a rhetoric that was stirring but often vague.

Meanwhile he endeavored "to make Princeton . . . a great university" and "an institution of purpose." He succeeded brilliantly in reforming and enlarging the curriculum, raising academic standards and entrance requirements, attracting new faculty, and establishing the preceptorial system, whereby he hoped "to transform [Princeton] from a place where there are youngsters doing tasks to a place where there are men doing thinking." Wilson's success in improving undergraduate instruction and in elevating Princeton's reputation as a university was achieved with little difficulty and with widespread approval. But Wilson was not satisfied. More changes were necessary before his dream of "Princeton in the nation's service" could be realized.

One of these, which he proposed in 1907, was designed to enrich and invigorate the social life of all students by abolishing the aristocratic "eating clubs," which were comparable to fraternities at other universities, and to which only the more socially and economically privileged of Princeton's upperclassmen could aspire. In the place of these clubs, which he opposed primarily because of their intellectual shortcomings, Wilson proposed to institute the quadrangle or college system whereby the entire student body would be assigned to a number of colleges under university supervision. Each college would include upper- and lower-class students, resident preceptors, and unmarried faculty members. Wilson hoped that the chief purpose of a university—to promote "vital, spontaneous intellectual life"—could be realized by bringing together older and younger men from different social and economic backgrounds. Representative student committees within each college would determine and administer their own rules, so that each college would "form a unit in itself, and largely a self-governing unit."

Wilson saw in his proposal the means to promote the ideal of the intellectual life and to foster what he called the spirit of "comradeship based on *letters*"; but the scheme was opposed by the clubs' friends, among whom were trustees, alumni, and wealthy friends of the university. Their combined pressure resulted in Wilson's defeat. Meanwhile his plans to remake Princeton into a "real university" brought him into conflict with Andrew F. West, dean of the graduate school. West's desire for a graduate school separate from the remainder of the university interfered with Wilson's plans for reorganization, which called for making the new graduate school an integrated part of the university. Personally the two men, as West once said, had never "hit it off"; they had differed over university policies before. The fight over the location of the graduate school served to focus all their previous differences, though the underlying causes of their quarrel were their mutual antipathy, mistrust, and jealousy, and their struggle for power and loyalty in the university. Unwilling to fight West on personal issues, Wilson chose instead to wage battle upon the more exalted level of democratic versus aristocratic education.[2] When West defeated him by securing a lavish endowment from the estate of a Princeton graduate, Wilson was forced to step down. On September 15, 1910, less than a month before he resigned from the presidency of Princeton, he accepted the Democratic party's nomination for governor of New Jersey.

Wilson's experience at Princeton discloses much of the man's character and many of the traits which were to influence his career as President and world statesman. Many of the very same qualities which brought him success and failure, and which caused him to be idolized and then repudiated at Princeton, revealed themselves on the national and international level. Wilson's ability to lead men to accomplish his purpose by inspiring them with words and visions which expressed and aroused their loftiest ideals brought him success in educational reform. These same qualities made possible many of the impressive legislative achievements of his first years in the White House, just as they served him well later in appealing to "the conscience of the world" for a peace embodying "the reign of law, based upon the consent of the governed and sustained by the organized opinion of mankind." His failure to achieve this—his most ambitious goal—like his defeat in his fight over the graduate school, was in part the result of his inflexibility and tactlessness, and his unwillingness to make compromises once he determined he was right.

[2] John A. Garraty, "The Training of Woodrow Wilson," *American Heritage*, VII (August 1956), 24–27, 94.

Wilson's nomination in 1910 was largely the work of George Harvey, a New York publisher with Wall Street connections, who had suggested Wilson as a presidential possibility as early as 1906. Although Harvey came from Vermont, he happened to be a Democrat. He was looking for a conservative leader who could oust Bryan and the western radicals from control of the party machinery. Harvey persuaded the powerful, corrupt, and ambitious New Jersey boss, James Smith, Jr., and the other Democratic party chieftains in the state to nominate Wilson for the governorship. In 1910 the bosses needed an honest, respectable, and safe candidate who could appeal to liberal and reform-minded voters and, at the same time, could be counted upon to cooperate with them in perpetuating their control over the party. Since Wilson appeared to fulfill their needs, the bosses endorsed Harvey's suggestion willingly and engineered Wilson's nomination. During the campaign Wilson, realizing the strength of the reform spirit that was sweeping the state and the nation that year, loosened his ties with the men who had promoted his candidacy, steered a less conservative course, and endorsed many of the liberal reform programs advocated by the state's progressives.

Elected governor by the party machine and the votes of liberals and progressives whom he had attracted by his promise to fight for reform and his claim that he was not beholden to any man, group, or interest, Wilson proceeded to assert his independence of the men who had been responsible for his nomination. He broke with Harvey, who considered Wilson his protégé and tried to dictate his policies, and he defeated Boss Smith's effort to get the legislature to elect him to the United States Senate. With remarkable political ability, by forceful leadership, and through astute use of the press and his own direct appeals to the people, Wilson succeeded in forcing through the state legislature a series of reforms which New Jersey progressives had been advocating since the turn of the century. The extent of Wilson's accomplishment (corrupt practices, direct primary, and simplified ballot legislation; workmen's compensation; and more effective laws regulating railroads and public utilities) won the applause of liberals and progressives throughout the country. Even though his concern with, and knowledge of, many of the specific reforms which the progressives advocated were often vague and recently acquired, Wilson was able to capture and synthesize the reform mood of the day and to associate with it man's highest moral principles and loftiest aspirations. Wilson entered the White House as the eloquent spokesman of reform, justice, and virtue. "This is not a day of triumph," he concluded his inaugural address; "it is a day of dedication. Here muster, not the forces of party, but the forces of humanity. Men's hearts wait upon us; men's lives hang in the balance; men's hopes call upon us to say what we will do."

Presidential Leadership

Through years of study and observation Wilson had arrived at the conclusion that effective government required strong national leadership and that it was the responsibility of the President to exercise this leadership. Always a great admirer of the British parliamentary system, he deplored what he termed "the clumsy misrule of Congress" and attributed the governmental inefficiency and irresponsibility which characterized the American system to the lack of cooperation between the Executive and the legislature, a consequence of permitting the principle of the separation of powers to operate with no regulation or restraint. "What we need," he declared, "is harmonious, consistent, responsible party government." [3] As President, Wilson was determined to provide it.

As the leader of his party and the spokesman of the people who had elected him to carry out their purposes, Wilson asserted direct leadership over the Congress from the very beginning of his administration, working closely with the leaders of his party in formulating legislation, devising compromises, and, when necessary, disciplining erring Democrats who failed to do his bidding. Those who questioned or opposed him would be reminded that he was "the instrument of the people . . . carrying out their wishes" and that if congressional Democrats refused to accept his interpretation of what the people wanted he would go to them directly for their "decision" on the matter.[4] A contemporary described Wilson's relationship with his party in Congress by saying: "The Democratic Party revolves around him. He is the center of it; the biggest Democrat in the country—the leader and the chief." [5]

While Wilson's techniques of party leadership stemmed largely from his admiration of the British parliamentary system, his concept of a strong President who spoke for, and was accountable to, the nation was strongly

[3] Quoted in Richard F. Fenno, Jr., *The President's Cabinet . . . from Wilson to Eisenhower* (Cambridge, Mass., 1959), p. 251.
[4] Quoted in Arthur S. Link, "Woodrow Wilson: The Philosophy, Methods, and Impact of Leadership," in Arthur P. Dudden, ed., *Woodrow Wilson and the World of Today* (Philadelphia [1957]), pp. 15–16
[5] Quoted in *ibid.*, p. 17.

influenced by two events at the turn of the century—the Spanish-American War and the Presidency of Theodore Roosevelt. Wilson realized early that the war and the problems of world power which followed from it provided many new opportunities for the kind of "constructive statesmanship" he had held to be impossible only fifteen years earlier when he dismissed the Presidency as a relatively insignificant office. Roosevelt's dynamic use and broad definition of presidential authority in domestic and foreign affairs caused Wilson to revise many of his earlier views. But Roosevelt's greatest impact upon Wilson was the way he handled public opinion, especially the effective use he made of the press to win public support for his proposals. Nor did Wilson fail to realize the use of Roosevelt's direct appeals to the public to influence Congress. To Wilson, who had studied and practiced "the arts of persuasion" since his days as an undergraduate in college and who so greatly admired the nineteenth-century English orator-statesman, the opportunities the Presidency offered for the kind of national leadership he so admired were unlimited, provided its occupant could make use of that "deep eloquence which awakens purpose" to earn the people's confidence for his program.[6] As President, Wilson exploited all of Roosevelt's techniques, revised old ones, such as addressing Congress in person, and introduced others of his own, probably the most notable being the regular press conference.

Wilson was also an astute politician who understood the people's mood at the time and used it to win support, just as he capitalized upon the progressive temper of Congress to achieve his program. In dealing with the members of his own party, Wilson had little trouble. The new ones dared not oppose him and the veterans realized the necessity to prove to the country that the Democratic party had not lost its capacity to govern. Wilson recognized this and was determined to take advantage of every favorable circumstance and, if necessary, to crack the whip to ensure discipline. The party would have to show a record of achievement before the midterm elections of 1914 in order to win.

In selecting his cabinet, Wilson relied heavily upon the advice and suggestions of Colonel Edward M. House, a wealthy Texan and an amateur in politics, who had met Wilson in 1912 and had quickly become his closest personal friend and confidant. For the next seven years, House exercised more influence in the Wilson administration than any holder

[6] *Ibid.*, pp. 4–5; John Morton Blum, *Woodrow Wilson and the Politics of Morality* (Boston [1956]), pp. 11–12.

of public office. In 1913 Bryan was still the most influential personality in the Democratic party and his support was necessary if Wilson was going to achieve his domestic reforms. Wilson, therefore, appointed him Secretary of State. Though the two men shared many similar ideas on foreign policy, Wilson had little confidence in Bryan's capacity to handle foreign affairs, and he acted as his own Secretary of State whenever any

Colonel Edward M. House, a Texas millionaire, became Woodrow Wilson's closest adviser. He is shown here with President Wilson in 1915. (Culver Pictures, Inc.)

important crisis occurred. Of the remainder of the cabinet, the most important member was William G. McAdoo, of Georgia and New York, who became Secretary of the Treasury. Except for his Secretary of Commerce, William C. Redfield, a New York manufacturer with a short and undistinguished record in Congress, most of the others were reasonably capable men. They included Lindley M. Garrison of New Jersey, Wilson's first Secretary of War; Franklin K. Lane, the Secretary of the Interior; Attorney General Thomas W. Gregory, the Texas trust-prosecuting lawyer who replaced James C. McReynolds when Wilson appointed the latter to the Supreme Court in 1914; David F. Houston, the Secretary of Agriculture; and William B. Wilson, the nation's first Secretary of Labor. The Navy Department was headed by the North Carolina newspaper editor Josephus C. Daniels, who, despite his inexperience with the ways and jargon of the sailors with whom he had to deal, proved his abilities by instituting long-needed reforms and in presiding over the navy building program authorized in 1916. Daniels' lack of understanding of naval traditions and the customs of seamen was more than offset by his youthful and enthusiastic Assistant Secretary, Franklin D. Roosevelt. Postmaster General Albert S. Burleson, charged with ensuring party loyalty in Congress and dispensing the administration's patronage, fulfilled effectively his duties of rewarding the faithful and strengthening the party organization.

As a group, Wilson's cabinet hardly represented what he claimed to want: "the best men in the nation." In 1913 he looked upon the cabinet as "an executive, not a political body." [7] He wanted to staff it with capable and loyal administrators who, when he chose to consult them, would provide him with expert advice in determining policy, but whose views were sympathetic with his own, for once he made up his mind, Wilson expected his lieutenants to fight for his program, regardless of what they thought of it. Choice and circumstance, however, caused him to settle for less. Since no Democrat had occupied the White House for the past sixteen years and the Democratic party in Congress, a minority most of the time since 1860, had produced few experienced administrators, the number of promising and knowledgeable government executives within its ranks was limited. Wilson, moreover, was reluctant to devote the time and energy necessary to study the requirements of each department and appraise the qualifications of the individuals who were available for it. As a result, most of the men in Wilson's first cabinet were there

[7] Fenno, *op. cit.*, p. 56.

for reasons other than the theoretical ones he claimed as his guide. To a considerable extent Wilson's first cabinet reflected the influence of House and Joseph P. Tumulty, Wilson's secretary, more than that of the man it was created to serve. The one man Wilson did want as a member of his "official family," Louis D. Brandeis, he failed to secure, largely because House, on two occasions, convinced him against it.

Tumulty, Wilson's private secretary from 1911, merits special note. Since he was devoted to his chief and conscientious in fulfilling his duties, Wilson relied heavily upon him, leaving many of the less important appointments to his discretion. Tumulty also supervised most of the contacts between Wilson and the American people outside Washington—a responsibility which he performed with integrity and loyalty.

THE LEGISLATION OF
THE NEW FREEDOM, 1913–1914

On April 8, 1913, Congress convened for a special session, with revision of the tariff as its first responsibility. For more than a quarter of a century Wilson had been declaring that the influence of pressure groups and private interests over the legislature could be checked by means of strong Executive leadership; and his resolution to put his own doctrines into practice became apparent when he reverted to the old custom, abandoned by Jefferson, in 1801, of the President's addressing Congress in person. In his inaugural he had restated the ideals of progressivism with the solemn and deeply moving eloquence characteristic of all his major speeches, and he went on to specify, as subjects where reform was most needed, the tariff, banking and currency, conditions of labor, conservation, and public health.

The Tariff

The tariff had been conspicuously a subject over which presidential leadership and party discipline had often proved ineffectual and in which private interests had prevailed over the public welfare. The success with which Wilson forced a genuine reduction through Congress was, therefore, unprecedented. Believing previous tariffs had served to strengthen the trusts by guaranteeing them against foreign competition, Wilson proposed to restore "effective competition." "We must," he declared, "abolish everything that bears even the semblance of privilege or of any kind of artificial advantage and put our business men and producers under the stimulus of a constant necessity to be efficient, economical and enterprising." A bill providing for drastic reductions, drafted primarily by Oscar Underwood of Alabama, passed the House of Representatives in May. Its acceptance by the Senate was endangered by the lobbyists of the wool, sugar, and other manufacturing interests; but Wilson rallied popular support by denouncing their activities publicly, and by exerting direct pressure upon individual Democratic senators he succeeded in preventing them from deserting the program of the party. In September the bill passed the Senate with only minor changes, and in October the Underwood-Simmons tariff became law.

As compared with the schedules of the Payne-Aldrich tariff, there were 958 reductions and only 86 increases, and the average duty was lowered from 36.86 per cent to 26.67 per cent. More than one hundred articles were transferred to the free list, many of which, such as raw wool, iron, and foods, were daily necessities. Since a considerable loss of revenue was anticipated, in compensation the act included an income tax, which had recently been legalized by the Sixteenth Amendment. Unmarried persons earning more than $3,000 and married persons earning more than $4,000 were to pay 1 per cent; on incomes above $20,000 the rates were increased, 6 per cent being levied on incomes above $500,000. The number of persons who paid income taxes was 357,515. These details were, in the main, the work of a young congressman from Tennessee, Cordell Hull. Thus, for the first time since the Civil War the tariff had been genuinely reduced. What effect tariff reductions would have on the American economic system, however, was never revealed, since shortly after the Underwood-Simmons tariff became law, international trade was disrupted by World War I.

The Federal Reserve System

On June 23, 1913, Wilson again appeared before the Congress and assigned it the task of revising the banking and currency system of the country. The need for financial reform had been generally admitted since the Wall Street crisis of 1907; and it was demonstrated still further in 1912 by the report of a congressional committee under the chairmanship of Arsène Pujo, which investigated the financial practices and alliances of the country's principal bankers.

The currency system of the United States in 1912 was regulated by the National Bank Act of 1863, under which the quantity of notes a bank might issue depended on the amount of government bonds it held. This system had two cardinal weaknesses. In the first place, the supply of currency had no relation to the need for it. No provision was made for increasing the supply of notes when there was an increase in the volume of business, despite the greater need for currency in prosperous years than in years of depression and in the autumn when the volume of business was normally greater with the harvesting of crops. To a considerable degree, in fact, prosperity caused the supply of currency to contract instead of expand, since the prices of government bonds increased when business was good and at such time the banks preferred to sell them rather than buy them. The second weakness was that no provision was made for mobilizing the nation's bank resources to save any particular bank which found itself in danger. The United States contained approximately 30,000 separate independent banking institutions, each of which had to maintain its own reserve and, at a time of crisis, to rely almost entirely on its own resources.

In 1908 Congress had passed the Aldrich-Vreeland Act, which permitted banks to issue notes on certain other kinds of securities in addition to government bonds and which set up a National Monetary Commission, with Senator Nelson W. Aldrich as chairman. After devoting four years to a study of the world's banking practices and issuing forty volumes of reports, the commission recommended the establishment of a single central bank with fifteen branches in different parts of the country. The National Reserve Association, the name of the proposed institution, was to be capitalized at $100 million or more, would be controlled by the bankers, and would be independent of the government. These recommendations, known as the Aldrich plan, had been prepared by Paul M. Warburg, a prominent and knowledgeable Wall Street banker, and they reflected the views of the leading commercial banking interests of the country.

For various reasons the Aldrich plan was unacceptable to the majority of Democrats. Carter Glass of Virginia, the chairman of the House Committee on Banking and Currency, who represented the views of the more conservative wing of his party, was strongly opposed to a central bank. Faithful to his party's Jacksonian tradition, he insisted that any reform of the banking system must provide for decentralization, so that financial power would not be concentrated in the Northeast. Progressive Democrats, on the other hand, insisted upon considerable public control, if not outright government ownership of the banks, while the more radical southern agrarian wing insisted upon a provision for short-term agricultural credit and another outlawing interlocking bank directorates. These fundamental conflicts in objectives, especially the one involving the crucial question of public or private control, precipitated a major intraparty crisis, which broke out when the progressive Democrats on Capitol Hill learned that Carter Glass, with the assistance of H. Parker Willis, a former professor of political economy and an associate editor of the New York *Journal of Commerce*, had drafted a preliminary bill providing for a decentralized reserve system controlled by the bankers. Glass's proposed bill was so vigorously opposed by the progressive and agrarian members of his party that Wilson was forced to intervene.

During the summer of 1913, while the Glass bill was being hotly debated in and out of Congress, Wilson worked energetically and very effectively with Bryan and other administration leaders to reconcile these conflicting views. He sought the advice of Louis D. Brandeis, who convinced the President that the government rather than the bankers should supervise the banking and currency system. Wilson then persuaded Glass to accept an amendment to his bill establishing government control over both the reserve banks and the currency they were to be empowered to issue. Having conciliated the progressives with this concession, the President, with Bryan's able assistance, then won the support of the southern agrarians by granting their demand for short-term agricultural credits and by assuring them that provision would be made to outlaw interlocking bank directorates in subsequent legislation. Originally, the banking interests had supported the Glass bill, but now they denounced it, objecting strongly to the powers it gave the federal government; and they predicted that it would ruin the financial system of the country. Most people, including many businessmen, however, praised the measure. Finally, the amended Glass-Owen bill passed both houses of Congress and became law when Wilson signed it on December 23, 1913.

By the Federal Reserve Act all national banks were required, and state banks were invited, to become members of the Federal Reserve System. The country was to be divided into twelve regions, in each of which a Federal Reserve bank was to be established. The stock of these Federal Reserve banks was to be subscribed by the member banks, and each of the Reserve banks was to be governed by nine directors. Three of these directors were to be appointed by the Federal Reserve Board, and the remainder were to be elected by the member banks. The Federal Reserve Board, which supervised the whole system, was to consist of the Secretary of the Treasury, the Comptroller of the Currency, and five other members, one of whom was to be Governor, appointed by the President for ten-year terms.

The Federal Reserve banks were given two duties of special importance. In the first place, they were to hold all the reserves of the member banks. Various devices were provided by which these reserves might be transferred in case of need from one region of the country to another. The Federal Reserve System thus made possible the mobilization of bank reserves at times and places where they were most needed. In the second place, the Reserve banks were to obtain Federal Reserve notes from the Federal Reserve Board in return for gold certificates, eligible commercial paper, or United States government bonds. The use of government bonds required the consent of a majority of the board, and according to the original act, it was allowable only until 1933. The Reserve banks could then pass these notes on to the member banks, in return for collateral of the same kind. These Federal Reserve notes were to take the place of the bank notes that had circulated under the previous system; and since their number was determined not merely by the holdings of the banks in government bonds but also by the quantity of gold certificates and commercial paper they might acquire, it was hoped that the supply of notes would expand or contract in proportion to the volume of business.

In addition to mobilizing reserves and providing for an elastic currency, a sound banking system must also perform one other function: it must provide for a check on excessive loan expansion during boom periods, in order to prevent a dangerous credit inflation. The directors of the Federal Reserve System could curb inflation in two ways. First, they could raise the rediscount rate on the commercial paper given them in return for notes by the member banks. This would be the equivalent of charging the member banks a higher rate of interest and would thus, it was hoped, compel the member banks in turn to raise the interest rates charged for their own loans to businessmen and also compel them to stop expanding the quantity of notes in circulation. Second, the directors could sell government bonds and commercial paper in the open market and then withdraw from circulation the money they obtained by these sales. These two powers in combination would make it possible, if sound banking practices were followed, for the directors of the system to exert a considerable degree of control over the movements of the business cycle.

By 1915, 7,615 banks, with about half of the total banking resources of the nation, had become members of the Federal Reserve System. By 1928 the proportion of the banking resources controlled by the system had risen to 80 per cent, and by 1938 it was 87 per cent. A large number of the smaller state banks preferred, nevertheless, to remain independent; even in 1938 only 11 per cent of the state banks had become members. The system proved to be a considerable improvement over previous banking practices and was especially valuable in facilitating the government's financial operations during World War I. It did not, however, prevent bank failures, even of member banks, or provide the country with effective central monetary management, or succeed in evening out the business cycle.

The chief weakness of the system, perhaps, was that a proper functioning of it depended primarily on the wisdom and integrity of the Federal Reserve Board. If its members were to perform their function of checking inflation by raising discount rates and selling bonds during a boom period, they must be capable of resisting political and business pressure in favor of continued easy money. The events of 1927–28 showed that to expect this might be to demand too much of human nature. Another deficiency of the Federal Reserve Act was that, in spite of recommendations by the Pujo committee, nothing was done to regulate the stock exchange and investment banking. Despite its shortcomings, many of which were not remedied until the 1930's and after, the act corrected many of the worst weaknesses in the structure and operation of the nation's banking system and provided the means, not entirely realized at the time, to improve and strengthen the system in the future. Once again, leadership and compromise had yielded victory and, in this case, an outstanding legislative accomplishment.

Antitrust Legislation

The third principal measure that Wilson asked of Congress was legislation to curb monopoly. Like the Underwood tariff and the Federal Reserve acts, the antitrust program he proposed reflected the convictions he had expressed when he elaborated his New Freedom, namely, that the government should be used to provide an economic climate which would allow laissez faire to flourish rather than to guarantee it. Wilson had demanded tariff reform so that "men of business will be free to thrive by the law of nature—the nature of free business—instead of the law of legislation and artificial arrangement"; and he had appealed for banking and currency reform to provide business with "the instrumentalities and conveniences of free enterprise." The fact that the Federal Reserve Act provided for more governmental authority than he had asked for was in considerable part forced upon him by the advanced progressives in Congress and by Louis D. Brandeis. The trust legislation he recommended was in the spirit and tradition of the New Freedom. "What we are purposing to do," he declared in his special message to the Congress, on January 20, 1914, "is . . . not to hamper or interfere with business as enlightened business men prefer to do it, or in any sense to put it under ban." The legislation he recommended should "give expression to the best business judgment in America" and "square business methods with public opinion and the law." It should "meet business half way in its process of self-correction and disturb its legitimate course as little as possible" and "see to it . . . that the penalties and punishments . . . fall not upon business itself . . . but upon individuals who use the instrumentalities of business to do things which public policy and sound business practices condemn."

Considerations of the program began at once and the debates which followed the introduction of the administration's bills indicated there was a considerable body of progressive opinion in the Congress which demanded much more regulation than Wilson had conceded was necessary or desirable. Moreover, influential spokesmen of organized labor, like Samuel Gompers, and farm groups, such as the Farmers' Union, were shocked to learn that no provision was made to protect labor unions and farm organizations from prosecution under the Sherman Act and to safeguard their rights. Ultimately, the administration yielded just enough to satisfy the most insistent demands of the labor and farm groups by including in the Clayton bill a provision (Section VI) which stated "That the labor of a human being is not a commodity or article of commerce" and that "Nothing contained in the anti-trust laws shall be construed to forbid the existence and operation of labor, agricultural, or horticultural organizations . . . nor shall such organizations . . . be held or construed to be illegal combinations or conspiracies in restraint of trade. . . ." Meanwhile other parts of Wilson's antitrust program were arousing debate and opposition.

One of the recommendations Wilson had suggested to the Congress was the creation of an "interstate trade commission" to provide the business community with "advice . . . definite guidance, and information." There was nothing in his original proposal that called for government regulation or control. Indeed, he made it specifically clear that it was to be no more than "an indispensable instrument of information and publicity . . . a clearing house for the facts by which both the public mind and the managers of great business undertakings should be guided." But such a commission was entirely unsatisfactory to the more progressive members of Congress who wanted to destroy all forms of concentration and to use the government to regulate business. The provisions of the Federal Trade Commission Act of September 26, 1914, indicated that Wilson's ideas on government regulation had changed considerably during the months the antitrust program was being debated in Congress. For one thing, Wilson had become less certain that a purely investigatory commission would achieve his purposes. He was dissuaded further from his original plan by his adviser Louis D. Brandeis, whose ideas had influenced his own thinking on economic problems before, notably during the campaign of 1912 and during the period that Congress was framing the Federal Reserve law. Brandeis impressed upon Wilson the need for a commission with broad authority to investigate and prevent "unfair methods of competition," rather than one which attempted to define and enumerate them. The result was that Wilson dropped his earlier idea and endorsed the Brandeis proposal for a powerful Federal Trade Commission, which was supported by the progressives also. The passage of the Federal Trade Commission Act, therefore, marks the beginning of Wilson's move toward the reform ideas and governmental interventionist principles expressed by Theodore Roosevelt in his New Nationalism.[8]

The Federal Trade Commission, superseding Roosevelt's Bureau of Corporations, consisted of five members, appointed for seven-year terms. Its functions were to investigate and publicize the business practices of corporations engaged in interstate commerce (except banks and railroads, which were regulated by the Federal Reserve and the Interstate Commerce Commission, respectively), to hear complaints of unfair methods of competition, and, when necessary, to issue "cease and desist" orders, the corporations having in these cases the right of appeal to the courts.

The Clayton Antitrust Act, signed on October 15, 1914, specified as illegal a number of practices which tended to prevent competition, among them being price discrimination, interlocking directorates in large indus-

[8] Arthur S. Link, *Woodrow Wilson and the Progressive Era, 1910–1917* (New York [1954]), pp. 70–71.

trial corporations which had previously been competitive, and "tying" contracts by which manufacturers prohibited dealers from handling commodities of rival firms. The act also provided methods by which injured persons might obtain redress and—unlike the Sherman Act in its original form—declared the penalties for violation were to be civil and not criminal. Besides the concessions to labor included in Section VI, a provision in Section XX restricted the use of injunctions in labor disputes and declared that strikes, boycotts, and picketing were not contrary to any federal law. Gompers, who had thrown the support of the AFL to Wilson during the presidential campaign and had demanded that these safeguards be included in the bill while it was being framed, now declared that these two sections constituted the "Magna Carta" of labor. They were, however, considerably weakened by the judicial interpretations of the courts after World War I, and throughout the 1920's employers continued to obtain injunctions against numerous union activities.

Under the Sherman Act the Wilson administration in eight years instituted legal proceedings in ninety-two cases, as contrasted with about the same number brought by the Taft administration in only four years. This decrease in trustbusting can be attributed to the weaknesses of the Clayton Act (which, in the words of James A. Reed, Democratic senator from Missouri, had started out as a "raging lion with a mouth full of teeth [and] . . . degenerated [in]to a tabby cat with soft gums, a plaintive mew, and an anaemic appearance" [9]); to the adoption of the rule of reason by the Supreme Court; to the avoidance by corporations of practices that might open them to legal attack; to the fact that many of the chief trusts had already been attacked by Roosevelt and Taft; and to the reluctance of the administration to disturb or frighten industry, especially at a time when the country was suffering from a business decline. This started in the last quarter of 1913 and, with increasingly threatening signs of degenerating into a serious depression, continued until after the outbreak of the European war in 1914. Wilson's willingness to placate the business community and his efforts to earn their confidence were reflected in his first appointments to the Federal Reserve Board and the Federal Trade Commission. Neither of these regulatory bodies included men whose views were unacceptable to bankers or businessmen. Indeed, it was the progressives in Congress and the men who had been most concerned about making these commissions into strong and effective regulatory agencies who were most disappointed with Wilson's appointments.

[9] Quoted in *ibid.*, pp. 72–73.

The process of reform, already impeded by the depression and by Wilson's belief that he had accomplished the Democratic party program of 1912, was checked still further by the outbreak of the European war. Attention now was concentrated on the economic disturbances caused by the war and on the problems of American foreign policy. By August, 1914, it appeared as if the administration had abandoned its progressivism.

FURTHER DOMESTIC REFORM,
1915–1917

The reform legislation enacted during the first session of the Sixty-third Congress fulfilled the major campaign pledges of the Democratic party and the fundamental objectives of Wilson's New Freedom. Both Congress and the President had reason to rejoice over their considerable accomplishments, which Wilson called a "great body of thoughtful and constructive work . . . in loyal response to the thought and needs of the country." But despite the administration's record, the 1914 midterm elections indicated that the voters, concerned with the recession at home and the war in Europe, felt no obligation to reward the Democratic party for its past efforts. While the Democrats were able to hold on to their six-seat majority in the Senate, they lost forty-eight seats in the House of Representatives, so that Democratic control of the lower house now rested in twenty-five votes. The results on the state level were equally disappointing; the Republicans recaptured nine states which had gone Democratic in 1912, including the governorships of New York and Ohio.

Following the congressional elections of 1914, while public attention was centered upon the war in Europe, the disturbances in Mexico, and the preparedness and defense campaigns at home, Wilson's ideas upon the extent and the proper course of the domestic reform program were undergoing profound and significant changes. Between 1914 and 1916 he all but abandoned the economic liberalism and cautious progressivism which had dominated his thinking for so long and had characterized almost all the administration's measures thus far. The first clear indication of his change of attitude came with the La Follette Seamen's Act of March 4, 1915, which regulated the conditions of labor and safety on board ship. Wilson endorsed this measure at a time when he was revising his earlier convictions about government intervention and his previously expressed fears about the dangers of paternalistic legislation. Here was a measure which protected men. His aim heretofore had been only to free them. By November, 1916, when he was campaigning for reelection, the transformation in Wilson's social and economic thought was complete. Not only did the crusader for the New Freedom largely jettison his own formulas for economic democracy, but he accepted those of his chief critic, Theodore Roosevelt. Whether this metamorphosis in Wilson's thought was due primarily to the need for securing the support of the advanced progressives, whose faith in Wilson had been shaken by his reluctance to accept many of their proposals and by the segregationist policies which he permitted in several government departments, as Arthur S. Link suggests,[10] or whether Wilson had realized the need for "social justice" legislation as early as 1912, but had been held back by uncertainty about the extent to which the federal government should sponsor such legislation, as John W. Davidson claims, is not entirely clear.[11] But whatever doubt remains as to the time when Wilson accepted the ideas expressed by the "social justice" and advanced progressive groups, or his reasons for doing so, none exists about his energetic and effective leadership in directing congressional Democrats after 1914 to adopt what Link has called "the most sweeping and significant progressive legislation in the history of the country up to that time."[12]

Wilson's first victory in his new role as an advanced progressive reformer occurred on June 1, 1916, when, after four months of fighting the combined opposition of influential members of the American Bar Association, most business leaders, and conservatives generally, he got the Senate to confirm the appointment of Louis D. Brandeis as an associate justice of the Supreme Court. Wilson's success in this "epic battle" was followed by a series of others. Because there was continued agrarian discontent, which found expression among the nation's organized farmers in various state and regional organizations, such as the Nonpartisan League of North Dakota, and because he was no longer opposed to using federal funds to provide easier credit facilities for farmers, Wilson, on July 17, 1916, signed the Federal Farm Loan Act. Two years earlier, when Congress was considering a similar measure, he said it was "unwise and unjustifiable to extend the credit of Government to a single class of the community."[13] The terms of the Federal Farm Loan Act provided for the very thing he had opposed in 1914. Under its authority twelve Federal Land banks were established, which were to raise money by selling bonds

[10] *Ibid.*, p. 224.
[11] John W. Davidson, ed., *A Crossroads of Freedom: The 1912 Campaign Speeches of Woodrow Wilson* (New Haven, Conn., 1956).
[12] Link, *Wilson and the Progressive Era*, 224–25.
[13] Quoted in *ibid.*, p. 58.

to the public and were to lend it to cooperative farm associations. The latter were to be formed and controlled by farmers and were to make long-term mortgage loans (from 5 to 40 years), at from 5 to 6 per cent, to individual members. By 1930 there were 4,659 such associations, which had loaned to farmers a total of $1.6 billion.

Wilson's new interest in using the authority of the federal government to promote social justice and to improve and safeguard the welfare of the workers resulted in the passage of three significant pieces of legislation, all within a month. On August 19, Congress provided workmen's compensation benefits to federal employees and, with Wilson's help, quickly enacted the Keating-Owen Federal Child Labor Act, which the President signed on September 1, 1916.[14] Two days later, Wilson signed the Adamson Act, which averted a general railroad strike by establishing an eight-hour day without a reduction in wages for the employees of interstate railroads and authorized the President to appoint a three-man commission to observe and study the effects of the Adamson law upon the operations and finances of the lines. Just as significant as his intervention on behalf of the workers is the fact that when Wilson asked Congress to accept the eight-hour day, he defended it as "a thing upon which society is justified in insisting as in the interest of health, efficiency, contentment, and a general increase of economic vigor."

If Wilson's efforts in 1916 to secure federal legislation to aid special groups, such as farmers and workers, violated principles he had enunciated in 1912 and had adhered to during the first two years of his administration, his policy toward some of the business community's efforts to secure the cooperation of the federal government appeared similarly in-

---

[14] The law, prohibiting from interstate commerce commodities produced in violation of its provisions concerning the ages and hours of children, was declared unconstitutional by the Supreme Court on June 3, 1918, in *Hammer v. Dagenhart*. By a 5 to 4 vote, the Court upheld the decision of the Federal District Court of western North Carolina, declaring, among other reasons, that the authority of Congress to regulate interstate commerce could not be used "to control the States in their exercise of the police power over local trade and manufacture." Defeated in its efforts to use the commerce clause to prohibit child labor, the following year the reform element in Congress tried to tax child labor out of existence by attaching a provision to the Revenue Act of February 24, 1919, which imposed a 10 per cent excise tax upon the net profits of anyone employing children under fourteen years of age. In 1922 the Supreme Court in *Bailey v. Drexel Furniture Company* invalidated the child-labor tax law on the ground that, in this instance, the intent of Congress was not to raise revenue but to regulate where it had no authority to do so. Chief Justice Taft concluded the majority opinion by saying that "the so-called tax [in this law] is a penalty to coerce people of a state to act as Congress wishes them to act in respect of a matter completely the business of the state goverenment."

consistent. In January, 1916, he abandoned his long-held opposition to the establishment of a nonpartisan tariff commission, which was supported by various influential groups of businessmen, and urged Congress to authorize such an agency, which it did by including a provision in the revenue act of that year. Designed to investigate the changes occurring in international trade affecting the domestic and foreign marketing of American goods and to recommend policies to safeguard and promote the economic interests of the United States, the commission was created to serve business as well as the government. The Wilson administration also approved other measures similarly aimed to satisfy business, such as an increase in tariff rates to protect certain industries suffering from foreign competition, and supported a bill to permit exporters to form associations and other combinations to secure and protect overseas markets without fear of being prosecuted under the antitrust laws. Such a measure was enacted in April, 1918, when Congress passed the Webb-Pomerene Act.

By the time of the presidential election of 1916, the Wilson administration had accomplished an impressive amount of significant legislation. Not only had it redeemed the major pledges of its own platform, but as Wilson pointed out in September, 1916, it had "opened its heart to comprehend the demands of social justice" with the result that it had "come very near to carrying out the platform of the Progressive Party." In the process of satisfying the progressives while assuring the businessmen that the policies of his administration were "not directed against big business but only against unfair business," Wilson had come very close to accepting the very essence of Roosevelt's New Nationalism. Under his forceful and energetic leadership, the Democratic party legislated most of the common objectives which progressives and liberals had been advocating since the turn of the century. Between 1912 and 1916, Wilson so altered the make-up and orientation of the Democratic party that for the first time in the twentieth century it represented an effective vehicle of national, liberal reform.

FOREIGN POLICY, 1913–1917

The Caribbean

Woodrow Wilson came into office as a convinced opponent of imperialism. He believed that the United States should use its influence and power in the world to promote democracy, justice, law, and peace. The Latin American republics, he claimed, should enjoy complete independence and self-government. In an address at Mobile, Alabama, on October 27, 1913, he declared that "morality and not expediency is the thing that must guide us." "It is a very perilous thing to determine the foreign policy of a nation in the terms of material interest." He added that "the United States will never again seek one additional foot of territory by conquest." Unfortunately, it was easier to preach these idealistic sentiments than to practice them. As a result of considerations of national security, his own belief in the necessity for the United States to expand its economic interests overseas, and pressure from financial interests who expected their government to protect their property and privileges abroad, Wilson found it impossible to abandon the Roosevelt Corollary, and his administration was actually responsible for more interventions than the Roosevelt and Taft administrations combined. Wilson endeavored to reconcile his policies with his ideals by intervening not in the interests of the United States but for the sake of the Latin Americans themselves and in order to promote democratic government and economic progress. Actually, however, the moral imperialism of Wilson differed little from the military and economic imperialism of his predecessors, and it was equally unpopular in Latin America.

The Haitian republic was unable to pay its debts, and in 1915 there were revolutionary disorders. President Vilburn G. Sam massacred 160 of his political opponents and he was then seized by a mob and literally torn limb from limb. American marines thereupon landed on the island in July, 1915, and forced the Haitians to accept a treaty which made the republic virtually a United States protectorate. Haiti was allowed to elect a new president, but the marines stayed to enforce order. While they brought an unprecedented peace and prosperity, they were confronted in 1918 by a peasant rebellion, in the suppression of which more than two thousand Haitians lost their lives.

A similar situation occurred the following year in the Dominican Republic. After a new president, who took power by revolution, refused to obey the Convention of 1905, marines took control of the republic and remained until 1924. During this period the American officials increased Dominican revenues from $700,000 to $4.5 million, reduced the cost of collection from 15 per cent to 5 per cent, and built schools and roads. They also imposed a strict press censorship and meted out justice sternly through naval courts.

Cuba again saw American marines in 1917, when a disputed election resulted in civil war. The marines stayed until 1922, although until 1920 native officials were free to govern the republic. During this period there was a rapid increase in American investments and in the sugar crop, while Cuban officials took advantage of the prosperity of the republic to enrich themselves. In 1920 when the price of sugar fell from 22½ cents a pound to 3¾ cents, the danger of economic collapse caused General Enoch H. Crowder to be sent as financial advisor. Crowder supervised Cuban finances until 1922, when the island resumed full self-government.

Continuing the Roosevelt policy of safeguarding and controlling the approaches to the Panama Canal, the Wilson administration, concerned with Germany's ambitions in the Caribbean, purchased the Virgin Islands from Denmark in 1916, at a price of $25 million.

The Mexican Revolution

The most difficult problems which confronted Wilson in Latin American affairs were those presented by the outbreak of revolution in Mexico. From 1876 until 1910, except for one four-year interlude, Mexico had been governed by Porfirio Díaz. In theory Díaz was merely president of the republic, and his powers were limited by a constitution, but actually he had ruled as a dictator. Díaz had given Mexico a long respite from civil war and revolution and had brought about an enormous economic development. Most of the capital had been supplied by foreign investors, chiefly citizens of the United States, who by 1910 had acquired ownership of mines, oil fields, railroads, public utilities, plantations, and cattle ranches with a total value of perhaps a billion dollars. After 1900 Díaz had become alarmed by the growth of American interests and had given preference, whenever possible, to British financiers, who became owners of a number of oil fields Americans had hoped to acquire.

The bulk of the Mexican people had, however, failed to benefit from Díaz's policies. The peasants had been expropriated for the benefit of a small group of aristocratic *hacendados,* so that by 1910 at least 95 per cent of the rural population owned no land. The working classes, suffering from excessively long hours and low wages, were crushed by government troops if they ventured to strike. All classes of Mexicans were angered and alarmed by the powers and privileges acquired by foreigners. Díaz, moreover, in spite of the fact that in 1910 he was eighty years of age, had refused to provide Mexico with a successor.

In November, 1910, there began an insurrection against Díaz, which was headed by Francisco Madero, an idealistic liberal of a wealthy family, who hoped to make constitutional government a reality. American financial interests, irritated by Díaz's pro-British policy, were sympathetic to Madero, and the United States government allowed him for several months to use Texas as his base of operations. In May, 1911, Díaz was overthrown and Madero became president. American businessmen, however, quickly began to oppose Madero, partly because he began to restrict the privileges enjoyed by foreign capitalists and partly because the Mexican workers and peasants were allowed to organize and demand reforms. The United States minister in Mexico, Henry Lane Wilson, became a fanatical enemy of Madero, telling the State Department that Mexico was in a state of anarchy. In February, 1913, Madero was overthrown by a group of reactionary generals, headed by Victoriano Huerta, and was subsequently murdered. Minister Wilson had been informed in advance of Huerta's plans; and when Huerta seized power, he hailed him publicly as "the savior of Mexico" and urged that the new government at once be officially recognized. Wilson also refused to intercede with Huerta to spare Madero's life.

Huerta's government was tyrannical and corrupt. He was, however, quickly recognized by the European powers, and following Díaz's later policy of giving preference to British interests, he was on friendly terms with the British minister in Mexico. Meanwhile movements to avenge Madero and restore constitutional government had been initiated in several parts of the country. In the north these movements were led by Venustiano Carranza and Pancho Villa, and in the south by Emiliano Zapata. Thus, when President Wilson assumed office Mexico was in a state of civil war.

Considerations both of economic interest and of morality caused the United States to be hostile to Huerta. Wilson proposed, however, to allow the Mexican people to settle their own affairs without interference; furthermore, he realized that they could never achieve permanent peace without fundamental changes in their economic system. He refused to recognize Huerta, whom he regarded as a "desperate brute" who had seized power illegally and did not represent the will of the people. To emphasize his displeasure with him, he recalled Henry Lane Wilson from the American embassy in Mexico and imposed an embargo on shipments of munitions. In the summer he sent John Lind, former governor of Minnesota, to Mexico as his personal representative; Lind endeavored, without success, to persuade Huerta to resign and allow a free election to determine his successor. The danger of a clash with Great Britain over Mexican affairs was averted by negotiation. In return for repeal of the law exempting American coastal ships using the Panama Canal from paying tolls and assurance that the United States would watch over its interests in Mexico, the British Foreign Office, unwilling to alienate the United States, agreed to give no support to Huerta and to follow President Wilson's lead.

Wilson's policy of "watchful waiting" proved increasingly irksome to American businessmen, who wanted peace and stability in Mexico and demanded that the United States government intervene to end the civil war. Meanwhile Wilson's decision "to teach the South American republics to elect good men" aroused considerable criticism at home and abroad. Wilson was therefore unable to leave Mexico to work out its own salvation. Actually, Wilson's pressure against Huerta, regardless of its laudable motives, was intervention. In February, 1914, the arms embargo was lifted for the benefit of the constitutionalists. But because Huerta was not overthrown so quickly as Wilson had hoped, Wilson then adopted more forceful measures. When some American marines who had landed at Tampico were placed under temporary arrest by one of Huerta's generals, the American admiral demanded that, by way of apology, the American flag be saluted; and when Huerta refused, Wilson decided to resort to force. Informed that a German ship was on its way to Vera Cruz with munitions for Huerta, Wilson ordered the American fleet to seize the town. On April 21 American marines occupied Vera Cruz, an episode which cost the lives of eighteen Americans and nearly two hundred Mexicans. This act was denounced by the constitutionalists, whom Wilson was trying to help, as vigorously as by Huerta. The Vera Cruz incident produced an impasse from which war seemed to be the only solution, until Argentina, Brazil, and Chile offered to mediate, thus providing Wilson with an opportunity to resolve the difficulty without abandoning national honor or going to war to defend it. After a month of conferences at Niagara Falls, which actually settled nothing, military events in Mexico forced Huerta into exile on July 15 and Carranza was installed as provisional president. On November 23, 1914, the marines were withdrawn from Vera Cruz, and Wilson could hope that peace was returning to Mexico.

Unfortunately the different constitutionalist factions now proceeded to fight one another. Villa and Zapata refused to accept the leadership of Carranza; and it was not until the end of 1915 that Carranza's victory was assured. Wilson recognized Carranza as *de facto* president and prohibited the sale of American munitions to Villa. Carranza, however, showed little consideration for the rights and interests of Americans in Mexico and strongly resented Wilson's suggestions that he make some return for the support the United States was giving him. Moreover, Villa, regarding the United States as primarily responsible for Carranza's victory, proceeded to exact vengeance, after he had been defeated by Carranza's generals. On January 10, 1916, a band of Villistas killed sixteen American citizens at Santa Ysabel, in northern Mexico; and on March 9 they raided the town of Columbus, New Mexico, and killed sixteen more Americans. Wilson ordered American militia to guard the border and sent General John J. Pershing with sixteen thousand troops into Mexico to capture Villa. Villa succeeded in evading his pursuers, while Carranza, though reluctantly consenting to the Pershing expedition, expressed great resentment. Numerous incidents and border clashes, in which both Mexicans and Americans lost their lives, appeared to be bringing the two countries to the brink of open war; and there were numerous demands in the United States for occupation of the entire country. The danger was, however, averted by the approach of the American entry into the war in Europe. Pershing left Mexico in February, 1917, without having captured Villa, and the following month the United States granted *de jure* recognition to the constitutionalist Carranza government.

Early in 1917 Mexico adopted a new constitution, under which the rights of aliens to own land were restricted and the subsoil was declared to be the inalienable property of the nation. Although these provisions were not put into force, they represented a threat to Americans who owned estates and oil fields in Mexico. Carranza, moreover, had failed to restore order, and large parts of the country were virtually in a state of anarchy. American oil interests organized an Association for the Protection of American Rights in Mexico; and Senator Albert B. Fall of New Mexico, a close friend of the oil magnate Edward L. Doheny, took the lead in demanding intervention. In the autumn of 1919, when an American consular officer at Puebla was seized by bandits, Secretary of State Lansing sent vigorous protests, and war again seemed imminent. Wilson was in virtual retirement as a result of his physical collapse during the League of Nations controversy; but he emerged to silence Lansing and work for peace, and after the consular officer had been released, the crisis ended. In the following spring Carranza was overthrown by forces headed by General Álvaro Obregón, whose new regime had considerable success in restoring order and appeared to be more friendly to American interests.

Wilson's sympathy with the plight of the Mexican people was sincere and his intention "to serve them" unselfishly was laudable. But because he failed to understand that the Mexicans resented being told what kind of government was best for them, because he neither appreciated nor took the trouble to learn the nature and complexities of the Mexican problem, and because he was almost exclusively preoccupied with the morality and justice rather than with the mechanics and reality of his foreign policy, Wilson's Mexican diplomacy resulted in the very kind of intervention which he deplored most and for which he had censured previous administrations. Many of the same qualities which characterized Wilson's Mexican policy are apparent also in his handling of Far Eastern problems.

The Far East

Wilson's first step in revising Taft's efforts at "dollar diplomacy" in the Far East was his announcement on March 19, 1913, that the United States government would no longer support the Six-power Consortium. Wilson's decision was based upon several considerations: the desire of the American bankers themselves to get out of the consortium, as well as Wilson's antiimperialism and his belief that there was "some better way" in which the United States could serve democracy and progress in China. His decision earned the United States the gratitude of China. Yet in the final outcome this "morally faultless" action only served to whet the appetite and strengthen the ambitions of Japan—the one nation whose intentions in the Far East were most inimical to the interests of the United States. By failing to take into account the internal weakness of China and the political and military realities of the Far East, the decision to withdraw the United States from the consortium facilitated Japan's expansionist program, and thus undermined the very principles which Wilson had tried to serve.

During World War I Japan took advantage of the preoccupations of the European powers to enlarge its holdings in the Chinese empire. The Wilson administration continued to support the Open Door, and in the hope of checking Japanese expansion it finally returned to the Taft-Knox policy Wilson had repudiated. Relations between Japan and the United

States suffered also as a result of laws, enacted after 1913 by a number of state governments, notably California, which prohibited Japanese from acquiring ownership of land. This policy of racial discrimination caused constant resentment in Japan and seriously embittered relations between the two countries, but under the American federal system the United States government had no power to prevent it.

On August 23, 1914, Japan, as the ally of Great Britain, declared war on Germany and proceeded to seize the German possessions in the Far East, including a number of islands (the Marshalls, Marianas, and Carolines) and certain economic and political rights in the Shantung peninsula, which was legally a part of China. Great Britain and France, fighting for survival in Europe and concerned lest Japan quit the war, were compelled to accept this growth of Japanese imperialism, and in secret treaties signed in 1916 and 1917 formally recognized Japan's claims to Germany's Far Eastern and Pacific possessions. In January, 1915, Japan took further advantage of the war by presenting China with her Twenty-one Demands. Japan wanted complete control of Manchuria and Shantung and far-reaching rights in the remainder of China. The United States, while acknowledging Japan's new position in the Shantung peninsula and recognizing its growing influence in southern Manchuria, protested against the demands in Article V, which called for military, administrative, political, and economic concessions that would have impaired Chinese independence. In May, Bryan advised the Japanese that the United States "cannot recognize any agreement or understanding which has been entered into or which may be entered into between the Governments of Japan and China, impairing the treaty rights of the United States and its citizens in China, the political or territorial integrity of the Republic of China, or the international policy relative to China commonly known as the open door policy." The United States, however, was in no position to check Japan.

In November, 1917, after the United States and Japan had technically become associates in the war with Germany, the Japanese diplomat Kikujiiro Ishii visited Washington; and by the Ishii-Lansing Agreement of November 2, 1917, the Open Door and the territorial integrity of China were—on paper—reaffirmed; but Japan's special interests in Manchuria and Shantung were admitted in suitably vague terms, since there was little else that could be done at the time without threatening seriously Japan's continued participation in the war against Germany. As soon as possible, however, the Wilson administration took more forceful measures to check Japanese expansion. In 1918 Wilson insisted that American bankers participate with Britain, France, and Japan in a new loan to the Chinese government, and in the same year the United States sent troops to Siberia. The latter move, while designed for other purposes, also served to keep Washington informed of Japanese activities in Siberia and Manchuria.

Suggested Readings

One of the most useful and convenient guides to the many books and articles on Wilson that have been published since 1947 is the excellent article by Richard L. Watson, Jr., "Woodrow Wilson and His Interpreters, 1947–1957," *Mississippi Valley Historical Review*, XLIV (September 1957), 207–36. See also Laura S. Turnbull, comp., *Woodrow Wilson: A Selected Bibliography* (Princeton, N.J., 1948) for references to Wilson's published writings.

Until the forthcoming comprehensive publication of the Wilson papers, the first volume of which is to appear in 1965, Ray Stannard Baker and William E. Dodd, eds., *The Public Papers of Woodrow Wilson* (6 vols., New York, 1925–27) remain the most useful collection. There are several short and useful editions of Wilson's writings, such as Donald Day, ed., *Woodrow Wilson's Own Story* (Boston, 1952); August Heckscher, ed., *The Politics of Woodrow Wilson: Selections from his Speeches and Writings* (New York, 1956); and John Welles Davidson, ed., *A Crossroads of Freedom* (New Haven, Conn., 1956), an annotated and more complete edition of Wilson's 1912 campaign speeches, which can be consulted with profit. The student should refer also to Charles E. Seymour, ed., *The Intimate Papers of Colonel House* (4 vols., Boston, 1926–28).

Among the numerous biographies of Woodrow Wilson, the old, detailed, and friendly one by Ray Stannard Baker, *Woodrow Wilson: Life and Letters* (8 vols., Garden City, N.Y., 1927–39), is still helpful. The first three volumes of Arthur S. Link's multivolumed biography, *Wilson: The Road to the White House* (Princeton, N.J., 1947), *Wilson: The New Freedom* (Princeton, N.J., 1956), and *Wilson: The Struggle for Neutrality, 1914–1915* (Princeton, N.J., 1960) cover the years through 1915. The most recent comprehensive biography is Arthur Walworth, *Woodrow Wilson* (2 vols., New York, 1958). Among the shorter, one-volume studies see Silas Bent McKinley, *Woodrow Wilson: A Biography* (New York, 1958); John M. Blum, *Woodrow Wilson and the Politics of Morality* (Boston [1956]), an especially perceptive interpretation; Herbert C. F. Bell, *Woodrow Wilson and the People* (Garden City, N.Y., 1945); and John A. Garraty, *Woodrow Wilson* (New York, 1956). Older and useful as indications of contemporary thought are William E. Dodd, *Woodrow Wilson and His Work* (rev. ed., New York, 1924); David Lawrence, *The True Story of Woodrow Wilson* (New York, 1924); William A. White,

Woodrow Wilson (Boston, 1924); and the quite critical account by Robert E. Annin, *Woodrow Wilson: A Character Study* (New York, 1924).

Wilson has been the subject of several efforts to explain his career in psychological terms. See, for example, Alexander L. George and Juliette L. George, *Woodrow Wilson and Colonel House: A Personality Study* (New York, 1956).

Biographies and studies of intimate members of the Wilson administration include Arthur D. H. Smith, *Mr. House of Texas* (New York, 1940) and George S. Viereck, *The Strangest Friendship in History* (New York, 1932). For Brandeis' influence, see the excellent biography by Alpheus T. Mason, *Brandeis: A Free Man's Life* (New York, 1946), and, on Tumulty, the equally good study by John M. Blum, *Joe Tumulty and the Wilson Era* (Boston, 1951). On Harvey's influence, see Willis F. Johnson, *George Harvey, "A Passionate Patriot"* (Boston, 1929). Many of the biographies and studies of important contemporary figures mentioned previously are also useful for the Wilson era, such as those on Roosevelt, Taft, Root, Hughes, and Bryan.

Memoirs were written by almost everyone associated with Wilson. The following are among some of the more important ones: William G. McAdoo, *Crowded Years* (Boston, 1931) for the years to 1917; Carter Glass, *An Adventure in Constructive Finance* (Garden City, N.Y., 1927) on the framing of the Federal Reserve law; David F. Houston, *Eight Years with Wilson's Cabinet* (2 vols., Garden City, N.Y., 1926); Joseph P. Tumulty, *Woodrow Wilson as I knew Him* (Garden City, N.Y., 1921) must be used cautiously; William F. McCombs, *Making Woodrow Wilson President* (New York, 1921), the bitter account of an influential Democratic boss who lost Wilson's confidence; Josephus Daniels, *The Wilson Era: Years of Peace, 1910–1917* (2 vols., Chapel Hill, N.C., 1944–46); William C. Redfield, *With Congress and Cabinet* (Garden City, N.Y., 1924) is not especially revealing; Edith B. Wilson, *My Memoir* (New York, 1938); and Thomas R. Marshall, *Recollections of Thomas R. Marshall* (Indianapolis, 1925) is no more than adequate. Many of the memoirs and autobiographies of contemporary figures cited previously are also useful, such as those of Bryan and Champ Clark.

There are several collections of essays covering various aspects of Wilson's career which the student should consult, such as Em Bowles Alsop, ed., *The Greatness of Woodrow Wilson, 1856–1956* (New York [1956]); Earl Latham, ed., *The Philosophy and Policies of Woodrow Wilson* (Chicago, 1958); and Arthur P. Dudden, ed., *Woodrow Wilson and the World of Today* (Philadelphia [1957]).

The best and most recent general account of the Wilson administration is Arthur S. Link, *Woodrow Wilson and the Progressive Era, 1910–1917* (New York [1954]). Older but still excellent for its detail is Frederic L. Paxson, *Pre-War Years, 1913–1917* (Boston, 1936), the first of three volumes entitled, *American Democracy and the World War*. See also Volume IV of Mark Sullivan's *Our Times* (6 vols., New York, 1926–35). A revealing "estimate of how Americans looked to themselves in 1913" is Alan Valentine, *1913: America between Two Worlds* (New York, 1962). The intellectual challenge of the times is appraised in Henry F. May, *The End of American Innocence: A Study of the First Years of Our Own Time, 1912–1917* (New York, 1959). A brief summary of the Wilson years is to be found in the first three chapters of William E. Leuchtenburg, *The Perils of Prosperity, 1914–1932* (Chicago [1958]).

Detailed studies of various aspects of Wilson's career include McMillan Lewis, *Woodrow Wilson of Princeton* (Narberth, Pa., 1952) and Hardin Craig, *Woodrow Wilson at Princeton* (Norman, Okla., 1960), which appraise Wilson's academic career; James Kerney, *The Political Education of Woodrow Wilson* (New York [1926]); and William Diamond, *The Economic Thought of Woodrow Wilson* (Baltimore, Md., 1943), which emphasizes the years before he became President.

On the tariff see Frank W. Taussig, *Some Aspects of the Tariff Question* (Cambridge, Mass., 1915) and other works cited in Chapter 6, such as Ida M. Tarbell, *The Tariff in Our Times* (New York, 1911).

There are many works on the Federal Reserve System from which to choose, but among the most useful are J. Lawrence Laughlin, *The Federal Reserve Act: Its Origins and Problems* (New York, 1933); H. Parker Willis, *The Federal Reserve System* (New York, 1923); Robert L. Owen, *The Federal Reserve Act* (New York, 1919) is important on the history of the act's origins and enactment; Paul M. Warburg, *The Federal Reserve System: Its Origin and Growth* (2 vols., New York, 1930) and, by the same author, *Essays on Banking Reform in the United States* (New York, 1914). See also Carter Glass, *An Adventure in Constructive Finance*, cited already. A convenient guide is Edwin and Donald L. Kemmerer, *The A.B.C. of the Federal Reserve System* (12th rev. ed., [1950]). Summaries of the purposes and operations of the system can be found in the standard financial histories, such as Davis R. Dewey, *Financial History of the United States* (12th ed., New York, 1934), and in Board of Governors of the Federal Reserve System, *The Federal Reserve System: Purposes and Functions* (3d ed., Washington, D.C., 1954). The best study of the history of the Federal Reserve to 1933 is Seymour E. Harris, *Twenty Years of Federal Reserve Policy* (2 vols., Cambridge, Mass., 1933). This should be supplemented now by Lester V. Chandler, *Benjamin Strong, Central Banker* (Washington, D.C. [1958]), the story of the first governor of the Federal Reserve Bank of New York, and, until his death in 1928, probably "the greatest influence on American monetary and banking policies."

The background of the trust problem is treated generally in Eliot Jones, *The Trust Problem* (New York, 1921); William Z. Ripley, ed., *Trusts, Pools, and Corporations* (rev. ed., Boston, 1916); Henry R. Seager and Charles A. Gulick, Jr., *Trusts and Corporation Problems* (New York, 1929); and John D. Clark, *The Federal Trust Policy* (Baltimore, 1931). Wilson's efforts on regulating the trusts is discussed in Oswald W. Knauth, *The Policy of the United States towards Industrial Monopoly* (New York, 1914). On the Federal Trade Commission, see Gerard C. Henderson, *The Federal Trade Commission*

(New Haven, Conn., 1924) and Thomas C. Blaisdell, *The Federal Trade Commission* (New York, 1932).

Efforts to extend rural credits to farmers are discussed in Clara Eliot, *The Farmer's Campaign for Credit* (New York, 1927); Earl S. Sparks, *History and Theory of Agricultural Credit in the United States* (New York [1932]); James B. Morman, *The Principles of Rural Credits* (New York, 1915); and Edna D. Bullock, *Agricultural Credit* (New York, 1915).

The struggle over a federal child labor law is discussed briefly in all of the standard labor histories mentioned previously and in greater detail in Miriam E. Loughran, *The Historical Development of Child-Labor Legislation in the United States* (Washington, D.C., 1921). More specialized is Elizabeth H. Davidson, *Child Labor Legislation in the Southern Textile States* (Chapel Hill, N.C., 1939).

Harley Notter, *The Origins of the Foreign Policy of Woodrow Wilson* (Baltimore, 1937) is a useful monograph which should be supplemented with Arthur S. Link, *Wilson the Diplomatist: A Look at His Major Foreign Policies* (Baltimore, 1957), a perceptive "analysis and interpretation." See also Edward H. Buehrig, *Woodrow Wilson and the Balance of Power* (Bloomington, Ind., 1955), which is primarily concerned with the European phases of Wilsonian diplomacy.

The Caribbean and Latin American policy of the Wilson administration is discussed in the standard general works cited previously, such as Samuel F. Bemis, *The Latin American Policy of the United States* (New York, 1943) and Dexter Perkins, *The United States and the Caribbean* (Cambridge, Mass., 1947).

For specialized works on the Caribbean, see the works cited in Chapter 5 as well as Arthur C. Millspaugh, *Haiti under American Control, 1915–1930* (Boston, 1931) and Charles C. Tansill, *The Purchase of the Danish West Indies* (Baltimore, 1932).

On the internal background of the Mexican crisis, Ernest H. Gruening, *Mexico and Its Heritage* (New York, 1928); Frank Tannenbaum, *Peace by Revolution* (New York, 1929); and Robert E. Quirk, *The Mexican Revolution, 1914–1915* (Bloomington, Ind., 1960) are all useful. The most recent account of the American intervention is Howard F. Cline, *The United States and Mexico* (Cambridge, Mass., 1953), which in many ways supersedes the older study by J. Fred Rippy, *The United States and Mexico* (New York, 1931). See also Chapters XIII and XIV in James M. Callahan, *American Foreign Policy in Mexican Relations* (New York, 1932), and Charles W. Hackett, *The Mexican Revolution and the United States, 1910–1926* (Boston [1926]). George M. Stephenson, *John Lind of Minnesota* (Minneapolis, 1935) is revealing on Wilson and Huerta; and Clarence C. Clenden, *The United States and Pancho Villa: A Study in Unconventional Diplomacy* (Ithaca, N.Y., 1961) is a detailed analysis of this subject.

The Far Eastern policy of the United States is treated generally in the surveys mentioned previously, such as A. Whitney Griswold, *The Far Eastern Policy of the United States* (New Haven, Conn., 1938); and briefly in John K.

Fairbanks, *The United States and China* (Cambridge, Mass., 1948); and similarly for Japan in Edwin O. Reischauer, *The United States and Japan* (Cambridge, Mass., 1950). Roy W. Curry, *Woodrow Wilson and Far Eastern Policy, 1913–1921* (New York, 1957) is a carefully researched, detailed study of the period.

More specialized accounts include Toyokichi Iyenaga and Kenoske Sato, *Japan and the California Problem* (New York, 1921) and Yamato Ichihashi, *Japanese in the United States* (Stanford, Calif., 1932). The Chinese crisis is treated superbly by Tien-yi Li, *Woodrow Wilson's China Policy, 1913–1917* (New York, 1952), and the documentation of the Japanese negotiations of 1915 is published in Carnegie Endowment for International Peace, *The Sino-Japanese Negotiations of 1915* (Washington, D.C., 1921).

PART **II** THE ERA OF

WORLD WAR I

1914–1921

8

From Neutrality to

Belligerency, 1914-1917

THE OUTBREAK OF WAR

World War I, which interrupted the progressive movement, dislocated the American economic system, and drew the United States out of its traditional noninterventionist policy vis-à-vis European political affairs, was the result of the historic rivalries and competing ambitions of various European peoples and nations. The emergence and development of a strong, unified Germany after 1871 aggravated these old conflicts and created new ones, most notably the threat posed by Germany's ascendancy upon the continental position of the other European states and the world balance of power. In addition to these larger causes, the confusion, dilemmas, and miscalculations which dogged the principal European chancellories during the Serbian crisis of June and July, 1914, also contributed materially to the outbreak of war in that they prevented the principal statesmen, despite the honest efforts of nearly all of them, from finding the kind of acceptable solution they had previously employed to resolve even more serious incidents without recourse to armed force. Regarding all these questions, however, most Americans were at first unaware, or indifferent, or certain that they were of no concern to them.

Europe in 1914 was divided into six great powers and a number of smaller states. The major nations were all competing with one another for position, recognition, and prestige, as well as for the control of colonial and other underdeveloped areas where they could obtain raw materials, invest capital, and find profitable markets for their surplus products. All of them, moreover, maintained large armies or navies; they feared or suspected one another; and each of them, afraid lest it be crushed by a combination of forces or by more powerful rivals, subscribed to the principle *si vis pacem para bellum*. Under such conditions the sentiment of nationality, among both the independent peoples and the minority groups who did not enjoy self-government, had developed into an explosive passion capable of destroying tolerance and rationality.

Of the various international rivalries, two were of special importance: that of Russia against Austria, and that of Germany against Great Britain and France. Austria and Russia, the former of which included a number of discontented minority groups, had for a long period been competing with each other for influence over the Slavic peoples in the Balkan peninsula. Meanwhile Germany, having defeated France in the Franco-Prussian War of 1870–71, had developed into the strongest military and industrial power in Europe. The Kaiser's government was eager that Germany should acquire the position which its strength and continental status warranted, and it resented Great Britain's traditional naval and commercial supremacy. The British and the French, having reconciled the many colonial disputes which had kept them apart for so many years, were drawn closer together by their growing concern with German power and by their unwillingness to allow it to become strong enough to threaten further their own status and interests in Europe and the rest of the world.

Late in the nineteenth and early in the twentieth centuries the European powers had become grouped into two increasingly hostile and approximately equal combinations—a situation which always increases the danger of war. Russia had allied itself with France in 1894. Then Great Britain, faithful to its traditional policy of preventing any one power from becoming strong enough to dominate the continent, formed an entente with the Franco-Russian combination and supported the French in several disputes with Germany. In opposition to this triple entente of the Allies was the more formal alliance of the Central Powers—Germany, Austria, and Italy—first formed in 1882. Italy's loyalty to the alliance was, however, very dubious, so that Austria, despite serious internal troubles, was Germany's most reliable friend, a fact which strengthened Vienna's ambitions and augmented Berlin's anxieties.

On June 28, 1914, Franz Ferdinand, the heir to the Austro-Hungarian throne, was murdered at Sarajevo by Gavril Princip, a nineteen-year-old student, who aspired to lead the liberation of the Slavic peoples from Austrian rule. Claiming that the activities of the Slav nationalists were being encouraged by officials of the Serbian government, the Austrian foreign minister, after having received reassurances from the Kaiser that Germany would "faithfully stand by Austria-Hungary," prepared to use the incident to fulfill one of Vienna's long-time objectives—the destruction of Serbian influence in the Balkans. On July 23, Austria presented Serbia with a stiff ultimatum. The Serbs, assured of Russia's support, accepted some of the Austrian demands, but others, which they regarded as incompatible with their independence, they courteously rejected, offering to submit them for arbitration either to the international court at The Hague or to a conference of the major European powers. Dissatisfied with this reply, on July 28 Austria declared war on Serbia. The next day Russia came to Serbia's support by ordering partial mobilization against Austria. This decision, however, was strongly contested by the Tsar's war chiefs and other advisers who, for various military and diplomatic reasons, persuaded him to replace it with one calling for general mobilization, which the Tsar announced on July 31.

The reaction of the German government to these events was divided, confused, and hesitant. Realizing more fully than previously the serious consequences of the Kaiser's earlier pledge to support Austria, some of the civilian members of the government still hoped it would be possible to limit the Austro-Serbian war to the Balkans; but while these officials welcomed Britain's efforts at trying to find a peaceful solution acceptable to both the Serbs and the Austrians, their ability and willingness to influence the course of events were now seriously limited by Germany's commitment to Austria, which neither government officials nor anyone else in the country was willing to abandon, and, even more important, by the military threat posed by Russia's mobilization. The latter was of special concern to Germany's army leaders, since their war plans, based on the idea of all-out war and not taking into account a contingency such as this, called for a quick and decisive victory over France before Russia was ready. Thus, when Russia announced its general mobilization order on July 31, Germany, according to its military leaders, must either attack France without delay or—unless war were averted—face a conflict on two fronts and probable defeat. Rather than gamble on the chances of peace, the high command of the German army insisted upon immediate action. The same day that Germany learned of the Tsar's proclamation of general mobilization, Berlin sent an ultimatum to Moscow, demanding that Russia cease all war preparations; and it sent another to Paris, calling upon France to declare its attitude should Germany find itself at war with Russia. The Tsar's government ignored the German ultimatum, and on August 1, after ordering its own forces mobilized, Germany declared war on Russia. That same day, France mobilized and replied to Berlin's ultimatum by declaring that French policy would be guided by the nation's interests. Two days later, on August 3, Germany declared war on France; and when Belgium denied the German armies "free passage" through its territory, the Kaiser's troops proceeded to violate that country's neutrality.

Meanwhile, on August 2, Great Britain, having sought and failed to prevent the crisis from precipitating a general war, promised France to protect its coast against a German naval attack. British public opinion, however, was still not convinced of the necessity of Britain's participation in the war. These doubts were ended by the German invasion of Belgium; and on August 4, Great Britain declared war on Germany. Britain's participation, really necessitated by the threat Germany's growing power posed to its security and interests, appeared to the British people as due also to a desire to protect the rights of small nations and the sanctity of international law. For British public opinion, therefore, the war became an idealistic crusade.

Subsequently a number of other nations, swayed by the hope of territorial gains, entered the war. Turkey and Bulgaria became allies of Germany. Japan, Italy, Rumania, and Greece, whose nationalistic and imperialistic ambitions could best be satisfied at the expense of the Central Powers, joined Great Britain, France, and Russia.

The war took most Americans by complete surprise, and the belief that the United States should and could remain neutral was, at first, almost universal. Even Theodore Roosevelt, who was soon to urge American participation on the side of the Allies, declared in September that he was in favor of neutrality. Wilson issued a neutrality proclamation on August 4, and two weeks later he urged Americans to remain "impartial in thought as well as in action." In his message to Congress in December, he referred to the European conflict as "a war with which we have nothing to do, whose causes cannot touch us." Wilson was no advocate of isolation; on the contrary, he believed that the United States could serve its own and humanity's best interests only by preserving its neutrality and thus making it possible for him to act as an impartial mediator in bringing both sides together in a just and enduring peace.

Initial Sympathies

On August 19, Wilson asked the American people to "act and speak in the true spirit of neutrality" so that the United States could fulfill its "duty as the one great nation at peace, the one people holding itself ready to play a part of impartial mediation and speak the counsels of peace and accommodation, not as a partisan, but as a friend." For various reasons, many Americans found it very difficult to adopt and adhere to such an attitude. As soon as the war broke out, the sympathies of most Americans, like those of the President himself, were on the side of Britain and France.

The initial sympathy toward these two countries was furthered by the fact that although the British-Americans residing in the United States composed less than half the total population, they outweighed all other groups in their economic and political influence. Moreover, most Americans, whatever their descent, were predisposed to sympathize with Great Britain because of ties of language and literature, of common political and legal traditions, and because of the defensive and basically pacific nature of British policy, at least in the recent past. On all major questions and at all times except when its own security was threatened, Britain respected international law and the rights of other nations. Furthermore, the United States had generally found it easy to cooperate with Great Britain; and a growing number of Americans had come to realize that the maintenance of the Monroe Doctrine had always depended on the control of the Atlantic by the British navy. France too enjoyed the strong sympathy of many Americans, because of both their admiration for its civilization and its role in the Revolutionary War.

On the other hand, the ambitious commercial designs and aggressive methods of German diplomacy and the bellicose utterances of the German Kaiser had offended and alarmed large segments of American opinion ever since the beginning of the century. Moreover, the actions of the German and Austrian governments during the crisis, their declarations of war against Russia and France, and the violation of Belgium's neutrality all seemed to confirm the suspicions of many Americans that the

Central Powers were responsible for the outbreak of hostilities and that they had little respect for treaty obligations and neutral rights. A few sophisticated observers also believed that if Germany succeeded in destroying British naval supremacy, the Kaiser's aggressive and expansive ambitions would pose a serious threat to the security of the United States, the American system of democratic government, and the independence of the Western Hemisphere. The United States, they argued, would then be compelled, in self-defense, to become a militaristic nation. Despite the sincerity and impressive size of this pro-Allied sentiment and the fact that it was expressed by many different groups and for different reasons, almost all these pro-British and pro-French partisans, nevertheless, supported Wilson's neutrality policies; and before 1917 only a very few of them called for America's intervention.[1]

In comparison with the varying intensity of this widespread, though widely dispersed, pro-Allied sentiment, the number of Americans who supported the cause of the Central Powers was considerably smaller. But whatever disadvantages the friends of Germany and the Dual Monarchy may have suffered from lack of numbers, they compensated for by their singleness of purpose and by the energy and stridency with which they expressed it. Americans of German and Irish descent were frequently inclined to sympathize with the Central Powers, and they were generally opposed to any measures which they believed to be of assistance to the Allies. In addition to these two groups, from which the largest number of pro-Germans were recruited, many American Jews were strongly sympathetic to Germany either because of their German or Austrian origin or because of their deep resentment against Russia's anti-Semitic policies. Jacob Schiff, for example, the head of the powerful investment banking firm of Kuhn, Loeb & Company and a leading spokesman of American Jewry, refused to participate in the $500 million Anglo-French loan of September, 1915, because neither Britain nor France would guarantee that none of the proceeds would be used to assist Russia. Dislike for Tsarist Russia also explained the considerable pro-German sentiment existing among the Swedish-Americans.

Belligerent Agencies

The initial advantage enjoyed by the Allies was ably cultivated by the British government; but even though the British controlled the Atlantic

[1] Arthur S. Link, *Wilson: The Struggle for Neutrality, 1914–1915* (Princeton, N.J., 1960), pp. 17–18.

cables and censored all mail between Germany and America, they were unable to prevent or effectively limit the Germans from stating their case to the American people. The British propaganda campaign was placed in charge of Sir Gilbert Parker; and under his direction well-known British writers made lecture tours in the United States, a weekly news-sheet presenting the British case was distributed to American newspapers, American libraries and clubs were supplied with British books and documents, and prominent Americans in every profession received letters from individual Englishmen. British efforts to publicize the atrocities allegedly committed by the German army in Belgium attracted considerable attention at first, especially since the British committee which gathered the evidence against the Germans was headed by Viscount James Bryce, a long-time student of American government and a former British ambassador in Washington. Despite the stir caused by this report and other atrocity stories, some of which were not wholly honest, their influence on American opinion was of minor importance, except to strengthen further the convictions of pro-Allied partisans. British propaganda certainly did not cause the American people to abandon their neutral status or antiwar feelings, much less drive them into the conflict.

The German government also subsidized several propaganda agencies in the United States, spending a total of some $35 million during the period of American neutrality. German money was spent to buy or establish newspapers in the United States, particularly *The Fatherland*, which was edited by George Sylvester Viereck. Such money was also contributed to various pro-German and pacifist organizations and committees in an effort to moderate popular sympathy for Britain and France and, with far more success, to feed the anti-Russian prejudices of many Americans. Considering the intrinsic weakness of the German case—the fact that Germany had initiated the war in western Europe, that its armies had invaded Belgium and were fighting on foreign soil, and that German statesmen sometimes spoke about treaties and rules of international law with a most injudicious cynicism—the Kaiser's agents in the United States displayed a remarkable skill in trying to persuade the American people that Germany was fighting in self-defense and that the war was "a struggle between western culture and Slavic barbarism." [2]

After the United States had developed into a vital source of supply for Allied war needs, German agents began to meddle in American internal affairs; worst of all, they committed the error of being found out. Public disclosure of these subversive activities occurred in the summer of 1915,

[2] Link, *op. cit.*, p. 41.

just after the *Lusitania* crisis, causing intense and widespread popular indignation against Germany. As early as May, 1915, the United States Secret Service began investigating the activities of German agents; and on July 24, a secret service officer succeeded in picking up a brief case belonging to Dr. Heinrich Albert, an official of the German embassy, which had been left by its owner on the Sixth Avenue elevated railroad in New York City. From the contents of the brief case, which were turned over by the government for publication in the New York *World*, it was discovered not only that the German government was spending large sums on propaganda but also that its agents were interested in promoting strikes and organizing sabotage in American munitions factories.

In August the British intercepted letters the Austrian ambassador Constantin Dumba had sent to Vienna, from which it appeared that the Austrian government also was encouraging strikes. Dumba's recall was requested in September; and in December the German military and naval attachés, Franz Von Papen and Karl Boy-Ed, were asked to leave because they had tried to buy American supply ships for the use of German raiders. These revelations caused widespread alarm, and many people began to think the United States was honeycombed with German secret service agents. Two serious fires in munitions plants, the Black Tom fire of July, 1916, and the Kingsland fire of January, 1917, were generally attributed to German agents.

German activities, moreover, not only provoked public antagonism against Germany; they also succeeded in weakening the pacifist movement. In addition to two avowedly anti-Ally groups—the National German-American Alliance and the American Truth Society (an Irish organization)—and Labor's National Peace Council, a German-sponsored organization, there also came into existence a number of committees for the preservation of American neutrality, such as the Friends of Peace, supported by William Jennings Bryan. Pro-Germans, however, promptly joined this and other similar organizations and provided them with money, thereby creating in the public mind a conviction that pro-Germanism and pacifism were the same thing.

Discredited by German propagandists, the pacifist movement was then made ridiculous by the fiasco of Henry Ford's well-intentioned but ill-planned peace ship. In 1915 an Emergency Peace Conference, headed by Jane Addams and David Starr Jordan, made plans to create an international organization at The Hague which would endeavor to mediate between the two groups of powers. In November a member of the conference, Rosika Schwimmer, asked Henry Ford for financial assistance; and Ford promptly chartered a ship for transporting various pacifist leaders to Europe. A publicity man employed by Ford informed the press that they would "get the boys out of the trenches by Christmas," and this absurd suggestion made the whole enterprise seem laughable. Serious leaders refused to join the Ford peace ship, which eventually left Hoboken with a party of idealists and eccentrics on December 4 and brought most of them home again after they had spent five days in Europe. Opponents of war thus became branded in the public mind as both pro-German and impractical. The result was that, after being defeated in their attempt to preserve neutrality, they were to be regarded as a public menace and deprived of their rights of free speech during the period of American participation in the war.

Exports to the Allies

The outbreak of war precipitated an immediate crisis in Wall Street. Fear that widespread selling by foreign holders of American securities would drive down prices to new lows and set off a serious panic forced the New York Stock Exchange to remain closed from July 31 until the second week in December, 1914. Moreover, the economy had generally been depressed during the first six months of the year; in August there were more than a million unemployed, and there was serious concern among businessmen and farm spokesmen that the war, by curtailing exports, would result in even greater price drops and loss of profits. Allied purchases, however, soon dispelled these fears, and less than a year later most branches of economic activity were booming.

Sales of munitions and foodstuffs to Britain and France increased by huge amounts and grew steadily throughout the entire war period. Between 1914 and 1916, while American commerce with the Central Powers shrank from nearly $169.3 to $1.6 million, trade with the Allies increased fourfold, from almost $825 million to more than $3.2 billion. The latter business was almost entirely handled by the House of Morgan which, at its own suggestion, was appointed, in December, 1914, commercial agents for the British government, with a commission of 2 per cent on the first $10 million worth of purchases and 1 per cent on all subsequent purchases.

Exports of munitions were especially important. Between August, 1914, and December, 1915, the Allies spent over $508 million on munitions in the United States; between January, 1916, and March, 1917, the value of their purchases amounted to $1.7 billion. Nearly one-third of these sums was used for explosives, most of which were supplied by E. I. Du Pont de Nemours. The firm of Du Pont, in fact, manufactured 40 per cent of all the ammunition used by the Allies during the war. The Allies, however, relied on their own factories for artillery and airplanes, the result being that these industries were not developed in the United States and that America's own war preparations after it entered the war were severely handicapped.

The result of these purchases was to bring about a general prosperity in the United States. The excess of exports over imports, for example, which had amounted to $438.8 million for the year 1913-14, rose to nearly $3.57 billion by the year 1916-17. And although the financiers and munitions makers certainly profited from this trade, it is equally important to recognize that all classes of the population benefited, just as they did from the other economic connections which developed between the United States and the Allies as a result of these exports. If the average profits of American steel companies rose from 7.4 per cent in 1913 to 28.7 per cent in 1917, the total profits of American wheat farmers increased from about $56.7 million in 1913 to more than $642.8 million in 1917. It was not the bankers, manufacturers, and munitions makers alone who had an economic interest in an Allied victory; nor, despite later charges, is there any evidence to indicate that these groups had any influence upon Wilson's subsequent decision to go to war against Germany.

Pacifists and pro-Germans denounced the munitions traffic as unneutral. In refusing to interfere with it, however, the administration had good legal and practical justification. In the Contraband Circular of October, 1914, the administration declared that while it would be "unneutral" for the United States government itself to engage in the munitions trade, it was not "within the power of the Executive to prevent or control" such traffic by "a private individual." [3] The following year, in August, 1915, Robert Lansing, who had by this time succeeded Bryan as Secretary of State, replied to official German protests by pointing out that to change the rules of international law by outlawing the munitions trade in the middle of the war would be unfair to the Allies, and that a general policy

[3] Quoted in Daniel M. Smith, "Robert Lansing and the Proclamation of American Neutrality Policies, 1914-1917," *Mississippi Valley Historical Review*, XLIII (June 1956), 68.

of embargoing munitions would benefit militaristic nations, discriminate against pacifistic ones, and compel each country to increase its own munitions manufactures. What Lansing's reply failed to reveal was equally important—namely, the fact that by this time the effectiveness of the British blockade against the Central Powers and its control on neutral commerce made America's trade prosperity heavily dependent upon Allied purchases.

Loans to the Allies

Almost as influential as the Allies' purchase of munitions and other goods was their borrowing of American money. At the outset of the war the Allies were able to buy for cash, partly by shipping gold to the United States, partly by selling American securities owned by their citizens. Altogether they sent about $1 billion in gold, and sold about $2 billion worth of securities. The United States government, moreover, refused at first to countenance loans to the Allies. Approached by the House of Morgan in August, 1914, Secretary of State Bryan declared that the floating of an Allied war loan would be unneutral.

It was, however, difficult to organize large-scale sales without short-term credits. The opposition of Bryan and the administration to credits soon began to weaken; and once credits were allowed, it was the logical next step to tolerate loans. By that time American prosperity had become dependent on Allied purchases; and when the cash reserves of the Allies began to be exhausted, loans became the only method by which this prosperity could be maintained.

In October, 1914, President Wilson agreed that American banks might make short-term credits to the Allies. Credits then began to accumulate, with no provision made for their liquidation; and by August, 1915, this financial problem had become acute. Pressed by Lansing and McAdoo, who in turn were being pressed by a number of influential Wall Street bankers, Wilson then agreed not to oppose loans to the Allies. The President's decision in this instance appears to have been especially influenced by two of McAdoo's arguments: the necessity of providing the Allies with financial assistance to preserve American prosperity, and, probably even more important, the fact that since the government maintained "it is lawful for our citizens to manufacture and sell to belligerents munitions of war," it follows then that this trade "is entitled to the same treatment at the hands of our bankers, in financing it, as any other part of our lawful commerce." [4] In other words, financing trade with the Allies was no more unneutral than the trade itself. On September 10, 1915, an Anglo-French mission arrived in New York and proceeded to float a $500 million loan to run for five years. The interest rate was set at 5 per cent, but when all syndicate charges were included the cost to Britain and France approximated 6 per cent. Raising this money, which was to be used to refund previous short-term obligations held by American creditors, proved difficult and required, in the words of one Morgan partner, the formation of "the largest [underwriting] group for distributing bonds ever organized in the United States." [5] The loan was bitterly denounced by various pro-German and other anti-Allied groups; and their views were given wide circulation by the newspapers of William Randolph Hearst, with the result that while Britain and France received their money, it was the large financial and business institutions rather than the small investor who purchased the bonds. After this flotation there were no more large loans for nearly a year. By August, 1916, however, the financial resources of the Allies were near exhaustion. Between that date and April, 1917, Allied borrowings in the United States totaled nearly $1.1 billion by Great Britain, $300 million by France, $400 million by Canada, and $50 million by Russia. Most of these bonds were subscribed by American commercial banks and "secured by such first-class American collateral as the banks were required by law to demand." [6]

Loans to the Allies strengthened further the already close trade relations existing between them and the United States. And while the pro-Allied sympathy of the Wall Street bankers was not universal, the House of Morgan, according to a statement in 1920 by one of its partners (Thomas Lamont), "had never for one moment been neutral; we did not know how to be. From the very start we did everything we could to contribute to the cause of the Allies." This admission, however, does not indicate that their views or economic considerations had any influence whatsoever upon Wilson's policies. In his opinion, as well as in that of Lansing and McAdoo, it would have been unneutral for the United States to prevent the belligerents from access to private American capital. The fact that the Central Powers were able to raise only about $20 million in the United States was not the fault of the administration.

[4] Quoted in Link, *op. cit.*, p. 619.
[5] Thomas W. Lamont, *Henry P. Davison: The Record of a Useful Life* (New York, 1933), p. 195.
[6] Link, *op. cit.*, p. 628.

AMERICAN DIPLOMACY, 1914–1916

Controversies with Great Britain

The primary official responsibility of the United States government after the outbreak of the war was to protect the rights of neutrals under international law against the warring powers. These rights had been codified in the Declaration of London in 1909, and at the beginning of the war the United States asked the belligerents whether they would obey it. Since it was to their advantage, the Germans agreed to abide by it; but Great Britain, whose Parliament had not ratified the declaration, announced that it required modification. Actually, the differences between the declaration and previous international law were of small importance. The Declaration of London declared, first, that "paper" blockades were illegal. To be legal a blockade of an enemy seaport must be effectively maintained by an adequate naval force. Second, the doctrine of "continuous voyage" was denied. In other words, goods other than war material could be shipped freely to neutral ports even if they were ultimately destined for a blockaded country. Third, goods were divided into absolute contraband, conditional contraband, and noncontraband, and the only goods which could be seized by a blockading force were war material (absolute contraband) and goods for the use of armed forces (conditional contraband). All goods destined for civilian use were exempt from seizure. By international law, therefore, the United States had the right to trade freely with the civilian populations of both Great Britain and Germany.

At the outset of the war the British government established a blockade of Germany, which grew steadily more comprehensive and which violated several rules of international law. The United States government, at first, sought to secure Britain's adherence to the declaration, but when the British explained that such a course would make it impossible for them to execute their blockade policies, the Wilson administration dropped the issue, declaring it would hold London accountable only for the "observance of traditional international law." [7]

The President did not wish to prevent the British from taking action they believed necessary to win the war. In spite of his sincere public

[7] Ernest R. May, *The World War and American Isolation, 1914–1917* (Cambridge, Mass., 1959), p. 21.

President Wilson's two most important secretaries of State: William Jennings Bryan (left), who served from 1913 to 1915, and his successor, Robert Lansing, who occupied the post until 1920. (Culver Pictures, Inc.)

professions of neutrality and his belief that the United States need not become involved in the war, Wilson's sympathy, like that of most Americans, was on the side of the Allies.[8] As early as September, 1914, he had come to the conclusion that, as he told Sir Cecil Spring-Rice, the British ambassador, a German victory would compel the United States to "give up its present ideals and devote all its energies to defense, which would mean the end of its present system of government." On another occasion, he told Joseph Tumulty, "England is fighting our fight. . . . I will not take any action to embarrass England when she is fighting for her life and the life of the world." Furthermore, as one commentator has pointed out, while it is true that the Wilson administration "adopted a double standard in the enforcement of the traditional principles of neutrality— that it was rigorous in dealing with Germany and generously lax in dealing with Great Britain," it is equally undeniable "that this partiality was

[8] William L. Langer, "From Isolation to Mediation," in Arthur P. Dudden, ed., *Woodrow Wilson and the World of Today* (Philadelphia [1957]), p. 25.

in a large measure a reflection of the drift of American opinion itself." [9]

Except for Bryan, whose strong pacifistic leanings caused him to oppose any policy which might threaten to involve the United States in the war, Wilson's other chief advisers on European affairs were, in varying degrees, all pro-Allied. Robert Lansing, the counsellor to the State Department before succeeding to Bryan's post in June, 1915, believed it was the duty of the United States to defend international law and protect and promote the wartime interests and rights of the business community. At the same time, he was also sufficiently aware of the realities of international life to become convinced that the security of the United States required that Germany should not be allowed to crush the Allies. Colonel House's understanding of international politics and of America's role and position in world affairs was even more sophisticated than Lansing's, and because of his intimate friendship with Wilson, his views carried great weight with the President. House's interpretation of foreign policy proceeded from two basic assumptions: the necessity of maintaining good Anglo-American relations and of extending the influence of the United States. Finally, Walter Hines Page, the American ambassador in London, was an even more enthusiastic partisan of the Allied cause.

These pro-Allied sympathies were ably cultivated by the English Foreign Secretary, Sir Edward Grey, whose personality was particularly sympathetic to the Americans. His policy toward the American government was guided, as he declared later, by the principle that while the "blockade of Germany was essential to the victory of the Allies . . . the ill-will of the United States meant their certain defeat. . . . It was better . . . to carry on the war without blockade, if need be, than to incur a break with the United States about contraband and thereby deprive the Allies of the resources necessary to carry on the war at all or with any chance of success. The object of diplomacy, therefore, was to secure the maximum of blockade that could be enforced without a rupture with the United States." [10]

Partly because of Grey's consideration for American feelings and partly because of the pro-Allied sympathies of Wilson and his chief advisers, the frequent protests Washington made against Britain's blockade practices during the first two years of the war never included threats to take action.

---

[9] Dexter Perkins, "American Wars and Critical Historians," in Glyndon G. Van Deusen and Richard C. Wade, eds., *Foreign Policy and the American Spirit* (Ithaca, N.Y. [1957]), p. 98.

[10] Quoted in Link, *op. cit.*, p. 116.

Robert Lansing afterward declared that the "notes that were sent were long and exhaustive treatises which opened up new subjects of discussion rather than closing those in controversy. Short and emphatic notes were dangerous. Everything was submerged in verbosity. It was done with deliberate purpose. It insured continuance of the controversies and left the questions unsettled." Both Page and House occasionally gave advice to the British government as to how the notes might most effectively be answered and what measures would both enable the British to maintain their blockade and at the same time appease the American traders whose goods were being confiscated. Sir Edward Grey recorded later that Page's "advice and suggestions were of the greatest value in warning us when to be careful or encouraging us when we could safely be firm."

As the war continued, the British in a series of Orders in Council steadily extended their contraband lists to include many raw materials, such as foodstuffs and cotton, declaring that almost all commodities were potentially war materials. They began to seize commodities being shipped to the neutral countries of northern Europe, except when the shipper could prove that they were not destined for German use; they declared that the whole of the North Sea was a military area and that all neutral vessels must stop at British ports for inspection; and finally, on March 11, 1915, they extended the blockade regulations to cover all commodities entering or leaving Germany. The blockade now completely prohibited all imports into Germany and northern Europe except when it could be proved they were for neutral consumption. Supplies shipped to neutral countries were limited to their normal peacetime needs, and all cargoes consigned to firms which traded with Germany were seized. These orders violated the rules of international law, which had declared that a blockade must be effective, that the theory of "continuous voyage" could be applied only to war materials, and that goods not destined for military use were exempt from seizure.

The United States government sent protests against these Orders in Council in September and December, 1914, and in March, 1915. These protests, however, were not worded in a manner likely to win concessions. That of December, for example, requested the British not to interfere with American trade "unless such interference is manifestly an imperative necessity to protect their national safety, and then only to the extent that it is a necessity." In February, 1915, moreover, in retaliation for the British blockade, the German submarine campaign had commenced; and the British government could then time its replies to the American protests so that they arrived during periods of controversy between the United States and Germany. The British reply to the American note of March, 1915, for example, arrived in July, in the middle of the *Lusitania* controversy.

Apart from the blockade itself, the necessity for which the United States government finally accepted, there were a number of other matters which provoked American complaints. American ships bound for neutral countries in northern Europe were often detained in British ports for months before they were finally searched and allowed to proceed. Meanwhile British trade with those same neutral countries was increasing. The United States sent a note of protest in October, 1915, to which the British did not reply until April, 1916, during the controversy with Germany over the sinking of the *Sussex*. The British searched all mail passing between the United States and Germany and northern Europe; and it was suspected that they used this practice in order to obtain American trade secrets for the benefit of their own traders. Controversy on this subject continued through 1916 with increasing seriousness. The British made a blacklist of neutral firms suspected of trading with Germany and attempted to prevent all other firms, British or neutral, from doing business with them. In July, 1916, the blacklist was extended to cover about thirty American firms. American protests, however, caused this order to be modified. Finally, the British held up shipments of German exports which were needed by American industry, and they offered to supply goods of their own manufacture in their place. A controversy about a consignment of German machine knitting needles continued from May, 1916, until February, 1917, when it was discovered that the British manufacturers were themselves importing German knitting needles of the same brand without interference by the British government.

The British attitude to these questions precipitated a serious crisis in Anglo-American relations, extracting from President Wilson, in October, 1916, the complaint: "How difficult it is to be friends with Great Britain without doing whatever she wants us to do."

Controversies with Germany

Meanwhile the United States government, having tolerated violations of international law by the British, was insisting that the Germans obey it. This difference not only reflected the pro-Allied sympathies of Wilson and his advisers, though the President himself does not appear to have been consciously inconsistent, but even more important, it revealed the very significant fact that it was impossible for the United States to remain genuinely neutral. By refusing to sell to the Allies or by insisting upon Britain's unqualified adherence to the Declaration of London, America would have deprived the Allies of employing their sea power effectively. Had the United States adopted such a position, it would have been an unneutral action against the Allies. After the war a number of Americans, despite ample evidence to the contrary, refused to recognize this fact, preferring to believe that since the British blockade of Germany was as much a violation of neutral rights as Germany's submarine warfare, the latter was merely a pretext for the United States' entry into the war.

On February 4, 1915, the Kaiser signed an order for submarine warfare on all enemy merchant ships in British waters. On February 10, the United States government declared that Germany would be held to "strict accountability" if any American ships or lives were lost; and when the submarines finally commenced action, on February 22, they were given strict orders not to attack neutral ships. The first American life was lost on March 28, when the British passenger ship *Falaba* was torpedoed after the passengers had been allowed twenty-three minutes in which to disembark, and one American, Leon C. Thrasher, was among the drowned. On April 28 the American ship *Cushing* was attacked by a German seaplane, and on May 1 the American tanker *Gulflight* was torpedoed with a loss of three Americans. These two attacks were accidental, and Germany at once apologized and offered compensation. Finally, on May 7, 1915, the British liner *Lusitania* was torpedoed off the Irish coast. The ship sank in eighteen minutes, and of 1,959 persons on board, 1,198 were drowned, 128 of these being Americans. This episode, which aroused widespread indignation in the United States, brought matters to a head. Wilson did not want war, and the great majority of the American people agreed with him when, three days after the sinking of the *Lusitania*, he declared: "There is such a thing as a nation being so right it does not need to convince others by force that it is right." A few people, however, were convinced that the latest German action made war necessary. To Theodore Roosevelt, the sinking of the *Lusitania* was "murder on the high seas": "I do not believe that the firm assertion of our rights means war, but, in any event," he went on to say, "it is well to remember there are things worse than war." The *Lusitania* incident further strengthened Lansing's conviction that the United States could never permit Germany to win the war. "American public opinion," he wrote in July, 1915, "must be prepared for the time, which may come, when we will have to cast aside our neutrality and become one of the champions of democracy." [11]

During the controversy with Germany over the use of the submarine, the United States government maintained that American citizens were under the protection of the American flag even when they chose to travel on enemy ships. This claim was opposed by Secretary Bryan, who declared that an American who lost his life while traveling on a British ship was guilty of contributory negligence and that it was wrong for "one man, acting purely for himself and his own interests, and without consulting his government" to create an international crisis. Wilson, however, preferred to follow the advice of Robert Lansing. In contending that American citizens traveling on British passenger ships should be immune from German attacks, the United States government failed to take account of the fact that those ships sometimes carried munitions. On board the *Lusitania* were 4,200 cases of cartridges and 1,250 cases of shrapnel; and although the liner was not an "auxiliary warship," the Germans had reason for believing that she was. Another significant feature of the episode was the failure of the ship's officers to take even the most elementary precautions to avoid a submarine attack. In the case of the *Lusitania*, therefore, Germany was not the only guilty party; the British were also to blame for transporting munitions on a passenger ship.

The American government insisted that submarines must search merchant ships and provide for the safety of the passengers and crew before torpedoing them. This was an established rule of international law, but it did not apply to the existing situation. From the beginning of the war the British government armed its merchant ships and ordered them, whenever possible, to ram submarines rather than submit to seizure; it also made a practice of luring submarines to their destruction by flying American flags on British vessels. For German submarines to conform to international law was, therefore, to invite their own destruction. Nor was such procedure legally necessary, since a merchant ship armed with offensive weapons—and against the submarine all weapons were offensive—lost its peaceful character and became legally a warship. The American government, nevertheless, continued to insist that the weapons carried by British merchant ships were purely defensive and that no such ships might be torpedoed without warning. In support of this claim it quoted the opinion of Chief Justice John Marshall in the *Nereide* case, declaring that merchant ships might legitimately arm themselves. Wilson's legal advisers,

[11] Quoted in Smith, *op. cit.*, p. 80.

however, omitted a paragraph from Marshall's opinion in which the Chief Justice had added that an armed merchant ship must be regarded as "an open and declared belligerent" and "subject to all the dangers of the belligerent character."

The only sound legal reason for protesting against the submarine campaign was that it violated the American right, under international law, to ship noncontraband articles to the Allies. The United States, had, however, weakened its case by waiving that right in the case of the British blockade of Germany. There was a strong feeling in the United States that the German submarine campaign differed from the British blockade in that it involved the destruction of lives and not merely of property. As Wilson declared in April, 1917, "property can be paid for; the lives of peaceful and innocent people cannot be." Such a distinction was, perhaps, not strictly fair to Germany, which was unable to adopt any other method of retaliating against the blockade. The truth was that the American government could never be strictly neutral or impartial, and its attitude can be justified only in terms of national policy and interest: American diplomacy was helping to prevent Germany from winning the war.

The first *Lusitania* note was sent on May 13. Germany replied by defending the sinking and, in July, by offering not to attack passenger ships if the United States would guarantee they did not carry contraband. Meanwhile, submarine commanders were secretly given orders not to attack large passenger ships. Since Wilson regarded the German replies as unsatisfactory, further notes were sent on June 9 and July 21. Meanwhile, believing that the American position was legally unsound and that it would inevitably lead to war, Bryan resigned from the State Department on June 8 and was succeeded by Robert Lansing, whose pro-Allied sentiments and more realistic conception of America's national interest and the world balance of power had been so instrumental in determining Wilson's neutrality policies.

On August 19 a German submarine, disobeying orders, sank the British passenger ship *Arabic* without warning, two Americans being drowned. On September 4 another British passenger ship, the *Hesperia*, was torpedoed; and on November 7 an Austrian submarine sank an Italian passenger ship, the *Ancona*, with the loss of about twenty American lives. Meanwhile the controversy about the *Lusitania* continued; and although in February, 1916, Germany admitted its liability for the loss of American lives and expressed its regret, it still refused to accept Wilson's contention that the sinking had been illegal. In the same month the German government ordered that all passenger ships should be spared but that armed merchant ships might still be sunk without warning. These orders were violated on March 24, when the French steamer *Sussex* was sunk without warning, the submarine commander having failed to recognize it as a passenger ship.

Wilson replied, on April 18, by threatening to break off diplomatic relations unless Germany would agree that neither merchant ships nor passenger ships should henceforth be torpedoed without warning. The German government decided to give way, and on May 4, 1916, it gave the required pledge. It added, however, that unless the United States induced Great Britain to relax its blockade, Germany might be compelled to reconsider this decision. In replying to the German government's acceptance of the American demands, Lansing stated that the responsibility of the German government to honor its pledge of May 4 was in no way "contingent upon the course or the result of diplomatic negotiations between . . . the United States and any other belligerent government. . . . Responsibility in such matters is single, not joint; absolute, not relative." This ended the controversy. Wilson had forced Germany to abandon unlimited submarine warfare and, by so doing, had made a considerable contribution to an Allied victory. He had, however, placed the United States in a position where, if Germany decided to abandon its agreement, the United States would have no alternative but to go to war.

In the course of the controversy Wilson and Lansing came to realize that the arming of merchant ships by the British was the crux of the matter and that it was unfair to ask the Germans not to torpedo these vessels without warning unless they also asked the British not to arm their merchantmen. "It is hardly fair," Wilson informed Colonel House in October, 1915, "to ask Submarine commanders to give warning by summons if, when they approach as near as they must for that purpose they are to be fired upon." On January 18, 1916, in the hope of avoiding further difficulties with Germany, Lansing, with Wilson's approval, suggested that both sides accept a new set of rules regulating naval warfare. The American proposal called upon the British to cease arming their merchantmen and asked the Germans to stop all surprise U-boat attacks against these vessels. The British, recognizing the grave dangers such a policy would impose upon their merchant fleet, opposed it strongly. Sir Edward Grey told the American ambassador that if the proposal were adopted the "sinking of merchant vessels shall be the rule and not the exception." [12] Thus, warned by House and Page of the serious difficulties Lansing's pro-

---

[12] Quoted in Arthur S. Link, *Woodrow Wilson and the Progressive Era, 1910–1917* (New York [1954]), p. 208.

posal would create in Anglo-American relations, especially upon Wilson's efforts at mediation, the President and the secretary quickly dropped the matter.

Meanwhile, the administration's retreat in the face of Britain's rejection of Lansing's armed-ship proposal caused considerable alarm on Capitol Hill, which was unaware of Wilson's sincere efforts at mediation. Many congressmen, believing that American interests were not involved in the European struggle, felt the United States should not go to war with Germany in order to defend the claim that American citizens traveling on armed belligerent ships should be immune from attack. In February, 1916, resolutions in repudiation of this claim were introduced by Senator Thomas P. Gore of Oklahoma and Congressman Jeff McLemore of Texas. Wilson protested against these resolutions in a letter to Senator William J. Stone of Missouri, chairman of the Senate Foreign Relations Committee, in which he insisted that Americans had a right under international law to travel safely on armed belligerent ships. "No nation, no group of nations," he asserted, "has the right while the war is in progress to alter or disregard the principles which all nations have agreed upon in mitigation of the horrors and sufferings of war. . . . For my own part I cannot consent to any abridgement of the rights of American citizens in any respect. . . . What we are contending for in this matter is of the very essence of the things which have made America a sovereign nation." Fear that Wilson's stand on the issue might lead the nation into war caused a group of Democratic leaders in the House of Representatives to call at the White House on the morning of February 25, 1916. At this meeting, the so-called "Sunrise Conference," Wilson reasserted his intention to defend the rights of American citizens regardless of McLemore's resolution. (Senator Gore did not introduce his resolution until later that day.) At the same time, Wilson also reassured the congressional leaders of his continued desire to keep out of the war. "In God's name," Wilson declared, "could any one have done more than I to show a desire for peace." [13] As a result of administration pressure and strong popular opposition to the resolutions, the Senate voted on March 3 to table the Gore resolution by a vote of 68 to 14. Four days later the House took similar action on the McLemore resolution by a vote of 276 to 142.

While the debate on these resolutions was in progress, Colonel House was in Europe exploring the possibility of American mediation between the two sides. At the same time he was bringing the United States ap-

[13] Quoted in *ibid.*, pp. 212–13.

preciably nearer to entering the war. Wilson had already sent House to Europe in January, 1915; but this visit had been fruitless apart from a suggestion by Sir Edward Grey that after the war a world parliament must be established to maintain peace and that the United States ought surely to exercise leadership in such an organization. House returned to Europe in January, 1916; and, after a visit to Berlin, he joined Grey in drafting the House-Grey memorandum, signed on February 22. The memorandum declared that when the Allied Powers should so request, President Wilson would invite the Allied and Central Powers to a peace conference, and that if Germany refused the invitation or if the conference failed to bring peace, the United States "would probably enter the war against Germany." But since each side still believed that total victory was possible, Wilson's efforts to mediate received a frigid reception. In Berlin, House recorded, the imperial chancellor "intimated that Germany would be willing to evacuate both France and Belgium if indemnity were paid," a condition which, as House said, "the Allies would not consider for a moment." [14] Ambassador Page summarized the British view of Wilson's proposal in a letter to Lansing: "They feel that the moral judgment of practically the whole civilized world is on their side except only the Government of the United States." [15]

When the Allies failed to respond to the House-Grey memorandum, Wilson became considerably disillusioned. In spite of his conviction that the Allies were fighting America's battle, he still believed that only a negotiated peace would make possible a lasting settlement. The Allied peoples, however, were so convinced of Germany's guilt in starting the war and so resentful of the deaths and suffering they had endured that they would not consider peace until Germany had been decisively defeated. Moreover, they continued to hope that their armies would win real victories in Flanders. They refused, therefore, to suggest a conference. Disappointed at his failure to bring about peace and increasingly angered by the extent and frequency of British violations of the rights of American trade, Wilson began to turn in the direction of real neutrality. The severity of Lansing's complaints against British search and seizure of American mail and the stern language the State Department used to reprimand the Foreign Office for including eighty-seven American firms on its blacklist of July 19, 1916, indicate the extent to which Anglo-American

---

[14] Charles Seymour, ed., *The Intimate Papers of Colonel House* (4 vols., Boston, 1926–28), II, 142.
[15] Quoted in *ibid.*, II, 204.

relations had deteriorated. When official protests failed to bring results, the administration employed more direct action. On September 7, 1916, the Shipping Board Act was amended to permit the President to withhold a ship's clearance papers if it refused to accept cargo from an American firm on the British blacklist.

Throughout the summer and autumn of 1916, while maritime and commercial controversies so embittered Anglo-American diplomacy as to threaten to disrupt relations altogether, public opinion also reflected the stormy course of official events. Many Americans were horrified at the bloodshed and ruthlessness with which the British crushed the Irish Rebellion of April 24, 1916, and with the trials and executions following it. At the very time when Britain and America appeared to be growing further and further apart, relations between the United States and Germany were becoming increasingly relaxed and amicable. The result of all this was that by the end of 1916 Wilson was more nearly impartial toward the war than at any time since it had started, while his interest in mediating the conflict was as strong as ever.

PREPAREDNESS

During the first two and a half years of the war, public opinion in the United States continued to be undecided on the question of American participation. Some people, particularly in the East, believed that war should have been declared after the sinking of the *Lusitania*. The most prominent and the most aggressive of these was Theodore Roosevelt, whose contempt for Wilson was unbounded. The advocates of neutrality, however, although they made considerably less noise than the interventionists, no doubt had a majority of the people on their side.

One of the most conspicuous and early results of the war on American politics was the controversy which arose over the issue of preparedness. Some observers, like Walter Hines Page and Harvard University's *emeritus* president Charles W. Eliot, predicted that if Germany won the war in Europe and destroyed British naval supremacy, the Kaiser would proceed next to intervene in Latin America in violation of the Monroe Doctrine and might even attack the United States. These possibilities, as well as the realization that unprepared nations, like Belgium, could not survive the aggressive designs of their neighbors, caused widespread alarm in small but influential quarters. Before 1917, the propaganda activities of these interventionists did not convince many people that it was necessary for the United States to become involved in the war. The warnings that these groups sounded and the fears they expressed about the safety of the Republic did serve, however, to arouse interest in the nation's defense. As a result, beginning late in 1914 and continuing throughout 1915, a number of organizations were established to advocate preparedness, among them being the Military Training Camp Association, the Junior American Guard, the National Society for Patriotic Education, the National Security League, the American Defence Society, the American Legion, and the American Rights Committee. Among the prominent champions of the movement were Theodore Roosevelt, Henry Cabot Lodge, Henry L. Stimson, and General Leonard Wood.

The campaign inaugurated by the preparedness groups and their spokesmen grew steadily and assumed many forms. Besides the usual speeches, lectures, and articles in national magazines and newspapers, numerous books and pamphlets were published, all of which aimed to awaken the people to the danger which would result from military weakness. For those who preferred a visual demonstration of what continued unpreparedness would mean for the United States, the infant motion picture industry provided alarming tales of a foreign invasion in such films as *The Fall of a Nation* and *The Battle Cry of Peace*. Wilson opposed the preparedness movement as long as he dared. Since the war in Europe was one "with which we have nothing to do, whose cause can not touch us," he saw no reason for special measures to increase the armed forces. "We shall not alter our attitude toward . . . [defense]," he told the Congress in December, 1914, "because some amongst us are nervous and excited." "The country," he declared, "has been misinformed." But Wilson's opposition did not deter the advocates of preparedness. Indeed, it served only to drive them on to new and greater efforts. With the sinking of the *Lusitania* on May 7, 1915, the defense issue assumed a new and greater urgency. The negotiations which followed the sinking, along with the diplomatic difficulties the United States was experiencing with German submarine policy, attracted even more attention to the status of American preparedness.

By mid-summer Wilson found it impossible, as well as politically inadvisable, to ignore entirely the demands of the preparedness groups, and, after much thought, he decided to support moderate measures of preparedness. In July he consulted Josephus Daniels and Lindley M. Garrison, the secretaries of the Navy and War, and asked them to study and appraise the country's defenses and to make suggestions. On the basis of their findings, he would devise a program to recommend to the Congress in December. Wilson, however, chose to announce his defense program publicly, and on November 4, 1915, he did so while speaking at New York City's Manhattan Club. "We have it in mind to be prepared," he declared, "not for war, but only for defense. . . . The mission of America in the world is essentially a mission of peace and good will among men. . . . But we feel justified in preparing ourselves to vindicate our right to independent and unmolested action by making the force that is in us ready for assertion." The following month he appeared before the Congress to recommend the adoption of his program. Besides increasing the size of the regular army from 108,008 to 141,843 enlisted men and officers and providing for a comprehensive five-year naval expansion program, Wilson's proposal also called for the establishment of an additional fighting force of 400,000 "disciplined citizens."

As soon as Wilson disclosed his plan, a bitter and protracted debate arose over it. Most of the country's progressives, with the exception of a few eastern spokesmen, opposed it. Much of the progressive movement, especially in the South and the Middle West, was provincial and isolationist. Much of it was pacifist; and almost all of it looked upon preparedness and war as useless, as a threat to continued reform at home, and as a means to strengthen and enrich the very same industrial and financial interests it sought to curb. Antipreparedness groups and peace societies campaigned energetically against Wilson's proposal, along with most of the spokesmen for the country's organized workers and farmers. As the nation debated the merits of preparedness generally, Congress was engaged in trying to resolve the controversies which arose in that body over the specifics of Wilson's program. On January 27, 1916, Wilson started on an eight-state speaking tour of the East and the Middle West to inform the nation "that new circumstances have arisen which make it absolutely necessary that this country prepare herself, not for war, but for adequate national defense." But the speaking tour had little effect upon the antipreparedness forces within the Democratic party in Congress, and Wilson was forced to make concessions. On February 10, he accepted the resignation of Secretary of War Garrison, who had aroused the enmity of the antipreparedness members of the House Military Affairs Committee by insisting that the volunteer citizen army Wilson had proposed should be controlled by the federal government rather than the National Guard. Garrison was succeeded by Newton D. Baker, the progressive mayor of

Cleveland, a former pacifist and a very recent convert to preparedness. Ultimately, after considerable debate and much compromise, and partly because of the crisis created by the *Sussex* sinking, the Congress enacted the National Defense Act on June 3, 1916. This measure called for an increase in the regular army to 175,000 men, with provisions to enlarge it to 223,000 within the next five years. The national guard was federalized and its strength increased to 450,000 men. The act also authorized the creation of a reserve corps for training civilians and officers and provided for the government's building and operating a plant to manufacture nitrates. Strong advocates of preparedness like Theodore Roosevelt criticized the bill for failing to provide an adequately trained and effective fighting force.

Meanwhile the Congress continued its work of enacting the remainder of the President's program. On August 29, in the Naval Appropriation Act, $313 million was voted to increase the strength of the navy at once by constructing four battleships, at the time still looked upon in most quarters as "the principal fighting ship of the Navy." The act also provided for the construction of four battle cruisers, which, according to other naval experts, had replaced the battleship as a result of their performance at the battle of Jutland (May 31–June 1, 1916). The act also included provisions for a large number of other warships, including cruisers, destroyers, submarines, and smaller craft, as well as for other naval construction during the next three years; increased appropriations for the naval air force; and authorization of a government-owned armor-plate factory.

On the same day that the President signed the Naval Appropriation Act into law, he also signed the Army Appropriation Act, which provided for the creation of a Council of National Defense, composed of six cabinet members and seven civilian experts, to plan and regulate the preparedness program. Among its other responsibilities it was to assay the nation's natural and industrial resources and devise the means to employ them effectively and efficiently. On September 7, Wilson secured the creation of a United States Shipping Board, with an appropriation of $50 million for building merchant ships. The measure, obviously necessary in view of the scarcity of American ships and the diminution of Allied vessels as a result of the submarine campaign, had been advocated by Wilson since the autumn of 1914 and was included also as a part of his defense program of 1915; but private shipping interests had hitherto succeeded in blocking it on the ground that it was socialistic.

Throughout 1915 and 1916, as the preparedness campaign gained strength, there was also a growing tendency to be intolerant toward the more recent immigrants and toward the use of foreign languages. This suspicion of foreigners, which sometimes manifested itself in ugly ways, was fed by the diverse fears and prejudices of numerous groups and individuals. Labor leaders, worried that the continued influx of immigrants would depress wages, demanded restrictive legislation; liberals and progressives, many of whom entertained strong racist and religious prejudices, looked upon the newcomers from southern and eastern Europe as "indigestible" foreigners and "inferior races" and blamed them for the evils and corruption of urban life; and antiunion businessmen attributed the demands of the workers to dangerous, alien ideologies. These and the other groups which saw in the foreigner or his culture the source of all their grievances, real or fancied, joined forces in demanding that everyone swear allegiance to a new code of "Americanism." A National Americanization Committee was formed to inculcate patriotism among these so-called "hyphenated Americans." Wilson himself neither approved nor knowingly contributed to this growing intolerance and demand for conformity. But whether because of his not being entirely immune from this antiforeign contagion himself or because of his own sense of patriotism, the fact remains that he did little to promote tolerance and respect for honest dissent.

In the summer of 1916 a number of preparedness parades were organized. During one such parade, in San Francisco on July 22, a bomb was exploded, and two California labor leaders, Thomas J. Mooney and Warren K. Billings, were convicted and sentenced to life imprisonment on what appeared later to have been fabricated evidence. This *cause célèbre* continued to excite controversy until the release of both men in 1939 and 1940.

THE ELECTION OF 1916

During the summer of 1916 as Congress was debating and enacting the administration's defense program and other Americans were marching in preparedness parades and participating in patriotic activities of one kind or another, the presidential election was approaching. On June 14, while Wilson was marching in a preparedness parade in Washington, the Democratic convention was meeting in St. Louis and preparing to renominate him by acclamation, but the opposition of a single Illinois delegate prevented it from doing so. Although the convention renominated Vice President Marshall by acclamation, Wilson was declared nominated by a vote of 1,092 to 1. Far more notable than the platform, which applauded Wilson and the Democratic party's domestic accomplishments and foreign policies and endorsed the administration's defense program, was the speech of former Governor Martin Glynn of New York. Glynn provoked enormous enthusiasm by praising Wilson for avoiding war, and the claim "He Kept Us Out of War" became the chief campaign slogan of the Democrats. Wilson tried to be careful not to make any commitment for the future. "I know that you are depending upon me to keep this nation out of the war," he had declared in a speech in January. "But you have laid another duty upon me. You have bidden me see to it that nothing stains or impairs the honor of the United States. . . . There may at any moment come a time when I cannot preserve both the honor and the peace of the United States. Do not exact of me an impossible and contradictory thing." Despite this and other similar statements, the zeal and energy with which Wilson searched for peace led him on occasion to speak as if he alone could keep the United States out of the war, a view which the Democratic party's orators propagated extensively later in the campaign with the slogan, "Wilson and Peace with Honor? or Hughes with Roosevelt and War?" As a result, many people voted for Wilson in the belief that the Democratic slogans were formal presidential commitments.

The Republican convention was notable chiefly for the return of Theodore Roosevelt to the fold. The nomination was given to Charles Evans Hughes, the former progressive governor of New York, and an associate justice of the Supreme Court since 1910. Since Hughes had kept himself sufficiently removed from the internal strife which had split the GOP in 1910 and had rendered the party ineffective since then, he was the only candidate with sufficient national stature who was acceptable to both wings of his party. When Roosevelt was nominated by a separate Progressive convention, he refused to be a candidate and urged the Progressives to vote for Hughes—a desertion which caused bitter resentment among many of those who had followed him out of the Republican party in 1912. The GOP then proceeded to carry water on both shoulders. While some of its orators, headed by Roosevelt, demanded immediate war with Germany, others appealed to the pro-German vote on the ground that Wilson had supported the Allies. Hughes himself, unable to reconcile these contradictory attitudes, made speeches about the tariff, a question which excited no enthusiasm. Wilson did not begin to campaign seriously until late in September, after a threatened railroad strike was averted. Once on the stump, however, he proceeded to portray himself and the Democratic party as the proven agents of reform and "social justice" legislation. By November, most of the advanced progressives who had supported the Roosevelt Bull Moose ticket in 1912 had turned to Wilson, along with a majority of the country's farmers and workers—two groups who had benefited considerably from the legislation of his first term. Many independent voters were attracted to Wilson too because of his liberal program and his proven ability to use the Democratic party as the vehicle of reform. But Wilson's greatest achievement in 1916 was, as Arthur S. Link has indicated, to bring about a "fusion of the peace cause with the ideal of progressive democracy." [16]

The election, nevertheless, was close, Wilson winning by an electoral vote of 277 to 254 and a popular vote of 9,129,000 to 8,538,200. The vote of California, which went to Wilson by a majority of only 4,000, was enough to decide the election. The Socialist party candidate, Allen L. Benson, polled 585,113 votes, nearly 313,000 fewer than Debs had received in 1912, while Arthur E. Reimer, the Socialist-Labor party candidate, received only 13,403, less than half the number of votes he had received four years earlier. Obviously, Wilson had attracted to the Democrats many of the people who had voted for these two parties in 1912. The Senate remained Democratic but with reduced strength. Of the 435 seats in the House, the Democrats captured 213 and the Republicans 217; the other 5 went to a Socialist, two Progressives, an Independent, and a Prohibitionist.

WAR

After the election Wilson made another, and more serious, effort to bring about a negotiated peace in Europe—a move quite necessary in view of the likelihood that Germany would resume unlimited submarine warfare. On December 18, 1916, he invited all the belligerents to formulate their peace terms, declaring that their war aims, as stated hitherto, appeared to be "virtually the same"—a statement which caused considerable indignation in Great Britain and France.

The replies of the belligerents showed, however, that peace was wholly

[16] Link, *Wilson and the Progressive Era*, p. 241.

impossible. The Allied peace terms, which included not only the evacuation of all conquered territories and the restoration of Belgium and northern France but also the dismemberment of Austria-Hungary and payment by Germany of compensation for the damages which its armies had inflicted, would never be accepted by Germany unless it were defeated. Germany, who had hitherto been victorious in military operations, was genuinely hopeful for peace, but only for a peace advantageous to itself, to which the Allied powers would never agree. On January 22, in an address to the Senate, Wilson stated his own conception of a satisfactory peace settlement. The peace terms must be arranged by mutual agreement and without a victory for either side; they must recognize the right of all nationalities to self-government; they must give every great nation access to the sea and must guarantee the freedom of the seas; and armaments must be limited and entangling alliances forbidden. The settlement must, moreover, be maintained by a system of collective security which would make aggression impossible. Wilson summarized his ideals by demanding a universal Monroe Doctrine.

Nine days later, on January 31, 1917, the German government announced that on the next day it would adopt unlimited submarine warfare. The seas around Great Britain and France were declared a war zone, and all ships, both neutral and belligerent, which entered the zone were liable to be sunk without warning. The United States was to be allowed to send one passenger ship a week to the British port of Falmouth, provided the ship was clearly marked with red and white stripes and carried no contraband. The German civilian government had consistently opposed submarine warfare, but early in January it had been overruled by the military leaders, who were convinced that they could starve Great Britain into submission and that, even if the United States entered the war, its military assistance to the Allies would be negligible and its economic assistance could not be greater than it was already.

At a meeting of his cabinet Wilson found that all his advisers felt that there was now only one course open to the United States and that, in the words of Secretary of Agriculture Houston, "nothing worse can ever befall us than what Germany proposes and no greater insult can be offered to any people." On February 3 diplomatic relations with Germany were broken, and the German ambassador was dismissed.

During the next two months Wilson slowly and reluctantly arrived at the conviction that war was unavoidable. On March 1, the Zimmermann note, sent by the Kaiser's foreign secretary to the German minister in

Mexico and intercepted and decoded by the British, was made public. In case the United States should declare war, Mexico was invited by Germany to become its ally and regain the territories of New Mexico, Texas, and Arizona taken by the Americans in 1848; and the Mexican government was urged to invite help from Japan and "at the same time, offer to mediate between Germany and Japan." This rather fantastic suggestion caused widespread indignation and alarm in the Southwest and along the Pacific coast.

On February 26 Wilson, still hoping to avoid war, asked Congress to appropriate money for arming American merchant ships. The United States was to adopt a policy of armed neutrality and await overt action by Germany before taking more drastic steps. A large majority of Congress was in favor of the proposal, but a small group of western senators, headed by La Follette, succeeded in killing it by filibustering until March 4, when the session ended. Wilson denounced the filibusterers as "a little group of wilful men, representing no opinion but their own," who had "rendered the great government of the United States helpless and contemptible." On March 12 he ordered merchant ships to be armed even without congressional assent.

The overt action which Wilson expected came on March 12, when a submarine sank the *Algonquin* by gunfire. During the following three weeks five other American vessels were sunk, the loss of life amounting to twenty-five Americans and thirty-nine of other nationalities. On March 20 Wilson found that his cabinet was unanimous for war, and Congress was summoned to meet on April 2. He was still reluctant to accept the necessity of war, because he realized how much harm it would do to American democratic ideals. On the evening before the meeting of Congress he told Frank Cobb of the New York *World:* "Once lead this people into war, and they'll forget there ever was such a thing as tolerance; to fight you must be brutal and ruthless, and the very spirit of ruthless brutality will enter into the very fiber of our national life." He sought justification for America's entry into the war in the belief that only American influence could bring about a just peace, without revenge, and that the Allies would not listen to America if it remained neutral. Unless the United States joined the Allies, he told Jane Addams, it could "only call through a crack in the door" when the peace conference was held. Further support for the belief that Wilson's ideals could be achieved through an Allied victory was provided by the Russian Revolution, which overthrew the Tsar in February, 1917. Wilson could now claim what had

formerly been impossible—that this was a war of the democracies against
the autocracies.

Wilson's war message, read to Congress on April 2, declared that the
submarine campaign, the sabotage plots of German agents in the United
States, and the Zimmermann note left no alternative but war. "It is a
fearful thing," he declared, "to lead this great peaceful people into war,
into the most terrible and disastrous of all wars, civilization itself seeming
to be in the balance. But the right is more precious than peace, and we
shall fight for the things which we have always carried nearest our hearts
—for democracy, for the right of those who submit to authority to have
a voice in their own governments, for the rights and liberties of small
nations, for a universal dominion of right by such a concert of free people
as shall bring peace and safety to all nations and make the world itself at
last free. To such a task we can dedicate our lives and our fortunes, everything that we are and everything that we have, with the pride of those who
know that the day has come when America is privileged to spend her
blood and her might for the principles that gave her birth and happiness
and the peace which she has treasured. God helping her, she can do no
other."

There was never any doubt that Congress would decide for war; the
only question was the size of the majority. In view of the inflamed state
of public opinion, a vote against war required considerable courage. In
the Senate the vote was 82 against 6, the dissenters being Robert La Follette of Wisconsin, George W. Norris of Nebraska, William J. Stone of
Missouri, James K. Vardaman of Mississippi, Asle J. Gronna of North
Dakota, and Harry Lane of Oregon. The viewpoint expressed by these
men was that the British violations of American rights were just as
deserving of condemnation as those committed by the Germans, and
that the United States was being drawn into the war on the Allied side
by the economic interests of bankers and munitions manufacturers. In
the House of Representatives the vote was 373 to 50. War was declared on
April 6 and the United States joined the Allies as an Associated Power.

The outcome was to show that Wilson's idealistic aspirations could
not be achieved by means of an Allied victory, and to this extent it justified
the small group of men who had voted against war. As Wilson himself had
realized, a peace dictated by the victors, at the end of four and a half years
of bitter conflict, could be a peace only of revenge, not of conciliation. It
is plain, moreover, that the United States had finally been driven into the
war by the German government because it had never been genuinely

neutral and had asked from Germany an obedience to international law which Washington had not required of the Allies. Realization of these facts was eventually to cause many Americans to feel that their entry into the war had been an error and that they had been tricked into it by the propaganda of the Allies and by those Americans who were financially interested in an Allied victory. Although, in the minds of some people, the United States may have gone to war for mistaken reasons, it is impossible to conclude that entrance into the war was itself a mistake. The cardinal question at issue was neither the rights and wrongs of the submarine campaign nor the relative honesty and idealism of the Allied and German governments, but whether it was desirable that the United States, as a democratic nation, interested both in its own security and in the maintenance of international order and world peace, should prevent a German victory. Whether the United States acted wisely or not can be determined only by comparing what actually happened after 1918 with what might have happened if the Allied nations, deprived of American assistance, had been compelled to capitulate to the German army.

Suggested Readings

Many of the biographies and general works covering the years 1913 to 1920 cited in Chapter 7, such as Link, *Woodrow Wilson and the Progressive Era, 1910–1917;* Baker, *Woodrow Wilson: Life and Letters;* Paxson, *The Pre-War Years, 1913–1917;* and Notter, *The Origins of the Foreign Policy of Woodrow Wilson* are all pertinent in evaluating the causes of America's participation in World War I. The influence of English liberals upon Wilson's foreign policy is the subject of the able study by Laurence W. Martin, *Peace Without Victory* (New Haven, Conn., 1958).

Among the many memoirs and diaries of the war years, the following are some of the more worthy ones: Johann H. von Berstorff, *My Three Years in America* (New York, 1920) and the same author's *Memoirs* (New York, 1936); Constantin Dumba, *Memoirs of a Diplomat* (Boston, 1932); James W. Gerard, *My Four Years in Germany* (New York, 1917); Edward Grey, *Twenty-Five Years, 1892–1916* (2 vols., London, 1925); Stephen Gwynn, ed., *Letters and Friendships of Sir Cecil Spring-Rice* (2 vols., Boston, 1929); Burton J. Hendrick, *The Life and Letters of Walter Hines Page* (3 vols., New York, 1922–25); David F. Houston, *Eight Years With Wilson's Cabinet, 1913–1917,* already cited in Chapter 6; Franklin K. Lane, *The Letters of Franklin K. Lane* (Boston, 1922); Robert Lansing, *War Memoirs of Robert Lansing, Secretary of State* (Indianapolis, 1935): Charles Seymour, ed., *The Intimate Papers of Colonel House . . .* (4 vols., Boston, 1926–28); and others cited in Chapter 7. For

a revealing personal memoir of Woodrow Wilson from the time he was inaugurated on March 4, 1913, until his death in 1924, see Cary T. Grayson,
Woodrow Wilson: An Intimate Memoir (New York, 1960).

Clarence H. Cramer, *Newton D. Baker: A Biography* (Cleveland, 1961)
covers the career of Wilson's second Secretary of War in considerable detail.

The best and most comprehensive guide to the literature of American participation in World War I is Richard W. Leopold, "The Problem of American
Intervention, 1917: An Historical Retrospect," *World Politics*, II (April 1950),
405–25. Two of the best studies are Arthur S. Link, *Wilson: The Struggle for
Neutrality, 1914–1915*, already cited, which is detailed and exhaustive for the
period it covers, and Ernest R. May, *The World War and American Isolation,
1914–1917* (Cambridge, Mass., 1959). The bibliographical references in May's
monograph are exhaustive and supplement the Leopold article cited above.
Also excellent and similar to May in its interpretation of the role of the submarine is Karl E. Birnbaum, *Peace Moves and U-Boat Warfare* (Stockholm
[1958]). Two other studies of real value are Arno J. Mayer, *Political Origins
of the New Diplomacy, 1917–1918* (New Haven, Conn., 1959) and Daniel M.
Smith, *Robert Lansing and American Neutrality, 1914–1917* (Berkeley, Calif.,
1958). Much of Smith's thesis on Lansing's influence upon Wilson is stated in his
article, "Robert Lansing and the Formulation of American Neutrality Policies,
1914–1915," *Mississippi Valley Historical Review*, XLIII (June 1956), 59–81.

Older general works on this subject which continue to serve are Newton D.
Baker, *Why We Went to War* (New York, 1936) and the two studies by
Charles Seymour, *American Diplomacy during the World War* (Baltimore,
1934) and *American Neutrality, 1914–1917* (New Haven, Conn., 1935). See
also the same author's briefer account in *The Chronicles of America* series,
Woodrow Wilson and the World War (New Haven, Conn., 1921). Alice M.
Morrissey, *The American Defense of Neutral Rights, 1914–1917* (Cambridge,
Mass., 1939) stresses the role of the submarine and defends the legality of
Wilson's position on this question. The case showing that the Wilson adminis-
tration was less than neutral is discussed in Edwin M. Borchard and William P.
Lage, *Neutrality for the United States* (New Haven, Conn., 1937). Consult
also Maurice Prendergast and Richard H. Gibson, *The German Submarine
War, 1914–1918* (New York, 1931). The influence of the isolationism of the
1930's in explaining American participation in World War I is revealed in
Walter Millis, *Road to War: America, 1914–1917* (Boston, 1935). Equally cen-
sorious of Wilson and American diplomacy are C. Harley Grattan, *Why We
Fought* (New York, 1929) and Charles C. Tansill, *America Goes to War*
(Boston, 1938).

Alex M. Arnett, *Claude Kitchin and the Wilson War Policies* (Boston, 1937)
discusses the policies and views of the House majority leader who succeeded
Oscar M. Underwood and who was one of the country's staunch antipreparedness spokesmen.

The story of the Zimmermann telegram and its influence in getting the United
States into the war is excitingly told in Barbara W. Tuchman, *The Zimmermann
Telegram* (New York, 1958).

The peace movement is discussed generally in Merle Curti, *The American Peace Crusade* (Durham, N.C., 1929) and more specifically in the same author's *Bryan and World Peace* (Northampton, Mass., 1931).

On the Germans in the United States during the War, see Carl Wittke, *German-Americans and the World War* (Columbus, Ohio, 1936) and Clifton J. Child, *The German-Americans in Politics, 1914–1917* (Madison, Wisc., 1939). The story of German intrigue and conspiracy is told in John P. Jones and Paul M. Hollister, *The German Secret Service in America, 1914–1918* (Boston [1918]) and by a master agent in Franz R. von Kleist, *The Dark Invader* (London, 1933).

Horace C. Peterson, *Propaganda for War* (Norman, Okla., 1939) is a good general account of the efforts of both sides to sway American opinion. More specialized studies include Harold D. Lasswell, *Propaganda Techniques in the World War* (New York, 1927); James M. Read, *Atrocity Propaganda, 1914–1919* (New Haven, Conn., 1941); George S. Viereck, *Spreading Germs of Hate* (New York, 1931), an account of German activities; and James D. Squires, *British Propaganda at Home and in the United States from 1914 to 1917* (Cambridge, Mass., 1935).

Certain segments of American opinion on the war and Wilson's diplomacy have been studied. See, for example, Harold C. Syrett, "The Business Press and American Neutrality, 1914–1917," *Mississippi Valley Historical Review*, XXXII (September 1945), 215–30. There is no published study of American newspaper opinion comparable to Armin Rappaport, *The British Press and Wilsonian Neutrality* (Stanford, Calif., 1951).

An interesting account of the war reporters and the stories they sent back from the front is Emmett Crozier, *American Reporters on the Western Front, 1914–1918* (New York, 1959).

9

The United States at War

1917-1918

THE TASK OF PREPARATION

Once the United States had abandoned neutrality, the overwhelming majority of the population loyally supported the government, and only a very small number of individuals dared to oppose the war. The task of placing American life on a war footing was, nevertheless, one of enormous difficulties. Modern war is not merely a war between armies and navies; it is also a war between economic systems, and the victory goes to the side which can command the greater economic resources and more effectively mobilize the efforts of its civilian population and maintain their morale. After the United States entered the war, the government was compelled to assume dictatorial powers over industry, regiment the lives and thoughts of the American people, and place restrictions on civil liberties. The United States nearly became, for the duration of the war, a totalitarian state.

In spite of the measures of preparedness which had been adopted in 1916, the country was unready for immediate participation in the war. The army, owing mainly to the reforms made by Elihu Root as Secretary of War between 1899 and 1904, was a much more efficient body than it had been at the time of the war with Spain; but it was too small to be of any immediate service to the Allies. Before the United States could reinforce the British and French in France, hundreds of thousands of civilians had to be drafted and trained. The army, moreover, had also to be equipped and transported; and the United States was deficient in many important branches of the munitions industry and lacked an adequate supply of both ships and yards for building them. The economic needs of the Allies had meanwhile to be supplied—a task the German submarine campaign made both vitally important and exceedingly difficult.

Hence, while the United States was drafting into the army a large part of the civilian population, it had to increase the productiveness of both agriculture and industry. It was therefore not surprising that the American war preparation should proceed so slowly that critics began to accuse the government of criminal negligence. Not until May, 1918—nearly fourteen months after the United States had officially entered the war—did American troops begin to participate in serious fighting on the Western Front.

The chief responsibility for war preparation belonged, under Wilson, to Secretary of War Newton D. Baker. As chairman of the Council of National Defense, Baker had the task not only of organizing the army but also of putting the American economic system on a war basis. Of the twenty months during which the United States was at war, the first six were unavoidably devoted mainly to formulating policies, the second six to organization and preparation, and only the last eight to action. At the outbreak of the war whatever suspicions the administration may have entertained against big business were abandoned, and leading industrialists were invited to come to Washington to serve the government at nominal salaries of a dollar a year.

The tasks of organization were at first entrusted to a number of committees, which were responsible to the Council of National Defense. Washington at this period was described as "a patriotic madhouse." As it became apparent that divided responsibility was incompatible with efficiency, single individuals, responsible to the President, were gradually given sole authority over the various branches of the American war effort. This process was hastened by the growth of discontent with the apparent slowness of war preparation, which came to a head in January, 1918. Many Republican leaders denounced the government as inefficient, and they were supported by Democratic Senator George E. Chamberlain, chairman of the Senate Committee on Military Affairs, who told a New York audience that "the military establishment of America has broken down. . . . It has almost ceased functioning." Instead of consenting to the Republican demand for a coalition, Wilson replied by asking that the government be given virtually dictatorial powers over industry and the various governmental agencies established to prosecute the war. These were granted by Congress in the Overman Act, passed on May 20, 1918. Within a few months the mobilization program was proceeding in an orderly and efficient manner and, equally important, without corruption. The Republican administration which followed that of Wilson spent more than $3 million in an effort to prove that its predecessor had been dishonest; and although not all the dollar-a-year men were blameless, there was no evidence of misconduct on the part of regular government officials.

As it turned out, however, America's war preparations were on a much more elaborate scale than was necessary. The administration made its plans on the assumption that the war would continue at least until the end of 1919, and that in its final stages the United States would bear the main burden of the struggle with Germany. The unforeseen early collapse of German resistance in November, 1918, made much of the American preparation unnecessary and caused the war to be much more costly than it need have been. The United States drafted at least four times as many soldiers as were needed and spent vast sums unnecessarily on ships, munitions, and equipment. The cost of the war was further increased by the sale after the war, particularly by the Harding administration, of ships, factories, and supplies for a small fraction of what the government had originally paid for them.

The Draft

Soon after the declaration of war, it was decided that an army should be sent to France and that it should be raised mainly by conscription. There was considerable opposition to conscription in Congress, but the experience of Great Britain showed it was necessary—not because of any lack of enthusiasm but because it would enable the government to choose which persons could best be spared for service in France and which were needed at home.

The Selective Service Act became law on May 18. The War Department had already made preparations for the draft, the officials mainly responsible being General Enoch H. Crowder, the Provost Marshal–General, and Captain Hugh S. Johnson. On June 5 all men between the ages of twenty-one and thirty, inclusive, were required to register. A year's imprisonment was the penalty for refusal, but every effort was made to treat the registration day as an occasion for patriotic enthusiasm and to avoid any emphasis on compulsion. On August 31, 1918, the registration ages were extended to from eighteen to forty-five. The total number who registered on June 5, 1917, and on June 5 and September 12, 1918, was 24,234,021. Local draft boards then gave exemption to men who had families dependent on them, who were physically incapacitated, who were needed for duties at home, or who belonged to religious organizations with pacifist principles. This left 6,373,414 persons available for service. The final choice was then made by lottery.

In June, 1917, 687,000 persons were called for service, and more than two million were called at later dates. Altogether more than 4,750,000 persons served in the armed forces. Of these about 750,000 were in the army, navy, and national guard at the outset of the war; more than 1,250,000 were accepted as volunteers; and the remainder were drafted.

Draft evaders numbered 337,649, only 163,738 being caught. Of those who, after being drafted, refused war service, a number whose objections were based on religious principles were assigned to noncombatant service; but 450 who refused service on political grounds were condemned to imprisonment. Some of these objectors were not released until November, 1920.

Finance

The total ultimate cost of the war to the United States government approached $50 billion. Of the $32 billion spent during 1917, 1918, and 1919, $10.34 billion represented credits to the Allies for purchases in the United States, of which $2.6 billion was subsequently repaid. About one-third of the cost of the war was paid for immediately by taxes; the remainder became part of the national debt.

Special excise and "nuisance" taxes on luxury articles were steadily increased and new ones added by successive acts of Congress; but it was the income tax, with its excess profits provisions, which provided nearly two-thirds of the tax revenue. By the end of the war there was an income tax of 2 per cent on all incomes above $1,000 and surtaxes on larger ones. Incomes above $4,000 paid a surtax of 12 per cent; those above $500,000 paid 65 per cent. The number of individuals, including trusts and estates, that were required to pay income taxes more than doubled between 1917 and 1920, increasing from 2.7 to 5.5 million in the latter year. Despite this large increase in the number of taxpayers, it was "the relatively well-to-do" who bore most of the income tax burden during the war years. The corporation income tax was increased to 6 per cent, and special excess profits taxes were imposed to check profiteering. Firms earning a profit of more than 15 per cent paid an excess profits tax of 20 per cent; those earning more than 33 per cent paid 60 per cent. The really significant features of these levies, however, were not in the money they raised but rather in the important precedents they established for the future. Within fifteen years the New Deal was to pick up where the Wilsonian progressives left off and to employ their tax ideas to pay for not only war and defense but also social reconstruction.

One of these precedent-setting innovations was the introduction of the excess profits tax. Equally important was the principle, strongly supported by Wilson and the progressives on Capitol Hill, and incorporated in the War Revenue acts of both October, 1917, and May, 1918, that personal income tax rates should be graduated in such a way as to impose the heavier burden upon those individuals most capable of carrying it. As with the excess profits tax, many of the wealthy and more conservative groups denounced the "discriminatory" provisions of these laws, just as some of the more advanced liberals opposed them for being too lenient. Most people, however, probably agreed with the opinion expressed by the Pittsburgh *Leader:* "Conscription of men for the Army will take those who are best able to fight the country's battles. Conscription of money will affect only those who are best able to bear the loss." [1]

The government also borrowed directly from the public to finance the costs of the war. Five war loans were raised, the first in June, 1917, and the last, a Victory Loan, in April, 1919. The total amount subscribed was nearly $21 billion. The interest rates varied from 3½ per cent on the first loan to 4¾ per cent on the last. The government sold its bonds directly instead of acting through the banks; and every effort was made to arouse popular enthusiasm, including some intimidation of those who seemed reluctant to subscribe. The results of this high-pressure salesmanship were remarkable: it was estimated that previously not more than 300,000 persons had been in the habit of buying stocks or bonds, yet the total number of subscribers to the fourth government war loan amounted to 21 million.

War Industries

The measures for the control of industry involved a direct reversal of previous government policies. Whereas the government had previously been endeavoring to maintain competition, it was now necessary to en-

[1] Quoted in Randolph E. Paul, *Taxation in the United States* (Boston, 1954), p. 113.

force coordination and combination. In the early months of the war the Council for National Defense appointed seven major committees composed chiefly of dollar-a-year men, which were to take charge of the more vital branches of economic activity. These committees were responsible for war industries, shipping, food, transportation, fuel, foreign trade, and labor.

The most important of the committees was the War Industries Board. Composed at first of a number of prominent businessmen, it was reorganized in March, 1918, and placed under the sole authority of Bernard M. Baruch, who henceforth functioned as a kind of economic dictator. A free-lance Wall Street operator who had made a fortune by speculation, Baruch was qualified for his position not only because he had great ability but also because he combined an intimate knowledge of business practices with personal independence. He was, moreover, personally congenial to President Wilson.

The first function of the War Industries Board was to determine priorities. With both the Allied governments and the various branches of the American government all competing with one another for supplies, it was necessary to decide in what order their different needs should be satisfied. The powers of the War Industries Board steadily increased. It finally took charge of all purchases by the government; and it could order that the production of some raw materials be expanded and others conserved, could standardize products (an activity which had a permanent effect on the American industrial system), and could fix prices.

The general policy of the government in buying supplies and in making contracts for construction was to avoid too much haggling about prices and to allow a rate of profit that would stimulate production and bring marginal mines and factories into operation. Such a policy had the additional advantage that by enabling manufacturers to pay higher wages it thereby avoided labor disputes. It resulted also in a rapid increase in both prices and profits, although it was hoped that much of the latter would be recaptured by the government through taxation. Baruch did, however, force down a number of prices. Steel plates, for example, were reduced from 4.25 to 3.25 cents a pound, and copper from 32.5 to 22.5 cents a pound, and the manufacturers of these commodities were still left a substantial profit. In making construction contracts the traditional method of competitive bidding was abandoned, and the government agreed to pay the cost of production—however much that might be—plus a reasonable profit. The profits allowed by the government under the cost-plus contracts varied between 2½ per cent and 15 per cent according to the size of the contract; but some manufacturers appear to have been able to increase their earnings illegitimately by exaggerating their costs of production. Between 1916 and 1919 the number of persons reporting incomes of more than $25,000 increased from 38,382 to 56,323. The large war profits caused much criticism, especially since many of the individuals responsible for the government's economic policies were dollar-a-year men who could hardly be expected to view the claims of business impartially.

Control over War Department purchases was given to General George W. Goethals, builder of the Panama Canal, who was appointed in April, 1918, as head of the purchase, storage, and traffic division of the General Staff. There was no serious difficulty in obtaining supplies of rifles, machine guns, and ammunition, although the government was compelled to build plants of its own in addition to relying on private industry. It constructed the $60 million powder plant at Nitro, West Virginia (subsequently sold for $8.5 million), the $90 million Old Hickory plant at Nashville, Tennessee (subsequently sold for $3.5 million), and a plant at Muscle Shoals on the Tennessee River, which became the subject of one of the major political controversies of the 1920's and 1930's. On the other hand, for its heavy artillery and tanks the American army was compelled to rely mainly on the British and French, and in one branch of production—aircraft—there was serious mismanagement.

At the outset of the war the American army possessed fifty-five planes, of which fifty-one were described as obsolete, the remainder as obsolescent. Since there was no aviation industry in the United States, one had to be created. Progress was exceedingly slow as a result of disagreement over policies, shortage of materials, and misconduct by those in charge of both the government program and the contracting corporations.

The navy spent $143 million on aviation and succeeded in acquiring 570 airplanes in time for service in Europe. The army, on the other hand, although it spent more than a billion dollars on aviation, shipped its first airplane to France in March, 1918, and by the time of the armistice had in active service in France no bombers and only 196 observation planes, all of a type officially described as "exceptionally dangerous to pilots and observers because of its defective construction." American aviators were compelled to use British and French airplanes. The individual mainly responsible for this fiasco was a dollar-a-year man who had been placed in charge of the War Department program. Apparently he was more interested in giving large contracts to corporations with which his friends and family were connected than in obtaining airplanes. A committee headed by Charles Evans Hughes investigated his activities, and after deciding there was not sufficient evidence for a criminal prosecution, recommended that, since he had accepted a commission as a colonel, he might appropriately be court-martialed.[2] In May, 1918, he was replaced by John D. Ryan, of the Anaconda Copper Corporation, and by November, 1918, 11,754 airplanes had been completed. Almost all of these, however, were too late to be shipped to France, and most of them were subsequently scrapped.

Shipping

The most vital of all the needs of the Allied powers was for shipping. In the spring of 1917 the German submarine campaign was so successful that Great Britain was in imminent danger of being starved into surrender. By June of that year the British had lost 5,360,000 tons of shipping, and sinkings were continuing at the rate of about 600,000 tons a month. Ships were being sunk more than twice as fast as they could be built, and at one point the British had supplies of food enough for only six or seven weeks. Later in the year the situation was still so serious that the British food controller cabled to the American government that the war was lost.

In 1914 the United States had had less than 1 million tons of shipping engaged in foreign trade. In 1916 Wilson had secured from Congress permission to create the United States Shipping Board, whose chairman in the latter stages of the war was Edward M. Hurley. The Shipping Board created the Emergency Fleet Corporation, with the function of purchasing and building merchant ships. In April, 1918, the steel magnate and former president of the Carnegie and United Steel corporations, Charles M. Schwab, was placed in charge of the program. This corporation, though government-owned, took out a charter in the District of Columbia and was thereby freed from much red tape and congressional interference—a legal device which was imitated by other government agencies and which was to be of considerable importance. The Emergency Fleet Corporation confiscated German ships interned in American ports, purchased a number of neutral ships, built four great shipyards with ninety-four launching ways, and contracted for the construction of mil-

[2] See the *Report of the Aircraft Inquiry*, issued by the Department of Justice in 1918.

lions of tons of shipping. Ten months after the United States entered the war the number of shipyard workers had increased from 50,000 to 350,000. On one day—July 4, 1918—one hundred ships were launched. In the year 1918 533 ships, totaling more than 3 million tons, were built; and by August 31 of that year the Emergency Fleet Corporation controlled more than 8,500,000 tons.

Most of this gigantic effort was, however, too late to be of service to the Allies. It was not until close to the end of the war that the dockyards built by the corporation began delivering ships in any quantity. The total new tonnage completed before September, 1918, amounted to less than half a million, the remainder of the ships controlled by the corporation having been confiscated or purchased from neutrals. The Hog Island yards near Philadelphia, for example, where the Emergency Fleet Corporation created a new city of 150,000 inhabitants, with eighty miles of railroads and fifty launching ways, did not deliver a single ship until December, 1918. It was therefore fortunate that the British navy had meanwhile discovered how to conquer the submarine. Sinkings of merchant ships began to decrease in the summer of 1917, and throughout 1918 they averaged only 200,000 tons a month. The British merchant fleet was able not only to keep Great Britain supplied with food but also to transport to France about half the American Expeditionary Force.

Food Production

Another vital necessity resulting from the submarine campaign was for an increase in food production. Herbert Hoover, who had earned a great reputation by his control of Belgian relief earlier in the war, was placed in charge of the problem in May, 1917, and was given legal authority by Congress in the Lever Act of August 10. Hoover supervised food imports and exports, arranged transportation priorities, was allowed (within limits) to fix prices, and organized a publicity campaign for strict economy, with meatless and wheatless days.

The problem of wheat was especially serious, since production had decreased from more than 1 billion bushels in 1915 to only 636 million bushels in 1916. By May, 1917, the price had risen to $3.45 a bushel. Congress therefore created a Grain Corporation, which promised to buy the total wheat crop. The price for 1917 was fixed at $2.20 a bushel. The Grain Corporation also bought the 1918 and 1919 crops at similar prices.

Assured of a market and urged to do their patriotic duty by the government, the farmers increased their wheat acreage from 45 million in 1917 to 75 million in 1919.

Total agricultural production increased during the war years by 24 per cent over 1913. As a result of greater production and decreased consumption, there was an enormous increase in the export of food: exports of breadstuffs averaged 3,320,000 tons before the war and 10,566,165 tons for the year 1918–19; exports of meats and fats rose from 645,000 tons to 2,369,630 tons; exports of sugar rose from 618,000 tons to 1,704,523 tons. American farmers thus helped defeat the German submarine campaign. The ultimate consequences to the farmers themselves were, however, disastrous. For a period they made big profits, which encouraged them to buy more land at swollen prices, to invest in more machinery, and to increase their mortgages. They also ploughed up millions of acres in the Great Plains which should have been left to grass. In 1920, when Europe resumed normal peacetime production, the agricultural boom collapsed, and the farmers found themselves caught between wartime debts and peacetime prices. The problem remained unsolved throughout the 1920's and was one of the causes of the general depression of the 1930's.

Transportation, Fuel, and Foreign Trade

The railroads were at first placed under a board of railroad men, which was supposed to coordinate their operations. This measure proved to be inadequate, and by the end of the year the roads were seriously congested. In December, 1917, the government leased the railroads from their owners, agreeing to pay them their average earnings during the previous three years, and began to operate them as a single system. William G. McAdoo, the Secretary of the Treasury, was placed at the head of the Railroad Administration. In August of 1918 the telephone and telegraph services were also taken over by the government on similar terms and were entrusted to the Post Office.

The Fuel Administration was created in August, 1917, by the same act which established the Food Administration, with Harry A. Garfield, the son of the former President and head of Williams College, as its chairman. The domestic use of fuel was severely curtailed, daylight saving was introduced, and a number of submarginal bituminous coal mines were opened, the result being a 37 per cent increase in production.

Foreign trade was supervised by the War Trade Board, headed by

Vance C. McCormick, the youthful chairman of the Democratic National Committee in 1916. The War Trade Board controlled all imports and exports, prohibiting those it regarded as unnecessary. Under the Trading-with-the-Enemy Act of October 16, 1917, the board helped to enforce the British blockade regulations, prohibited trade with neutral countries which might be of assistance to Germany, and adopted the British practice of blacklisting certain neutral firms. All enemy properties in the United States, the total value of which was estimated at about $500 million, were entrusted for the duration of the war to an alien property custodian.

Labor

The government paid special attention to the interests of the working class both because of the liberal sympathies of Wilson and Baker and because of the need for increasing production and preventing strikes. At the beginning of the war, labor was restless as a result of the rapid increase in the cost of living. In 1916 there were 3,789 strikes involving 2,275,000 workers, and in 1917 the numbers increased to 4,450 and 2,349,600. While Gompers and the other AFL leaders supported the war policies of the government, believing that the defeat of Germany was necessary for the preservation of democracy, the more radical branches of the labor movement, including especially the IWW, opposed the war as the work of bankers and munitions makers. In the Far West there were labor disputes accompanied by violence on both sides. In July, 1917, during a strike in a copper mine at Bisbee, Arizona, the employers kidnaped 1,186 of the strikers, transported them into the deserts of New Mexico, and left them there. In August an IWW organizer, Frank Little, was lynched in Montana. And in September the U. S. Department of Justice arrested 113 IWW leaders. These men were put on trial for sedition before Judge Kenesaw Mountain Landis in April, 1918, and 93 of them were given prison sentences, William D. ("Big Bill") Haywood being condemned to twenty years.

Although there was some danger that the war might be used as an excuse for crushing the labor movement, the administration maintained its sense of justice; nor did Gompers and the AFL leaders regret the suppression of the radicals. In 1917 the Council for National Defense appointed a Committee on Labor under the chairmanship of Gompers. Later in the year a National War Labor Conference Board worked out a program that proved very advantageous to the more conservative branches of the labor movement. The labor leaders agreed there should be no more strikes; and in return they were promised an eight-hour day, a raise in wages to keep pace with the rise in prices, collective bargaining, and the right of all workers to belong to unions. A National War Labor Board, headed by former President Taft and the labor lawyer Frank P. Walsh, was appointed to arbitrate labor disputes; and a War Labor Policies Board, headed by Felix Frankfurter of Harvard University, supervised the details of the program.

The final result was that wages actually rose as quickly as prices. In 1916 average real wages had been 5 per cent greater than in 1913. In 1917 they decreased by 4 per cent, but in 1918 they began to increase; and by the end of the war, although prices were almost double what they had been in 1913, real wages were as high as in 1916. After the war, prices fell sharply while wage rates remained relatively stable, with the result that by 1922 real wages were 16 per cent above the 1913 level. This was the most rapid rise in real wages in American history. The chief sufferers from wartime prices were not the working class but the middle classes, whose money earnings were slower to change.

There was, moreover, a decrease in hours of labor during the war years, which proved to be no impediment to an increase in production. Industrial production in 1918 was 38 per cent higher than in 1913, yet the proportion of workers who had gained a forty-eight-hour week had increased from 11.8 per cent to 48.6 per cent. There was also a rapid increase in unionization, which for the first time was receiving the support of the federal government. In 1914, 2,716,000 workers had belonged to unions. By 1920 the number had risen to 5,111,000, about 4 million of whom belonged to the AFL.

The Control of Public Opinion

The control of public opinion and the maintenance of popular enthusiasm were regarded by all the belligerent governments as vital parts of their war policies. In the United States this function was entrusted to the Committee on Public Information, which was headed by a progressive journalist of a remarkably colorful and exuberant personality, George Creel. Creel declared that his object was not censorship but "unparalleled openness"; he set out to acquaint the American people with every aspect of America's war effort. The Committee on Public Information distributed 75 million pamphlets, sent out 75,000 "four-minute men" who made

7.5 million four-minute speeches to audiences totaling more than 300 million, gave news to 16,000 local and foreign-language newspapers, and published a daily *Official Bulletin of the United States*. Having thus popularized the war in the United States, Creel went on, in 1918, to advertise the personality and ideals of Woodrow Wilson to the entire world—a publicity effort which has never been equaled in history and which had extraordinary and in some ways tragic consequences. By contrast with the propaganda agencies of some other belligerent governments, Creel displayed considerable integrity. He never indulged in conscious lying, and he did not allow atrocity stories unless he believed they were true.

Creel's activities, however, helped to increase the popular hysteria, the most lamentable feature of the whole war period in the United States. The intolerance displayed by the American public was, with much less excuse, fully as great as that which prevailed in any of the other belligerent nations. The number of Americans who opposed the war or who sympathized with Germany was far too small to be dangerous. Of that large body of Americans who were of German descent, the overwhelming majority were wholly loyal to the United States government. A few radicals opposed the war for political reasons, but they won no support. In April, 1917, the Socialist party, in a convention at St. Louis, voted against the war; but when a considerable number of both the leaders and the rank and file refused to accept this decision, the party began to disintegrate. These radical opponents of the war were, however, generally regarded as pro-Germans—an identification due partly to the support given by German agents to pacifism and to labor sabotage in 1915 and 1916.

In November, 1917, moreover, the Russian Revolution passed into a more radical phase, with the Bolshevik seizure of power. The Bolsheviks were believed by many Americans to be agents of the German government, and those American radicals who approved of them came under the same condemnation. Popular opinion, therefore, failed to discriminate between pro-Germanism and political radicalism; and the result was a wave of intolerance which threatened to destroy all the traditional guarantees of civil liberty. Journalists, businessmen, college professors, and ministers of religion vied with one another in propagating hatred; and they began to condemn not only pacifism and radicalism but also the use of foreign languages, the publication of foreign-language newspapers, and the most harmless deviations from orthodox customs and beliefs.

Congress retained rather more sanity than the remainder of the population, so that the limitations it imposed on civil liberties were due at least partly to a desire to restrain the popular hysteria. If the government had not undertaken to restrict the liberties of those who opposed the war, many of them might have been lynched. In June, 1917, Congress passed the Espionage Act, which imposed penalties for interfering with recruiting or making false statements that might obstruct the successful prosecution of the war, and also prohibited the use of the mails for treasonable literature. In May, 1918, the limitations on free speech were increased by the Sedition Act; the penalties were made more severe, and the list of offenses was extended, including, for example, the uttering of abusive language about the government, Constitution, armed forces, or flag of the United States.

These laws were enforced with excessive severity by the officials of the Post Office Department and the Department of Justice and by judges and juries who had totally lost their capacity for giving impartial verdicts. Albert Sidney Burleson, Postmaster General, forbade the use of the mails to a large number of Socialist periodicals, including particularly *The Masses* and *The Milwaukee Leader;* and the Department of Justice almost indiscriminately arrested persons suspected of radicalism and demanded that they be given prison sentences which would far exceed the duration of the war. To assist the government in protecting the country from radicalism and pro-Germanism, the department organized 250,000 volunteer patriots into an American Protective League. There were 1,597 arrests under the Sedition Act. Twenty-year prison sentences were given to twenty-four persons, including Victor Berger, formerly Socialist congressman from Milwaukee; fifteen-year sentences were given to six persons; and ten-year sentences were given to eleven persons, including the presidential candidate of the Socialist party, Eugene Debs. The repressive activities of the Department of Justice continued, moreover, for more than a year after the armistice, long after all excuse for them had disappeared.

A number of cases under the Espionage and Sedition acts reached the Supreme Court in 1919. The Court generally affirmed the convictions, thus showing that it could not be relied upon to defend civil liberties in a time of popular hysteria, but the cases were made memorable by the dissenting opinions of Justice Oliver Wendell Holmes. In the Schenck case (involving an attempt to obstruct recruiting) he upheld the conviction but took occasion to declare that only "a clear and present danger" could justify abridgment of free speech. In *Abrams v. United States* (in which five persons were sentenced to jail, three of them for twenty years, for circulating a Communist leaflet), he wrote a dissenting opinion which was one of the most eloquent defenses of free speech in American history.

AMERICAN NAVAL AND
MILITARY ACTIVITIES

The most valuable contributions of the United States to the cause of the Allies were economic and political rather than military. It is very probable that the Allies would have been unable to defeat the Central Powers if they had not been allowed to rely on the United States, both before and after April, 1917, as a source of supplies and financial assistance. The American government aided them also by inducing the German government not to adopt unlimited submarine warfare during the first two and a half years of the war, and—after April, 1917—by representing the war as a crusade for a better world and thereby helping to raise the hope and determination of the Allied peoples and undermine the morale of the Germans.

By contrast, as noted previously, the military contributions of the United States were less important. Still, without American reinforcements the Allied armies would probably have been unable to repel the German offensive of July, 1918, or to bring the war to a successful conclusion a few months later. And while it may have been unnecessary for the United States to raise an army of 4 million men, the military preparations of the American government, like its industrial policies, were based on the urgent needs of the Allies in April, 1917, and on the assumption that the war would last a year longer than it actually did.

The importance of the economic contributions of the United States is shown by the fact that of the total direct cost of the war to all the countries engaged in it, calculated at $186 billion, about one-sixth was paid by the United States. Of the lives lost in the war, on the other hand, only one in every eighty-nine was American, with 48,909 men killed in action and 63,513 dying from other causes. The total loss of life to all countries was about 10 million, of which 1,385,300 were French and 947,023 British.

The American navy began to cooperate with that of Great Britain soon after the United States declared war; and soon thereafter 300 ships and 75,000 men, under the command of Admiral W. S. Sims, were serving in European waters, where they assisted the British in defeating the submarine campaign. The most important activity of the American navy was in

General John J. ("Black Jack") Pershing (right), the Commander
in Chief of the American Expeditionary Forces in France (1917–
19), is shown here with General Henri Philippe Pétain of France,
the "Hero of Verdun." (Brown Brothers)

convoying supplies and troops across the Atlantic. The remarkable success of this operation is shown by the fact that about 2 million American
soldiers were transported to France before the end of the war and that
only one ship and 100 lives were lost on the eastbound passage. Next to
its convoy duties, the American navy also made a material contribution

in laying an enormous mine barrage, 245 miles long and 20 miles wide, across the northern end of the North Sea. This project, the inception of which was partly due to Assistant Secretary of the Navy Franklin D. Roosevelt, was, along with the convoy system, an important factor in the defeat of the submarine.

American military assistance, on the other hand, was much slower in reaching the Allies. It was on May 28, 1917, that the first American troops left the United States, and on October 21 that Americans for the first time occupied frontline trenches in a quiet sector of the Western Front, near Toul. But during the first eleven months after the United States entered the war, American troops sent to France averaged only about 700 a day. By March, 1918, there were in France only 300,000 Americans, all inadequately equipped. The delay was due not only to the fact that the Americans had first to receive military training but also to the scarcity of ships. This was a problem not merely of transporting men but also of bringing to France the equipment, munitions, and food supplies needed to support them.

General John J. Pershing had been selected to command the American armies in France. Pershing's qualifications were generally admitted, although it was felt in some circles that General Leonard Wood had a better claim and that he had been rejected because of his political activities as an adherent of the Republican party. Other generals who occupied important positions were Peyton C. Marsh, who became chief of the General Staff in Washington in December, 1917, and J. G. Harbord, who assisted Pershing as head of the Services of Supply, with headquarters at Tours. A general who was also a banker, Charles G. Dawes, took charge of the General Purchasing Board in France. Wilson and Baker gave Pershing complete freedom of action; he was to have full responsibility for American activities in France, and the function of the War Department in Washington was, as far as possible, to carry out his recommendations. Baker told Pershing on his departure that he was giving him only two orders: to go to France, and to come home again. Until March, 1918, when American troops began to arrive in large numbers, Pershing's most prominent activity was to insist, in opposition to the British and French, that the Americans should eventually constitute a separate army, fighting independently under their own commanders, and that they should not be used merely as reserves and reinforcements, wherever they might be needed, by the British and French generals. Believing that the British and French were too exhausted ever to take the offensive, Pershing decided it would be the task of the Americans to win the war, and he trained his troops for attack.

Since the autumn of 1914 the fighting on the Western Front had become a matter of trench warfare, the advantages being with the defense rather than with the attack. The Germans had taken the offensive in 1916, and the Allies in both 1916 and 1917. Gains of a few miles had been purchased with enormously heavy losses, and it seemed impossible for either side to win a decisive victory. The rival armies faced each other in lines extending from the North Sea to the Swiss border, and each of them hoped to wear down the other by a slow and very costly process of attrition.

The Germans, however, were capable in 1918 of one last effort. They had made peace with the Bolshevik government of Russia, had forced Rumania out of the war and occupied most of the Balkans, and had inflicted a crushing defeat on Italy at Caporetto. In March, 1918, they brought all their available men to the Western Front in the hope of winning a decisive victory before American reinforcements should arrive in large numbers and before the morale of the German people should begin to crack under the strain of the Allied blockade. The German offensive began on March 21 with a crushing attack on the British Fifth Army, which drove a deep salient into the Allied line in the region of the Somme. This was followed by other equally vigorous German attacks in Flanders and in the region of the Aisne and Marne. The initiative remained with the Germans until July 17; and the Allies, driven back in three different areas, seemed in imminent danger of defeat.

The crisis compelled the Allies, for the first time, to adopt unity of command. In April the British consented to accept French leadership, and General Ferdinand Foch was appointed to command all the Allied armies in France. Pershing assented to this decision; and although he still insisted that the Americans should finally become a separate army, he agreed on March 28 that during the crisis they might be used as reinforcements by the British and French. The transportation of American troops was hastened, the British supplying the majority of the ships; and for the next six months American arrivals averaged 263,000 a month. Wilson promised that by June of 1919 there should be 3,200,000 American soldiers in France.

The Americans saw their first real fighting on May 28, when the American First Division, brigaded with the British in the region of the Somme, captured Cantigny. The success of this operation convinced the British and French generals, hitherto skeptical, of the fighting capacity of the Americans. In June the Second and Third Divisions were used to reinforce the French in the region of the Aisne and Marne, now the scene of the main German offensive. The Americans stopped the German advance to Château Thierry, thereby checking a movement which threatened to capture Paris, and subsequently drove the Germans out of Belleau Wood.

The German offensive was exhausted by July 17. The initiative then passed to the Allies, and Foch immediately ordered a series of counterattacks. At this period the American troops were scattered along the whole Allied line from Ypres to near the Swiss border. An American army corps had been organized around Château Thierry, under the command of Hunter Liggett, and on July 18 this First Army Corps participated with the French in a successful offensive. In August the Allied offensive became general; the British under General Douglas Haig attacked along the Somme, and French troops under General Charles Mangin advanced up the Oise, a number of American divisions taking part in both these operations. Meanwhile the bulk of the American troops were being concentrated further east, between Verdun and the Moselle, where on August 30 Pershing took command of a First American Army.

Contrary to the wishes of Foch, who believed the Allied attacks should be concentrated on the regions further west, Pershing insisted that the Americans should undertake an independent operation under their own leaders and that it should take the form of an attack on the German salient at St. Mihiel. The attack on September 12 was a complete success; and it might perhaps have been followed by an advance upon Metz and the Rhineland and the cutting of the German lines of communication if Foch had allowed Pershing to follow up his advantage.

Subsequently the American troops were moved somewhat farther to the west, into the region of the Argonne and the Meuse, where they launched an attack on September 26. This region was the main scene of American operations for the remainder of the war, two separate armies, under Hunter Liggett and Robert Lee Bullard, being organized on October 12. The terrain was singularly difficult, because of—as Pershing described it—"the vast network of uncut barbwire, the deep ravines, dense woods, myriads of shell craters and a heavy fog." In this region the American armies made a series of attacks and continued slowly to advance throughout October, threatening finally to cut the railroads by which the Germans in Flanders maintained contact with their sources of supply. At the same time the British and French armies farther to the west, with American divisions participating, were also advancing; and by the second week in November the retreat of the Germans had become a rout.

WILSON'S WAR AIMS

Meanwhile services equal in importance to those of the American armies were being performed by Woodrow Wilson, whose eloquent advocacy of a just peace helped to convince the German people they ought to surrender. In a series of speeches Wilson insisted that the United States was not fighting against the people of Germany but only against their government, that the war ought not to be followed by punitive annexations or indemnities, and that peace should henceforth be maintained by the establishment of the rule of law in international affairs and of a League of Nations to enforce it. Wilson had probably made a mistake in not requiring that the British and French governments formally adopt his war aims as a condition of America's entrance into the war, because they had never accepted them. But most people assumed that Wilson was speaking for all the Allies, even though officially the United States was an Associated rather than an Allied Power.

On January 8, 1918, in a message to Congress, Wilson outlined the war aims of the United States in a series of fourteen points. This was done at the suggestion of George Creel, who pointed out that a brief and concrete summary of Wilson's program could effectively be publicized inside Germany. The fourteen points were as follows: open convenants of peace, openly arrived at; freedom of the seas, both in peace and in war; no economic barriers between nations; the reduction of armaments to the lowest point consistent with domestic safety; an impartial settlement of claims to colonies, in which the interests of the colonial populations would be considered equally with those of the great powers; evacuation of the Russian territory held by the Germans; evacuation and restoration of the Belgian territory held by the Germans; evacuation and restoration of the French territory held by the Germans, with the return of Alsace-Lorraine to France; an adjustment of the frontiers of Italy in accordance with the lines of nationality; autonomous development of the peoples making up the Austro-Hungarian empire; a reorganization of frontiers in the Balkans along ethnic lines, with access to the sea for Serbia; self-determination for the peoples in the Turkish empire; independence and access to the sea for Poland; and a "general association of nations." In another speech, delivered on July 4, Wilson summarized his international ideals as including the destruction of arbitrary power everywhere, the right of all peoples to self-determination, the rule of law in international affairs, and the organization of peace.

Wilson's speeches and war aims were then publicized throughout the world by George Creel and the Committee on Public Information. By the end of the war Creel had agents in every Allied and neutral capital in the world, and he was supplying news not only to the belligerents but to all the leading neutrals. Wilson's speeches were translated into every major language within twenty-four hours of delivery, and peoples of the war-torn countries began to regard Wilson as a kind of world saviour, endowed with a wisdom and a sanctity that were more than human. Peasants in Catholic countries put up pictures of Wilson beside the images of their local saints. Extracts from Wilson's speeches and information about America's war preparations were, moreover, distributed by airplane throughout Germany.

By October the German High Command knew that they had lost the war and that the only way to prevent an Allied invasion of Germany was to sue for peace immediately. There was a change in the German government, and a liberal, Prince Max of Baden, became chancellor. On October 5 Germany informed Wilson that it was willing to accept a peace based on the Fourteen Points, and on October 8 he asked whether the German acceptance was unconditional and whether the German armies would evacuate all invaded territories. On October 14 he declared that the Allied military leaders would fix armistice terms and that submarine warfare must end immediately, and he asked for further confirmation that the new German government was genuinely representative of the German people. Germany agreed to these conditions, so that on October 23 Wilson gave the correspondence to the Allied governments. The Allies now declared they were willing to accept the Fourteen Points with two amendments: the doctrine of the freedom of the seas must be modified, and Germany must agree to pay reparations for all the damage done to the civilian populations of the Allied countries by land, sea, and air. Foch was then appointed to arrange terms of armistice. Meanwhile Bulgaria had sued for peace in September and Austria on November 3; and there were beginning to be revolutionary disturbances inside Germany. On November 9 the Kaiser abdicated and the Social Democrats took over the government. On November 11 Foch's armistice terms were accepted, and fighting ceased.

Suggested Readings

Since the volume in the *New American Nation* series covering the years 1917 to 1920 has not yet been published, Frederic L. Paxson's *America at War, 1917–1918* (Boston, 1939), the second volume of his *American Democracy and the World War*, continues to be the single best volume on this subject. See also Mark Sullivan, *Our Times*, volume V and the more recent and well-written account by Pierce G. Fredericks, *The Great Adventure: America in the First World War* (New York, 1960). Among the older and still useful works covering various aspects of the war years, see especially John S. Bassett, *Our War With Germany: A History* (New York, 1919) and John B. McMaster, *The United States in the World War* (2 vols., New York, 1918–20) for their contemporary flavor. Pertinent and useful material is also to be found in the standard biographies of Wilson and in the personal accounts of other administration leaders, all cited previously. Richard O'Connor, *Black Jack Pershing* (Garden City, N.Y., 1961) is a recent biography of America's most famous World War I soldier.

The literature on American participation in World War I, including the "home front," is large and the works cited here are no more than indication of the kinds and extent of the studies available.

On economic mobilization, the detailed account by Benedict Crowell and Robert F. Wilson, eds., *How America Went to War* (6 vols., New Haven, Conn., 1921) is in many respects standard. Among the one-volume surveys, see Bernard M. Baruch, *American Industry in the War: A Report of the War Industries Board* (New York, 1941); the story as seen by the secretary of the Council of National Defense is told by Grosvenor B. Clarkson, *Industrial America in the World War* (Boston, 1923); and the contemporary account by Arthur Bullard, *Mobilizing America* (New York, 1917). On Baruch, see his own account in *My Own Story* (New York, 1957) as well as the biographies of William L. White, *Bernard Baruch, Portrait of a Citizen* (New York [1950]) and Margaret L. Coit, *Mr. Baruch: The Man, The Myth, The Eighty Years* (Boston, 1957). Also useful is William C. Mullendore, *History of the United States Food Administration, 1917–1919* (Stanford, Calif., 1941). On Herbert Hoover's role in aiding the Belgians before 1917, see his own detailed story, *An American Epic: The Relief of Belgium and Northern France . . .* (3 vols., Chicago, 1959–61). The organization of the government for war is told in William F. Willoughby, *Government Organization in War Time and After* (New York, 1919).

On the financing of the war, consult the excellent study by John M. Clark, *The Cost of the World War to the American People* (New Haven, Conn., 1931). Also useful are two older works by Ernest L. Bogart, *Direct and Indirect Costs of the Great World War* (New York, 1919) and *War Costs and their Financing* (New York, 1921). See also Alexander D. Noyes, *The War*

Period in American Finance (New York, 1926) and Jacob H. Hollander, *War Borrowing* (New York, 1919). A brief statement on wartime finance based on considerable research is Charles Gilbert, "How the United States Financed World War I," *The Journal of Finance*, X (December 1955), 510-11. Useful also are the memoirs of Treasury Secretary McAdoo, *Crowded Years*, cited in Chapter 8.

On labor during the war years, see John Steuben, *Labor in Wartime* (New York [1940]); Edward Berman, *Labor Disputes and the President of the United States* (New York, 1924); and Samuel Gompers, *American Labor and the War* (New York [1919]).

The effect of the war upon railroad transportation is discussed in Walker D. Hines, *War History of the American Railroads* (New Haven, Conn., 1928); Frank H. Dixon, *Railroads and Government: Their Relations . . . 1910-1921* (New York, 1922); and Albert R. Ellingwood and Whitney Coombs, *The Government and Railroad Transportation* (Boston [1930]).

Federal activity in moulding public opinion and the role of the government in dispensing information are told by the director of the chief agency created for these purposes in George Creel, *How We Advertised America* (New York, 1920) and the same author's *The War, The World and Wilson* (New York [1920]) and *Rebel at Large: Recollections of Fifty Crowded Years* (New York [1947]). See also the more detached accounts by Harold D. Lasswell, *Propaganda Technique in the World War* (New York, 1927), and James R. Mock and Cedric Larson, *Words that Won the War: Story of the Committee on Public Information* (Princeton, N.J., 1940). See also George G. Bruntz, *Allied Propaganda and the Collapse of the German Empire in 1918* (Stanford, Calif., 1938). For the effect of the war on personal liberty, the older works by Zechariah Chafee, *Freedom of Speech* (New York, 1920) and Norman Thomas, *The Conscientious Objector in America* (New York, 1923) are still useful, as is the more general account of the antiwar groups by Horace C. Peterson and Gilbert C. Fite, *Opponents of War, 1917-1919* (Madison, Wisc., 1957). Harry N. Scheiber, *The Wilson Administration and Civil Liberties, 1917-1921* (Ithaca, N.Y. [1960]), is an excellent, brief account "of the formulation and enforcement of federal policies affecting freedom of speech and press."

The effect of the war upon American education is told in Parke R. Kolbe, *The Colleges in War Time and After* (New York, 1919) and Lewis P. Todd, *Wartime Relations of the Federal Government and the Public Schools, 1917-1918* (New York, 1945).

The story of the War Department is competently told in Frederick D. Palmer, *Newton D. Baker: America at War* (2 vols., New York, 1931), but see also the pertinent sections of Clarence H. Cramer, *Newton D. Baker*, already cited.

The official and most detailed account of the American army during the war is U. S. Department of the Army, *United States Army in the World War, 1917-1919* (17 vols., Washington, D.C., 1948). Early brief accounts include Shipley Thomas, *The History of the A.E.F.* (New York [1920]); Leonard P. Ayres, *The War With Germany* (Washington, D.C., 1919); Thomas G. Frothingham, *The American Reinforcement in the World War* (Garden City, N.Y., 1927); Richard J. Beamish and Francis A. March, *America's Part in the World War* (Philadelphia [1919]); Frederick D. Palmer, *America in France* (New York, 1919); Peyton C. March, *The Nation at War* (Garden City, N.Y., 1932); and Girard L. McIntee, *Military History of the World War* (New York, 1943), a brief account told with reference to its excellent collection of maps.

Memoirs of American officers include John J. Pershing, *My Experiences in the World War* (2 vols., New York, 1931); James G. Harbord, *The American Army in France, 1917–1919* (Boston, 1936); and the same author's, *America in the World War* (Boston, 1933). See also Hunter Liggett, *Commanding an American Army: Recollections of the World War* (Boston [1925]); Robert L. Bullard, *Personalities and Reminiscences of the War* (Garden City, N.Y., 1925); and William Mitchell's revealing *Memoirs of World War I* (New York, 1960) for the story of the American air force in France between 1917 and 1919. Maurice P. A. H. Hankey, *The Supreme Command, 1914–1918* (2 vols., London [1961]) is the exceptionally perceptive and well-told story of an important participant.

On the draft, see Enoch H. Crowder, *The Spirit of Selective Service* (New York, 1920).

For the role of the American navy in World War I, see Thomas G. Frothingham, *The Naval History of the World War* (3 vols., Cambridge, Mass., 1925–26). An excellent account of the commander of American naval forces is Elting E. Morison, *Admiral Sims and the Modern American Navy* (Boston, 1942). The activities of the Navy Department are detailed by Secretary Josephus Daniels, *The Wilson Era: Years of War and After, 1917–1923* (Chapel Hill, N.C., 1946). See also William S. Sims and Burton J. Kendrick, *The Victory at Sea* (Garden City, N.Y., 1920) and Louis Guichard, *The Naval Blockade, 1914–1918* (New York, 1930). The latter should be supplemented by the more recent study by Marion C. Siney, *The Allied Blockade of Germany, 1914–1916* (Ann Arbor, Mich. [1957]).

The story of wartime shipping is told by Edward N. Hurley, *The Bridge to France* (Philadelphia, 1927). See also the same author's, *The New Merchant Marine* (New York, 1920). Older but still of value are J. Russell Smith, *Influence of the Great War upon Shipping* (New York, 1919) and Willis J. Abbott, *Story of Our Merchant Marine* (New York, 1919).

The American side of wartime diplomacy is covered in Charles Seymour, *American Diplomacy During the World War* (Baltimore, 1934). David F. Trask, *The United States in the Supreme War Council: American War Aims and Inter-Allied Strategy, 1917–1918* (Middletown, Conn., 1961) is exactly what its subtitle states. The diplomacy of the United States with Russia during the critical months between November, 1917, and March, 1918, is carefully and brilliantly detailed in George F. Kennan's first volume of *Soviet-American Relations, 1917–1920*, subtitled *Russia Leaves the War* (Princeton, N.J., 1956).

The best analysis of the armistice is Harry R. Rudin, *Armistice, 1918* (New Haven, Conn., 1944).

IO

Peace and the Return
to "Normalcy," 1919-1921

WILSON'S TASK

Wilson had led the United States into the war hoping that American influence would induce Great Britain and France to accept a just peace, one which would satisfy the legitimate interests of both the victorious and the conquered nations. The Fourteen Points were to be the basis of such a peace, the League of Nations the means to achieve and preserve it. But after the victory of the Allies such a peace was impossible. The peoples of Great Britain and France, convinced that Germany had deliberately started the war, and embittered by the sufferings and deaths of the past four and a half years, were determined on vengeance. No government which attempted to treat Germany leniently could have stayed in office. The governments of Great Britain, France, Italy, Rumania, and Japan had, moreover, made a series of secret treaties by which they had promised one another certain territorial gains at the expense of Germany, Austria, and Turkey. The Allied governments had never fully accepted Wilson's war aims, and it was natural that they should resent any attempt on the part of the United States to dictate the details of the settlement in Europe. It was the Allied Powers, not the United States, that had borne the brunt of the conflict and had suffered most of the losses; and it was their right, they believed, to draft the peace treaty. During the peace negotiations Wilson was therefore compelled to concede to most of the Allied demands, even when they conflicted with his Fourteen Points. In compensation, he could insist that the establishment of a League of Nations should be an integral part of the peace treaty, and he could hope that the benefits of the League would outweigh the injustices of the remainder of the treaty.

Wilson was, moreover, handicapped in his negotiations with the British and French by the fact that the Republicans had won control of Congress. Before the congressional elections of 1918 Wilson had been attacked by certain prominent Republicans, notably by Theodore Roosevelt, whose desertion of the party in 1912 had now been forgiven and forgotten, and by Henry Cabot Lodge, Republican leader in the Senate. Wilson had retaliated by issuing, on October 24, a request that a Democratic Congress be elected as an expression of confidence in his own leadership. This intervention in party politics, though hardly novel, proved to be a tactical mistake of which the Republicans made good use. The defeat of the Democratic party in the election of November, 1918, however, was probably due more to other factors than Wilson's partisan appeal. Businessmen and the wealthy were angry for the high taxes they were forced to pay; most urban voters were offended by the Eighteenth Amendment, which many rural Democrats had endorsed; middle-western farmers, a number of whom had voted for Wilson in 1916, returned to their traditional GOP allegiance because of the President's failure to approve an increase in the price of wheat; liberals were shocked by the Justice Department's repression of civil liberties; and many others simply were dissatisfied with the failure of the Democrats to take a stand on the many domestic issues of the day. The result was that the Republicans captured the Senate, and with it the Foreign Relations Committee, by 49 to 47, and the House of Representatives by 239 to 194.

During the campaign, moreover, it had become apparent that the Republicans were planning to oppose Wilson's peace aims. Earlier in the war it had seemed that almost all groups in America were in favor of a League of Nations. In 1915 a League to Enforce Peace had been formed, under the presidency of former President Taft, to work for the creation of a League of Nations; and a number of prominent Republicans, including Henry Cabot Lodge, had made speeches in support of it. In 1918, however, some of the Republican leaders decided that the most effective method of attacking Wilson and winning the election was to demand vengeance on Germany and to denounce the League as a superstate that would deprive America of its independence.

On November 18 Wilson announced he would go to Europe himself as chief of the American delegation. Two weeks later, in his sixth annual address to the Congress, he explained to that body that he was going to Paris to make certain "that no false or mistaken interpretation is put upon . . . [the ideals for which America fought] and no possible effort omitted to realize them." Wilson's decision to go to Paris was bitterly criticized by the Republicans on various grounds, some of which re- flected political partisanship. When he failed to take with him any prom- inent Republican or any member of the Senate—an error of judgment that strengthened the GOP's opposition to the peace treaty—the Republi- cans were outraged. The American delegates, in addition to Wilson him- self, were House, Lansing, General Tasker H. Bliss, and Henry White. White, a career diplomat who was qualified for appointment by his very wide experience with European diplomacy, belonged to the Republican party, but since he had not for a long time been active in American poli- tics, his membership on the delegation did not placate the party regulars.

Wilson reached Europe on December 13. During the next month he made visits to Paris, London, and Rome, during which he was received with a popular enthusiasm which probably surpassed that given to any other figure in human experience. The people of the Allied countries might not share Wilson's belief in fair treatment for their enemies, but they felt, nevertheless, that he was the embodiment of a new world order in which war would somehow be made impossible. Liberals in all coun- tries, moreover, recognized that all their hopes for a just settlement de- pended upon him. The moral leadership Wilson exercised at this period has no parallel in all history.

THE PEACE CONFERENCE

The peace negotiations began on January 18 at Versailles. Wilson's be- lief in open diplomacy was abandoned at the outset, and the more im- portant decisions were made in secret conclaves by a council of four, consisting of Wilson, Georges Clemenceau of France, David Lloyd George of Great Britain, and Vittorio Orlando of Italy. Clemenceau, represent- ing a nation whose soil had been invaded by the German army twice within half a century, was determined to achieve security for France;

Most of the important decisions at the Paris Peace Conference of 1919 were made in secret conclaves by the "big four," consisting of (from left) the premiers of Italy (Vittorio Orlando), Great Britain (David Lloyd George), and France (Georges Clemenceau), and President Wilson. (U. S. Signal Corps)

and he believed this could not be accomplished unless Germany was so weakened and humiliated as to make the Reich incapable of waging another war against France. The negotiations were largely a conflict between the realism of Clemenceau and the idealism of Wilson. Orlando's primary concern was to win territorial gains for Italy. Lloyd George was more sympathetic to Wilson, but his hands were tied by his Tory supporters and by the fact that the government he headed had just won a general election by promising to hang the Kaiser and to make Germany pay for the costs of the war. German delegates were not invited to the peace conference until the treaty had been drafted and it was time for them to sign it (June 28, 1919).

At the beginning of the conference Wilson won two victories by insisting that the German colonies should not be annexed by the Allied Powers but should be held by them as mandates, under international supervision, and that the Covenant of the League of Nations should be drafted immediately. Wilson became chairman of a League commission, which finished its work on February 13. Because liberal leaders in Great Britain and France, as well as in the United States, had been advocating a League since the early months of the war, the League commission had several different drafts upon which to work. The Covenant of the League, as finally agreed upon, provided for an Assembly representing all member-nations and a Council containing representatives of the United States, Great Britain, France, Italy, Japan, and four other nations to be elected by the Assembly. Most decisions of the Council were to be unanimous. The articles of greatest importance in the Covenant were Article 10, which guaranteed all member-nations against loss of territorial integrity and political independence through external aggression; Article 11, which declared that a war was a matter of concern to the whole League and that any circumstance which seemed likely to result in war might be brought up for discussion; Article 12, which provided that all disputes should be submitted either to decision by a Permanent Court of International Justice or to investigation by the Council; and Article 16, which declared that economic sanctions should automatically be applied by all League members against any nation resorting to war in violation of the Covenant, and also that, if the Council so recommended, economic sanctions might be followed by military action.

After presenting the draft of the League Covenant to the peace conference, Wilson returned to the United States for a two-week visit, during which time he hoped to sign the bills passed by the outgoing Sixty-fifth Congress and to explain to it the provisions of the Covenant. Its details, however, became known in the United States before Wilson's arrival, and its provisions were immediately denounced by a number of Republican senators. On February 26, two days after he had arrived from France, Wilson entertained the members of the House and Senate Foreign Relations committees at a White House dinner to discuss the Covenant and to answer questions; he also sought the advice of former President Taft and Elihu Root, two Republicans who favored some kind of League. The degree of senatorial opposition to the League among the Republican members of that body became ominously apparent when, on March 2, 1919, thirty-seven senators and two senators-elect—enough to prevent ratification—signed the Lodge-Brandegee round robin, a statement declaring they would vote against the League. But Wilson refused to be frightened by this senatorial opposition, and on the day before he was to return to France, in an address in New York City's Metropolitan Opera House, he accused his critics of "careful selfishness" and "comprehensive ignorance of the state of the world." Defying his opponents, he declared that the peace treaty "will find the covenant not only in it, but so many threads of the treaty tied to the covenant that you cannot dissect the

covenant from the treaty without destroying the whole vital structure."
Then he went on to say that "The structure of peace will not be vital
without the League of Nations, and no man is going to bring back a
cadaver with him." [1] Wilson's discussions in the United States at this time
caused him to conclude that four amendments to the Covenant were
needed to ensure the support of American public opinion: maintenance
of the Monroe Doctrine must be guaranteed, domestic questions such as
immigration and the tariff must be specifically excluded from League
control, and nations must be assured of freedom to withdraw from the
League and to refuse to accept colonial mandates. After returning to
France on March 14, Wilson persuaded the other powers to agree to
these amendments. In return for these concessions, however, France,
Italy, and Japan demanded that Wilson yield to some of their territorial
ambitions.

The details of the peace were worked out in April. Wilson, suffering
at the time from a severe attack of influenza, engaged in a prolonged
struggle to save his Fourteen Points and to prevent the secret treaties
from becoming the basis of the settlement. By threatening to withdraw
from the conference, he won two important victories with respect to the
European peace structure. France abandoned its demand that Germany
be deprived of the Rhineland, accepting in return a joint guarantee from
Great Britain and the United States to protect it from German aggression. Italy was not allowed to annex Fiume, and it did not receive the
African colonies the secret treaties had encouraged it to expect.

Wilson also succeeded in moderating Japan's ambitions in the Far East,
but he was compelled to allow Japan to retain the German islands in the
Pacific and to recognize Japan's acquisition of the economic suzerainty
Germany had previously exercised in the Shantung peninsula. All that
he was able to do was to prevent Japan from annexing this area, which remained under Chinese sovereignty. Though Wilson's sympathies were
with the Chinese and though he understood it was to America's advantage
to support China on the Shantung issue, Japan's threat to boycott the
League caused him to compromise. Incensed at this concession at its expense, China, also at war with Germany since August, 1917, refused to
sign the Treaty of Versailles.

Despite Wilson's efforts to moderate Allied demands against Germany,

[1] Quoted in John Morton Blum, *Woodrow Wilson and the Politics of Morality* (Boston
[1956]), p. 171, and Thomas A. Bailey, *A Diplomatic History of the American People*
(2d ed., New York, 1942), p. 661,

the treaty which came out of the Versailles Palace was designed to maintain Franco-British supremacy over Europe, and with few exceptions the Germans regarded it as punitive. Germany was stripped of its colonies and its navy, forbidden to maintain an army larger than 100,000 men, deprived of Alsace-Lorraine in the west and the Polish territories in the east, declared guilty of having caused the war, and condemned to pay the Allied powers the full cost of it. The amount of reparations was fixed two years later at $33 billion, payment of which was to continue for generations. Allied armies were, moreover, to occupy the Rhineland for fifteen years. Four new or newly enlarged "succession states"—Czechoslovakia, Rumania, Yugoslavia, and Poland—were created out of the former Austro-Hungarian empire, which had fallen apart even before the armistice was signed. These states subsequently became the guardians of Franco-British supremacy in eastern Europe, but since all of them contained large minority groups whose rights to self-determination were mostly denied, the discontent among these peoples constituted a perpetual threat to the stability of the peace settlement. The Turkish empire was similarly broken up, and much of its territory, along with the former German colonies, became British and French mandates. These arrangements, except those pertaining to Germany, were formalized in a series of separate treaties with Austria, Bulgaria, Hungary, and Turkey, all of which were signed between September, 1919, and August, 1920.

The statesmen who drafted the eastern European settlements were forced to contend with numerous difficulties. Some, such as the question of deciding upon the frontiers of the new "succession states," involved complex issues with roots deep in the past; others resulted from the collapse of the Hapsburg and Turkish empires; and still others arose out of the postarmistice unrest and turmoil which swept the region. But whatever the origins of these problems, their solution was made more difficult by the events which had occurred in Russia.

Torn by internal strife and discontent, burdened by governmental intrigue and incompetence, and crippled by the backwardness of its economy, Tsarist Russia had broken under the strain of nearly three years of fighting. After Nicholas II abdicated on March 15, 1917, a provisional government was formed; but the Russian people, tired of years of suffering and privation and disgusted by the mounting war casualties, which they attributed to governmental incompetence, were attracted to the Bolshevik promise of "peace, bread, and land." On November 6, 1917, the Bolsheviks overthrew the provisional government and on the next day issued a decree on peace (written by Nicolai Lenin), calling upon all belligerents to end the war by agreeing to "a just and democratic peace," one involving "no annexations and no indemnities." When neither the Allies nor the Central Powers showed any serious interest in ending hostilities on these terms, the Bolsheviks negotiated a separate armistice with the Germans. Shocked by the extent of Germany's territorial demands and surprised by the indifference with which the belligerent peoples of Europe greeted their revolutionary appeal, the Bolsheviks tried to delay formal peace talks as long as possible. The Germans tolerated the equivocation and subterfuges of the Russian negotiators long enough to serve their purpose. Then, on February 10, 1918, after the Bolshevik delegation refused to continue the peace talks, the Germans launched an offensive against Petrograd which quickly convinced the Russians of the futility of further procrastination. Three weeks later, on March 3, 1918, they accepted Germany's terms and signed the Treaty of Brest-Litovsk, whereby Russia, in addition to accepting the loss of the Ukraine, was deprived also of Poland, its Baltic provinces, and considerable other territory.

Meanwhile the Allies had agreed upon tentative plans to prevent the vast quantities of military supplies they had shipped to Russia from being seized by the Germans. During the spring of 1918, British, French, and American forces were sent to Murmansk and Archangel; and in August, the United States participated in an Allied expedition to Siberia, sending 7,000 American soldiers under General William S. Graves. At Wilson's orders, the American forces in Siberia were only to assist the Czechoslovakian garrison stationed at Vladivostok and "to guard military stores." Three months after the first of General Graves's troops had arrived in Siberia, Germany surrendered; but for various reasons—anti-Bolshevik sentiment in the State Department, suspicion of Japanese intentions in northern Manchuria, and Wilson's preoccupation with the problems of the peace conference and the fight for Senate ratification of the treaty—the American forces remained in Siberia until January, 1920.

The Allied intervention in Russia was undertaken primarily as a military move against Germany, but it was motivated also, as one student of these events has asserted, by "an active distaste for Soviet power and a strong desire to see it replaced by one more friendly to the Allies." [2] These considerations, along with fear of the spread of Bolshevik ideology

[2] George F. Kennan, *Russia and the West under Lenin and Stalin* (Boston [1960]), p. 119.

throughout Europe, lack of agreement among the Allies on how to deal with the new Soviet regime, and French resentment against Russia's defection, combined to exclude Russia from participating in the peace conference and to complicate the problems of the Allied leaders.

Whatever the errors Wilson, Clemenceau, and Lloyd George committed at Paris, they should not be blamed too severely for the treaty. Its two most indefensible features were the exaction of reparations and the fixing of the frontier lines in eastern Europe. Payment of reparations, however, was demanded by an enraged public opinion in the Allied nations, and the swollen boundaries of such countries as Poland and Rumania were largely due to the fact that the governments of those states were already seizing what they wanted and could not be dislodged except by force. The primary error here lay with Wilson's own principle of self-determination. In eastern Europe, races were so intermingled that to fix frontiers along ethnic lines was impossible; any kind of settlement must create a minorities problem. Permanent peace in this area was impossible unless nationalistic hatreds were forgotten, armaments and trade barriers abandoned, and some form of political and economic confederation created. After World War I, however, this was totally impossible. The Fourteen Points had promised disarmament and the abolition of trade barriers, but Wilson had no practical scheme for accomplishing these objectives.

The effect of the Versailles settlement was to divide Europe into satisfied and dissatisfied powers. In the former category were Great Britain, France, and some of the states in eastern Europe; in the latter were three defeated countries—Germany, Austria, and Hungary—and one victorious country, Italy. Russia was also dissatisfied with the Versailles peace structure, but because of its internal troubles, both economic and political, the Soviet regime was concerned primarily with its own survival. Peace under such conditions would endure only as long as the satisfied powers retained decisive military supremacy. It might have been maintained permanently if the European powers had accepted Wilson's ideals of just treatment for all nationalities, disarmament, abolition of trade barriers, freedom of the seas, and collective security through the League of Nations. It might have been maintained longer than proved to be the case if the conference had accepted Clemenceau's thesis that nothing but force could prevent German aggression and if the makers of the settlement had therefore set out to give an overwhelming military superiority to those powers who had profited by it. Actually, however, the Treaty of Versailles was neither one thing nor the other; and unless the United States was prepared to intervene constantly in Europe to maintain the settlement, it made another war almost inevitable.

Nor did the League of Nations, which Wilson hoped would outweigh the injustices of the remainder of the treaty, prove to be a remedy. Germany was excluded from membership until 1926. Any revision of the treaty by peaceful negotiation proved to be impossible, and the dissatisfied powers and minority races soon came to believe that they could obtain their demands only by force or the threat of it. The League settled a number of minor disputes and provided for valuable international co-operation on nonpolitical matters, but on the major political questions it functioned primarily as an instrument for maintaining the Versailles settlement. Nor did the British and French governments give much support to its ideals except where they coincided with their own political interests.

THE FIGHT FOR RATIFICATION

The treaty was signed by the German delegates on June 28, and Wilson left for the United States on the next day. The treaty and the League were submitted to the United States Senate on July 10. Wilson had deliberately seen to it that the League Covenant should be a part of the Versailles Treaty, so that the Senate could not reject one without rejecting the other.

Of the members of the Senate, there were forty, all Democrats, led by minority leader Gilbert M. Hitchcock of Nebraska, who were for ratification. Thirteen or fourteen, headed by the Republicans Borah of Idaho and Johnson of California and the Democrat Reed of Missouri were for unconditional repudiation. These were the isolationists, the "irreconcilables." The remainder, the "reservationists," held views probably shared by most of the American people in that they were for ratificationa with reservations.

The viewpoint of Borah and Johnson was that Article 10 of the League Covenant committed the United States to defense of the existing territorial arrangements throughout the world, and that these territorial arrangements contained many injustices and must inevitably cause future wars. The United States, they believed, should not commit itself to perpetual involvement in European conflicts, nor should it pledge itself, as in fact would be the case, to go to the defense of the British and French empires. In most instances, this isolationist attitude represented a sincere conviction, but in some it reflected anti-British or other prejudices. Whatever its origins, it might be condemned as impractical, for experience had shown that the United States did become involved in European wars even against its will (neither Borah, nor Johnson, nor Reed had voted against war in 1917).

The attitude of the reservationists was more complex. Their chief objections to the Covenant were that it might limit the independence of the United States by requiring it to go to war with aggressor nations against its will, and that the League might deprive America of the suzerainty it exercised over the weaker Latin American countries under the Monroe Doctrine. Some of the reservationists felt that the Versailles Treaty had been too severe; others denounced Wilson for not having yielded to all the demands of the Allied Powers, indicating that they would have been willing to substitute for the League a pledge on the part of the United States to go, when necessary, to the defense of Great Britain and France. Elihu Root criticized the Covenant as impractical. He argued that nations would not, in practice, be willing to obey Article 16 requiring them to apply economic sanctions against any aggressor, and that this article would, by raising false hopes, do more harm than good.

Mingled with these legitimate considerations of foreign policy were a desire to assert the powers of the Senate over the Presidency, much personal dislike of Woodrow Wilson, and a willingness to use a vital international question as a football of party politics. If the Republicans were to win the next election, Wilson must be discredited; Republican politicians who wanted office, and business leaders who wanted to end progressive legislation and return to the practices of the McKinley era, therefore set out to destroy Wilsonism by defeating the League which Wilson had created. The fact that Wilson refused to announce he would not be a candidate for reelection in 1920 also alienated many people, especially businessmen, and caused them to use their influence against him. Throughout the spring there had been an elaborate anti-League campaign, financed chiefly by the two Pennsylvania business magnates Henry Clay Frick and Andrew Mellon. The American people had been told that the League would be a superstate which might compel them to accept unrestricted Japanese and Chinese immigration, which might deprive them of their army and navy and put them at the mercy of Mexican bandits, which might enable the colored races of the world to outvote and dominate the white races, and which might cause the whole world to become subjected to the Roman Catholic Church. The anti-League propagandists omitted to point out that according to the Covenant of the League, important decisions of the Council had to be unanimous and that the United States would be a perpetual member of the Council. The campaign soon began to take effect; and public sentiment, which—in the opinion even of the enemies of the League—had been strongly in favor of it in 1918, swung slowly toward isolationism.

The isolationists, irreconcilably opposed to American participation in a League of any kind, and the reservationists, with their conflicting views, were marshaled for common action with consummate political clever-ness by the strongly nationalistic senator from Massachusetts, Henry Cabot Lodge, who was himself a reservationist, but whose principal motive seems to have been hatred of Wilson. Of the other Republican leaders, Roosevelt had died in January, and Taft, as head of the League to Enforce Peace, continued to support Wilson and to urge American entry into the League. Lodge worked in close cooperation with George Harvey, who nine years before had started Wilson on his political career but who had now become one of his bitterest enemies. The Senate de-bate on the treaty continued through the summer and autumn of 1919, and every possible objection to the Versailles settlement was thoroughly aired.

Meanwhile Wilson determined to carry his case to the American peo-ple. On September 3 he left Washington for the West, and in twenty-two days he delivered thirty-seven speeches and traveled eight thousand miles. Warning the American people of the possible consequencs of isolation, he declared that: "To play a lone hand now means that we must always be ready to play by ourselves. It means that we must always be armed, that we must be always ready to mobilize the man strength and the manufacturing resources of the country. That means that we must continue to live under not diminishing but increasing taxes and be strong enough to beat any nation in the world." His audiences, at first apathetic, especially in the Middle West, grew steadily more enthusiastic as he approached the Rocky Mountains and the Pacific Coast. Wilson's hopes to arouse public support for the treaty, however, were cut short by his physical breakdown. Never a man of very good health, Wilson had endured in succession the responsibilities of domestic reform and war leadership, the struggle to achieve his ideals at Versailles, and now the fight with the Senate. During the night of September 25, after having delivered at Pueblo, Colorado, one of his most inspired and moving addresses, Wilson's dwindling physical reserve gave out and, against his protests, he was forced to abandon the rest of his trip and return to Washington. On October 2, he had a paralytic stroke, and for the remainder of his Presidency he was compelled to remain inactive.

In November the Foreign Relations Committee adopted fifteen reservations to the League Covenant, the most important of which were that the United States would not undertake to employ economic or military sanctions by order of the League Council unless Congress consented, and that the United States alone could interpret its powers and responsibilities under the Monroe Doctrine. Other reservations condemned the Japanese control over Shantung and (with Lodge dissenting) urged independence for Ireland. Taft and the League to Enforce Peace advocated acceptance of the reservations as the only method of bringing the United States into the League. Wilson, however, believed that the reservations would fatally weaken the League's authority and that, if the United States refused to enter the League except on its own terms, every other power would claim similar privileges. He recommended that the Democratic senators vote against the reservations, a decision that was probably a mistake.

When a vote was taken, 39 senators voted for the treaty with the reservations; 55, including both Democrats and isolationists, voted against it. In a second vote 38 senators voted for the treaty without the reservations and 53 voted against. The question was then adjourned until March, by which time some of the Democrats had decided that the treaty with the reservations was better than no treaty at all. Lodge and some Democratic senators attempted to devise a compromise which would permit ratification, but since neither Wilson nor the irreconcilables would allow it, the effort had to be abandoned. In a final vote, on March 19, 1920, 49 voted for the treaty with the reservations; 35, of whom 23 were Democrats, voted against it. The treaty with reservations thus failed by seven votes to secure the necessary two-thirds majority. Rejection of the treaty meant that the United States was still legally at war with Germany, and a resolution by Congress declaring that the war was ended was vetoed by Wilson, so that not until July, 1921, after Harding had become president, did the war officially end.

The responsibility for "this costly failure of American statesmanship" probably rests as much with Wilson as it does with Lodge. In addition to the inflexibility of these two men must be considered the unwillingness or the inability of the American people to understand their new responsibilities in world affairs.[3] Finally, had Wilson not insisted upon tying the treaty to the League Covenant, it might have been possible to secure enough votes to permit the ratification of each independently.

Whether the American people in 1920 were for the Wilson League or against it cannot be determined with certainty, but as Thomas A. Bailey has argued, it is probable that "an overwhelming majority of the people wanted the treaty with some kind of reservations."[4] The Republican victory in the election of the autumn was due to many causes other than hostility to the League, and many persons who voted for Harding did so in the belief that they were voting not against the League but for the League with the reservations. The defeat of Cox and the Democrats proved, however, to be a victory for the isolationists, and throughout the 1920's and 1930's they continued to be strong enough to prevent any intimate participation by the United States in the affairs of Europe.

Time has shown this attitude was unwise. That the United States could remain aloof from future European conflicts and could preserve its freedom and its democracy no matter what happened in other parts of the world was a dubious proposition even then. Wilson knew this and warned the American people in 1919 that if they refused to exercise the diplomatic leadership required of them, they would be forced to defend their freedom and security again in another great and more costly war. But whether American participation in the League would have altered the course of world affairs is debatable. By supporting the League, the United States might at least have attempted to reinforce those elements in Europe which were working for a permanent peace. The enemies of the League were wrong in declaring it would become a superstate which would deprive America of its independence. Although their suspicions of British and French diplomacy may have had some justification, it is probable that continued American participation in European affairs would have strengthened those groups in Europe who believed in justice and in collective security against aggression.

One of the most significant features of world politics in the 1920's and 1930's was the manner in which isolationists in the United States

---

[3] Thomas A. Bailey, "Woodrow Wilson Wouldn't Yield," *American Heritage,* VIII (June 1957), 106.
[4] Thomas A. Bailey, *Woodrow Wilson and the Great Betrayal* (New York, 1945), p. 274

and conservatives in Great Britain and France played into each others'
hands. America's refusal to support the League served to justify those
European statesmen who believed that a new world order was impossible and that international affairs must be conducted by the old methods
of power politics and secret diplomacy. And on every occasion when
the British and French governments acted in terms of self-interested power
politics rather than of Wilsonian idealism, the American isolationists had
a new argument for urging that the United States had been right in not
supporting the League. The United States had enabled the Allies to win
the war; but by refusing to use its influence in behalf of a new world
order and shirking its responsibilities as a great power, it lost the peace
and—in the final outcome—sacrificed all the objectives it had professedly
entered the war to achieve.

THE RETURN TO "NORMALCY"

Postwar Hysteria

From September, 1919, until March, 1921, the United States was virtually without a President. Wilson continued to head the administration,
and he occasionally asserted his will on important issues; but he was incapable of performing most of the functions of his office and, at the same
time, unwilling to allow them to be performed by anybody else.
Throughout this most important period, when the adjustment from wartime to peacetime conditions had to be made, the United States therefore
had no leadership. Congress relaxed the war regulations, and industry
returned to production for civilian needs; but little attempt was made
to plan the transition. The end of government controls, the public's
demand for consumer goods which could not be satisfied during the
war, speculation in scarce commodities, and European purchases in the
United States all combined to bring about a runaway inflation. Meanwhile
there was a continuance of the war hysteria which constitutes one of
the most shameful episodes in American history.

The popular fear of alien influences which had developed during the
war now expressed itself in hostility to any form of liberalism or radicalism. The crusading idealism Wilson had infused into America's war
preparations was replaced by cynicism and conservatism, bordering on
reaction. Meanwhile the working class was becoming restless, and some

members were affected by the radical tendencies that flourished for a short period in postwar Europe. The Bolshevik government in Russia was maintaining itself in power, despite efforts to overthrow it by Russian reactionaries and Allied armies. And while conservatives regarded Bolshevism as a menace to civilization, radical idealists saw in it the promise of a new and better social order. In 1919 a number of former members of the Socialist party, one of the best known of whom was the journalist John Reed, organized the Communist party in the United States on a basis of cooperating with the Russian government in the Communist International and working for a proletarian revolution in the United States. And although the Communists were far too few to constitute any real danger to American capitalism, they provoked hysterical alarm among many American conservatives who were frightened by the changes brought about by the war and longed to undo them and return to the "good old days" of prewar America.

Throughout 1919 there were many conflicts between capital and labor, and in the course of the year more than 4 million workers participated in strikes. From September, 1919, until January, 1920, 300,000 steel workers were on strike, under the leadership of William Z. Foster, demanding union recognition, higher wages, and the abolition of the twelve-hour day. In spite of much popular sympathy for the strikers, Judge Elbert H. Gary and the other steel magnates made no concessions. By importing Negro strikebreakers and playing upon nationalistic antagonisms among the workers, such as that between Serbs and Italians, they defeated the strike. It was not until 1923 that, as the result of a personal request by President Harding, the steel corporations finally conceded the eight-hour day. During the same period a coal strike, involving 450,000 workers, was defeated by means of an injunction obtained by the federal government. On the west coast the IWW was again active in labor conflicts, and in February, 1919, there was a five-day general strike in Seattle.

The growth of labor militancy even began to infect city employees, such as policemen and firemen; and at Boston, where the police had numerous legitimate grievances, there occurred a strike that gave the United States a future President. The cause of the strike was the refusal of the Boston Police Commission to allow the men to join a union. On the third day of the strike, following some minor rioting which the press greatly exaggerated, the governor of Massachusetts, Calvin Coolidge, called out the state guard to assist the state troops the mayor had previously called into action. After the strike had been broken, Coolidge upheld the police commissioner in refusing to reinstate the strikers. Samuel Gompers intervened on their behalf, whereupon Coolidge defended his attitude in a singularly forceful telegram, one sentence of which—"There is no right to strike against the public safety by anybody, anywhere, any time"—was widely applauded. As to the wisdom of Coolidge's actions there has been considerable controversy; but the political effectiveness of his message to Gompers was indisputable.

The authorities reacted to this wave of labor militancy by adopting sternly repressive measures. A. Mitchell Palmer, Wilson's Attorney General, arrested numerous individuals suspected of radicalism, often with little or no legal justification, and expelled from the country those of them who were not American citizens. In December, 1919, 249 alien radicals were deported to Russia. On New Year's Day, 1920, the offices of the Communist party throughout the United States were raided, and 6,000 Communists were arrested, most of them being subsequently released for lack of evidence of any criminal activity. A number of state governments enacted criminal syndicalism laws, under which Communist and IWW organizations were declared illegal and many of their leaders given long prison sentences. Under these laws it became illegal to make statements which tended to provoke violence, or to uphold the desirability of a proletarian dictatorship. Although such laws appeared to be inconsistent with the Bill of Rights, they were upheld in a number of cases by the Supreme Court. Meanwhile radical meetings were frequently broken up, and radical leaders were attacked and occasionally lynched by mob action, in which ex-soldiers frequently took the leading part. Socialists, as well as Communists and members of the IWW, were attacked, despite the belief of Socialists in peaceful and constitutional methods of change. Five regularly elected Socialist assemblymen were expelled from the New York State legislature.

One episode of this period was to become particularly notorious. On April 15, 1920, two men were murdered at South Braintree, Massachusetts, and $150,000 which they were carrying was stolen. Two Italians who held radical opinions, Nicola Sacco and Bartolomeo Vanzetti, were accused of the crime, convicted, and sentenced to death. Many people believed that the evidence against them was wholly inadequate and that their conviction had been due to their radicalism, which had been emphasized during the trial both by the prosecution and by the judge. Sacco and Vanzetti were finally put to death on August 23, 1927, after their conviction had provoked bitter controversies and had been denounced as judicial murder by liberal, radical, and labor organizations not only in the United States but throughout the civilized world.

THE ELECTION OF 1920

The presidential election of 1920 registered the general desire of the American people to abandon wartime sacrifices and crusading idealism, both in foreign policy and at home, to forget that they lived in a world of change to which their ideas and institutions must constantly be readjusted, and to return to an earlier, more familiar, and simpler age. It was a rejection not only of Wilsonism but of the whole movement of twentieth-century progressivism. The outcome of the election reflected also a weariness with the wartime regulations of the government and a disillusionment with the outcome of the war. Democratic candidates suffered from the fact that the economy was heading toward a depression. Among the first to feel the pinch were the farmers, but after May, 1920, industry and business generally were being effected. Commodity prices began falling in May and thereafter rapidly registered a sharp drop. The Democrats, first blamed for the inflation of 1919, now were being censured for the deflation.

The Republican convention met at Chicago on June 8. The two leading candidates were General Leonard Wood, who had been a close friend of Theodore Roosevelt, and Governor Frank Lowden of Illinois, whose support came chiefly from the large farmers of the Middle West. Hiram Johnson of California also controlled a number of delegates, but his progressivism and isolationism, as well as his bitter anti-League position, made him unsuitable to the party bosses, though he enjoyed considerable popular support. Herbert Hoover, a popular favorite with the female voters and the crowds at the convention, was another possible candidate, once he had declared himself a Republican. But Hoover had few delegates and no influence with the senators who were running the convention. Since neither Wood nor Lowden would yield to the other, and since both men had spent embarrasingly large sums of money to capture the nomination, it became necessary to find a compromise candidate. During the evening of June 11, this task was undertaken by a group of senators and party bosses who were anxious to weaken presidential authority and restore to Congress much of the power which, under Roosevelt and Wilson, had been assumed by the Executive. With this end in view, they agreed to swing the nomination to Senator Warren Gamaliel Harding of Ohio. His nomination, however, was not just the result of the intrigues of senators and party bosses, important as some of these maneuvers were. Harding was nominated because of a deadlocked convention, because he "was the most complete antithesis to Wilson that . . . [the delegates] could find, and [because he] represented a relaxation from wartime fanaticisms and a return to a sentimentalized 'normalcy.' "[5]

Harry M. Daugherty, an Ohio lawyer with a dubious reputation, was Harding's manager at the Chicago convention; and having sized up the situation very shrewdly, he had predicted to newspapermen what might happen. A journalist, paraphrasing Daugherty, had announced that Harding's friends expected him to be nominated for the Presidency by fifteen men in a smoke-filled room at eleven minutes past two in the morning. This was not exactly what happened, but it proved to be at least partly true. On the day after the party leaders made their decision, the convention began to turn to Harding, and he was nominated on the tenth ballot. In retaliation for obeying their leaders as to the presidential nomination, the rank and file of the convention insisted on making their own decision for the Vice Presidency. Ignoring the senatorial cabal's choice, Senator Irwin Lenroot of Wisconsin, they gave the nomination to Calvin Coolidge of Massachusetts.

The Democratic convention, which met at San Francisco three weeks later, was deadlocked for an even longer period. Wilson, though an invalid since October, 1919, continued to refuse to say he was not a candidate for a third term. While the Democrats were meeting in San Francisco, Wilson was in Washington quietly working through his friends at the convention to get himself nominated. When these maneuvers failed, largely because most of the delegates refused to consider the incapacitated President, the convention proceeded with the business of selecting a candidate from the nominees.[6] The leading contenders were two members of Wilson's cabinet—William G. McAdoo, Wilson's son-in-law, and A. Mitchell Palmer—and James A. Cox, a newspaper publisher who had been an efficient and moderately liberal governor of Ohio for three terms. Close to the state's Democratic machines, which approved of his stand in favor of liberalizing the Volstead Act, Cox's "wetness" made

---

[5] Wesley M. Bagby, "The 'Smoke Filled Room' and the Nomination of Warren G. Harding," *Mississippi Valley Historical Review*, XLI (March 1955), 674.
[6] Wesley M. Bagby, "Woodrow Wilson, a Third Term, and the Solemn Referendum," *American Historical Review*, XL (April 1955), 567-75.

him popular with a large number of urban voters all over the country. Because of these considerations and the fact that while he was loyal to Wilson and his policies, he had not been associated with the outgoing administration or the fight over the League, Cox was finally nominated on the forty-fourth ballot, with Franklin D. Roosevelt of New York, Wilson's Assistant Secretary of the Navy, as vice presidential candidate.

The Farmer-Labor party of this year was composed largely of four groups: disgruntled farmers (many of whom were supporters of Arthur C. Townley's Nonpartisan League of North Dakota), former Progressives of 1912, middle-class liberals disillusioned with the conservatism of the two major parties, and left-wing urban workers, who found the Socialist and Communist parties too radical or doctrinaire. Meeting in Chicago, the party nominated the prolabor Utah lawyer Parley P. Christiansen for President and the former Ohio Socialist printer and editor Max Hayes for Vice President. The new party's platform, a mildly Socialist document, called for greater control and public ownership of certain industries and other liberal reforms, including a demand for more vigilant protection of freedom of speech. The effort of the Farmer-Labor party to ally rural and urban workers into an effective national party proved shortlived. Many of the farmers and liberals, who were represented by the Committee of Forty-eight, a group of former Roosevelt progressives, withdrew from the new party before the election.

For President, the Socialists nominated Eugene V. Debs, at the time serving the first of a ten-year sentence in the federal prison at Atlanta for having violated the wartime Espionage Act. For Vice President, the party chose Seymour Stedman of Ohio, Debs's attorney. Three other parties—Socialist-Labor, Single Tax, and Prohibition—also ran candidates for the Presidency and Vice Presidency that year.

The only issue in the campaign was Wilsonism. Little was said about domestic questions, and attention was concentrated on the League of Nations. The Democratic convention declared that the election was a "solemn referendum," and Cox and Roosevelt toured the country advocating adherence to the League. The Republican position, however, was much less clear cut. The Republican party included both isolationists and reservationists; and in order to retain the support of both groups, the platform had deliberately been made vague. The Republicans were opposed to Wilson's League, but they declared that they were not opposed to every kind of League; their platform promised support for an "association of nations" which would fulfill the same purposes as Wilson's

League but which would safeguard American sovereignty. While John-son and Borah urged the election of Harding on isolationist grounds, a group of thirty-one Republican supporters of the League (including Elihu Root, Charles Evans Hughes, Herbert Hoover, and Nicholas Mur-ray Butler) declared that they would vote for Harding because he would take America into the League on the basis laid down by the Senate reservationists. From the viewpoint of reconciling these contradictory attitudes, Harding was an ideal candidate. He had such a fondness for soothing, sonorous, and empty phraseology, and his mental processes were so cloudy and so imprecise, that it was possible to interpret his speeches as meaning almost anything one wished. The strongest impres-sion to be derived from his utterances was that he would give the country an era of placid conservatism. "America's present need," he declared, "is not heroics but healing; not nostrums but normalcy; not revolution but restoration; . . . not surgery but serenity."

The result was a landslide for the Republicans. Supporting Harding were conservative Republicans who wanted to return to McKinleyism, war-weary citizens who were disillusioned by the outcome of the crusade in Europe and wanted to forget about the world outside America, repre-sentatives of the racial groups—German, Italian, and Irish—who resented the Treaty of Versailles, and all those who for one reason or another had come to dislike Woodrow Wilson. Harding was elected president by a popular vote of 16,152,200 to 9,147,353 and an electoral vote of 404 to 127. The Republicans also strengthened their control of both houses of Congress. The vote for the imprisoned Debs was 919,799, the largest number he had ever polled. All of the other parties together polled 252,-961, of which 189,408 went to the Prohibitionist candidate, A. S. Watkins, who headed the ticket after William Jennings Bryan refused to be con-sidered for the nomination. With Harding's election the voters looked to what they hoped would be a return to prewar America.

Suggested Readings

The literature on the peace conference is voluminous, and research on the subject continues. Harold W. V. Temperley, ed., *A History of the Peace Conference of Paris* (6 vols., London, 1920–24) is a long-time standard work containing many of the essential documents. On American participation, see the friendly account by Ray S. Baker, *Woodrow Wilson and World Settle-ment* (3 vols., Garden City, N.Y., 1922) and the same author's *What Wilson*

Did at Paris (Garden City, N.Y., 1919). The American side is defended in Edward M. House and Charles Seymour, eds., *What Really Happened at Paris* (New York, 1921). Charles H. Haskins and Robert H. Lord, *Some Problems of the Peace Conference* (Cambridge, Mass., 1920) is good on the territorial problems debated at Versailles; George H. Noble, *Policies and Opinions at Paris, 1919* (New York, 1935) analyzes the views of the principal figures; and Seth P. Tillman, *Anglo-American Relations at the Paris Peace Conference of 1919* (Princeton, N.J., 1961) is careful and revealing on this aspect of the negotiations. A number of important issues are presented briefly in the Amherst booklet, Theodore P. Greene, ed., *Wilson at Versailles* (Boston [1957]).

Among the numerous memoirs and diaries by participants and others at the Paris meetings, the following are especially useful: Harold G. Nicolson, *Peacemaking, 1919* (New York, 1939), the lively memoir of an observant and knowledgeable English diplomat; David Lloyd George, *Memoirs of the Peace Conference* (2 vols., New Haven, Conn., 1939); Robert Lansing, *The Big Four and Others of the Peace Conference* (Boston, 1921), good on personalities; Lansing's own side of the story and his criticisms of Wilson's role, his *The Peace Negotiations: A Personal Narrative* (Boston, 1921); James T. Shotwell, *At the Paris Peace Conference* (New York, 1937); Bernard M. Baruch, *The Making of the Reparations and Economic Sections of the Treaty* (New York, 1920); David H. Miller, *My Diary at the Conference of Paris* (21 vols., New York, 1924) and the same author's *The Drafting of the Covenant* (2 vols., New York, 1928); Edith B. Wilson, *My Memoir* (Indianapolis, 1929), the reminiscence of the second Mrs. Wilson; and the friendly and perceptive account by Herbert Hoover, *The Ordeal of Woodrow Wilson* (New York, 1958).

John M. Keynes, *The Economic Consequences of the Peace* (London, 1920), a widely influential and controversial book, should be compared with Étienne Mantoux, *The Carthaginian Peace, or the Economic Consequences of Mr. Keynes* (New York, 1952).

Among the other more specialized works, see especially the retrospective and interpretative account by Paul Birdsall, *Versailles Twenty Years After* (New York, 1941); Thomas A. Bailey, *Woodrow Wilson and the Lost Peace* (New York, 1944), which cites Wilson's errors at Paris; Allan Nevins, *Henry White* (New York, 1930), a careful biography of the GOP career diplomat who served on the peace commission; Frederick Palmer, *Bliss, Peacemaker: The Life and Letters of General Tasker Howard Bliss* (New York, 1934), the soldier on the peace commission. The conflict of interests within the Allied countries between March, 1917, and November, 1918, in determining the kind of peace that should be drafted is revealed in Arno J. Mayer, *Political Origins of the New Diplomacy, 1917-1918* (New Haven, Conn., 1959). See also Herbert Feis, *The Diplomacy of the Dollar* (Baltimore, 1950), on the period 1918-22.

The Far Eastern problems at Paris are ably treated by Russell H. Fifield, *Woodrow Wilson and the Far East: The Diplomacy of the Shantung Question* (New York, 1952). The thesis that the real purpose of the American intervention in Siberia was "to preserve the open door in Siberia and North

Manchuria" is carefully developed in Betty M. Unterberger, *America's Siberian Expedition, 1918–1920: A Study of National Policy* (Durham, N.C., 1956). This whole subject is superbly analyzed in more comprehensive fashion in the second volume of George F. Kennan's, *Soviet-American Relations, 1917–1920*, subtitled *The Decision to Intervene* (Princeton, N.J., 1958). See also William S. Graves, *America's Siberian Adventure, 1918–1920* (New York, 1941), the account of the military leader of the American forces. An older work on this subject is Leonid I. Strakhovsky, *The Origins of American Intervention in North Russia* (Princeton, N.J., 1937).

On the League and the fight in the Senate, see Denna F. Fleming, *The United States and the League of Nations, 1918–1920* (New York, 1932), a detailed and pro-Wilson account; scholarly and more critical of Wilson is Thomas A. Bailey, *Woodrow Wilson and the Great Betrayal* (New York, 1945). Some of the author's conclusions are summarized briefly in his article, "Woodrow Wilson Wouldn't Yield," *American Heritage*, VII (June 1957), 21–25, 105–06. Henry Cabot Lodge tells his own story with no quarter given to Wilson in *The Senate and the League of Nations* (New York, 1925). Lodge is also the subject of two biographies, the highly critical one by Karl Schriftgiesser, *The Gentleman from Massachusetts: Henry Cabot Lodge* (Boston, 1944) and the more recent and carefully researched one by John A. Garraty, *Henry Cabot Lodge: A Biography* (New York, 1953), some of which is summarized in the author's article, "Spoiled Child of American Politics," *American Heritage*, VI (August 1955), 55–59. The activities of another isolationist in the League fight are told in Marian C. McKenna, *Borah*, already cited. The details of the Senate fight are ably analyzed in W. Stull Holt, *Treaties Defeated by the Senate: A Study of the Struggle Between President and Senate in the Conduct of Foreign Relations* (Baltimore, 1933). On this subject, see also Kenneth Colgrove, *The American Senate and World Peace* (New York, 1943). Ruhl J. Bartlett, *The League to Enforce Peace* (Chapel Hill, N.C., 1944) is a history of this organization.

Herbert Hoover's overseas activities in trying to ease war-caused suffering is detailed in the third volume of his *An American Epic: Famine in Forty-five Nations: The Battle on the Front Line, 1914–1923* (Chicago, 1961).

On the transition from war to peace see Frederic L. Paxson, *Post-War Years: Normalcy, 1918–1923* (Berkeley, Calif., 1948) and the same author's more selective essay in *The Great Demobilization and Other Essays* (Madison, Wis. [1941]). A brief and perceptive explanation of the "boom and collapse of 1919–1920" is John D. Hicks, *Rehearsal for Disaster* (Gainesville, Fla., 1961). James R. Mock and Evangeline Thurber, *Report on Demobilization* (Norman, Okla., 1944) is standard.

The hysteria of 1919–20 is well treated in Robert K. Murray, *Red Scare: A Study in National Hysteria, 1919–1920* (Minneapolis, 1955), but see also Jane P. Carey, *Deportation of Aliens from the United States to Europe* (New York, 1931); Felix Frankfurter, *The Case of Sacco and Vanzetti* (Boston, 1927); and G. Louis Joughin and Edmund M. Morgan, *The Legacy of Sacco and Vanzetti* (New York, 1948). The most recent review of this famous case is

Robert H. Adair, *Sacco-Vanzetti: The Murder and the Myth* (Chicago, 1960).

The rise and history of the postwar Communist party to 1923 is well detailed in Theodore Draper, *The Roots of American Communism* (New York, 1957), a volume in the *Communism in American Life* series sponsored by the Fund for the Republic. See also the same author's *American Communism and Soviet Russia: The Formative Period* (New York, 1960), volume II, which covers the years 1923-29. James Oneal and Gustave A. Werner, *American Communism* (new rev. ed., New York, 1947) and William Z. Foster, *From Bryan to Stalin* (New York, 1937) are also useful. On the Socialists, David A. Shannon's *The Socialist Party of America* and Ray Ginger's *The Bending Cross*, both already cited, are very useful, as is Granville Hicks, *John Reed* (New York, 1936), the biography of an important figure; and for a left-wing Socialist's own account, see Benjamin Gitlow, *I Confess* (New York [1940]).

The story of labor's strife during demobilization is told in Samuel Yellen, *American Labor Struggles* (New York [1936]) and in volume IV of John R. Commons, *et al., History of Labour in the United States* (4 vols., New York, 1918-35). See also the important work by the Interchurch World Movement, *Report on the Steel Strike of 1919* (New York, 1920) and Vincent W. Lanfear, *Business Fluctuations and the American Labor Movement, 1915-1922* (New York, 1924). On the decline of the IWW, see John S. Gambs, *The Decline of the I.W.W.* (New York, 1932).

The most recent account of the rise and fall of the Nonpartisan League is Robert L. Morlan, *Political Prairie Fire: The Nonpartisan League, 1915-1922* (Minneapolis, 1956). Older studies include Herbert E. Gaston, *The Nonpartisan League* (New York, 1920); the hostile account by Andrew A. Bruce, *Non-Partisan League* (New York, 1921); and the sympathetic one by Charles E. Russell, *The Story of the Nonpartisan League* (New York, 1920).

An older, but still interesting, account of the election of 1920 is to be found in volume VI of Mark Sullivan, *Our Times*, already cited. This needs to be corrected in places by the much more detailed and comprehensive study by Wesley M. Bagby, *The Road to Normalcy: The Presidential Campaign and Election of 1920* (Baltimore, 1962) and by the same author's two articles "The 'Smoke Filled' Room and the Nomination of Warren G. Harding," *Mississippi Valley Historical Review*, XLI (March 1955), 657-74, and "Woodrow Wilson, A Third Term, and the Solemn Referendum," *American Historical Review*, LX (April 1955), 567-75. On Lowden, see the detailed biography by William T. Hutchinson, *Lowden of Illinois: The Life of Frank O. Lowden* (2 vols., Chicago, 1957). Also useful is James M. Cox, *Journey through My Years: An Autobiography* (New York, 1946).

For further references on the politics and politicians of the 1920's see the suggested readings at the end of the next chapter.

PART **III** THE REPUBLICAN ERA

1920–1933

II

Republican Politics
and Policies, 1921-1929

STALWARTS AND PROGRESSIVES
IN CONGRESS

From the inauguration of Warren G. Harding until the beginning of
Franklin D. Roosevelt's first term, conservative Republicanism was in
control of the federal Executive. During these years there was little of
the strong presidential leadership which had characterized Wilson's two
terms or of the efforts to use the prestige and power of the Presidency
to continue and extend the progressive movement. This return to Mc-
Kinleyism in the White House was in conformity with the predominantly
conservative opinions of the times and was reflected also in many of the
policies of the divided and strife-ridden Democratic party, which became almost as conservative as the Republican. The only effective opposition to the conservative administrations which controlled the federal
Executive during the decade was provided by a group of progressive
senators and congressmen, belonging to both parties, most of whom came
from the western agricultural states. These men, joined by a few others,
such as Congressman Fiorello La Guardia of New York City, kept progressive ideals alive on Capitol Hill and, in some instances, achieved
significant results for the cause of reform. Since this progressive coali-

tion in Congress frequently held the balance of power between the two major parties, it was often able to exercise an influence out of proportion to its numbers. Not only did these congressional progressives prevent the administration from achieving some of its more conservative proposals, but they were at times strong enough to secure the passage of some important liberal legislation of their own or to force the stalwarts to accept significant compromises.

The Railroads

The progressive coalition which existed in Congress during the Republican administrations of the 1920's made its influence felt even before Harding was inaugurated. Business interests, anxious to rid themselves of wartime controls as fast as possible, were forced to accept a compromise in finding a solution to the problem of the nation's railroads. William Gibbs McAdoo, who had been running the railroads for the government since December, 1917, proposed that the lines be operated by the government for five more years in order to test the value of unification. The workers, on the other hand, had put forward a plan, suggested by Glenn E. Plumb, by which the government should purchase the railroads from the stockholders and transfer control to a corporation in which the managers, the workers, and the public should have representation. The conservative Republicans in Congress and general opposition of the business community to any form of socialism prevented the adoption of either of these proposals. In February, 1920, Congress passed the progressive-sponsored Esch-Cummins Transportation Act. The railroads were given back to their owners, but the powers of the Interstate Commerce Commission were considerably enlarged. The commission, which was to consist henceforth of eleven members chosen from both parties and having seven-year terms, was to fix rates which would yield "a fair return upon the aggregate value of the railway property of the country." A profit of 5½ per cent was indicated as a fair return. By the "recapture clause" railroads earning more than 6 per cent were to transfer half their excess earnings to the commission, which would lend it to the less prosperous railroads. The commission was also to plan the consolidation of the railroads into a small number of integrated systems, which would be exempt from antitrust prosecutions, and it was to supervise the issuance of new securities. A Railway Labor Board was created to deal with labor disputes, and the employees of the railroads were guaranteed the right to belong to unions. The labor board, however, did not succeed in preventing strikes, several of which occurred as a result of wage cuts in 1921 and 1922; and in 1926 it was replaced by boards of arbitration.

The Interstate Commerce Commission was, in practice, unable to enforce the recapture clause or to bring about consolidation; and its rate-fixing powers were incomplete unless it could also determine the capital value of the railroad properties. But the method by which capital value was to be assessed remained indefinite. The method preferred by the commission was to take the reproduction cost of the railroads in 1914 and then make allowance for improvements and depreciation. The railroad corporations, on the other hand, insisted on the rule of reproduction cost new in terms of 1920 price levels, declaring that "it is that property and not the original cost of it, of which the owner may not be deprived without due process of law." In the case of the *St. Louis and O'Fallen Railway Company v. United States*, decided by the Supreme Court in 1929, the commission fixed the capital value at $850,000, while the railway corporation insisted on a figure of $1,350,000. In this case the Supreme Court, following the precedent of *Smyth v. Ames* (1896), decided against the commission, although it did not lay down any clear-cut rule as to how values were to be calculated.

Shipping

A similar opposition to government ownership and operation was displayed by the Republican leadership with respect to shipping. Since, however, the shipping industry was unable to stand on its own feet, it finally became necessary for even the most stalwart Republicans to accept a compromise. In June, 1920, the Congress passed the Jones Merchant Marine Act, whereby the vast fleet of merchant ships built and acquired during the war was to be sold by the Shipping Board to private operators. Until the sales had been completed the government-owned Merchant Fleet Corporation was to continue to operate certain of the ships and shipping routes. The Shipping Board began by selling ships at from $200 to $250 a ton. In 1921, however, Albert D. Lasker, who became head of the board by appointment of President Harding, proceeded to sell a large part of the government fleet to private corporations at $30 a ton, about one-eighth of what the ships had cost the government. Buyers were allowed to take their pick, and all sales were made in private. But even such governmental largesse as this was not enough for American owners to operate their ships profitably, so that in 1928 the Coolidge administration had to come to their rescue.

Power

In 1920 the progressives in Congress succeeded in introducing a bill to provide federal regulation of the rapidly growing power industry. Power production was a public utility, constituting a natural monopoly. Like the railroad corporations in the 1870's and 1880's, the power companies were becoming a field for unscrupulous manipulation by financiers; and as with the railroads, so much power crossed state lines and so much of the business was controlled by a few corporations that only the federal government could establish effective regulation. In June, 1920, the progressives in Congress succeeded in passing the Water Power Act, which created the Federal Power Commission, a body composed of three cabinet members and a secretary. The law empowered the commission to issue licenses to power corporations wishing to build plants on navigable rivers and streams on the federal public lands. The corporations were to pay annual fees, and the commission in the absence of state laws was to regulate the rates charged to consumers and pass upon new stock issues by the companies. Preference was to be given to enterprises owned by states or municipalities. This law was an important beginning in federal regulation and, like the Esch-Cummins Transportation Act, indicated the continuing strength of progressive ideals and programs in the Congress; but after a decade of experience, in which the commission granted 449 licenses, it was obvious that it was unable to regulate or supervise the power companies effectively. In 1930 the commission was changed into a body of five full-time members and given status similar to that of the Interstate Commerce Commission and the Federal Trade Commission.

The domestic record of the Republican Congress elected in 1918 indicated that the progressives, though in a minority, were strong enough to influence the course of legislation in that body. At the same time, as Arthur S. Link has suggested, progressivism as a national force was suffering from too many internal divisions, from significant defections from its own ranks which deprived it of much of the middle-class support which had previously helped to sustain it, and from the fact that it had no recognized national leader who could reconcile its warring factions, adopt a realistic program, and forge the loose liberal coalition into an effective

President Harding, shown here with his wife and father, owed much of his popularity to his physical appearance. (Brown Brothers)

and modern instrument of reform.[1] If the progressives could not agree upon a national policy, the same cannot be said of the leaders of the newly elected administration.

WARREN GAMALIEL HARDING

Harding had been nominated for the Presidency by a deadlocked convention. The Republican bosses believed he would be an amiable, unassuming, and popular figurehead, who would allow the major decisions to be made by the trusted Old Guard leaders of his party, many of whom were in the Senate. This anticipation proved to be correct. Unfortunately, Harding's intellectual equipment and weaknesses of character made him totally unsuited for high office. The son of a small-town homeopath of limited means, Harding left high school a year before graduation. He

[1] Arthur S. Link, "What Happened to the Progressive Movement?," *American Historical Review*, LXIV (July 1959), 833–51.

attempted to study law but gave it up quickly. After trying his hand at teaching school and selling insurance, he turned to journalism, and at nineteen, with three hundred dollars earned by playing the alto horn in the Citizen's Coronet Band of Marion, Ohio, and managing the local ensemble's bookings, he bought a third interest in his small-town's moribund newspaper, the Marion *Star*. Soon thereafter he became its sole owner and editor. Unambitious himself and aware of his own limitations, he was pushed from journalism into Republican state politics partly by his wife and partly by his friend Harry M. Daugherty.

Beginning as county auditor, Harding rose to the state senate, where he spent four years, and then served a term as lieutenant governor. Defeated for the governorship in 1910, he succeeded in 1914 in winning a seat in the United States Senate, where he remained until he became President. His career in the Senate was utterly undistinguished. In six years he did not introduce one important measure. Of the 134 bills he was responsible for placing before that body, only twelve were remotely, and in a very minor way, concerned with national problems. The rest were strictly bills dealing with "vote-bait, pension, or local measures." [2] Harding avoided work as much as possible; when he did attend the Senate's sessions he either refused to vote on measures before discussion or followed without question the orders of his party's bosses. Whenever possible, he avoided committing himself on major public issues. When forced to take a stand, he would not hesitate to reverse himself later if party politics or public opinion required him to do so. Not only was Harding's public record, crowded with inconsistencies, devoid of any indication of the intelligence and strength of will needed for the Presidency, but also his speeches revealed nothing suggesting he understood the problems of the day. Pompous, verbose, banal, and ridden with clichés, Harding's "big bow-wow style of oratory" confused rather than clarified any subject he chose to discuss. Commenting upon him as a speaker, William Gibbs McAdoo declared that Harding's "speeches left the impression of an army of pompous phrases moving over the landscape in search of an idea; sometimes these meandering words would actually capture a struggling thought and bear it triumphantly, a prisoner in their midst, until it died of servitude and overwork." [3] H. L. Mencken claimed that

---

[2] Samuel Hopkins Adams, *Incredible Era: The Life and Times of Warren Gamaliel Harding* (Boston [1939]), p. 86.

[3] Quoted in Mark Sullivan, *Our Times* (New York, 1943), VI, 31.

Harding spoke "the worst English" he had ever heard, and then went on to say: "it reminds me of a string of wet sponges."[4]

As an individual, Harding was pleasant, warm-hearted, and very likable. Indeed, his physical appearance, good nature, friendliness, and willingness to please appear to have been his greatest assets. Personally honest and well-meaning, though naïve and gullible, Harding was easily victimized by unscrupulous associates. He admitted his easy-going ways himself. Speaking to the members of the National Press Club in 1922, he said that his father had once told him, "Warren, it's a good thing you wasn't born a gal. Because you'd be in the family way all the time."[5] Harding craved affection and prized the friendliness of his old-time Ohio cronies. In background, temperament, and outlook, he was in many ways a typical citizen of a middle-western small town; and if he had never entered politics, he would probably have lived and died with the affection of all his neighbors.

The Politics of "Normalcy"

During Harding's administration an extraordinary collection of corrupt and disreputable adventurers assembled in Washington and were able to use their acquaintance with the President for private profit. Harding's unfitness for the Presidency—a fact he recognized himself when he told Columbia University President Nicholas Murray Butler, "I am not fit for this office and should never have been here"—was strikingly illustrated by the quality and behavior of his guests at White House parties. Alice Roosevelt Longworth, Theodore Roosevelt's oldest daughter and the wife of an Ohio congressman, once visited Harding's study and found it "filled with cronies . . . the air heavy with tobacco smoke, trays with bottles containing every imaginable brand of whiskey . . . cards and poker chips ready at hand. . . ." All in all, it was "a general atmosphere of waistcoat unbuttoned, feet on desk, and spittoons alongside."[6] Only at public White House receptions did Harding conform with the Volstead Act, which it was his constitutional duty to enforce at all times.

Of the ten members of Harding's cabinet, only three were outstanding figures. Andrew Mellon, the Pittsburgh multimillionaire with interests in coal, iron, aluminum, oil, and banking, who had previously been largely unknown to the general public, became Secretary of the Treasury—a

[4] Quoted in Adams, *op. cit.*, p. 115.   [5] Quoted in *ibid.*, pp. 7–8.
[6] Alice Roosevelt Longworth, *Crowded Hours* (New York, 1933), p. 324.

position he retained until 1931; Charles Evans Hughes became Secretary of State and served in this post until 1925; and Herbert Hoover became Secretary of Commerce, staying on at this job through the Coolidge administration. These three men determined most of the policies of the administration. Two other departments were entrusted to reasonably competent men: Henry C. Wallace, the editor of *Wallace's Farmer*, was appointed Secretary of Agriculture; and John W. Weeks, a former Boston broker and congressman, took over the War Department. Will

Secretary of Commerce Herbert Hoover (1921–28) and Secretary of State Charles Evans Hughes (1921–25) were the most widely respected members of the Harding and Coolidge cabinets. (Culver Pictures, Inc.)

H. Hays, the chairman of the Republican National Committee, became Postmaster General, but resigned after a year to take over the moral guardianship of the nation's movies. For Secretary of Labor, Harding chose James J. Davis, whose only association with labor was that he had joined a union when he worked as a puddler in an ironworks during his youth. His money came from banking, and his main interest was in guiding the destinies of the Loyal Order of Moose, an organization in which Harding was an active member. The Navy Department was entrusted to Edwin Denby, a veteran of the Spanish-American War and World War I and a former congressman. Denby's record looked good, but he proved to be incompetent. Harding's dearest wish, however, had been to give high office to his personal friends. He accordingly appointed his friend Senator Albert B. Fall of New Mexico as Secretary of the Interior, with charge over conservation, and his close friend Harry M. Daugherty as Attorney General, with charge over law enforcement. These two proved to be Harding's worst cabinet choices.

Other appointments, outside the cabinet, were equally unsuitable. Harding's boyhood friend Daniel R. Crissinger, a small-town lawyer who had once presided for a few months over a bank at Marion, Ohio, first became Comptroller of the Currency and then head of the Federal Reserve System. Colonel Charles R. Forbes, whom Harding had met and liked on a trip to Honolulu, became director of the newly created Veterans' Bureau, greatly to the profit of himself and his friends.

The conservatism and business-oriented policies which characterized the three Republican administrations of the 1920's were designed, in general, to assist big business, in the belief that if corporations earned large profits and were encouraged to expand their capital equipment, they would pay higher wages and provide greater employment, so that all sections of the nation would benefit. This attitude was especially noticeable in the financial policies of Treasury Secretary Mellon, whose influence upon fiscal affairs and programs continued for a decade and was largely undisputed. Besides working to reduce the national debt, which he did by some $7.19 billion by the time he left office in 1931, Mellon's chief desire was to reduce taxes, especially in the higher brackets. He maintained that this was necessary to release capital for business expansion. In the Revenue Act of 1921 the excess profits tax imposed during the war was repealed. The corporation income tax was, however, raised from 10 to 12½ per cent and, in spite of Mellon's recommendations, Congress, responding to the protests of the progressive-farm coalition, refused to reduce the maximum surtax paid by millionaires to less than 50 per cent. The Budget and Accounting Act of June, 1921, which established the Bureau of the Budget with the Chicago banker and former purchasing agent of the American Expeditionary Forces in France, Charles G. Dawes, as its first director, was one of the more constructive financial reforms of the Harding administration. For the first time now, it was possible to establish a more integrated control of federal expenditures. Businessmen and the administration's leaders approved of this law, just as they did of any measure which aimed to bring about economies and reduce federal expenditures.

During the war the government had made what it considered adequate provision for veterans' relief. Disabled veterans were to have hospital treatment; pensions were to be paid to all totally disabled men and to their dependents at the rate of $30 a month per person, and life insurance was sold by the government on easy terms. At the end of the war a discharge bonus totaling $256 million was paid to all veterans. The pension demands of the Grand Army of the Republic had played an important part in American politics after the Civil War, and it was hoped that this experience would not be duplicated in the case of the American Expeditionary Forces. This hope, however, was frustrated. The veterans' lobby soon became one of the strongest pressure groups in Washington. When the veterans tried to get the government to increase their benefits in the form of "adjusted compensation," Harding, in one of his rare examples of Executive leadership, appeared before the Senate to register his disapproval of any measure which would threaten the balanced budget. But few congressmen were able to resist its demands, so that in 1922, just before the congressional elections, the House and the Senate ignored Harding's appeal of the previous year and passed a "bonus" bill in the form of "paid-up insurance." Harding vetoed it on September 19, 1922, and defended his action by stating that no means had been provided to raise the money required and that to pay the veterans by increasing the public debt "would undermine the confidence on which our credit is builded and establish the precedent of distributing public funds whenever the proposals and numbers affected make it seem politically appealing to do so." [7]

If the administration's financial and fiscal policies won for it the applause of the business community, the return to a protective tariff received the support of both businessmen and farmers. During the 1920's there was considerably less opposition than formerly to tariff increases,

[7] Quoted in Adams, *op. cit.*, p. 259.

since industries which wanted protection were now developing in the South and West. Most of the nation's farmers, moreover, had never accepted the idea that the tariff should be used only to raise revenue. To be sure, they protested against levies which curbed competition and permitted domestic manufacturers to charge monopoly prices for goods the farmers needed, but they were not at all opposed to use of the tariff to protect themselves against foreign competition. Neither the administration, nor the progressives in Congress, nor the farmers, nor most businessmen realized that tariff protection was inconsistent with America's new status as a creditor nation. Few realized that if foreign nations were denied access to American markets, they could pay neither their war debts nor the interest on American private investments, and that since nations could not buy unless they could sell, the curtailment of American imports would eventually result in a decline of American exports.

In May, 1921, an Emergency Tariff Act, supported by the protectionists of both parties and the farm bloc in Congress, raised the duties on agricultural commodities, wool, sugar, and chemicals. In September of the following year, after prolonged studies by committees of both houses of Congress, the Fordney-McCumber Tariff was passed, which restored many of the rates to the levels of the Payne-Aldrich Tariff, and also imposed prohibitive duties to protect a number of new industries. The average ad valorem duty was 33.22 per cent. The principle on which the tariff was supposedly based was to equalize the manufacturing costs of foreign industry with those of American industry, and a Tariff Commission was appointed to investigate differences in costs. On recommendations from the commission the President was empowered to change the rates by not more than 50 per cent either upward or downward. Actually, however, the proposals of the commission resulted in thirty-two increases and only five very unimportant decreases. Protectionism was the accepted principle and, as the vote on the Fordney-McCumber bill indicated, it was not only the conservative representatives of industry who supported it, but most farmers and progressives, like Senator Hiram W. Johnson of California, as well.

The farmers had hoped that tariff protection would increase the price of their products, but they did not stop here in trying to resolve the problems arising out of the agricultural depression which started in 1920. The interests of the farmers were ably presented by their spokesmen in Congress, where a bipartisan agricultural bloc had been organized under the Senate leadership of William S. Kenyon of Iowa and Arthur Capper of Kansas. Guided by this group, the Congress, in August, 1921, passed the Packers and Stockyards Act, prohibiting monopolistic practices by the meat-packing corporations and requiring stockyards and meat and poultry packers to file price schedules with the United States Department of Agriculture, which was empowered to enforce the law. This measure was followed in February, 1922, by the Capper-Volstead Cooperative Marketing Act, which exempted cooperatives for the marketing of farm products from prosecution under the Sherman Antitrust Act. In September, 1922, after the Supreme Court had declared the Grain Futures Trading Act of 1921 unconstitutional, a second one was enacted to regulate practices on the grain exchanges. To facilitate and promote agricultural credits, in March, 1923, Congress passed the Intermediate Credit Act, which created twelve banks, one for each Federal Reserve District, with capital subscribed by the government, which were to lend money to cooperatives, with crops stored in warehouses as collateral. These measures, many of which had been part of the populist program of the 1890's, did not meet the basic farm problem of low prices and overproduction, as the next few years were to indicate. Still, the farm legislation of the Sixty-seventh Congress represented a considerable achievement for the progressive-farmer coalition, while the results of the midterm elections of 1922 gave them cause to hope for even greater success in the next session.

When the conservative wing of the Republican party suffered a serious defeat at the polls in November, 1922, its leadership in the Sixty-eighth Congress was more seriously threatened than before. In the House of Representatives the Republican majority was reduced from 300 to 225, and in the Senate the GOP lost eight seats. Although the Democrats increased their numbers in both houses, the election was not a Democratic party victory. It was, as one labor journal stated, "a Republican defeat" and not "a vote of confidence in the Democratic Party . . . [which] is the accidental beneficiary of popular resentment against Old Guard Republicanism." [8] The real victors in 1922 were the progressives in both parties, for they were, as *The Nation* asserted, in a position to control both houses of Congress and to determine the course of federal legislation. Republican stalwarts would now have to come to terms with the liberal bloc, for, as the election revealed, "the farmer-labor alliance . . . in the Middle West is a political fact." [9]

The rebuke the administration received at the polls in 1922 stunned

[8] *Journal of the Brotherhood of Locomotive Engineers*, LVI (December 1922), 890.
[9] "The Third Party Is Born," *The Nation*, CXV (November 22, 1922), 540.

and disappointed Harding; the events of the next few months would humiliate him. Incontestable evidence of corruption in the Veterans' Bureau came to his attention late in 1922 and, in order to avoid scandal, Harding, after accepting Charles R. Forbes's resignation, ordered him to take a trip to Europe. On March 11, 1923, Charles F. Cramer, the bureau's legal adviser, returned home from his office and committed suicide. These and other events, along with the rumors of corruption in high government circles which were circulating in official Washington, depressed and embarrassed Harding. He realized that he had been betrayed by a number of his friends and that he would be lucky if he escaped impeachment. The public, however, was as yet unaware of the corruption that was going on in the government and Harding still enjoyed widespread popularity. Partly to escape from his troubles and partly to explain his policies to the people, Harding left Washington on June 20, 1923, for a cross-country trip and a visit to Alaska. On his way back, he fell ill in Seattle. His hometown friend and personal physician, a homeopath, diagnosed Harding's trouble as a stomach disorder, but Dr. Joel T. Boone, the United States navy's medical officer who accompanied the presidential party, suspected a heart attack and, when Harding arrived in San Francisco, Dr. Boone insisted the President be examined by two recognized cardiologists, who confirmed his suspicions. Harding's difficulties were complicated by pneumonia, and on August 2, he died suddenly of a blood clot on the brain.

Corruption and Scandal

Five months after Harding's death the corruption and scandals which had disgraced his administration began to come to light. The most important of this spectacular series of disclosures had to do with oil. Presidents Taft and Wilson had set aside certain oil fields on public land for permanent government ownership so that the navy might be assured a supply of oil. Among these oil fields were Naval Oil Reserve Number One, at Elk Hills, California, and Naval Oil Reserve Number Three, at Teapot Dome, Wyoming. These oil fields had been placed under the control of the Secretary of the Navy. In May, 1921, by an Executive order signed by Harding and approved by Secretary of the Navy Edwin Denby, control was transferred to the Secretary of the Interior, Albert B. Fall. In April, 1922, Fall leased the Teapot Dome field to Harry F. Sinclair, and in December of the same year he leased the Elk Hills field to Edward L. Doheny. These leases were made secretly and without any competitive bidding by rival oil producers. Fall justified them on the plea that the oil was being drained off into diggings on adjoining land. Sinclair and Doheny agreed in return to store a part of the oil in tanks for the use of the navy.

The secrecy with which these transactions had been made aroused criticism among old-time conservationists, like Gifford Pinchot, and their progressive friends in the Senate, particularly La Follette. The suspicions of these individuals increased when they discovered that Secretary Fall had been spending money much more freely than formerly. Senator Thomas J. Walsh of Montana was appointed chairman of a Senate committee of investigation; and after eighteen months of preparation, he began hearings in October, 1923. His activities were at first bitterly denounced by the press and throughout the country as a partisan attempt to smear the administration; but he gradually extracted from a series of very unwilling witnesses evidence of corruption which could not be confuted. Fall had received $260,000 in Liberty bonds from Sinclair, while Doheny had "loaned" him $100,000 without interest or security. Among the discoveries incidentally made during the investigation was that the Liberty bonds given by Sinclair had been part of the profits of the Continental Trading Company, a corporation which had been formed by several oil executives in order to buy oil at $1.50 a barrel and subsequently sell it at $1.75 a barrel to the companies they controlled. By this device the oil executives had mulcted the stockholders, whose interests they supposedly represented, of more than $8 million. Out of the profits of the Continental Trading Company Sinclair had not only bribed Fall but had also made loans to the campaign fund of the Republican party—a fact which was known to Andrew Mellon and to Will H. Hays, chairman of the Republican National Committee, but which they succeeded in keeping secret until 1928.

Fall resigned from the cabinet in 1923. In 1929 he was convicted of accepting bribes and sentenced to a year in prison and a fine of $100,000. In another trial, however, Sinclair and Doheny were acquitted of bribing Fall, though Sinclair was subsequently sentenced to prison for contempt of the Senate and for hiring detectives to shadow members of the jury selected to try him. After Walsh had proved that Sinclair and Doheny had obtained the oil fields corruptly, President Coolidge appointed Atlee Pomerene and Owen J. Roberts to serve as government prosecutors, and the oil fields were recaptured by the government through a Supreme Court decision in 1927.

Other scandals occurred in the Department of Justice, headed by Harding's friend Daugherty, who antagonized the progressives by refusing to prosecute businessmen accused of fraud in connection with government contracts during the war, by refusing to enforce the antitrust laws, and—in 1922—by obtaining a sweeping injunction to break a

IT'S WASHDAY EVERY DAY IN WASHINGTON
The widespread scandals of the Harding administration were widely advertised by cartoonists. (Brown Brothers)

railroad strike. In 1924 a Senate committee, with Smith W. Brookhart of Iowa as chairman and Burton K. Wheeler of Montana in charge of the investigation, examined the activities of the department. It was discovered that the enforcement of the prohibition act was corrupt, with officials selling liquor permits on a large scale to bootleggers, and that the alien property custodian, Thomas W. Miller, had been defrauding the government by selling properties confiscated from German citizens during the war for much less than their value.

Daugherty retaliated by ordering government detectives to investigate the previous activities of Wheeler and Brookhart, in the hope of discovering something discreditable; and he subsequently declared that the Department of Justice had been the victim of a Communist conspiracy. Daugherty's complicity in the misconduct of his subordinates was never definitely proved, although it was significant that his closest friend, Jess Smith, who had assisted him in administering the department and with whom he lived in Washington, had committed suicide in May, 1923. In 1927 Miller was sentenced to eighteen months in prison and a fine of $5,000. Daugherty, tried on the same charge, was acquitted after he had refused to testify and had defended his refusal in a statement which implied that his testimony would have incriminated Harding. Daugherty's enemies, however, thought it more probable that he was using the reputation of the dead President in order to shield himself.

Another Harding official who found his way to the penitentiary was Colonel Charles Forbes, of the Veterans' Bureau. Forbes was guilty of wholesale corruption in making contracts for the construction of hospitals and in the sale and purchase of supplies. Out of $1 billion appropriated for the bureau in two years, about $200 million was stolen. In 1924, after a Senate committee had made an investigation, Forbes was sentenced to two years in prison and a fine of $10,000.

CALVIN COOLIDGE

Calvin Coolidge, who succeeded to the Presidency, saved the reputation of the Republican party. While there was no spectacular housecleaning, Harding's friends gradually disappeared from office, and there was a marked and salutary change in the tone of White House society. "It was my desire," Coolidge wrote, "to maintain about the White House . . . an attitude of simplicity and not engaging in anything that had an air of pretentious display." [10] It would have been difficult, indeed, to find a successor to Harding so unlike the dead President as Calvin Coolidge. Honest, shrewd, parsimonious, and taciturn, Coolidge carried into the Presidency the characteristic traits of the Yankee farmers of his native Vermont. On the night of Harding's death, Coolidge was near Plymouth, Vermont, visiting his father on the farm where he was born. As was his custom, Coolidge had retired early and was awakened and notified that he had succeeded to the Presidency by his father, who, as a notary public, administered the presidential oath in "the sitting room by the light of the kerosene lamp." [11] Modern and urban America seized upon this example of the "good old days" of rural America, and, with few exceptions, made Coolidge into a symbol of old-time American virtue.

A graduate of Amherst College, Coolidge began his career as an attorney in Northampton, Massachusetts. Within two years of being admitted to the bar, he began his slow and highly successful climb up the political ladder. Few Presidents have matched the range of his political experience: in 1899 he was elected to his first public office, the Northampton city council; from there he moved on to become city solicitor, mayor, a member of the Massachusetts house of representatives and of the state senate, then lieutenant governor, and in 1918 governor, from which post he was nominated for the Vice Presidency. In all these positions he displayed considerable political ability, unimpeachable integrity, and a remarkable capacity for selling himself to the public and for winning popular support. He believed in private enterprise, individual initiative, no government interference with business, and strict economy; and he could express these ideals with a forcefulness and a clarity which were proofs of his sincerity.

Coolidge's conception of the Presidency was in keeping with his economic beliefs. Two years after leaving the White House, when the nation was in the throes of the worst economic crisis in its entire history, the responsibility for which his administration must bear not little of the blame, he declared that one of the "most important" duties of the President "consists of never doing anything that someone else can do for you." [12] Coolidge's doctrines were perhaps a century behind the times and had little relation to the world of huge corporations and stock exchange speculation in which he lived, but they were doctrines which

[10] Calvin Coolidge, *The Autobiography of Calvin Coolidge* (New York, 1931), p. 216.
[11] *Ibid.*, p. 176.   [12] *Ibid.*, p. 196.

still had great popular appeal and which squared well with the temper of the times. Americans liked to believe the Coolidge philosophy, just as they enjoyed the wry Yankee humor of many of his utterances. It was part of the good fortune which accompanied Coolidge's whole career that he left office before the inadequacy of his program to twentieth-century conditions became apparent.

Administration Policies, 1923–1925

Because Coolidge believed it was not the function of the President to initiate policy, hardly a single significant domestic measure originated directly from the White House during his term. He kept on all of Harding's cabinet until death or resignation forced him to make new appointments; and because he shared many of Treasury Secretary Mellon's ideas on what was best for the country, Coolidge relied heavily on him for advice on domestic policy. When Coolidge declared that "the business of America is business," he was speaking not only as an individual but as the spokesman of the majority of the American people, who looked upon business as the provider of the material comforts to which they aspired. "I have been greatly pleased to observe," Coolidge once said with complete sincerity, "that the attitude of the Chamber of Commerce . . . very accurately reflects that of public opinion generally." [13]

In fiscal affairs Coolidge supported Mellon's program of reducing taxes and helping business. In 1924, the minimum income tax was reduced from 4 to 2 per cent; the minimum income liable to surtaxes was raised from $6,000 to $10,000; and the maximum surtax was reduced to 40 per cent. Many wartime excise duties were abolished. Congress, however, increased the estate taxes, imposed a new tax on gifts, and ordered publicity for income tax returns. In the Revenue Act of February, 1926, Mellon secured the repeal of these three measures, the maximum surtax was reduced to 20 per cent, and the exemption figure for heads of families was raised from $2,500 to $3,500. Finally, in 1929, the minimum income tax was reduced to 0.5 per cent, and the corporation income tax was reduced to 11 per cent. Another conspicuous feature of Mellon's administration of the Treasury Department was the willingness of its officials to allow wealthy men to take advantage of loopholes in the laws in order to reduce their tax payments. Yet in spite of the drastic tax reductions, the

[13] Quoted in Richard F. Fenno, Jr., "Coolidge: Representative of the People," *Current History*, XXXIX (October 1960), 210.

Sitting on the front porch of his father's Plymouth, Vermont, home, President Calvin Coolidge is shown here in 1925 conferring with GOP Senator Reed Smoot of Utah (left) and Treasury Secretary Andrew Mellon (right). (Wide World Photos)

national debt was reduced from $24,298,000,000 in 1920 to $16,185,000,000 in 1930, and there was always a surplus of receipts over expenditures.

Mellon was hailed by his admirers as the greatest Secretary of the Treasury since Alexander Hamilton. Actually, however, his program of surtax reductions probably helped to cause the surplus of capital savings, in excess of the investment needs of the country, which appears to have been an important factor in provoking the overspeculation of 1929 and the depression of the 1930's.

Closely related to the administration's policy of lowering taxes was its determination to promote economy, but on this question, despite Coolidge's declarations that he was "for economy" and "After that for more economy," the Congress refused to support him when economy involved thwarting the incessant demands of the World War veterans. In 1924 veterans suffering disabilities of various kinds which had developed prior to January 1, 1925, were given pensions, and the compensation scales were increased.[14] The veterans, moreover, demanded an additional bonus which would compensate them for the difference between their pay as soldiers and the high wages which had been received during the war by civilian workers. Congress passed a bonus bill, over Coolidge's veto, in 1924. By this bill veterans received twenty-year endowment policies, at the rate of $1.25 for each day they had spent in the army overseas and $1.00 for each day of home service, with compound interest at 4 per cent. Veterans could borrow up to 22½ per cent of the value of these policies. By the end of 1930 about 3.5 million persons held policies, and the total value amounted to about $3.5 billion; the total cost of veterans' relief, including the unpaid bonus certificates, amounted to about $6.5 billion; and the annual cost of hospital and other services provided by the Veterans' Bureau was $500 million.

The most serious problem of the Coolidge administration was the continuing agricultural depression. Neither the protective tariff nor the credit-marketing legislation of the Harding administration proved adequate to the twin problems of overproduction and declining prices. Farm leaders hoped to solve their problems by securing new foreign markets. One of the ways they advocated to attain this objective was the McNary-Haugen bill, first introduced in the Congress on January 16, 1924. The principal author of this proposal was George N. Peek, president of the Moline Plow Company. The McNary-Haugen bill proposed that a federal farm board be created with a revolving fund of $400 million which it was to loan to cooperatives to assist them in keeping the surpluses of a number of basic crops off the home market. Protected by the American tariff, the domestic price of these crops would increase sufficiently to assure the farmer "a fair value of exchange" between the prices of his commodities and those of nonagricultural producers. The surpluses would then be marketed abroad by the cooperatives for whatever they would bring, and the difference between what the cooperatives had paid to the farmers and what they had received from these foreign sales was to be met subsequntly by requiring the farmers to pay an "equalization fee." Besides trying to achieve "equality for agriculture," Peek and the sponsors of the McNary-Haugen bill also sought to increase the farmers' purchasing power to what it had been before World War I, thus introducing the idea of parity prices, "a concept which formed the basis of all subsequent farm legislation." [15]

[14] In 1930, the pension system was again extended to cover disabilities acquired before the beginning of that year.

[15] Gilbert C. Fite, "George N. Peek: Equality for Agriculture," *Current History*, XXVIII (June 1955), 354.

The McNary-Haugen bill had the support of the Secretary of Agriculture and the farm bloc in Congress, but this was not enough to see it through the House of Representatives. Coolidge and most other administration leaders, such as Hoover and Mellon, opposed it, and on June 3, 1924, eastern Republicans joined with Democrats from the South to defeat it. Four days later, the first session of the Sixty-eighth Congress came to an end; the legislators left Washington to prepare for the presidential nominating conventions, and the debate on farm relief was postponed until after the elections.

IMMIGRATION

The most important measure to be passed by the Republicans of this Congress remains to be mentioned. Reversing the policies which had prevailed since the first colonization of the United States three hundred years before, Congress imposed drastic limitations upon immigration. The propaganda carried on against unrestricted immigration since the 1880's had now begun to permeate public opinion. There was a widespread fear, especially among the labor organizations, that the postwar poverty of Europe might result in such an extensive migration to America as would seriously lower the American standard of living. The justification for restriction was that excessive immigration would make it impossible for the newcomers to be assimilated into American civilization and the American way of life. The authors of restriction were, however, influenced to some extent by the very narrow and intolerant conception of Americanism which had developed during the war and by the belief that certain racial groups were more desirable than others.

Between 1916 and 1920 immigrants averaged about 300,000 a year. In the year 1920–21 the number increased to more than 800,000, about two-thirds of whom came from southern and eastern Europe. In 1921 Congress passed the Emergency Quota Act, limiting the number of immigrants of each nationality to 3 per cent of the persons of that nationality resident in the United States in 1910. Since the act did not apply to persons born in the Old World but resident in the Western Hemisphere, it was followed by a very rapid growth of immigration by way of Canada and Mexico. From 1921 to 1925 immigration averaged 650,000 a year.

Finally, in May, 1924, Congress passed the Immigration Quota Act. Immigration was to be immediately restricted to 2 per cent of the persons of each nationality resident in the United States in 1890. Meanwhile a committee was to determine the racial composition of the American people in 1920. When the committee finished its work, immigration from the Old World was to be limited to 150,000 a year, and it was to be distributed among the various national groups in proportion to the number of persons descended from that national group in the American population of 1920. Persons born in the Western Hemisphere might enter the United States without quota restrictions; and the children and wives of American citizens, as well as teachers, students, and ministers of religion, were also allowed to enter freely. The purpose of this act was to limit immigration from southern and eastern Europe and to increase the proportion of immigrants from northern and western Europe. In spite of the fact that the quota requirement would have permitted only a negligible immigration from Japan, the admission of Japanese for permanent residence was totally prohibited. This insult to Japan, strongly criticized by Secretary of State Hughes, resulted in a most dangerous increase of Japanese hostility. The committee which was studying the racial composition of the American people reported, after several years of work, that it was unable to arrive at any scientifically accurate figures. Congress, however, insisted that it do the best it could, with the result that the national origins quota was finally put into effect on March 22, 1929.

The immigration acts limited entries from Europe but did not restrict immigration of persons born in the Western Hemisphere. Throughout the 1920's large numbers of French Canadians and Mexicans took advantage of the fact that American employers could no longer obtain cheap labor from Europe. French Canadians had already entered the United States in considerable numbers in the 1880's; the new wave of immigration in the 1920's brought the total number of entries from French Canada to more than 1.5 million. More than a million of these settled in New England, where they became, for the most part, factory workers. During the same period more than a million Mexicans came to the United States, half of them to Texas. Mexican standards of living were very much lower than those in the United States, and Mexican immigrants were paid excessively low wages. Largely of Indian descent, they were also the victims of color prejudice. The exploitation of Mexican workers by American employers created labor problems, especially in Texas, which occasionally resulted in bitter conflicts.

After 1930 the depression reduced immigration of all kinds drastically. Many persons wishing to come to America were refused visas lest they become public charges, and many aliens either left the United States voluntarily or were deported by the Department of Labor. In 1933 there were only 23,068 immigrants, as contrasted with 80,081 departures. Departures continued to exceed arrivals until 1936, when the growth of persecution in some of the European countries caused immigration to increase.

Most Americans felt that the continuance of unrestricted immigration would tend to weaken American traditions and institutions. Restriction, however, was by no means an unmixed benefit. Temporarily, it meant that the rate of increase of the population was sharply reduced. And since the American economic system, both in industry and in agriculture, had always been keyed to rapid expansion, such a reduction would eventually necessitate considerable economic readjustments. It would, for example, increase the problem of agricultural overproduction. The new American policy had, moreover, most deleterious consequences on Europe. The density of population in some of the European countries was ten times as great as in the United States; and the inability of the European nations to dispose of their surplus population through emigration to the United States was one of the factors which helped to cause the international hostilities of the 1930's.

The adoption of policies of racial, religious, and political persecution by certain European governments created, moreover, a refugee problem which constituted one of the greatest tragedies of world history in recent times. The most valuable citizens of Germany and Italy found life under fascism intolerable. Those who secured admission to the United States included such world-famous figures as Thomas Mann and Albert Einstein, who could make a great contribution to American culture and science. But many thousands of others were denied admission under the American immigration laws. Prior to the enactment of the laws of 1921 and 1924 no such problem could have occurred. Considerable areas of America had been first colonized by refugees, and hospitality to the victims of persecution had been the oldest, and one of the noblest, of American traditions.

The restriction of immigration was supported by religious fundamentalists, nativists, and racists, but it was also one of the goals of many progressives who felt that the nation's ills were directly attributable to the great influx of foreigners. What purpose, the progressives argued, did it serve to save the nation from the monopolists, if its moral values and standards were to be diluted by unassimilable foreigners? Immigration restriction was thus as much a part of the liberal and progressive reform program of the 1920's as its demand for federal farm relief and government-sponsored and operated regional power projects.

The Election of 1924

When the Republicans met in Cleveland on June 10, Coolidge and his business friends dominated the proceedings. Neither the Senate cabal which had been so influential in nominating Harding nor the Republican leadership in the Senate commanded any influence this time. Henry Cabot Lodge, who had been the convention chairman in 1920, did not even address the delegates in 1924, and in his own state of Massachusetts, William M. Butler, a Boston businessman and long-time friend of Coolidge, replaced him as GOP leader. The results of the first ballot were no surprise. Coolidge won the nomination with 1,065 out of a total of 1,109 votes. Only two farm states, with 44 votes, failed to support him. Wisconsin endorsed La Follette and South Dakota supported California's Hiram W. Johnson. When both Senator William E. Borah, Coolidge's choice, and Governor Frank O. Lowden of Illinois, also a Coolidge favorite, refused to accept the vice presidential nomination, the convention nominated the financier and former Director of the Budget, Charles G. Dawes. The Republican platform praised the Coolidge prosperity and policies and promised more of the same. It recognized the plight of the farmers and indicated its interest in alleviating their distress, but proposed no specific remedies. All in all the convention was a cut and dried affair and in three days it was over. In a letter to his son commenting upon the events at the convention, Hiram Johnson wrote: "I think Coolidge will be able to buy the election. The amount of money behind him will be greater than in all previous campaigns during our lives." [16]

Disorder, bitterness, and strife marked the Democratic convention which met in New York City's Madison Square Garden on June 24. The division between the rural, Protestant, and conservative South and the urban, Catholic, and liberal North developed into an open conflict which lasted for twelve days. The differences were now intensified by the growth of the Ku Klux Klan, with its program of preserving Protestant supremacy, and by the question of prohibition. A total of sixty candidates were nominated, but the two leading ones were William Gibbs McAdoo

[16] Quoted in John D. Hicks, *Republican Ascendancy, 1920–1933* (New York [1960]), p. 91.

and Alfred E. Smith. McAdoo, formerly of Wilson's cabinet, was the candidate of the South. For a time he had also enjoyed the support of many progressives and of the railroad brotherhoods, but when a Senate investigation disclosed that he had been retained by Doheny at $50,000 a year, these two groups quickly abandoned him.[17] Smith, born of Irish Catholic parentage in a New York East Side slum, had been elected governor of New York in 1918 and again in 1922 by way of Tammany Hall. An opponent of prohibition, he was the representative of the urban and immigrant population of the Northeast. Balloting continued for nine days, neither of the two chief candidates being willing to give way to the other. Finally both of them agreed to withdraw, and on the 103rd ballot the nomination went to John W. Davis, a conservative Jeffersonian Democrat and a New York corporation lawyer who had been born in West Virginia and had served in Congress for three years, then as Solicitor General, and, between 1918 and 1921, as Wilson's ambassador to Britain. To balance the ticket and placate the western progressives, the convention nominated William Jennings Bryan's brother, Charles W. Bryan, the governor of Nebraska, for the Vice Presidency.

The dissension within the Democratic party precluded a strong platform. The most bitterly debated issue—whether to repudiate the Ku Klux Klan by name—dramatized the party's division between the urban North and the rural South and West. In the end, the South and West carried the day with an inoffensive declaration in favor of civil liberties, but only by some five votes. On the question of American participation in the League of Nations, the platform deferred to the people by declaring it was up to them to state their intention in a national referendum. As for prohibition, apart from accusing the Republicans of poor enforcement, the Democrats did no more than announce that they intended "to respect and enforce the Constitution and all laws." The agricultural plank accused the Republicans of neglecting the interests of the farmers, but gave no clue as to what the Democrats intended to do for them. The Democrats attacked the extreme protectionism of the Republicans and called for a return to the Wilsonian principle of a competitive tariff, but this aroused little interest or enthusiasm. What at first appeared to be the best issue for the Democrats—the corruption of the Harding administration—was compromised by the fact that a number of prominent Demo-

[17] J. Leonard Bates, "The Teapot Dome Scandal and the Election of 1924," *American Historical Review*, LX (January 1955), 309.

crats, such as McAdoo, were also implicated in the oil scandals. The Senate oil investigation made it difficult for the Democrats to stand firmly on the issue of clean government.

Since both Coolidge and Davis were conservatives and the platforms of the two major parties provided little hope or comfort to the liberals, progressive leaders and the chiefs of the powerful railroad unions resolved to nominate a third candidate who would appeal to the farmers and organized labor. The Conference for Progressive Political Action, which had been formed in 1922 and had taken an active part in promoting liberal candidates in the midterm elections of that year, met in Cleveland on July 4 and offered the presidential nomination to La Follette. In his letter of acceptance to the convention, La Follette insisted upon running as an independent and not as a candidate of a new third party. The convention agreed, and then La Follette and the national committee of the CPPA chose the progressive Democratic senator from Montana, Burton K. Wheeler, for Vice President. The platform, largely written by La Follette, reflected the program which the CPPA had been advocating for the past two years and demanded—in the style of nineteenth-century populism and prewar progressivism—more political democracy and more federal control of business. It condemned the Republican agricultural policies, but went no further than to "advocate the calling of a special session of Congress to pass legislation for the relief of American agriculture" and to demand that the Interstate Commerce Commission "reduce . . . to pre-war levels . . . freight rates on agricultural products . . . and upon the materials required upon American farms for agricultural purposes." To placate labor, the platform contained a plank advocating "abolition . . . of injunctions in labor disputes" and "the right of farmers and industrial workers to organize [and] bargain collectively through representatives of their own choosing." Among its more radical proposals were the ones which called for the development of publicly owned power systems to supply electricity to the people at cost; eventual public ownership of the railroad system; "the election of all Federal Judges, without party designation" for ten-year terms; and a constitutional amendment to permit Congress to override a judicial veto. The Republicans predicted the most dire consequences for the country should La Follette be elected and portrayed him as a radical who wanted to destroy the independence of the judiciary and to overthrow the Constitution.

La Follette's candidacy was endorsed by the officials of the American Federation of Labor, but the union's membership was far from enthusiastic. Furthermore, individual leaders, like John L. Lewis of the miners, supported Coolidge. The loyalty to La Follette of the membership of other unions, except for the railroad brotherhoods and the clothing workers, was also mixed. The Socialist party endorsed the La Follette–Wheeler ticket, not because it had abandoned its principles, but in the hope that a new national party would emerge out of the groups which had come together under the banner of the CPPA.

Despite the three-cornered race, there was little popular interest in the campaign, and only half the electorate took the trouble to vote. Most of the nation was satisfied with Coolidge, and he was careful to avoid any semblance of partisanship. He campaigned little, kept to his desk in the White House, and, with great success, portrayed himself as a national symbol. The election results were a landslide for Coolidge. He polled 15,725,000 votes (54.2 per cent) and carried every northern and western state except Wisconsin, which went to La Follette. Only twelve southern states remained Democratic. Davis failed to carry even his native state of West Virginia, and he lost Kentucky, Maryland, Delaware, and Missouri. His popular vote was 8,385,586. La Follette's popular vote was 4,826,471. Though La Follette carried only his home state, he ran second in the eleven mountain and Pacific states. The division of the electoral vote was 382 for Coolidge, 136 for Davis, and 13 for La Follette. Five other minor parties, including the Prohibitionists and the Communists, entered candidates, but their combined total vote was less than 160,000.

In February, 1925, the CPPA, divided between the Socialists who wanted to form an independent third party and the railroad brotherhoods which wanted it to continue on a nonpartisan basis as in the past, voted to postpone making a decision as to its future. It was never made. The CPPA passed out of existence, and its leaders returned to their previous party allegiances. La Follette himself died in 1925, and his policies were inherited by his sons, Robert, who succeeded him in the Senate, and Philip, who served as governor of Wisconsin from 1931 until 1933 and again from 1935 to 1939.

President in His Own Right

During the last four years of Coolidge's presidency, most Americans were too busy enjoying the prosperity of the new era or searching for personal success to pay much attention to the politics of the times. Progressives and farmers, however, continued to fight for legislation they believed to be in the national interest.

PUBLIC POWER

From 1921 on, the progressives in Congress recommended federal regulation of all interstate power corporations, and some of them advocated outright government ownership. The chief enemy of the power corporations was Senator George W. Norris of Nebraska. Norris believed that the American people could derive almost unlimited benefits from the development of cheap electrical power if the rivers of the country were harnessed and developed, and he was convinced that these benefits could never be fully realized as long as the industry was controlled by a few financiers for private profit. He believed that only government ownership could ensure rates low enough for a widespread use of power by farmers and workers. Throughout the 1920's Norris conducted, almost singlehanded, a long crusade against the power corporations. He chose as his test case the question of Muscle Shoals, on the Tennessee River in Alabama. During the war the government had built at Muscle Shoals two nitrate plants for the manufacture of explosives and had begun to construct dams on the Tennessee River to provide power for the plants. The total cost had been $145 million. After the war the nitrate plants were no longer used, and the power plants, which had never been completed, were operated by the U. S. Army Corps of Engineers, the power being sold to local corporations. The Republican administration proposed to transfer the whole enterprise, both nitrate plants (which were to be used for fertilizer) and power plants, to private operation on very easy terms. In July, 1921, Henry Ford proposed to take over the project and submitted a bid to this effect.

Norris succeeded in blocking this proposal and in 1926 and 1927 introduced bills which recommended instead that the power plants be completed and that a government-owned corporation operate the plants and sell the nitrates and the surplus power. Congress passed a bill embodying Norris' ideas in May, 1928, but Coolidge pocket-vetoed it. In 1931 Congress passed a similar bill, which was vetoed by Hoover. In a vehement protest to Congress, Hoover declared that he hesitated "to contemplate the future of our institutions, of our country, if the preoccupation of its officials is to be no longer the promotion of justice and equal opportunity but is to be devoted to barter in the market. That is not liberalism; it is degeneration." The efforts of the progressives during the 1920's to achieve legislative recognition of the principle of public power and regional development were not to be realized until 1933.

AGRICULTURE

Progressives and farmers were defeated by Coolidge again when they renewed their effort to secure agricultural relief from the federal government. When the farm representatives in Congress failed to muster enough strength to pass the McNary-Haugen bill in May and June, 1926, they tried again in February, 1927, and succeeded in getting it through both houses of Congress only to have Coolidge veto it. The President was not indifferent to the plight of the farmers; he believed that the protective tariff was "a great benefit to agriculture as a whole," but he was entirely opposed to any measure which interfered with the individual through government controls. "The ultimate result to be desired," he said, "is not the making of money, but the making of people. Industry, thrift, and self-control are not sought because they create wealth, but because they create character. These are the product of the farm. We who have seen it, and lived it, know." [18] With no visible signs that the Coolidge prosperity was improving the lot of the farmers, the agricultural group in Congress determined to try to enact a modified McNary-Haugen bill. Once again the measure passed both houses of Congress by large majorities (53 to 23 in the Senate, 204 to 121 in the House), only to meet a similar fate at the hands of the President. Coolidge disapproved of almost every single provision of the bill. He claimed that the equalization fee called for an illegal use of the federal tax power; that the price-fixing provision was economically unsound and interfered with the liberties of the individual; that the bill discriminated against the diversified farmer and favored only the producers of certain staples; and that the price increase it sought to bring about would entice farmers to produce even greater surpluses, which, if dumped abroad at low prices, would invite retaliation. There was much in the McNary-Haugen bill that deserved criticism and required revision, but neither Coolidge nor the other administration leaders showed any interest in improving the bill or offering a comprehensive alternative of their own to meet the problems facing agriculture. The farmers were indignant, but they had no hope of overriding the presidential veto.

Another proposal the farmers advanced in the hope of raising prices was

[18] Quoted in Claude M. Fuess, *Calvin Coolidge: The Man from Vermont* (Boston, 1940), p. 384.

the export debenture scheme, under which export bounties in the form of "debentures" were to be paid to the exporters of the chief agricultural commodities. These debentures could be used to pay import duties, and they would thus be returned to the government. A federal farm board was to control production by reducing the debenture rates or canceling them if production increased. The export debenture scheme passed the Senate in 1926, 1928, and 1929, but it was always rejected by the House of Representatives. When Hoover indicated he too would veto the measure, the Senate was forced to abandon it and to accept the administration's marketing program, which became law on June 15, 1929.

SHIPPING

Although Coolidge and the Republican leaders were unwilling to use federal funds to help the farmers, they showed themselves quite ready to subsidize American shipping. Under the provisions of the Jones Merchant Marine Act of 1920, the federal government made a virtual gift of millions of tons of shipping to private operators. When this proved insufficient to enable them to hold their own against foreign competition —by 1928 the proportion of American foreign trade carried in American ships had decreased from 42.7 per cent to 32.2 per cent—Congress came to the rescue with the Jones-White Merchant Marine Act of May 22, 1928. The law provided for a government loan of $250 million to American firms for new construction, and it was to pay them an annual subsidy by means of mail-carrying contracts. Meanwhile the Shipping Board continued to sell them ships at very low prices. In spite of these measures it was still necessary to continue the Merchant Fleet Corporation. The Merchant Marine Act of 1928 resulted in some increase in the number of new and reconstructed American ships, but because the subsidy provisions of the law favored the construction of luxury liners, more of these were built than of any other type, among them the United States Line's trans-Atlantic flagships *Washington* and *Manhattan* and the Matson Navigation Company's Hawaii and Pacific cruise ships *Lurline, Mariposa,* and *Monterey,* which were among the first ships built in the United States since 1922.[19] By the end of 1930 there were 1,778 ocean-going ships of more than one thousand tons, with a total tonnage of about 9.5 million, flying the American flag. Of these, 1,345 were owned by private corporations and 433 by the Merchant Fleet Corporation. The Jones–White Act proved

[19] John G. B. Hutchins, "The American Shipping Industry since 1914," *Business History Review,* XXVIII (June 1954), 115.

to be only a stop-gap measure; it did not solve the basic problems of the industry. Within less than a decade, the entire shipping industry had to be salvaged from near bankruptcy and reorganized.

Despite the administration's obviously pro-business policies and its reluctance to use the federal government's authority to help the farmers as it had done in the case of the businessmen, Coolidge was very popular with the majority of the American people. The industrial prosperity was running smoothly and, since low farm prices reduced food costs, many workers found themselves sharing some of the benefits of the business boom. The fact that prices were relatively stable during the Coolidge years also helped to remove much of the workers' resentment against the infrequency of wage increases. To be sure, there were setbacks during Coolidge's term in the White House, such as the bursting of the Florida real estate bubble in 1926, but by and large most Americans agreed with the President when, on December 4, 1928, in his last message to Congress, he declared that the United States was enjoying "the highest record of years of prosperity" and that the people could "regard the present with satisfaction and anticipate the future with optimism." The majority of the American people believed him. And they had good reason to do so, for the economic developments and progress of the postwar years were truly remarkable.

Suggested Readings

Two recent interpretive articles on the 1920's serve as useful bibliographical introductions to the newer works on this period. Arthur S. Link, "What Happened to the Progessive Movement?," *American Historical Review*, LXIV (June 1959), 833–51 suggests several new insights into some of the decade's problems, while indicating also many of the newer works. Henry F. May, "Shifting Perspectives on the 1920's," *Mississippi Valley Historical Review*, XLIII (December 1956), 405–27 is an equally revealing and informative piece.

The most recent general synthesis of the decade is John D. Hicks, *Republican Ascendancy, 1921–1933* (New York [1960]). Shorter and more selective, though equally up-to-date, is William E. Leuchtenburg, *The Perils of Prosperity, 1914–1932* (Chicago [1958]). The first volume of Arthur M. Schlesinger, Jr., *The Age of Roosevelt: The Crisis of the Old Order* (Boston, 1957) emphasizes the political shortcomings of the decade and foreshadows Franklin D. Roosevelt. Harold U. Faulkner, *From Versailles to the New Deal* (New Haven, Conn., 1951) is the brief, factual account of these years in the *Chronicles of America*. Karl Schriftgiesser, *This Was Normalcy* (Boston, 1948) is caustic in its criticisms of the Republican administrations; more favorably disposed toward the GOP during these years is Malcolm Moos, *The Republicans* (New York, 1956).

Older general works include the sixth and last volume of Mark Sullivan, *Our Times* (New York, 1935), which covers the years 1920 to 1925, the briefly-written account with many useful insights by Frederick Lewis Allen, *Only Yesterday* (New York, 1931), and parts of the same author's more general survey, *The Big Change* (New York, 1952). See also the very lucid topical summaries in James C. Malin, *The United States after the World War* (Boston, 1930). The Marxist view of these years is to be found in Bruce Minton and John Stuart, *The Fat Years and the Lean* (New York, 1940).

The politics of the decade are analyzed with considerable insight by William Allen White, *Masks in a Pageant* (New York, 1930) and *Autobiography* (New York, 1946). See also Walter Johnson, ed., *Selected Letters of William Allen White, 1899–1943* (New York [1947]) and the same author's *William Allen White's America* (New York [1947]). Many of the works cited previously are also useful for the 1920's. Consult, for example, the pertinent sections of Hofstadter, *The Age of Reform*; Nye, *Midwestern Progressivism*; Goldman, *Rendezvous with Destiny*; and Ekirch, *The Decline of American Liberalism*, among others. Politics on the congressional level between 1917 and 1932 is well told in Howard Zinn, *La Guardia in Congress* (Ithaca, N.Y., 1958) and in the first of a proposed two-volume biography by Arthur Mann, *La Guardia: A Fighter against His Times, 1882–1933* (Philadelphia, 1959). On the insurgents in Congress see Ray Tucker and Frederick R. Barkley, *Sons of the Wild Jackass* (Boston, 1932) and also Grant McConnell, *The Decline of Agrarian Democracy* (Berkeley, Calif., 1953).

On the Harding administration the third volume of Frederic L. Paxson's, *American Democracy and the World War: The Post-War Years, Normalcy, 1918–1923* (Berkeley, Calif., 1948) is quite full. Samuel Hopkins Adams, *Incredible Era: The Life and Times of Warren Gamaliel Harding* (Boston, 1939) is serious journalism but sensational in tone. Harding is defended in Harry M. Daugherty and Thomas Dixon, *The Inside Story of the Harding Tragedy* (New York, 1932) and in Joe Mitchell Chapple, *Life and Times of Warren G. Harding* (Boston, 1924), both of which should be read with much caution.

On the men in Washington and around Harding there are numerous memoirs and autobiographies. Among the most useful are *The Memoirs of Herbert Hoover* (3 vols., New York, 1951–52); Bernard M. Baruch, *My Own Story* (New York, 1957); James M. Cox, *Journey through My Years*, cited previously; George W. Norris, *Fighting Liberal*, also cited before.

Biography also offers a rich selection in this decade. On Charles Evans Hughes see the excellent study by Merlo J. Pusey, *Charles Evans Hughes* (2 vols., New York, 1951) and the much shorter one by Dexter Perkins, *Charles Evans Hughes and American Democratic Statesmanship* (Boston [1956]). Mellon is criticized strongly in Harvey O'Connor, *Mellon's Millions: The Life and Times of Andrew W. Mellon* (New York, 1933) and he is overly praised in Philip H. Love, *Andrew W. Mellon: The Man and His Work* (Baltimore, Md., 1929).

Other relevant biographies include Willis F. Johnson, *George Harvey* (Boston, 1929); Claudius O. Johnson, *Borah of Idaho* (New York, 1936), which should be compared with Marian C. McKenna, *Borah*, already cited; William T. Hutchinson, *Lowden of Illinois: The Life and Times of Frank O. Lowden* (2 vols., Chicago, 1957); and Bascom N. Timmons, *Portrait of an American: Charles G. Dawes* (New York, 1952). On Norris see Alfred Lief, *Democracy's Norris* (New York, 1939) and Richard L. Neuberger and Stephen B. Kahn, *Integrity: The Life of George W. Norris* (New York, 1937). Alfred E. Smith has been the subject of a number of studies and biographies. One of the earliest efforts was the precampaign portrait by Henry F. Pringle, *Alfred E. Smith* (New York, 1927). A popular reconsideration of the "Happy Warrior" appeared with Frank Graham, *Al Smith, American, An Informal Biography* (New York [1945]). The most recent effort to tell the Smith story is Emily S. Warren, *The Happy Warrior: A Biography of My Father, Alfred E. Smith* (Garden City, N.Y., 1956). Although there is much new detail here, especially on Smith's early life, the book becomes less reliable as Smith assumes more importance as a national figure. A much more satisfying, though brief, analysis is Oscar Handlin, *Al Smith and His America* (Boston [1958]). Consult also the second and third volumes of Frank Freidel, *Franklin D. Roosevelt: The Ordeal* (Boston, 1954) and *Franklin D. Roosevelt: The Triumph* (Boston, 1956), and Ray Ginger, *The Bending Cross*, already cited.

Biographical sketches of prominent Americans of the 1920's are to be found also in several other works, including Oswald G. Villard, *Prophets True and False* (New York, 1928); this should be supplemented by D. Joy Humes, *Oswald Garrison Villard, Liberal of the 1920's* (Syracuse, N.Y., 1960), which attempts to depict the editor of *The Nation* from 1918 to 1932 in the vanguard of the liberal tradition of the 1920's and to show his relationship to the reform urge of the progressives and of the New Deal. Morris R. Werner, *Privileged Characters* (New York [1935]); Walter Lippmann, *Men of Destiny* (New York, 1927); and Henry F. Pringle, *Big Frogs* (New York, 1928) are all useful.

The oil scandals are treated in Marcus E. Ravage, *The Story of Teapot Dome* (New York, 1924) and most fully in the more recent account based upon Secret Service reports by Morris R. Werner and John Starr, *Teapot Dome* (New York, 1959). See also Burl Noggle, "The Origins of the Teapot Dome Investigation," *Mississippi Valley Historical Review*, XLIV (September 1957), 237–66. There is a good section on the Harding scandals, along with those in the Truman and Eisenhower administrations, in Blair Bolles, *Men of Good Intentions* (Garden City, N.Y., 1960).

Apart from his *Autobiography*, which is not very revealing, there are two good biographies of Calvin Coolidge, William Allen White, *A Puritan in Babylon: The Story of Calvin Coolidge* (New York, 1938), which is excellent, and Claude M. Fuess, *Calvin Coolidge: The Man from Vermont* (Boston, 1940), which is adequate but not always as informative as White. The most recent collection of what thirty-eight of Coolidge's contemporaries thought of him is Edward C. Lathem, ed., *Meet Calvin Coolidge: The Man behind the Myth* (Brattleboro, Vt., 1960). Older biographies include William Allen White, *The*

Man Who Is President (New York, 1925) and Cameron Rogers, *The Legend of Calvin Coolidge* (Garden City, N.Y., 1928).

Fiscal policies and developments are discussed in part in the biographies of Mellon and in Hoover's *Memoirs*, already cited, but also in three specialized studies by William F. Willoughby, *The Problem of a National Budget* (New York, 1918); *The National Budget System* (Baltimore, 1927); and *Financial Conditions and Operations of the National Government, 1921–1930* (Washington, D.C., 1931). See also Charles G. Dawes, *The First Year of the Budget of the United States* (New York, 1923).

Postwar railroad problems and efforts to remedy them are treated in Rogers MacVeagh, *The Transportation Act, 1920* (New York, 1923); William N. Leonard, *Railroad Consolidation under the Transportation Act of 1920* (New York, 1946); D. Philip Lochlin, *Railroad Regulation since 1920* (Chicago, 1928); Harry D. Wolf, *The Railroad Labor Board* (Chicago [1927]); and Isaiah L. Sharfman, *The Interstate Commerce Commission* (4 vols., New York, 1931–37).

On the shipping industry see the excellent review article by John G. B. Hutchins, "The American Shipping Industry since 1914," *Business History Review*, XXVIII (June 1954), 105–27. More detailed and emphasizing the problems facing postwar shipping is the National Industrial Conference Board, *The American Merchant Marine Problem* (New York, 1929). Consult also Darrell A. Smith and Paul V. Betters, *The United States Shipping Board* (Washington, D.C., 1931) and Paul M. Zeis, *American Shipping Policy* (Princeton, N.J., 1938).

The tariff program of the Harding administration is discussed in a chapter of Frank W. Taussig, *The Tariff History of the United States* (8th ed., New York, 1931); and more in detail by Abraham Berglund, "The Tariff Act of 1922," *American Economic Review*, XIII (March 1923), 14–33. The consequences of protection are detailed in Joseph M. Jones, *Tariff Retaliation* (Philadelphia, 1934). An interesting aspect of tariff legislation is told in Elmer E. Schattschneider, *Politics, Pressures and the Tariff* (New York, 1935).

The first postwar depression in agriculture is well told with much detail in James H. Shideler, *Farm Crisis, 1919–1923* (Berkeley, Calif., 1957). For the politics and programs of the discontented farmers between 1915 and 1922 see Robert L. Morlan, *Political Prairie Fire: The Nonpartisan League*, already cited, and Alice Christensen, "Agricultural Pressure and Government Response, 1919–1929," *Agricultural History*, XI (January 1937), 33–42. Two other general works are also very useful on the problems of agriculture during the decade of prosperity. Theodore Saloutos and John D. Hicks, *Agricultural Discontent in the Middle West, 1900–1939* (Madison, Wis., 1951), which is quite thorough and analytical, and Murray R. Benedict, *Farm Policies of the United States, 1790–1950* (New York, 1953), which contains much useful data. Older but still valuable is John D. Black, *Agricultural Reform in the United States* (New York, 1929). The opinions of one farm spokesman are summarized in Malcolm Sillars, "Henry A. Wallace's Editorials on Agricultural Discontent, 1921–1928," *Agricultural History*, XXVI (October 1952), 132–40. Among other specialized works, see the following: James E. Boyle, *Farm Relief: A Brief on the McNary-*

Haugen Plan (Garden City, N.Y., 1928); Arthur Capper, *The Agricultural Bloc* (New York [1922]); Joseph S. Davis, *The Farm Export Debenture Plan* (Stanford, Calif., 1929); Clara Eliot, *The Farmers' Campaign for Credit* (New York, 1927); Gilbert C. Fite, *George N. Peek and the Fight for Farm Parity* (Norman, Okla., 1952), which is especially good on McNary-Haugenism; Orville M. Kile, *The Farm Bureau Movement* (New York, 1921); Wilson Gee, *The Place of Agriculture in American Life* (New York, 1930); Edwin G. Nourse, *Government in Relation to Agriculture* (Washington, D.C., 1940); Edwin R. A. Seligman, *The Economics of Farm Relief* (New York, 1929); Earl S. Sparks, *History and Theory of Agricultural Credit in the United States* (New York [1932]); and Ellis A. Stokdyk and Charles H. West, *The Farm Board* (New York, 1930). On Agriculture Secretary Henry C. Wallace see the pertinent sections of Russell Lord, *The Wallaces of Iowa* (Boston, 1947). Henry A. Wallace reviews the agricultural plight of the farmers during the 1920's in his own *New Frontiers* (New York, 1934).

On the development and regulatory problems of the power industry see Hugh L. Elsbree, *Interstate Transmission of Electric Power* (Cambridge, Mass., 1931) and Jerome G. Kerwin, *Federal Water-Power Legislation* (New York, 1926). Gifford Pinchot, *The Power Monopoly* (Milford, Pa., 1928), is an indictment by a conservationist; see also the pertinent chapters in Forrest McDonald, *Let There Be Light: The Electric Utility Industry in Wisconsin, 1881–1955* (Madison, Wis., 1955), which is more specialized and less hostile. Carl D. Thompson, *Confessions of the Power Trust* (New York, 1932) is a somewhat sensational study. The growth of the idea of a regional power system in various parts of the country between 1919 and 1924 is outlined in William S. Murray, *Superpower: Its Genesis and Future* (New York, 1925).

The efforts of the veterans to secure government relief in the form of a bonus is told in Katherine Mayo, *Soldiers, What Next!* (Cambridge, Mass., 1934) and in the National Industrial Conference Board, *The World War Veterans and the Federal Treasury* (New York, 1932).

An excellent historical account of the nativist groups which helped sponsor the restrictions in the immigration acts of 1921 and 1924 is John Higham, *Strangers in the Land* (New Brunswick, N.J., 1955). The restrictive quota system is defended by Robert De C. Ward, "Our New Immigration Policy," *Foreign Affairs*, III (September 15, 1924), 99–111. See also Roy L. Garis, *Immigration Restriction*, already cited, and Manuel Gamio, *Mexican Immigration to the United States* (Chicago, 1930).

12

Economic Developments, 1921-1929

AN ERA OF PROSPERITY

The end of World War I and the return to power of conservative Republicanism inaugurated a period which in some respects resembled the epoch of McKinley. By the year 1920 war conditions were ending and business was able to return to peacetime methods. The war had raised all prices; and when it ended, the prices of raw materials fell much more sharply than those of manufactured goods. Hence, the manufacturers' margin of profit was larger. Industry, moreover, had a large market for its goods because of the numerous needs, both in the United States and in Europe, which had been left unsatisfied during the war years. There was an acute but brief economic depression in 1921; but the years from 1922 until 1929 were, with the exception of a minor setback in 1925, a period characterized by an industrial and business prosperity unexampled in the previous history of the United States. The average profit of the 2,046 leading manufacturing corporations during these years was 11.25 per cent a year.

Throughout this period business leaders enjoyed the admiration and applause of the general public; government officials held that their chief function was not to police business but to assist it and cooperate with it; and critics of the economic system were few in number and exercised little influence. It was widely believed that business had reformed itself and had abandoned the antisocial practices characteristic of the age of the trusts, that prosperity would continue indefinitely without any of the cyclic periods of depression which had recurred throughout the nineteenth century, and that poverty was steadily being abolished. These hopes ended abruptly in the autumn of 1929, when the American economic system entered the most acute depression in its history. It then became apparent that throughout the 1920's the system had many weaknesses which were overlooked. In the opinion of many economists the most important of these weaknesses were the prevalence of monopolistic practices resulting in price rigidities, the relatively restricted purchasing power of the farmers and of many sections of the working class, the rapid growth of savings as contrasted with the relatively slower growth of consumption, the increase in debts, and the dependence of important branches of production on consumer credit at home and on an export trade which was largely financed by American loans.

The most remarkable feature of the decade and the chief cause for the prevalent spirit of optimism was the rapid growth of the national wealth and the national income. Between 1920 and 1929 production in all branches of the economic system increased by no less than 46 per cent. The total national income, which had been about $27 billion in 1909, had risen to $66 billion in 1922 and to $82 billion in 1929. If allowance is made for the decreased value of money, the real increase was 44 per cent between 1909 and 1922, and an additional 31 per cent between 1922 and 1929. Throughout the whole period from 1900 to 1929 population rose from nearly 76 million to nearly 123 million, while the national wealth increased from $88 billion to $361 billion. In 1929 the per capita wealth was $2,977, and the per capita income was $692.

The chief cause for the growth of wealth was the increase in the productivity of labor, brought about by new mechanical inventions, the development of new sources of power, and the application of new techniques for promoting efficiency. Between 1922 and 1929, population increased by 1.4 per cent a year, production increased by 3.8 per cent a year, and production per capita increased by 2.4 per cent a year. The growth of productivity was especially great in manufacturing. According to the National Resources Board the output of American factories increased between 1920 and 1929 by 40.6 per cent, while the man-hours worked decreased by 1.9 per cent and the unit-labor requirement decreased by 30.2 per cent. The result was that, in spite of the growth of population, the number of factory workers decreased during the decade by a figure estimated at between 200,000 and 600,000. Sixty-nine workers in 1929, and fifty-five workers in 1934, could produce as much as a hundred workers could in 1920. In mining and transportation there were similar tendencies. Between 1920 and 1929 the number of miners decreased by about 250,000, whereas the output of the mines increased by 5.5 per cent; and on the railroads the number of workers decreased by about 100,000, while output decreased by only 0.8 per cent.

THE DEVELOPMENT OF
THE CORPORATION

In spite of the trustbusting activities of the progressive era, the giant corporations which had been formed a quarter of a century earlier continued to dominate the economic system. Such industrial empires as United States Steel, American Telephone and Telegraph, the various Standard Oil companies, General Electric, and the leading railroads retained leadership in their respective fields. And although the House of Morgan exercised less control over the business of selling securities than it had in 1913, it still occupied its position at the apex of the economic pyramid; in 1932 it was estimated to have connections with one-quarter of all corporate wealth. Meanwhile a number of new monster corporations had appeared in new fields of activity. Some of the most notable were General Motors and the Ford Motor Company in automobiles; Du Pont in chemicals; and Commonwealth and Southern, Electric Bond and Share, United States Electric Power, and Samuel Insull's Middle West Utilities in the production of electricity.

A few figures will illustrate the dominance of the large corporations. In 1929, according to figures compiled by the Bureau of Internal Revenue, there were 456,000 corporations actively engaged in business. These did about 95 per cent of all manufacturing, and their total net income was $8.74 billion. No less than 80 per cent of this sum was earned by those corporations, only 1,349 in number, whose incomes exceeded $1 million each. According to one study, the 200 largest nonfinancial corporations owned 49.2 per cent of all corporate wealth and 22 per cent of the total national wealth.[1] The combined assets of these 200 corporations amounted to $26 billion in 1909, $43 billion in 1919, and $81 billion in 1929. Their growth had thus kept pace with the growth of the national wealth.

[1] Adolph A. Berle and Gardiner C. Means, *The Modern Corporation and Private Property* (New York, 1934).

The internal organization of these great industrial empires was, however, undergoing important changes. The individual entrepreneurs of the age of the trusts, who had combined ownership with management, were disappearing; and the corporations were developing into collective enterprises in which ownership and management were divorced from each other. Ownership was becoming diffused among a considerable number of stockholders, while effective control was frequently assumed by salaried executives. The trend toward the increase of stockholders was constant; and the larger the corporation, the more widely diffused its ownership was likely to be. It was, however, during the years from 1916 until 1921 that the most rapid extension of ownership occurred. In 1909 nearly three-fifths of all stocks were the property of the 25,000 richest individuals; by 1927 the proportion had decreased to a little over one-third. Of the 200 largest corporations, only 11 per cent by number and 6 per cent by wealth were, in 1930, controlled by single stockholders who owned a majority of the stock. At least 71 of them, on the other hand, had more than 20,000 stockholders each.

The most conspicuous example of this trend was American Telephone and Telegraph Company, the largest corporation in the country, whose assets amounted in 1930 to more than $4 billion and whose employees numbered more than 450,000. In 1901 AT&T had 10,000 stockholders; by 1930 the number had increased to nearly 570,000, none of whom owned as much as 1 per cent of the stock. The second and third largest corporations, United States Steel and the Pennsylvania Railroad, also had no stockholder owning more than 1 per cent.

Similar tendencies prevailed in the smaller corporations. In 1925, according to the Federal Trade Commission, the officers and directors of more than four thousand typical medium-sized corporations owned, on an average, only 10.7 per cent of their firm's common stock and 5.8 per cent of its preferred stock.

The diffusion of ownership, important as it was, did not, however, mean that the American people were becoming a nation of capitalists. The total number of stockholders, variously estimated at between 3 and 12 million, was probably closer to the former figure; and the bulk of the dividends were paid to a relatively small group. According to the Bureau of Internal Revenue, total dividend payments amounted in 1929 to $5.75 billion. More than one-third of this sum went to about 17,000 individuals, and more than three-fifths of it to about 150,000 individuals. The profits of American corporate enterprise were thus going, in a large degree, to a small body of absentee owners, many of whom belonged to a privileged leisure class.

There were still in the 1920's a few outstanding entrepreneurs who combined ownership with control, among them being Henry Ford and the three Du Pont brothers. In general, however, the control of corporate business was exercised either by financial promoters or by salaried managers. Financial promoters were able to dominate corporations in which they owned a minority of the stock by means of various legal devices, such as control of proxy votes and voting trusts, and the pyramiding of holding companies. Notable examples of the holding company technique were afforded by the Van Sweringen brothers, who controlled railroads worth more than $2 billion by means of an investment of less than $20 million, and by Samuel Insull, who constructed a system in which one dollar invested in Middle West Utilities controlled $1,750 invested in the Georgia Power Company.

The most significant development, however, was toward management control. This prevailed in 44 per cent by number and 58 per cent by wealth of the two hundred largest corporations. Management control was rendered possible by the large diffusion of stock holdings. Individual stockholders rarely had detailed information as to the policies pursued by the management; and even when some of them disapproved of those policies, it was almost impossible for them to gather enough support to demand a change. The management thus had almost complete power and tended to become self-perpetuating. The state laws regarding incorporation were, moreover, becoming laxer, especially in Delaware, which had become the chief source of corporation charters after 1912, when Woodrow Wilson brought about a reform of the New Jersey corporation laws. The executives of some corporations used their freedom from control to develop a sense of responsibility to the interests of the general public, but there were others who did not resist the temptation to secure financial advantages for themselves at the expense of the stockholders.

In the opinion of A. A. Berle, Jr., and Gardiner C. Means the substitution of management control for ownership control constituted a minor revolution. "There has resulted," they declared, "the dissolution of the old atom of ownership into its component parts, control and beneficial ownership. This dissolution of the atom of property destroys the very foundation on which the economic order of the past three centuries has rested." "Those who control the destinies of the typical modern corporation own so insignificant a fraction of the company's stock that the returns from running the corporation profitably accrue to them in only a very minor degree. The stockholders, on the other hand, to whom the profits of the corporation go, cannot be motivated by those profits to a more efficient use of the property, since they have surrendered all disposition of it to those in control of the enterprise. The explosion of the atom of property destroys the basis of the old assumption that the quest for profits will spur the owner of industrial property to its effective use. It consequently challenges the fundamental economic principle of individual initiative in industrial enterprise."

Other observers felt that the closest analogies to the position held by corporation managers were to be found in the sphere of politics. The executives of a big corporation resembled the rulers of an empire in that the principal motive which determined their policies was not primarily the quest for personal profits, as in the individualistic capitalism of earlier periods, but rather the ambition to win greater power and prestige both for themselves and also for the enterprises to which they belonged. The big corporations, both in their impetus toward expansion and in their alliances and hostilities with one another, resembled independent political entities.

MONOPOLY PRACTICES

Despite the phenomenal growth of the corporation, there was less monopoly, in the strict sense of the word, in the 1920's than there had been at the beginning of the century. This was a result not only of the trustbusting of the progressive era but also of the rapid growth of production, which made it more difficult for any one corporation to acquire complete control of any branch of industry. Thus, for example, the various Standard Oil companies, which had controlled 80 per cent of the oil business in 1911, controlled only 43.1 per cent in 1926; the share of International Harvester in the agricultural machine industry dropped from 80 to 64 per cent; the proportion of the steel industry controlled by United States Steel declined from 70 to 40 per cent.

One monopolistic practice, however, of the greatest importance, tended to increase. Rival corporations adopted the habit of maintaining uniform prices and of competing with one another not by reducing prices but by improving quality and by advertising. When an industry was controlled by a small number of corporations, it was easy for them to agree on uni-

form price schedules; and none of them had any sufficient motive for resorting to price competition, which would result only in a price war and
no profits for any of them. Uniform price schedules, which sometimes
remained unchanged for a decade, became the rule in many of the more
important branches of industry. These were sometimes achieved by means
of trade associations, of which there were about two thousand, although
only about a hundred seem to have adopted effective price-control policies.
More frequent was price leadership by a large corporation, the price
policies of which were imitated by its smaller competitors. Among the
firms exercising price leadership were United States Steel, Standard Oil,
International Harvester, Philadelphia and Reading (in anthracite), American Can Company, International Paper Company, and National Biscuit
Company.

Even in many industries in which there was neither a trade association
nor a price leader it became customary for prices to be uniform. This was
conspicuously the case with cigarettes and milk. Businessmen in general
strongly favored price stability and felt that any resort to price cutting
was an unfair form of competition. Although, however, price stability
tended to stabilize business conditions during prosperity periods, the
prices appear often to have been made unduly high, thus restricting production and consumption for the sake of higher profits. The results during periods of depression were disastrous. Another incidental consequence
was an excessive growth of advertising. In 1929 the money spent on advertising amounted to about $2 billion, representing an increase of nearly
500 per cent since 1915.

Attitude of the Federal Government

The federal government, under Republican control, made little attempt to restrict monopoly practices and pursued policies designed to assist business development. The tariff was raised to protect American industries, and taxation was lowered to provide capital for expansion. The
Department of Commerce, under Herbert Hoover, promoted industrial
efficiency and encouraged the standardization of products in accordance
with the methods first adopted during the war. In ten years, by diminishing
unnecessary variations in different commodities, it enabled business to
make economies amounting to $250 million a year. Hoover also encour-
aged the growth of trade associations, and sponsored two hundred "codes
of fair practice" drawn up by the associations and other groups of business-

men. Big business was no longer regarded with suspicion, and trustbusting was not revived. The Federal Trade Commission attempted to prohibit certain unfair forms of competition, such as fraudulent advertising and the misbranding of commodities, but the more important provisions of the Sherman and Clayton acts became almost a dead letter. The commission took no action against holding companies or against interlocking directorates, nor did it interfere with the various devices by which corporation managers protected themselves from stockholder interference.

Similar policies were adopted by the courts. Former President Taft became Chief Justice of the Supreme Court in 1921, and he was succeeded in 1930 by Charles Evans Hughes. The Court abandoned the mild tendency toward liberalism it had shown between 1905 and World War I; and throughout the 1920's a majority of the justices were conservative, liberalism being represented only by a minority consisting of Oliver Wendell Holmes, Louis D. Brandeis, and (after 1925) Harlan F. Stone. The acquittal of United States Steel in 1920 meant that bigness was no longer regarded as a violation of the Sherman Act. Since the Court decided for acquittal on the ground, among others, that the dissolution of the corporation would injure the public interests and the development of foreign trade, it seemed to some observers that the "rule of reason" had been replaced by a "doctrine of business expediency." In 1925 the Court further weakened the Sherman Act by declaring, in the cases of the Maple Flooring Manufacturers' Association and the Cement Manufacturers' Protective Association, that trade associations were not illegal. Meanwhile the courts were again granting injunctions against labor unions, in spite of the apparent prohibition of this practice by the Clayton Act; and they were again using the Fourteenth Amendment to protect business against interference by state legislatures and public utility commissions.

It was widely believed that government regulation of business had become unnecessary because business had reformed itself. Business, it was said, had become a profession, and its primary purpose was to serve the public. Numerous organizations of businessmen, particularly the Rotary Clubs, preached the ideal of service, and in 1925 the United States Chamber of Commerce adopted fifteen "principles of business conduct" which businessmen were supposed to follow. This attitude was accepted by many former muckrakers, especially by Ida Tarbell. It is true that a number of the forms of unfair competition which had prevailed in the late nineteenth century had almost disappeared; and it is true also that businessmen now realized the need for conciliating public opinion and that they devoted considerable money and attention to securing popular approval. Business, nevertheless, was still carried on to make profits, and the quest for profits was still likely to result in activities contrary to the public interests.

Numerous episodes during the 1920's suggested that the reform of business had been relatively superficial. Many corporations still pursued oppressive and tyrannical labor policies. The telephone and power corporations carried on extravagant and unscrupulous propaganda campaigns against government regulation. Businessmen condoned the bribery of government officials, as was shown when Sinclair and Doheny were elected directors of the American Petroleum Institute after it had been proved that they had obtained oil fields from the federal government by bribing the Secretary of the Interior. There were certain wealthy financiers who enriched themselves at the expense of the stockholders of the corporations they controlled. And the belief that rich men were justified in taking advantage of loopholes in the income tax laws in order to evade payment was widely prevalent.

Nor was the maintenance of honesty and of obedience to the law the only problem presented by the new economic structure. The most significant feature of business development was that in those industries with managed or fixed prices, laissez-faire principles were no longer fully operative. There were corporation executives who were scrupulously honest but who, nevertheless, adopted price and wage policies which were probably detrimental to the public interest.

CHANGES IN THE CHARACTER
OF ECONOMIC ACTIVITY

Another important aspect of economic development was the increasing importance of durable and semidurable commodities. The production of basic necessities, such as food and clothing, was becoming relatively less important, while there was a rapid growth in the production of articles which had formerly been considered luxuries, such as automobiles, refrigerators, telephones, electrical equipment, and plumbing fixtures. There was also a marked increase in the production of capital equipment—of machinery, factories, and office buildings. Between 1922 and 1929, according to one study by the National Bureau of Economic Research, the production of nondurable consumption goods increased by 24 per cent;

on the other hand, durable consumption goods (housing excluded) grew by 72 per cent, and capital equipment (buildings included) grew by 70 per cent.[2] In 1899 food and clothing constituted 57.9 per cent by value of all production, while durable goods amounted to only 26.5 per cent. By 1929, on the other hand, food and clothing had dropped to 43.6 per cent, and durable goods had risen to 35.21 per cent.

Such a tendency was a sign of economic progress: it indicated a rapid rise in the general standard of living. Unfortunately it also increased the instability of the economic system. The market for durable consumption goods, unlike that for basic necessities, could easily become glutted; and the attempt of manufacturers to maintain sales by means of constant changes in style—by, for example, urging the public to buy a new car every year—could not wholly surmount this problem. Nor could the production of new capital equipment continue indefinitely. The building of new factories required a constantly expanding consumers' market for the commodities which these factories would produce. When, moreover, a depression started, the sale of durable goods, unlike that of basic necessities, was liable to fall sharply. The increasing importance of the durable goods industries was thus likely to make depressions more acute. An added cause of instability was the growth of installment selling. A large proportion of the durable consumers' goods were sold on the installment plan instead of for cash, the effect being to increase purchasing capacity in the present but to curtail it in the future. Between 1923 and 1929 the volume of installment selling was estimated at $5 billion a year.

A parallel tendency, which had similar causes and comparable effects, was the movement of labor away from production and into service and distribution. As the productivity of industry increased, a smaller proportion of the nation's labor resources was needed for farming and manufacturing and a larger proportion could be transferred to various white-collar occupations. By 1930, according to estimates made by Alfred Bingham, 34.5 per cent of the employed population were industrial workers, and 21.5 per cent were either farmers or farm laborers; professional, clerical, and service occupations accounted for 30.5 per cent, while 8 per cent were businessmen and 5.5 per cent were in domestic service. Thus only 58 per cent were engaged directly in production, whereas in 1920 the proportion had been 65 per cent.

The growth in the number of clerical workers (nearly half of whom were women) and of workers engaged in retail trade was particularly

[2] F. C. Mills, *Economic Tendencies in the United States* (New York, 1932).

rapid. The result was that consumers received better service; but on the other hand there was a rapid growth of distribution costs and an increasing price spread between what the producer received and what the consumer paid. According to estimates made by the economist Robert R. Doane, persons engaged in distribution received 3 per cent of the national income in 1860, 7.6 per cent in 1904, 9.5 per cent in 1922, and 12.6 per cent in 1929. Between 1913 and 1929 the cost of distributing food rose by 90 per cent. In 1929, according to the Department of Agriculture, consumers paid nearly $21.2 billion for articles of food, and of this sum only some $8.8 billion was received by the farmers who produced them. Paul D. Converse estimated that in the same year more than half the total retail prices of all commodities was represented by distribution costs. The growth of chain-store systems was an important feature of economic development in the 1920's. In 1909 chain stores were responsible for perhaps 15 per cent of all retail sales, and in 1925 for 30 per cent. This development made distribution more efficient, but it does not appear to have reduced its costs as much as might have been expected. It had, moreover, the disadvantage that profits from retail selling did not remain in the communities where they were made but were diverted to stockholders living elsewhere.

The high cost of distribution was responsible for one of the more significant economic development of the 1920's and 1930's—the growth of consumer cooperatives. Originating in Great Britain, the cooperative movement was strongly established in the Scandinavian countries. Under the leadership of J. P. Warbasse, it was introduced into the United States in 1915 and began to grow rapidly after 1926. It was strongest among the farm populations, especially those of Scandinavian descent, in the Middle and Far West. By 1936 there were 20 wholesale cooperatives and 3,600 retail cooperatives; they had 677,750 members and were doing an annual business of $182,685,000. The leaders of the movement preached cooperation with great fervor and believed that its general adoption would remedy most of the economic weaknesses of capitalism.

Inequality and Debt

Monopolistic price-fixing, the growth of the durable goods industries, and the increase of distribution costs could not be regarded as altogether healthy tendencies. Economic weaknesses of more fundamental importance, however, were the prevalence of inequalities of income and the growth of debt.

Throughout the 1920's the wage-earning class made substantial gains; and it was widely believed that a new economic order was being created, characterized by high wages and a large-scale consumers' market. Actually, however, poverty and inequality continued to a much greater extent than most observers realized, the result being that the purchasing power of the American people remained considerably smaller than the productive capacity of American agriculture and industry. It might perhaps be considered that $2,500 was the minimum annual income on which an urban family of normal size could enjoy an adequate standard of living; but in 1929 71.2 per cent of the employed population were receiving less than this figure, and 42 per cent of all American families were earning less than $1,500 a year. In that year, according to estimates made by the Brookings Institution, the income distribution was as follows:

INCOME GROUP	FAMILIES IN THOUSANDS	PER CENT	INCOME IN MILLIONS	PER CENT
Under $1000	5,899	21.5	$ 2,900	3.8
$1000–1999	10,455	38.0	$15,364	19.9
2000–2999	5,192	18.9	$12,586	16.3
3000–4999	3,672	13.4	$13,866	18.0
5000–9999	1,625	5.9	$10,820	14.0
10,000 and over	631	2.3	$21,580	28.0

Thus the 631,000 richest families were receiving a total income substantially greater than that of the 16 million families at the bottom of the scale.[3]

The tendency throughout the 1920's, moreover, was toward an increase in inequality. The prices of raw materials tended to fall, thus decreasing the earnings of the farm population; the prices of consumers' goods tended to rise, thus lowering the living standards of persons with fixed incomes. This divergence in price movements meant larger gross earnings per unit for the industrial corporations. The bulk of the increase went to profits rather than to wages. Between 1922 and 1929 the real wages of industrial workers increased, on an average, by 1.4 per cent a year. Since, however, production per capita was increasing by 2.4 per cent a year, the gains of the workers were not proportionate to the increase in what they produced. Certain sections of the working class, moreover, especially in bituminous

[3] Maurice Leven, et al., America's Capacity to Consume (New York, 1934).

coal and in textiles, were receiving wages very much below the national average.

The largest gains were made by salaried executives and by stockholders. Whereas the money wages of all industrial workers increased between 1922 and 1929 by 33 per cent, salaries increased by 42 per cent, corporation net profits by 76 per cent, and dividends paid to stockholders by 108 per cent. Labor costs per unit (estimated in dollars of constant purchasing power) fell by 9.5 per cent, but overhead expenses and profits rose by 10.6 per cent. Out of the value added by manufacturing, the proportion received by all wage and salary earners dropped from 58.7 per cent in 1921 to 47.7 per cent in 1929. While, therefore, the wage earners were receiving larger incomes, their share in the total national income was decreasing.

Another unhealthy tendency was the growth of debt. Between 1912 and 1930 long-term debts, both public and private, increased at the rate of 12.2 per cent a year, considerably faster than the national wealth and the national income. During the period of the war, for example, there was a rapid growth of farm mortgages, which totaled $3.8 billion in 1912, $8.9 billion in 1922, and $9.2 billion in 1930. There was also a steady increase in the indebtedness of state, county, and municipal governments, which were expending large sums on roads, public buildings, and other improvements, and financing them by borrowing. The net public debt (excluding that of the federal government) amounted to $4.3 billion in 1912, $9.9 billion in 1922, and $17.6 billion in 1932. By 1930, according to the estimates of John Blair, the total private long-term debt was $84.5 billion, and the total public debt was $31.9 billion.[4] If to these sums are added the debt of financial institutions ($21.9 billion), all short-term debts ($112.4 billion), and the value of all corporation stocks ($86 billion), the total invested capital upon which interest and dividend payments were being made amounted to $336.7 billion. Interest payments (not including dividends to stockholders) totaled $2.1 billion in 1913 and $7.6 billion in 1929.

This disproportionate growth of debt tended to increase economic inequality since it meant that the rentier class was receiving a larger share of the national income; and it made the economic system less able to withstand the effects of a depression. The development of a complicated structure of interlocking debt obligations, in which farmers, businessmen,

[4] John M. Blair, *Seeds of Destruction* (New York, 1938).

railroads, industrial corporations, banks, insurance companies, and government bodies were all dependent on one another, meant that if any of these groups became unable to make their interest payments, the chain of bankruptcies was liable to spread with the speed of a forest fire.

Surplus Money and Idle Men

The primary economic justification for inequality was that the richer families would save a large proportion of their incomes and thus provide capital for industrial expansion. Almost all saving was done by the richer families. Those who earned more than $300,000 a year saved, on an average, more than half their incomes. Two-thirds of all saving by individual families, according to Harold G. Moulton, was done by the 2.3 per cent with incomes above $10,000. On the other hand, 59 per cent of the families having incomes below $2,000 were responsible for only 1.6 per cent of all saving.[5] The 60,000 richest families saved as much as the 25 million poorest families. There was also a rapid growth during the decade in the saving made by corporations. Corporation executives began to set aside considerable surpluses for expansion and for security against depression, in preference to distributing them among stockholders. Between 1922 and 1927, when the big corporations saved 29.4 per cent of their profits, it was estimated that 40 per cent of all saving was done by corporations.

During the 1920's it appears that the supply of savings was in excess of the economic need for it. According to Harold G. Moulton, the total savings available for investment amounted to 8 or 9 billion dollars in 1923 and had risen to 15 billion by 1929. Between 1922 and 1929 the rate of increase in savings was 4.7 per cent a year, whereas production was increasing by only 3.8 per cent a year. Of these savings, however, only about 5 billion dollars a year was invested in industrial expansion or in mortgages. Of the remainder, part was loaned to foreign countries and the remainder was diverted into investment trusts or holding companies or used for speculation on the stock exchange. There was consequently a very rapid rise in the prices of stocks, amounting to an average of 19.4 per cent a year. After stocks had been pushed far above their real values (as measured by their capacity to earn dividends), a sudden and catastrophic fall became inevitable.

Meanwhile the fact that these large sums were being diverted into spec-

[5] Harold G. Moulton, *The Formation of Capital* (Washington, D.C., 1935).

ulation, instead of being used to buy new consumers' goods or invested in new capital equipment, meant that the system of production was unable to operate at its full capacity. Throughout these years a part of the nation's industrial equipment and of its labor resources was lying idle. Even in 1929, near the height of prosperity, it would have been possible (according to the estimates of the Brookings Institution) for production to be 19 per cent greater than it actually was. Unemployment existed throughout the 1920's; and although there are no exact figures, it has been generally estimated that there were never less than about 2 million men looking for work. The mobility of labor was increasing, and workers were constantly being displaced by machinery. Although eventually such workers were usually able to find employment elsewhere, they frequently had to move from one part of the country to another or to adopt occupations for which they had not been trained, so that the interval of unemployment was liable to be unduly long. It was, moreover, increasingly difficult for men past the age of forty-five, once they had been displaced, to find jobs of any kind.

The combination of surplus savings, idle factory equipment, and unemployed workers proved that the economic system was not functioning as it should. Although it was not until the 1930's that the problem became acute, it was present on a smaller scale throughout the 1920's. Considered from the viewpoint of human needs, the economic system was still capable of great expansion. Very much more wealth was required by the American people than was actually being produced, because a large number of American families still lacked basic necessities. If these needs were to be satisfied, idle money, factories, and men must be kept at work, and the purchasing power of the mass of the people must be increased. Alhough the nature of the problem was evident, there was no agreement as to its solution. While defenders of capitalism maintained that business leaders, if left free from political interference, would continue to increase the national income, reformers argued that the government must promote economic planning and, when necessary, intervene directly in order to regulate the investment of capital and increase mass purchasing power.

In view of the many factors at work undermining the stability of the economy during this decade, what then helped to promote and sustain the business and industrial prosperity of the Coolidge era? A large part of the answer to this question is to be found in the development of certain new industries and the expansion of older ones.

SOME NEW INDUSTRIES

Automobiles

Unquestionably the most important industry of the postwar period was the manufacturing of automobiles. Originating near the end of the nineteenth century, it developed into spectacular proportions in the 1920's. By 1928 it was giving direct employment to 5 per cent of all industrial workers and paying 6 per cent of all industrial wages. It had, moreover, stimulated the gasoline, leather, plate glass, rubber, steel, paint, and cement industries; and it had created jobs for thousands of mechanics, chauffeurs, and filling-station attendants. The number of cars that had been manufactured was 24.5 million, and the total number of workers directly or indirectly dependent upon the industry was probably close to 4 million. The growth of this industry was the most important single factor in creating the prosperity of the 1920's.

The first gasoline-driven vehicles were made in Europe in the 1870's and 1880's, the most important pioneers being Jean Lenoir, Carl Bery, and the Daimler brothers, and until 1905 there were more automobiles in Great Britain than in the United States. The first Americans to make automobiles were Charles Duryea, Elward Haynes and the Apperson brothers, and Henry Ford, all of them in the 1890's. Ford's first car, made in 1893, traveled twenty-five miles an hour, had a wooden flywheel and a cylinder made of a piece of gas pipe, and was mounted on a carriage with bicycle wheels. The period of experimentation lasted until 1910. After that date the standard cheap car was shaft-driven, magneto-equipped, and water-cooled; it had four cylinders and a three-speed sliding-gear transmission. In 1912 appeared the electric starter, first adopted by Cadillac. The chief subsequent improvements were the adoption of stronger bodies and tires.

The growth of the industry would have been impossible without the building of hard-surfaced roads. Roads were at first built by the county governments. Then, starting with New Jersey in 1892, the state governments began to assume responsibility. Finally, by acts of Congress passed in 1916 and 1921, the federal government entered the field. The Department of Agriculture began to organize a national system of numbered highways, the cost of which was to be divided equally between the federal government and the states. After 1920 federal expenditures on roads varied between $65 million and $100 million a year. This sum, however, was only a small fraction of the total amount spent on roads. The increase of automobiles made it necessary for roads to be built at least partly of cement, for automobiles quickly ruined roads made merely of water-bound macadam. The cost of a cement highway was from $33,000 to $44,000 a mile, and the upkeep also was expensive. By 1922 there were about 200,000 miles of cement roads. The total expenditure on roads in 1921 was $1.14 billion, most of which was paid by the state governments. Only a small proportion of this sum was raised by automobile fees and gasoline taxes. In other words, the whole community was virtually being taxed to subsidize the automobile industry. Whereas the railroads had been required to construct their own lines of track, the automobile industry received roads as a gift from the state.

The development of the automobile industry exhibited the usual transition from competition to combination. Altogether nearly 200 independent firms undertook, at one time or another, to manufacture automobiles, of which 44 were still in existence in 1927. By that date, however, at least 60 per cent of the industry was controlled by two corporations, General Motors Corporation and Ford Motor Company. Some of the evils of competition had, moreover, been avoided by the standardization of thousands of the small parts of which automobiles were composed, and subsequent to 1915 the automobile manufacturers adopted the policy of pooling all patents.

General Motors was the creation of William C. Durant, who began his career as a drugstore clerk and was subsequently a patent medicine salesman and a wagon manufacturer. Winning control of the Buick Company, Durant expanded it into General Motors, but lost control of it to a group of bankers in 1910. He then organized the Chevrolet Company and was able to recapture General Motors in 1915. In the postwar depression he lost control again, this time permanently, and General Motors became a subsidiary of the Du Pont and Morgan empires, which had formed an alliance. Effective control remained henceforth with the Du Pont family, who owned about 30 per cent of the stock. Throughout the 1920's General Motors was the most spectacular money-maker of all American corporations. Anyone who had invested $25,000 in it in 1921 was a millionaire by 1929; and during 1927, 1928, and 1929 its profits exceeded $200 million a year. The corporation not only manufactured cars of all prices, but it

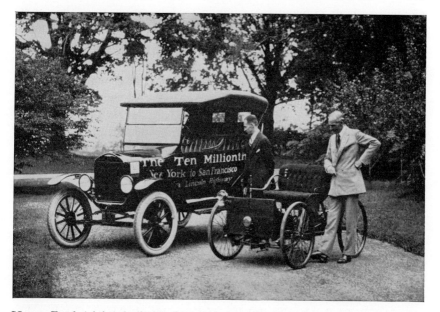

Henry Ford (right) built his first motor car in 1896. On June 4, 1924, when his son Edsel (left) presided over the largest automobile manufacturing company in the world, the ten millionth car rolled off the Ford Motor Company's Highland Park assembly line. (Brown Brothers)

also extended its activities into the fields of radio, aviation, electric refrigeration, and power and light production. Ranking eighth among all corporations in capital value, it was exceeded in the average volume of its profits only by American Telephone and Telegraph.

Henry Ford was almost the last survivor of the kind of individual entrepreneur who had dominated American industry in the 1870's and 1880's. In 1903 he entered into partnership with the Dodge brothers and with James Couzens. In 1907, however, he bought out his associates and became the owner of a majority of the stock in the Ford Motor Company. His policy henceforth was to retain personal control and not to surrender his independence to bankers or stockholders. More fully, perhaps, than any of his contemporaries, he grasped the essential elements of the new industrial system—standardization, division of labor, high wages, and mass production at low prices for a popular market. From 1909 until 1927 he made only one type of car, the famous Model T. By adopting the assembly line, on which division of labor was carried to an almost fantastic extreme, he reduced the time required for making the chassis from 12 hours 28 minutes to 1 hour 33 minutes. Starting in 1908, he set out to sell his car at a price which the average middle-class American could meet. He paid, moreover, wages considerably above the average. On January 5, 1914, he created a sensation by announcing that henceforth Ford workers would receive five dollars a day for an eight-hour day. For a number of years his profits reached 100 per cent a year. As a result of these policies Ford was regarded in Europe as the principal spokesman and symbol of American industrial civilization. In America, on the other hand, he incurred considerable antagonism on account of his paternalistic attitude to his employees, his stubborn opposition to trade unionism, and the naïve eccentricity of many of his pronouncements on political and social questions.

Aviation

Human beings had dreamed of flying for thousands of years; but the first persons who actually constructed a successful flying machine were Wilbur and Orville Wright, the owners of a bicycle shop at Dayton, Ohio, who began to study flying in 1896. Choosing as the scene of their experiments the desolate sand dunes of Kitty Hawk, North Carolina, by 1902 they had built a successful glider, after which they proceeded to the application of power. They made their first successful flight on December 17, 1903, traveling 852 feet and staying in the air for 59 seconds. Two years later they could travel a distance of 24 miles. So successfully had they solved the problems involved that the machine of today is, in many essentials, identical with the one they built. Because the Wrights discouraged publicity and because there was thus general scarcity of news regarding their achievement, those reports that did appear in the papers were received with skepticism. It was not until 1908 that the public became aware that flight had become possible.

The aviation industry remained backward in the United States until 1927. Ninety per cent of the factories built during the war were scrapped in 1919, and the government made little effort to develop military aviation. Brigadier General William Mitchell, who had commanded the American air force in France, insisted that future wars would be won by aviation, but his superior officers paid no attention to him.[6] During the early 1920's, aviation was carried on by numerous small companies and by independent barnstormers who sold rides to persons interested in the experience.

[6] When Mitchell's protests became disrespectful, he was court-martialed, and in January, 1926, he resigned after being suspended from the army for five years. Ironically, in 1942, six years after his death, the army returned him to the service and granted him the rank of major general.

The development of aviation into a major industry began with the Air Mail Act of 1925, by which the government was empowered to subsidize the industry through granting contracts for carrying mail. Charles Lindbergh's flight across the Atlantic in May, 1927, aroused further popular enthusiasm. These events were followed by a boom in aviation stocks, which had reached a value of a billion dollars by the autumn of 1929. The industry rapidly became consolidated. Although in the 1930's there were thirty-four different companies manufacturing airplanes, the bulk of the business was controlled by three major groups: North American Aviation, which was connected with General Motors, Curtiss-Wright, and United Aircraft and Transport Corporation. Most of the leading transportation lines were connected with these three groups. The process of consolidation was assisted by the federal government. In 1930, under the Air Mail Act, Walter F. Brown, Postmaster General under President Hoover, allotted 90 per cent of the air mail contracts to the three major groups without competitive bidding, thereby eliminating many of the smaller companies which lacked political influence. The War Department also made three-quarters of its purchases from the same groups. In spite of lavish subsidies, however, the companies reported small profits, chiefly because they paid high salaries and were milked by holding companies. A congressional committee commented in 1933 that "although the air transport industry is a very young one its intercorporate relationships have rapidly assumed a degree of complexity which would do credit to long established industries such as the utilities and the railroads."

Later, the Roosevelt administration attempted, by the Air Mail Act of 1934 and the Civil Aeronautics Act of 1938, to cleanse the industry of its financial abuses. The air mail subsidies were reduced, and an effort was made to separate manufacturing from transportation and to prevent interlocking directorates. Meanwhile there was a steady growth in air transportation services, particularly those of Pan American Airways, which covered 63,000 miles in 1939. There was also a growth in sales of airplanes, the majority of which were made to the United States government or to foreign governments for war purposes.

Chemicals

Ranking third among all American corporations in the postwar period with respect to net profits, surpassed only by American Telephone and Telegraph and General Motors, was the original Du Pont corporation of E. I. Du Pont de Nemours, which was unique in that it had been controlled by the same family for more than a century. The Du Pont firm originated as early as 1802, when a French immigrant, Eleuthère Irénée du Pont, built a gunpowder factory on the Brandywine in Delaware. Exactly one hundred years later the firm passed under the ownership of three Du Pont cousins, Coleman, Pierre, and Alfred, associated with whom was a young French-Irish stenographer, John Jacob Raskob. During the next four years the cousins created a gunpowder trust, acquiring control of 70 per cent of the business in the United States; but when the government sued under the Sherman Act, the Supreme Court, because of legal technicalities, found it impossible to dissolve the trust into its constituent units.

During the war the Du Ponts made 40 per cent of all explosives used by the Allies. They built fourteen square miles of factories, increased the capital value of the corporation from $83 to $308 million, and earned net profits of $237 million. At the end of the war the corporation had $90 million in its treasury. Turning from the manufacture of explosives to that of chemicals, and creating a large and very efficient staff of research experts, the Du Ponts began to produce numerous coal tar and cellulose products. By 1930 they were making eleven hundred separate articles and owned eighty different factories in thirty different states. A large number of the more spectacular applications of science to industrial processes during the 1920's and 1930's were the work of the Du Pont laboratories. Coleman and Alfred had retired before the end of the war, after which the firm was controlled by three brothers, Pierre, Irénée, and Lammot. The family dominated the state of Delaware; and genuine political conflicts rarely occurred in that state except when different branches of the family espoused different policies. Normally Republican, the family was persuaded by their business associate, John Jacob Raskob, to support the Democratic candidates in the elections of 1928 and 1932, chiefly because of their opposition to prohibition. Subsequently the Du Ponts returned to Republicanism and were among the most vigorous opponents of the New Deal.

Power

Another industry which grew rapidly during the 1920's was the production of electrical power. Between 1902 and 1929 the kilowatt hours of energy produced increased from about 4.8 billion to 97.4 billion. In terms of horsepower the increase was from 7.5 billion in 1912 to 20.3 billion in 1922 and 43.2 billion in 1930. By 1931 the capital invested in the industry totaled about $12 billion. The manufacture of electrical equipment was still dominated by the two corporations which had been founded before the end of the nineteenth century, General Electric and Westinghouse Electric. The production of power, however, originally handled by numerous small companies, became in the 1920's a field for ambitious and unscrupulous financing.

By 1930 more than half the power produced in the United States was controlled by four billion-dollar corporations—Electric Bond and Share, Middle West Utilities, Commonwealth and Southern, and United States Electric Power. A number of extraordinarily complex systems of pyramided holding companies had been constructed, and financiers were dominating large aggregations of capital through relatively small initial investments. The most notorious example of the holding company technique was Middle West Utilities, by means of which the English-born Samuel Insull, formerly an employee of Thomas A. Edison, controlled no less than 150 different public utility corporations.

Power production was a natural monopoly and presented the same problems of public control as had the railroads a generation earlier. Critics of the industry believed that rates were generally too high; that the financiers who controlled it had not learned the lesson taught by the automobile industry; and that by lowering rates, power producers would stimulate a wider use of electrical equipment and actually earn larger profits, in addition to benefiting society. That this opinion was justified was proved after 1933 when the TVA began to force down the rates of the private power companies operating in the Tennessee Valley, the result being that those companies increased their earnings.

Meanwhile the state governments, following the lead of Wisconsin and New York, attempted to regulate the industry, but with little success. The state public utility commissions were hampered by the fact that much power crossed state lines, and by the difficulty of determining capital values, in terms of which the rate of profit allowed to the companies had to be assessed. The courts, moreover, declared that holding companies were not public utilities and were therefore not subject to regulation. Effective control over the industry could be established only by the federal government, which took little action until 1933. Meanwhile all the public utility corporations fought government control by means of extensive propaganda campaigns, which were financed not by individual owners but out of corporate profits. The different branches of the industry combined to form state committees to watch their interests in the state legislatures and a National Joint Committee on Utilities to represent them at Washington. It set out to educate the American public as to the benefits of private ownership through the medium of school and college textbooks and by subsidizing journalists, teachers, and public lecturers.

Motion Pictures

Another new major industry was the production of motion pictures. A new art form of the greatest importance, both as a means of aesthetic expression and as a vehicle of propaganda, the motion picture was also a branch of big business, and its history exhibited the usual development from competition to combination.

The first attempts to photograph motion by taking a succession of pictures were made in the 1880's. In 1882, for example, the railroad magnate Leland Stanford adopted this method to discover whether a galloping horse lifted all its feet from the ground at the same time. The use of celluloid instead of glass for making such pictures originated with George Eastman and Hannibal Goodman. Finally, in 1889, Thomas A. Edison discovered how to reflect a series of pictures on a screen by using perforated film and a sprocket wheel which ensured regularity in starting and stopping. Similar inventions were being made independently at the same period in Europe.

Edison had already invented the phonograph; and having patented both inventions, he exploited them commercially in penny arcades where people could simultaneously listen to a phonograph and watch a brief moving picture. He regarded both inventions as cheap toys which could never become important. The public, however, quickly became interested in "vitascopes," as the first motion pictures were called; and when, in 1896, the Edison Company exhibited a vitascope at Koster and Biall's Music Hall in New York, it created a sensation. The Edison Company sold projection machines to numerous individuals who had perceived the financial possibilities of the invention, among them being two furriers, Marcus Loew and Adolph Zukor; a New York garment worker, William Fox; and the manager of a clothing store, Carl Laemmle. Since Edison was unable to satisfy the demand for vitascopes, numerous independent producers entered the field, in violation of Edison's patent rights. Vitascopes steadily grew longer, they began to tell stories, and the leading performers in them became well known.

The first film to tell a story was *The Great Train Robbery*, produced by E. S. Porter in 1903. In 1908 David Wark Griffith, the first American who fully grasped the aesthetic potentialities of the motion picture, became a producer, and in 1909 the career of the first motion picture star, Mary Pickford, began. The motion picture had, moreover, developed beyond the penny arcade and the music hall and had created its own theater, the "nickelodeon," of which there were nearly 10,000 by 1909. During the same period the motion picture was also being developed in Europe, especially in France and Italy, where it was treated from the beginning as a serious art form and not merely as a popular toy. In 1913 the Italian picture *Quo Vadis* was shown in New York in a regular theater with seats priced at a dollar—an event which marked an epoch in motion picture history.

Meanwhile Edison was fighting to maintain a stranglehold over the new industry by means of his patent rights. In 1909 he combined with nine of his leading competitors to form the Motion Pictures Patents Company, which was to handle production, and the General Film Company, which was to control distribution. All independents were to be totally excluded from the business. There followed a long battle between Edison and the independents, fought partly in the courts and partly by hired strong-arm men. Edison and his associates, however, consistently underestimated the possibilities of the motion picture and the tastes of the public. The independents captured the market by steadily improving the quality of their pictures and by developing such stars as Mary Pickford, Charlie Chaplin, Tom Mix, Broncho Billy, Theda Bara, and John Bunny. By 1914 the Motion Pictures Patents Company, rejected by the public and threatened with prosecution under the Sherman Act, had to accept defeat. One incident of the struggle was the removal of most of the independents to Hollywood, from which they could more easily escape into Mexico in case of pursuit by Edison's lawyers and detectives.

After the defeat of Edison the leading figure in the industry was Adolph Zukor, who joined Jesse Lasky and Samuel Goldfish (later called Goldwyn) in 1916 in forming Famous Players' Lasky, which was allied with the distribution company known as Paramount Pictures Corporation. Zukor aspired to dominate the industry; but he was fought by a number of rival producers. Since the chief desire of the public was to see their favorite stars, the producers began to bid against one another for control of the stars, and thus drive up salaries. By 1916 both Chaplin and Mary Pickford were probably earning a million dollars a year. The same process brought about higher admission prices, more luxurious theaters, and a steady improvement in the technique of production. In 1921 Paramount was still in the lead, but its supremacy was contested by William Fox, First National, and United Artists. There were half a dozen medium-sized production companies, and between thirty and forty small producers on "Poverty Row."

After World War I the motion picture rapidly developed into a major industry. By 1926 there were 20,000 theaters in the United States, with an average attendance of 100 million persons a week. Hollywood, moreover, had defeated its European competitors and captured the market of the entire world. Some $2 billion was invested in the business, and enormous sums were passing through its treasuries. The men who had developed the industry—most of them immigrants from eastern Europe who had started in the clothing trades—had not only become rich; they also controlled an instrument for molding popular customs and beliefs to which there was no parallel in world history.

This period saw the consolidation of most of the theaters into a few major chains. Zukor attempted to squeeze out his competitors in production by establishing a monopoly of distribution—a project which was checked by the Federal Trade Commission in 1922. In order to fight Zukor the other leading producers began to acquire theaters, while a number of independent exhibitors were combined into a rival chain by Marcus Loew. Loew subsequently joined forces with a group of producers to form Metro-Goldwyn-Mayer, while his chain of theaters passed under the control of William Fox. Another chain of theaters was created by RKO, formed in 1928 as an affiliate of the Radio Corporation of America. The result was that the exhibitors lost their independence. Production and exhibition passed under the control of the same individuals; and under the system of block-booking those theaters which remained nominally free were required to show whatever pictures were sent them by the producers—a practice which made it difficult for the smaller producers who did not control theaters to stay in business.

The chief subsequent event in motion picture history was the appearance of the sound or talking picture. The first sound picture, *The Jazz Singer*, was made in 1927 by the four Warner brothers, who had hitherto been on Poverty Row, but who developed into producers of major importance as a result of their initiative. The development of the sound picture was at first impeded by patent difficulties, most of the patents being the property of AT&T. By 1929, however, the victory of the talking picture was complete.

In the 1930's attendance at motion picture theaters in the United States averaged 85 million a week—a decrease from the high figure of the 1920's—and American producers had a world audience estimated at 250 million a week. The industry made between five hundred and seven hundred feature pictures a year, of which there were usually about forty costing more than a million dollars each. Most of the theaters in the United States were combined into four chains, Paramount, Warner Brothers, RKO, and Fox-Loew. The leading production corporations were Paramount, MGM, Warner Brothers, Twentieth-Century-Fox, RKO, United Artists, Universal, and Columbia. These eight companies made 90 per cent of all American pictures.

Since, however, the motion picture industry was more directly dependent on popular favor than any other form of big business, it was difficult for any small group of producers to establish a permanent monopoly. The history of the industry showed again and again that the leading production companies were likely to underestimate both the aesthetic tastes of motion picture audiences and their desire for novelty. Smaller producers continued, from time to time, to achieve importance by displaying more courage and a greater respect for their public.

Radio

Radio had been made possible early in the twentieth century by the inventions of Guglielmo Marconi and Lee De Forest. Commercial broadcasting, however, did not begin until November 2, 1920, when Westinghouse Electric began regular broadcasts over KDKA at Pittsburgh, beginning with the returns of the Harding-Cox election, in order to promote the sale of receiving sets. The sale of advertising became the regular method by which broadcasting was financed in 1923.

The industry then grew rapidly, and by 1938 there were about 30 million receiving sets in use and 700 broadcasting stations. Although most of these were small local stations, the industry was dominated by three large companies with national networks, the National Broadcasting Company, the Columbia Broadcasting System, and the Mutual Broadcasting System. There were also twenty-five regional networks. Radio was closely affiliated with the motion pictures, Columbia being partially owned by Paramount, while NBC was under the same control as RKO.

The fact that wave lengths had to be allotted to various stations in such a way as to prevent interference made some kind of government supervision necessary. Wave lengths were at first distributed by the Department of Commerce, which claimed authority under an act of Congress passed in 1912. In 1926 the department was denied power by a court decision, the result being that by the following year there were 732 different stations and the air was overcrowded. Congress then established the Federal Radio Commission, with power to allot wave lengths, and in 1934 this was replaced by a Federal Communications Commission, which had seven members. The FCC was authorized to give broadcasting stations licenses which would run for not more than three years; but in practice it limited licenses to six-month periods and used its power to refuse renewal in order to compel stations to devote part of their time to educational programs and to prohibit programs which violated accepted moral standards. Since radio was thus considerably less free than the press, there were occasional complaints of government censorship. On the other hand, the radio was much more nearly impartial on political questions, as a result particularly of a government regulation that rival candidates for political offices must be allowed equal radio facilities. Even the Communist party, whose policies rarely received fair treatment in the newspapers, was allowed to state its case over the air. Since the political influence of the radio was probably greater than that of the press, this enforcement of impartiality was of great importance for the preservation of democratic processes.

The new industries, and those related to them, were the ones that prospered most in the 1920's. Benefiting from the surge of technology, the increased standardization and simplification of production, and improved corporate management, the producers of these goods profited from the public's almost insatiable demand for automobiles, radios, and a host of new electric household products, like refrigerators, toasters, washing machines, and vacuum cleaners. But while the manufacturers of these new consumer durables prospered, as did certain producers of the older industries for a time, such as the manufacturers of producer durables and the builders of private and nonresidential construction, a number of industries did not share in the prosperity of Coolidge's New Era. Coal, for example, suffering from oil competition, remained depressed throughout the decade, just as did the woolen and cotton textile industry which faced competition from the producers of rayon and silk. The consequences of the industrial development of the 1920's and the changes they wrought upon the living habits of the people not only affected the economic and social status of the workers, but also helped to explain the course of the trade union movement during the decade.

THE LABOR MOVEMENT

The Decline of Trade Unionism

During the 1920's the working class enjoyed a higher standard of living than at any previous period. The workers continued, however, to have real grievances. Wages, though higher than formerly, were still too low to provide an adequate standard of living; the average working-class family earned less than $1,500 a year. Insecurity and unemployment were increasing, one out of every twenty workers being required to change his job in each two-year period; and workers who were displaced by machinery after they had passed the age of forty-five often found it impossible to obtain new jobs. Many forms of labor, particularly on the assembly lines of the automobile factories, were becoming more intense and more exhausting. And in certain industries, such as coal mining in Kentucky and West Virginia and textile manufacturing in North Carolina, hours remained abnormally long and wages subnormally low. The employers were still able, through their ownership of the workers' houses and their control over the local governments and police authorities, to exercise a feudal domination.

There was, nevertheless, a marked decline in labor militancy and in the power of the trade unions. Strikes were relatively rare, and many unions adopted a policy of cooperating with the employers by helping to reduce costs and prevent waste. The total number of union members decreased from 5.1 million in 1920 to 4.3 million in 1929, only about two-thirds of whom belonged to the AFL. The membership of some of the larger unions decreased with special rapidity. This was particularly true of the United Mine Workers, defeated in a series of strikes in 1922 and weakened by the growth of nonunion coal fields in West Virginia and Kentucky.

The AFL retained control over the skilled crafts; but under the leadership of William Green, who succeeded Gompers in 1924, it became a decidedly conservative organization. The chief function of the federation officials was to settle jurisdictional disputes between different craft unions and to be the official representatives of labor at public meetings. There was, moreover, a marked growth of corruption among some of the unions affiliated with the AFL. Certain union locals, whose leaders devoted themselves primarily to establishing the closed shop and compelling workers to become members in order that they might collect dues from them, became almost indistinguishable from criminal rackets.

The decline of trade unionism was due, in the first place, to the decrease in the importance of skilled labor. Since in many of the newer highly mechanized industries, such as the automobile industry, almost all labor was only semiskilled, there was no place for the trained and privileged workers who had always composed the bulk of AFL membership. The AFL, however, made little attempt to adapt itself to these conditions. It continued to represent mainly the skilled workers in the craft unions, and it still set out to benefit its members by establishing labor monopolies, limiting the numbers of the skilled workers by insisting on long apprenticeships and high union initiation fees. It scarcely attempted to organize the unskilled workers, nor did many of its affiliated unions admit Negroes to membership. Yet between 1915 and 1930 more than 1 million Negroes became industrial workers in the North, and being excluded from the unions, they were willing to work for low wages and could be used as strikebreakers.

In the second place, many employers in the 1920's both carried on an elaborate campaign for the open shop and also adopted a policy of outbidding the trade unions by instituting various measures of welfare capitalism. They remedied many of the grievances of the workers by adopting safety devices and improving sanitation in the factories, building hospitals and workers' houses, and establishing playgrounds, athletic teams, and orchestras. United States Steel, for example, continued to pay low wages and require long hours, yet between 1915 and 1923 alone it spent $60 million on welfare work. By 1926 nearly 250 corporations, employing nearly 3 million workers, had adopted pension plans. Three hundred corporations were encouraging their employees to become stockholders by selling them stock on credit and at less than the market price. Although less than 1 per cent of all outstanding stock was held by workers, this measure had some influence on working-class psychology. The works' council, or company union, was, moreover, spreading rapidly. By 1926 there were 430 company unions; and although they did not intervene in questions of wages and hours, they enabled the workers to voice their grievances on matters of smaller importance.

Meanwhile employers in the basic industries were still strongly opposed to the formation of independent unions. "Yellow-dog contracts," by which workers pledged themselves not to join unions, were frequently employed. In 1907 a federal court in West Virginia had enjoined the United Mine Workers from attempting to unionize workers under yellow-dog contracts, and in 1917 this use of the injunction was upheld by the Supreme Court in the case of *Hitchman v. Mitchell*. Throughout the 1920's the courts frequently granted injunctions limiting the powers of the unions, particularly with reference to the boycotting of firms employing nonunion labor. It was not until 1932 that Congress made another attempt to restrict this practice. By the Norris–La Guardia Federal Anti-injunction Act of that year, the federal courts were forbidden to issue injunctions for the purpose of breaking strikes, destroying unions, or upholding yellow-dog contracts. It was declared that an injunction could be issued only after a hearing in open court and that labor leaders accused of violating an injunction must have a jury trial. In addition to obtaining help from the courts, many corporations continued also to spend considerable sums on labor spies provided by private detective agencies. The result of these activities, along with the general indifference of the public and reformers toward labor's problems, brought about a decline in the number of union members and in organized labor's influence.

Communism in the Labor Movement

The IWW never recovered from the repressive measures inflicted upon it during the war period, and by 1924 it was virtually dead. Its leader, William D. Haywood, who had been condemned to prison in 1918, forfeited his bail to escape to the Soviet Union, where he died a few years later. The place of the IWW as the principal sponsor of radicalism in the labor movement was then taken by the Communist party. The chief Communist trade unionist was William Z. Foster, who joined the party after the defeat of the steel strike of 1919, which he had led.

The Communists provided leadership in several strikes, particularly in the furriers and cloakmakers strikes in New York in 1926, the textile workers strike at Passaic, New Jersey, in the same year, and the textile workers strike at Gastonia, North Carolina, in 1928 and 1929. In these strikes there was considerable use of violence, by both employers and workers. During the Gastonia strike the local chief of police was killed in a riot; and seven Communist organizers, although there was no reliable evidence directly implicating them, were condemned to prison sentences of from five to twenty years. All of them forfeited the bail put up on their behalf and fled to the Soviet Union. Two of them, Fred Beal and Red Hendricks, subsequently returned to serve their sentences, having decided they would rather face imprisonment in the United States than live under a Communist dictatorship.

The Communists, however, did not succeed in gaining any real strength in the American labor movement, the Fur Workers' Union being the only important union which retained Communists among its officials. Their primary purpose was not to win immediate gains for the workers but to overthrow capitalism; and for this reason they were often unwilling to allow strikes to be settled, even on terms advantageous to the workers. They were, moreover, required to obey the instructions of the Communist International, the leaders of which lived in Moscow and had little understanding of American conditions.

After the Passaic and Gastonia strikes they retained little support among the textile workers; and after the cloakmakers strike they lost the positions they had won in the International Ladies' Garment Workers. This union was subsequently reorganized under the more conservative leadership of David Dubinsky, who brought it quickly to the position of one of the strongest, best managed, and most genuinely progressive unions in the country. The Communists failed also in a long campaign to capture the United Mine Workers. For a number of years they supported a dissident group among the miners, which was led by John Brophy and which attempted to oust John L. Lewis from leadership. There was a prolonged, unscrupulous, and sometimes violent conflict between the two groups, Lewis being denounced by the Communists as an agent of the capitalist class. He succeeded, nevertheless, in retaining leadership of the union.

This phase of Communist activity ended abruptly in 1929, after the Sixth Congress of the Communist International, meeting in Moscow, had ordered the American Communists to abandon their policy of seeking the capture of established unions and to start organizing new rival unions. As their instrument for carrying out this new program of dual unionism and for splitting the labor movement, the Communists organized in 1929 the so-called Trade Union Unity League. This new policy, however, failed even more completely than did its predecessor. Discontented American workers might be willing temporarily to accept Communist leaders during a strike but they would not permanently adopt Communist ideals or follow all the deviations of the Communist policies.

AGRICULTURE

If the industrial workers were somewhat better off in the 1920's than they had been before the war, the farmers were distinctly worse off. During the war years they had increased the acreage under crops in order to raise food for Europe, and there had been a rapid rise in farm prices, land values, and the quantity of farm mortgages. The end of the war was followed by a catastrophic fall in prices. European countries no longer needed American farm products to the same degree; and there developed a condition of chronic agricultural overproduction, from which the farmers were never able to recover. In 1921 the index of farm prices registered a drop of nearly 44 per cent; and although prices subsequently rose slowly, the increase was not enough to redress the balance. In terms of the ratio of farm prices to other prices, the farmers were 9.1 per cent better off in 1929 than they had been in 1921; on the other hand, they were 11 per cent worse off than they had been in 1913.

Although the war had intensified the problems of American agriculture, it must not be supposed that it created them. The fundamental causes of the agricultural depression were to be found in the development of the economic system. There was a steady increase in agricultural production. Between 1910 and 1930 the acreage under crops increased from 331.3 million to 369.1 million, while at the same time output per acre was also increasing. The 1920's, moreover, were years of especially rapid mechanization in agriculture. As the tractor replaced the horse and the mule, the acreage formerly employed to raise feed for these animals was now used to grow food and other products for human consumption, and thus even more was added to the agricultural surplus. Between 1919 and 1932 productivity per acre increased by 16 per cent, and productivity per agricultural worker increased by 25 per cent. Meanwhile the markets for American agricultural products were diminishing. The internal market was limited by the decrease in the rate of population growth (because of immigration restriction and the fall in the birth rate) and by a steady shift in consumption habits away from such agricultural staples as meat and grain toward poultry, fruit, and vegetables. The external market grew

smaller for a number of reasons, the most important being the development of new agricultural areas in Argentina and the British Dominions,
the policy of encouraging economic self-sufficiency which was adopted
by many European governments, and the expansion of American exports
of manufactured goods, as a result of which the nations purchasing
them had less dollar exchange with which to buy agricultural goods.

As a result of these factors, total farm incomes decreased from about
$15 billion in 1919 to about $12 billion in 1929. During the same period
the total value of all farm properties decreased from $78 billion to $57
billion, while the total value of farm mortgages, which had amounted to
$3.8 billion in 1912, had risen by 1930 to $9.2 billion. Whereas in 1912
the farmers were paying 3 per cent of their total gross income as interest
on mortgages, by 1930 they were paying 6 per cent. During the same
period their real estate taxes also rose from 3 per cent to 6 per cent of
gross income. The result was that farm tenancy continued to increase,
the proportion of farms operated by tenants reaching 42.4 per cent by
1930. The figures were very much higher in the cotton-growing area of
the South; and the southern cotton sharecroppers, 750,000 in number,
continued to be the most poverty-stricken group of people in the entire
country. Outside the South a majority of the landlords were themselves
farmers, not absentee businessmen. Many tenants were relatives or former
employees of their landlords, and they had reasonably stable and prosperous lives. There were, however, a large number who were migratory,
incompetent, and miserably poor, rarely staying on the same farm for
more than two or three years at a time. In 1935, according to a committee
of Congress, one-third of all tenant farmers had moved within the previous twelve months.

The result of the increase of farm mortgages and farm tenancy was that
much of the gross income from agriculture did not become purchasing
power for the farmers but flowed back immediately to the cities. To a
considerable degree urban America was exploiting rural America. In
this connection the steady flow of population from the country into the
cities was also of significance. Since the population of the urban areas
did not fully reproduce itself, young men and women from rural areas,
where the birth rate was always higher, moved to the cities. The cost
of rearing and educating these workers, which may be estimated at $2,000
each, had, however, been carried by the agricultural communities where
they were born. O. E. Baker, of the U. S. Department of Agriculture, has
calculated that the total wealth which flowed from the farms into the

cities as a result of these various factors amounted between 1920 and 1929 to perhaps $25 billion.

Another significant feature of agricultural development was the increase of economic differences among the farmers themselves. The better trained and more vigorous farmers were very much more prosperous than their less fortunate neighbors. By 1929, 11 per cent of all farmers were receiving half the total farm income, while 49 per cent were receiving only 11 per cent of the income. Half the farm families each produced less than $1,000 worth of products a year, while there were 750,000 families, two-thirds of them in the South, who produced less than $400 worth a year each.

In a smoothly working economic system, functioning in accordance with the rules of supply and demand, there should have been a considerable reduction in the size of the farm population. Several million of the less successful farmers should have been stimulated by falling farm prices to seek jobs in industry. Throughout the 1920's, however, industrial employment did not expand sufficiently for this to be possible. There was unemployment in the cities as well as poverty on the farms. The actual decrease in the number of males employed in agriculture amounted to less than 900,000 for the entire period from 1910 to 1930, the figures being 10.4 million for 1910 and 9.5 million for 1930. The depression period of 1930–35 saw, moreover, an actual increase in the farm population, since unemployed workers turned to subsistence agriculture and the children of farmers were unable to find city jobs. Between 1930 and 1935 the number of farms increased by 523,702, and the total farm population increased by no less than 2.3 million.

Under such conditions the remedies which had been adopted during the progressive era—government control of railroad rates, easier credit facilities, and the organization of cooperative grain elevators and cooperatives for the marketing of farm products—were no longer adequate. The farmers themselves hoped for an increase in their foreign markets, but there was little likelihood that such a reversal of economic trends would take place. Their leaders put forward various proposals for federal government assistance; but the Republican administration rejected the more drastic of them. Meanwhile the depressed condition of agriculture, which limited the internal market for American industry and caused a steady increase in indebtedness, weakened the whole economic system of the United States, and by doing so helped to precipitate the crisis of 1929.

FOREIGN TRADE AND INVESTMENTS

The United States as a Creditor Nation

During World War I the United States had changed from a debtor into a creditor nation; and for ten years after the war American capital investments abroad continued to increase. There was also a steady growth in the volume of American export trade, although at the same time the ratio between exports and total production was declining. The American economic system had a surplus of capital and of goods; and until 1929 the policy of both the American government and American industrial leaders was to find outlets for these surpluses in foreign countries. Such a policy, however, created certain problems, the importance of which was not fully grasped by American public opinion.

In the first place it is impossible for a nation to continue indefinitely both to invest capital abroad and at the same time to export more goods than it imports. This, however, was what the United States did between 1919 and 1928. Foreign nations that were in debt to American investors could not pay either the principal or the interest on those debts unless America would consent to buy a sufficient quantity of goods from them. Such a policy, however, would be detrimental to American industry and agriculture, which would have to admit foreign competitors into the home market. Foreign lending was thus incompatible with the maintenance of a high protective tariff, and sooner or later the United States would have to decide which of them should be abandoned.

In the second place, the growth of American investments in Europe, South America, and the Far East meant that the United States had become a world power, vitally interested in the maintenance of peace and prosperity and in the defense of its economic interests in all parts of the world. The United States, in fact, was moving into the position which had been occupied by Great Britain during the nineteenth century. This development, however, involved an abandonment of the doctrine of isolation from European entanglements, and American public opinion was by no means prepared to accept the consequences of such a change. Three possible courses presented themselves. First, the United States could accept the responsibilities of a world power and intervene in Europe and the Far East for the purpose of maintaining peace and thereby promoting

American trade and protecting its investments. Second, the United States could sacrifice its economic connections with other parts of the world and attempt to reorganize its internal economic system on a basis of self-sufficiency. Third—as a compromise between these two extremes—the United States could concentrate on maintaining peace and extending its economic ties in the Western Hemisphere. Throughout the 1920's and 1930's American public opinion remained undecided among these three courses; nor was there any general realization of the responsibilities and sacrifices which each of them would involve.

IMPORTS AND EXPORTS

Down to 1929 there was a steady increase in the volume of imports, although there was a decline in the proportionate value of imports to exports. Between 1901 and 1905 the average annual value of imports had been $972 million; between 1926 and 1930 it was slightly more than $4 billion. During the latter period 49.4 per cent were raw materials and 50.6 per cent were manufactured goods; 29.9 per cent came from Europe, 29.7 per cent from Asia, 24.9 per cent from Latin America, 11.9 per cent from Canada, 2.3 per cent from Africa, and 1.3 per cent from Oceania. The most significant trend was the declining importance of Europe, which had contributed 52.6 per cent of American imports at the beginning of the century, and the rising importance of the Far East. The United States bought its silk from Japan and its rubber and much of its tin from the British and Dutch East Indies. Although luxury or nonessential articles of this import trade could be sacrificed without serious losses, it included also a number of mineral products not available at home, which were of vital importance to American industry. The steel industry, for example, required forty different commodities, which were imported from fifty different countries.

Between 1901 and 1905 the average annual value of American exports had been $1.45 million; between 1926 and 1930 it was $4.77 million. The proportion of exports to total production had, however, declined from 12.8 per cent in 1899 to 9.8 per cent in 1929. Between 1926 and 1930, 36.1 per cent of exports were agricultural goods, and 63.9 per cent were mineral products or manufactured goods. Of the exports, 46.8 per cent went to Europe (as contrasted with 76.7 per cent in 1900), 17.8 per cent to Latin America, 17.4 per cent to Canada, 12.0 per cent to Asia, 3.7 per cent to Oceania, and 2.3 per cent to Africa. In spite of the decreasing importance of exports, from the viewpoint of the economic system as a whole, there were certain branches of production the prosperity of which was mainly dependent on it. In 1929 the United States exported 54.8 per cent of its cotton, 41.2 per cent of its tobacco, and 17.9 per cent of its wheat. The value of the cotton export averaged $765 million a year.

Throughout the 1920's American industrialists vigorously pushed their exports in all parts of the world and received assistance from the federal government, especially from the enlarged and reorganized Department of Commerce under Secretary Hoover. In 1921 a Bureau of Foreign and Domestic Commerce was organized in the Department of Commerce, and commercial attachés were added to the American diplomatic service. William R. Castle, Assistant Secretary of State, told an exporters' convention in 1928 that "Mr. Hoover is your advance agent and Mr. Kellogg is your attorney."

THE EXPORT OF CAPITAL

Meanwhile the Republican administration under Hoover's leadership was also encouraging the growth of American private investments abroad, apparently without realizing that this policy would ultimately prove to be incompatible with its tariff policy. A considerable part of the exports of American manufactured goods was, in fact, financed by loans extended by American bankers. American foreign investments consisted partly of the acquisition of mines and factories in foreign countries, and partly of the purchase of foreign securities. Investments of the former kind, which Hoover tried to discourage because of their adverse effect upon the domestic economy, were motivated, in part, by a desire to burrow under the tariff walls erected by foreign countries. In some instances they were detrimental to American producers. Thus, the American meat-packing corporations acquired factories in Argentina, which tended to injure American cattle raisers; and American capital helped to rebuild the German merchant marine, which competed with American shipping.

The purchase of foreign securities by American citizens was encouraged by American bankers, who collected commissions on such transactions; but many of the foreign loans floated in the United States, particularly those issued by some of the Latin American countries, were very unsound and were soon in default. By 1938, 66 per cent of all Latin American loans were no longer paying interest. American bankers were so eager to acquire more foreign bonds which they could sell to American investors at a profit to themselves that they paid lavish commissions to the relatives of Latin American presidents who were willing to borrow American capital. Thus, the son of the president of Peru received $415,000 from J. & W. Seligman and Company, and the son-in-law of the president of Cuba received $500,000, in addition to a regular salary of $19,000 a year, from the Chase National Bank.[7] Many of the Latin American loans were not spent on productive economic investments, but helped to keep dictatorial regimes in power. The ultimate result was that Latin American dictators got the money and the bankers got their commissions; but the American investors who had been induced to buy the bonds in many instances came out with nothing. In 1922 the State Department asked to have advance information about all foreign loans; but it does not appear to have exercised any real supervision over the export of capital. The Commerce Department was far more effective in formulating and implementing America's foreign economic policy than the State Department.

By 1930 American capital invested abroad (exclusive of the war debts due to the American government) amounted to about $16 billion. Of this sum $8.23 billion represented American holdings of foreign securities, and $7.86 billion represented American ownership of properties in foreign countries. Of the latter figure, $1.61 billion was invested in transportation, $1.53 billion in factories, $1.18 billion in mines, $1.11 billion in oil fields, and $874 billion in agricultural properties. Since foreigners held about $4.5 billion worth of investments in the United States, America's credit balance was about $11.6 billion.

Nearly $5 billion was invested in Europe, especially in Germany and Great Britain. German industry after World War I was largely rebuilt with the aid of American capital. Many of the leading American corporations, including General Motors, Ford, General Electric, Standard Oil, and American Telephone and Telegraph, built factories in Europe and established financial alliances with German and British corporations.

Nearly $4 billion was invested in Canada. By 1930 Americans owned one-third of all the capital in Canadian industry and one-twelfth of the total wealth of the Dominion. There was a greater volume of trade between Canada and the United States than between any other two countries in the world. Fortunately the relations between the two peoples remained amicable. The result was that Canada became an important link between the United States and Great Britain.

More than $5.5 billion was invested in Latin America. United States capital had become predominant in Mexico and the Caribbean before

[7] See the *Hearings before the Senate Committee on Finance*, investigating the sale of foreign bonds in the United States, 1932.

1914; during and after the war United States investments rapidly increased throughout South America, and United States corporations acquired ownership of South American mines, oil fields, and fruit and rubber plantations. Parts of South America, however, particularly Argentina, which exported chiefly meat and food stuffs that competed with the products of United States farms, remained within the British orbit. Certain political problems resulted from this development. In the first place, the United States found itself in competition for trade and control of raw materials with Great Britain and with Germany. In the second place, because many of the Latin American governments were financially unstable, they were likely to repudiate their obligations. The peoples of Latin America, moreover, suffered from acutely low standards of living and were beginning to resent the high profits which often accrued to foreign investors, and to demand that foreign corporations either pay higher wages or undergo expropriation. This occurred particularly in Mexico. The United States government was, in consequence, under pressure from businessmen with Latin American interests to use force to protect these interests and to intervene in the internal affairs of the Latin American countries.

Investments in Asia and the Pacific totaled about $1.5 million. Of this sum about $300 million was invested in Japan, and $130 million in China. China had been regarded since 1898 as a suitable field for American investments, but this hope had never materialized. In spite of the Open Door policy, the bulk of the foreign capital in China was contributed by Great Britain and by Japan.

The export of American capital reached its peak in 1928, the figure for that year being $944 million. The flow of capital abroad throughout the 1920's enabled foreign countries to buy American goods, thus providing markets for American industry. It also contributed to the recovery of Europe from World War I and made it possible for Germany to pay reparations and for the Allies to pay the war debts. Sooner or later, however, the interest payments on the total investment must exceed the amount of new investments; and when this happened, American industry would lose some of its foreign markets, the recovery of Europe would be endangered, and there would be difficulty in maintaining the structure of reparation and war debt payments. This point was reached in 1929. In that year new investments abroad totaled only $306 million, whereas the interest payments made to the United States on previous investments amounted to $408 million. This was an important contributory cause to the worldwide economic depression which began in the autumn of that year.

During the depression there was no revival of foreign lending, and the existing American investments abroad were drastically cut down, many securities held by Americans being canceled or reduced in value by foreign governments, particularly by the Nazi government in Germany. By 1936 American foreign investments totaled only about $11.5 billion. Many of the securities included in this figure were, moreover, in permanent default. What had virtually happened in the case of many foreign securities, therefore, was that foreign countries had received free gifts of American goods, while the bills had been paid out of American capital contributed by American investors. American industry during the 1920's had been given the stimulus of a kind of public works program conducted for the benefit of Europe and Latin America.

Some critics of the economic system deduced from this experience that the money should have remained at home and been used to increase the purchasing power of the American workers and farmers. Others argued that the export of capital was a beneficial process which tended to promote world unity and world peace and to improve the standard of living of backward countries. They held that these foreign loans would not have gone into default if the United States had lent its money more intelligently, had changed its tariff policies in order to make possible an increase in its imports, and had conducted its foreign policy in order to promote effective world peace and an increase in international trade.

International Trade Rivalries

The growth of American foreign trade and investments involved the United States in economic and diplomatic conflicts with other nations. On a number of occasions countries which controlled raw materials needed by American industry adopted plans for restricting production and raising prices. One of the Commerce Department's policies under Hoover was to fight all kinds of foreign combinations which restricted or interfered with American traders. Such policies aroused the enmity of the governments against whose nationals they were directed. There was, moreover, constant rivalry between the leading powers for control of mineral resources and for export markets. Hoover, for example, wanted to assure access to raw materials needed by industry in the United States by getting American businessmen to develop their own sources of supplies. This too aroused bitterness abroad and cries of imperialism.

In the 1920's when the chief competitor of the United States was Great Britain, it was sometimes suggested that the two nations would eventually go to war with each other. American and British oil companies were constantly in conflict; and while the Americans secured control of the oil fields in Venezuela and Colombia, the British won victories in Iran and Iraq and and obtained the more valuable of the Mexican oil fields. The British controlled the world's chief source of rubber in the East Indies; and in 1922, by the Stevenson Restriction Act, they set out to raise prices. The project failed, however, because of competition from rubber producers outside the British Empire, so that it was abandoned in 1928.

The industrialists of the two nations competed with each other for control of the export markets in South America, and their governments supported them by endeavoring to win popularity. Herbert Hoover (when President-elect) and the Prince of Wales paid goodwill visits to the more important Latin American republics. The British, moreover, endeavored to prevent American financiers from winning control over British industries, attempting occasionally to disfranchise American stockholders. This British-American rivalry ended, however, in the 1930's, when the rise of Nazi Germany, which adopted much more aggressive methods of pushing its trade and excluding foreigners from its export markets, caused Great Britain and the United States to draw together.

The United States was alarmed also by the growing power and aggressiveness of Japan. Yet the United States had much closer economic ties with Japan than with any other country of the Far East. In 1927 Japan supplied 10 per cent of all American imports, silk being the chief item, and bought 5 per cent of all American exports. The relation between the two nations was even more important to the Japanese: one-third of all Japanese trade, both import and export, was with the United States. In this instance, there was some discrepancy between the strategic and the economic interests of the United States.

Suggested Readings

The general economic development of the United States during the 1920's is ably presented in the comprehensive and cooperative study prepared by the President's Conference on Unemployment, *Recent Economic Change in the United States* (2 vols., New York, 1929) and more briefly in volume VIII of *The Economic History of the United States* series by George Soule, *Prosperity Decade: From War to Depression, 1917-1929* (New York [1947]), the best single volume on the entire period. The business point of view is expressed in Economic Principles Commission of the National Association of Manufacturers, *The American Individual Enterprise System* (2 vols., New York, 1946). Brief and worthwhile is the article by Joseph Schumpeter, "The American Economy in the Interwar Period: The Decade of the Twenties," *American Economic Review*, XXXVI (May 1946), 1-10. Louis M. Hacker, *American Problems of Today* (New York, 1938) contains pertinent chapters on economic developments during these years. Frederick Lewis Allen, *The Lords of Creation* (New York, 1935) surveys the expansion of business from the depression of the 1890's to the one of the 1930's, with emphasis upon the great industrial and financial figures of these years. Thomas C. Cochran, *The American Business System* (Cambridge, Mass., 1957) briefly but excellently appraises the changes in the structure and operation of the business system during the twentieth century.

Indispensable for the economic ideas of the period and their influence are volumes IV and V of Joseph Dorfman, *The Economic Mind in American Civilization* (New York, 1959). The business ideas of the 1920's as expressed by the National Association of Manufacturers and the United States Chamber of Commerce are summarized in James Prothro, *Dollar Decade: Business Ideas in the 1920's* (Baton Rouge, La., 1954). See also Charles Chapman, *The Development of American Business and Banking Thought, 1931-1936* (London, 1936).

A number of contemporary works continue to merit attention, among which consult Thomas N. Carver, *The Present Economic Revolution in the United States* (Boston, 1925), which reflects the New Era psychology and optimism; William Z. Ripley, *Main Street and Wall Street* (Boston, 1927), which points out certain corporate malpractices and suggests "individualization of responsibility within a corporation" as a possible remedy; Paul M. Mazur, *American Prosperity: Its Causes and Consequences* (New York, 1928); Rexford G. Tugwell, *Industry's Coming of Age* (New York, 1927); and the collection of essays in Rexford Tugwell, ed., *The Trend of Economics* (New York, 1924). Edgar L. Heermance, *The Ethics of Business: A Study of Current Standards* (New York, 1926) and James Truslow Adams, *Our Business Civilization* (Boston, 1929) have both been frequently cited.

The number of specialized studies analyzing various aspects of the industrial developments of the 1920's is exceptionally large. Those listed here suggest only some of the more important ones available. Two studies by Arthur R. Burns are especially worthwhile, *Production Trends in the United States since 1890* (New York, 1934) and the *Decline of Competition* (New York, 1936). Frederick C. Mills, *Economic Tendencies in the United States* (New York, 1936) analyzes prices, costs, and production, as well as other factors from 1914 to 1929. Willford I. King, *The National Income and Its Purchasing Power* (New York, 1930) is an excellent quantitative study sponsored by the National Bureau of Research, Inc., as are the two works by Solomon Fabricant, *The Output of Manufacturing Industries, 1899-1937* (New York, 1940) and *Employment in Manufacturing, 1899-1939* (New York, 1942). Consult also Charles A. Bliss, *The Structure of Manufacturing Production in the United States* (New York, 1939); Ralph C. Epstein, *Industrial Profits in the United States* (New York, 1934); Harold Barger, *Outlay and Income in the United States, 1921–*

1938 (New York, 1942); Robert F. Martin, *National Income in the United States* (New York, 1939); Spurgeon Bell, *Productivity, Wages, and National Income* (Washington, D.C., 1940); and Evans Clark, ed., *The Internal Debts of the United States* (New York, 1933), a summary "of the amount of indebtedness of the various classes of debtors in the United States in relation to their 'capacity to pay' at certain times between the immediate pre-war period to 1933." Maurice Leven, *et al.*, *America's Capacity to Consume* (Washington, D.C., 1934) analyzes income distribution between 1900 and 1930. Two important studies by Harold G. Moulton are *Income and Economic Progress* (Washington, D.C., 1935) and *The Formation of Capital* (Washington, D.C., 1935); the latter is an analysis of the growth of capital in the United States since the Civil War. Edwin G. Nourse, *et al.*, *America's Capacity to Consume* (Washington, D.C., 1934) is a revealing study. Three works by Simon Kuznets —*National Income and its Composition, 1919–1938* (New York, 1941), the standard work on this subject, *National Product since 1869* (New York, 1946), and *Economic Change* (New York, 1953)—are all carefully prepared studies published under the auspices of the National Bureau of Economic Research, Inc.

Business concentration during the 1920's is appraised in Harry W. Laidler, *Concentration of Control in American Business* (New York, 1931); Adolph A. Berle and Gardiner C. Means, *The Modern Corporation and Private Property* (New York, 1933) a major interpretation; James C. Bonbright and Gardiner C. Means, *The Holding Company: Its Public Significance and Regulation* (New York, 1932), an analysis of this form of corporate control; National Industrial Conference Board, *Mergers and the Law* (New York, 1929); Henry R. Seager and Charles A. Gulick, Jr., *Trust and Corporate Problems* (New York, 1929); Frank A. Fetter, *The Masquerade of Monopoly* (New York [1931]), a critical, though analytical, study of concentration in metals, steel, and oil. Hilary A. Marquand, *The Dynamics of Industrial Combination* (London, 1931), analyzes "the motives which lie behind the outward act of combination and the problems of administration and control to which that act gives rise."

On trade associations in the 1920's see William J. A. Donald, *Trade Associations* (New York, 1933); Federal Trade Commission, *Open-price Trade Associations* (Washington, D.C., 1929); Joseph H. Foth, *Trade Associations: Their Services to Industry* (New York [1930]); and National Industrial Conference Board, *Trade Associations* (New York, 1928), all of which cover the subject from varying points of view.

Thurman W. Arnold, *The Folklore of Capitalism* (New Haven, Conn., 1937) is critical of the business practices of the 1920's, as are the following: John M. Blair, *Seeds of Destruction* (New York, 1938); Lewis Corey, *The Decline of American Capitalism* (New York, 1934), a left-wing attack on business practices and economic policies; Lawrence Dennis, *Is Capitalism Doomed?* (New York, 1932); John T. Flynn, *Graft in Business* (New York, 1931); Ferdinand Lundberg, *America's 60 Families* (New York, 1937); Stuart

Chase, *Prosperity: Fact or Myth?* (New York, 1929); and Edward D. Kennedy, *Dividends to Pay* (New York [1939]).

What Americans thought of six of their business leaders at the time each died is appraised by Sigmund Diamond, *The Reputation of the American Businessman* (Cambridge, Mass., 1955). The three twentieth-century businessmen included are J. P. Morgan, John D. Rockefeller, and Henry Ford.

On the automobile industry generally see the early account by Herbert L. Barber, *The Story of the Automobile* (Chicago, 1917); Edward D. Kennedy, *The Automobile Industry: The Coming of Age of Capitalism's Favorite Child* (New York, 1941), which emphasizes finance; Carl B. Glasscock, *The Gasoline Age* (Indianapolis [1937]); Ralph C. Epstein, *The Automobile Industry: Its Economic and Commercial Development* (Chicago, 1928); Lawrence H. Seltzer, *Financial History of the American Automobile Industry* (Boston, 1928), which emphasizes the industry's sources of capital; and Merrill Denison, *The Power to Go: The Story of the Automobile Industry* (New York, 1956), a recent general survey; and David L. Cohn, *Combustion on Wheels: An Informal History of the Automobile Age* (Boston, 1944). The best study of a single firm is Allan Nevins and Frank Ernest Hill, *Ford: Expansion and Challenge, 1915-1933* (New York, 1957), the second of a three-volume study. Aside from its detailed account of the Ford empire, this work contains also much general automotive history. Ford himself has attracted a number of biographers. Keith Sward, *The Legend of Henry Ford* (New York, 1948), which is critical, and Johathan N. Leonard, *The Tragedy of Henry Ford* (New York, 1932) are of some merit. Ford himself tells his own story in *My Life and Work* (Garden City, N.Y., 1922). Wayne G. Broehl, Jr., *Trucks, Trouble, and Triumph: The Norwalk Truck Line Company* (New York, 1954) details the events in the growth of an important regional carrier.

General histories of aviation include Elsbeth E. Freudenthal, *The Aviation Business: From Kitty Hawk to Wall Street* (New York, 1940); Jeremiah Milbank, Jr., *The First Century of Flight in America: An Introductory Survey* (Princeton, N.J. [1943]); Edward P. Warner, *Early History of Air Transportation* (Northfield, Vt., 1938); Henry L. Smith, *Airways: The History of Commercial Aviation in the United States* (New York, 1942); George L. Wilson and Leslie A. Bryan, *Air Transportation* (New York, 1948); Eric Hodgins and F. Alexander Magoun, *Sky High: The Story of Aviation* (Boston, 1929); and John Goldstrom, *Narrative History of Aviation* (New York, 1930). The history of the Boeing Airplane Company, with a background of industry developments, is told in Harold Mansfield, *Vision: A Saga of the Sky* (New York [1956]).

The story of the Wright brothers is told in their own words in Fred C. Kelly, ed., *Miracle at Kitty Hawk: The Letters of Wilbur and Orville Wright* (New York [1951]) and in a biography by Fred C. Kelly, *The Wright Brothers* (New York [1943]).

The best biography of Charles A. Lindbergh is Kenneth S. Davis, *The Hero: Charles A. Lindbergh and His American Dream* (New York, 1959). The aviator's own account of the famous 1927 flight is told in Charles A. Lindbergh, *We* (New York, 1927) and in more detail, and with greater perspective, in his later book, *The Spirit of St. Louis* (New York, 1953). On the implications of that flight, John W. Ward, "The Meaning of Lindbergh's Flight," *American Quarterly*, X (Spring 1958), 3–16, is very good.

The growth and development of the radio industry is revealed in Paul Schmidt, *The Electric Word: The Rise of the Radio* (New York, 1928); more thoroughly in *The Annals of the American Academy of Political and Social Science*, CLXXVIII (January 1935), 1–219; and Federal Council of the Churches of Christ in America, *Broadcasting and the Public* (New York [1938]).

The motion picture industry is surveyed in several works, of which Albert R. Fulton, *Motion Pictures: The Development of an Art Form from Silent Films to the Age of Television* (Norman, Okla. [1960]) is the most recent scholarly account; but see also Harold B. Franklin, *Sound Motion Pictures* (Garden City, N.Y., 1929); Lewis Jacobs, *The Rise of the American Film: A Critical History* (New York, 1939); and Arthur Mayer, *Merely Colossal* (New York, 1953). One of the more important references is the symposium published in *The Annals of the American Academy of Political and Social Science*, CCLIV (November 1947), 1–172. The personal intrigues of the industry and financial maneuverings are interestingly told by *The New York Times'* motion picture reviewer, Bosley Crowther, *Hollywood Rajah* (New York [1960]), the biography of Louis B. Mayer.

Besides the references on the power industry cited in Chapter 11, see also Federal Trade Commission, *The Electric Power Industry* (Washington, D.C., 1927); Charles O. Hardy, *Recent Growth of the Electric Light and Power Industry* (Washington, D.C. [1929]); and Marion L. Ramsay, *Pyramids of Power: The Story of Roosevelt, Insull and the Utility Wars* (Indianapolis [1937]); the criticism of the power interests in Ernest Guening, *The Public Pays* (New York, 1931); and Jack Levin, *Power Ethics* (New York, 1931).

Frank Presbrey, *The History and Development of Advertising* (New York, 1929) covers some of the developments in the early 1920's, but see also J. Rorty, *"Our Master's Voice": Advertising* (New York [1934]). The inside story of an important firm is Ralph M. Hower, *The History of an Advertising Agency: N. W. Ayer & Sons at Work, 1869–1939* (rev. ed., Cambridge, Mass., 1949).

The basic and most comprehensive reference on the chemical industry is William Haynes, *American Chemical Industry* (6 vols., New York, 1945–54), covering developments to 1939. On the Du Ponts see John K. Winkler, *The Du Pont Dynasty* (New York [1935]), a lively and accurate account written without access to the family records. A more sympathetic portrait of the firm is William S. Dutton, *Du Pont: One Hundred and Forty Years* (3d ed., New York, 1951).

On labor in the 1920's see Irving Bernstein, *The Lean Years: A History of the American Worker, 1920–1933* (Boston, 1960), the most recent analysis; the first several chapters of Philip Taft, *The A.F. of L. from the Death of Gompers to the Merger* (New York, 1959); Jacob B. S. Hardman, ed., *American Labor*

Dynamics . . . (New York [1928]), which analyzes the labor movement in the decade between 1918 and 1928; and the following articles: Lyle Cooper, "The American Labor Movement in Prosperity and Depression," *American Economic Review*, XXII (December 1932), 641–59; David Saposs, "The American Labor Movement since the War," *Quarterly Journal of Economics*, XLIX (February 1935), 236–54; and Sumner Slichter, "The Current Labor Policies of American Industries," *Quarterly Journal of Economics*, XLIII (May 1929), 393–435.

All of the general comprehensive one-volume histories of American labor, such as Joseph G. Rayback, *A History of American Labor*, cited previously; Carroll R. Daugherty, *Labor Problems in American Industry* (Boston, 1933); and the final chapters of Leo Wolman, *The Growth of American Trade Unions, 1880–1923* (New York, 1924) are also useful.

Among the more relevant specialized works on labor violence, see Louis Adamic, *Dynamite: The Story of Class Violence in America* (rev. ed., New York, 1934); John A. Fitch, *The Causes of Industrial Unrest* (New York, 1924); Paul M. Angle, *Bloody Williamson* (New York, 1952), which details the 1922 Herrin massacre; and Grace Hutchins, *Labor and Silk* (New York, 1929), which tells the story of the Paterson strike.

The Socialist view is ably presented in two volumes by Norman Thomas, *What Is Industrial Democracy?* (New York, 1925) and *Human Exploitation in the United States* (New York, 1934).

Radicalism and communism in the United States among the working class are specifically detailed in John S. Gambs, *The Decline of the I.W.W.* (New York, 1932); David S. Saposs, *Left-wing Unionism* (New York, 1926); Benjamin Gitlow, *I Confess* (New York, 1939); William Z. Foster, *From Bryan to Stalin* (New York [1937]); and James Oneal, *American Communism* (new rev. ed., New York, 1927). All of these should be supplemented with the more recent detailed study by Theodore Draper, *The Roots of American Communism* (New York, 1957) for the early years of the Communist party, from 1919 to 1923; and the same author's second volume, *American Communism and Soviet Russia: The Formative Period* (New York, 1960), which brings the story down to 1929, when Earl Browder took over.

Thomas D. Clark, *The Emerging South* (New York, 1961) is an excellent study of that region since 1920. Among the more specialized works see George S. Mitchell, *Textile Unionism and the South* (Chapel Hill, N.C., 1932) and Tom Tippett, *When Southern Labor Stirs* (New York, 1931), both of which are on the textile industry.

On the Negro worker in industry see Sterling D. Spero and Abram L. Harris, *The Black Worker* (New York, 1931).

Among other specialized works covering various aspects of labor activities in the 1920's see Robert W. Dunn, *Company Unions* (New York [1927]); Harold Seidman, *Labor Czars: A History of Labor Racketeering* (New York [1938]); and Leo Huberman, *The Labor Spy Racket* (New York, 1937). Statistical syntheses of labor's earnings include National Industrial Conference Board, *Wages in the United States, 1914–1927* (New York, 1928); Willford I.

King, *Employment, Hours and Earnings in Prosperity and Depression . . . 1921–1922* (2d ed., New York, 1923); Paul H. Douglas and Aaron Director, *The Problem of Unemployment* (New York, 1931), which is primarily concerned with technological unemployment during the depression; Paul H. Douglas, *Real Wages in the United States, 1890–1926* (New York, 1932), which is standard. Matthew Josephson's biography, *Sidney Hillman* (New York, 1952) is basic for studying labor in the clothing industry.

Almost all the references cited in Chapter 11 on the agricultural discontent and policies of the Harding and Coolidge administrations are relevant in trying to understand the problems and postion of agriculture in the economy of the 1920's. In addition to those, see also Oliver E. Baker, *et al., Agriculture in Modern Life* (New York, 1939); Russell C. Engberg, *Industrial Prosperity and the Farmer* (New York, 1927); Edwin G. Nourse, *American Agriculture in the European Market* (New York, 1924); Bernhard Ostrolenk, *The Surplus Farmer* (New York, 1932); and Harold G. Barger and Hans Landsberg, *American Agriculture, 1899–1939: A Study of Output, Employment and Productivity* (New York, 1942), primarily a statistical synthesis.

The two best general studies of American foreign economic policy in the 1920's are Herbert Feis, *The Diplomacy of the Dollar, First Era, 1919–1932* (Baltimore, 1950) and Cleona Lewis, *America's Stake in International Investments* (Washington, D.C., 1938), which summarizes America's debtor-creditor position up to World War II, and is more detailed than the long-time standard reference by James W. Angell, *Financial Foreign Policy of the United States* (Washington, D.C., 1933), which emphasizes the post-1929 period. Of the older works see John T. Madden, *et al., America's Experience as a Creditor Nation* (New York, 1937); Benjamin H. Williams, *Economic Foreign Policy of the United States* (New York, 1929); Muriel F. Jolliffe, *The United States as a Financial Centre, 1919–1933* (Cardiff, Wales, 1935); William S. Culbertson, *International Economic Policies* (New York, 1925); Paul M. Mazur, *America Looks Abroad* (New York, 1930); Hiram Motherwell, *The Imperial Dollar* (New York [1929]); and Scott Nearing and Joseph Freeman, *Dollar Diplomacy* (New York, 1925).

On the export of American capital Robert W. Dunn, *American Foreign Investments* (New York, 1926) is very useful, but see also some of the more specialized studies, such as Max Winkler, *Investments of United States Capital in Latin America* (Boston, 1928); Margaret A. Marsh, *The Bankers in Bolivia* (New York [1928]); and J. Fred Rippy, *The Capitalists and Colombia* (New York [1931]).

Herbert Marshall, *et al., Canadian-American Industry* (New Haven, Conn., 1936) remains useful for American economic expansion above the forty-ninth parallel, as does Frank A. Southard, *American Industry in Europe* (New York, 1931) for that phase of the subject. The rivalries and cooperation in the overseas economic expansion of the 1920's are told in Ludwell Denny, *America Conquers Britain* (New York, 1930), and in the more general study by Benjamin B. Wallace and Lynn R. Edminster, *International Control of Raw Materials* (Washington, D.C., 1930), which analyzes the agreements and cartel arrangements of the 1920's. Also useful on this subject are Irvin Hexner, *International Cartels* (Chapel Hill, N.C., 1945) and the official, more contemporary appraisal by William F. Notz, *Representative International Cartels, Combines and Trusts* (Washington, D.C., 1929).

The rivalry to secure oil is told generally in Ludwell Denny, *We Fight for Oil* (New York, 1928) and more specifically in such studies as Raymond F. Mikesell and Hollis B. Chenery, *Arabian Oil: America's Stake in the Middle East* (Chapel Hill, N.C., 1949); Benjamin Shwadran, *The Middle East: Oil and the Great Powers* (New York, 1955); and Edwin Lieuwen, *Petroleum in Venezuela: A History* (Berkeley, Calif., 1955). A number of oil company histories also include chapters on the international politics and economics of the oil industry. See, for example, George S. Gibb and Evelyn H. Knowlton, *The Resurgent Years, 1911-1927* (New York [1956]), volume II in the *History of the Standard Oil Company (New Jersey)*.

The views of a close associate of Herbert Hoover in the Commerce Department on foreign economic policies are expressed in Julius Klein, *Frontiers of Trade* (New York [1929]).

13

Social and Cultural Trends

AN AGE OF MATERIALISM

From some points of view the decade of the 1920's appears, in retrospect, as a golden age. In contrast with the 1930's, it was a period when money was relatively easy to acquire and when men had few doubts or fears about the future. It was also a period of steady cultural advance, in which the literature and art of the United States appeared for the first time to have passed beyond the stage of colonialism or provincialism and to have achieved maturity. Yet the tone of American society in the 1920's was in many ways very unhealthy, and the American people were left dangerously unprepared to face the catastrophic events of the period which followed. There was probably more materialism, more illiberality, and more cynicism than ever before in American history. Ideals lost their meaning as more and more people became increasingly disillusioned with the results of World War I and Versailles. The number of international incidents following the peace treaties which threatened or led to violence made it obvious that the war to end wars had fallen far short of its goal and that peace and democracy were no safer afterward than they had been before. Meanwhile the war had accelerated numerous changes in the American way of life. Though many of these changes were already becoming apparent when Wilson first entered the White House in 1913, their impact came in the 1920's and caused many Americans to believe that their effort to save the world had resulted only in losing what they held most dear at home.[1] Disillusionment with the postwar world abroad and at home caused many Americans to supplant reform and idealism with materialism and cynicism. For a considerable proportion of the population, financial success became the only objective worth striving for, and much of the spirit of the era might be summarized in the word *debunk*, coined by William E. Woodward, the novelist and historian.

The most trusted leaders of America were unanimous in agreeing with President Coolidge that "the business of America is business." Such a sentiment was unexceptionable insofar as business meant the making and distribution of goods. But business also included speculation, advertising, and pressure salesmanship; and these activities, which involved the making of money rather than the making of goods, assumed in the 1920's an exaggerated importance.

Speculation had always been a favorite American occupation, but it had never before been pursued so vigorously or by a larger number of people. The hope of getting something for nothing culminated in the stock exchange fever of 1928 and the catastrophe of October, 1929; but throughout the decade there were numerous epidemics of speculative excitement. The most extraordinary of these was perhaps the Florida land boom of 1924 and 1925. Thousands of hopeful individuals from all over the country swarmed into Coral Gables, Miami, and Palm Beach to buy real estate on the installment plan, with hopes of selling it again within a few weeks before the next installment was due. Thousands of others bought land without even seeing it. The price of a lot in the business section of Miami rose from $800 to $150,000. The Florida realtors dexterously stimulated the fever by such methods as hiring William Jennings Bryan, former champion of agrarian radicalism and Secretary of State of the United States, to make speeches in praise of the Florida climate. The inevitable collapse began in 1926, and was completed by a hurricane which killed four hundred persons along the Florida coast. But many gullible persons who had lost their savings were undaunted by the experience and only too willing to transfer their hopes the following year from Miami to Wall Street.

Meanwhile the salesman and the advertising man seemed to be replacing the engineer as the key figures in the economic system. Confronted by a consumers' market which was apparently too small to absorb all the

---

[1] Henry F. May, "Shifting Perspectives on the 1920's," *Mississippi Valley Historical Review*, XLIII (December 1956), 405–27 and the same author's "The Rebellion of the Intellectuals, 1912–1917," *American Quarterly*, VIII (Summer 1956), 114–26.

products of American industry, corporation managers found that their principal problem was not the improvement of production but the capture of new customers. Qualities which made for successful salesmanship—aggressiveness and lack of scruple—acquired a new value; and the ability to "sell oneself," which had formerly denoted dishonesty, now indicated a desirable accomplishment. The glorification of business and the advertising man reached its peak in a widely read book, *The Man Nobody Knows*, written by the New York advertising agent Bruce Barton. Jesus Christ, declared Mr. Barton, "would be a national advertiser today," and he was "the founder of modern business." The appeal of the salesman and the advertising man was largely to motives of envy and cupidity. Luxuries began being represented as necessities, and millions of American families were induced to emulate their neighbors by running into debt in order to maintain a higher standard of living than they could afford. In this popularization of luxury the advertising man received valuable assistance from the motion pictures and from the best-selling magazines.

The desire for material satisfactions, which was stimulated by all the new propagandist devices of salesmanship, expressed itself in a general relaxation of traditional ethical standards. Moral taboos, both in speech and behavior, grew rapidly weaker. In every age, of course, the older generation has viewed with alarm the conduct of the young; but since there is no statistical evidence, it may be doubted whether there have been any considerable variations in the amount of immorality in different periods. Two generalizations, however, may safely be made about the so-called "jazz age" of the 1920's: conversation was freer than for a number of generations, and—largely as a result of the automobile—the traditional double standard was breaking down. Obsession with the problems of sex among persons who considered themselves emancipated ended abruptly in the 1930's, when they turned instead to the problems of economic reform or revolution.

A more indubitable symptom of a weakening of moral fiber was the series of waves of popular excitement whipped up by the ballyhoo of sensationalist newspapers. Motion picture stars, sports champions, celebrated criminals, and successful gangsters occupied in turn the spotlight of national attention. College football, played by teams of semiprofessionals, became a big business in which a single university could collect a million dollars in admission fees in a single season; $1.5 million was paid to see Jack Dempsey beat Georges Carpentier, and ten persons died of excitement while listening to radio reports of the fight between Dempsey and Gene Tunney. The most popular motion picture idols were almost deified, and the death of Rudolph Valentino caused astonishing outbursts of feminine hysteria. Among the different figures who attained the rôle of a national hero, it seemed refreshing to find one, Colonel Charles A. Lindbergh, who had earned his fame by genuine achievement and who clearly hated the publicity he received. The enthusiastic acclaim which greeted Lindbergh's flight expressed the American people's desire to identify themselves with his accomplishment, to celebrate it as a great feat of the promises of the new technology, and, at the same time, to revere him as a symbol of the old-time individualism which had made America great.[2]

THE INCREASE OF CRIME

Many tendencies which appeared to some people as indicating a growth of materialistic standards of value and a decay of morality might be regarded by others as unimportant or not wholly reprehensible. There was, however, one feature of American life in the 1920's which provoked the most justified alarm and which indicated a genuine danger of social disintegration: the extraordinary increase of lawlessness.

Disrespect for the law, always an American characteristic, was especially widespread during the 1920's. Encouraged by examples on Wall Street and—during the Harding regime—in Washington, the officials of numerous state and city governments reverted to the ways of the post–Civil War period. Outstanding among the examples of municipal misgovernment were the Democratic regime of Mayor James J. Walker of New York, which combined a corruption reminiscent of the Tammany of Boss Tweed with a polished sophistication appropriate to the richest city in the world, and the Republican regime of Mayor William Hale Thompson of Chicago, who won his election by appealing to the German and Irish vote with a promise to keep "King George's snoot" out of the city.

Law enforcement being frequently in venal hands, organized crime flourished as never before in American history. Thanks to the Eighteenth Amendment, criminal groups were able to take over the very lucrative business of supplying the American people with liquor. They were aided

[2] John W. Ward, "The Meaning of Lindbergh's Flight," *American Quarterly* (Summer 1958), 15–16.

also by corrupt connections with local politicians; by the deficiencies of the American legal system, which enabled shyster lawyers to prevent convictions by means of technicalities; and by the extraordinary tolerance of public opinion, which sometimes treated a clever criminal as a figure of national importance. Another factor in the growth of crime was the American system of states' rights; whereas law enforcement was local, crime, thanks to the automobile, was organized on a national scale. The jurisdiction of the police stopped at state lines, but murderers and bank robbers often traveled a thousand miles from the scene of their activities.

Bootlegging necessarily involved many criminal activities in addition to the manufacture and sale of liquor. Since the liquor gangs could not claim legal protection against their business competitors, they were compelled to provide for their own defense, using machine guns to guard against the theft of their property by hijackers and to intimidate retailers into buying their liquor. The growth of the liquor gangs, armed with the most modern weapons of warfare and earning revenues equal to those of all but the largest corporations, stimulated crimes of other kinds—particularly the organizing of rackets so that retail storekeepers were compelled to pay for "protection," the robbing of banks, and the kidnaping and holding of members of wealthy families for ransom. The crime statistics of the United States in the 1920's far exceeded those of any other nation in the world. Homicides averaged 10,800 a year, a rate twice that of Italy, sixteen times that of England, and thirty-six times that of Switzerland. Thefts cost the American people a direct sum of $250 million a year, while the indirect costs of crime ran into many billions of dollars. By the year 1935 there were no less than 3 million persons in the United States who either had been convicted or had been under arrest on criminal charges.

Chicago had the greatest notoriety as a center of criminal activity. In 1920 a young New Yorker, Alphonse Capone, established himself in Chicago as the organizer of a liquor gang. By 1927 his group was earning an annual revenue of $60 million from the sale of liquor, while Capone himself had accumulated a private fortune of $20 million, which enabled him to control the town of Cicero and to own an estate in Florida. Numerous battles were fought between the Capone gang and the rival gang of Dion O'Banion; and when O'Banion was killed he was buried in a casket worth $10,000 and accompanied by twenty-six truckloads of flowers. By 1929 there had been more than five hundred gang murders in Chicago, many of which had occurred on the public streets and in open daylight, and for which there had been virtually no convictions. In addition to the liquor business the gangs had organized ninety-one rackets which cost the law-abiding citizens of Chicago a total of $136 million a year. Conditions in a number of other cities were probably almost as bad. Nor was it only the immigrant groups in the big cities which produced criminals: gangsters from rural and Anglo-Saxon stock, of the type of "Baby Face" Nelson and John Dillinger, were quite as vicious as the big-city racketeers.

After 1929 crime decreased. The revenues of the gangs were diminished first by the depression and subsequently by the repeal of prohibition. The federal government also discovered several legal devices which enabled it to assume more responsibility for law enforcement. A number of leading criminals, headed by Capone, were sent to jail on the charge of income tax evasion; while the Dyer Act, making it a federal offense to transport stolen automobiles across state lines, could be applied to most of the gangs. The Federal Bureau of Investigation, founded in 1924 and headed by J. Edgar Hoover, became one of the most efficient detective agencies in the world. Thus, during the 1930's the leading "public enemies" were systematically hunted down and eliminated.

THE GROWTH OF INTOLERANCE

While American society was paying rewards in an increasing degree to the qualities of egotism, aggressiveness, and lack of scruple, it was at the same time encouraging timidity and conformity in intellectual questions. The wartime fear of radicalism continued, and persons who doubted the merits of business civilization provoked considerable antagonism.

Certain economic developments, particularly the growth of debt, strengthened the pressure toward conformity. Creditor interests, enjoying economic power, began also to claim rights of intellectual supervision. The ability to borrow depended on a sound credit status; and credit status, as interpreted by small-town bankers, was likely to be assessed not only by strictly economic considerations but also by adherence to the established political and ethical conventions. The intellectual control thus acquired by bankers was especially important when it affected the publishers of newspapers.

Meanwhile the national habit of speculation was making optimism appear a patriotic duty. Speculative profits, whether in real estate or on

Wall Street, depended on rising values, and rising values were impossible if any public exposure of abuses caused confidence to be impaired. Critics of the economic and social system were thus a menace to its financial stability. The exhortations, frequently expressed in the 1920's, that one should "boost" one's native city instead of "knocking" it, and that one should be a "bull upon the United States," were not merely an indication of a homely patriotism; they expressed also a fear lest an injudicious honesty check the rise of monetary values.

The hostility toward anything radical, alien, or "un-American" assumed also more dangerous forms—movements of organized intolerance and repressive legislation. The most formidable of these threats to the ideals upon which America had been built was the Ku Klux Klan. The postwar Klan, which had no connection except its name with the Klan of the Reconstruction Period and which was dedicated to the prevention of any changes threatening what it chose to interpret as traditional standards of behavior and to the suppression of Negroes, Catholics, Jews, foreigners, and organized labor, had been founded in 1915 by William J. Simmons. In 1921 the "Imperial Kleagle," Edward Y. Clarke, embarked on an aggressive membership campaign, sending out "kleagles" who sold membership cards for ten dollars apiece and kept for themselves 40 per cent of the proceeds. By 1924 the Klan had a membership of perhaps 4.5 million, most of whom were small farmers, storekeepers, and wage earners. It was elaborately organized into "dominions" headed by "Grand Goblins" and "realms" headed by "King Kleagles." From its headquarters at Atlanta, Georgia, it exercised considerable political power throughout the black belt in the South, as well as in Texas, Oklahoma, Ohio, Indiana, Oregon, and California. It was responsible for much intimidation and suppression of persons and activities it chose to regard as "un-American." Fortunately for American democracy, the Klan had lost most of its influence before the onset of the depression. When David C. Stephenson, the corrupt and powerful Klan organizer in the Middle West and the boss of the Indiana Republican party, was arrested for abducting and assaulting a young woman, who committed suicide while his captive, the Klan's downfall was accelerated by the disclosure of its brutality, commercialism, and corruption which accompanied the trial. Other exposés of its nefarious activities, plus the fact that it was opposed to so many groups and relied upon an artificially created fear to attract its members, combined finally to subdue the Klan for a number of years, until the 1950's, when it reappeared as an aspect of the white supremacy movement in the South.

The same fear of anything new or unusual showed itself in numerous restrictions on cultural and intellectual freedom. There was much censorship of books and plays regarded as immoral, particularly in Boston, where laws originally enacted by Puritans were being enforced by Catholics. On several occasions American customs officials made their country ridiculous by refusing to allow the importation of European classics they held might endanger the morals of American citizens. State legislatures displayed considerable faith in their capacity to make men virtuous and God-fearing by law; and in three southern states—Tennessee, Oklahoma, and Mississippi—the teaching of the Darwinian theory of evolution in the public schools was prohibited. In the Tennessee town of Dayton a high school teacher, John Thomas Scopes, defied the law; and in the subsequent trial in July, 1925, Clarence Darrow appeared for the defense and William Jennings Bryan for the prosecution. Scopes was convicted, although the supreme court of the state later released him on a technicality; and the law remained on the statute books. Bryan's cross-examination by Darrow as to his belief in the Garden of Eden and in Jonah and the whale was his last public appearance. He died a week after the trial.

The Scopes trial involved more than a question of academic freedom. To Bryan and the prosecution, Scopes represented all the alien forces threatening to destroy the foundations of American civilization. Though there were radicals in the country and stalwart conservatives in the city, rural Americans by and large were more tradition-conscious than their urban counterparts. Rural and small-town America blamed the moral decay, the lawlessness, and the social disintegration they claimed to see all about them upon the corrupting influence of the city, where foreigners, radicals, and racketeers congregated and where they propagated the alien and immoral ideologies which were undermining traditional virtue, morality, and loyalty.

The first reaction of all those who opposed change was to strike down, often indiscriminately, everything new, including honest and well-intentioned criticisms of the social and economic scene. The "Red scare" of 1919–20, the antilabor crusades, the advocacy of conformity in all sectors of American life and culture, and the Ku Klux Klan had the common goal of preventing change and strengthening the *status quo*. One of the purposes of the immigration act of 1924 was to keep out undesirable and unassimilable foreigners, with their alien ideas, religion, and customs. The same attitude motivated many of the intolerant and repressive laws enacted on the state and local levels, such as the law in Oregon which, had the state courts not invalidated it, would have closed Catholic parochial schools on the ground they were un-American.[3] In other states and cities local school boards tried to inculcate "real Americanism" by insisting upon textbooks which satisfied their "patriotic" sensibilities rather than historical objectivity. The Scopes trial reflected the social insecurities which lay at the root of all these conflicts, especially the religious one centering on the issue of fundamentalism versus modernism in interpreting the Bible.

The research of biologists, psychologists, anthropologists, and biblical scholars had raised serious questions as to the validity and accuracy of the churches' interpretation of the Bible, while the distractions of modern life and the movement of people away from their traditional environment, especially the trek from the country to the city, loosened church ties still further. People continued to go to church in the 1920's, but it appears that a great many attended for reasons other than the fear of hell. The Protestant churches, which suffered most from the religious controversy, generally reacted in one of two ways. The modernists, most of whom were eastern, upper middle-class urbanites, found no difficulty in reconciling science and religion. To them the importance of the Bible was in its ethical message. Dogma, literal interpretation of the Scriptures, and the divine inspiration of the Bible were of secondary importance. Their chief concern, wrote André Siegfried, was with "moral sincerity and social welfare." Religion, the modernists argued, "should adapt itself to the conditions of the time, in order to fill its appointed *rôle* as guiding factor of the community." This was far "more important than formal belief in hidebound doctrines."[4]

The fundamentalists, most of whom lived on the farms and in the small towns of the South and West, saw in the modernist's approach to religion another alarming example of the alien and secular forces which were undermining traditional virtues and standards. They accepted the Bible as divine truth and argued that to question any part of it was to weaken the whole structure of Christian religion and morality. Their message was carried across the land by evangelists like William A. "Billy" Sunday, a former baseball player who became an ordained Presbyterian minister,

[3] John D. Hicks, *Republican Ascendancy, 1921–1933* (New York [1960]), pp. 182–83.
[4] André Siegfried, *America Comes of Age* (New York [1927]), pp. 40–41.

and the Los Angeles revivalist and faith-healer Aimee Semple McPherson; but none of these spokesmen had as much influence and prestige as William Jennings Bryan. A son of the rural Middle West, a devout Presbyterian who took the religious teachings of his youth most seriously, and a stern moralist who distrusted cities and too much education, Bryan was sincere and completely honest in his defense of fundamentalist principles. "It is better," he once stated, "to trust in the Rock of Ages than to know the age of rocks; it is better for one to know that he is close to the Heavenly Father than to know how far the stars in the heavens are apart." [5]

PROHIBITION

The most striking example of the American faith in moralistic legislation was the thirteen-year attempt to enforce prohibition. In January, 1920, it became illegal by the Volstead Act to sell liquor containing more than 0.5 per cent alcohol, except for medicinal purposes or as sacramental wine. Enforcement was at first entrusted to the Bureau of Internal Revenue in the Treasury Department, and the prosecution of offenders was handled by the Department of Justice.

The number of federal prohibition agents was only 1,520 in 1920 and 2,836 in 1930; and since their salaries were generally lower than $2,000 a year, they were under considerable temptation to increase their incomes illicitly, particularly while Harry Daugherty was Attorney General. These men were expected to police the personal habits of the American people and to enforce a law which perhaps a third of the population had no intention of obeying. To what extent the law actually diminished the consumption of alcohol is impossible to say. In 1930 the director of the Prohibition Bureau calculated that the domestic production of liquor for sale was about 40 per cent of the figure for 1914, but this did not include smuggling from abroad, the diversion of industrial alcohol and of medicinal and sacramental wines, and home brewing. The law was enforced in some rural areas, but there was probably no city of any size which was not adequately supplied with speakeasies and staffed with bootleggers. The most conspicuous results of the Eighteenth Amendment were to encourage disrespect for the law, increase the revenues of criminals, add a

[5] Quoted in William E. Leuchtenburg, The Perils of Prosperity, 1914–1932 (Chicago [1958]), p. 219.

spice of adventure to the consumption of liquor, and strengthen the preference of the American people for hard liquor rather than for beer or wine.

For a period the Anti-Saloon League was strong enough to prevent any politicians from publicly admitting that prohibition had failed. In 1928, however, Alfred E. Smith advocated repeal, and in 1930 a number of candidates for Congress, notably Dwight Morrow in New Jersey, were bold enough to run as wets and were elected. In May, 1929, President Hoover appointed the Wickersham commission to consider the problem of crime and law enforcement; and, although the commission as a whole was induced to recommend continuance of prohibition, five of its eleven members came out individually for modification and two for repeal. Opposition to prohibition was further strengthened by the depression; rich men, who feared a rise in the income tax, began to advocate the legalization and taxation of liquor as a revenue measure. In the campaign of 1932 the Democratic platform demanded repeal. Congress voted for repeal in February, 1933, and amended the Volstead Act to allow 3.2 per cent beer in March. By December repeal had been ratified by two-thirds of the states. States which wished to continue dry were to be protected by the federal government against the importation of liquor from wet states; but by 1937 only seven states were still dry. Of the remainder, fifteen made the sale of liquor a state monopoly, and twenty-six established central licensing bodies with strict rules which would, it was hoped, prevent any return of the evils of the saloon.

CRITICS OF AMERICAN SOCIETY

American society in the 1920's did not lack critics. Never before, in fact, had American intellectuals been so nearly unanimous or so bitter in condemning their environment. Unfortunately their attitude was almost wholly destructive; for the most part, it encouraged escape or cynical acquiescence rather than effort toward constructive change.

Movements for economic reform or revolution had very little support. A few small groups continued to denounce the capitalist system. The Socialist party, headed after the death of Eugene Debs by Norman Thomas, was still functioning, although seriously weakened by the appearance of the Communist party. Hopefully prophesying revolution in the near future, the Communists won some adherents among metropolitan intellectuals, but they were largely occupied by conflicts among the various factions which aspired to party leadership. These controversies were referred to Moscow which—in 1929—awarded control of the party machinery to the group headed by William Z. Foster and Earl Browder, their rivals being expelled from the party and subsequently declared fascistic counterrevolutionaries.

But the opposition to capitalism was considerably weaker than before World War I. Business prosperity appeared firmly established and likely to continue for an indefinite period; and very few individuals, either conservative or radical, were acute enough to predict the debacle of 1929. There was little comprehension of the real weaknesses of the economic system and, consequently, little attempt to prepare a constructive program which might have been applied in the 1930's. Many of the intellectual leaders of the progressive era—such men as Veblen, Brandeis, Dewey, Beard, Steffens—were still active, but no social critics of comparable weight appeared among the younger generation.

Most critics of the American scene now thought primarily in terms not of politics and economics but of aesthetic experience and the life of the individual. American society was no longer denounced because it was insufficiently democratic; some of the more influential figures of the 1920's were, in fact (like H. L. Mencken), disposed to ascribe its deficiencies to too much democracy. The Americans were now denounced as a people who were blind to aesthetic values and among whom civilized and cultured living was impossible. The terms of the indictment were emphatic and comprehensive. The United States was a country of dollar-chasing materialism, of standardized mediocrity, of a repressive puritanism, and of hypocrisy; it did not understand the values of aesthetic experience or of leisure or of personal freedom. The ablest and most plausible statement of these opinions was in the writings of Van Wyck Brooks; but they first achieved notoriety in 1922 in *Civilization in the United States,* edited by Harold Stearns, in which thirty different contributors examined thirty different aspects of American life and found almost all of them unsatisfactory.

Harold Stearns subsequently fled to Paris, where he was joined by numerous other refugees from prohibition, while other dissidents from the civilization of the Coolidge era retired to Majorca, Vienna, Mexico, or the Pacific islands. Meanwhile this attitude of supercilious disgust was popularized by H. L. Mencken, who founded the *American Mercury* in 1924 and who enjoyed considerable influence, particularly among college undergraduates, until 1927, when he made the mistake of ridiculing the campaign to save Sacco and Vanzetti. Contempt for almost all that America stood for continued to be the correct attitude for intellectuals until almost the middle of the 1930's, when the rise of fascism in Europe, coupled with a new hopefulness in the United States, caused a rediscovery of national traditions and ideals.

The flight of the intellectuals from America was in many ways deplorable; but similar viewpoints expressed themselves, on a higher plane, in a considerable cultural achievement. And although much of the work of this period was vitiated by a lack of sympathy and a tendency toward satire, by a desire to debunk ideals and expose the falsity of accepted traditions, and by an ivory-tower aloofness and intellectuality, it produced a number of commentaries on American life which seem of lasting importance.

LITERATURE AND THE ARTS

During the early twentieth century there was a remarkable growth in both the quantity and the quality of American contributions to all the various arts and an equally significant improvement in the standards of popular taste. It can plausibly be argued that during the first half of the century more good work in literature and painting was produced in the United States than during the whole of the preceding three hundred years.

Since the time of Emerson, critics had frequently urged American intellectuals to break away from European influences and to develop an indigenous American culture. It was suggested that the United States was in need of an artistic Declaration of Independence. In accordance with this recommendation, twentieth-century American writers and painters set out to depict the American environment more realistically than did their predecessors, they abandoned European forms and conventions which did not seem to be adapted to American material, and they repudiated the traditional belief in the artistic superiority of Europe. It would, however, be an error to attach too much importance to nationalistic influences in the arts. The arts, like the sciences, have always been international, and the writers and artists of different nations have always borrowed freely from one another. Throughout the twentieth century there has been a constant and fruitful interchange between the United

States and Europe; new techniques and new ideas, first conceived on one continent, have been adopted and developed on the other; and the transit of influences across the Atlantic has been by no means a one-way passage.

The artistic interchange between the United States and Europe was paralleled by a similar interchange among the different regions of the United States. Since the end of the nineteenth century New York City had been the cultural capital of the country, so that it often seemed to attract too large a proportion of the nation's intellectuals and to exercise too powerful an influence over the nation's artistic development. In the early 1900's, however, groups of writers and artists established themselves in other cities, or set out to record the distinctive physical and cultural characteristics of the regions from which they had sprung. Good novels were written and good pictures were painted in every part of the United States; and the growth of cultural activities was by no means confined to the great metropolitan centers.

The arts in America were also enriched by the interplay of ethnic differences. In the nineteenth century most of the leading American intellectuals were of British descent, but after 1900 the children of the immigrants and the descendants of the slaves played an increasingly important part in American development. American writers, painters, and musicians were German, Irish, Jewish, Italian, Negro, Slavic, Scandinavian, Spanish, and Portuguese as well as Anglo-Saxon.

Perhaps the two main tendencies in American aesthetic development after 1900 were realism and intellectualism. The realists set out to tell the whole truth about American society, with special emphasis on those dark features of it that appeared to contradict the more optimistic beliefs cherished by conservatives. They often adhered to a materialistic and deterministic philosophy of life and were usually sympathetic to some form of political and economic radicalism. Meanwhile, writers and artists with more intellectual inclinations endeavored to record complex experiences with the greatest possible subtlety and precision, and in so doing they frequently produced works of such obscurity that their audiences were very limited. Both these tendencies were vigorously denounced by academic conservatives, who remained faithful to the traditions established in the nineteenth century. The realists were condemned for their unrestricted frankness, while the work of the intellectualists was dismissed as unintelligible and nonsensical. The conservatives, however, were fighting a losing battle, and the influence of the modernists steadily increased.

Although the origins of the more important new trends can be traced back to the 1880's and 1890's, they made little headway during the first decade of the twentieth century, when intellectuals were largely preoccupied with political reforms. The most decisive turning point in the history of the arts in America occurred during the years 1912 through 1915. These four years saw the first appearance of a large number of the new poets and novelists who were to be dominant figures during the 1920's. In 1912 the magazine *Poetry*, edited by Harriet Monroe, began publication, and in 1914 appeared the first *Imagist Anthology*. These and other noncommercial "little magazines" enabled young experimental writers to find a hearing. In the other arts the same period was notable for the Armory Exhibition of modern painting in New York in 1913, which introduced to America the leading European modernists; the foundation in 1915 of both the Washington Square Players and the Provincetown Players, who were to vitalize the American theater; and the completion in the same year of D. W. Griffith's *Birth of a Nation*, the first motion picture to demonstrate the aesthetic potentialities of this new art form.

This artistic activity was accompanied by the advent of a number of young critics, especially Randolph Bourne and Van Wyck Brooks. These men sympathized with the political aspirations of the progressive era; and while they were severe in indicting the deficiencies of American society and traditions, they accepted American democratic ideals and were not unduly pessimistic about the future. In their opinion the American people had too little esteem for aesthetic and intellectual activities, were governed by largely utilitarian, materialistic, and narrowly puritanical standards of value, and were inclined to consider the arts as merely superficial adornments, not as vital elements in daily life. Bourne died in 1918; but Brooks, who remained the most influential spokesman of the group, continued his critical career into the 1960's, though his later writings were much more optimistic about American life.

The hopefulness expressed by this group of writers was not maintained after American entry into World War I. The ten years from the Treaty of Versailles to the Wall Street debacle were perhaps the most fruitful period in artistic activity that the United States had ever known, but it was a period in which the leading writers either set out to expose and condemn the failures of American civilization or else aloofly declared that the function of the artist was to give pleasure only to himself and his friends. The tone of disillusionment was reflected in almost all the important writing of the period. It was apparent at one extreme in the best-selling realistic novels of Sinclair Lewis, who published *Main Street* in 1920 and *Babbitt* in 1922; it found expression in a totally different manner in the highly intellectual poetry of T. S. Eliot, whose *The Waste Land* appeared in 1922.

Meanwhile Americans were learning about many new techniques and ideas from Europe. Such innovators as Marcel Proust and James Joyce in the novel, Pablo Picasso in painting, and Igor Stravinsky in music were studied in the United States; and new currents of thought, particularly those represented by Sigmund Freud and psychoanalysis, by Marx and Russian communism, and by the revival of the Thomist philosophy, began to have considerable influence among intellectuals. An influential movement of native origin was the humanism of Irving Babbitt and Paul Elmer More, largely a restatement of the academic and moralistic conservatism of earlier generations. Another new development was the reformulation of the agrarian ideals of the South by a group of southern writers headed by John Crowe Ransom and Allen Tate. This group, whose members wrote some of the best poetry and ablest criticism of the period, was opposed to industrialism and the pretensions of modern science and was sympathetic to traditional religion.

Poetry

The only important writer of poetry whose career spanned the entire period from the 1890's to the 1930's was Edwin Arlington Robinson, a native of a Maine seaport, whose best works were marked by intellectual depth and clarity and precision in the expression of emotion. His writings were pervaded by an ironic bitterness which reflected the twentieth-century loss of faith in both religious ideals and the American achievement. Another New England poet was Robert Frost of New Hampshire, who published his first book in 1913. Frost, whose writing was simple and colloquial, wrote realistic descriptions of rural people and places which were also philosophical commentaries on human life in general. These two men, who were little influenced by the technical experiments of the modernists, were often regarded as the leading American poets of the twentieth century.

Most of the poets who appeared after 1912 abandoned the verse forms and the conventions of nineteenth-century poetry and experimented with various kinds of free verse, derived partly from Whitman and partly from the symbolist poets of nineteenth-century France. Much of their work displayed a bold use of apparently incongruous metaphors and images, as well as an attempt to extend the subject matter of poetry to include the phenomena of industrial civilization. For these reasons their work frequently seemed obscure or unpoetic to conservative readers and thus provoked considerable antagonism. Their most vigorous champion was Amy Lowell of Boston. Miss Lowell, whose own "imagist" poetry was mediocre but who was a very formidable personality, conducted an elaborate campaign to win recognition for the new poetry.

The leading poets of the 1920's can be roughly divided into the realists and the intellectualists. The most prominent of the realists were three middlewesterners: Vachel Lindsay, who expressed the beliefs of American evangelical Protestantism; Carl Sandburg, who celebrated the industrial civilization of Chicago; and Edgar Lee Masters, whose *Spoon River Anthology* delineated the life of a small midwestern town. A younger writer who resembled the realists in style, though not in his subject matter, was Robinson Jeffers of California. His narratives of crime and incest reflected a most pessimistic attitude toward the future of the human race.

The most prominent representatives of the intellectualist trend were two Americans who had settled in Europe before the war, Ezra Pound and T. S. Eliot. A leader in evolving new techniques of writing verse, Pound often seemed more concerned with the manner of his poetry than with his matter. His most ambitious work, the *Cantos*, was a confused *mélange* of history and anecdote, notable chiefly for the virtuosity of its craftsmanship. T. S. Eliot, on the other hand, who derived much of his verse technique from Pound, used it to convey a repudiation of twentieth-century civilization and an acceptance of religious tradition which influenced numerous disciples. He was probably the most important figure in the Anglo-American literature of the 1920's and 1930's. Among the other poets whose work displayed a similar intellectual sophistication were Wallace Stevens and several members of the southern agrarian group, especially John Crowe Ransom and Allen Tate, while Archibald MacLeish combined the technical innovations of Pound and Eliot with a more popular appeal. Less complex but equally baffling to conservatives were E. E. Cummings, whose impulse was mainly lyrical; William Carlos Williams, who was primarily an observer of the American scene; and Hart Crane, who endeavored in his *The Bridge* to convey a unified vision of American civilization.

Fiction and the Theater

The novelists of twentieth-century America were so numerous and their audience was so large that the writing of fiction could almost be regarded as a branch of big business. And although the bulk of what was written, intended merely for entertainment, was quickly forgotten, there was a notable increase in the number of novels with artistic value. It is impossible, in any brief discussion, to convey the extraordinary richness and variety of modern American fiction.

The novel was dominated by the trend toward sociological realism, of which the oldest leading representative was Theodore Dreiser. Dreiser's work had little subtlety and was marred by its clumsy prose style; but his delineation of contemporary American life had a massive strength and honesty, and his insistence on his right to tell the truth as he saw it in defiance of accepted conventions removed many obstacles from the path of his successors. Other novelists who began publishing before World War I included Sinclair Lewis, Sherwood Anderson, and Willa Cather. Lewis' bent was primarily toward satire, and his strength lay in his talent for accurate observation. His first successful novels, *Main Street* and *Babbitt*, were generally considered denunciations of American middle-class society, though Lewis himself, as was shown in his later and weaker books, had considerably more sympathy with the average American businessman than had most other writers of the period. He was awarded the Nobel prize, the first American writer to be so honored, in 1930. Anderson's leanings were mystical rather than sociological; most of his novels dealt with middle-class Americans who were seeking a new and more emotionally satisfying way of life. Miss Cather's work had more positive affirmation, as well as more artistry, but she found values in the pioneer background more easily than in contemporary American society.

Some of the writers who first appeared during the 1920's achieved even higher levels. The most widely acclaimed was probably Ernest Hemingway, who specialized in studies of simple characters confronting inevitable defeat. More successful as a writer of short stories than as a novelist, he developed a deceptively simple style, filled with concrete imagery, which had many imitators. Almost equally skillful was F. Scott Fitzgerald, who was fascinated by the life of the wealthy leisure class but at the same time very aware of its corrupting influences. Almost forgotten during the 1930's, he was rediscovered by readers and critics after World War II. Meanwhile John Dos Passos won attention with a disillusioned war novel, *Three Soldiers*, and went on to write equally bitter descriptions of American society as a whole, the most ambitious being his trilogy, *U.S.A.* The South, which was now producing major writers for the first time, was represented by Thomas Wolfe, who wrote the story of his own life in four long volumes notable for vividness and vitality, and by William Faulkner, who dealt mainly with crime, degeneracy, and insanity in his native state of Mississippi. Oxford, Mississippi, remained Faulkner's home for the greater part of his life. He wrote about southerners, and his work presented a symbolic picture of southern history, but essentially he was dealing with problems that were universal. In order to write about humans he used those he knew best in the setting he knew best. Thus he could focus dramatically and with rich detail on such questions as man's loss of community and his isolation.

Shifting critical judgments may eventually cause a reassessment of the novelists of postwar America. Certain revisions have already become accepted. Recent critics have refused to give high rank to the romances of James Branch Cabell, to the historical and society novels of Joseph Hergesheimer, or to the novels in which Booth Tarkington portrayed American middle-class life, all of which were highly praised during the 1920's. Some other novelists who displayed a delicate artistry rather than breadth and vigor, such as Elinor Wylie and Thornton Wilder, may prove to have an enduring audience. But certainly the American novel had passed beyond any taint of provincialism and was now dealing with all important aspects of American experience.

A similar coming-of-age was to be seen in the American theater. Prior to 1915 the drama had not been considered a serious art form. Leading playwrights, such as Clyde Fitch and Augustus Thomas, had been interested merely in producing competent entertainment; and except in the work of William Vaughn Moody, who died before he was able fully to realize his talents, there had been little attempt to use the stage as a vehicle for genuinely creative work. A new era in the history of the American theater began in 1915, when two groups of amateurs founded two "little theaters" for the production of serious plays. These were the Washington Square Players, which later became the Theater Guild, and the Provincetown Players. The existence of these two groups encouraged serious writers to turn to writing for the theater. Good plays found steadily increasing audiences; and although musicals continued as the main stock-in-trade of Broadway theaters, there was also room for work of genuine artistic value.

The best-known of the new American dramatists was Eugene O'Neill, who was discovered by the Provincetown Players. Always dissatisfied with the limitations imposed by traditional stage techniques and experimenting constantly with new methods of expression, O'Neill evolved from a realist into a mystic concerned primarily with spiritual salvation. Many critics, however, preferred his early studies of working-class character to the more pretentious explorations into complex emotions which filled his later work. Although no other dramatist of the 1920's reached comparable levels, significant work was done by Maxwell Anderson, who attempted to reestablish the poetic drama; by George Kelly and Sidney Howard, who were primarily realistic recorders of American life; by S. N. Behrman, Robert Sherwood, and Philip Barry, who excelled in sophisticated comedy; and by George S. Kaufman, who wrote comedies with a broader and more colloquial humor.

Another art form which began to come to life was the dance. Early in the twentieth century the United States produced one of the greatest dancers of modern times in Isadora Duncan, who introduced a greater naturalness into ballet technique in Europe as well as in America. During the 1920's there was a rapid growth of interest in stage dancing, and a number of American performers, such as Martha Graham and Ruth St. Denis, became widely known.

Other Arts

In painting leadership continued to belong to the realists of the so-called "ashcan school." Most of the original group remained productive until the 1940's, and their delight in recording the vigor and color of urban life was transmitted to younger men like George Bellows and Reginald Marsh. Another development of the realistic tradition was the growth of regionalism, as exhibited by Thomas Benton of Missouri, Grant Wood of Iowa, and John Steuart Curry of Kansas. Meanwhile European painters were beginning to repudiate the belief that the artist should copy nature, declaring instead that his proper task was to create significant forms, not necessarily resembling anything in the external world, which would be expressive of emotional states. This nonrepresentational art became widely known in America as a result of an exhibition held in 1913 at the 69th

Regiment Armory in New York. The most famous art show ever held in America, this made it evident that a revolutionary change of artistic standards was occurring. Its most vigorous champion was the photographer Alfred Steiglitz, while its earliest important American practitioner was Max Weber. Probably the most satisfying American work of the 1920's was done by men and women who recorded American subjects but who had also been influenced by the newer European schools and had been able to achieve a fusion of the descriptive and the expressive. Outstanding examples were the seascapes of John Marin, the landscapes and seascapes of Marsden Hartley, the flower studies of Georgia O'Keefe, and the portraits of urban scenes and of the American countryside by Edward Hopper and Charles Burchfield.

Meanwhile American art museums and private collectors were becoming more receptive to native contemporary work and were no longer spending all their available money on European old masters. Art was still hardly a paying profession for most of its practitioners, but there was a healthy growth of interest among the general public in the work of American artists.

In architecture the newer trends were slower to win acceptance. In the 1920's the functionalist methods developed by Louis Sullivan and Frank Lloyd Wright made little further headway in the United States, though they wielded a wide influence in other parts of the world. The best known American architects of the period were men like Cass Gilbert and Raymond Hood, who had picked up some of the ideas of the functionalists but did not understand their spirit. Skyscrapers were built in increasing numbers in most large cities, and their designs improved after civic authorities began to make zoning ordinances requiring setbacks above a certain number of floors. But most of them were still disfigured by much irrelevant ornamentation; and since all of them added to the congestion of urban areas, they could not be regarded as aids to humane living. Meanwhile most government buildings continued to be classical, like the Supreme Court building designed by Gilbert; and Gothic was still the favorite style of churches and university campuses.

In music, at least in its more serious forms, the United States was even slower to achieve a native idiom. The history of American music remained largely a history of the growth of appreciation. Symphony orchestras, of which there had been less than half a dozen in 1900, increased both in number and in quality, and American audiences now demanded the best possible conductors, concert artists, and vocalists, most of whom were Europeans. The invention first of the phonograph and then of radio did much to diffuse higher standards of musical taste. But though there was a rapid increase in the number of native composers, none of them achieved levels comparable to the best of the Europeans.

In popular music, on the other hand, America had a rich tradition, and its influence was almost worldwide. Earlier generations had contributed Negro spirituals and a wide variety of folk songs sung by cowboys, sailors, and other groups. The repertory of popular music was steadily increased by composers for the theater, from Stephen Foster in the 1840's to men like Irving Berlin and Jerome Kern in the 1920's. But the most significant American musical product was the idiom variously known as ragtime, jazz, and swing. Originating among Negro performers in cabarets in Memphis and New Orleans late in the nineteenth century, it was introduced by southern bands to northern audiences during World War I. The merits of jazz remained controversial, but some gifted American composers, notably George Gershwin, showed that it could be used as a foundation for more serious work.

Twentieth-century Americans enjoyed a wide variety of other entertainment arts, all of which deserved sociological study, though their aesthetic merits were usually low. Most Americans read the comics in their morning and evening newspapers and were connoisseurs of various forms of radio entertainment. But unquestionably the most important of the new popular art forms was the motion picture. Invented in the 1890's and achieving maturity with the films directed by D. W. Griffith before and during World War I, motion pictures during the later 1920's had an audience in the United States of 100 million persons a week, and comparable numbers in most other Western countries. It had immense aesthetic potentialities, but these were more often realized by European producers, who were less concerned with box-office results than were the Americans. Some American pictures, notably the comedies of Charlie Chaplin, pleased audiences on all cultural levels. For the most part American producers concentrated on providing popular entertainment, remaining faithful to the time-worn themes of love and adventure, with a strong preference for characters in the upper income brackets.

Suggested Readings

Apart from the general surveys of the 1920's, like John D. Hicks, *Republican Ascendancy, 1920–1933* and William E. Leuchtenburg, *The Perils of Prosperity, 1914–1932*, both of which cover social and cultural trends along with other developments during the decade, see Preston W. Slosson, *The Great Crusade and After, 1914–1928* (New York [1930]), a volume in the *History of American Life* series. Charles A. and Mary R. Beard, *America in Midpassage* (New York, 1939) also contains much pertinent social history. Frederick Lewis Allen, *Only Yesterday*, cited previously, continues to be useful, but see also André Siegfried's perceptive *America Comes of Age* (New York [1927]); Denis W. Brogan, *The American Character* (New York, 1944); and George H. Knoles, *The Jazz Age Revisited: British Criticism of American Civilization during the 1920's* (Stanford, Calif., 1955). Robert S. and Helen M. Lynd, *Middletown: A Study in Contemporary American Culture* (New York [1929]) is, what the foreword claims it to be, "a pioneer attempt to deal with a sample American community after the manner of social anthropology."

On the intellectual developments and history of the 1920's, Alfred Kazin, *On Native Ground* (New York, 1942) and more specifically the interpretation of the decade on the basis of its writers in Frederick J. Hoffman, *The Twenties* (New York, 1955) are especially good, but the older study by Oscar Cargill, *Intellectual America* (New York, 1941) continues to be useful.

Among the more popular accounts of American life in the 1920's, see Lawrence Greene, *The Era of Wonderful Nonsense* (Indianapolis, 1939); Isabel Leighton, ed., *The Aspirin Age, 1919–1949* (New York, 1949), a good collection of pieces on various facets of American life; Edmund Wilson, *The American Earthquake: A Documentary of the Twenties and Thirties* (Garden City, N.Y., 1958); and Paul Sann, *The Lawless Decade: A Pictorial History of a Great American Transition: From the World War I Armistice and Prohibition to Repeal and the New Deal* (New York [1957]).

Critical accounts of American society during the 1920's include James Truslow Adams, *Our Business Civilization* (New York, 1929); Walter Lippmann, *A Preface to Morals* (New York, 1929), which deals with the problems of religion and morality; Van Wyck Brooks, *Three Essays on America* (New York [1934]); Waldo Frank, *The Rediscovery of America* (New York, 1929); Harold E. Stearns, *America and the Young Intellectual* (New York [1921]); and the famous collection by Harold Stearns, ed., *Civilization in the United States: An Inquiry by Thirty Americans* (New York, 1922).

Henry L. Mencken is the subject of two studies within the past decade, Edgard Kemler, *The Irreverent Mr. Mencken* (Boston, 1950) and William R. Manchester, *Disturber of the Peace: The Life of H. L. Mencken* (New York [1951]). Consult also Alistair Cooke, ed., *The Vintage Mencken* (New York, 1955).

The intolerance of the 1920's is discussed generally in many works, including Ernest S. Bates, *This Land of Liberty* (New York, 1930); Winfred E. Garrison, *Intolerance* (New York, 1934) and more specifically in Morris L. Ernst and Alexander Lindley, *The Censor Marches On* (Garden City, N.Y., 1940); Norman Hapgood, *Professional Patriots* (New York, 1927); the two books by Arthur Garfield Hays, *Let Freedom Ring* (New York, 1928) and *Trial by Prejudice* (New York [1933]); Walter Lippmann, *American Inquisitors: A Commentary on Dayton and Chicago* (New York, 1928), a searching analysis of the Scopes and McAndrew trials; and M. Shipley, *The War on Modern Science* (New York, 1927).

On the Ku Klux Klan, see John M. Mecklin, *The Ku Klux Klan: A Study of the American Mind* (New York, 1924) and the more specialized study on the Klan's activities in one state by Emerson H. Loucks, *The Ku Klux Klan in Pennsylvania* (New York, 1936).

The religious crisis in the 1920's is treated in the survey by Herbert W. Schneider, *Religion in Twentieth Century America* (Cambridge, Mass., 1952) and more specifically in Robert M. Miller's scholarly *American Protestantism and Social Issues, 1919–1939* (Chapel Hill, N.C., 1958). Consult also the careful study by Paul A. Carter, *The Decline and Revival of the Social Gospel, 1920–1940* (Ithaca, N.Y., 1956) and Donald B. Meyer, *The Protestant Search for Political Realism, 1919–1941* (Berkeley, Calif., 1960). Norman Furniss, *The Fundamentalist Controversy, 1918–1931* (New Haven, Conn., 1954) is a penetrating and sound study which largely replaces the older work by Stewart G. Cole, *The History of Fundamentalism* (New York, 1931). Besides the various works cited above and the sections in Clarence Darrow, *The Story of My Life* (New York, 1932), all pertinent on the Scopes trial, there is Ray Ginger, *Six Days or Forever?* (Boston [1958]), the most recent reappraisal.

William G. McLaughlin, *Billy Sunday Was His Real Name* (Chicago, 1955) is a good study of this popular evangelist, while Nancy Barr Mavity, *Sister Aimee* (Garden City, N.Y., 1931) describes this southern Californian's appeal. Lately Thomas, *The Vanishing Evangelist* (New York, 1959) details one of the more striking episodes in Aimee McPherson's life.

Prohibition is discussed generally in the popular but entirely sound accounts by Herbert Asbury, *The Great Illusion: An Informal History of Prohibition* (Garden City, N.Y., 1950) and Kenneth Allsop, *The Bootleggers and Their Era* (Garden City, N.Y., 1961); and more seriously in the contemporary study of the Federal Council of the Churches of Christ in America, *The Prohibition Situation* (New York, 1925). A contemporary account is David L. Colvin, *Prohibition in the United States* (New York [1926]), and a long-time standard reference is Charles Merz, *The Dry Decade* (Garden City, N.Y., 1931); but see also Herman Feldman, *Prohibition: Its Economic and Industrial Aspects* (New York, 1927) and Irving Fisher, *Prohibition at Its Worst* (New York, 1926). A well-documented and detailed account of the prohibition experiment in the nation's leading wine-producing state is Gilman M. Ostrander, *The Prohibition Movement in California, 1848–1933* (Berkeley, Calif., 1957). Two good biographies of leading "drys" are Justin Steuart, *Wayne Wheeler: Dry Boss* (New York, 1928) and Virginius Dabney, *Dry Messiah: The Life of Bishop Cannon* (New York, 1949).

On the decade's lawlessness, see Frank Tannenbaum, *Crime and the Community* (Boston, 1938). The work of the FBI in the 1920's is well-told in Max Lowenthal, *The Federal Bureau of Investigation* (New York, 1950) and in several chapters of Don Whitehead, *The F.B.I. Story: A Report to the People* (New York [1956]). Contemporary accounts include Marcus A. Kavanagh, *The Criminal and His Allies* (Indianapolis, 1928); Richard W. Child, *Battling the Criminal* (Garden City, N.Y., 1925); and, because of the high competence with which it treats the subject, Andrew A. Bruce, *The Administration of Criminal Justice in Illinois* (Chicago, 1929).

Among the biographies of leading citizens who did not permit the law to interfere with their activities, see Fred D. Pasley, *Al Capone: The Biography of a Self-Made Man* (Garden City, N.Y., 1931) and Gene Fowler, *Beau James: The Life and Times of Jimmy Walker* (New York, 1949).

Robert E. Spiller, *et al.*, *Literary History of the United States* (3 vols., New York, 1948), is the standard reference, and volume II contains well-presented material on the 1920's. On what the people read in the 1920's, see the pertinent chapters of Alice P. Hackett, *Fifty Years of Best Sellers, 1895–1945* (New York, 1945). Maxwell Geismar, *The Last of the Provincials* (Boston, 1947) is also a useful and sound analysis. On the "lost generation," see Malcolm Cowley's excellent account in his *Exile's Return* (new ed., New York, 1951). Consult also the useful collection of pieces in John K. Hutchens, ed., *A Literary Panorama: The American Twenties* (Philadelphia, 1952) and Cleveland Amory and Frederic Bradlee, eds., *Vanity Fair: A Cavalcade of the 1920's and 1930's* (New York, 1960), an anthology of pieces from *Vanity Fair*, which was established in 1914. One of the finest magazines of the 1920's, it ceased publication in 1936.

Among the older more specialized works, consult Malcolm Cowley, ed., *After the Genteel Tradition* (New York [1937]); Walter F. Taylor, *A History of American Letters* (Boston [1936]); the left-wing interpretation by Granville Hicks, *The Great Tradition* (rev. ed., New York, 1935); Morton D. Zabel, ed., *Literary Opinion in America* (rev. ed., New York [1951]); and, on the contribution of the Negro, the sample selections in Sterling A. Brown, *et al.*, *The Negro Caravan* (New York [1941]).

More specifically on the novel, see Frederick J. Hoffman, *The Modern Novel in America, 1900–1950* (Chicago, 1956) and Arthur Mizener's article, "The Novel in America, 1920–1940," *Perspectives, U.S.A.*, XV (Spring 1956), 134–47. Carl Van Doren, *The American Novel* (rev. and enl. ed., New York [1955]); Fred L. Pattee, *The New American Literature, 1890–1930* (New York, 1930); and Joseph W. Beach, *American Fiction, 1920–1940* (New York, 1941) are older but continue to be useful. A sympathetic biography of F. Scott Fitzgerald is Arthur Mizener, *The Far Side of Paradise* (Boston, 1951); Andrew Turnbull, *Scott Fitzgerald* (New York, 1962) is a "biography-memoir" of a friend.

On the drama in the 1920's, consult Joseph Wood Krutch, *The American Drama Since 1918* (New York [1939]) and Glenn Hughes, *History of the American Theater* (New York, 1951), a good survey of its subject.

On poetry, see Horace Gregory and Marya Zaturenska, *History of American Poetry* (New York, 1946), the standard reference. But also helpful are the pertinent chapters in David Daiches, *Poetry and the Modern World* (Chicago [1940]). F. O. Matthiessen, *The Achievement of T. S. Eliot* (2d rev. and enl. ed., New York, 1947) is satisfactory.

On the short story after the outbreak of World War I, see the collection by Martha Foley, ed., *The Best of the Short Stories, 1915–1950* (Boston, 1951).

On twentieth-century developments in art, see Oliver W. Larkin, *Art and*

Life in America (New York, 1949), the standard work on art and architecture. Consult also the excellent collection in Holger Cahill and Alfred H. Barr, Jr., *Art in America* (New York [1935]) and the account by John I. Baur, *Revolution and Tradition in Modern American Art* (Cambridge, Mass., 1951). Older but still useful is the treatise by Frederick P. Keppel and Robert L. Duffus, *The Arts in American Life* (New York, 1933). See also Suzanne LaFollette, *Art in America* (New York, 1929) and Martha C. Cheney, *Modern Art in America* (New York [1939]). Virgil Barker, *American Painting: History and Interpretation* (New York, 1950) and James M. Fitch, *American Building* (Boston, 1948) are both excellent on their respective subjects.

American music is treated in Henry Cowell, ed., *American Composers on American Music* (Stanford, Calif., 1933), and John T. Howard, *Our Contemporary Composers: American Music in the Twentieth Century* (3d ed., New York, 1946) is excellent. A recent survey of one kind of American music is Barry Ulanov, *A History of Jazz in America* (New York, 1952). Helen L. Kaufmann, *From Jehovah to Jazz* (New York, 1937); Claire R. Reis, *Composers in America* (New York, 1938); Aaron Copland, *Our New Music* (New York, 1941); Paul Rosenfeld, *An Hour with American Music* (Philadelphia [1929]); Winthrop Sargeant, *Jazz, Hot and Hybrid* (New York, 1938); Sidney W. Finkelstein, *Jazz: A People's Music* (New York, 1948); and Isaac Goldberg, *Tin Pan Alley* (New York, 1930) are of varying merit but a convenient place to start.

On the dance, see John J. Martin, *American Dancing* (New York [1936]).

On architecture, consult Sheldon Cheney, *The New World Architecture* (London, 1930); George H. Edgell, *The American Architecture of Today* (New York, 1928); Henry R. Hitchcock, *Modern Architecture* (New York, 1929); Sidney F. Kimball, *American Architecture* (Indianapolis, 1928); the two works by Lewis Mumford, *Sticks and Stones* (2d rev. ed., New York [1955]) and *The Brown Decades* (2d rev. ed., New York [1955]); Louis H. Sullivan, *Autobiography of an Idea* (New York, 1924); Thomas E. Tallmadge, *The Story of Architecture in America* (2d rev. and enl. ed., New York [1936]); Frank Lloyd Wright's own accounts in *Modern Architecture* (Princeton, N.J., 1931) and in *An Autobiography* (New York [1943]); and Carl W. Condit, *The Rise of the Skyscraper* (Chicago [1952]).

Besides the works cited in Chapter 11, the history of motion pictures is surveyed in a number of works, including Maurice Bardèche and Robert Brasillach, *The History of Motion Pictures* (New York [1938]); Lewis L. Jacobs, *The Rise of the American Film* (New York [1939]); Paul Rotha and Richard Griffith, *The Film Till Now* (3d rev. and enl. ed., New York [1960]); and Rotha's more specialized account, *Documentary Film* (3d rev. and enl. ed., London [1952]).

The contemporary collection by Freda Kirchwey, ed., *Our Changing Morality: A Symposium* (New York, 1924) is still very worthwhile, while Charles Merz, *The Great American Bandwagon* (New York, 1928) satirizes the conventions, fads, and social ideas of the period. Henry F. May, *The End of American Innocence*, already cited, is a useful and suggestive reference for the early background of the cultural changes that occurred in the 1920's.

14

Foreign Policy, 1921-1933

ISOLATION OR COOPERATION?

Although a majority of the Senate had been in favor of entry into the League of Nations, either with or without the reservations, and although many people had voted for Harding in the belief that he was in favor of the League with reservations, the inability to work out a satisfactory compromise which would have resolved the impasse between the Senate leaders and the administration permitted the extremists (those who were irreconcilably opposed to any League and those who, like Wilson, refused to consider any further compromise) to block passage of the treaty and thus allow the isolationist view to prevail. After the rejection of the treaty in 1920 the question of American entry into the League was not revived, and isolationism became the official American policy. Harding set the pace of America's foreign policy in his inaugural address: "Confident of our ability to work out our own destiny and jealously guarding our right to do so," the new President announced, "we seek no part in directing the destinies of the Old World. We do not mean to be entangled. We will accept no responsibility except as our own conscience and judgment may determine." Public opinion endorsed Harding's position and accepted the isolationist doctrine that the United States must never again become entangled in the traditional rivalries of the European nations, that America must not pledge its resources to support any program for checking war by measures of collective security, and that, if war came, the United States must keep out of it. This attitude was frequently expressed in a tone of self-righteous complacency which aroused considerable indignation in Europe.

It was, however, the State Department that actually conducted American foreign policy; and successive secretaries of State—Charles Evans Hughes (1921–25), Frank B. Kellogg (1925–29), and Henry L. Stimson (1929–33)—found themselves unable to adopt complete isolationism. State Department officials were necessarily aware of the degree to which the safety and prosperity of the United States were dependent upon the maintenance of peace and tranquillity in other parts of the world. They realized, moreover, that if Europe were again plunged into war, the economic and psychological ties of the United States with European nations would make it difficult for us to preserve neutrality, for which reason it was desirable that we should participate in measures likely to prevent war. But although the State Department favored international cooperation, it was always prevented by an indifferent public opinion and by the Senate isolationists from asserting effective United States leadership and from making binding pledges of United States support in any program for maintaining peace by collective security. American officials had to content themselves, therefore, either with making futile pacifistic declarations which did not commit the United States to any kind of action or with trying to persuade other nations to take action against aggressors. Thus, during the twenty-year period in which Europe first failed to organize peace and then plunged into a second catastrophic war, the most powerful nation in the world, and the only nation capable of viewing European rivalries with relative impartiality, refused to undertake any of the responsibilities of leadership.

The isolationists justified their position by pointing to the narrowly selfish policies pursued by all the European nations and to the manner in which the League of Nations was used to maintain Franco-British supremacy. The deficiencies of the League were, however, partly due to the rejection of it by the United States. Lacking any assurance of United States support in the maintenance of peace, none of the European nations felt secure; nor did they have any confidence that the League of Nations could effectively check aggression by economic sanctions if the cooperation of the United States remained doubtful. It was this universal insecurity which made a lasting European peace impossible.

As soon as the United States Senate rejected the Treaty of Versailles, including not only the League of Nations but also the pledge of support against German aggression which had been promised by Wilson during the dispute over the Rhineland, the French government began to build up a system of alliances with the succession states of eastern Europe. In 1923, after Germany had defaulted on the reparations payments, the French army occupied the Ruhr, and thereby precipitated the crisis of inflation which ruined the German middle classes. The attempt of the French to achieve security by such methods aroused bitter resentment in Germany and contributed eventually to the rise of the Nazis. The British, on the other hand, favored conciliation with Germany. Great Britain was, however, no longer strong enough to exercise the leadership which had belonged to London during the nineteenth century, nor did the British produce men capable of the statemanship which Europe required. After World War I, except for two brief intervals, Britain had conservative governments whose primary concern was with economic stability at home and imperial interests abroad. Britain thus used America's rejection of the League as a pretext for giving the new world organization's objectives only lukewarm support.

Moves toward International Cooperation

At first, the United States even refused to acknowledge the fact that the League existed. The State Department did not answer letters sent to it by the League, and when the League officials wanted information from the American government, they had to ask the government of the Netherlands to serve as intermediary. The Senate isolationists were deeply suspicious of any American cooperation with the League, even when it concerned merely control of the opium and white-slave traffics.

After 1922, however, the fear of contamination began to subside, and the State Department began to send "unofficial observers" to a number of the League conferences. Secretary Hughes, moreover, declared in a speech at New Haven in December of that year that on both economic and humanitarian grounds the United States was interested in European peace, and he offered American help in settling the reparations problem. In December, 1923, Coolidge appointed Charles G. Dawes, the American banker who had served as Harding's first Director of the Budget, along with two other Americans, to a ten-member international committee of financial experts to study Germany's internal finances under the Versailles Treaty's Reparations Commission. The recommendations of the committee, of which Dawes became chairman, proposed a plan which led to a reduction in reparations payments and the stabilization of German finances. Another American, S. Parker Gilbert, was appointed agent-general to supervise the payments. This settlement, which came to be known as the Dawes Plan, was followed by the French evacuation of the Ruhr and in 1925 by the Locarno treaties, which, it was hoped, would put an end to Franco-German hostility and create a lasting peace. In 1928, when Germany again had difficulty in meeting its obligations, another international commission—this time headed by Owen D. Young, one of the Americans who had served under Dawes in 1923 and 1924, with J. P. Morgan serving as the second representative of the United States—met in Paris on February 11, 1929, to modify the schedule of reparations established by the Dawes Plan. By the end of August, 1929, the commission had agreed upon a formula to lessen Germany's burden of reparations: the amount Germany owed was fixed at some $8 billion, the year 1988 was fixed as the date when the payments were to be completed, and the interest rate was set at 5½ per cent.

Americans, especially Elihu Root, assisted also in the establishment of the World Court of International Justice, set up by the League in 1921. One of the nine judges of the court was always an American. In 1923, at the suggestion of Secretary Hughes, Harding recommended American adherence to the court, but without result. Coolidge, who had endorsed American adherence to the World Court in his annual messages to the Congress in 1924 and 1925, took up the question again in 1926, after the House of Representatives, by a vote of 303 to 28, had approved American participation. This time the Senate, by a vote of 76 to 17, consented to American adherence, but laid down five reservations and declared that each of the forty-eight nations which had signed the World Court protocol must agree to them. Five nations, all of them small ones, declared that they would accept the reservations, while the other forty-three accepted four of the American conditions but refused to accede to the one which denied the court "without the consent of the United States [to] entertain any request for an advisory opinion touching any dispute or question in which the United States has or claims an interest." In 1929 Elihu Root worked out a formula to which he thought both the forty-eight nations in the World Court and the isolationists in the United States Senate could agree; but the Senate took no action on this proposal until 1935, and then rejected it.

The most conspicuous gesture made by the United States in the cause of world peace was its sponsorship of the Pact of Paris, better known as the Kellogg Pact. For a number of years a Chicago lawyer, Salmon O. Levinson, had been urging that all nations pledge themselves to outlaw war and to settle disputes only by pacific means. Similar ideas were espoused by the Columbia University historian James T. Shotwell, who, in March, 1927, discussed the subject with French Minister of Foreign Affairs Aristide Briand. The following month Briand suggested that France and the United States sign a bilateral pact renouncing any resort to war between each other. Secretary of State Kellogg at first paid no attention; but Senator William E. Borah, President Nicholas Murray Butler of Columbia University, and Professor Shotwell began to arouse public opinion in favor of the proposal and to urge that Briand's suggestion be adopted and enlarged into a multilateral pact of the kind advocated by Levinson. In December, Kellogg began negotiations with the governments of other great powers; and on August 27, 1928, the representatives of fifteen nations signed the Pact of Paris promising never to resort to war. The pact was subsequently accepted by forty-seven other nations, the first of which was the Soviet Union. Almost every nation, however, made reservations which deprived the pact of its meaning, and no method was provided for enforcing obedience upon nations which violated it. When it ratified the pact by the nearly unanimous vote of 85 to 1, the United States Senate, for example, declared that the pact did not curtail the right of the United States to self-defense or the powers the Washington government exercised under the Monroe Doctrine, and that the pact did not commit the United States to take any positive action to check aggression. A few Americans declared at once that the Kellogg-Briand Pact was, in the words of Senator Carter Glass of Virginia, "worthless, but perfectly harmless." Outside the United States it was generally regarded as a peculiarly futile and meaningless moral gesture. Its only visible consequence was that thereafter when nations resorted to war, they sometimes omitted to make any formal declaration of it.

DISARMAMENT

In promoting disarmament, American diplomacy was somewhat less ineffectual, if not always completely realistic. During the war the United States had made plans for enlarging its navy until it would be at least equal to that of Great Britain. After the war, however, the leaders and business interests of both countries were economy minded and anxious to avoid any expensive and dangerous race for naval supremacy. The United States was, moreover, alarmed by the growing power of Japan in the Far East and by the possibility that the Anglo-Japanese alliance, originally directed against Russia and Germany, might be continued and, as certain Britishers and Canadians feared, used by Japan to force Great Britain to join Tokyo in case of a war against the United States. Canadian opposition to the alliance, as well as that of Australia, made Great Britain anxious to find some method of abandoning it which would not offend Japan. It was therefore easy for the British and American governments to agree on a conference. The United States was primarily interested in meeting with the British for the purposes of naval disarmament, while the British wanted a meeting which would result in easing the tension in the Far East and securing peace in the Pacific. While the State Department was making plans to call a disarmament conference, the British Foreign Office was engaged in trying to arrange a meeting on the Far East and the Pacific. The result of these efforts, after preliminary discussions between the United States and Britain, was the Washington Conference, to which President Harding, on August 11, 1921, invited all the principal naval powers and the nations with Asiatic interests, except Russia, which resented and protested the fact that it had been excluded. While agreeable to limiting naval armaments, the Japanese were reluctant to enter upon any negotiations which interfered with or threatened their interests and ambitions in the Far East. After indicating their reservations on these questions, they prepared to attend the meetings.

The Washington Conference, which met from November 12, 1921, until February 6, 1922, resulted in nine separate treaties. The leading delegates were Hughes for the United States, Arthur Balfour for Great Britain, and Baron Tomosaburo Kato for Japan. As soon as the conference opened, Hughes, much to the surprise of everyone present, took the bull by the horns and made specific proposals, as carefully prepared as they were daring, for naval reductions. He recommended that the various powers scrap a total of sixty-six ships, built or under construction, with a total tonnage of 1,878,043. In the words of the English journalist, Colonel Repington, "Secretary Hughes sank in thirty-four minutes more ships than all the admirals of the world have sunk in a cycle of centuries." Secretary Hughes's proposals were incorporated into a Five Power Treaty signed on February 6, 1922, by the United States, Great Britain, Japan, France, and Italy. According to the chief provisions of this treaty, Britain and the United States accepted the principle of naval equality, each power limiting the tonnage of its capital ships (defined as those exceeding 10,000 tons or equipped with guns larger than eight-inch caliber) to 525,000 tons. Japan was allowed a capital-ship tonnage of 272,000 tons, whereas France and Italy were each to have 175,000 tons. The signatories also agreed to build no new capital ships for ten years and to limit the total tonnage of their aircraft carriers as follows: the United States and Great Britain, 135,000 tons each; Japan, 81,000 tons; and France and Italy, 60,000 tons each.

To placate Japan, which resented its inferior ratio, and to assure its adherence to the treaty, the United States and Britain agreed with Japan to uphold the *status quo* in their Pacific possessions. Insofar as the United States was concerned, this meant that the American government would not construct any "new fortifications or naval bases" in any of its insular possessions west of Hawaii. The British were barred from enlarging or improving their defense facilities at Hong Kong and prohibited from fortifying any of their other possessions "east of the meridian of 110° east longitude," except for Singapore and the islands off the coasts of Australia, New Zealand, and Canada. The Japanese, in turn, agreed not to fortify their recently acquired German possessions. Since no agreement could be made about smaller ships, the question was left for future negotiation. The British, recalling vividly their struggle against the submarine during World War I, wanted to outlaw it entirely and to scrap the ones in service. But the proposal fell on deaf ears and the British were forced to settle for a second treaty, signed by the same five naval powers, establishing certain rules of submarine warfare. But because France rejected it, the treaty was defeated before it went into effect.

American naval experts were considerably disturbed by the provisions of the naval limitation treaty. Without fortified bases in the Pacific, it would be impossible for the United States navy, despite its greater capital-ship strength, to operate effectively west of Hawaii. Britain was similarly handicapped. Anglo-American cooperation might have achieved an added degree of strength, but it never materialized. The fact that naval limitation proved more advantageous to Japan than the United States was not generally appreciated in 1922 because most Americans believed their interests and peace in the Pacific had been secured by the guarantees which Britain, France, the United States, and Japan had agreed to in the Four Power Treaty of December 13, 1921.[1] Public interest in Pacific affairs, except to preach the necessity of upholding the Open Door policy, was small; and only a very few people were willing to assume the expense and responsibility involved in establishing and maintaining an effective

[1] See page 442.

naval power capable of defending the nation's strategic interests. The majority of the American people wanted peace and security; they believed that with the signing of the Four Power Treaty and the naval limitation agreement they had achieved both without expensive naval armaments. Those who warned against such illusions were in a minority, and their opinions carried small weight. The Washington Conference, as its spokesmen quickly pointed out, was the only one of the postwar disarmament conferences that actually achieved disarming, even if only in limited categories.

Subsequent international meetings at Rome in 1924 and at Geneva in 1927 endeavored to forestall a race to build cruisers by reaching agreements about them and also about other smaller ships, including submarines, which the less affluent powers could afford to build; but without success. The failure of the second of these conferences, which was called by President Coolidge and to which all the signatories of the Washington naval limitation treaty were invited, was due to several reasons: the refusal of France and Italy to attend the meeting; the inability of the Anglo-American naval chiefs to agree on size of the ships and other technicalities, public indifference, and the activities of William B. Shearer, the hired agent of certain American corporations engaged in warship construction. The Geneva Conference broke up in August, with the United States and Britain resentful and blaming each other for failing to achieve an agreement.

Nationalists and strong-navy advocates in the United States were determined that the country should not be second to Britain; and in February, 1929, they succeeded in getting Congress to authorize a naval expansion program which would give the United States fifteen new 10,000-ton cruisers, the largest warships which could be built without violating the Washington naval treaty. Since Britain could not afford such a building program, it made efforts to renew negotiations. In January, 1930, there was another conference in London, which had been preceded by more careful preparations, including a visit of British Prime Minister Ramsay MacDonald to the United States. No settlement could be made which included France and Italy; but the United States, Great Britain, and Japan agreed to build no more battleships until 1936, while the building of smaller ships was to be regulated by a series of ratios. These ratios, however, permitted considerable extra construction by all three powers. By an "escalator clause" the treaty was to be modified if other countries began to build in excess of their relative strength at the time of the treaty.

The rapid increase of the German and Italian navies after 1933 soon brought the "escalator clause" into effect and made the treaty a dead letter. Equally futile was a general disarmament conference which met at Geneva in February, 1932, and in which the United States participated. Planned in the hope of limiting land and air armaments, the conference could not overcome the desire of the European nations for more security, and was abandoned after the establishment of the Nazi dictatorship a year later.

WAR DEBTS

Meanwhile the United States was endeavoring to secure payment of the war debts, which represented credits extended to the Allied Powers for purchases of goods in the United States during the war and in 1919. At the time the credits were made, little thought had been given to the question of repayment, and a number of congressmen had declared, without being rebuked, that the United States should not insist on being repaid. The credits, it was said, represented America's contribution to the common cause and were a recognition of the fact that the losses and expenditures of the Allied Powers had been far greater than those of the United States and that America's military assistance had been negligible for twelve months after its entry into the war.

In February, 1922, however, Congress decided to demand repayment and appointed the World War Foreign Debt Commission. Few Americans realized that payment of the debts was rendered difficult by the high protective tariff of the United States, and that the attempt to enforce payment without opening American markets to European goods would result in a flow of gold to the United States which might disrupt the monetary systems of Europe. The insistence on payment of the debts made America acutely unpopular in Europe, which began to refer to the United States as "Uncle Shylock."

Between 1923 and 1930 the debt commission made agreements with fifteen out of the sixteen nations who had received credits, the only exception being Russia. The total credits had been $10.35 billion; with accrued interest these credits were funded at $11.67 billion. Payment was to be extended over more than sixty years, and the average rate of interest was 2.1 per cent. Since the interest rate originally provided for had been 5 per cent, this represented a considerable reduction. Total payments, including both principal and interest, would, however, amount to almost twice the original credits. Some nations received much more favorable terms than others: of the three principal debtors, Great Britain owed $4.6 billion and was to pay 3.3 per cent interest; France owed a little more than $4 billion and was to pay 1.6 per cent interest; Italy, now governed by the fascist dictatorship of Benito Mussolini, owed some $2 billion, but was asked to pay only 0.4 per cent interest.

Meanwhile the Allies were extracting reparations from Germany; and although the United States refused to recognize any connection between reparations and war debts, the Allies would not reduce reparation payments as long as the war debt payments continued. In practice all these payments were rendered possible only by large-scale lending to Germany by Allied and American bankers. By 1931 the world depression made a continuance of payments impossible. In June of that year the Hoover moratorium suspended payments for twelve months; and in the following year, at the Lausanne Conference, Great Britain and France agreed to remit 90 per cent of their claims to reparations on condition that a "satisfactory settlement" could be made with reference to the war debts. Although in December, 1931, the United States Congress refused to consider cancellation, Germany, under the rule of Adolf Hitler, abandoned all reparation payments in 1933, and the Allies then ceased payment of the debts. France stopped payment in 1932; Great Britain, which had already canceled debts due it from other nations that were considerably larger than its own debt to the United States, made a last "token" payment in June, 1933. Of the fifteen debtor nations Finland alone, whose debt totaled $9 million, continued payments. These defaults aroused much indignation in America, and in April, 1934, Congress passed the Johnson Debt Default Act forbidding any government whose debt to the United States was in default from floating fresh loans.

Throughout the period during which reparation and war debt payments had been made, Germany had borrowed about $6 billion from foreign investors, of which about $2.5 billion had come from the United States; and it had paid some $4.4 billion in reparations. The Allies had paid a little more than $2 billion on their war debts. After 1933 the Nazi dictatorship in Germany ceased to pay interest on German foreign debts, and proceeded to repatriate German bonds held by foreigners at a discount rate in some cases as high as 70 per cent. By this method the Third Reich repudiated most of Germany's foreign debt. Thus, the paradoxical result of the attempt to maintain the structure of international debt payments was that, taking into consideration both public and private debts, the payments and receipts of each nation during the postwar period almost balanced each other. Germany seems to have gained more than it paid out; the United States paid out almost as much as it received.

The Far East

In the Far East, secretaries Hughes, Kellogg, and Stimson continued the Roosevelt-Wilson policies initiated before the war. American diplomacy sought to protect the Philippines against attack and to preserve the Open Door in China, and it opposed the imperialist policies pursued by Japan. But the American people in the 1920's, like the administrations in Washington, were too preoccupied with domestic affairs, and with enjoying and extending the benefits of their industrial prosperity, to assume the diplomatic and naval burdens which were required if the Far Eastern policy of the United States was to be effective.

One indication of the American people's unwillingness to pay the price to secure their interests in the Far East was the naval limitation treaty, whereby they hoped to curb future Japanese expansion by a naval agreement. Faith in disarmament was strengthened further by negotiating a series of other multilateral treaties. At the Washington Conference the Anglo-Japanese alliance, which now embarrassed and worried Britain and the British dominions, was enlarged into a ten-year Four Power Treaty, signed in December, 1921, by the United States, Great Britain, France, and Japan. The four nations agreed to respect one another's possessions in the Pacific and to consult with one another in case any of them was endangered by attack from any nation not included in the treaty. When the treaty was presented to the Senate for ratification, a number of senators, among them the three who had been most opposed to Article X of the League Covenant—Borah, Johnson, and Reed—criticized it on the ground that it was an entangling alliance which might involve the use of American military power. Secretary Hughes and the administration, however, had assured themselves of Senate support by including senators Lodge and Underwood, the latter a Democrat, among the delegates to the conference. Harding, moreover, reassured doubters by expressing, in verbiage less cloudy than was usual with him, that "nothing in any of these treaties commits the United States, or any other power, to any kind of an alliance, entanglement, or involvement. It does not require us or any power to surrender a worth-while tradition." And he specified further that the treaty provided for "no commitment to armed force, no alliance, no written or moral obligation to join in defense, no expressed or implied commitment to arrive at any agreement except in accordance with our constitutional methods." [2] But the Senate was not satisfied with the assurance of the President of the United States and other government leaders that although the administration had promised to maintain the *status quo* in the Pacific, it had not really committed itself to anything. The Senate insisted upon incorporating the principle of nonresponsibility into the treaty, and did so when, by a unanimous vote, it added the Brandegee Reservation, which stated that "under the terms of this treaty there is no commitment to armed force, no alliance, no obligation to join in any defense." [3] In spite of all these guarantees, the Senate vote on the treaty (67 to 27) was just four votes in excess of the required two-thirds, whereas the Brandegee Reservation, which for all practical purposes rendered the treaty worthless, passed without dissent. Without effective force to implement the treaty, peace in the Pacific rested upon "moral force" and "the conscience of the world."

Besides curbing Japan, American policy aimed at supporting China and, in the Nine Power Treaty, signed on February 6, 1922, the United States, Great Britain, France, Japan, Italy, Belgium, Holland, Portugal, and China reaffirmed the Open Door and the territorial integrity of China. Japan was allowed to retain its economic predominance in Manchuria and in the Shantung peninsula, but Tokyo agreed to withdraw its troops from Shanghai and also to restore to the Soviet Union territories it had occupied in eastern Siberia. The treaty did not, however, provide any method for enforcing its provisions; and the result of the disarmament provisions of the conference and the failure of Britain and America to cooperate on naval strategy was that the Japanese fleet could, if it chose, dominate the Asiatic end of the Pacific. Maintenance of the treaty would depend, therefore, on the good faith of the Japanese.

A Far Eastern power not included in any of the Washington settlements was the Soviet Union. Throughout the 1920's the United States refused to recognize the Communist government in Russia, chiefly because of the Soviet government's refusal to repay $75 million lent by American citizens in 1916 to the government of the Tsar and $192 million lent by the American government in 1917 to the government of

[2] Quoted in J. Chal Vinson, "The Parchment Peace: The Senate Defense of the Four-Power Treaty of the Washington Conference," *Mississippi Valley Historical Review*, XXXIX (September 1952), 309, fn. 23.
[3] Quoted in *ibid.*, fn. 42 and the same author's article, "Military Force and American Policy, 1919–1939," in Alexander DeConde, ed., *Isolation and Security: Ideas and Interests in Twentieth Century American Foreign Policy* (Durham, N.C., 1957), p. 69.

Alexander Kerensky. The Soviet Union also refused to give compensation for private properties with an estimated value of $430 million which had belonged to American citizens and which the Communists had confiscated. The United States government was, moreover, strongly opposed to the principles of the Soviet government and to the encouragement it gave, through the Communist International, to Communists in the United States. As long as Russia remained Communist, American officials did not believe it could become a market for American goods. The United States was the only great power which had no official relations with the Soviet Union.

The most important development in the Far East in the 1920's was the clash which resulted from the imperialistic ambitions of Japan on the Chinese mainland and the growth of the Chinese Nationalist party, the Kuomintang, under the leadership first of Sun Yat-sen and later of Chiang Kai-shek. The Kuomintang established a government at Nanking in June, 1928, and set out to extend its authority over the rest of China, much of which was controlled by various war lords, and to restrict the privileges that had been acquired by the citizens of European nations. It began also to assert Chinese sovereignty over Manchuria, a province that had always been legally Chinese and which had a large Chinese population, but which had passed under the economic control partly of Russia and partly of Japan. In 1929 the Soviet government, which had not discarded all the imperialist policies of Tsarist Russia, resorted to armed force to defend its control over the Chinese Eastern Railway in northern Manchuria. Secretary of State Henry L. Stimson denounced this violation of the Kellogg Pact, but the Soviet authorities refused to listen to protests from a country which had refused to give them official recognition.

A more serious crisis began in 1931. The Japanese, hard-hit by the worldwide depression, believed that their prosperity was largely dependent on their economic control of southern Manchuria, which they had come to look upon as their special sphere of interest and where they had invested considerable capital. When the Chinese government, resenting Japan's extensive rights and concessions in an area over which it was nominally sovereign, began to curtail Nippon's privileges there, and when the local Chinese war lord who exercised effective control over Manchuria indicated that he intended to strengthen his authority in the area still further, the Japanese used a railway explosion at Mukden (September, 1931) as an excuse for undertaking the military conquest of the entire province. Domestic politics in Japan, which strengthened the influence of the military in the government, facilitated Japan's plans to take over Manchuria. By February, 1932, it had achieved its goals and organized Manchuria into a puppet state, under the name of Manchukuo, which Nippon formally recognized in September of that year. In January, Japan had also attacked the Chinese city of Shanghai, hundreds of miles to the south of Manchuria, by merciless bombing. Meanwhile China appealed to the League of Nations and to the government of the United States.

Since Secretary Stimson did not want to "excite nationalistic feeling in Japan in support of the military," he avoided, at first, any action which might embarrass the moderates in the Japanese government.[4] He informed China that the United States was "playing no favorites," and he urged the Japanese to settle the dispute peacefully themselves. At the same time, Stimson's caution was tempered by the fact that he was anxious Japan be checked, not so much because of his interest in the Open Door policy as because he believed that successful violation of the Covenant of the League of Nations, the Kellogg Pact, and the Washington treaties would destroy all hope of establishing the rule of law in international affairs, would encourage aggression by other nations, and would lead inexorably to another world war. Although the Senate isolationists had refused to allow any teeth to be put into the Washington treaties or the Kellogg Pact, Stimson felt that if those documents meant anything at all, they meant that the United States should not only obey them itself but should also require other nations to honor them.

Joint action against Japan could, however, be organized only through the League of Nations, and since the United States was not a member of the League, Stimson was unable to exert much influence on its proceedings or to coordinate United States policies successfully with those adopted by the League powers. But even more important in frustrating Stimson's efforts to force Japan to cease hostilities and to adhere to its treaty obligations was President Hoover's opposition to any American action which might increase the risk of war, a position strongly endorsed by the great majority of the American people. As much as they deplored Japan's aggression in Manchuria, Americans disapproved even more of the possibility of war. To add still further to Stimson's burden was the lack of unanimity among the members of the League. While nearly all the smaller members of that body wanted action, some of the great powers, particularly Great Britain, were sympathetic to Japan. Sir John Simon, the British foreign secretary, had no faith in the ideal

[4] Henry L. Stimson, *The Far Eastern Crisis: Recollections and Observations* (New York, 1936), pp. 5–6.

Secretary of State under Herbert Hoover, Henry L. Stimson was a leading Republican. He later joined Franklin Roosevelt's cabinet as Secretary of War in 1940 in a gesture of bipartisan support for a vigorous anti-Axis foreign policy. (Culver Pictures, Inc.)

of collective security, which he believed would tend to promote wars rather than to prevent them. The British Foreign Office, moreover, disliked Chinese nationalism, which might endanger British economic interests in the Yangtse valley, and since Japan was not threatening the British there, it was inclined to regard Japan as a useful ally.

In September Stimson embarked upon a course of "parallel action" with the League by urging Japan to cease fighting; in October he authorized Prentiss Gilbert, the American consul at Geneva, to attend meetings of the League Council, and he asked the League to "assert all the pressure and authority within its competence." To Stimson this meant the enforcement of economic sanctions, if necessary. Hoover, however, firmly rejected this idea. "Neither our obligation to China nor our interest nor our dignity require us to go to war over these questions," he declared in a cabinet meeting. While the United States should "cooperate with the rest of the world" in employing "moral pressure," the President asserted, this should be "the limit" of American action. "We will not go along on any of the sanctions, either economic or military, for these are roads to war." [5] In the end, the League merely urged both

[5] Quoted in Richard N. Current, *Secretary Stimson: A Study in Statecraft* (New Brunswick, N.J., 1954), p. 81.

Japan and China to abandon military operations, and appointed a commission, headed by Britain's Lord Lytton, to study the situation.

In January, 1932, after the military had taken over the Japanese government and had "destroyed the last remnant of Chinese authority in Manchuria," Stimson went beyond the League by declaring that the United States would not recognize any territorial changes made in violation of treaties—a policy which became known as the Stimson Doctrine. The British government, doubtful of the extent to which the United States would go to implement its pledge, replied by publishing a communique in which it refused to support the Stimson Doctrine, declaring it had no reason to believe that the Japanese would exclude other nations from the trade of Manchuria and making no mention of the questions of Chinese territorial integrity and protection against aggression. In February Stimson held several telephone conversations with Sir John Simon, asking for joint action under the Nine Power Treaty, but Simon remained noncommittal. Stimson, hoping to "encourage China, enlighten the American public, exhort the League, stir up the British, and warn Japan," then wrote an open letter to Senator Borah, in which he pointed out that the United States had accepted the naval limitations of the Washington treaties only because all the other signatories to the treaties had promised to maintain the *status quo* in the Far East.[6] In March the Assembly of the League of Nations met, and the representatives of the smaller nations joined in denouncing the refusal of the British government to take action. Since the Japanese were now becoming active in the Yangtse valley, where Britain's interests were concentrated, London was more willing to oppose them. Japan was induced to evacuate Shanghai, and the League accepted the policy of nonrecognition of changes in the *status quo* by force.

Nothing, however, was done to discipline Japan for its seizure of Manchuria. Faced with an economic crisis at home and imperial troubles overseas, the British were interested only in the defense of their own interests; and despite Stimson's efforts, the attitude of President Hoover and most Americans was against the use of any forceful action. Whereas Hoover looked upon nonrecognition as an end in itself, Stimson viewed it as "a preliminary to economic and military sanctions"; and though he hoped war could be avoided, he believed the United States should be prepared to fight if necessary.[7] So long as Hoover was President, how-

[6] Stimson, *op. cit.*, p. 175.
[7] Richard N. Current, "The Stimson Doctrine and the Hoover Doctrine," *American Historical Review*, LIX (April 1954), 542.

ever, Stimson was forced to subordinate his views to those of the President. Meanwhile, the United States navy was afraid lest sanctions lead to a Japanese attack on the Philippines; and the isolationists in the Senate were demanding that the United States remain strictly neutral. No further action was taken by the League until October, when the report of the Lytton Commission was published. The report admitted that the Japanese had had grievances, but it condemned unequivocably their resort to war, and it worked out a solution which might satisfy the legitimate claims of both China and Japan. At the next Assembly of the League Sir John Simon eloquently pointed out all the extenuating circumstances for the Japanese action and declared that the only purpose of the League was conciliation. The League, however, adopted the report on February 24, 1933. The following month Japan notified the League that it was withdrawing from its membership. No further attempt was made to stop the Japanese, who continued their program of aggression at the expense of China, moving into Mongolia early in 1933.

It is possible, as critics of Secretary Stimson have argued, that any serious action against Japan would have extended the conflict instead of checking it and would have committed the British and American navies to war in the Far East at a time when the people of neither country were prepared or willing to fight. It is, however, certain that the failure of Britain, France, and the United States to act together permitted Japan's successful defiance of the Covenant of the League of Nations and of the Kellogg Pact. By showing would-be aggressors that the great powers were unwilling to maintain peace by measures of collective security, the Manchurian crisis set an example which was subsequently followed by Italy and Germany. And while some Americans thought the failure of the League to act was due primarily to the government of Great Britain, it was caused as much by the fact that the Japanese knew the policies enunciated by the American Secretary of State could not be implemented. Neither the President, nor the Congress, nor the American people were willing to go beyond words, and Stimson himself was unable to win approval of his policy to endorse economic sanctions and support them by force if necessary. Subsequent events were to indicate that Manchuria was only the first of a series of successful attacks against the peace system that had been established at Paris in 1919 and at Washington in 1921-22.

The Philippines

In the Philippines the Republican administration reversed the trend toward independence which had been instituted by the Democrats in the Jones Act of August, 1916. Harding sent to the islands the Wood-Forbes Commission, which declared that the Filipinos were misusing the powers which had been entrusted to them. General Leonard Wood was then appointed governor general, and he set up what was almost a military dictatorship: he controlled every branch of the executive, allowed little power to the legislature, and turned over to private capital the economic enterprises the Harrison regime had placed under government ownership. When the Filipinos began to protest, Coolidge in 1926 sent a commission headed by Carmi A. Thompson to investigate the situation. The commission recommended more self-government, and steps in this direction were taken in 1927, when Wood died and was succeeded by Henry L. Stimson. In 1929, when Stimson became Secretary of State, he was followed by Dwight F. Davis.

Meanwhile early in the 1930's, sentiment in favor of Philippine independence was increasing in the United States. The islands were a military liability which might involve us in a war with Japan, and they had brought few economic benefits. In 1930 American capital invested in the Philippines amounted to only $160 million; exports from America to the islands amounted in that year to $89.7 million; imports from the islands into America amounted to $113.5 million. Two-thirds of all the trade of the Philippines was with the United States, but to the United States the value of the trade was negligible. The Philippines, moreover, sold more than $50 million worth of sugar each year to the United States. This sugar, grown mostly by Filipino and Spanish planters, was admitted duty free and hence competed with sugar grown in the United States. Another factor of importance was popular opposition, especially in California, to the admission of Filipino immigrants. The sugar producers and the enemies of oriental immigration joined, therefore, with the isolationists and the antiimperialists in demanding that the United States abandon the islands. This combination of idealism and self-interest caused Congress to pass, over the veto of President Hoover, the Hawes-Cutting Act of January, 1933, by which the islands were to become independent in twelve years. The act was, however, unacceptable to the Filipinos, and a definite settlement was not made until the Tydings-McDuffie Act of 1934.

Latin America

The chief tendency between the United States and Latin America in the 1920's was toward abandonment of the Roosevelt Corollary to the Monroe Doctrine, which had justified armed intervention by the United States in order to forestall the danger of European intervention. The policy of intervention, whether pursued for political and economic reasons, as had been the case during the Roosevelt and Taft administrations, or undertaken for moral and idealistic purposes, as was true of Woodrow Wilson, had alarmed and alienated all the Latin American nations, and thereby had impeded the growth of United States trade and investments. Latin American protests were particularly vehement at the Pan-American Congress, which President Coolidge opened in Havana on January 16, 1928. The American delegation to the meeting, headed by former State Secretary Hughes, succeeded in preventing the conference from adopting a resolution stating that "no state has the right to intervene in the internal affairs of another." On the surface, this appeared to be a reassertion of the old-time "police diplomacy." Actually, however, it was to be the last time the United States would assert this right, for a new policy was to emerge out of the Havana conference.[8]

The new attitude of the United States was expressed most clearly in a memorandum by J. Reuben Clark, Under Secretary of State, written in 1928 and published in 1930. Clark declared that the sole purpose of the Monroe Doctrine was to protect the American hemisphere from European imperialisms, and that the Roosevelt Corollary was not justified by the terms of the doctrine. "So far as Latin America is concerned," said Clark, "the Doctrine is now, and always has been, not an instrument of violence and oppression, but an unbought, freely bestowed and wholly effective guaranty of their freedom, independence, and territorial integrity against the imperialist designs of Europe." This repudiation of the right of intervention was strengthened by a Pan-American Arbitration Conference, which met at Washington in 1929, and at which the United States and the Latin American nations agreed to the compulsory arbitration or conciliation of all disputes with one another.

The United States continued, however, to assert special interests in

[8] Alexander DeConde, *Herbert Hoover's Latin-American Policy* (Stanford, Calif., 1951), p. 124.

the Caribbean region, in order to guard the approaches to the Panama Canal. The Roosevelt Corollary was replaced by the Isthmian Doctrine, formulated by Secretary Stimson, which meant that the United States must claim certain rights of supervision over the small Caribbean and Central American republics. "The failure therefore of one of these Republics to maintain the responsibilities which go with independence," said Stimson, "may lead directly to a situation imperiling the vital interests of the United States in its seagoing route through the Panama Canal. Out of this situation has followed our national policy—perhaps the most sensitive and generally held policy that we have—which for half a century has caused us to look with apprehension upon even the perfectly legitimate efforts of European nations to protect their rights within this zone."

The retreat from the Roosevelt Corollary was a gradual process which did not become immediately effective everywhere. Cuba resumed full self-government in 1922, and the marines left the Dominican Republic in 1924. In Haiti, on the other hand, American rule was in 1922 made stronger; but in 1930 President Hoover promised eventual withdrawal, a promise that was honored in 1934. In both the Dominican Republic and Haiti an American receiver-general continued to exercise financial supervision after the departure of the American officials and marines.

Nicaragua was of special concern to the American government, both because of American financial interests and because of its proximity to the Panama Canal. The marines were withdrawn in 1925, but were sent back, as a result of civil war, in the following year. By 1927 there were 5,000 American troops and marines in the republic, who were apparently enforcing the rule of conservative President Adolfo Díaz, whose policies were favorable to American financial interests. This large-scale intervention, which verged on war, had never been sanctioned by Congress, and was vigorously opposed by Democratic and progressive senators.

In 1927 President Coolidge sent Henry L. Stimson to Nicaragua. Stimson succeeded in persuading almost all the different factions in Nicaragua to agree that an election should be held in 1928 under American supervision. The election resulted in a victory for the liberals, who accordingly took over the government. Similar American-controlled elections were held in 1930 and 1932. One Nicaraguan leader, Augusto Sandino, refused to agree to American supervision; and for some years the American troops were engaged in an attempt to capture or suppress him and his small band of followers. Nicaragua finally resumed complete independence in 1933.

Mexico presented the United States government with more serious problems. The regime which had taken power in Mexico in 1920, after the fall of Venustiano Carranza, set out to achieve the purposes of the Mexican revolution. These were to restore the land to the peasants, to improve the living conditions of the workers, to limit the privileges of foreign capital, to regain Mexican ownership of oil fields and other natural resources, and to reduce the powers of the Catholic Church. Such a program was inevitably distasteful to Americans who had economic interests in Mexico, and was opposed by the Catholic Church in both countries. President Alvaro Obregón, however, who governed Mexico from 1920 until 1924, proceeded along this revolutionary path very slowly and cautiously; and in 1923, in order to obtain United States recognition, he promised not to interfere with American mineral and subsoil rights which had been acquired before 1917. At the end of the year, when the Obregón regime was threatened by a rebellion, it was allowed to purchase munitions in the United States.

In 1924, when Obregón was succeeded by Plutarco Elias Calles, the Mexican government became more radical. Calles pursued the program of land distribution with greater vigor, ordered the foreign oil companies to exchange their titles of ownership for fifty-year leases, and by insisting on some measure of government control of the Church, provoked the Catholic priests into open opposition. The result was a diplomatic conflict with the United States. American oil magnates and some American Catholics asked the United States government to take a firm stand against the Calles policies; and William Randolph Hearst, who owned large estates in northern Mexico, published a series of forged documents purporting to show that four United States senators who had advocated conciliation were in the pay of Mexico. The situation became worse when Secretary Kellogg, wholly without evidence, publicly accused the Mexican government of working in alliance with Soviet communism.

Most Americans, however, favored a peaceful settlement, particularly since some of the oil magnates clamoring for protection had been involved in the oil scandals of the Harding regime. Early in January, 1927, the United States Senate passed a unanimous resolution urging that every effort be made to end the dispute by negotiation. In September, Coolidge sent as minister to Mexico his friend Dwight Morrow, a Wall Street investment banker and attorney. Morrow set out to win Mexican friendship by showing sympathy and understanding, and was scrupulously careful to respect Mexico's rights as a sovereign power. His unconventional diplomatic methods brought rapid and substantial results. Two months after his arrival the Mexican supreme court declared that the constitution of 1917 could not be interpreted retroactively. In accord with the constitution the oil companies must accept leases rather than titles of ownership, but these leases must be perpetual for all fields on which the companies had performed some "positive act" of exploitation before 1917. For the time being this settlement satisfied everybody except the oil companies, who remained reluctant to make the slightest concession to the Mexican authorities. Morrow then went on to negotiate a settlement between the Mexican government and the Church, and used his influence with Calles to urge more conservative policies. The whole Mexican revolutionary program was, in fact, slowed down, and was not resumed with full vigor until the accession of Lázaro Cárdenas to the presidency in 1934.

The settlement Morrow had helped to bring about proved to be short-lived. The oil companies were expropriated in 1938, after they had refused to obey government orders for wage increases. Morrow, moreover, was sometimes criticized for failing to appreciate the need for drastic reforms in the Mexican economy. But the atmosphere of friendship he had created was lasting. Mexicans and Americans might disagree about specific policies, but their arguments were much less acrimonious than in the past, and relations between the two countries grew increasingly close and harmonious.

Whatever shortcomings Morrow's policies would reveal for the future of Mexican-American relations, the fact remains that by the close of Hoover's term in the White House the bases for a new Latin American policy had been firmly established. Beginning with his six-week goodwill tour to Latin America in November, 1929, which he described as "a courtesy call from one good neighbor to another," Hoover worked hard to restore the amicable relations which existed with the Latin American states before the Spanish-American War. The principles of friendship, understanding, and cooperation Hoover did so much to promote as President were to be strengthened still further under Franklin D. Roosevelt's policy of "the good neighbor." To be sure, suspicion as to American motives continued, but the road to hemispheric solidarity was indicated and some real efforts made to travel it.

Suggested Readings

On general developments in American foreign policy during the 1920's, besides the pertinent chapters in the survey volumes cited previously, see chapters 7 and 8 in Foster Rhea Dulles, *America's Rise to World Power, 1898–1954* (New York [1955]) and Allan Nevins, *The United States in a Chaotic World* (New Haven, Conn., 1951), which covers briefly the major developments of the 1920's. The same author's *America in World Affairs* (New York, 1941) is also useful here. Perceptive and authoritative accounts of some of the important world figures of the period are included in Gordon A. Craig and Felix Gilbert, eds., *The Diplomats, 1919–1939* (New Haven, Conn., 1953). See also, on the years 1920–39, Geoffrey M. Gathorne-Hardy, *A Short History of International Affairs* (New York, 1950); J. H. Jackson, *The Post-war World, 1918–1939* (New York, 1939), which emphasizes Europe more than the United States; Frank H. Simonds, *American Foreign Policy in the Post-war Years* (Baltimore, 1935), the appraisal of a competent journalist; and Quincy Wright, ed., *Interpretations of American Foreign Policy* (Chicago [1930]). Alexander DeConde, ed., *Isolation and Security: Ideas and Interests in Twentieth Century American Foreign Policy* (Durham, N.C., 1957) contains some useful and suggestive essays. Selig Adler, *The Isolationist Impulse: Its Twentieth Century Reaction* (New York, 1957) is an excellent study. A suggestive article is William A. Williams, "The Legend of Isolationism in the 1920's," *Science and Society*, XVIII (Winter 1954), 1–20.

The biographies of the men who helped make the history cited previously are also useful on foreign policy, but see especially the brief and very excellent study by Dexter Perkins, *Charles Evans Hughes and American Democratic Statesmanship* (Boston [1956]) and the pertinent sections of Pusey, *Charles Evans Hughes*, already cited. L. Ethan Ellis, *Frank B. Kellogg and American Foreign Relations, 1925–1929* (New Brunswick, N.J., 1961) is valuable for both its account of Kellogg as Secretary of State and its review of the events of the period.

On American efforts at international cooperation, consult the able presentation of United States achievements and failures in cooperating with the League of Nations by Denna F. Fleming, *The United States and World Organization, 1920–1933* (New York, 1938) and the same author's *The United States and the World Court* (Garden City, N.Y., 1945), which censures the country's isolationist trends in this field. Also useful is the study by Manley O. Hudson, *The Permanent Court of International Justice, 1920–1942* (New York, 1943), but consult also Russell M. Cooper, *American Consultation in World Affairs* (New York, 1934) and Council on Foreign Relations, *The United States in World Affairs* (New York, 1931–). There is more useful material in Allan Nevins and Louis M. Hacker, *The United States and Its Place in World Affairs, 1918–1943* (Boston [1943]) and the authoritative study by Francis P. Walters, *A History of the League of Nations* (2 vols., New York, 1952).

On disarmament generally, see Benjamin H. Williams, *The United States and Disarmament* (New York, 1931) and the newer works by Merze Tate, *Disarmament Illusion* (New York, 1942) and *The United States and Armaments* (Cambridge, Mass., 1948). J. Saxon Mills, *The Genoa Conference* (London [1922]) is adequate on the proceedings of this meeting, as is Richard Hooker, "The Geneva Naval Conference," *Yale Review*, n.s., XVII (January 1928), 263–80, on its subject. Giovanni Engely, *The Politics of Naval Disarmament* (London, 1932) covers the London Naval Conference of 1930.

The efforts to outlaw war are carefully detailed in Robert H. Ferrell, *Peace in Their Time: The Origins of the Kellogg-Briand Pact* (New Haven, Conn., 1952). An older work is David H. Miller, *The Peace Pact of Paris* (New York, 1928), while James T. Shotwell, *War as an Instrument of National Policy and Its Renunciation in the Pact of Paris* (New York, 1929) and John E. Stoner, *S. O. Levinson and the Pact of Paris: A Study in the Techniques of Influence* (Chicago, 1943) are accounts of important participants in promoting the treaty. Harold G. Moulton and Leo Pasvolsky, *War Debts and World Prosperity* (Washington, D.C., 1932) is the standard work on the subject, but see also the same authors' earlier *World War Debt Settlements* (New York, 1926). Wildon Lloyd, *The European War Debts and Their Settlement* (New York, 1934); George P. Auld, *The Dawes Plan and the New Economics* (Garden City, N.Y., 1928); and James T. Gerould and Laura C. Turnbull, eds., *Selected Articles on Interallied Debts and Revision of the Debt Settlements* (New York, 1928) all contain competent information on the question.

Two studies that merit special attention for the scholarship and insights they bring to their analyses of the Washington Conference are Harold and Margaret Sprout, *Toward a New Order of Sea Power: American Naval Policy and the World Scene, 1918–1922* (Princeton, N.J., 1946) and John C. Vinson, *The Parchment Peace: The United States Senate and the Washington Conference, 1921–1922* (Athens, Ga. [1955]). Some of Vinson's views are summarized in his article, "The Parchment Peace: The Senate Defense of the Four-Power Treaty of the Washington Conference," *Mississippi Valley Historical Review*, XXXIX (September 1952), 303–14. Older works that are still adequate include Raymond L. Buell, *The Washington Conference* (New York, 1922) and Yamato Ichihashi, *The Washington Conference and After* (Stanford, Calif., 1928). The temper of the times is captured in Mark Sullivan, *The Great Adventure at Washington* (Garden City, N.Y., 1922) and is appraised in its effect upon the diplomacy of the meetings by Charles L. Hoag, *Preface to Preparedness: The Washington Disarmament Conference and Public Opinion* (Washington, D.C. [1941]).

On the Far East diplomacy of the 1920's, a number of the more comprehensive general accounts remain useful, such as A. Whitney Griswold, *The Far Eastern Policy of the United States* (New York, 1938), which is critical of American policy; George H. Blakeslee, *The Pacific Area* (Boston, 1929); and Harold S. Quigley and George H. Blakeslee, *The Far East: An International Survey* (Boston, 1938). For a detailed and thorough account of developments in China, see Dorothy Borg, *American Policy and the Chinese Revolution, 1925–1928*

(New York, 1947). Helpful supplements include Conrad Brandt, *Stalin's Failure in China, 1924–1927* (Cambridge, Mass., 1958) and Frederick L. Schuman, *American Policy toward Russia since 1917* (New York [1928]), which should now be corrected and supplemented with the pertinent chapters of George F. Kennan's brilliantly analytical, *Russia and the West under Lenin and Stalin* (Boston [1960]), and Jane T. Degras, ed., *Soviet Documents on Foreign Policy* (2 vols., New York, 1951–52), the first volume of which contains selected documents on the years 1917–24.

The developing crisis with Japan after the Washington Conference is discussed in various works already cited and in Eleanor Tupper and George E. McReynolds, *Japan in American Public Opinion* (New York, 1937). The second volume of Herbert Hoover, *The Memoirs of Herbert Hoover: The Cabinet and the Presidency, 1920–1933* (3 vols., New York, 1951–52) contains useful information on Far Eastern developments specifically and foreign policy generally. This should be supplemented with William Starr Myers, *The Foreign Policies of Herbert Hoover, 1929–1933* (New York, 1940); Charles P. Howland, ed., *Survey of American Foreign Relations, 1928–1930* (4 vols., New Haven, Conn., 1928–31); and Robert H. Ferrell, *American Diplomacy in the Great Depression: Hoover-Stimson Foreign Policy, 1929–1933* (New Haven, Conn., 1957).

The various developments leading to the Manchurian crisis are explained in a number of works, including Westel W. Willoughby, *The Sino-Japanese Controversy and the League of Nations* (Baltimore, 1935); Henry L. Stimson, *The Far Eastern Crisis: Recollections and Observations* (New York, 1936); and in Stimson and McGeorge Bundy, *On Active Service in Peace and War* (New York, 1948), which contains material from Stimson's diary and private papers. The best account of the incident and its repercussions is Sara R. Smith, *The Manchurian Crisis, 1931–1932: A Tragedy in International Relations* (New York, 1948), but see also Robert H. Ferrell, *American Diplomacy during the Great Depression*, already cited; Richard N. Current, "The Stimson Doctrine and the Hoover Doctrine," *American Historical Review*, LIX (April 1954), 513–42, and the same author's fuller and more detailed account in *Secretary Stimson: A Study in Statecraft* (New Brunswick, N.J., 1954); Paul H. Clyde, "The Diplomacy of Playing No Favorites: Secretary Stimson and Manchuria, 1931," *Mississippi Valley Historical Review*, XXXV (Spring 1948), 187–202; and the pertinent sections in Elting E. Morison, *Turmoil and Tradition: A Study of the Life and Times of Henry L. Stimson* (Boston [1960]), the most recent full-length reappraisal.

On the Philippines, Grayson Kirk, *Philippine Independence* (New York, 1936) is the standard work.

The Latin American policy of the United States is discussed generally in Graham H. Stuart, *Latin America and the United States* (New York, 1955); Arthur P. Whitaker, *The Western Hemisphere Idea: Its Rise and Decline* (Ithaca, N.Y., 1954); and Samuel F. Bemis, *The Latin American Policy of the United States* (New York, 1943). More specialized are Chester L. Jones, *The Caribbean since 1900* (New York, 1936) and Alexander DeConde, *Herbert*

Hoover's Latin-American Policy (Stanford, Calif., 1951). The latter is especially good on the background of the new Latin American policy, but see also J. Reuben Clark, *Memorandum on the Monroe Doctrine* (Washington, D.C., 1930).

Other specialized studies include Henry L. Stimson, *American Policy in Nicaragua* (New York, 1927); Isaac J. Cox, *Nicaragua and the United States, 1909–1927* (Boston, 1927); and Sumner Welles, *Naboth's Vineyard: The Dominican Republic, 1844–1924* (2 vols., New York, 1928).

The background to the Mexican problem of the 1920's is discussed in Ernest Gruening, *Mexico and Its Heritage* (New York [1928]) and in Frank Tannenbaum, *Peace by Revolution* (New York, 1933). The best statement of American involvement in Mexican affairs is Howard F. Cline, *The United States and Mexico* (Cambridge, Mass., 1953). Morrow's efforts at reconciliation are expertly detailed in the biography by Harold Nicolson, *Dwight Morrow* (New York, 1935).

15

Herbert Hoover and the
"Great Depression," 1929-1933

THE ELECTION OF 1928

Coolidge's good fortune continued throughout his second term, and there were no setbacks to the prosperity of business and no breaks in the rising trend of stock market prices. There was talk of a third term, and Coolidge could easily have had the nomination, but on August 2, 1927, while on vacation in the Black Hills of South Dakota, he curtly declared that he did not "choose to run." The wording of the announcement provoked speculation, and since he had not discussed the question with any of the administration or party leaders, some of them suggested that Coolidge hoped for another nomination. Coolidge, however, refused to discuss the question further. Three years later, he wrote that he could not "conceive how one man can successfully serve the country for a term of more than eight years." He had served only a little more than five years and seven months, but he was anxious "to be relieved of the pretensions and delusions of public life" and "to return to the people." [1]

As soon as Coolidge declared himself unavailable for another term, the support of the administration went to Herbert Hoover, still serving as Secretary of Commerce. Coolidge himself, however, endorsed neither

[1] Calvin Coolidge, *Autobiography* (New York, 1931), pp. 240, 242.

Hoover nor any of the other hopefuls. He simply kept quiet. There were numerous favorite sons, such as senators Charles Curtis of Kansas and James E. Watson of Indiana and Vice President Charles G. Dawes, but Hoover's chief rival candidate was Frank Lowden, the former governor of Illinois, who, unlike Hoover, had favored the McNary-Haugen bill, the kind of farm relief legislation which Coolidge had vetoed. But when the Republican convention met in Kansas City, Missouri, on June 11, it was obvious that Hoover's lead and support would be decisive, and he received the nomination on the first ballot. Senator Charles Curtis was nominated for the Vice Presidency, in the hope his name on the ticket would placate the disgruntled farmers, who had little liking for Hoover. One farm leader called Hoover "the arch-enemy of a square deal for agriculture."

As was to be expected, the Republican platform was a conservative document reflecting GOP domination by the big business interests. It applauded the Coolidge policies and attributed the country's prosperity to them. Allegiance to the protective tariff was reaffirmed and the party went on record to uphold the principle and enforcement of the Eighteenth Amendment, notwithstanding the opposition of a number of influential antiprohibitionists from the East, including Columbia University President Nicholas Murray Butler. The Republicans claimed credit for labor's high wages and, in order to attract its support, suggested that legislation to curb the unfair use of the injunction might be necessary and perhaps forthcoming, though no specific promises were made. The spokesmen and representatives of the farmers at Kansas City had hoped to get the convention to endorse the principle embodied in the McNary-Haugen bill, but their efforts proved futile and they were forced to settle for a plank which provided for the creation of "a Federal farm board clothed with the necessary powers to promote the establishment of a farm-marketing system of farmer owned and controlled stabilization corporations or associations to prevent and control surpluses through orderly distribution." This was as far as the Republican party went to meet the farm crisis.

When the Democrats convened at Houston, Texas, on June 26, 1928, it was almost a foregone conclusion that they would nominate New York's governor, Alfred E. Smith. Since 1924, when Franklin D. Roosevelt had dubbed him the "Happy Warrior," Smith had been twice re-elected governor of his state and had been widely applauded for the efficiency and liberality of his administration. He had earned the approval of liberals by his defense of civil liberties and minority rights during the "Red scare" of 1919–20, and he had won the support of social and political reformers for his success in pushing through a reorganization of the New York State government, opposing private ownership of power sites, and securing from a conservative legislature the passage of a number of social welfare laws providing for better public schools, roads, parks, and legislation safeguarding women and children factory workers. To be sure, he was forced to raise taxes, but he was convinced that the voters were willing to pay for the services provided. "What the people want," he wrote, "is an honest accounting for every dollar appropriated." Because of his remarkable capacity for winning votes and his great political skill, the politicians and party workers respected and trusted him. But Smith had numerous handicaps, the most important of which was that he was an entirely new kind of presidential aspirant.

The son of a poor, Irish-Catholic family from the slums of New York City, Smith represented what Richard Hofstadter, Samuel Lubell, and others have designated as the first serious challenge by the offspring of the urban immigrant to the long-time Protestant upper middle-class domination of American politics.[2] There were many prominent Democrats, especially from the South and the border states, whose nativistic prejudices caused them to recoil at the thought of nominating an Irish-Catholic from New York City. To many of these men New York City was about as "foreign" a metropolis as you could find within the continental limits of the United States. If all this were not enough to dampen enthusiasm for Smith in some quarters, the New York governor was an outspoken wet, who despised the hypocrisy and prejudices of the drys, many of whom associated drinking with the immigrant, the city, and the saloon. But despite their prejudices against him, the southern and other rural leaders of the Democratic party were compelled to recognize the fact that in 1928 Smith was probably the only Democrat capable of winning the election. To be sure, there was still widespread opposition throughout the South to the nomination of a Catholic and a wet, but neither the South nor the West had a candidate to offer who enjoyed a national reputation and could reconcile the party's internal differences. The names of several favorite sons were placed before the convention, but when the first roll call was completed and Smith came within ten votes of the nomination, the Ohio delegation shifted its support to the New Yorker

[2] Richard Hofstadter, *The Age of Reform: From Bryan to F.D.R.* (New York, 1955) and Samuel Lubell, *The Future of American Politics* (New York, 1953).

to put him across. Several other states quickly followed Ohio's lead, thereby assuring Smith the nomination. To appease the South the convention chose Senator Joseph T. Robinson of Arkansas as Smith's running mate. Since he was a Protestant, a dry, and a son of the rural South, the Democrats hoped that Robinson would appeal to the groups that Smith would probably alienate.

The Democratic platform, once the difficult prohibition issue was settled with a statement which called for "an honest effort to enforce the Eighteenth Amendment," was somewhat more outspoken than the Republican one, though it could hardly be called progressive. In the hope of capturing the farm vote, the Democrats flirted with a number of the provisions which had been proposed in the McNary-Haugen bill, but without endorsing the measure itself. The agricultural planks called for legislation which would bring about the "economic equality of agriculture with other industries," increased financial assistance to cooperatives, and government help in marketing agricultural products through a farm board established for this purpose. The Democrats tried to appear more interested than the Republicans in the farmer's welfare, but with the exception of Smith's personal endorsement of the McNary-Haugen farm relief program during the campaign, there was little in the platform itself that was

Governor Alfred E. Smith of New York, the first Roman Catholic to run for President (1928), represented many of the hopes and aspirations of the new immigrant and urban groups who were striving for recognition. (Brown Brothers)

markedly different from what the Republicans were promising. The same was true of the Democratic stand on the tariff. While they decried the extreme protectionism the Republicans had embraced, the Democratic platform proposed rates which would protect the American workers and producers from foreign competition. In no sense could their proposal be construed to mean a lower tariff. Apart from the provision calling for government-sponsored public projects to provide work for the unemployed when necessary, there was little in the Democratic platform which went beyond the Republican one, insofar as labor was concerned. The Democratic party had no intention to alienate or frighten the business interests.

On most basic economic questions, moreover, there was very little difference between the two candidates. Citing the record of the Republican party since 1921, Hoover claimed that his election would mean continued prosperity. "We in America today," he declared in his acceptance speech, "are nearer to the final triumph over poverty than ever before in the history of any land. The poorhouse is vanishing from among us. We have not reached the goal, but given a chance to go forward with the policies of the last eight years, we shall soon, with the help of God, be in sight of the day when poverty will be banished from this nation. There is no guaranty against poverty equal to a job for every man. That is the primary purpose of the policies we advocate." Smith was somewhat less conservative than Hoover, as his record in New York indicated. During the campaign he denounced the use of injunctions in labor disputes and promised farm relief. On the other hand, his stand on the tariff and his friendliness to big business, proved by the choice of millionaire John J. Raskob, of Du Pont and General Motors, as chairman of the Democratic National Committee, indicated that he was no fiery progressive. Moreover, almost nothing in Smith's campaign showed he intended to depart from what Hoover liked to call "our American system."

The campaign of 1928, nevertheless, was one of the most bitter in American history. Hoover, born of poor Quaker parents on a farm in West Branch, Iowa, had been left an orphan at nine years of age. From that time on, largely through his own initiative and hard work, he provided for his own needs, and in 1891 he enrolled as a freshman at Leland Stanford University, in Palo Alto, California, graduating four years later as a mining engineer. From 1895 until 1914, when he became chairman of the American Relief Committee in London, Hoover worked as a mining engineer and consultant all over the world—in North America, Asia,

Africa, Europe, and Australia. His career was highly successful and Hoover had amassed a considerable personal fortune by the time he was forty years old. "Had it not been for the first World War," he wrote in his *Memoirs*, "I should have had the largest engineering fees ever known to man." Everything in Hoover's life and career squared well with what the American people liked to believe—the story of a poor boy who had made good on his own. To his success in private life Hoover added a distinguished record of selfless public service, so that by 1928 his career made him a shining example of the opportunities the American system provided for self-improvement, while his heritage made him the symbol of the rural Anglo-Saxon Protestant tradition.

Social snobbery and religious prejudice played a prominent role in the campaign. Smith was denounced because of his mannerisms, his attire, his East Side accent, and his associations with Tammany Hall, all of which offended the rural and small-town folk of the South and West. Smith was aware of all this, but he was proud of his heritage and too honest to want to disguise any of it. To add to his troubles in 1928, Smith, who was exciting and eloquent when speaking before a live audience, proved incapable of mastering the radio, while Hoover was far more effective when speaking into a microphone than when talking from a platform. The fear that Smith's election would put the American government under the control of the Vatican was widely propagated, along with other more vicious, scurrilous, and unfounded rumors of a Catholic conspiracy, especially in the areas where rural Protestantism was strong. The candidates were, moreover, in opposition over the issue of prohibition. Hoover described prohibition as "a great social and economic experiment, noble in motive and far-reaching in purpose." Smith, disavowing the Democratic platform, recommended repeal of the Eighteenth Amendment and the return of liquor control to the state governments. If Smith's religion and his outspoken stand against prohibition, along with the fact that he was the symbol of the urban, immigrant, machine-sponsored politician, were not enough to frighten the voter, the widespread prosperity which, with the exception of farmers and a few others, was being enjoyed by almost everyone, and for which Hoover and the Republicans claimed sole responsibility, virtually guaranteed his defeat.

In the cities of the Northeast Smith received a popular acclaim probably unprecedented in American history, but even in this section of the country, where he was best known, he carried only two states—Massachusetts and Rhode Island, whose large urban, Catholic, wet, and immigrant populations voted for him. Though he carried New York City by a large majority, he lost the state by some 103,000 votes, and five states of the hitherto "solid South" (Texas, Virginia, North Carolina, Tennessee, and Florida) rejected him. Smith received the largest popular vote ever given to a Democratic candidate up to that time, but in the electoral college he was defeated by an unprecedented margin. Hoover won 21,392,-000 popular votes, or 58.12 per cent, and 444 electoral votes. Smith, with a popular vote of 15,016,000, or 40.8 per cent, carried only six southern states besides Massachusetts and Rhode Island, with an electoral vote of 87. Norman Thomas, the Socialist candidate, received 267,420 votes, and William Z. Foster, the Communist party's standard-bearer, polled only 48,770 votes. The Republicans also carried both houses of Congress by comfortable majorities: in the House of Representatives there were 267 Republicans to 163 Democrats and in the Senate the division was 56 to 39. Only eighteen state houses had Democratic governors.

Despite Smith's defeat, the Republican triumph of 1928 indicated some serious weaknesses which were to prove disastrous for the party in subsequent presidential elections. The two most notable trends which emerged were the growing number of urban voters, especially among the immigrants and their descendants, who were attracted to the Democratic party for the first time in 1928, and the increase in the size of the farm vote which went to the Democrats. Most of the middle-western farmers voted against the Catholic, wet, and city-bred Smith in 1928, but as John D. Hicks points out, "enough of them were drifting over to the Democrats to indicate a trend." [3] It would be out of these groups, along with the South and the liberal vote throughout the country, that the Democratic party under Franklin D. Roosevelt would forge a new coalition which would defeat the Republicans repeatedly.

HERBERT HOOVER

Herbert Hoover, who became President seven and a half months before the beginning of the worst depression in American history, took office with a great reputation for administrative efficiency and humanitarian sympathies, which he had earned by his work as supervisor of Belgian relief (1915–18), as food controller during the war, as chairman of the Supreme Economic Conference at Paris in 1919, as chairman of the Euro-

[3] John D. Hicks, *Republican Ascendancy, 1921–1933* (New York [1960]), p. 214.

pean Relief Council the next year, and as Secretary of Commerce from 1921 to 1928. Yet he left the White House after four years with a larger body of more bitter opponents than any previous President since Andrew Johnson. This unpopularity may be regarded as Hoover's misfortune rather than his fault, but there is no doubt that he lacked certain of the qualities needed for the position to which he had been elected. Hardworking and widely experienced, with a remarkable grasp of detail and a strong sense of the dignity of the presidential office, he had little ability to work with people, to conciliate opponents, or to win popularity. Having spent most of his early life as a mining engineer and businessman in the Far East and in Europe, and having never been elected to any office previous to the Presidency, he was tragically lacking in the practical experience of American politics and in an appreciation of the importance of Executive leadership. Besides being politically inept, he was totally unfamiliar with the legislative process on Capitol Hill and he found it difficult to secure cooperation from Congress—a fact which became obvious immediately after his accession to office, during the debates on the Hawley-Smoot tariff bill. Nor could he successfully dramatize his personality and his program in such a way as to obtain popular support. According to one close White House observer, "There was always a frown on . . . [Hoover's] face and a look of worry," giving the impression "of a fellow who was always afraid of losing his job . . . ." [4] Hoover's relationship with the press, which had been good while he was Secretary of Commerce, started to deteriorate shortly after his nomination and worsened as his term continued. It soon became apparent that he was highly sensitive to criticism and that opposition to his plans was apt to make him irritated and resentful.

Hoover was, moreover, a strong believer in the American system of individualistic capitalism, as it had operated in the 1920's. He believed government should assist business and should avoid any measures tending toward socialism or toward bureaucratic control. Hoover maintained that "the proper job of Government" was "to investigate, call conferences, and make suggestions that would increase the efficiency of business and agriculture." He was convinced that if unemployed or needy persons acquired the habit of expecting financial assistance from the federal government, the American system would soon be destroyed. He was therefore sternly opposed to any grants of direct relief by the federal government. Unemployed persons must be supported by private charity or by the local governments.

[4] Irwin [Ike] Hoover, *Forty-two Years in the White House* (Boston, 1934), pp. 184, 188.

"The moment responsibilities of any community, particularly in economic and social questions, are shifted from any part of the nation to Washington," he declared on February 12, 1931, "then that community has subjected itself to a remote bureaucracy. . . . It has lost a large part of its voice in the control of its own destiny. . . . Where people divest themselves of local government responsibilities they at once lay the foundations for destruction of their liberties. . . . At once when the government is centralized there arises a limitation upon the liberty of the individual and a restriction of individual opportunity . . . [which] can lead but to the superstate where every man becomes the servant of the State and real liberty is lost." Hoover's faith in private enterprise, "rugged individualism," and voluntary cooperation was the expression of a clearly integrated philosophy of government, and to persist in such a position during the depression years required considerable courage. But such an attitude, whatever merits it may have had, inevitably caused him to be regarded as callously indifferent to human suffering and unaware of the realities of the crisis.

AGRICULTURAL RELIEF

As soon as Hoover entered the White House, he was faced with the continuing problem of the farm crisis, which had disturbed the smooth and peaceful course of the two previous Republican administrations. Farm fortunes had been deteriorating steadily since 1921, and the amount of farm mortgages outstanding had jumped from $4 billion in 1917 to $9 billion in 1928. If this were not enough reason to call for governmental action, Hoover and the Republicans had promised the farmers relief during the campaign. Hoover had assured Senator Borah of this fact and the Idaho progressive endorsed him in his campaign speeches. Now the time had come for the new administration to make good its promises. The agricultural interests still hoped to resolve their difficulties by enacting the principles expressed in the oft-debated McNary-Haugen bill, but because Hoover agreed with Coolidge, he rejected all schemes which involved government subsidies. The farm legislation of his administration would have "no equalization fees, price fixing, or any other such nonsense." Hoover, who had become intimately associated with the farm problem during the Harding and Coolidge administrations and had expressed himself on the question and its solution often throughout his term as Secretary of Commerce, recognized that overproduction might occasionally exist, and he believed that the federal government might legitimately assist the farmers in limiting production by voluntary and cooperative methods. The government could help the farmer also by raising the tariff, but the main burden of the responsibility for bringing prosperity to agriculture should be borne by the farmers themselves. Price stability, Hoover maintained, should be achieved by the "orderly marketing" of farm produce through marketing cooperatives established for this purpose.[5] On June 15, 1929, the special session of Congress which Hoover had called to raise the tariff to benefit the farmers passed the Agricultural Marketing Act, which embodied Hoover's recommandations. A Federal Farm Board with eight members and the Secretary of Agriculture was established; it was to encourage the organization of co-operatives for marketing farm products, and it was to have a fund of $500 million, which was to be loaned to cooperatives. When overproduction occurred, the cooperatives would buy and hold surplus crops until the market adjusted itself. Special stabilization corporations might be established for handling particular commodities. In 1930, three of these—one each for cotton, grain, and wool—were organized.

Hoover's assumption was that agricultural overproduction was occasional and not chronic. He believed that, when there was overproduction of one particular crop, the Agricultural Marketing Act would assist farmers to transfer their land to a different crop for which there was greater demand. The Federal Farm Board might have worked had prosperity continued, but it began functioning during a depression period when the prices of all farm commodities were dropping catastrophically for lack of markets and when the decrease in farm incomes made it impossible for the farmers to reduce production. The Grain Stabilization Corporation bought 330 million bushels of wheat in 1930 and 1931, but it could find no purchasers and, after accumulating huge stores of wheat and corn, it was finally compelled to stop buying. The price of wheat then dropped, and the storage charges for the wheat held by the corporation soon exceeded its cash value. The history of the Cotton Stabilization Corporation was similar. It bought 3.25 billion bales of cotton; then it stopped buying and the fall of prices resulted in a loss to the corporation of $150 million. By the spring of 1932, the Cotton Corporation was urging the growers to plow under a third of that year's crop.

[5] James H. Shideler, "Herbert Hoover and the Federal Farm Board Project, 1921–1925," *Mississippi Valley Historical Review*, XLII (March 1956), 710–29.

The onset of the depression nullified every effort of the Farm Board to stem the tide of falling prices, and in the end it was engulfed by the economic crisis which beset the country. The failure of Hoover's farm policy, however, was not due only to the depression. Its chief fault lay in assuming that farmers could help themselves and that the role of the federal government would be minimal, limiting itself largely to recommending policies with which the farmers would comply voluntarily. The experience with marketing cooperatives, for example, indicated that the farmers who needed the most help—the producers of staples—received the least, while fruit growers and poultry farmers who could brand, advertise, and market their products regionally or nationally gained the most. But the Farm Board's greatest weakness was its inability to control production effectively. Hoover, of course, was opposed to any such invasion of individual liberty, just as he disapproved of the board's increasing role in trying to stabilize prices. Before it passed out of existence, the Farm Board recommended that the government abandon its effort to solve the farm problem by looking for solutions which would improve the distribution of agricultural commodities and concentrate its energies upon measures which would permit the effective control of production. The New Deal's farm policies began with this recommendation.

THE TARIFF

By 1933 Hoover's farm policy also indicated that the protective tariff was hardly the answer to higher agricultural prices, but in 1928 neither Hoover nor the Republican party was prepared to admit to this. During the campaign, refusing to take warning from the bitter experience of former President Taft, Hoover promised Borah that upon his election he would ask Congress to revise the tariff, especially the rates which applied to farm products. True to his word, Hoover immediately called a special session of the Congress, which met on April 15, 1929. Hoover and Borah had hoped that the Congress would limit itself to giving the farmers greater protection, but the Senate rejected Borah's proposal to this effect by one vote and thereby opened the door to a general tariff revision. This was precisely what Hoover did not want, but because he did not believe that the President should interfere with the will of the legislature, he did nothing to prevent Congress from ignoring his expressed intentions. Once the debate on the Hawley-Smoot bill began, it soon became apparent that the proponents of lower duties, principally the spokesmen of the investment banking and foreign trade interests, could not withstand the demands of the powerful protectionist lobby which had come to Washington to safeguard and extend the interests of the country's manufacturers. Big industry, whose chief spokesman in Congress was the president of the Pennsylvania Manufacturers' Association, Senator Joseph R. Grundy of Pennsylvania, dictated most of the changes; and wherever Grundy's influence was felt, the duties were almost always raised. When the progressives in Congress realized that industry rather than agriculture was receiving most of the protection, they attempted to secure special benefits for the farmers by including a provision which would have revived the export debenture plan and another which would have transfered to Congress the power to change rates by as much as 50 per cent of the established duty, if the tariff commission recommended it. The Fordney-McCumber Act of 1922 had granted this authority to the President.

These two amendments, both of which Hoover strongly disapproved, extended the debate on the bill. Hoover now stepped into the battle and, apparently not at all concerned in this case with using the power of the Executive to influence the legislature, worked hard to get the Senate to remove the offending amendments. When the tide seemed to be going against him, he threatened to veto the bill. This extraordinary example of presidential leadership on Hoover's part proved sufficient to force the Congress to drop the amendments, and the bill passed the Senate by 44 to 42 and the House by 222 to 153. The bill, which increased duties on the average by 40.08 per cent, was not at all what Hoover had wanted, and 1,038 of the leading economists in the country urged him to veto it, declaring that it would raise prices, protect inefficiency, prevent the payment of international debts, reduce exports, and compel foreign nations to raise their own tariffs against American goods. Even though Hoover called the bill "vicious, extortionate, and obnoxious," he signed it into law on June 17, 1930. His chief reason for doing so was that the bill gave increased powers to the tariff commission, which would, he hoped, be able gradually to reduce the excessive schedules and to make the tariff a nonpolitical question. Within a year twenty-five nations retaliated by either raising their own tariffs or threatening to do so; and the results were a general decrease in world trade. Thus the Hawley-Smoot Tariff Act, which had started out as a measure to provide relief to the American farmer during a period of prosperity, went into effect just in time to intensify the rapidly growing world depression.

THE WALL STREET CRASH AND
THE ONSET OF THE DEPRESSION

The Stock Exchange

The factor immediately responsible for the stock market collapse of October, 1929, and the widespread economic depression of the 1930's which followed it was an example, in the words of John Kenneth Galbraith, of "the seminal lunacy which has always seized people who are seized in turn with the notion that they can become very rich." [6] This desire to get rich quickly, which came to possess so many Americans in the 1920's, attracted thousands to the stock market, producing the "speculative orgy" which fed the bull market of 1927, 1928, and 1929. During these years stock prices rose continuously and by leaps and bounds, with only few interruptions. The index of common stock prices (1926 = 100) was 118.3 in 1927; by 1929 it had risen by more than 50 per cent to 190.3. The index price for utilities more than doubled during the same period, jumping from 116 to 234.6. Yet while it is true that by 1929 more people were directly involved in the stock market than ever before, and that a considerable number of these were engaged in speculation on a scale hitherto unprecedented, still the fact remains, as a Senate investigating committee was to disclose later, that no more than 1.5 million people were actually engaged in buying and selling stocks. This is a very small number when compared with a total population of 121.7 million. Numbers in this instance, however, are unimportant. What is significant is the extent to which the speculative psychology which characterized the Wall Street market dominated so much of American life. The stock market no longer existed primarily as a means of providing capital for productive enterprise; it had become a place where men expected to make fortunes by gambling on the prices of stocks. Billions of dollars were diverted from investment into speculation; and stock values, pushed upward by competitive bidding, ceased to bear any relation to their real capacity for earning dividends.

Certain orthodox economists, conservative bankers, and other prominent public officials who at the time were opposed to any governmental action which interfered with the free operation of the economy later

[6] John Kenneth Galbraith, *The Great Crash, 1929* (Boston [1955]), p. 4.

attributed the speculative frenzy which precipitated the crash to the easy money policy pursued by the Federal Reserve Board, and particularly to its lowering of the rediscount rate in 1927. As Winthrop W. Aldrich, chairman of the board of the Chase National Bank, declared in 1938: "The real trouble in 1928 and 1929 was, I believe . . . an excess of bank credit going into capital uses and speculative uses due to the cheap money policies of the Federal Reserve System during the nineteen-twenties. When a prolonged period of artificially cheap money generates a volume of bank credit which outruns the needs of commerce and industry and runs over on a grand scale into capital and speculative uses, we inevitably lay the foundation for a crisis and depression, because we inevitably create a situation in which debt outruns production."

The Federal Reserve System had lowered its rediscount rate at the request of European bankers, who wished to check the drain of gold from Europe to America; but its failure to abandon the easy money policy the following year was due chiefly to pressure from the financial community in New York, many of whose leading members were making enormous profits through the rise in stock prices. And even if the Federal Reserve had been able to raise the rediscount rate in 1928, it is highly questionable whether this action alone would have reduced significantly the funds being attracted to the stock market. For one thing, money was not especially cheap in 1928 and 1929 and the speculator, intent upon getting rich from a substantial rise in the market price of the securities which he planned to acquire, would not have been stopped from buying stock simply because he had to pay a little more interest on the money he may have had to borrow.[7] To curb speculation, much more was needed than the Federal Reserve's manipulation of the rediscount rate. The speculative craze continued with increasing momentum because almost no one wanted to stop it. When some of the more sober members of the banking and financial communities recommended caution or suggested that the Federal Reserve take some action, they were shouted down by most of their colleagues on Wall Street, who deprecated any talk that a break in the market was inevitable. Far more important in explaining the continuing stock market joy ride is the failure of President Coolidge and Treasury Secretary Mellon to take any action to discourage speculation. Coolidge was aware of the dangerous course in which the market was heading. He had been informed of this fact on several occasions, but he

[7] *Ibid.*, pp. 36, 174 and the same author's "The Days of Boom and Bust," *American Heritage*, IX (August 1958), 101–2.

was wedded to the principle that the federal government should do as little as possible, especially when it concerned the operation of the economy. As a result he refused to do or say anything which might have slowed down the madness. When he did speak out, it was only to say the wrong thing, as the time he declared early in 1928 that in his opinion brokers' loans were not too large.

While conservative financiers thus blamed the Federal Reserve System, and by inference the federal government, other observers attributed the bull market to more fundamental causes. They argued, for example, that the income of the American people was very poorly divided, and that a small group of men and corporations with excess capital savings, for which —as a result of the restricted purchasing power of farmers and certain workers—they could find no outlet in productive investment, were using their money to speculate in the market.

In 1928 and 1929 the profits to be derived from "playing the market" were widely and vigorously publicized by many of the leading bankers, who were themselves engaged in speculation but who omitted to point out that when the inevitable crash occurred it would be the individuals without inside knowledge who would take most of the losses. The National City Company, for example, an affiliate of the National City Bank, combed the whole of the United States for possible buyers of stocks. It divided the country into seventy districts, used contests to stimulate its salesmen to sell more stocks, and made use of eleven thousand miles of private telegraph wires. Many members of the general public were induced to put their savings into Wall Street through the medium of investment trusts, which conducted speculative operations on a large scale.

Between January and September of 1929 investment trusts sold to the public more than $2 billion worth of their own securities. Many speculators, later estimated at about 600,000, were buying on margin, which meant that the purchaser would pay only a small part of the price of his stocks and would borrow the remainder from his broker. The broker, in turn, would borrow from the bank, leaving the speculator's stocks as collateral. This practice greatly increased the instability of the financial system, since a fall in the value of stock would compel the banks to demand additional collateral or payment of the brokers' loans. This, in turn, would cause the brokers to sell their customers' stocks for whatever they would bring in order to cover themselves. By September, 1929, loans to brokers totaled more than $8.5 billion.

In March, 1929, the Federal Reserve Board put pressure on the banks to limit brokers' loans. This action, which would tend to check speculation and thereby prevent stock prices from continuing to rise, was bitterly resented by a number of New York bankers; and Charles Mitchell, chairman of the board of National City Bank and one of the directors of the Federal Reserve Bank of New York, promptly declared that his bank would increase its loans to brokers by $25 million. "We feel," Mitchell said, "that we have an obligation which is paramount to any Federal Reserve warning, or anything else, to avert a dangerous crisis in the money market." Mitchell, one of Wall Street's most vociferous apostles of optimism, was far more popular in New York financial circles than the few bankers who, like Paul M. Warburg of the Kuhn, Loeb investment house, had been suggesting caution and advocating restraint. When Warburg, also in March, 1929, declared that the wild speculation going on that spring would result in "a general depression involving the entire country," he was accused, among other things, of "sandbagging American prosperity."[8] Many industrial corporations, moreover, were pouring their savings into Wall Street, and these reserves of money could not be controlled by the Federal Reserve System. In August, 1929, the board raised its rediscount rate from 5 to 6 per cent, hoping thus to curtail some of the supply of bank credit. This action, however, was too late to prevent the approaching crisis.

By this date there were already a number of indications that the economy, despite public assurances, was far from healthy. Building had fallen off in 1928; production was now beginning to decline in the steel and automobile industries. Stock prices reached their peak early in September and then showed a tendency to fall. Since, however, so many persons had bought stocks they could not afford in the expectation of selling them at a profit, any gradual decline of prices was impossible. As soon as it became obvious that the bull market had ended, there would be a frenzied rush to sell. October 19 was the first bad day; but the real break came on the morning of what came to be known as "Black Thursday," October 24, when nearly 13 million shares were traded. That afternoon a group of powerful and influential Wall Street bankers (National City Bank's Mitchell, Chairman Albert H. Wiggin of the Chase National Bank, Thomas W. Lamont of J. P. Morgan, and men of like station from the Guaranty Trust Company and Bankers Trust Company) endeavored to restore confidence by duplicating what J. P. Morgan had done in 1907, namely, buying stocks at more than their market prices. Later in the day,

[8] Quoted in Galbraith, *The Great Crash*, pp. 42, 77.

Lamont explained to the press that the "little distress selling" that had occurred in the morning was nothing more than "a technical condition of the market." Lamont's assurances were accepted and it was optimistically believed the situation had been saved. Faith and confidence survived the weekend, but they were hard hit again on Monday, October 28. The next day, however, came still another and even more acute crisis: nearly 16.5 million shares were traded, and the bankers, who had temporarily stemmed the tide of sales the previous Thursday, abandoned all hope of checking the stampede. Stock prices dropped in some cases as much as 80 per cent below their September levels. At the end of the day, it was impossible to determine how much money had been lost. *The New York Times* called it "the most disastrous trading day in the stock market's history." On the New York Stock Exchange alone, 880 issues registered a loss of $8 or $9 billion. No buyers could be found for many stocks, and thousands of margin accounts were liquidated.

Subsequently the stock market coasted slowly downward for two and a half years, with occasional brief rises which were not maintained. In September, 1929, the stock market index of *The New York Times* had stood at 311.90; by July, 1932, it had dropped to 34.43.

Some Statistics of the Depression

The break in the stock market meant only a decline in paper values which did not directly affect the productive capacity of American industry and agriculture; the real wealth of the American people was as great in November, 1929, as it had been in September. It was therefore believed by President Hoover and by the majority of the American people that the economic system would quickly adjust itself and that prosperity would continue. Actually, however, the economy in 1929 was suffering from a number of serious weaknesses which made it impossible for the stock market to recover from the great shock it had just experienced. The result was that what had happened on Wall Street put in motion a chain of events which was to cause the greatest depression in American history.

By mid-November, paper wealth had decreased by $30 billion. (By the summer of 1932 another $45 billion would be wiped out.) The consequence was that the people who had incurred these losses—and they were the ones with most of the disposable income—began to limit their purchases of new goods, particularly of the durables which had played such an important role in sustaining the prosperity of the 1920's. Moreover, because of lack of both capital and confidence, businessmen began to invest less money than formerly in industrial expansion. The result was that production of capital goods and durable consumption goods declined, workers in these industries were laid off, and the growth of unemployment caused further contractions of purchasing power, which led in a vicious cycle to still more unemployment. After the stock market crash, the economic system could have righted itself only through a reduction in all other monetary values, including prices and debts, in proportion to the decrease in stock prices. That, however, was impossible.

The country did not feel the full effects of the crash for several years. Economic conditions slowly deteriorated during 1930 and the early months of 1931, and by the summer of that year many people believed the corner had been turned. What had happened on Wall Street had, however, caused repercussions in Europe, which reacted back upon the United States. The cessation of American loans and the decline of American foreign trade, coupled with the intrinsic weaknesses of the European economic system due to the war, led in the summer of 1931 to the collapse of central Europe—an event which was to help bring about the emergence of the Nazi dictatorship. From Austria and Germany the chain of disaster then spread to Great Britain and returned to the United States. According to President Hoover, "there came to us a concatenation of catastrophes from abroad such as we have not experienced in the whole of our economic history." The depression continued to deepen until July, 1932. Then after a slight recovery in the autumn, the trend turned downward again until March, 1933.

The production of national income decreased from $82.69 billion in 1929 to $40 billion in 1932, and the total output of goods decreased by 37 per cent. The decrease of production was very much greater in industry than in agriculture: agricultural production declined by only 6 per cent; industrial production, on the other hand, declined by 48 per cent. The decline in construction was 86 per cent.

The total income of labor decreased between 1929 and 1932 by 40 per cent. The number of unemployed in March, 1933, was variously estimated at between 12 and 15 million. Factory employment fell off by 38 per cent. Although the reductions in hourly wage rates were relatively small and were more than counterbalanced by the fall in prices, a considerable number of the workers still in employment were working on a part-time basis. The real wages of the average employed wage earner decreased by about 16 per cent. In 1929 industry had paid $10.9 billion in wages; in

1932 it paid only $4.6 billion. Meanwhile the farmers had suffered from a sharp drop in farm prices, which were 61 per cent lower in 1933 than in 1929. Farm incomes in 1929 totaled about $12.79 billion; in 1932 they amounted to $5.56 billion. In March, 1933, the purchasing power of the farmers was exactly half what it had been ten years before.

The total incomes from property decreased between 1929 and 1932 by 31 per cent. In 1929, 269,400 corporations had reported profits, and 186,600 corporations reported deficits; the net profits of all corporate enterprise had totaled $8.74 billion. In 1932 only 82,600 corporations reported profits, whereas 369,200 corporations reported deficits. The net deficits of all corporate enterprise amounted to $5.64 billion. The number of bank failures in 1930, 1931, and 1932 was 4,377, involving deposits totaling $2.75 million.

Reasons for the Severity of the Depression

For more than a hundred years the American economic system had suffered from periodic depressions which had always been followed by a return to prosperity. Recovery, moreover, had been due primarily to economic causes and not to any action taken by the American government. For a number of reasons, however, the depression which began in 1929 was exceptionally acute and eventually affected almost everyone. In terms of the mass unemployment, the extremely depressed conditions of the economy generally, and the hardships inflicted upon so many people who had never experienced economic distress before, such as the white collar salariat and professional men and women, the "great depression" was qualitatively as well as quantitatively more serious than any previous one. Recovery was so long delayed that the American people finally insisted the government intervene. To this day, economists differ in trying to explain what brought about this extended economic crisis, which left such an impress upon the American people and gave rise to new economic, political, and social ideas and practices. The following are among the generally accepted explanations of what aggravated the instabilities in the economy and delayed recovery.

In the first place, the expansion of the capital and durable goods industries in the 1920's had been on a wholly unprecedented scale. By 1929 the supply of factories, machinery, office buildings, automobiles, and other durable goods appears to have been out of all proportion to the effective purchasing power of the nation's consumers. In the case of consumer durables, for example, many sales had been possible only by installment selling, which, by providing the means for immediate acquisition, tapped future demand. The result was that the revival of these industries was exceptionally slow. Many observers, indeed, doubted whether any revival was possible without government intervention.

In the second place, the price-fixing policies of the big corporations meant that in the capital and durable goods industries prices remained high, while production and employment were drastically reduced. In agriculture and in the more competitive consumption goods industries, on the other hand, prices were reduced while production was maintained. According to Gardiner C. Means, "the whole depression might be described as a general dropping of prices at the flexible end of the price scale and a dropping of production at the rigid end with intermediate effects between." With the exception of the railroads, most of the large corporations continued to make profits, though on a reduced scale, all through the depression. Their policy of maintaining prices, however, tended to delay any real recovery in the capital goods industries, while their drastic reduction of employment prolonged the depression by decreasing consumer purchasing power. Means illustrates his statement by the following figures, showing percentage decreases in prices and production between 1929 and the spring of 1933:

	FALL IN PRICES	FALL IN PRODUCTION
Agricultural implements	6%	80%
Motor vehicles	16	80
Cement	18	65
Iron and steel	20	83
Textile products	45	30
Food products	49	14
Leather	50	20
Agricultural commodities	63	6

Price maintenance was particularly conspicuous in the case of certain mineral products. Throughout the depression nickel remained at 35 cents a pound; sulfur remained at $18 a ton, its leading producer, Texas Gulf, making a 50 per cent profit on every sale; aluminum sold for 24 cents a pound in 1929 and 23 cents in 1932. The effects of price fixing on a consumption goods industry are illustrated in the case of cigarettes. By maintaining prices and taking advantage of decreased costs of production, the seven leading cigarette corporations were able to increase their profits from $85 million in 1929 to $105 million in 1932.

In the third place the depression deprived American industry of many of its foreign markets. In 1929 American exports had a total value of $5.24 billion; by 1932 the value had decreased to $1.61 billion. Recovery of these foreign outlets for American surpluses proved to be impossible. Much of the American export trade before 1929 had been financed by American loans; since, however, many of these loans went into default during the depression, American investors were unwilling to continue foreign lending. Other nations, moreover, began to raise tariff barriers, to use import quota systems, and to adopt policies of economic nationalism, partly in retaliation for the Hawley-Smoot Tariff and partly in the hope of shielding their own industries from the force of the world depression.

In the fourth place, the severity of the depression was increased by the extraordinarily intricate system of debt obligations. Interest payments which could be handled easily in 1929 were a crushing burden in the deflationary conditions of 1932, and these payments could not be scaled down except through bankruptcies. In the early stages of the depression the share of the national income going to the creditor classes was increased, which meant that the purchasing power of the remainder of the population was proportionately reduced. As one banker put it, "capital kept too much and labor did not have enough to buy its share of things." [9] In addition to the workers who "did not have enough," he could have added most of the farmers who were always pinched for money during the 1920's. In 1930 the total amount of interest and dividend payments was actually greater than in 1929. Even in 1932 interest payments (though not dividend payments) were only 3.5 per cent less than in 1929. The concentration of industry which had occurred in the 1920's created a complex corporate structure where in certain areas, such as public utilities and banks, one holding company was pyramided upon another. Many of these intricate holding company structures were created for no other reason than to provide opportunity to secure monopoly privileges or to issue new stocks for the insiders to manipulate to their own advantage. But once defaults and bankruptcies began on any level of these pyramids, they threatened to spread so widely and to involve so many institutions in a common ruin that even the government of President Hoover, which professed to believe in laissez-faire principles, was compelled to intervene.

[9] Quoted in Hicks, *op. cit.*, p. 230.

Rather than allow economic mechanisms to take their natural course, the government began to give support to the financial structure. Such an intervention moderated the severity of the depression; but by preventing debt obligations from being wiped out, it probably delayed any genuine recovery.

In the fifth place, there was neither the desire nor the means to regulate the banking system effectively and to curb the flow of Federal Reserve credit from going into speculative transactions on the stock market. The country's banks had encouraged borrowing on all levels. Businessmen and corporations borrowed to expand production or to speculate in securities, while individuals, in the hope of getting rich quickly and in order to satisfy their desire to acquire the many new products of the new technology, borrowed to gamble on the market and to buy on installment.

In the sixth place, the tremendous strides which had occurred in the efficiency of industry resulted in technological unemployment; fewer workers were required to produce a greater amount of goods. The new industries, like the manufacturing of automobiles and radios and those affected by them, did not take up all the workers displaced by machines in the older ones. The result was that throughout the 1920's the number of unemployed fluctuated from a low of about 464,000 in 1926 to more than 2 million in 1922 and 1924. The psychology of optimism which prevailed during the 1920's caused most people to overlook the effects of technological unemployment and the other danger signals which were undermining the prosperity. And because so many Americans had come to believe that the United States had discovered the secret of perpetual "good times," the social and human effects of the depression were even more devastating than the actual economic losses, great as they were. Facts and figures cannot begin to describe the deepening despair which gripped the American people as they passed from what had been for most of them an era of striking prosperity to one of severe depression. As the distinguished journalist Anne O'Hare McCormick wrote at the time, the depression was "the worst in the extent to which it . . . caught people unprepared." [10]

Human Effects of the Depression

Statistics chart the growth of the depression, but they only hint at the extraordinary degradation, misery, and suffering that it caused—the wide-

[10] Anne O'Hare McCormick, *The World at Home* (New York, 1945), p. 78.

spread malnutrition; the devastation of savings, homes, and properties; and the humiliation and the loss of self-respect on the part of men and women who found themselves unemployed and dependent upon charity. The total of human misery was slowly growing through 1930, 1931, and 1932. For about a year after the stock market crash, although unemployment was steadily increasing, no unusual measures were taken to meet the crisis. Private charity was considered adequate for feeding the unemployed. The autumn of 1930, however, brought the first catastrophic bank failures —the failure in November of the brokerage house of Caldwell and Company in Nashville, Tennessee, which carried down with it 129 banks; and the failure of the Bank of the United States in New York in December. In Arkansas, moreover, the man-made crisis of the depression was coupled with a severe drought which brought many thousands of farmers to the verge of starvation. During the winter of 1930–31 most of the city governments were giving direct relief, and unemployed persons selling apples and shining shoes at street corners became a familiar sight.

By the summer of 1931 the treasuries of New York, Chicago, Philadelphia, Detroit, and Boston were all close to bankruptcy. Compelled to borrow from large financiers in order to continue paying relief, they were, in return, required to reduce payments to a minimum. Detroit, for example, was able to obtain funds from the automobile corporations only on condition that relief be limited to 7½ cents a day for each individual. In May, 1932, Philadelphia's 55,000 families on local relief received $4.23 a week, of which $3.93 was to buy food. Thousands of the unemployed began to build themselves huts out of refuse timber on vacant city lots. These colonies became known ironically as "Hoovervilles." Thousands of other unemployed persons were drifting about the country, walking the roads and taking possession of railroad boxcars in such numbers that railroad detectives were unable to eject them. According to the testimony of one railroad official, the number of these "unemployed transients" on the Missouri Pacific Railroad alone increased from 13,745 in 1928 to 186,028 in 1931. In Pennsylvania and Kentucky, hundreds of thousands of bituminous coal miners went on strike against starvation wages; conditions of virtual civil war prevailed, and the miners and their families lived on payments averaging 4 cents a day per person which were contributed by the Socialist Relief Fund.

By the end of 1931 the resources of private charity and of the city governments were almost exhausted, and most of the state governments had been compelled to appropriate money for relief. The year 1932 brought new financial disasters: the suicide of Ivar Kreuger, the Swedish match king, in March, and the subsequent discovery that the company of Kreuger and Toll, to which American investors had contributed $250 million, was nothing but a gigantic fraud; the break-up of the Insull public utilities empire with its 150 interlocked corporations; and more epidemics of bank failures which threatened by the end of the year to engulf even the strongest institutions in the country. By September, 1932, it was estimated that the total number of unemployed was about 13 million, that 1 million of them were living in Hoovervilles, and that nearly 2 million more, including 200,000 children, had become undernourished, hungry, homeless migrants. Mrs. Elizabeth A. Conkey, Chicago's commissioner of public welfare, reported in September, 1931, "that no fewer than 200 women . . . [were] sleeping in Grant and Lincoln Parks, on the lake front, to say nothing of those in the other parks." Another large body of unemployed had returned to the land and were endeavoring to support themselves by subsistence agriculture. During the depression the number of farmers increased by more than half a million. Moreover, 154 different organizations in twenty-nine states had established barter and scrip systems, under which unemployed persons, having virtually seceded from the established economic system, exchanged the products of their labor with one another without the use of legal money. One such system, in California, had 200,000 members; another, in Minneapolis, included factories, restaurants, and stores.

Probably the most remarkable feature of the depression was the docility with which most of its victims accepted their fate. As the economic historian George Soule pointed out in August, 1932, in an article in *Harper's*, "If you want to hear discussions of the future revolution in the United States, do not go to the breadlines and the mill towns, but to Park Avenue and Wall Street, or to the gatherings of young literary men." To most Americans the depression had been caused by the mechanisms of society and not by the forces of nature; the families who lived on the verge of starvation were surrounded by plenty. Yet throughout the depression the American people displayed an extraordinary respect for law, order, and the established rights of property. Only on three or four occasions was there any organized resort to violence. In July, 1931, the starving farmers of Arkansas seized food from the local storekeepers. Later in the year there were demonstrations of unemployed workers outside the Ford plant at Dearborn, Michigan, which ended in a riot and the killing of four men by the police. In August, 1932, a National Farmers' Holiday Association, headed by Milo Reno, was organized in Iowa, with the purpose of raising prices by preventing farm products from being shipped into the cities. For about a month farmers in Iowa barricaded roads and forcibly held up shipments. Finally, in January, 1933, opposition to mortgage and tax foreclosure sales developed on a large scale throughout the middle-western farm belt. Farmers forcibly prevented courts from hearing fore-closure cases or saw to it that the foreclosed land and chattels were sold for trifling sums and subsequently returned to their original owners. This technique, reminiscent of Shays's Rebellion 150 years before, proved to be successful; and state governors finally intervened to prevent further sales. Along with the Pennsylvania coal strike, these appear to have been the only major cases of organized resistance to the workings of the eco-nomic system. In the larger cities labor conflicts were conspicuous by their absence, and to quote George Soule again, "searching for actual flesh-and-blood revolutionary proletarians is a thankless job. Most of those who really suffer from the depression are . . . simply struck dumb by it." The American people, in the words of another contemporary com-mentator, appeared to be simply "waiting, waiting for something to turn up."

Political Repercussions

In the European countries the depression caused a rapid growth of Communist and fascist parties; it destroyed democracy in Germany and Austria, and seriously weakened it elsewhere. No such development, how-ever, was visible in the United States. Most Americans remained faithful to the traditional two-party system, and the only considerable shift of sentiment was from the Republicans to the Democrats.

The Socialist party made gains, but in spite of the able leadership of Norman Thomas, its voting strength remained smaller than it had been in 1912 and 1920. A growing number of litterateurs became converts to communism, as Russia's experiments with a planned economy attracted much attention in the United States. The Soviet Union at this period was apparently undergoing a rapid economic development; and the much-advertised triumphs of its Five Year Plan seemed to present a startling contrast to the chaotic conditions which prevailed in the United States. But although there was much interest in the Russian experiment and con-siderable talk about the "crisis of capitalism," and although books in de-fense of communism began to appear in considerable numbers and the probability of a proletarian revolution became a favorite subject of conversation in middle-class intellectual and university circles, particularly in New York, the Communist party continued to be a small, weak organization with very few working-class supporters. Its membership increased from 7,545 in 1930 to 25,000 in 1934. It organized a number of unemployed demonstrations and hunger marches, but such importance as it seemed to have was due chiefly to the excessive precautions taken to check its activities by the police authorities, especially in New York City and in the District of Columbia.

The demands for action which Communist leaders advocated caused some government officials and conservative spokesmen to fear revolution. The insecurity of the times and the inability of the political and economic leaders of the country to develop any real plans to meet the crisis caused many people to question whether the political and economic system which had served them in the past was capable of surviving this crisis. The fact that the country's leaders themselves were timid and frightened hardly inspired confidence, and some people began to consider whether communism or fascism might not be the system of the future. Because there were those who found a certain attraction in the fascist program, a number of fascist organizations appeared at this time, especially in the South. The best known of these was William Dudley Pelley's Silver Shirts, although there were others who extolled Mussolini's experiment with the corporate state and advocated a fascist America. In the end, these groups, despite the stir they created at the time, proved to be as weak as the Communists.

The insecurity, fear, and humiliation which were increased by the continually deepening depression attracted many people to demagogues and political activists of the extreme right and left who promised immediate solutions to all the country's problems. But not all the depression-born radical movements looked to European communism and fascism for their inspiration. A number of them—among the more important ones being the movements started by Senator Huey Long of Louisiana, Dr. Francis E. Townsend of Long Beach, California, and Father Charles E. Coughlin of Royal Oak, Michigan—were at first purely American in their inspiration and ideals. To many observers, however, they shortly began to present alarming analogies to the fascist parties of Europe. The three chief movements, which gained increasing importance and attracted a considerable following in the early 1930's, reflected the discontent and the demand for action which was stirring throughout the country. The effectiveness of the campaigns of these prophets of a new day cannot be minimized, for it was to have much bearing upon the orientation, policies, and programs of Franklin D. Roosevelt's New Deal.

THE FIRST TWO YEARS OF
THE HOOVER ADMINISTRATION

For nearly two years after the Wall Street debacle Hoover appears to have taken the view that the economic system would quickly adjust itself without large-scale government action. The chief thing needed, he felt, was a revival of confidence. In the autumn and winter of 1929–30 the Federal Reserve System lowered the rediscount rate to 4½ per cent and made possible a credit expansion of $500 million; the Farm Board set up under the Agricultural Marketing Act took action to keep agricultural surpluses off the market; and on December 2, 1930, Hoover increased government expenditures on public works by asking Congress for an appropriation of $100 to $150 million. The total federal spendings on public works, which had averaged $275 million a year before the depression, amounted to $410.42 million in 1930, $574.87 million in 1931, and $670.29 million in 1932. The number of persons employed increased from 180,000 in 1929 to 760,000 in 1932. But despite these increases in federal expenditures and employment, the government's effort did not begin to meet the problems created by 10 million or more unemployed.

The most important piece of construction begun under Hoover's initial program was the building of a dam at Boulder City on the Colorado River. Hoover also called several conferences of business leaders, at which he urged them not to reduce wages and to undertake capital expansion. Business carried out the Hoover program to the extent of making no serious wage cuts until the autumn of 1931; but it was unable to undertake expansion, nor was anything done to check the growth of unemployment. In October, 1930, Hoover appointed New York City's former police commissioner, Colonel Arthur Woods, to supervise the collection of money for relief under the President's Committee for Unemployment Relief which had just been established. Woods was succeeded in 1931 by Walter S. Gifford, who worked to keep the federal government out of the relief business by trying to secure money "to aid the private relief agencies." Local and state efforts proved entirely inadequate, and neither Woods, Gifford, nor their successor, Fred C. Croxton, who took over the President's agency in 1932, was able to cope with the problems of relief and unemployment.

Otherwise Hoover's chief activity during the first two years of the depression was the making of reassuring statements designed to restore business confidence. Unfortunately the causes of the depression were not merely psychological, and the constant reiteration by members of the administration that prosperity was just around the corner soon began to seem ridiculous. Republican Senator Simeon Fess of Ohio, complaining that "every time an administration official gives out an optimistic statement about business conditions the market immediately drops," even suggested that there must be a Wall Street plot to discredit President Hoover by prolonging the depression.

Meanwhile the Arkansas drought provoked the first of many conflicts between the President and Congress on the question of relief. In December, 1930, Hoover asked Congress to vote $45 million to save the animals of the Arkansas farmers, but he insisted that none of the money be used to provide food for human beings, who were to be assisted by such private organizations as the Red Cross. When members of the Senate urged government aid for men as well as for animals, Hoover replied that they were "playing politics at the expense of human misery." Eventually Congress compromised by voting an additional $20 million to feed the farmers, but stipulated that this money was to be a loan and not a gift. In approving this measure, Hoover declared that for the federal government to give money for relief "would have injured the spiritual responses of the American people." "We are dealing with the intangibles of life and ideals. . . . A voluntary deed is infinitely more precious to our national ideals and spirit than a thousandfold poured from the Treasury." Hoover's view, however, was repudiated by Harvard University economist Sumner Slichter, who told a Senate subcommittee in 1932 that "the need for national assistance . . . has become so self-evident that it would seem to me to be a waste of your time for me to offer anything along that line."

Hoover Takes Action

The thesis of the administration was that during the summer of 1931 the American economic system was beginning to recover but that the depression was subsequently prolonged by catastrophes abroad. In May of that year the financial structure of central Europe began to crumble. From this date on Hoover began to act vigorously and quickly.

His first measure, taken on June 20, was to recommend a moratorium on all payments of war debts and reparations. This proposal was designed to save Austria and Germany from financial collapse and to protect the large investments of American and British financiers in those countries. Private debts were to have precedence over government debts. Unfortunately the French government, still hostile to Germany and indignant over a proposed customs union of Germany and Austria, delayed acceptance until July 23, by which time it was too late to prevent financial disaster. Catastrophe spread throughout central Europe, and from it emerged, eighteen months later, the Nazi dictatorship.

In the autumn of 1931 Hoover began to put into effect a program for ending the depression. He proposed to give financial aid to business institutions, particularly banks and railroads; to refinance mortgages on farms and houses to check foreclosures; to increase the volume of money in circulation; and to balance the federal budget by reducing expenditures and increasing taxes. Unfortunately for him, the Democrats had made considerable gains in the congressional elections of 1930. The Republican majority in the Senate and the House was reduced to one in each chamber, and with the two parties now almost equal in both houses, the administration was faced with new difficulties in securing approval of its program. Since a number of the Republicans were western progressives, the opponents of the administration were actually in the majority. Democrats and progressives from both parties criticized Hoover's program of pouring in money at the top of the economic system, and they demanded that it be distributed instead among the unemployed workers at the bottom, whose needs were more desperate. Some of Hoover's opponents were not averse to playing politics with the situation in order to improve the chances of the Democratic party in the 1932 election. There were, therefore, a series of conflicts between the President and Congress, so that it was a number of months before Hoover's recommendations were put into effect.

In December, 1931, the National Credit Corporation (NCC) was organized with a capital of $500 million, which was subscribed by large banks and designed to aid small banks in danger of failure. When the NCC proved inadequate, Congress, largely as a result of the efforts of Eugene Meyer, the chairman of the Federal Reserve Board, and Ogden Mills, the Secretary of the Treasury, established the Reconstruction Finance Corporation (RFC) in January, 1932.

Modeled after the War Finance Corporation of 1918, the RFC was empowered to lend money to banks, insurance companies, building and loan associations, and other institutions in the need of financial help. The corporation, with the Chicago banker and former Vice President Charles G. Dawes as its first president, was established with an original capitalization of $500 million, but it could borrow up to $2 billion. The initial sum was to be raised by selling the RFC's stock to the United States Treasury, and the remainder was to be subscribed by the federal government. To permit the RFC to expand its activities, such as lending to state and local governments so that they could finance new, self-liquidating public works, such as bridges and dams, Congress provided the RFC with an additional $1.5 billion in July, 1932, of which $300 million was set aside to lend to state governments who were unable to meet all their relief needs from their own funds. The chief purpose of the RFC, according to administration spokesmen, was to lend money to banks, insurance companies, and other strategic organizations which, if permitted to default, would threaten the savings and investments of many individuals. Ogden Mills, for example, declared that he thought the RFC would be "an insurance measure more than anything else. I think its very existence will have a great effect psychologically, and the sooner it is created, the less use we will have to make of it." [11] The severity of the economic crisis and the dangerous condition of many of the country's banks forced bankers to call upon the RFC for help. Under the leadership of Eugene Meyer, who was appointed chairman after Dawes, the RFC set out to alleviate business distress, and by the end of March, 1933, it had assisted 7,411 institutions with $1.78 billion in loans, of which about $1 billion went to financial institutions and $331 million to save the country's railroads.[12] During the same thirteen-month period, the RFC also lent $223.7 million to state and municipal governments for self-liquidating public works and another $201 million for relief.

When the RFC was established, Hoover announced that its purpose was not to come to "the aid of big industries or big banks," though he believed it was necessary to help secure these institutions, for if they collapsed, then the whole economic structure would go down with them. So long as the RFC's transactions were kept secret, most people believed the agency was concerned primarily with helping small business rather than the corporate giants. The Democrats, however, insisted upon Con-

[11] Quoted in Arthur M. Schlesinger, Jr., *The Age of Roosevelt: The Crisis of the Old Order* (Boston, 1957), p. 236.
[12] Harris Gaylord Warren, *Herbert Hoover and the Great Depression* (New York, 1959), p. 146.

gress' being informed of all RFC loans. Hoover opposed this proposal on the ground that if the public learned the names of the institutions receiving loans, it would lose confidence in those institutions, and in the case of banks, precipitate the very kind of crises an RFC loan aimed to prevent. But Hoover was unable to persuade the Congress upon the necessity of secrecy, so that in July, 1932, a Democratic-sponsored amendment required the RFC to inform the Congress of its loans. It was not long before the public knew about the RFC's lending policies. Publication of the RFC's loans proved somewhat embarrassing to the administration, for it indicated that while the number of loans to the small banks far exceeded those made to large financial institutions, most of the RFC's money went to save a few of the great metropolitan banks. The loan which attracted the most public attention was the $90 million made available to the Chicago bank which had been founded by Charles G. Dawes, the recently retired president of the RFC. There was nothing illegal in this loan or in any of the others which were made during Hoover's last year in the White House, but they underscored the fact that while the administration was quite willing to use public funds to save the large banks and the other big business institutions of the country, it was not similarly disposed when it had to use federal funds to alleviate individual suffering. As a result, the impression quickly spread that the RFC, despite Hoover's assurance that it was established "to stop deflation in agriculture and industry and thus to increase employment by the restoration of men to their normal jobs," was what Congressman Fiorello La Guardia of New York had called it, "the millionaire's dole."

The RFC was one of Hoover's major attacks upon the worsening depression, and despite public criticism against its policy of favoring financiers and industrialists, it was a constructive and beneficial action on his part. It did little, however, to mitigate human suffering, but as Hoover had asserted earlier, "The sole function of government is to bring about a condition of affairs favorable to the beneficial development of private enterprise." [13] Once the business community was out of the doldrums, the rest of the economy would recover too, so Hoover believed. In keeping with this philosophy, he took a series of other steps to fight the depression.

Less than a month after the RFC went into effect, Congress passed the Glass-Steagall Act, which liberalized the discount requirements of the Federal Reserve System and made possible an extension of bank credit

[13] Quoted in Schlesinger, *op. cit.*, p. 238.

amounting to $2.5 billion. Meanwhile the Federal Land Banks had been given $125 million for the refinancing of farm mortgages. In April, to offset a decrease in federal revenue amounting to about $2 billion, taxes were increased to provide an additional revenue of $1 billion; the income tax exemption was reduced to $1,000 for single persons and $2,500 for married persons, and the initial tax was increased to 2 per cent. Congress also authorized federal economies of about $300 million. These figures meant a deficit for 1932 of $2.68 billion and a total deficit for the Hoover administration of $3.59 billion, against which could be set recoverable loans made by the RFC amounting to about $2.5 billion. In July Congress passed the Federal Home Loan Bank bill, authorizing the establishment of twelve banks with a total capital of $125 million for the relief of home owners in danger of foreclosure. Here was a positive and strong measure which provided real help to suffering home owners, aimed to stimulate the construction of new private dwellings, and thus indirectly helped reduce unemployment in the building trades.

Meanwhile progressives in both parties in Congress tried to steer the administration to accept the principle of direct federal relief to the needy and to embark upon a large public works program designed to reduce unemployment. However, Hoover opposed various Democratic and progressive programs which called for spending up to $2 billion of federal money for such purposes, and these and other similar proposals were either defeated in Congress or killed by presidential veto. Hoover described all projects of this kind as "the most gigantic pork barrel ever proposed to the American Congress" and as "an unexampled raid on the public treasury." Hoover's opposition to the use of federal money to help the needy and the unemployed made him appear callous and indifferent to human suffering, just as his actions toward the veterans in June and July, 1932, caused him to lose whatever goodwill he still had with the American people.

Hoover and the Veterans' Bonus

As the depression grew in intensity, the veterans of World War I began to demand, first, that the percentage which might be borrowed on their insurance policies be increased to 50 per cent of the value of the bonus and, subsequently, that the whole bonus which had been voted them in 1924 be paid immediately. Congress passed the first of these proposals over Hoover's veto in February, 1931, but on June 17, the Senate rejected the House-sponsored Patman bill calling for the immediate payment in full of the remaining bonus. The money to meet these payments was to be raised by issuing $2.4 billion of fiat money. During May and June some seventeen to twenty thousand unemployed veterans, who called themselves the Bonus Expenditionary Force (BEF) and were headed by a former sergeant from Oregon, Walter W. Waters, arrived in Washington, many of them with their wives and children, and, like Coxey's army of 1894, started to agitate for payment. With little or no money to pay for room and board, some of the veterans set up their own tents in empty lots in and around Washington, while others found refuge wherever they could, in shacks and in old vacant government buildings along Pennsylvania Avenue which were to be razed to make room for new ones. After the Senate rejected their demand, Congress prepared to raise the money to send the veterans and their families back home. The government would collect this transportation money by deducting it from the veterans' bonus which, according to the 1924 law, would be paid to them in 1945. Most of the men accepted the government's loan and returned to their homes, but about two thousand of them, having no other

During the "great depression," beginning in 1929, an appreciable part of the working population was reduced to living in homemade shanties, known ironically as "Hoovervilles." The one shown above (Anacostia, May, 1932) was established by the "Bonus Marchers." (U. S. Information Agency)

place to go, stayed in Washington, living as before in their makeshift Hooverville constructions on Pennsylvania Avenue and on the flats of the Anacostia River. Up to this point, the veterans had maintained exemplary discipline, giving the administration no cause to evict them from the city by force. Even when the Senate rejected the Patman bill, the veterans, who were awaiting the result of the vote outside the Capitol, accepted their defeat and serenaded the legislators with "America." At no time during these trying weeks did Hoover or any other administration spokesman make any effort to hear their cause or to speak to them. Publicly, the administration acted as if the two thousand veterans who had refused to go home were no longer in Washington. Privately, however, their presence in the capital caused some administration leaders serious concern.

On July 28, the authorities decided to eject them from the city. After the Washington police had met with some resistance in forcing the veterans out of the government property they occupied on Pennsylvania Avenue, during which two veterans and two policemen were killed, the city government asked the President for federal troops. Hoover passed the request on to his Secretary of War, Patrick J. Hurley, who called upon General Douglas MacArthur, Chief of Staff of the United States Army, to complete the ejection. With the help of his aide, Major Dwight D. Eisenhower, MacArthur led four troops of cavalry, four companies of infantry, a machine gun squadron, and six tanks to clear out the veteran encampments in downtown Washington and along the Anacostia. The veterans were expelled by means of drawn sabers, bayonets, and tear-gas bombs. Then their encampment was burned. By 10 P.M. the army reported its mission completed without deaths and with only fifty-five injuries. MacArthur described the BEF as "a bad looking mob animated by the essence of revolution" and intent upon overthrowing orderly government, and President Hoover told the press that he had decided to use federal troops because most of the men were not defenseless and unarmed veterans but "Communists and persons with criminal records." Subsequent investigations proved Hoover wrong.

Probably no incident of his administration contributed more to make the President unpopular or to reveal his profound misunderstanding of the psychology of the American people than his action against the BEF. Hoover was not indifferent to the plight of the veterans, but he was disturbed and shocked that they should take such action and, unable to think of any other course to follow, he chose the one which allowed for the greatest criticism against him and his administration, an especially unfortunate course at a time when there was so much tension throughout the country and a presidential election less than four months away.

THE ELECTION OF 1932

The presidential nominating conventions in 1932 were held at one of the most critical times in American history. As Anne O'Hare McCormick, reflecting on the spirit of these days, wrote in *The New York Times* for June 26, 1932, the Republican and Democratic party conventions were occurring "in one of the real crises in human history, a crisis not only economic but political." Since the business giants of the country were more frightened and bewildered at the course of events than the common citizen, the entrepreneurial leaders, to whom everyone had deferred with respect during the prosperous 1920's, now gave no indication that they knew what to do to reverse the tide of the depression that was engulfing everybody. As a result, the people turned to Washington for help and guidance. The administration, however, was as worried and as timid as the business community. It was this political and governmental "pussyfooting and resourcelessness" that was most difficult to accept. With everyone looking hopefully to Washington, neither the President nor his advisers provided anything which warranted or received the people's confidence. The interest and attention which so many people focused upon the conventions and the campaign which followed them seemed to indicate that many Americans agreed with Anne O'Hare McCormick when she declared that the election of 1932 "may be our last chance to prove that there is initiative enough left in democracy to make it worth saving and spirit enough left in Americans to turn . . . sentimental, agitated but uninformed Americanism into positive and adventurous citizenship." [14]

Even before the two major parties met to choose their candidates, considerable interest was attracted to the proceedings of the more radical minor parties, which agreed in denouncing the capitalist system as the root cause of the economic distress but differed in the degree to which they believed reform was necessary and in the way it was to be achieved. During April and May the Socialist-Labor, Socialist, and Communist parties, along with the Prohibition, Farmer-Labor, and Liberty parties, convened to nominate presidential and vice presidential candidates.

When the Republicans met in Chicago on June 14, few of them were

[14] McCormick, *op. cit.*, p. 116.

overly optimistic about the GOP's chances for victory. In 1930 the Democrats had reduced the Republican majority in the Senate and in the House of Representatives to one in each chamber. Meanwhile, during the spring of 1932, the depression, which according to the administration was always just about to turn into recovery when some unforeseen event intervened to interfere, showed no indication of getting any better. In fact, there was ample evidence to show it was actually worse. If all this were not enough to dampen Republican spirits, the collapse of the Ivar Krueger and Samuel Insull empires early in 1932, with all their attendant losses and scandal, were dramatic refutations of Republican claims that business was "fundamentally sound" and that it would soon come out of its doldrums. Since no one was determined to admit publicly that the GOP had failed to resolve the problems arising out of the depression by denying Hoover the opportunity to run again, he was renominated almost unanimously on the first ballot, winning 1,126½ out of 1,140 votes. There was some talk of finding a new running mate for him and several candidates were proposed, but nothing came of it, and Vice President Curtis won renomination on the first ballot, after Pennsylvania switched to his side at the end of the first roll call.

The Republican platform, as was to be expected, exonerated the GOP of any blame for the economic disaster of October, 1929, and the subsequent depression; it hailed Hoover's leadership in helping the farmers by securing the passage of the Agricultural Marketing Act and in protecting them from foreign competition; it called for economy and a balanced budget; and it advocated international cooperation to protect the gold standard. It also stood for continued immigration restriction and tariff protection. On the ticklish question of prohibition, the GOP platform agreed to the need to revise the Eighteenth Amendment, but in order to straddle the serious intraparty differences on the subject, offered an ambiguous proposal which called for the people to vote whether they wanted to allow the states to decide on permitting the sale of alcoholic beverages within their own borders. At the same time the GOP made this concession to the wets, it reassured the drys by proclaiming that the federal government would continue to "safeguard our citizens everywhere against the return of the saloon and its attendant abuses." With minor exceptions, the Republican platform stood on the party's record and, while it recognized the economic plight facing the country, it proposed little to alleviate human suffering or to suggest that it was the federal government's responsibility to do so.

The leading contender for the Democratic nomination was Governor

Franklin Delano Roosevelt of New York, whose chief assets included a popular name which many believed "still worked magic" with the electorate and a warm, outgoing personality that had gained him many friends and a host of supporters across the country. Roosevelt had proved his ability to win votes in 1928 by capturing New York's state house while Hoover carried the state. In 1930 he was reelected by a majority nearly twice as large as any ever polled by the popular Alfred E. Smith. As governor, Roosevelt also had a good record which attracted reformers and liberals without alienating the independent and moderately conservative voters. His stand on water power and conservation, for example, was popular in the West, while his anti-Tammany policies endeared him to old-time progressives. He was politically astute and he got along very well with the press. He spoke well before large audiences and his charm captivated small groups. Roosevelt also possessed an unusual ability to communicate his ideas and sincerity over the radio, a fact which was to be of major importance throughout his years as President. Not the least of his assets in 1932 were the loyal, dedicated, and energetic efforts of his two closest political advisers, Louis McHenry Howe, his private secretary and confidante, and James A. Farley, the New York boxing commissioner and chairman of the state Democratic committee. Farley had been at work selling Roosevelt as a presidential candidate for the past four years, traveling throughout the country making friends, winning delegates, and guiding Roosevelt carefully in and out of the primaries. By convention time, Farley had secured a considerable bloc of votes, mostly from the rural South and West.

One of Roosevelt's chief rivals was John Nance Garner, representative from Texas since 1903 and Speaker of the House since 1931, whose proposal to balance the budget by imposing a federal sales tax won him notoriety but few friends among Democratic party politicos. Garner was essentially a conservative Jeffersonian Democrat, opposed as much to big government as he was to big business. His candidacy posed a real threat to Roosevelt, since the Texan enjoyed the support of two influential and prominent Californians, William Gibbs McAdoo and William Randolph Hearst.

Next to Garner, Roosevelt's other major rival was the still widely popular Alfred E. Smith, whose ties of friendship with F.D.R. had already begun to loosen. After reconsidering his decision made in 1928 not to run again, Smith arrived in Chicago for the convention early and, though he declared that his only purpose was "to get myself nominated," his supporters were determined to prevent Roosevelt's nomination. Smith's strength lay in the urban Northeast and, with the exception of the Bronx, in nearly every city where strong party machines dominated local politics. Smith also had the support of the Scripps-Howard newspapers.

There were other Democrats besides Garner and Smith who would have been quite disposed to take on the job of leading the party to victory in 1932. Among these leading hopefuls, to whom the convention could always turn in case the three popular contenders should deadlock themselves, stood the antiprohibitionist governor of Maryland, Albert Ritchie; Wilson's Secretary of War, Newton D. Baker; Missouri's perennial choice, Senator James Reed; governors George White and William Murray of Ohio and Oklahoma, respectively; and for those who still had confidence in bankers, the Chicago financier Melvin Traylor.

The Democratic convention which opened on June 27 confirmed at once Anne O'Hare McCormick's observation, "To the Republicans politics is a business, while to the Democrats it's a pleasure." Reasonably certain that the odds for victory this year were on their side, the Democrats presented a marked contrast to the GOP which had left the city less than a fortnight earlier. Noisily, exuberantly, with few inhibitions and still fewer restraints against parading the personal animosities and sectional differences which divided the party, the Democrats ultimately succeeded in agreeing upon an acceptable platform, which turned out to be a rather conservative document. It promised, among other things, a balanced budget, a 25 per cent reduction in government expenditures, a sound currency, and no government interference with private enterprise. It differed from the Republican platform, however, in its demands for regulation of the stock exchanges to safeguard investors, separation of investment from commercial banking, federal supervision of power companies, enforcement of the antitrust laws, and a restoration of international trade by reciprocal tariff agreements. The Democrats also approved state-regulated unemployment and old age insurance laws and, in somewhat vaguer terms, promised to appropriate federal funds for direct relief and to extend the public works program. The farmer was promised that efforts would be made to control agricultural surpluses so that the prices he received "for basic farm commodities [would be] in excess of the cost of production," and the veterans who suffered injuries while in the armed services were assured a pension. Whereas the Republicans had been vague on prohibition, the Democrats overruled the drys within their own ranks and in a clear statement supported outright repeal of the Eighteenth

Amendment. Independents, liberals, and progressives were not entirely pleased with the conservatism of many of the Democratic planks, but at least the platform allowed for more hope in the direction of progressive reform and governmental responsibility for the general welfare than the Republican one.

With the platform out of the way, the convention turned to the more exciting business of picking the Democratic standard-bearer. As everyone expected, the outstanding lead which Roosevelt commanded from the beginning was registered on the first ballot, which gave him 666¼ votes, Smith 201¾, and Garner 90¼. The minor candidates received the rest. Two more ballots and Roosevelt reached 682¾. This was still 88 votes less than the required 770 for nomination under the two-thirds rule. At this point Frank Hague, the boss of Jersey City and the convention strategist of the Smith supporters, attacked Roosevelt in a bitter statement, saying: "Governor Roosevelt, if nominated has no chance of winning. . . . He cannot carry a single state east of the Mississippi. . . ." Hague concluded his appeal that the delegates reject Roosevelt by pointing out to them that with "the wealth of material before this convention," they should not "consider the one man who is weakest." Meanwhile, James A. Farley, aware that Roosevelt could not afford to risk another roll call unless he was sure of winning the nomination, was busily trying to win more delegates. Realizing that the Smith forces would not shift their support, Farley concentrated his efforts on securing the Garner vote from Texas and California. While the convention was adjourned, following the all-night session which resulted in the inconclusive third ballot, Farley and other Roosevelt lieutenants succeeded in reaching an agreement with the two most powerful men behind the Garner forces—McAdoo and Hearst—which would give Roosevelt the nomination on the fourth ballot and assure Garner second place on the ticket. When the convention reconvened nine hours later for the fourth roll call, it appeared to the uninformed that Roosevelt was through, until the clerk called for California to cast its 44 votes. McAdoo, the leader of the California delegation, asked to be permitted to explain his state's vote. "California came here," McAdoo told the attentive delegates, "to nominate a President of the United States. She did not come here to deadlock this convention or to engage in another disastrous contest like that of 1924." So that the convention might make its choice known without further delay, California, McAdoo announced, was switching its support to Roosevelt. With this announcement, the convention, with the exception of the booing and hissing Smith forces, broke out into a wild demonstration. Roosevelt won over all of the delegates except 190—the votes of the Smith supporters from New York, Massachusetts, Connecticut, Rhode Island, and New Jersey, who refused to make the nomination unanimous. The next day, the convention ratified the remainder of the Farley arrangement by nominating Garner for Vice President by acclamation. Walter Lippmann analyzed the convention maneuvers which resulted in Roosevelt's nomination by concluding that the New Yorker owed his success "to the descendants of Bryan and the living influence of William Randolph Hearst." [15] Will Rogers put it more simply when he said that it was the "victory of the country boys over the city slickers."

In a telegram to the convention chairman, Roosevelt announced that he was flying to Chicago to accept the nomination in person. "The appearance before a National Convention of its nominee for President, to be formally notified of his selection, is unprecedented and unusual," Roosevelt admitted to the assembled delegates, "but these are unprecedented and unusual times." He then went on to say that it should be "the task of our Party to break foolish traditions." In general terms he outlined what he thought needed to be done to give the American people what they "want more than anything else. . . . Work and security . . . ." He concluded his acceptance address with the now famous statement: "I pledge you—I pledge myself to a new deal for the American people. Let us all here assembled constitute ourselves prophets of a new order of competence and of courage. This is more than a political campaign; it is a call to arms. Give me your help, not to win votes alone, but to win in this crusade to restore America to its own people."

Hoover's campaign was depressingly somber, stiffly dignified, and largely ineffectual. He argued that the chief causes of the depression were world conditions over which the American government had no control and that the measures which he had adopted would soon bring about recovery. But the people had heard all this before. A short-lived upswing on the stock market during the summer seemed to give a little more support to GOP assertions, but when stock prices turned down again in the autumn, what little hope Hoover's statement had produced was quickly shattered. Few believed the Republican claim that the drop in the market was due to fear of a Democratic victory or shared Hoover's fear that if Roosevelt were elected "the grass will grow in the streets of a hundred cities, a thousand towns; the weeds will overrun the fields of millions of

[15] Walter Lippmann, *Interpretations, 1931–1932* (New York, 1932), p. 314.

farms." The Republican cause was damaged considerably also when a group of progressive GOP senators, including Bronson Cutting of New Mexico, Hiram W. Johnson of California, George W. Norris of Nebraska, and Robert M. La Follette, Jr., of Wisconsin, repudiated Hoover and endorsed Roosevelt.

Since a Democratic victory was almost a foregone conclusion, Roosevelt's chief task during the campaign was to avoid making any damaging mistakes. In contrast to the solemnity and gloom which accompanied Hoover's public appearances, Roosevelt carried on a vigorous, militant, and strenuous personal campaign. Wherever he went he cultivated local politicians, exuded charm and affability, and to the tune of his theme song, "Happy Days Are Here Again," won votes and friends. In his speeches he gave expression to the main principles of what afterwards became the New Deal, but often in such vague and general phraseology that it was difficult for his opponents to attack him. But on at least three occasions he was quite specific. On September 14, while speaking at Topeka, Kansas, he outlined a broad program of farm relief and called for "national planning in agriculture." Nine days later, in a speech before the Commonwealth Club, in San Francisco, he declared that the epoch of rapid business expansion had ended and that the task now to be undertaken was to solve the problem of underconsumption. It was in this speech, which some people denounced as radical but which many others came to regard as "the most important statement of political philosophy Roosevelt ever made," that he declared: "Every man has a right to life; and this means that he has also a right to make a comfortable living . . . . Every man has a right to his own property; which means a right to be assured, to the fullest extent attainable, in the safety of his savings." The time had come when the "princes of property" must safeguard the public welfare by exercising "the responsibility which goes with . . . power," or else "the government must be swift to enter and protect the public interest." Several weeks later, in a speech at Pittsburgh, Pennsylvania, he denounced Hoover's failure to balance the budget, but was careful to say: "If starvation and dire need on the part of any of our citizens make necessary the appropriation of additional funds which would keep the budget out of balance, I shall not hesitate to tell the American people the full truth and ask them to authorize the expenditure of that additional amount."

The hope and confidence Roosevelt inspired in so many people with his promise to do something resulted in an overwhelming victory. He won a popular vote of 27,821,857 and an electoral vote of 472. Hoover, with a popular vote of 15,761,841, carried only the six states of Maine, New Hampshire, Vermont, Connecticut, Pennsylvania, and Delaware, having an electoral vote of 59. Considering the depths to which the economic fortunes of the country had sunk during the past three years and with some 14 million people out of work, the radical vote was extremely small. Norman Thomas, the Socialist candidate, polled 884,781 votes, some 35,000 fewer than Debs in 1920. William Z. Foster, the Communist candidate, won 102,991 votes, and all of the other minor candidates together received less than 216,000.

The Interregnum

The election was followed by a deterioration of financial conditions which threatened finally to ruin every bank in the country. Republicans ascribed this development to a fear lest the coming Democratic administration adopt an unsound money policy, as well as to the refusal of the Democratic Congress to cooperate with the "lame duck" administration or to adopt Hoover's proposals for banking reform. Roosevelt, busy in

The victor and the vanquished in the 1932 election ride together to the inaugural ceremonies, March 4, 1933. (Brown Brothers)

Albany preparing to assume responsibility in March, refused to declare what he intended to do. Democrats meanwhile pointed out that there were good reasons for believing many of the banks were genuinely unsound. Since the start of the depression, 18 per cent of the banks in the country had already failed, although most of them had been small institutions in western and southern farming communities. In January, 1933, it became known that total bank resources had decreased from $74 billion in 1930 to $57 billion in June, 1932, and that during 1931 and 1932 bank deposits had decreased by $12 billion. In February it was revealed that the Reconstruction Finance Corporation had made large loans to a number of banks. For nearly a year, moreover, the Senate Committee on Banking and Currency had been conducting inquiries into banking practices during the boom and had brought to light a number of astonishing cases of dishonesty and unscrupulousness on the part of leading New York financiers. The public had, therefore, good reasons for distrusting the banks and began to remove their deposits in such quantities that the state governments were compelled to intervene. On February 14 Michigan decreed a bank holiday, and other states quickly followed this example. By March 4, when the new administration took office, every bank in the country was closed; the economic crisis reached its lowest point, the index of industrial production having dropped eight points since December to an all time low of 56. All the other economic indicators registered what so many people could see all about them—how dangerously near the economic system was to total collapse. Commenting upon the Washington scene on inauguration morning, *The New York Times* declared that the "sense of depression [which] had settled over the capital . . . could be felt." Arthur Krock, of the same newspaper, likened the city to "a beleaguered capital in war time." The despair and fear in the faces of the people watching the inaugural parade was duplicated over and over again across the country. The meek and the strong, the propertied and the dispossessed, all seemed to be equally frightened and anxious to hear what the new President would have to say to them, realizing that what they would hear that noon might very well determine the course of their lives for a long, long time to come.

Suggested Readings

The general surveys of the 1920's cited previously, such as John D. Hicks, *Republican Ascendancy, 1921–1933;* William E. Leuchtenburg, *The Perils of*

Prosperity, 1914-1932, and Harold U. Faulkner, *From Versailles to the New Deal,* all contain pertinent information on Hoover's term in the White House, as does George Soule, *Prosperity Decade, 1917-1929.* The latter should be supplemented with the first three chapters of Broadus Mitchell, *Depression Decade, 1929-1941* (New York [1947]), the ninth volume in *The Economic History of the United States* series. The pertinent chapters of Louis M. Hacker, *American Problems of Today* (New York, 1938) are also useful. The general survey of social developments in the *History of American Life* series by Dixon Wecter, *The Age of the Great Depression, 1929-1941* (New York, 1948) is still an excellent and perceptive analysis of these years, as are the two accounts by Frederick Lewis Allen, *Only Yesterday,* cited previously, and its companion volume on the 1930's, *Since Yesterday* (New York, 1940). See also Charles A. Beard, *America in Midpassage* (New York, 1939). An important reappraisal of the 1920's is the first volume of Arthur M. Schlesinger, Jr., *The Age of Roosevelt: The Crisis of the Old Order* (Boston, 1957).

The best work on the election of 1928 is Edmund A. Moore, *A Catholic Runs for President: The Campaign of 1928* (New York, 1956), which largely supplants the older study by Roy V. Peel and Thomas C. Donnelly, *The 1928 Campaign* (New York, 1931). See also the pertinent sections in Oscar Handlin's *Al Smith and His America* (New York [1958]). For Smith's ideas on issues, see his own statement in *Progressive Democracy* (New York [1928]) and his book, *Campaign Addresses* (Washington, D.C., 1929). On Hoover's campaign, see his own, *The New Day: Campaign Speeches of Herbert Hoover, 1928* (Stanford, Calif., 1929). The best contemporary discussion of the Catholic question in 1928, insofar as it was aimed to clarify the issue rather than to appeal to emotion and prejudice, is to be found in two articles, Charles C. Marshall, "An Open Letter to the Honorable Alfred E. Smith," *The Atlantic Monthly,* CXXXIV (April 1927), 540-49 and Smith's own answer, "Catholic and Patriot: Governor Smith Replies," *ibid.* (May 1927), 721-28.

There is no entirely adequate biography of Hoover, largely because access to his papers has been restricted. This being the case, the most useful place to survey Hoover's career to 1941 is in his own account, *The Memoirs of Herbert Hoover* (3 vols., New York, 1951-52), of which the second volume covers the years 1920-33. The best brief account of Hoover's career, including an excellent interpretation of his presidential years, is the essay, "Herbert Hoover and the Crisis of American Individualism," in Richard Hofstadter, *The American Political Tradition and the Men Who Made It* (New York, 1951). On Hoover as President, see also the article by Victor L. Albjerg, "Hoover: The Presidency in Transition," *Current History,* XXIX (October 1960), 213-19. Among the early Hoover biographies that are available, only the first two of which cover the presidential years in part, see Edwin Emerson, *Hoover and His Times* (Garden City, N.Y., 1932); Walter W. Liggett, *The Rise of Herbert Hoover* (New York, 1932); Will Irwin, *Herbert Hoover* (New York, 1928); Samuel Crowther, *The Presidency vs. Hoover* (Garden City, N.Y., 1928); John Hamill, *The Strange Career of Herbert Hoover under Two Flags* (New York, 1931); and John Knox, *The Great Mistake: Can Herbert Hoover Explain His Past?* (Baltimore, 1930). A historian's contemporary appraisal of Hoover's term in the White House is Allen Nevins, "President Hoover's Record," *Current History*, XXXVI (July 1932), 385–94, while an eminent journalist's approach to the same subject is William Allen White, "Herbert Hoover: The Last of the Old Presidents or the First of the New," *The Saturday Evening Post*, CCV (March 4, 1933), 6–7 and 53–56. For a different point of view, see the article by Hoover's favorite newspaperman, Mark Sullivan, "The Case for the Administration," *Fortune*, VI (July 1932), 35–39 and 83–88. Important biographical information is included in the more recent account by Eugene Lyons, *Our Unknown Ex-President: A Portrait of Herbert Hoover* (Garden City, N.Y., 1950).

The official documentation of the Hoover record is to be found in William Starr Myers and Walter H. Newton, *The Hoover Administration: A Documented Narrative* (New York, 1936); William Starr Myers, ed., *The State Papers and Official Public Writings of Herbert Hoover* (2 vols., Garden City, N.Y., 1934); and the detailed and difficult work by Ray Lyman Wilbur and Arthur M. Hyde, *The Hoover Policies* (New York, 1937). Hoover explains his political and economic ideas in three works: *American Individualism* (Garden City, N.Y., 1922); *The Challenge to Liberty* (New York, 1934); and *Addresses upon the American Road, 1933–1938* (New York, 1938). Theodore G. Joslin, *Hoover off the Record* (Garden City, N.Y., 1934) is an incomplete account by one of Hoover's former secretaries, and the brief piece by William Starr Myers, *The True Republican Record* (New York, 1939) defends the Hoover regime, while Rexford G. Tugwell, *Mr. Hoover's Economic Policy* (New York [1932]) criticizes it.

A recent study of Hoover's domestic policies while he was in the White House is Harris Gaylord Warren, *Herbert Hoover and the Great Depression* (New York, 1959). Detailed and sympathetic to Hoover, though not to many of his policies, it is about as complete a record as can now be put together from public sources.

Hoover's agricultural policy is discussed in Saloutos and Hicks, *Agricultural Discontent in the Middle West, 1900–1939*, cited previously. A more detailed account of the conflicting ideas of agricultural relief and the triumph of the Hoover plan is James H. Shideler, "Herbert Hoover and the Federal Farm Board Project, 1921–1925," *Mississippi Valley Historical Review*, XLII (March 1956), 710–29. An older but still useful work is Ellis A. Stokdyk and Charles H. West, *The Farm Board* (New York, 1930).

The Hawley-Smoot Tariff is discussed in all of the economic histories of the period, such as George Soule, *Prosperity Decade* and Broadus Mitchell, *Depression Decade*, both cited above, and in more detail in Frank W. Taussig, *The Tariff History of the United States* (8th ed., New York, 1931). The effect of the measure is appraised in Joseph M. Jones, Jr., *Tariff Retaliation: Repercussions of the Hawley-Smoot Bill* (Philadelphia, 1934).

The best general account of the stock market crash is the lively written and sound analysis by John Kenneth Galbraith, *The Great Crash, 1929* (Boston [1954]), which largely replaces the older work by the Yale economist, Irving Fisher, *Stock Market Crash—and After* (New York, 1930). Other important works on the stock market debacle and the events which brought it about and followed it include Lionel C. Robbins, *The Great Depression* (London, 1934), an Englishman's view that is good on America's role in world affairs, and Joe Alex Morris, *What a Year!* (New York, 1956), which tells what happened in 1929 "in the field of politics, entertainment, agriculture, sports, and business."

More specialized economic discussions of the causes for the collapse, besides those contained in the general economic histories already cited, include James G. Bonbright and Gardiner C. Means, *The Holding Company* (New York, 1932); Francis W. Hirst, *Wall Street and Lombard Street* (New York, 1931); Gardiner C. Means, *Industrial Prices and Their Relative Inflexibility* (Washington, D.C., 1935); Raymond B. Fosdick, *Companions in Depression* (Pittsburgh, Pa., 1930), on the international implications of business slumps; Charles E. Persons, "Credit Expansion, 1920 to 1929, and Its Lessons," *The Quarterly Journal of Economics*, XLV (November 1930), 94–130; and John Jewkes, "Stock Dividends in Large and Small Companies," *The Quarterly Journal of Economics*, XLV (February 1931), 352–57. Ferdinand Pecora, *Wall Street under Oath* (New York, 1939), though not aimed primarily at the crash, reveals much on the stock market and the operations of the investment banking community. Among the works treating various aspects of the depression, but not limited to the Hoover years, see Alvin Hansen, *Fiscal Policy and Business Cycles* (New York, 1950), on some of the long-term problems the depression left for future generations to face; Grace Adams, *Workers on Relief* (New Haven, Conn., 1939) and Louise V. V. Armstrong, *We Too Are People* (Boston, 1938), is concerned with the unemployed. See also Max Lowenthal, *The Investor Pays* (New York, 1933); James G. Smith, ed., *Facing the Facts: An Economic Diagnosis* (New York, 1932); James D. Mooney, *Wages and the Road Ahead* (London, 1931); Mary S. Calcott, *Principles of Social Legislation* (New York, 1932); William C. Schluter, *Economic Cycles and Crisis: An American Plan of Control* (New York, 1933); and Rexford G. Tugwell, *The Industrial Discipline and the Governmental Acts* (New York, 1933), all of which reveal some of the thinking of the depression years.

The social and human impact of the depression is fully documented in such books as Gilbert Seldes, *The Years of the Locust: America, 1929–1932* (Boston, 1933); Jonathan Leonard, *Three Years Down* (New York [1939]); Edmund Wilson, *American Jitters: A Year of the Slump* (New York, 1932); T. J. Woofter and E. Winston, *Seven Lean Years* (Chapel Hill, N.C., 1939); Mauritz A. Hallgren, *Seeds of Revolt* (New York, 1933); Maxine Davis, *The Lost Generation* (New York, 1936); James Rorty, *Where Life Is Better* (New York [1936]); Robert S. and Helen M. Lynd, *Middletown in Transition* (New York, 1937); and David A. Shannon, ed., *The Great Depression* (Englewood Cliffs, N.J. [1960]), an excellent collection of contemporary observations, from which a number of the quotations in this chapter have been taken.

Some valuable insights into the spirit of the times can be gleaned from such interpretative works as Anne O'Hare McCormick, *The World at Home* (New York, 1945), which includes in its early chapters some of this brilliant newspaperwoman's columns in *The New York Times* dating from 1925; Walter

Lippmann's *Interpretations, 1913-1932* (New York, 1933); and Felix Morley, ed., *Aspects of the Depression* (Chicago, 1932). Roger W. Babson, *Cheer Up! Better Times Ahead!* (New York, 1932) is an example of the cult of optimism which was similar to many of the administration's statements, while Edward Angly, comp., *O Yeah?* (New York, 1931) contains a collection of pieces reflecting popular doubts as to the nearness of the corner around which lay the oft-proclaimed prosperity.

The depression gave rise to much talk about the necessity for planning. The views of the professional economists on this subject are expertly analyzed in volume V of Joseph Dorfman, *The Economic Mind in American Civilization*, already cited, but see also the essays in Charles A. Beard, ed., *America Faces the Future* (New York, 1932); Gerard Swope, *The Swope Plan* (New York, 1931); George Soule's two books, *A Planned Society* (New York, 1932) and *The Coming American Revolution* (New York, 1934); and Norman Thomas, *America's Way Out* (New York, 1931).

On the Reconstruction Finance Corporation, see, in addition to the general economic histories cited above, the first five chapters of Jesse H. Jones and Edward Angly, *Fifty Billion Dollars: My Thirteen Years with the R.F.C., 1932-1945* (New York, 1951), as well as the relevant sections of Bascom N. Timmons' biography of Charles G. Dawes, *Portrait of an American* (New York, 1953), and the same author's biography, *Jesse Jones* (New York [1956]). Gerald D. Nash, "Herbert Hoover and the Origins of the Reconstruction Finance Corporation," *Mississippi Valley Historical Review*, XLVI (December 1959), 455-68, is an excellent appraisal of Hoover's role in establishing the RFC.

The details of the bonus marchers of 1932 are told in Walter W. Waters and William C. White, *B.E.F.: The Whole Story of the Bonus Army* (New York [1933]).

The politics generally of the Hoover years is discussed in Robert S. Allen and Drew Pearson, *Washington Merry-go-round* (New York, 1931) and in greater detail in Roy V. Peel and Thomas C. Donnelly, *The 1932 Campaign* (New York, 1935); Edgar E. Robinson, *They Voted for Roosevelt* (Stanford, Calif. [1947]), which analyzes the Roosevelt vote between 1932 and 1944; the first three chapters of Ernest K. Lindley, *The Roosevelt Revolution* (New York, 1933); and Henry L. Mencken, *Making a President* (New York, 1932). Of the numerous reminiscences left by Roosevelt's associates, only a few that are especially pertinent on the 1932 election are cited here. Among these, see Raymond Moley, *After Seven Years* (New York, 1939), in which the first five chapters discuss the activities of an important member of the original brain trust during the events of 1932-33. The story of the preconvention activities and strategy of F.D.R.'s campaign manager is told by the man himself in James A. Farley, *Behind the Ballots: The Personal History of a Politician* (New York, 1948). Almost of equal importance is the story told by Roosevelt's floor leader at Chicago, Arthur F. Mullen, *Western Democrat* (New York, 1940). Edward J. Flynn, *You're the Boss* (New York, 1947) is the anecdotal reminiscences of the New York Bronx boss. See also the pertinent chapters of Daniel C.

Roper, *Fifty Years of Public Life* (Durham, N.C., 1941) on McAdoo's activities. On Garner and the election of 1932, the best account is in Bascom N. Timmons, *Garner of Texas: A Personal History* (New York, 1948).

The transition of government from Hoover to Roosevelt and its accompanying problems during the critical months of the interregnum are expertly discussed in the Brookings Institution study by Laurin L. Henry, *Presidential Transitions* (Washington, D.C., 1960), which includes accounts of the Taft-Wilson, Wilson-Harding, and Truman-Eisenhower changeovers as well as the one of 1932–33.

Index

Abrams v. United States, 286
absentee ownership, 32, 362
accidents, industrial, 31, 32
Adams, Henry, 105
Adams, Samuel Hopkins, 111
Adamson Act (1916), 220
Addams, Jane, 82, 116, 244, 268
Addyston Pipe Company, 61
Adkins v. Children's Hospital, 124
advertising, 95, 97, 111, 144, 363, 407, 408
  fraudulent, 365
  growth of, 364
  radio, 383
agrarian reform, 58–60
agricultural machinery, 22, 363
Agricultural Marketing Act (1929), 467, 484, 493
agriculture
  conflict of interest between business and, 50, 58, 59
  Coolidge administration and, 342–43, 351–52
  development of, 36–37
  during 1920's, 389–91
  farm income, 390
  farm legislation during 1920's, 333–34, 342, 351–52
  Harding administration and, 333–34
  Hoover administration and, 466–68
  in late 1700's, 3–4

agriculture (*cont.*)
  mechanization of, 37, 389
  in Middle West, 14–15
  in 1900, 4, 6
  in Northeast, 16
  Pacific Coast, 20, 21
  problems of, 36–42
  Rocky Mountain region, 19
  southern, 17, 18, 40–41, 87
  western, 141
  World War I and, 281–82
Agriculture Department, U. S., 37, 144, 334, 368, 373
  forestry division, 145
Aguinaldo, Emilio, 69–70, 72
Air Mail acts, 377
Alabama, political reform in, 121
Alabama Midland case, 61
Alaska
  boundary dispute with Canada, 162
  purchase of, 4, 73
  statehood, 74
  territorial status, 74, 186
Albert, Heinrich, 244
Aldrich, Nelson W., 57, 136, 151, 175, 176, 177, 178, 181, 185
  National Monetary Commission chairman, 211
Aldrich, Thomas Bailey, 103
Aldrich, Winthrop W., quoted, 471

Aldrich-Vreeland Act (1908), 149, 211
Algeciras Convention, 164
Algonquin (American ship), 268
Allen, Frederick Lewis, 148
Alsace-Lorraine, 303
amendments (U. S. Constitution)
  Fifth, 26
  Fourteenth, 26, 365
  Sixteenth, 186, 210
  Seventeenth, 124, 187
  Eighteenth, 90, 125-26, 298, 409, 415, 416,
    459, 461, 493, 495-96
  Nineteenth, 126-27
American, The, 111
American Bar Association, 219
American Can Company, 364
American Defence Society, 261
American Economic Association, 99
American Federation of Labor (AFL), 33-
  36, 139, 173, 283, 284, 348, 385, 386
American Legion, 261
American Mercury, 417
American Petroleum Institute, 366
American Protective Association, 91
American Protective League, 286
American Railway Union, 61
American Rights Committee, 261
American Sugar Refining Company, 185
American Telephone and Telegraph Com-
  pany, 360, 361, 375, 383, 395
American Tobacco Company, 138
American Truth Society, 244
Ancona (Italian ship), 256
Anderson, Maxwell, 425
Anderson, Sherwood, 423
Anderson, W. H., 126
Anglo-American relations, 68, 162
  World War I and, 249-53, 258, 259-60
Anthony, Susan B., 127
anti-Catholicism, 90-91
Anti-Saloon League, 90, 125, 126, 416
antitrust laws, 25, 27, 61, 221, 337, 365
  see also Clayton Antitrust Act; Sher-
  man Antitrust Act
Apperson brothers, 373
Arabic (British ship), 256
arbitration
  of labor disputes, 140-41, 284
  settlement of international disputes by,
    164, 165, 450
architecture, 105, 426

area, of United States, 11
  in 1789, 3
  in 1900, 4
Arena, The, 110
Arizona, admission to the Union, 186
Armstrong Committee, 122
Army, U. S.
  reforms, 70
  World War I and, 279, 287, 289, 290-91
Army Appropriation Act (1916), 263
art
  "Ashcan School" of, 104, 425
  trends in, 102-5, 418-27
Asia
  immigrants from, 86, 160, 344
  U. S. investments in, 396
  see also Far East; names of countries
assembly line, 375, 385
Associated Press, 95
Association for the Protection of Amer-
  ican Rights in Mexico, 226
Atlantic, The, 97, 201
Austria, World War I and, 239
automobile industry, 13, 366, 373-76, 385,
  386
aviation
  development of, 376-77
  World War I and, 279

Babbitt, Irving, 421
Babbitt (Lewis), 421, 423
Baer, George F., 140
Bailey, Thomas A., quoted, 310
Bailey v. Drexel Furniture Company,
  220 n.
Baker, George F., 23
Baker, Newton D., 117, 262, 274, 283, 289,
  495
Baker, O. E., 390
Baker, Ray Stannard, 111
Balfour, Arthur, 437
Ballinger, Richard A., 178-79
Ballinger-Pinchot controversy, 178-79
Baltimore, Maryland, 3 n., 15
Bank of Massachusetts, 3 n.
Bank of New York, 3 n.
Bank of the United States, 480
Bankers Trust Company, 473
banks
  Aldrich-Vreeland Act and, 149, 211
  failures, 480, 481

banks (*cont.*)
  Federal Land, 219, 489
  Federal Reserve, 212–14, 473
  Federal Reserve Act, 150
  Glass-Steagall Act and, 488–89
  in 1900, 4
  panic of 1907 and, 146–50
  in 1789, 3
  see also Federal Reserve System
Barry, Philip, 425
Baruch, Bernard M., 278
baseball, 94
basketball, 94
Battle Cry of Peace, The (film), 261
Beal, Fred, 388
Beard, Charles A., 114, 417
Behrman, S. N., 425
Belgium, World War I and, 240, 260
Bellamy, Edward, 100
Bellows, George, 425
Belmont, August, 194
Benson, Allen L., 266
Benton, Thomas, 425
Berger, Victor, 286
Berle, A. A., Jr., 362
Berlin, Irving, 427
Bery, Carl, 373
Beveridge, Albert J., 151, 176, 184, 192
Bible, 89, 414
Bidlack-Mallarino Treaty, 155
big business
  government regulation of, 60–62
  opposition to, 110, 114, 120
  Republican era and, 331
  Theodore Roosevelt and, 136–39, 142
  see also industry
Billings, Warren K., 264
Bingham, Alfred, 367
Birmingham, Alabama, 12
Birth of a Nation, 420
"Black Thursday," 473
Blaine, James G., 68, 133
Blair, John, 370
Bland-Allison Act (1878), 59
Bliss, Tasker H., 299
blue laws, 90
Bok, Edward, 96
bolshevism, 312
bonds, war, 277
Bonus Expeditionary Force (BEF), 490, 491

Boone, Joel T., 335
bootlegging, 410
Borah, William E., 306, 307, 317, 346, 436, 442, 466, 468
bosses, political, 49, 51, 52, 53, 55, 56, 117–18, 123, 133–34
Boston, Massachusetts, 3 n., 15, 82
  censorship in, 413
  police strike, 312–13
  progressive movement in, 116
Boston and Maine Railroad, 121
Boulder (Hoover) Dam, 484
Bourne, Randolph, 420
Boxers, 74–75
boycotts, 217
Boy-Ed, Karl, 244
Brandegee Reservation to Four Power Treaty, 443
Brandeis, Louis D., 102, 115, 122, 195, 209, 212, 215, 216, 365, 417
  appointment to Supreme Court, 219
Brest-Litovsk, Treaty of, 304
Briand, Aristide, 436
Bridge, The (Crane), 422
Bristow, Joseph L., 176
British Guiana, boundary dispute with Venezuela, 68
Brookhart, Smith W., 338
Brookings Institution, 372
Brooks, Van Wyck, 417, 420
Brophy, John, 388
Browder, Earl, 417
Brown, Robert E., 114 n.
Brown, Walter F., 377
Bryan, Charles W., 347
Bryan, William Jennings, 42, 59, 60, 68, 70, 138, 142, 184, 204
  election of 1908 and, 173–74
  election of 1912 and, 193, 194
  election of 1920 and, 317
  Florida land boom and, 407
  Friends of Peace supported by, 244
  fundamentalism and, 415
  peace negotiations, 165
  picture of, 250
  resigns as Secretary of State, 256
  Scopes trial and, 413
  Secretary of State, 155, 189, 207, 212, 228, 247, 251, 255
Bryce, James, 243

Bucks' Stove and Range Company case (1907), 36
Budget, Bureau of the, 332
budget, national, 187
Budget and Accounting Act (1921), 332
Buffalo, New York, 14
Bull Moose movement, 192–93
Bullard, Robert Lee, 291
Bunau-Varilla, Philippe, 154–55
Burchfield, Charles, 426
Burleson, Albert S., 208, 286
Burlington Railroad, 121
Burns, William J., 118
business
    conflict of interest between agriculture and, 50, 58, 59
    see also big business; industry
business cycle, 100
Butler, Edward R., 117
Butler, Nicholas Murray, 317, 329, 436, 459
Butler, William M., 346

Cabell, James Branch, 424
cabinet (see names of Presidents)
Caldwell and Company, 480
California, 20
    political reform in, 121
    progressive movement in, 116
    racial discrimination in, 228
Calles, Plutarco Elias, 452, 453
Cameron, Simon, 54
Canada
    boundary dispute with Alaska, 162
    negotiation of reciprocity agreement with, 184–85
    U. S. investments in, 395
Cannon, Joseph G., 56, 136, 175, 180, 194
Cantos (Pound), 422
capitalism, 98, 112, 113, 135, 312, 368, 372, 465
    opposition to, 417
    welfare, 386
Capone, Alphonse, 410, 411
Capper, Arthur, 333
Capper-Volstead Cooperative Marketing Act (1922), 334
Cárdenas, Lázaro, 453
Caribbean area
    U. S. intervention in the, 156–59, 450–51
    Wilson and, 222–23

Carnegie, Andrew, 22, 23, 29, 113, 151
Caroline Islands, 228
Carranza, Venustiano, 224, 225–26, 452
Castle, William R., 394
Cather, Willa, 423
Catholic Church (see Roman Catholic Church)
Catt, Carrie Chapman, 127
cattle, 19
caveat emptor, principle of, 144
Cement Manufacturers' Protective Association, 365
Central America, 188
centralization of government, trend toward, 11
Chaffin, Eugene W., 196
Chamberlain, George E., 274
Charleston, South Carolina, 3 n.
Chase National Bank, 395, 473
chemical industry, 377–78
Chiang Kai-shek, 444
Chicago, Illinois, 13, 14, 82
    political corruption in, 119, 409
Chicago, Burlington and Quincy Railroad, 137
Chicago Exposition (1893), 105
child labor, 18, 31, 32, 63, 125, 220
Children's Bureau, 187
China
    Japanese imperialism and, 159, 228, 444–45
    Open Door policy in, 74–76, 159, 160, 161, 227, 228, 442, 443, 445
    spheres of influence in, 74
    Versailles Treaty and, 302
Chinese immigrants, 86
Christianity and the Social Crisis (Rauschenbusch), 90
Christiansen, Parley P., 316
churches, 414
    architecture of, 105, 426
    public opinion and, 89–91
Churchill, Winston, 103, 104, 112
Cincinnati, Ohio, 14
cities
    growth of, 4, 7–8, 82
    in 1789, 3
city government (see government, local)
city manager plan, 119
Civil Aeronautics Act (1938), 377
Civil War, 4, 7, 14, 17, 50

Civilization in the United States, 417
Clapp, Moses, 176
Clark, Champ, 184, 193, 194
Clark, J. Reuben, 450
Clarke, Edward Y., 412
class inequalities, 30
Clayton Antitrust Act, 215, 216–17, 365
Clayton-Bulwer Treaty, 152
Clemenceau, Georges, 299, 300, 305
Cleveland, Grover, 49, 55, 59, 65, 142, 145, 196
  election of 1892, 133
  Pullman strike and, 140
Cleveland, Ohio, 82
  municipal reform in, 117
closed shop, 34, 35, 386
clothing industry, 16
coal, 12, 74, 282, 384
Cobb, Frank, 268
Colby, Everett, 121
collective bargaining, 33, 34, 35, 284
collective security, 446
colleges
  growth of, 93, 94
  Negro, 87
  sports and, 94
Collier, Robert J., 111
Collier's, 111, 179
Colombia, 153–56
colonial policy, U. S., 70–74
Columbia Broadcasting System, 383
Columbus, New Mexico, 226
combinations, industrial, 27–28, 39, 62, 137, 138
comic strips, 95
Commerce and Labor Department, U. S., 141
Commerce Department, U. S., 384, 394, 395, 397
  Bureau of Foreign and Domestic Commerce, 394
commission plan of city government, 119
Committee of Forty-eight, 316
Committee on Public Information, 284, 293
Commons, John Rogers, 100
Commonwealth and Southern Corporation, 360, 379
communication
  development of, 7, 11, 37
  in late 1700's, 3

communism, 482–83
  labor movement and, 387–89
Communist International, 312, 388, 444
Communist party, 112, 312, 313, 349, 387, 416–17, 464, 483, 492
"community of interest," 24, 27, 138
company unions, 386
competition, 24, 60, 61, 62
  decline of, 27–28
  unrestricted, 98
Conference for Progressive Political Action, 348–49
Congress, U. S.
  Hoover and, 465, 468, 469, 485, 486
  Taft and, 180–84, 186, 187
  Wilson and, 205, 206, 209, 221
Congressional Government: A Study in American Politics (Wilson), 201
Coniston (Churchill), 112
Conkey, Mrs. Elizabeth A., 481
conscription, World War I, 275–76, 277
conservation, 6
  Ballinger-Pinchot controversy over, 178–79
  Theodore Roosevelt and, 145–46
Constitution, federal, 3, 4
  commerce clause in, 26
  corporations protected by, 25
  protection of property rights, 24
  see also amendments
consular service, 65
Continental Trading Company, 336
control, government (*see* government control)
Converse, Paul D., 368
Coolidge, Calvin, 407
  administration of, 338–53
  agriculture and, 342–43, 351–52
  biographical sketch, 339–40
  Boston police strike and, 312–13
  cabinet, 340
  disarmament and, 439
  election of 1924 and, 346, 348
  failure to discourage speculation, 471–72
  fiscal affairs and, 340
  Latin America and, 451
  Mexico and, 452
  nomination for Vice President, 315
  Philippines and, 449
  picture of, 331

Coolidge, Calvin (*cont.*)
  popularity of, 353
  public power and, 350–51
  re-election as President (1924), 349
  second term, 458
  shipping and, 352–53
  succeeds Harding, 338–39
  Teapot Dome scandal settled by, 336
  veterans bonus bill vetoed by, 342
  World Court supported by, 435
cooperatives, 42, 220, 334, 467
consumer, 368
copper, 19, 74
corn belt, 14
corporations, 21–31
  decline of competition caused by growth of, 27–28
  development and growth of, 115, 360–63
  financial abuses, 28–29
  government and, 24–27
  ownership, 361
  pension plans, 386
  powers of, 54, 56
  Theodore Roosevelt and, 136–39
Corporations, Bureau of, 141, 216
corruption
  attack on, during progressive era, 115 ff.
  in federal government, 55, 335–38
  Harding administration and, 335–38
  labor unions and, 386
  in local government, 52–53, 54
  muckrakers and, 110–12
Cortelyou, George, 148
Cosmopolitan, The, 111
cotton, 40, 467
cotton belt, 17, 18, 41
Cotton Stabilization Corporation, 467
Coughlin, Father Charles E., 483
Council of National Defense, 263, 274, 278, 283
courts, 101–2
Couzens, James, 375
cowboys, 19
Cox, James M., 310, 315–16
Cramer, Charles F., 335
Crane, Hart, 422
Crane, Stephen, 103
Crawford, F. Marion, 103
credit, farm, 39
Creel, George, 284–85, 292, 293

crime, 82, 85, 111, 409–11
Crissinger, Daniel R., 331
Croly, Herbert, 114, 151, 194
Cromwell, Thomas Nelson, 154–55
Crowder, Enoch H., 223, 275
Croxton, Fred C., 484
Cuba
  autonomy, 71
  Platt Amendment and, 71
  Spanish-American War and, 68–70
  U. S. colonial policy and, 70–71
  U. S. intervention in (1906), 159; (1917), 223
Cummings, E. E., 422
Cummins, Albert B., 121, 176, 191, 192
Cunningham syndicate, 178
currency, 58, 59
Curry, John Steuart, 425
Curtis, Charles, 459, 493
Curtiss-Wright, 377
Cushing (American ship), 254
Cutting, Bronson, 498
Czechoslovakia, 303
Czolgosz, Leon, 131, 134

Daimler brothers, 373
dairy centers, 14
Danbury Hatters' case (1908), 36
dance, 425
Daniels, Josephus C., 208, 261
Darrow, Clarence, 413
Darwin, Charles, 24, 89, 98
Daugherty, Harry M., 315, 328, 331, 337–38, 415
Davidson, John W., 219
Davis, Dwight F., 449
Davis, James J., 331
Davis, Jefferson, 121
Davis, John W., 347–49
Dawes, Charles G., 289, 332, 434, 459, 487, 488
  nomination for Vice President, 346
Dawes, Henry G., 142
Dawes Plan, 435
Dayton, Ohio, commission plan in, 119
Debs, Eugene, 100, 142, 174, 196, 266, 286, 316, 317, 416, 499
debt, growth of, 370
debt, national, 57
  reduction of, 331, 341

Declaration of London (1909), 249, 254
De Forest, Lee, 383
DeLesseps, Ferdinand, 153–54
democracy, 5, 14, 57, 109, 113, 114, 135, 151, 406, 412, 417
education and, 92
Democratic party
primary system originated by, 123
in the South, 63–64
see also elections; political parties
Denby, Edwin, 331, 335
Depew, Chauncey, 56
depression of 1930's (see Great Depression)
Des Moines, Iowa, commission plan in, 119
Detroit, Michigan, 13, 82
Dewey, George, 69
Dewey, John, 92, 101, 417
Díaz, Adolfo, 451
Díaz, Porfirio, 223–24
Dill, James B., 26
Dillinger, John, 411
Dingley Act (1897), 175, 177
diplomatic service, 65
direct primary, 123
disarmament, 436–40
discrimination, 88
racial, in California, 228
Doane, Robert R., 368
Dodge brothers, 375
Doheny, Edward L., 226, 335–36, 347, 366
dollar-a-year men, 274, 278, 279
"dollar diplomacy," 151, 188, 189, 227
Dolliver, Jonathan P., 176, 177, 179
Dominican Republic, 222
U. S. intervention in, 158–59, 451
Dos Passos, John, 424
draft, World War I, 274, 275–76, 277
Drago, Luis, 157
Dreiser, Theodore, 103–4, 423
Dubinsky, David, 388
DuBois, W. E. Burghardt, 88
Dumba, Constantin, 244
Duncan, Isadora, 425
Du Pont family, 138, 246, 360, 362, 374, 377–78
Durant, William C., 374
Duryea, Charles, 373
Dyer Act, 411

Eakins, Thomas, 103
Eastman, George, 380
economic activity, changes in character of, 366–72
economic development, 25, 29, 358–405, 411
Economic Interpretation of the Constitution (Beard), 114
economic planning, 372
economic system
in early 1900's, 5, 6, 7
in late 1700's, 5
Edison, Thomas A., 380, 381
Edison Company, 380
education
compulsory, 91
democracy and, 92
free public, 91–92
progressive, 92–93
public opinion and, 91–94
reform in, 63, 65, 93
see also colleges; teachers; universities
Eighteenth Amendment, 90, 125–26, 298, 409, 415, 416, 459, 461, 493, 495–96
repeal of, 416
Einstein, Albert, 345
Eisenhower, Dwight D., ejection of bonus marchers from Washington, D.C., 491
elections
1892, 59, 64, 133
1896, 59–60, 64
1900, 70
1904, 142
1908, 172–74
1912, 100, 189–96
1916, 264–66
1920, 100, 307, 310, 314–17, 383
1924, 120, 346–49
1928, 91, 378, 458–64
1932, 378, 492–500
1960, 91
Electric Bond and Share Corporation, 360, 379
Eliot, Charles W., 93, 94, 260
Eliot, T. S., 421, 422
Elkins Act (1903), 141
Ellis Island, 84
Ely, Richard T., 99
Emergency Fleet Corporation, 280–81
Emergency Peace Conference (1915), 244
Emergency Quota Act (1921), 343

Emergency Tariff Act (1921), 333
England (see Great Britain)
entrepreneurs, 22–24, 25, 30, 95, 96, 361, 362, 375
Erie Canal, 15
Erie Railroad, 54
Esch-Cummins Transportation Act, 324, 326
Espionage Act (1917), 286
Europe
    U. S. foreign policy and, 161–65
    U. S. investments in, 395
    see also names of countries
Everybody's (magazine), 111
evolution, theory of, 98, 99
excess profits tax, 277, 331
exports, 393-94

factories, 5, 6, 13, 367
    sabotage in, 244
Falaba (British passenger ship), 254
Fall, Albert B., 226, 331, 335–36
Fall of a Nation, The (film), 261
Far East
    U. S. policy in, 159–61, 189, 227–29, 442–48
    see also Asia; names of countries
Farley, James A., 494, 496, 497
farm credit, 39
Farmer-Labor party, 316, 492
Farmers' Union, 215
farming (see agriculture)
fascism, 482, 483
Fatherland, The (newspaper), 243
Faulkner, William, 424
Federal Bureau of Investigation, 411
Federal Council of Churches, 89, 90
Federal Farm Board, 467, 468, 484
Federal Farm Loan Act (1916), 219
federal government (see government, federal)
Federal Home Loan Bank Act, 489
Federal Land banks, 219, 489
Federal Power Commission, 326
Federal Radio Commission, 384
Federal Reserve Act (1913), 150, 212, 214, 215
Federal Reserve Banks, 212–14, 473
Federal Reserve Board, 212–14, 217, 471, 472, 473

Federal Reserve System, 210–14, 331, 471, 472, 473, 484, 488
Federal Trade Commission, 216, 217, 361, 365, 382
Federal Trade Commission Act (1914), 216
Fess, Simeon, 485
Fifth Amendment, 26
financiers, 23, 29, 122, 155, 188, 326, 366, 379, 472, 480, 500
Finlay, Carlos, 71
First National Bank of New York, 23
First World War (see World War I)
Fitch, Clyde, 424
Fitzgerald, F. Scott, 423
Fiume, 302
Florida, land boom in, 407
Flower, Benjamin O., 110
Foch, Ferdinand, 290, 291, 293
Folk, Joseph W., 117, 121, 193
food production, during World War I, 281–82
football, 94, 408
Forbes, Charles R., 331, 335, 338
Ford, Edsel, 375
Ford, Henry, 244, 245, 350, 362, 373, 375–76
Ford Motor Company, 360, 374, 375–76, 395, 481
Fordney-McCumber Tariff, 333, 469
foreign investments (see investments, foreign)
foreign policy
    aggressive, 67
    during 1920's, 432–57
    Harding and, 432
    imperialist, 70
    intervention in the Caribbean, 156–59
    isolationist, 6, 7, 14, 65, 432–33
    Open Door (China), 74–76, 159, 160, 161, 227, 228, 442
    pacifistic, 65
    Panama Canal and, 152–56
    State Department and, 433
    Taft administration and, 151, 152, 187–89
    Theodore Roosevelt and, 150–65
    Wilson and, 151, 152
foreign trade
    during 1920's, 392–98
    increase in, 67

foreign trade (*cont.*)
  international rivalries and, 397–98
  in late 1700's, 3
  in 1900, 4
  World War I and, 282–83
Forest Reserve Act (1891), 145
Forest Service, 145, 179
Forestry, Bureau of, 145
forests, 145
Forum, The, 97
Foster, Stephen, 427
Foster, William Z., 312, 387, 417, 464, 499
Four Power Treaty (1921), 438–39, 442–43
Fourteen Points, Wilson's, 292–93, 297, 298, 302, 305
Fourteenth Amendment, 26, 365
Fox, William, 382
France
  Morocco and, 163–64
  World War I and, 240
Franco-Prussian War (1870–71), 238
Frankfurter, Felix, 284
Franz Ferdinand, 239
freedom, 5, 109
freight rates, 30, 39, 60, 61, 121, 141, 142, 144
Frenzied Finance (Lawson), 111
Freud, Sigmund, 421
Frick, Henry, 22, 149, 307
Friends of Peace, 244
Frost, Robert, 421
Fuel Administration, 282
functionalism, in architecture, 105, 426
fundamentalists, 89–90, 414
Fur Workers' Union, 388

Galbraith, John Kenneth, quoted, 470
Galveston, Texas, commission plan instituted at, 119
gangsterism, 85, 410–11
Garfield, Harry A., 282
Garfield, James R., 145, 178
Garner, John Nance, 494, 495, 496, 497
Garrison, Lindley M., 208, 261, 262
Gary, Elbert H., 112, 149, 312
Gary, Indiana, 13
General Electric Company, 185, 360, 379, 395
General Federation of Women's Clubs, 116

General Film Company, 381
General Land Office, 145, 178
General Motors Corporation, 360, 374–75, 377, 395
Gentlemen's Agreement (1907), 86, 160
George, Henry, 100, 117
Georgia, political reform in, 121
Georgia Power Company, 362
Germany
  Morocco and, 163–64
  reparations (World War I), 303, 305, 434, 435, 441
  Versailles Treaty and, 302, 303, 306
  World War I and, 237 ff.
Gershwin, George, 427
ghost towns, 19
Gifford, Walter S., 484
Gilbert, Cass, 426
Gilbert, Prentiss, 446
Gilbert, S. Parker, 435
Gilder, Richard Watson, 103
Gilman, Daniel Coit, 93–94
Glasgow, Ellen, 104
Glass, Carter, 64, 211, 212, 436
Glass-Owen bill (*see* Federal Reserve Act)
Glass-Steagall Act, 488
Glavis, Louis R., 178–79
Glynn, Martin, 265
Gobineau, Arthur de, 98
Goethals, George W., 156, 279
gold, 19, 20, 59, 74
gold standard, 142
Gold Standard Act (1900), 60
Goldman, Eric F., quoted, 195
Goldwyn, Samuel, 381
Gompers, Samuel, 33, 34, 35, 173, 215, 217, 283, 313, 385
Goodman, Hannibal, 380
Gore, Thomas P., 258
Gorgas, William C., 71, 156
Gould, Jay, 54
government, federal, 55–58
  corporations and the, 24–27
  monopoly practices and the, 364–66
  trend toward centralization, 11
government, local, 51–53, 82
  new ideas in, 119
  progressive movement and, 115–19
  reform, 115–19

government, state, 26, 53–55
new ideas in, 123–25
reform, 119–25
government control, 5, 6, 26
of railroads, 60
government ownership, 26, 58
government regulation
of big business, 60–62
of insurance companies, 122–23
of power industry, 326
of railroads, 58, 63
Graham, Martha, 425
Grain Corporation, 281, 467
Grain Futures Trading Act, 334
"grandfather clause," 64
Grange Laws, invalidation of, 60
Granges, 58
Graves, William S., 304
Great Britain
boundary dispute between Venezuela
and British Guiana, 68
Clayton-Bulwer Treaty, 152
Open Door policy in China proposed
by, 74
Panama Tolls Act denounced by, 156
Spanish-American War and, 162
U. S. relations with, 68, 162, 249–53,
258, 259–60
World War I and, 240, 242–43, 249–53
Great Depression, 359, 396–97, 470–84, 493
human effects of, 479–82
onset of, 470–74
political repercussions, 482–84
severity of, reasons for, 476–79
statistics, 474–76
Great Northern Railway, 23, 137
Great Train Robbery, The (film), 381
Green, William, 385
Gregory, Thomas W., 208
Grey, Sir Edward, 251, 252, 257, 259
Griffith, David Wark, 381, 420, 427
Gronna, Asle J., 269
Grundy, Joseph R., 469
Guam, acquisition of, 70, 73
Guaranty Trust Company, 248, 473–74
Gulflight (tanker), 254
Gummere, Samuel R., 163

Hague, Frank, 496
Hague machine, 119
Hague Tribunal, 158, 162

Haig, Douglas, 291
Haiti, 222, 451
Hamilton, Alexander, 50
Hammer v. Dagenhart, 125, 220 n.
Hampton's (magazine), 111
Hanna, Mark, 57, 59, 60, 134, 136, 139,
142, 154
Hapgood, Norman, 111
Harbord, J. G., 289
Harding, Warren G., 182
administration, 329–38
appointments by, 329–31
biographical sketch, 327–29
cabinet, 329–31
corruption during administration of,
335–38
death of, 335
elected President, 317
election of 1920 and, 310, 315, 317
foreign policy, 432
inaugural address, 432
Philippines and, 449
picture of, 327
strikes and, 312
World Court supported by, 435
Harmon, Judson, 184, 193
Harper's, 97, 201, 481
Harriman, Edward H., 122, 137, 142
Harrison, Benjamin, 133, 145
Harrison, Francis Burton, 73
Hartley, Marsden, 426
Harvard University, 93, 132
Harvey, George, 204, 308
Hatch Act (1887), 37
Hawaii
annexation, 4, 74
statehood, 74
territorial rights, 74
Hawes-Cutting Act (1933), 449
Hawley-Smoot tariff, 465, 468–69, 478
Hay, John, 67, 136, 152, 154, 159, 160, 163,
189
Open Door policy in China, 74–75
Hay-Bunau-Varilla Treaty, 155
Hay-Herran Convention, 154
Hay-Pauncefote Treaty, 152–53, 156, 162
Hayes, Max, 316
Haynes, Elward, 373
Hays, Will H., 330–31, 336
Haywood, William D. ("Big Bill"), 283,
387

Hearst, William Randolph, 67, 69, 95, 174, 184, 248, 452, 494, 496, 497
Hemingway, Ernest, 423
Hendricks, Red, 388
Heney, Francis J., 118
Henri, Robert, 104
Henry Street Settlement, 82, 116
Hepburn Act (1906), 143
Hergesheimer, Joseph, 424
Herrick, Robert, 112
Hesperia (British ship), 256
Hewitt, Abram S., 133
Hicks, John D., quoted, 464
Hill, James J., 22, 23, 137
History of the Great American Fortunes (Myers), 114
History of the Standard Oil Company (Tarbell), 110
Hitchcock, Gilbert M., 306
Hitchman v. Mitchell, 387
Hitler, Adolf, 441
Hofstadter, Richard, 460
Hogg, James Stephen, 122
holding companies, 27, 29, 121, 137, 362, 365, 371, 377, 379
Holmes, Oliver Wendell, 102, 138, 286, 365
Homer, Winslow, 103
Homestead Act (1862), 37
homestead regulations, 27
Honduras, 188
Hood, Raymond, 426
Hoover, Herbert, 416
  administration, 484–92
  biographical sketch, 462–63, 464–65
  Congress and, 465, 468, 469, 485, 486
  elected President, 464
  election of 1920 and, 314, 317
  election of 1928 and, 458, 462–64
  election of 1932 and, 493–99
  Far East policy, 446, 447
  farm crisis and, 466–68
  food controller during World War I, 281, 464
  foreign trade and, 397
  Latin America and, 451
  Latin American goodwill tour, 398, 453
  Memoirs, 463
  pictures of, 330, 499
  relations with the press, 465
  Secretary of Commerce, 330, 343, 364, 394, 458, 467

Hoover, Herbert (*cont.*)
  stock market crash and, 470–84
  tariff and, 465, 468–69
  unpopularity of, 465, 491
  veterans' bonus and, 489–92
Hoover, J. Edgar, 411
Hoovervilles, 480, 490, 491
Hopper, Edward, 426
House, Edward M., 206, 207, 209, 251, 252, 257, 258–59, 299
House-Grey memorandum, 259
House of Morgan, 24, 190, 245, 247, 248, 360, 473
House of Representatives, U. S., 55–56
housing, discrimination in, 88
Houston, David F., 208, 267
Howard, Sidney, 425
Howe, Frederick C., 117
Howe, Louis McHenry, 494
Howells, William Dean, 103, 112
Huerta, Victoriano, 224–25
Hughes, Charles Evans, 122–23, 172, 182, 191, 280, 365, 433, 434, 442
  election of 1916 and, 265
  election of 1920 and, 317
  Pan-American Congress and, 450
  picture of, 330
  Secretary of State, 330, 344
  Washington Conference delegate, 437
Hull, Cordell, 210
Hull House, 82, 116
humanism, 421
Hurley, Edward M., 280
Hurley, Patrick J., 491

Imagist Anthology, 420
immigrants (*see* immigration)
immigration, 83–86
  Americanization process and, 84–85
  during nineteenth century, 7, 16, 22, 33, 37, 83
  Japanese, 86, 160, 344
  opposition to, 264
  restriction of, 83, 99, 343–46
Immigration Act (1907), 160
Immigration Quota Act (1924), 343–44, 413
imperialism
  advocates of, 99
  Japanese, 159, 228, 442, 444–45
  opposition to, 67, 70

imperialism (*cont.*)
Russian, 159
Theodore Roosevelt and, 136, 151–52, 161
Wilson's attitude toward, 221–22
imports, 393–94
In the Arena (Tarkington), 112
income
farm, 390
inequalities of, 369
national, 4, 6, 31, 359, 475
income taxes, 210, 276–77, 331, 340
individualism, 97, 98, 99, 466
Industrial Workers of the World (IWW), 283, 312, 313
industry
after World War I, 311
growth of, 22, 30, 81
in Middle West, 12–14
in Northeast, 16
Pacific Coast, 21
in the South, 18
World War I and, 275, 277–80
see also big business; business; manufacturing; names of industries
inflation, after World War I, 311
initiative, 58, 123, 183, 193
injunctions, 35, 61, 217, 312, 337, 365, 387
instrumentalism (*see* pragmatism)
Insull, Samuel, 360, 362, 379, 481, 493
insurance companies, regulation of, 122–23
intellectual trends, 97–102, 113, 416–27
Interior Department, U. S., 145, 179
interlocking directorates, 24, 27, 56, 365
Intermediate Credit Act (1923), 334
International Harvester Company, 39, 138, 185, 363, 364
International Ladies' Garment Workers Union, 388
International Paper Company, 364
International Workers of the World, 283, 387
interstate commerce, 26
Interstate Commerce Act, 60, 61
Interstate Commerce Commission, 61, 143, 144, 186, 216, 324, 325, 348
inventions, 7, 21, 37, 380
investment trusts, 472
investments, foreign, 392–98
Iowa, political reform in, 121

Irish Rebellion (1916), 260
iron deposits, 12–13, 74
irrigation, 19, 20, 141
Ishii, Kikujiiro, 228
Ishii-Lansing Agreement (1917), 228
isolationism, 6, 7, 14, 65, 161, 308, 432–33
Isthmian Doctrine, 451

James, Henry, 103
James, William, 101, 102
Japan
imperialism, 159, 228, 442, 444–45
plan to purchase land in lower California, 188
Root-Takahira Agreement, 160
Russo-Japanese War, 159
Twenty-one Demands, 228
U. S. relations with, 159–61, 227–29, 398
Versailles Treaty and, 302
World War I and, 228
Japanese immigrants, 86, 160, 344
"jazz age," 408
Jazz Singer, The (film), 382
Jeffers, Robinson, 422
Jefferson, Thomas, 50, 59, 136, 196, 209
Jersey City, New Jersey, Hague machine in, 119
"Jim Crow" laws, 87
Johns Hopkins University, 93, 201
Johnson, Hiram W., 118, 121, 192, 306, 307, 314, 317, 442, 498
election of 1924 and, 346
Fordney-McCumber Tariff supported by, 333
Johnson, Hugh S., 275
Johnson, John A., 121
Johnson, Tom, 117
Johnson Debt Default Act (1934), 441
Johnston, Mary, 103
Jones, "Golden Rule," 118
Jones Act (1916), 73, 449
Jones Merchant Marine Act (1920), 325, 352
Jones-White Merchant Marine Act (1928), 352
Jordan, David Starr, 244
Joyce, James, 421
Jungle, The (Sinclair), 112, 144
Junior American Guard, 261
jurisprudence, 101–2

Justice Department, U. S.
  enforcement of Espionage and Sedition acts during World War I, 286
  IWW leaders arrested by, 283
  prohibition and, 415
  repression of civil liberties, 298
  scandals in, during Harding administration, 337–38
  trusts and the, 138
Jutland, battle of, 263

Kansas City, Missouri, 14
  Pendergast machine in, 119
Kato, Tomosaburo, 437
Kaufman, George S., 425
Keating-Owen Act (1916), 125, 220
Kellogg, Frank B., 433, 436, 442, 452
Kellogg-Briand Pact, 436, 444, 445, 448
Kelly, George, 425
Kennedy, John F., 91
Kenyon, William S., 333
Kerensky, Alexander, 444
Kern, Jerome, 427
Kern, John Worth, 173
Kipling, Rudyard, 67
Kitty Hawk, North Carolina, 376
Knickerbocker Trust Company, 146, 148
Knight case (1895), 62
Knox, Philander C., 137, 188, 189
Korea, Japanese control of, 159
Kreuger, Ivar, 481, 493
Kreuger and Toll, 481
Krock, Arthur, quoted, 500
Ku Klux Klan, 91, 346, 347, 412–13
Kuhn, Loeb & Company, 242, 473
Kuomintang, 444

labor
  after World War I, 312
  child, 18, 31, 32, 63, 125, 220
  Communists and, 387–89
  composition of, change in, 367–68
  convict, 63
  disputes, arbitration of, 140–41, 284
  division of, 22, 375
  hours of, 31, 32, 35, 90, 385
  immigrant, 83
  legislation, 124
  "Magna Carta" of, 217
  migrant, 14, 20
  mobility of, 372

labor (cont.)
  Negro, 88
  in 1900, 4
  women and, 31, 32, 126–27
  working conditions, 13–14, 31–36, 386
  World War I and, 283–84
  yellow-dog contracts and, 387
Labor Department, U. S., 186
labor unions (see trade unions)
Labor's National Peace Council, 244
Laemmle, Carl, 380
La Follette, Philip, 349
La Follette, Robert M., 115, 120–21, 136, 143, 144, 175, 176, 177, 182, 184, 268, 269, 336, 498
  death of, 349
  election of 1912 and, 190, 191, 192
  election of 1924 and, 346
  presidential candidate (1924), 348–49
La Follette, Robert M., Jr., 349
La Follette Seamen's Act (1915), 218
La Guardia, Fiorello, 323, 488
laissez faire, doctrine of, 5, 24, 25, 26, 27, 60, 82, 91, 97, 98, 99, 175, 214, 366, 478
Lamont, Thomas W., 248, 473–74
Landis, Kenesaw Mountain, 141, 283
Lane, Franklin K., 208, 269
Lansing, Robert, 226, 246–47, 248, 251, 252, 254, 255, 256, 257, 258, 259, 299
  picture of, 250
Lasker, Albert D., 325
Lasky, Jesse, 381
Latin America, 67, 68, 152, 450–53
  attitude toward U. S. intervention in the Caribbean, 156–59
  Taft administration and, 187–88
  U. S. investments in, 395–96
  Wilson and, 222
  see also names of countries
Lawson, Thomas W., 111
lead, 19
League of Nations, 292, 297–302, 305–11, 316–17, 347, 432
  anti-League propaganda, 307–8
  controversy over, in U. S., 306–7
  Covenant of, 300–302, 306–9
  Far East crisis and, 445–48
League to Enforce Peace, 298, 308, 309
Lenin, Nicolai, 304
Lenoir, Jean, 373
Lenroot, Irwin, 315

Lever Act (1917), 281
Levinson, Salmon O., 436
Lewis, John L., 349, 388
Lewis, Sinclair, 421, 423
Liberty party, 492
Liggett, Hunter, 291
Lind, John, 224
Lindbergh, Charles A., 377, 409
Lindsay, Ben, 111
Lindsay, Vachel, 422
Link, Arthur S., 326
    quoted, 196, 219, 266
Lippmann, Walter, 114, 497
literature, trends in, 102–5, 112, 406, 417,
    418–25
Little, Frank, 283
Lloyd, Henry Demarest, 110
Lloyd George, David, 299, 300, 305
local government (see government, local)
Locarno treaties, 435
Lochner case, 124
Lodge, Henry Cabot, 67, 133, 165, 182,
    188, 261, 298, 346, 442
    League of Nations opposed by, 301,
    308, 309
Lodge Corollary, 188
Loew, Marcus, 380, 382
London, Declaration of (1909), 249, 254
London, Jack, 104, 112
Long, Huey, 483
Longworth, Alice Roosevelt, 329
Looking Backward (Bellamy), 100
Los Angeles, California, 82
Lowden, Frank, 314, 346, 459
Lowell, Amy, 422
Lubell, Samuel, 460
lumbering, 21
Lusitania, 244, 253–56, 260, 261
lynchings, 87–88, 313
Lytton, Lord, 447
Lytton Commission, 447, 448

MacArthur, Douglas, ejection of bonus
    marchers from Washington, D.C.,
    491
MacDonald, Ramsay, 439
machines, political, 49, 50, 51, 52–55, 117,
    119, 120, 121, 125, 134
MacLeish, Archibald, 422
Madero, Francisco, 224

magazines, 96–97, 105, 110–11, 417, 420
    see also names of magazines
Mahan, Alfred T., 67, 162
Main Street (Lewis), 421, 423
Maine (battleship), 69
Man Nobody Knows, The (Barton), 408
Manchukuo, 445
Manchuria, 159, 160, 189, 228, 229, 443,
    444–45, 447, 448
Mangin, Charles, 291
Manila Bay, battle of, 69
Mann, Thomas, 345
Mann White Slave Traffic Act, 187
Mann-Elkins Act (1910), 143, 185
manufacturing
    development of, 4, 6, 11, 12
    in late 1700's, 3
    see also industry
Maple Flooring Manufacturers' Associa-
    tion, 365
Marconi, Guglielmo, 383
Mariana Islands, 228
Marin, John, 426
Marine Corps, U. S.
    in Cuba (1917), 223
    in Dominican Republic, 158, 222, 451
    in Haiti, 222
    in Nicaragua, 188, 451
    Vera Cruz occupied by, 225
Marion (Ohio) Star, 328
Marsh, Peyton C., 289
Marsh, Reginald, 425
Marshall, John, 255–56
Marshall, Thomas R., 193, 194
Marshall Islands, 228
Marx, Karl, 421
mass production, 21, 96, 375
Masses, The, 286
Masters, Edgar Lee, 422
materialism, age of, 406–9
Max, Prince, of Baden, 293
McAdoo, William G., 208, 247, 248, 282,
    315, 494, 496
    presidential candidate (1924), 346–47,
    348
    quoted on Harding, 328
McClure, S. S., 96, 110–11
McClure's Magazine, 96, 111
McCormick, Anne O'Hare, quoted, 479,
    492, 495
McCormick, Cyrus, 22

McCormick, Vance C., 283
McKinley, William, 59, 60, 133, 134, 136, 145
  assassination of, 131
  coal strike and, 139
  colonial policy, 72
  election of 1900, 70
  Panama Canal project and, 153
  Spanish-American War and, 69
McLemore, Jeff, 258
McNary-Haugen bill, 342, 351, 459, 461, 466
McPherson, Aimee Semple, 415
McReynolds, James C., 208
Means, Gardiner C., 362, 477
Meat Inspection Act (1906), 112, 144
mechanization, 21, 37, 389
Mellon, Andrew, 307, 329, 331, 336, 340–41, 343, 471
  picture of, 341
Memoirs of an American Citizen (Herrick), 112
Mencken, H. L., 417
  quoted on Harding, 328–29
Merchant Fleet Corporation, 325, 352
Merchant Marine Act (1928), 352
mergers, 27, 29
  newspaper, 96
Mexico
  revolution in, 223–27
  U.S. relations with, 452–53
  war with, 65
  Zimmermann note, 268, 269
Meyer, Eugene, 486, 487
Middle West
  agriculture, 14–15
  industry, 12–14
  labor conditions in, during late 1800's, 13–14
  politics controlled by, in late 1800's, 13
Middle West Utilities, 360, 362, 379
Midway Island, U. S. occupation of, 4
militarism, Theodore Roosevelt and, 151
Military Training Camp Association, 261
Miller, Thomas W., 338
Mills, Ogden, 486, 487
Milwaukee, Wisconsin, municipal reform in, 118
Milwaukee Leader, The, 286
mineral deposits, 12, 19
minimum wage law, 124

mining, development of, 4, 12, 19
Minneapolis, Minnesota, 14
Minnesota, political reform in, 121
Mississippi, political reform in, 121
Missouri, political reform in, 121
Missouri Pacific Railroad, 121, 480
Mitchell, Charles, 473
Mitchell, John, 139, 140
Mitchell, S. Weir, 103
Mitchell, Wesley Clair, 100
Mitchell, William, 376
modernism, 90
Mongolia, 448
monopolies, 25, 27, 121
  attitude of federal government toward, 364–66
  labor, 386
  natural, 28, 62, 326, 379
  practices of, 363–66
Monroe, Harriet, 420
Monroe Doctrine, 67, 152, 164, 188, 241, 260, 267, 302, 307, 309, 436, 450
  Lodge Corollary, 188
  Roosevelt Corollary, 157, 222, 450, 451
Moody, William Vaughn, 424
Mooney, Thomas J., 264
Moore and Schley (brokerage house), 148
Moose, Loyal Order of, 331
More, Paul Elmer, 421
Moreland Act, 123
Morgan, J. P., 137, 139, 140, 148, 149, 178, 435, 473
  picture of, 147
Mormons, 19
Morocco, 163–64
Morrill Act (1862), 37, 87, 93
Morrow, Dwight, 416, 452–53
motion picture industry, 261, 380–83, 408, 409, 420, 427
Motion Pictures Patents Company, 381
Moulton, Harold G., 371
Mowry, George E., quoted, 150, 187
muckrakers, 96, 110–12, 113, 145, 365
municipal government (see government, local)
Munsey, Frank A., 96, 190
Murray, William, 495
Muscle Shoals, 146, 279, 350
Mutual Broadcasting System, 383

music, American, 426–27
Myers, Gustavus, 114

Nation, The, 97, 334
National Academy of Design, 103
National Americanization Committee, 264
National Association for the Advancement of Colored People (NAACP), 88
National Bank Act (1863–64), 39, 211
National Biscuit Company, 364
National Broadcasting Company, 383
National Bureau of Economic Research, 366
National Cash Register Company, 185
National City Bank, 472, 473
National City Company, 472
National Credit Corporation (NCC), 486
national debt (*see* debt, national)
National Defense Act (1916), 263
National Farmers' Holiday Association, 481–82
National German-American Alliance, 244
national government (*see* government, federal)
national income (*see* income, national)
National Independent party, 174
National Joint Committee on Utilities, 380
National Monetary Commission, 149, 211
National Progressive Republican League, 189, 190
National Reserve Association, 211
National Resources Board, 359
National Security League, 261
National Society for Patriotic Education, 261
National War Labor Board, 284
National War Labor Conference Board, 283
natural resources, 6, 26–27
  conservation of, 145–46
  exploitation of, 22
Naval Appropriation Act (1916), 263
Navy, U. S., 67, 152
  increase in strength of, 263
  Theodore Roosevelt and, 133, 151
  world tour (1907), 160

Navy, U. S. (*cont.*)
  World War I and, 279, 287–89
Nazis, 434
Negroes
  discrimination against, 88
  disfranchisement of, 64
  education of, 87
  labor unions and, 386
  lynching of, 87–88
  number of, in United States, 86
  problem presented by emancipation of, 7, 17, 18
  segregation of, 87
  southern, 86–88
  status of, 5, 7, 86–88
  voting by, 63, 64
Nelson, "Baby Face," 411
Nereide case, 255
neutrality, Wilson's proclamation of (1914), 240
New Deal, 30, 99, 102, 115, 277, 468, 484, 498
  opposition to, 378
New Democracy (Weyl), 114
New England, 16
New Freedom, 195, 209 ff.
New Granada, 155
New Hampshire, political reform in, 121
New Jersey, political reform in, 121
New Mexico, admission to the Union, 186
New Nationalism, 150, 182, 194, 195, 216, 221
New Panama Company, 153–55
New Republic, The, 97, 151
New York, New Haven & Hartford Railroad, 122
New York City, 3 n., 15–16, 82
  city government, 51–52
  political corruption in, 119, 409
New York *Journal,* 95
New York *Journal of Commerce,* 212
New York State, political reform in, 122–23
New York Stock Exchange, 5, 245, 474
New York *Sun,* 65
New York Times, The, 96, 474, 492, 500
New York *World,* 95, 122, 244, 268
Newell, Frederick H., 145
Newfoundland fisheries dispute, 162
Newlands Act (1902), 141

newspapers, 67, 94–96, 411
  growth of, 95
  see also names of papers
Nicaragua, 153–54, 188, 451
Nicholas II, Tsar, 164, 303
Nine Power Treaty (1922), 443, 447
Nineteenth Amendment, 126–27
Nonpartisan League of North Dakota, 219, 316
Norris, Frank, 103, 104
Norris, George W., 175, 180, 269, 498
  public power advocated by, 350
Norris-La Guardia Federal Antiinjunction Act (1932), 387
North American Aviation, 377
Northeast, 15–16, 30
Northern Pacific Railroad, 137
Northern Securities Company, 137, 138
Northwestern Alliance, 58

O'Banion, Dion, 410
Obregón, Alvaro, 227, 452
Ochs, Adolph Simon, 96
Official Bulletin of the United States, 285
oil, 12, 16, 22, 56, 335–36, 363, 366, 384, 398
O'Keefe, Georgia, 426
Old Order Changeth, The (White), 112
Older, Fremont, 118
Olney, Richard, 68, 156
O'Neill, Eugene, 425
Open Door policy, 74–76, 159, 160, 161, 164, 189, 227, 228, 438, 442, 443, 445
open shop, 34, 386
Oregon, 21
Oregon (battleship), 152
Organic acts, 71, 72
Origin of Species, The (Darwin), 24, 89
Orlando, Vittorio, 299, 300
Outlook, The, 182
Overman Act (1918), 275

Pacific Coast, 20–21
  see also West, the
Packers and Stockyards Act (1921), 334
Pact of Paris (see Kellogg-Briand Pact)
Page, Thomas Nelson, 103
Page, Walter Hines, 251, 252, 257, 259, 260
Palmer, A. Mitchell, 313, 315
Panama, 152–56
Panama Canal, 152–56, 162, 223, 225, 451

Panama Tolls Act, 156
Pan American Airways, 377
Pan-American Arbitration Conference (1929), 450
Pan-American Congress, 450
Pan-Americanism, 68
panic, of 1907, 146–50
Pankhurst, Emmeline, 127
paper money, 58
parcel post system, 186
Paris
  Pact of (see Kellogg-Briand Pact)
  Treaty of (1898), 70
Paris peace conference, 299 ff.
Parker, Alton B., 142, 173, 193
Parker, Sir Gilbert, 243
patent medicines, 144
patronage, 49, 55, 208
Patten, Simon Nelson, 99
Paul, Alice, 127
Payne, Henry C., 180
Payne-Aldrich tariff, 177, 182, 184, 210
Peabody Foundation, 87
Peek, George N., 342
Peirce, Charles Sanders, 101
Pelley, William Dudley, 483
Pendergast machine, 119
Pendleton Act (1883), 133
Pennsylvania Railroad, 54, 361
Penrose, Boies, 54
Perdicaris, Ion, 163
Periodical Publishers Association of America, 190
Perkins, George W., 190
Pershing, John J.
  Mexican expedition, 226
  picture of, 288
  World War I and, 289–91
Pétain, Henri Philippe, 288
petroleum (see oil)
Phelan, James D., 118
Philadelphia, Pennsylvania, 3 n., 15, 82
  political corruption in, 119
Philadelphia and Reading, 364
Philippines, 449
  Japanese threat to, 159, 161, 448
  Spanish-American War and, 69–70
  U. S. colonial policy and, 71, 72–73
Phillips, David Graham, 104, 111
philosophy, 101
Picasso, Pablo, 421

picketing, 34, 35, 217
Pinchot, Amos, quoted, 192
Pinchot, Gifford, 145, 178–79, 181, 336
Pittsburgh, Pennsylvania, 12
Pittsburgh *Leader*, 277
Platt, Orville, 71
Platt, Tom, 133, 134
Platt Amendment, 71, 159
Plessy v. Fergusson, 87
Plumb, Glenn E., 324
Poetry (magazine), 420
poetry, American, 103, 104, 421–22
Poland, 303, 304, 305
political bosses (*see* bosses, political)
political machines (*see* machines, political)
political parties
    structure and organization, 49–58
    see also names of parties
politics, international, 6–7
poll tax, 64
Pomerene, Atlee, 336
population
    migratory habits of, 11
    in 1900, 4
    in 1789, 3
Populist (People's) party, 59, 60, 62–64, 142, 174
Porter, E. S., 381
Portsmouth, Treaty of, 159, 160
Post Office Department, U. S., 282, 286
postal savings bank bill, 186
Pound, Ezra, 422
Pound, Roscoe, 102
poverty, in the South, 17–18, 41
power industry, 326, 378–80
    Coolidge administration and, 350–51
pragmatism, 100–102
Preface to Politics (Lippmann), 114
President's Committee for Unemployment Relief, 484–85
press, the
    Hoover and, 465
    public opinion and, 94–97
    see also newspapers
prices
    control of, 363–64
    World War I and, 284
primary system, 123–24
Princeton University, 200, 201, 202–3
Princip, Gavril, 239

production
    food, during World War I, 281–82
    increase in, during 1920's, 359–60
    mass, 21, 96, 375
    wheat, 14, 281–82
Progress and Poverty (George), 100
Progressive party, 120, 191–93, 221
progressives, southern, 64–65
progressivism, 109–30
    muckrakers and, 110–12
    municipal reformers, 115–19
    political theory and, 113–15
    prohibition movement and, 125–26
    state reformers, 119–25
    Taft and, 185
    women's rights and, 126–27
prohibition, 90, 125–26, 415–16, 459, 461, 463, 493, 495–96
    repeal of, 411, 416
Prohibition party, 174, 196, 316, 317, 349, 492
Promise of American Life (Croly), 114, 195
prosperity (1922–1929), 358 ff.
prostitution, 125
Protestantism, 14, 89–91, 97, 113, 125, 414, 422, 463
Proust, Marcel, 421
public opinion
    churches and, 89–91
    control of, during World War I, 284–87
    education and, 91–94
    formation of, 89–97
    muckrakers and, 110–12
    press and, 94–97
public power (*see* power industry)
public utilities, 28, 42, 58, 117, 118, 119, 326, 379
public utility commissions, 124
public works, 484
Publicity Act (1910), 186
Puerto Rico
    acquisition of, 70
    U. S. colonial policy and, 71–72
Pujo, Arsène, 210, 214
Pulitzer, Joseph, 67, 69, 95
Pure Food and Drug Act (1906), 144
Pure Food, Drug and Cosmetic Act (1938), 144
Puritanism, 24

Quay, Matthew, 54
Quo Vadis (film), 381

racists, 98
radicalism, 286, 311, 313, 387, 411
Radio Corporation of America, 382
radio industry, 383–84
Railroad Administration, 282
railroad brotherhoods, 34, 36
railroads, 4, 11, 15, 22, 24, 28, 37, 42, 54–
    55, 56, 61
    Adamson Act and, 220
    after World War I, 324–25
    corrupt practices of, 119, 121, 122
    Elkins Act and, 141
    Esch-Cummins Transportation Act
        and, 324
    freight rates, 30, 39, 60, 61, 121, 141,
        142, 144
    government control of, 60
    government regulation of, 58, 63
    Hepburn Act and, 143
    holding companies and, 362
    Mann-Elkins Act and, 185
    Philippine, 73
    World War I and, 282
    see also names of railroads
Railway Labor Board, 324–25
Raisuli, Mulai Ahmed er, 163
Rankin, Jeanette, 127
Ransom, John Crowe, 421, 422
Raskob, John Jacob, 378, 462
Rauschenbusch, Walter, 90
realism, 103, 105, 419, 423
recall, 123, 183, 193
Reclamation Service, 141
Reconstruction Finance Corporation
    (RFC), 486–88, 489, 500
Reconstruction period, 17
Record, George, 121
Redfield, William C., 208
Reed, James A., 306, 307, 442, 495
    quoted on the Clayton Act, 217
Reed, John, 312
Reed, Thomas, 56
Reed, Walter, 71
referendum, 58, 123, 183, 193
reform
    in education, 63, 65, 93
    local government, 115–19
    progressive era and, 109–30

reform (cont.)
    state government, 119–25
    Taft administration and, 185–87
refugees, 345
regions of the United States, 11–21
    agricultural Middle West, 14–15
    industrial Middle West, 12–14
    inequalities between, 30
    Northeast, 15–16, 30
    Pacific Coast, 20–21
    Rocky Mountain, 18–20
    South, 17–18, 40
regulation, government (see government
    regulation)
Reid, Whitelaw, 67
Reimer, Arthur E., 196, 266
religion, 414–15, 421
    see also churches; Protestantism; Ro-
        man Catholic Church
Reno, Milo, 482
reparations
    moratorium on, 486
    World War I, 303, 305, 434, 435, 441
Republican party
    controlled by Middle West, 13, 14
    formation of progressive blocs within,
        15
    in late 1800's, 13, 14
    in the South, 63
    Taft and the split in the, 175, 179, 180,
        183
    see also elections; political parties
research, 22
Rhineland, 302, 303, 434
Riis, Jacob, 85
Ritchie, Albert, 495
roads, 373–74
    see also transportation
Roberts, Owen J., 336
Robinson, Edwin Arlington, 104, 421
Robinson, Joseph T., 461
Rochester Theological Seminary, 90
Rockefeller, John D., 22, 23, 112
Rocky Mountain region, 18–20
Rogers, Will, quoted, 497
Roman Catholic Church, 90–91, 308, 452,
    463
romanticism, 103
Roosevelt, Franklin D., 115, 459, 464
    Assistant Secretary of the Navy, 208,
        289

Roosevelt, Franklin D. (*cont.*)
elected President, 498
election of 1932 and, 494–500
"good neighbor" policy, 453
governor of New York State, 494
New Deal, 484, 498
nominated for President, 494–97
personality, 494
picture of, 499
vice presidential candidate (1920), 316
Roosevelt, Theodore, 55, 67, 99, 104, 110, 115
achieves nomination of Taft as his successor, 172
administration of (1901–1909), 131–71
Assistant Secretary of the Navy, 69
attitude toward the Philippines, 73
Autobiography, 131, 139
biographical sketch, 131–36
books written by, 134 n.
coal strike and, 139–41
congressional elections of 1910 and, 182–84
conservation and, 145–46
contempt for Wilson, 260
death of, 308
election of 1904 and, 142
election of 1912 and, 190–91
election of 1916 and, 265
Far East policy, 159
foreign policy, 150–65
Holmes appointed to Supreme Court by, 138
impact on Wilson, 206
imperialism and, 136, 150–52, 161
intervention in the Caribbean, 156–59
legislation enacted (1901–1905), 141
Lusitania incident, 254, 260
navy and, 133, 151
New Nationalism, 194, 195, 216, 221
Panama Canal and, 152–56
panic of 1907 and, 146–50
peace negotiations, 164–65
presidential leadership, 134–36
pure food legislation, 144
resentment against Taft, 190–91
second term, 142–44
Spanish-American War and, 69
succeeds McKinley, 131
treaty concerning Cuban sugar negotiated by, 71

Roosevelt, Theodore (*cont.*)
trusts and, 136–39
visit to Africa and Europe, 174, 181
woman suffrage supported by, 127
World War I and, 261, 263
Roosevelt Corollary, 157, 222, 450, 451
Root, Elihu, 54, 70, 71, 136, 140, 157, 159, 165, 172, 273
election of 1912 and, 191
election of 1920 and, 317
on League of Nations Covenant, 301, 307
picture of, 158
World Court and, 435
Root-Takahira Agreement (1908), 160
Rosenwald Foundation, 87
Rotary Clubs, 365
Ruef, Abraham, 118
rule of reason, 138, 217, 365
Rumania, 303, 305
Russell, Charles E., 111
Russia
Allied intervention in, 304
Brest-Litovsk, Treaty of, 304
economic development, 482
imperialism, 159
Revolution (1917), 268, 285, 303–4
Russo-Japanese War, 159
World War I and, 239–40
Russo-Japanese War, 159, 164
Ryan, John D., 280
Ryan, Thomas Fortune, 122, 194

sabotage, 244
Sacco, Nicola, 313, 418
St. Denis, Ruth, 425
St. Louis, Missouri, 14
municipal reform in, 117
St. Louis and O'Fallen Railway Company v. United States, 325
St. Paul, Minnesota, 14
Sakhalin Island, 159, 160
Salem, Massachusetts, 3 n.
Salisbury, Lord, 68
Sam, Vilburn G., 222
Samoa, 73
Sandburg, Carl, 422
Sandino, Augusto, 451
San Francisco, California
municipal reform in, 118
segregation of Oriental children in the

San Francisco, California (*cont.*)
  public schools, 160
San Francisco *Bulletin*, 118
Santo Domingo, 188
Saturday Evening Post, The, 96
savings, 371, 472, 480
Schenck case, 286
Schiff, Jacob, 242
Schmitz, Eugene R., 118
schools (*see* colleges; education; universities)
Schwab, Charles M., 280
Schwimmer, Rosika, 245
scientific research, 22
Scopes trial, 413, 414
Scribner's (magazine), 97
Scripps, Edward W., 95
sealing, regulation of, 162
Sedition Act (1918), 286
segregation, 87
  of Japanese children in San Francisco schools, 160
Selective Service Act, World War I, 275
Seligman, J. & W., and Company, 395
Senate, U. S., 56
senators, direct election of, 124, 187
Serbian crisis (1914), 237
settlement houses, 82, 116
Seventeenth Amendment, 124, 187
Shantung, 228, 302, 309
sharecroppers, 87, 390
Shaw, Anna Howard, 127
Shearer, William B., 439
Sherman, James S., 173, 191
Sherman Antitrust Act, 28, 61, 114, 137, 138, 149, 185, 215, 217, 334, 365, 378, 381
Sherman Silver Purchase Act (1890), 59
Sherwood, Robert, 425
shipping
  after World War I, 325-26
  Coolidge administration and, 352-53
  World War I and, 280-81
Shipping Board, 325, 352
Shipping Board Act, 260
Shotwell, James T., 436
Shurman, Jacob Gould, 72
Siberia, 229, 304, 443
Siegfried, André, 414
silver, 19, 59
Silver Shirts, 483

Simmons, William J., 412
Simon, Sir John, 445, 447, 448
Sims, W. S., 287
Sinclair, Harry F., 335-36, 366
Sinclair, Upton, 104, 112, 144
Single Tax party, 316
Sister Carrie (Dreiser), 103
Sixteenth Amendment, 186, 210
skyscrapers, 426
Slichter, Sumner, quoted, 485
Sloan, John, 104
slums, 32, 82, 85, 88
Smith, Adam, 25
Smith, Alfred E., 91, 416, 459-64, 494-95, 496, 497
  election of 1924 and, 347
  picture of, 461
Smith, Hoke, 121
Smith, J. A., 114
Smith, James, Jr., 204
Smith, Jess, 338
Smoot, Reed, 341
Smyth v. Ames, 325
social Darwinism, 24, 97-99
social gospel, 90, 113
social justice, 219, 220-21, 266
social legislation, 113-14, 116, 119, 121, 143
social work, growth of, 116
socialism, 100, 112
  opposition to, 91, 109, 465
Socialist party, 100, 142, 174, 196, 266, 316, 349, 416, 482, 492, 499
  disintegration of, 285
Socialist-Labor party, 174, 196, 266, 316, 492
Socialist Relief Fund, 480
society, changes in, 81 ff.
Soule, George, quoted, 481, 482
South, 17-18, 40
  Negroes in, 86-88
  political changes in, 62-65
Southern Alliance, 58, 62, 63
Southern Pacific Railroad, 116, 118, 121, 137
Spanish-American War, 4, 68-70, 75, 95, 152, 162, 206
speculation, 407, 411-12, 470-73
Spencer, Herbert, 25, 98, 113
Spirit of American Government (Smith), 114
Spoon River Anthology (Masters), 422

Spooner, John C., 69
Spooner Act (1902), 154
Spreckels, Rudolph, 118
Spring-Rice, Sir Cecil, 250
"Square Deal," 182
standard of living, 6, 32, 37, 82, 367, 369, 385, 408
Standard Oil companies, 110, 138, 141, 142, 360, 363, 364, 395
standardization, 375
Stanford, Leland, 380
Stanton, Elizabeth Cady, 127
State Department, U. S.
    disapproval of Japanese plans to pur-
        chase land in lower California, 188
    foreign policy and, 433
    League of Nations and, 434
    Moroccan affairs and, 163
    Panama revolution and, 155
    World War I and, 259
state government (see government, state)
states' rights, 50, 195, 410
Stearns, Harold, 417
Stedman, Seymour, 316
steel, 12, 13, 22, 56, 57
Steele, Charles F., 23
Steffens, Lincoln, 110, 111, 112, 417
Steiglitz, Alfred, 426
Stephenson, David C., 412
Stevens, Wallace, 422
Stevenson Restriction Act (1922), 398
Stimson, Henry L., 182, 184, 261, 433, 449, 451
    Far East policy and, 442, 444–48
    Isthmian Doctrine and, 451
    picture of, 446
Stimson Doctrine, 447
stock market crash (1929), 470
Stone, Harlan F., 365
Stone, William J., 258, 269
Storey, Moorfield, 54
Straight, Willard D., 151, 189
Strasser, Adolph, 33, 34
Stravinsky, Igor, 421
strikes, 34, 217, 385
    after World War I, 312–13
    coal, 139–41, 312, 480, 482
    communism and, 387–88
    Pullman (1894), 61, 140
    railroad, 325, 338
    steel, 312, 387

strikes (cont.)
    textile, 387, 388
    World War I and, 244, 283, 284
Strong, William L., 133
suffrage, woman, 125, 126–27
sugar, 22, 40, 62, 282
    Cuban, 71, 222
    Hawaiian, 74
    Philippine, 449
    Puerto Rican, 72
Sullivan, Louis, 105, 426
Sullivan, Mark, 111, 180
Sumner, William Graham, 24, 98, 113
Sun Yat-sen, 444
Sunday, William A. "Billy," 414
"Sunrise Conference," 258
Supreme Court, U. S.
    Adkins v. Children's Hospital, 124
    Brandeis' appointment to, 122, 219
    cases involving Espionage and Sedi-
        tion acts, 286
    child labor legislation and, 220
    conservatism and, 365
    Grain Futures Trading Act (1921) de-
        clared unconstitutional, 334
    "grandfather clause" invalidated by,
        64
    Hughes's appointment to, 123
    labor legislation and, 124–25
    Nereide case, 255
    Northern Securities Company case,
        137, 138
    Plessy v. Fergusson, 87
    railroad cases, 325
    Teapot Dome scandal and, 336
    trade associations upheld by, 365
    U. S. colonial policy and, 71
    use of injunctions upheld by, 387
    Sussex (French steamer), 253, 257, 263
Swift meat-packing trust, 138

Taft, Charles P., 174
Taft, William H.
    administration (1909–1912), 174–96
    antitrust suit against U. S. Steel, 149
    Ballinger-Pinchot controversy and,
        178–79
    biographical sketch, 174–75
    Canadian reciprocity and, 184–85
    Chief Justice, 365
    Congress and, 180–84, 186, 187

Taft, William H. (*cont.*)
  congressional elections of 1910 and, 182–84
  elected President, 174
  election of 1912 and, 189–96
  Far East policy, 159, 189
  foreign policy, 151, 152, 187–89
  Hughes appointed to Supreme Court by, 123
  League to Enforce Peace and, 298, 308, 309
  League of Nations favored by, 301
  National War Labor Board chairman, 284
  nomination for President, 172
  peace efforts, 165
  Philippines and, 72–73
  postal savings bank bill and, 186
  reforms under, 185–87
  Secretary of War, 136
  tariff issue and, 175–78, 184
  Theodore Roosevelt's resentment against, 190–91
  trustbusting by, 185
Taft-Katsura memorandum, 159
Tammany machine, 50, 54, 194
Tangier, 163
Tarbell, Ida, 110, 112, 365
tariff, 26, 30, 38, 50–51, 55, 57, 71, 72, 98, 462
  Dingley, 175, 177
  during the 1920's, 332–33
  Fordney-McCumber, 333, 469
  Hawley-Smoot, 465, 468–69, 478
  Hoover and the, 465, 468–69
  Payne-Aldrich, 177, 182, 184, 210
  Republican era and, 364
  Taft and the, 175–78, 184
  Underwood-Simmons, 210
  Wilson and, 209–10, 214–15, 221
Tarkington, Booth, 112, 424
Tate, Allen, 421, 422
taxes
  excess profits, 277, 331
  income, 210, 276–77, 331, 340
  poll, 64
  Sixteenth Amendment, 186
  World War I and, 276
Taylor, Zachary, 196
teachers, 92
Teapot Dome scandal, 335–36

technology, 4, 76, 84, 112, 384, 409
Tennessee Coal and Iron Company, 138, 148–49, 185, 190
Tennessee River, 146, 279, 350
Tennessee Valley Authority, 379
Tennyson, Alfred, 103
Texas, 17
  political reform in, 122
  textile industry, 16, 384, 385
  theater, 424–25
13th District, The (Whitlock), 112
Thomas, Augustus, 424
Thomas, Norman, 416, 482, 499
Thompson, Carmi A., 449
Thompson, William Hale, 409
Thrasher, Leon C., 254
Three Soldiers (Dos Passos), 424
Through the Eye of the Needle (Howells), 112
tobacco, 22, 40
  Puerto Rican, 72
Toledo, Ohio, municipal reform in, 118
Tolstoy, Leo, 103
Townley, Arthur C., 316
Townsend, Francis E., 483
trade (*see* foreign trade)
trade associations, 364, 365
Trade Union Unity League, 388
trade unions
  corruption and, 386
  decline of, 385–87
  growth of, 33–36
  Negroes and, 386
  opposition to unrestricted immigration, 85
Trading-with-the-Enemy Act (1917), 283
Trans-Missouri Freight Association case (1897), 62
transportation
  development of, 7, 37
  in late 1700's, 3
  World War I and, 282
  see also automobile industry; aviation; roads; shipping
Traveller from Altruria (Howells), 112
Traylor, Melvin, 495
Treason of the Senate, The (Phillips), 111
Treasury Department, U. S., prohibition and, 415

trustbusting, 28, 137–38, 185, 217, 363, 365
trusts, 27, 39, 60, 61, 62, 111, 378
    investment, 472
    Theodore Roosevelt and the, 136–39
Tumulty, Joseph P., 209, 250
Tuskegee Institute, 88
Tutuila, 73
Twain, Mark, 103
Tweed, Boss, 172, 409
Tydings-McDuffie Act (1934), 449

"un-American" activities, 412–14
Underwood, Oscar W., 193, 194, 210, 442
Underwood tariff, 73, 210
unemployment, 32, 97, 149, 245, 372, 465,
    479, 480, 481, 484–85, 489
Union Labor party, 118
Union Pacific Railroad, 137
unions (see trade unions)
United Aircraft and Transport Corpora-
    tion, 377
United Christian party, 174
United Mine Workers, 139–41, 385, 387,
    388
United States Chamber of Commerce,
    365
United States Electric Power Company,
    360, 379
United States Geological Survey, 145
United States Secret Service, 244
United States Shipping Board, 263, 280
United States Steel Corporation, 112, 138,
    149, 185, 190, 360, 361, 363, 364, 365,
    386
universities, 94
    architecture of, 105, 426
    see also names of universities
urbanization, 7–8, 16, 81–82, 390
U'Ren, William S., 123
U.S.A. (Dos Passos), 424

Vanderbilt, Cornelius, 22
Van Sweringen brothers, 362
Vanzetti, Bartolomeo, 313, 418
Vardaman, James K., 121, 269
Veblen, Thorstein, 100, 417
Venezuela
    blockade of coast (1902), 157–58
    boundary dispute (1895), 68, 156
Vera Cruz incident, 225
Vermont, political reform in, 121

Versailles Treaty, 300–310, 317, 406, 433
    fight for ratification of, in U. S., 306–11
veterans (see war veterans)
Veterans' Bureau, 331, 335, 338, 342
Viereck, George Sylvester, 243
Villa, Pancho, 224, 225–26
Virgin Islands, purchase of, 223
Virginia, University of, 201
Volstead Act (1919), 126, 329, 415, 416
Von Papen, Franz, 244
voting
    "grandfather clause" and, 64
    literacy tests and, 63, 64
    see also suffrage

wages
    during 1920's, 370, 385, 386
    World War I and, 284
Wald, Lillian D., 82, 116
Walker, James J., 409
Walker, John Brisben, 96
Walker, John G., 153
Wallace, Henry C., 330
Walsh, Frank P., 284
Walsh, Thomas J., 336
war bonds, 277
war debts, 440–42
    moratorium on, 486
War Department, U. S., 279, 289
War of 1812, 65
War Finance Corporation, 486
War Industries Board, 278
War Labor Policies Board, 284
War Trade Board, 282–83
war veterans
    Coolidge and, 341–42
    Harding and, 332
    Hoover and the bonus for, 489–92
Warbasse, J. P., 368
Warburg, Paul M., 211, 473
Ward, Lester Frank, 99
Washington, Booker T., 88
Washington, George, 3
Washington (state), 21
Washington Conference (1921–22), 437–
    39, 442
Waste Land, The (Eliot), 421
Water Power Act (1920), 326
Waters, Walter W., 490
Watkins, A. S., 317
Watson, James E., 459

Watson, Thomas E., 63, 142, 174
wealth
  national, 4, 359
  ownership and control of, 15
  sources of, 22
Wealth against Commonwealth (Lloyd), 110
Weaver, James B., 59
Webb-Kenyon Act (1913), 126
Webb-Pomerene Act (1918), 221
Weber, Max, 426
Weeks, John W., 330
welfare state, trend toward, 99–100
West, Andrew F., 203
West, the
  agriculture in, 141
  natural resources in, 26–27
  see also Pacific Coast
Westinghouse Electric Company, 379, 383
Wetmore, Claude H., 110
Weyl, Walter, 114
Wharton, Edith, 104
wheat production, 14, 281–82
Wheeler, Burton K., 338, 348, 349
Wheeler, Wayne B., 126
White, George, 495
White, Henry, 299
White, William Allen, 112
Whitlock, Brand, 112, 118
Whitman, Walt, 421
Wickersham, George W., 149, 179
Wiggin, Albert H., 473
Wilder, Thornton, 424
Wiley, Harvey W., 144
Wilhelm II, Kaiser, 163, 164
Willard, Frances, 125
Williams, William Carlos, 422
Willis, H. Parker, 212
Wilson, Henry Lane, 224
Wilson, William B., 208
Wilson, Woodrow, 115
  antitrust program, 214–18
  biographical sketch, 199–205
  books written by, 201 n.
  Brandeis appointed to Supreme Court by, 122
  cabinet, 206–9
  Congress and, 205, 206, 209, 221
  elected President, 196
  election of 1912 and, 192–96

Wilson, Woodrow (cont.)
  election of 1916 and, 264–66
  election of 1920 and, 315, 316
  Far East policy, 159, 189, 227–29
  financial reform, 210–14
  foreign policy, 151, 152, 221–29
  Fourteen Points, 292–93, 297, 298, 302, 305
  governor of New Jersey, 121, 184, 204
  inaugural address, 205, 209
  League of Nations and, 292, 297–302, 305–11, 316–17, 432
  Mexican revolution and, 223–27
  neutrality proclamation (1914), 240
  New Freedom, 195, 209 ff.
  Paris peace conference and, 299 ff.
  Philippines and, 73
  physical breakdown, 308–9
  picture of, 207, 300
  presidential leadership, 205–9
  reform of New Jersey corporation laws, 362
  social justice and, 219, 220, 221, 266
  tariff and, 209–10, 214–15, 221
  Theodore Roosevelt's contempt for, 260
  Theodore Roosevelt's impact on, 206
  Versailles Treaty and, 300–310
  Volstead Act vetoed by, 126
  woman suffrage and, 127
  World War I and, 237 ff.
Wisconsin, political reform in, 120–21
Wisconsin Idea, 120–21
Wolfe, Thomas, 424
women
  education and, 93
  labor force and, 31, 32, 126–27
  suffrage, 125, 126–27
Women's Christian Temperance Union, 125
Wood, Grant, 425
Wood, Leonard, 70, 261, 289, 314, 449
Wood-Forbes Commission, 449
Woods, Arthur, 484
Woodward, William E., 407
workmen's compensation, 124, 220
workshops, 5
World Court of International Justice, 435
World War I, 237 ff.
  American diplomacy and, 249–60

World War I (*cont.*)
British blockade of Germany, 249–53, 256, 257
Central Powers, 238, 242, 245, 247, 248, 259, 287
control of public opinion during, 284–87
cost of, to United States, 275, 276–77, 287
end of, 293, 309
German submarine warfare, 252, 254, 255–57, 261, 266, 267, 269, 280, 282, 287, 293
initial U. S. sympathies, 241–42
Japanese entry into, 228
Lusitania incident, 244, 253–56, 260, 261
outbreak of, 237 ff.
peace treaty, 298
propaganda and, 243–45, 260–61
U. S. entry into, 269
U. S. exports to the Allies, 245–47
U. S. loans to the Allies, 247–48
U. S. naval and military activities, 287–91

World War I (*cont.*)
U. S. participation in, 273–96
U. S. preparedness, 260–64
World War Foreign Debt Commission, 440
Wright, Frank Lloyd, 105, 426
Wright brothers, 376
Wylie, Elinor, 424

Yale University, 174
yellow-dog contracts, 387
yellow fever, 70–71
"yellow journalism," 95
Young, Owen D., 112, 435
Youngstown, Ohio, 13
Yugoslavia, 303

Zapata, Emiliano, 224, 225
Zelaya, José S., 188
Zimmermann note, 267, 269
Zola, Emile, 103
Zukor, Adolph, 380, 381, 382